LEGAL WRITING AND SKILLS FOR FOREIGN LL.M. STUDENTS

MAIN ASSIGNMENT FILE BOOK

■ ■ ■

Karen Lundquist

Assistant Professor of ESL and Legal Skills
University of Minnesota Law School

WEST ACADEMIC PUBLISHING

The publisher is not engaged in rendering legal or other professional advice, and this publication is not a substitute for the advice of an attorney. If you require legal or other expert advice, you should seek the services of a competent attorney or other professional.

West, West Academic Publishing, and West Academic are trademarks of West Publishing Corporation, used under license.

Printed in the United States of America

ISBN: 978-1-68328-766-7

Acknowledgments

This book would never be without my alma mater, William Mitchell College of Law (now Mitchell Hamline School of Law), and John Sonsteng, Professor of Law at Mitchell Hamline and long-time beloved figure at the law school for nearly four decades. It was first at Mitchell, where I was a law student from 2002-2005, that I was introduced to the "practicum method" of law and the philosophy of "learning by doing" that Mitchell is well known for. The basic premise of this book — that we learn best by doing and by being engaged in active-learning exercises — is the foundation upon which John and other professors at Mitchell have based the legal writing and advocacy programs at the school. I have been inspired by those teaching materials and by the courses that I took at Mitchell.

If John had not given me the opportunity, as an overly green attorney, to co-direct the Small Business Practicum course in 2007, I don't believe this book would have taken the shape that it has or that I would have even written it. It was under John's tutelage and guidance that I learned about teaching law and about writing effective and engaging classroom materials. Unit I in Section III in the book (restrictive covenants and preliminary injunctions) is in fact inspired by materials that John wrote for the National Institute of Trial Advocacy (Superior Speech and Hearing Center v. Baines). Thank you, John, for the faith and confidence that you placed in me.

Likewise, thank you to my boss, Khary Hornsby at the University of Minnesota Law School, for the support he has given me in writing this book. He has always made it clear that the book should be of prime importance for me in organizing my time and schedule, which I always seem to overbook, and has always reminded me of that. At the University of Minnesota, I also have to extend my thanks to Professor Brad Clary, whose fact pattern for one of the J.D. legal writing classes provided the basic facts for the apparent authority unit (Section I, Unit 2).

Aside from these two fact patterns inspired by those already created by John and Brad, all the other units in this book are based either on real-life stories that I heard or read about, on cases that I read as I carried out research for the book, or are creations of my imagination.

I also must express my thanks to my teaching and research assistants who helped me in drafting sample memos, editing and proofreading, and providing their feedback on the book: Milene Porchetto Carvalho, Brittany Johnson, Toshi Moran, Cara Tang, Minhquang Trang, and Shuang Xu. Chuquin Xing deserves special mention. It was with her that the brainchild of the ESL Workbook and the commented cases came to life, and her creativity and legal acumen were instrumental in the book coming together as we collaborated on the contract formation/promissory estoppel unit.

The book would also not look as handsome as it does without the skills and creativity of Denis Vorobiov, who worked with me without complaint and who created the attractive layouts and design for all the books that make up Legal Writing and Legal Skills for Foreign LL.M. Students. David Walcott of Getty Creations also added to the creative look of the book with his logos, illustrations, and website designs.

On a personal level, thank you to my mom, Carol Lundquist, for her support and her proofreading and revision skills, and also my husband Alejandro Anaya who patiently waited while I was absorbed in this project and provided his unwavering support as well.

Karen Lundquist

Minneapolis, February 2017

Table of Contents

**INTRODUCTION TO LEGAL WRITING AND LEGAL SKILLS
FOR FOREIGN LL.M. STUDENTS**

SECTION I. Beginning Legal Issues

SECTION II. Intermediate Legal Issues

SECTION III. Advanced Legal Issues

LEGAL WRITING AND LEGAL SKILLS FOR FOREIGN LL.M. STUDENTS

MAIN ASSIGNMENT FILE BOOK

Book Overview

This book — Legal Writing and Legal Skills for Foreign LL.M. Students — replicates as much as possible the real-life practice of law and provides interactive exercises that will develop not only your legal reasoning and analysis skills but also your English language skills.

The learning objectives of the book and its exercises are:
- To deepen your understanding of the U.S. legal system
- To improve your ability to carry out common-law legal analysis
- To improve your skills in all areas of English (speaking, listening, reading and writing)

You will achieve these objectives by:
- Playing the role of an associate attorney at a fictitious law firm in the state of Jefferson. Depending on the unit and the legal issue, you will work at one of four law firms: Lincoln, Adams and Washington, PLLC; the Law Office of Bennett, Elliot and Darcy; Anthony, Ross and Tubman; or the Baldwin and Bell Law Firm
- Carrying out client matters that replicate the real-life practice of law in the United States
- Being engaged with your classmates in interactive exercises that will allow you to practice and improve all language skills (reading, writing, speaking and listening), as well as legal skills such as analysis

The book is divided into three sections; each section represents a different level of difficulty of the legal issues included in the section. Each section — Beginning, Intermediate and Advanced — includes four units, each of which includes:
- The Main Assignment File that presents your client assignment and includes all documents and correspondence relevant to the client matter
- An Assignment Email from the senior partner describing what task you are to accomplish for the client
- Commented and edited cases and other legal authority
- ESL Worksheets that assist you in reading the cases and present grammar, vocabulary and other language-related information from the cases
- Skills-Building Exercises that will deepen your knowledge of the legal issue(s) presented in the unit and provide you opportunities to improve your language skills, in particular speaking

Each section has two common-law and two statutory legal matters. The book also provides additional resources that are available online at the website www.legalwritingforllms.com and that will deepen your understanding of the law, of legal writing in the American system, and of the skills presented in the book.

The units in the beginning section involve predictive legal writing assignments, and for these assignments, you will provide to the senior partner your prediction about what you think will happen in a client matter if a claim is filed. For these units, all students will be working at the Lincoln, Adams and Washington Law Firm and will receive assignments from one of the senior partners: Amy Lincoln, Jack Adams or Georgina Washington. Your client for all of these units is one of the most important clients of the law firm, a local advertising agency, Stray Dog Advertising.

In the intermediate and advanced sections, all but one of the units involve litigation and motion practice, either a motion to dismiss, motion for a preliminary injunction or a motion for summary judgment. For these units, only half of the students will work for the Lincoln, Adams and Washington Law Firm and represent Stray Dog Advertising. The other half will work for another law firm — the Law Office of Bennett, Elliot and Darcy; the Baldwin and Bell Law Firm; or Anthony, Ross and Tubman — and represent opposing party in that specific case, for which your instructor will assign roles to you and your fellow classmates.

Sources and Citations

Since the jurisdiction of Jefferson does not exist, you will read statutes and cases from different states, as well as federal statutes and cases. Since many students pursue an LL.M. degree in the United States with the intention of sitting for the New York bar exam, many of the cases that you will read for the different units were issued by New York courts. Other states represented in the book include Massachusetts, Illinois and Minnesota, as well as others.

Regardless of the state from which the sources (case law or statutes) are actually from, for purposes of this book and your class you must assume that all of cases were issued by the Jefferson courts and that the statutes were passed by the Jefferson state legislature and signed into law by the Jefferson governor, unless otherwise indicated. Because you are practicing in the jurisdiction of Jefferson, you must change the citations of the legal sources you use to Jefferson.

Thus, when you cite a statute, follow this pattern:

Minn. Stat. §181.953   *N.D. Cent. Code §25–01.2–01*

Jeff. Stat. §181.953   *Jeff. Cent. Code §25–01.2–01*

In other words, replace the state identifier with Jefferson.

If you are citing to a court case, do the same.

State v. Johnson, 237 N.W. 2d 155 (Minn. 1983).   *Gallegos v. Yeargin W. Constructors, 725 P. 2d 599 (N.M. Ct. App. 1986).*

State v. Johnson, 237 N.W. 2d 155 (Jeff. 1983).   *Gallegos v. Yeargin W. Constructors, 725 P. 2d 599 (Jeff. Ct. App. 1986).*

Time References

In the materials, you will find time references expressed in different ways. Some emails, memos and communications are written as April 10, **THIS YEAR**. When you write your assignment, you must write the actual year in place of **THIS YEAR**. For example, if the actual date is April 13, 2018 and if the date in the materials is written as June 23, **THIS YEAR**, the date for the exercise is June 23, 2018.

Some references to time are in the past, and they are indicated, for example, as **YEAR −10**. In this case, the calculation is simple, and you subtract 10 from the actual year. If the actual date is April 13, 2018 and the date of the exercise is June 23, **YEAR −10**, then the date for the exercise is June 23, 2008.

Likewise, if the time reference is in the future, the date will be written **YEAR +10** and the date for the assignment is June 23, 2028.

Factual Background of the Players in the Book

The Lincoln, Adams and Washington Law Firm, PLLC

You are an associate attorney at the law firm of Lincoln, Adams and Washington, PLLC (LAW Law Firm), a business law firm in the state of Jefferson. The firm's clients are small and medium-sized businesses from around the state, as well as others outside of Jefferson.

One of the firm's most important clients is a local business, Stray Dog Advertising, LLC (SDA). SDA is an advertising agency that was founded by a Jefferson resident, Pamela Park, ten years ago. Since its founding SDA has grown to one of the most influential and successful advertising agencies in Jefferson.

The LAW Law Firm was founded five years ago by the senior partners Amy Lincoln and Jack Adams, who had been working together at another local law firm and decided to break off and form their own firm. When they left, several associates came with them, as did many clients (including SDA).

Senior partner Georgina Washington joined the firm two years ago after working for nearly fifteen years with a nation-wide firm, Rivers Stoehr, which works with and defends some of the largest corporations in the country. Because of her extensive professional experience, Washington was offered a partnership immediately to entice her to join the firm.

Instead, for most associates, partnership is offered after six or seven years of working as an associate attorney. To be offered partner status, associate attorneys are expected to show sharp advocacy skills and also a penchant for business development.

You have been assigned many of the matters that SDA is facing. You work closely with Pamela Park and enjoy helping SDA as well as other clients.

Lincoln, Adams and Washington
LAW FIRM

Lincoln, Adams and Washington
LAW FIRM

HOME   ABOUT   PRACTICES   OUR LAWYERS   NEWS   CONTACT

Let us take care of the

legal matters.

So you can focus on

what you do best:

Run your business.

Our Attorneys Work with Jefferson Business Owners

Business owners need trusted advisors who are on their side and can help them make the tough decisions that they face. The experienced business attorneys at the Lincoln, Adams and Washington Law Firm are the trusted advisors that you need. We counsel and advise our clients on the law and in doing so, help protect what is most valued to them: their business. Contact us today for a consultation to learn how the Jefferson business attorneys at Lincoln, Adams and Washington can help you.

TESTIMONIALS

"Working with attorneys at the LAW Law Firm helps me sleep at night knowing that they are on my side. They keep the interests of my business foremost in their mind."

— A. Gomez, owner El Nostro Mexican Restaurant

WHY CHOOSE US?

OUR LAWYERS
Our lawyers have dedicated their careers to working with business owners like you. They understand the law and know what they need to do to help your business succeed.

READ MORE

GET TO KNOW US MORE
We offer a discounted initial consultation for all new clients. Call us today to set up an appointment.

READ MORE

WHAT WE OFFER
We offer services for all areas of law that affect you as a business owner, from contract drafting to litigation.

READ MORE

GET IN TOUCH WITH US
Call us or send us an email to learn more about how we can help you and your business.

READ MORE

LATEST NEWS
Jack Adams was recently awarded a 20___ Pro Bono Publico Award from the Jefferson State Bar Association.

CONTACT US
ADDRESS: 8600 Winston Boulevard, Suite 1225 West Rapids, Jefferson 66435
TEL: 623-861-7500
EMAIL: info@lawlawfirm.com

SEND US A MESSAGE
Send us an email to schedule a consultation with one of our business attorneys.

CLICK TO SEND US AN EMAIL

The Law Office of Bennett, Elliot and Darcy

Advanced Section:

- <u>Singh v. Stray Dog Advertising, LLC</u> (Title VII of the Civil Rights Act of 1964/religious accommodations and motion for summary judgment)
- <u>Stray Dog Advertising, LLC v. Winsted</u> (restrictive covenants and motion for preliminary injunction)

You have left your job as an associate at the Lincoln, Adams and Washington Law Firm. You decided that your heart was not in working with business owners and dealing with the various matters that they face. Instead, you have realized that your true passion lies in advocating for "the little guy," those individuals who have been injured and need an advocate's help to receive fair compensation for their injuries.

You interviewed with a firm that specializes in civil rights cases, as well as one that focuses on worker's compensation before finally accepting a position at the Law Office of Bennett, Elliot and Darcy, one of the most highly-respected law firms in the state of Jefferson that handles only plaintiff-side employment cases. You are excited to take on the corporations and businesses that take advantage of their employees.

Like most plaintiff-side law firms, Bennett, Elliot and Darcy handles cases on a contingency basis, meaning that the clients don't pay an hourly fee and don't pay costs and expenses. Instead, the firm advances the costs and expenses and then takes a percentage (usually 40%) of any recovery obtained, such as a settlement. If the case goes to trial and if the firm prevails, the employment statutes allow for the recovery of reasonable attorney's fees, and the defendant has to pay the firm's costs and expenses.

The partners at Bennett, Elliot and Darcy were all law firm classmates who were in the same 1L section and remained friends throughout their law school and professional careers until they opened the firm nearly twenty years ago. There are now nearly fifteen associate attorneys at the firm, as well as six partners (including the founding partners).

The firm's reputation has grown as one that tenaciously fights for its clients' rights, and the attorneys have won the respect of other attorneys around the state. The founding partners and the other attorneys in the firm enjoy a friendly and respectful working relationship with the attorneys at the Lincoln, Adams and Washington Law Firm.

Anthony, Ross and Tubman

Intermediate Section:
- <u>Estate of Ahmed v. Stray Dog Advertising, LLC</u> (duty to warn/negligence and motion to dismiss)
- <u>Beaumont v. Park</u> (defamation and motion to dismiss)
- <u>Mudd et al. v. City of Longworth state</u> (constitutional right to privacy and motion for preliminary injunction)

Advanced Section:
- <u>Gateway West Development, Inc. v. Stray Dog Advertising, LLC</u> (premises liability and motion for summary judgment)

You have recently been hired at Anthony, Ross and Tubman, located in the city of Charlestown, Jefferson. Anthony, Ross and Tubman (ART) is a civil litigation law firm, representing both plaintiffs and defendants in many types of civil matters ranging from personal injury to contract disputes and business litigation.

Anthony, Ross and Tubman was founded just three years ago when Suzanne Anthony, Martha Ross and Harry Tubman, all colleagues at a large, national law firm, decided to leave that firm and start their own firm based on their beliefs, different from the mainstream, of how a law firm should operate, recognizing that the traditional law-firm model wasn't working for all clients.

The ART law office offers non-traditional payment options and compensation models for its clients and its attorneys, and the firm's structure is not the hierarchical one employed at most law firms, but rather a collaborative, team-based approach. Billable hours aren't rewarded but rather results. The firm's unique approach to practicing law has been noticed and appreciated as the firm has grown over the three years in operation.

Last year, the firm hired two new associate attorneys to work on the growing number of clients who have hired the firm, and this year, you are one of three new associates. The firm's model for new hires is that the new attorneys work with all three of the partners and gain experience in different areas of law rather than working with just one partner and becoming pigeon-holed into one practice area.

This is the law firm's logo and website.

Introduction

Baldwin & Bell Law Firm

Advanced Section:

- <u>Groovia, Inc. v. Stray Dog Advertising, LLC</u> (personal jurisdiction and motion to dismiss)

Located in the State of Franklin, the Baldwin & Bell Law Office prides itself on tradition. The firm was founded in Silver Falls, Franklin in **YEAR −83** by George Baldwin and William Bell, the grandfathers of Rose Baldwin and Oliver Bell, the current owners and partners. The firm is the longest continually operating law firm in the state, something both partners are extremely proud of.

Both families have a long tradition of practicing law and the firm has been passed down to now the third generation of the Baldwin and Bell families. Both families are deeply rooted in the Franklin legal communities, and members of both families have served as judges in the state courts.

Although the capital of Franklin, Silver Falls is not a large city and has a population of only 65,000. Consequently, the Baldwin & Bell Law Firm is more of a general practice firm that serves the various legal needs of the members of the community, and the attorneys thus deal with matters ranging from family law to criminal and civil law. Senior Partner Baldwin has developed a reputation as a skilled attorney for matters involving Internet law, while Senior Partner Bell has focused his attention on criminal law. The firm employs four other full-time attorneys and three support staff.

Over the past few years, the legislature and governor of the State of Franklin have offered various tax incentives to new and established businesses to encourage them to establish their business there. As a result, businesses like Groovia, the organic energy drink company, have started up in or moved to Franklin and helped spur on economic growth, thus helping other businesses such as the Baldwin & Bell Law Firm, which has worked with many of these companies, including Groovia in the litigation matter against Stray Dog Advertising.

Stray Dog Advertising

Pamela Park is the owner of Stray Dog Advertising (SDA), an advertising agency located in the city of West Rapids in the state of Jefferson. Park founded SDA in **YEAR −10**; since its inception, the agency has grown rapidly and is now the largest and most successful advertising agency in Jefferson, boasting both out-of-state and international clients.

Park graduated from Chickasaw State University in **YEAR −16** with a degree in Mass Communication. Chickasaw is a neighboring state to Jefferson. Upon graduation, Park went to work for a small advertising agency in Riverside, the capital of Chickasaw. She worked there for three years before moving back to Jefferson City, which is just across the Aster River from West Rapids. She worked for another agency for three years before leaving and founding SDA.

Park is the sole owner of SDA. The company is a limited liability company (LLC), properly organized under the laws of Jefferson. Currently, SDA has 22 employees:

1 creative director	2 production managers
2 art directors	1 customer service representative
2 copywriters	4 sales representatives
2 account executives	4 administrative assistants
2 media buyers	1 office manager
1 media analyst	

SDA's original sweet spot was television advertising; Park had made a name for herself as someone who was willing to take risks to get people talking about her clients and their products and services. SDA now works routinely in television, radio, print, and digital platforms.

Park recently landed important new clients such a nationwide fast-casual food chain named Serrano, which is looking to revamp its image and attract a younger clientele; Zenith, a local micro-brewery that is looking to expand its brand nationally; and Canopy, Inc., a corporation that owns and operates many successful restaurants in the West Rapids/Jefferson City metropolitan area.

Recently, SDA has had to work with a local temporary employment agency to ensure that it can handle the increased client demands with its new clients, as well as the agency's solid base of existing clients. It has also taken on unpaid interns from the local university, Jefferson State University. With the challenging job market for recent graduates, the students have been happy to receive work experience, while SDA has been happy to have the extra help, without charge.

The SDA offices are located in an office complex in West Rapids named Gateway West. The owner of Gateway West and SDA's landlord is Greg Blackman. SDA also has a second office located in Sweetwater, another city in Jefferson. The office is located in a one-hundred-year-old building, which SDA purchased and renovated, in the historic downtown of Sweetwater. SDA opened up this second office to better serve clients in other parts of the state. SDA uses the first floor for its own offices and leases out the second floor to other professional businesses.

The part of town where SDA's West Rapids office is located is along the Aster River, which divides West Rapids from Jefferson City. SDA has been successful in marketing its services and acquiring clients from both cities, as well as from the surrounding metropolitan area. On the next page is a map of the West Rapids/Jefferson City metropolitan area.

The Aster River is the river to the east of the other river, the Loon River, and West Rapids occupies the areas numbered 3, 6, 7 and 8 on the map. The Loon River empties into the larger Aster River. Jefferson City, the capital of Jefferson, is located to the west of West Rapids and occupies the areas numbered 1, 2, 4, 5 and 9 on the map.

Together, the Jefferson City and West Rapids metropolitan area has a population of 2,220,000 people. West Rapids has 800,000 people while Jefferson City has 1,420,000.

On the next page you will also find Stray Dog's logo.

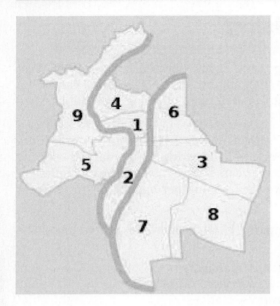

The office manager, Juan Gonzalez, was hired by SDA two years ago. SDA could not run without Gonzalez as he keeps the agency well organized. He often deals with clients and vendors, although Park remains the only person in the agency with authority to sign checks, make deposits at the bank, sign contracts on behalf of the agency, and hire and fire employees.

The two media buyers, Emily Johnson and Russell Wang, are both recent graduates from the Jefferson State University. Johnson is a skilled employee who maintains close relationships with Park's connections in TV advertising. Wang, on the other hand, focuses on digital media channels.

One of the two copywriters, Jasmine Singh was hired eight years ago and has been a productive and reliable employee. Singh is married and recently became a vegetarian. The other copywriter, Anthony DiGennaro, has been working for SDA for the past three years. They work very closely with each other. Park is very satisfied with the quality of their work.

The three account executives working for SDA are Wally Schwartz, June Tam and Amy Vanderbilt. All three have many years of experience working in advertising. As account executives, they maintain the relationship between SDA and the client, ensuring that the client's needs and expectations are being met on every project. All three excel at their job.

The agency has also begun looking for a new position within the company: Manager of Hispanic Client Accounts. The position is one that Park has created to serve a growing need of meeting the demands of the Latino population, which is growing in Jefferson as in many other states.

In addition, SDA works with many independent contractors to meet the demands of its clients and has created new positions to fill its changing needs.

Names and Addresses

Stray Dog Advertising, LLC
45 Sunrise Boulevard
West Rapids, Jefferson 66412
623–901–4585

Stray Dog Advertising, LLC
210 Main Street Northwest
Sweetwater, Jefferson 68910
517–510–3680

**Lincoln, Adams and
Washington Law Firm, PLLC**
8600 Winston Boulevard, Suite 1225
West Rapids, Jefferson 66435
623–861–7500
Senior Partners:
    Amy G. Lincoln (Atty. #0256090)
    Jack G. Adams (Atty. #0559811)
    Georgina Washington (Atty. #025609)

Anthony, Ross and Tubman
6001 Tulip Boulevard, Suite 1550
Charlestown, Jefferson 66490
624–600–9810
Senior Partners:
    Suzanne B. Anthony (Atty. #798916)
    Bethany Ross (Atty. # 821670)
    Harry Tubman (Atty. # 576208)

**The Law Office of Bennett,
Elliot and Darcy**
125 South 5th Street, Suite 1450
West Rapids, Jefferson 66402
612–555–1212
Senior Partners:
    Jim Bennett (Atty. #035469)
    Sara Elliot (Atty. # 045698)
    Graham Darcy (Atty. # 035469)

The Law Firm of Baldwin & Bell
5004 Excelsior Drive
Silver Falls, Franklin 07601
414–555–0101
Senior Partners:
    Rose Baldwin (Atty. # 0986511)
    Oliver Bell (Atty. # 083469)

SECTION I

Beginning Legal Issues

Statutory Law

Unit 1 Damages
Dog Bite Dilemma

For this Unit, you will learn about the legal issues of damages and *respondeat superior*. You will provide your opinion on a matter involving Pamela Park of Stray Dog Advertising. She has turned to the LAW Law Firm for advice about whether she should bring a claim against the owner of the dog that tragically killed her dog, Honey. You will analyze and determine what type of damages Pamela can recover if she prevails in bringing a claim, and whether she should also bring a claim against the owner's employer. You will also analyze an ethical issue.

Learning Objectives of this Unit:

This Unit will build your skills to:

- Explain complex legal matters clearly and concisely
- Use appropriate technical terminology
- Identify and analyze the applicable case law and facts for the relevant legal issues
- Efficiently read and understand legal authority (statute and case law)
- Articulate legal arguments in support of client's position
- Analyze possible outcomes for legal dispute, evaluate and articulate strengths and weaknesses of such outcomes
- Efficiently and effectively communicate in a written and oral format
- Respond to questions about the relevant law

To achieve these learning objectives, you will complete the following tasks:

- Draft a predictive memo to senior partner about the legal issues and potential damages
- Draft a client advice letter about your client meeting and the legal issue
- Carry out a client meeting with Pamela Park

To complete these tasks, you will use the following materials in the book:

- Assignment email from Senior Partner (pages 17-18; 21-22)
- Main Assignment File (pages 19-24)
- Statutes: Minnesota Chapter 347 (selected)
- Damages Commented Cases:
    - <u>Soucek v. Banham</u>, 524 N.W.2d 478 (Minn. Ct. App. 1994).
    - <u>State v. Graham</u>, No. C1-02-887, 2003 WL 282470 (Minn. Ct. App. Feb. 11, 2003).
    - <u>State v. Weber</u>, No. C4-94-1145, 1995 WL 238940 (Minn. Ct. App. Apr. 25, 1995).
    - <u>Jensen v. Walsh</u>, 623 N.W.2d 247 (Minn. 2001).
- ESL Workbook (pages 1-13).

Your instructor will also assign you additional skills-building exercises to bolster your understanding of the legal issues and further develop your legal reasoning and language skills. You will find an icon with each exercise that indicates which skills the exercise will focus on.

ICON	SKILL
	Speaking — in particular about the legal issues and the law presented in the Unit
	Oral comprehension
	Legal analysis and reasoning
	Analysis of the legal issue(s) presented in the Unit
	English grammar, syntax, and vocabulary
	Legal ethics and professional responsibility
	Legal research

In this Unit, the additional skills-building exercises that accompany the Main Assignment File include:

- Ethics Dilemma (page 25)
- Damages Analysis Exercise (pages 26-29)
- Professional Presentation: *If Pamela Park Were Your Client...* (pages 30-31)

Before beginning the Unit, you should read and be familiar with the Stray Dog Advertising Factual Background (pages 7-8) and the Factual Background of the Lincoln, Adams and Washington Law Firm (pages 2-3).

You will also find online at the website www.legalwritingforllms.com the following online resources that accompany this Unit. The additional online resources will help you deepen your mastery of the skills presented in the Unit and also provide additional understanding about the U.S. legal system and legal writing.

- Additional Resources:
  - Sources of American Law
  - Writing Professional Emails
  - Writing Predictive Memos
  - Writing E-memos
  - IRAC
- Additional Skills-Building Exercises:
  - Issues and Issue Statements
  - Stating the Rule
  - Analysis
  - Ethical Spotlight Exercises

Damages

Unit 1

Section I, Unit 1 Legal Issue
Damages

Main Assignment File	Damages Cases	ESL Workbook	Additional Exercises	Additional Online Resources
Introduction to File and Client Matter Pages 12-16	Soucek v. Banham, 524 N.W.2d 478 (Minn. Ct. App. 1994).	Soucek v. Banham, 524 N.W.2d 478 (Minn. Ct. App. 1994).	Ethics Dilemma Page 25	Writing Professional Emails
Documents Related to Client Matter Pages 17-24	State v. Weber, 1995 WL 238940 (Minn. Ct. App. April 25, 1995).	State v. Weber, 1995 WL 238940 (Minn. Ct. App. April 25, 1995).	Damages Analysis Exercise Pages 26-29	Business Correspondence (with sample letters)
Assignment Information Pages + Rubrics Pages 32-39	State v. Graham, 2003 WL 282470 (Minn. Ct. App. Feb. 11, 2003).	State v. Graham, 2003 WL 282470 (Minn. Ct. App. Feb. 11, 2003).	Presentation: If SDA Were Your Client... Pages 30-31	Writing Memos (office memos and e-memos)
	Jensen v. Walsh, 623 N.W.2d 247 (Minn. 2001).	Jensen v. Walsh, 623 N.W.2d 247 (Minn. 2001).		IRAC (including the various exercises for each element)
				Skills-Building Exercises for Rules, Issues and Issues Statements, Analysis and Ethical Dilemmas

Introduction — Damages

Damages are the "[m]oney claimed by, or ordered to be paid to, a person as compensation for loss or injury."[1] The types of damages that a litigant can recover in a lawsuit depend on the claim filed (personal injury (tort) vs. contract, for example), as well as the jurisdiction. The term damages encompasses monetary compensation for harm that the plaintiff has already suffered, as well as harm which the plaintiff is reasonably certain to suffer in the future because of the defendant's conduct.[2] Damages can also be non-economic. For example, a plaintiff in a personal injury case may be awarded damages for pain and suffering, while a plaintiff in a wrongful death claim may be awarded damages for loss of consortium (i.e. loss of the victim's companionship).

The Black's Law Dictionary entry for damages lists 105 different types of damages, too many to cover in this short introduction. In this Unit, you will analyze and learn about two types of damages: compensatory damages, which include both economic and non-economic damages, and punitive damages.

The goal of compensatory damages, also known as actual damages, is to fully compensate an individual for a legally recognized loss.[3] You often hear that compensatory damages aim "to make the plaintiff whole," meaning that the damages should reimburse, compensate or indemnify the injured party for the loss or harm suffered, to the extent that it is possible to measure his or her injury in terms of money.[4] The term covers all loss recoverable as a matter of right, and includes all damages (beyond nominal damages) other than punitive or exemplary damages.[5] Compensatory damages may include economic damages such as lost wages or lost profits, or non-economic damages such as pain and suffering, as mentioned above.

> "Damages have been defined to be the compensation which the law will award for an injury done, and are said to be exemplary and allowable in excess of the actual loss where a tort is aggravated by evil motive, actual malice, deliberate violence, or oppression. While some courts and text writers have questioned the soundness of this doctrine, it has been accepted . . . in most of the states of this Union, and has received the sanction of this court." <u>Scott v. Donald</u>, 165 U.S. 58, 86 (1897).

Punitive damages, on the other hand, are those awarded to a plaintiff to punish the defendant, make an example of his actions and serve as a deterrent for future wrongdoers.[6] Punitive damages are limited in certain ways, however. For example, in a general breach of contract claim they are not allowed, although they may be recoverable in cases in which the defendant's actions are actionable as a tort.[7] Moreover, the Supreme Court has held that punitive damages cannot violate constitutional due process, which can occur when the punitive damages awarded greatly exceed the compensatory or actual damages awarded.[8]

As also stated above, the types and amounts of damages that an injured party can recover depend on the claim and the jurisdiction. For example, awards of damages for claims of employment discrimination brought under the federal law Title VII of the Civil Rights Act of 1964 are limited depending on the size of the employer. If an employer has fewer than 100 employees, the damages are limited to $50,000; the

---

[1]   *Damages*, BLACK'S LAW DICTIONARY (10th ed. 2014).

[2]   25 C.J.S. *Damages* § 10 (Westlaw database updated Sept. 2016).

[3]   <u>Brokaw v. Winfield-Mt. Union Cmty. Sch. Dist.</u>, 788 N.W.2d 386, 389 (Iowa 2010) ("Compensatory damages or actual damages are intended to compensate the victim for the injury sustained by another party's wrongful acts.").

[4]   <u>Stamp v. Vail Corp.</u>, 172 P.3d 437, 448 (Colo. 2007) ("Compensatory damages are intended to make the plaintiff whole.").

[5]   <u>Manning v. Pounds</u>, 199 A.2d 188, 190 (Conn. Cir. Ct. 1963).

[6]   25A C.J.S. *Damages* § 222 (Westlaw database updated Sept. 2016).

[7]   <u>See</u> <u>generally</u>, Timothy J. Sullivan, *Punitive Damages in the Law of Contract: The Reality and the Illusion of Legal Change*, 61 MINN. L. REV. 207, 207 (1977); <u>Conocophillips v. 261 E. Merrick Rd. Corp.</u>, 428 F. Supp. 2d 111, 129 (E.D.N.Y. 2006) (stating that "New York law permits a plaintiff to recover punitive damages in tort actions arising from the parties' contractual relationship if the plaintiff demonstrates (1) that the defendant's conduct is actionable as an independent tort; (2) the tortious conduct [is] of [an] egregious nature; (3) the egregious conduct [is] directed to plaintiff; and (4) it [is] part of a pattern directed at the public generally.").

[8]   <u>See</u> <u>State Farm Mut. Auto. Ins. Co. v. Campbell</u>, 538 U.S. 408, 429 (2003) (holding that award of $145 million in punitive damages on $1 million compensatory judgment violated due process).

amount increases to a statutory maximum of $300,000 for employers with 501 or more employees.[9] As another example, California limits the amount of non-economic damages (pain, suffering) in medical malpractice claims to $250,000.[10] The federal Racketeer Influenced Corrupt Organizations (RICO) Act allows injured parties to bring civil claims (in addition to criminal claims brought by the government) against those who have harmed someone's property or business due to racketeering activities.[11] If the plaintiff is successful, he can recover three times the actual damages suffered (called "treble" damages), in addition to attorney's fees, costs and expenses.[12] As is often the case in the law, the damages that a plaintiff can recover will depend on many factors.

Thus when meeting with a client and discussing the viability of bringing a claim, assessing potential damages is an important part of the attorney's work. If damages are low, the client might decide that it is not worth the time and expense to bring a claim; if damages don't exist, the attorney might not bring the claim since for some causes of action, such as torts, a plaintiff must suffer damages for a claim to be actionable. If the plaintiff suffered no damages, the claim will likely be dismissed for failure to state a claim.

In this Unit, you will analyze a matter that Pamela Park of Stray Dog Advertising is facing. Rather than a business issue involving her company, you will provide her advice about a personal legal issue after her dog is attacked and killed by another dog. The main legal issue presented in this Unit is damages, and you will analyze what damages Pamela could recover if she were successful in bringing a claim against the owner whose dog killed her dog. In addition, you will learn about *respondeat superior*, a doctrine within agency law. Respondeat superior is a Latin term that means "*let the master answer.*"

Under *respondeat superior*, an employer can be held liable for the actions of his employees if those actions are carried out within the scope of employment. You will assess and determine whether the employer of the owner of the dog that killed Pamela's dog can be held liable for his employee's actions and whether the employee's actions were done within the scope of employment. Finally, you will analyze an ethical matter and learn about the ethical duties that attorneys have towards third parties who are not attorneys.

---

[9]   42 U.S.C. § 1981a(b)(3) (2012).

[10] Cal. Civ. Code § 3333.2 (West 2016).

[11] 18 U.S.C. § 1964(c) (2012).

[12] Id.

Main Assignment File: Damages

You have received the following email from Senior Partner Washington about a personal issue that Pamela Park of Stray Dog Advertising is facing. The senior partner would like you to assess the matter and advise Pamela on what she should do.

From: Georgina Washington <g.washington@lawlawfirm.com>
To: Associate Attorney <a.attorney@lawlawfirm.com>
Sent: Monday, November 23, THIS YEAR 8:32
Subject: Client Matter: Dog Bite

Dear Associate Attorney,

We have an interesting new matter that we will be dealing with. It involves Pamela Park, the owner of Stray Dog Advertising. This issue doesn't directly involve her business and is instead a personal matter. Nevertheless, given the amount of work that Pamela brings to the firm, the matter is very important.

I am attaching here an article about an unfortunate incident that happened to Pamela just a few weeks ago. As you will read in the article, Pamela's beloved Maltese dog, Honey, was attacked and killed in the driveway of her home by a dog belonging to an employee of a local construction company, Stone Arch Construction. Pamela had recently contracted with Stone Arch to build an addition to her home, and the employees were working there that morning when the tragedy happened.

Pamela and her wife, Jordan, loved their dog and wanted to be sure that whichever attorney in the firm worked on this matter knew what Honey looked like. This is a picture of the dog.

Pamela wants to know what legal actions she can take against the individual whose dog killed Honey, or against Stone Arch Construction. As you will read, Pamela was present when Honey was attacked and has suffered greatly as a result. She told me that she has been depressed, has lost weight and has not been able to work at 100% capacity since this occurred.

After Honey was attacked, Pamela and Jordan took Honey to the vet for emergency surgery, which ultimately was unsuccessful. But not before they incurred $5,150.00 in vet bills for emergency surgery and care.

These are my thoughts with regard to this matter and what I need you to tell me:

- What, if any, liability the owner has for the dog's action. Look to the Jefferson statutes and find those that address this issue.
- Is the owner responsible for the medical bills that Pamela incurred?
- Under Jefferson law, is the dog's owner required to pay for a replacement dog? Pamela had bought Honey from a breeder about two years ago and paid approximately $1,200 for her. Can the court order the employee to pay for the cost of replacing Honey?
- Can the owner be ordered to pay anything else?
- Are there any other issues that you can identify?

I have attached to this email the Jefferson statutes regarding dogs. I have not had the time to review them to determine which of the statutes (if any) are relevant. You will be responsible for that.

After you analyze the Jefferson law, I want you to also provide counterarguments. If we do bring a claim on Pamela's behalf, what possible defenses could be raised? Let's focus right now on bringing the claim just against the individual, Andrew Weisman. Later, we can research whether we should also bring a claim against Weisman's employer, Stone Arch Construction. I would also like you to provide some recommendations to Pamela on what she should do. In the end, she wants advice and guidance to help her through this difficult time.

Pamela is coming to our office next week and I would like you to prepare a memo for me with your research conclusions.

Georgina

Georgina Washington

Senior Partner

Lincoln, Adams and Washington Law Firm, PLLC

952-350-1100

gwashington@lawlawfirm.com

As you have read, you have been asked to write a predictive memo to Senior Partner Washington about the types of damages that Pamela could likely recover if she were to bring a claim against the owner of the dog that killed Honey.

Washington has asked you to write a memo about the following:

- A summary of what has happened with Pamela and her dog Honey
- The legal issue at hand (damages)
- A summary and analysis of the law that applies (statutes and case law)
- Your opinion about what damages Pamela would be able to recover if she were to bring a claim against Andrew Weisman

You will find complete information about this assignment on the Information Page on pages 32-33.

You will be analyzing the client matter using the damages cases that you read and review in class, the short case summaries included in the email from Senior Partner Washington, as well as the assigned statutes.

Dogs maul man, kill Maltese dog in separate incidents in West Hampton

*November 13, **THIS YEAR** at 11:50am*

By John Marrone

West Hampton - Uncontrolled vicious dogs mauled a man and killed a Maltese dog in two separate incidents in West Hampton over the weekend.

In the first incident, a man was attacked in the Nokomis area of West Hampton and was later admitted to the West Hampton Medical Center, where he had surgery. Hospital spokeswoman Sheila McCarthy said the man was bitten on his arms and left leg. "He could only recall that it was a big dog that attacked him," McCarthy said.

In the second incident, in north West Hampton, local businesswoman Pamela Park, owner of the advertising agency Stray Dog Advertising, watched in horror as her beloved Maltese dog, Honey, was mauled by another dog. Honey died from her injuries the day after the attack. The dog belonged to one of the employees of Stone Arch Construction, LLC, another local business that has been constructing an addition at Park's home over the past months.

Park said she was returning home after a short trip to the supermarket on Saturday morning, and that Stone Arch's employees were working at her home to finish the construction project. Park was greeted by one of her dogs, Sheeba, whom she had left inside earlier that morning after taking a walk with the dogs.

The dog that attacked and killed the Maltese dog belonging to local businesswoman Pamela Park.

On Sheeba's heels was Honey, who came rushing out to greet her owner when she heard Park at the door. What Park did not realize was that the door to one of the Stone Arch Construction trucks had been left open and that inside were two dogs belonging to Andrew Weisman, one of the firm's employees. The dogs ran out of the truck towards Honey.

The big male dog grabbed and bit Honey, who managed to escape and take shelter under Park's car, only to be followed by Weisman's dog, who continued to attack her. The incident was a "gross act of negligence," Park said. Although heroic efforts to save Honey were made by Dr. Veronica Downey of Happy Animals Pet Hospital, the dog died the next day from the injuries suffered in the attack.

However, the owner of the dog denies negligence. He claims that Park should have known that the dogs were present when she returned home and that she should have taken steps to keep her dogs inside her home. "My dogs are not murderers. They are guard dogs that guard the expensive equipment and truck that Stone Arch entrusts us with when we are working," he said.

From: Georgina Washington <g.washington@lawlawfirm.com>
To: Associate Attorney <a.attorney@lawlawfirm.com>
Sent: Tuesday, November 24, THIS YEAR 13:18
Subject: Re: Client Matter: Dog Bite

Associate Attorney,

Two cases were just issued yesterday by the Jefferson Court of Appeals, and they both seem to apply to Pamela's recent case about Honey. You might want to use them in your analysis.

The primary limitation on consequential damages is that a party is only liable for damages that, at the time a harm is suffered, are reasonably foreseeable to the parties. The harmed party has the burden to demonstrate such damages with a reasonable degree of certainty and exactness. The harmed party also has an obligation to take reasonable measures to mitigate damages. Applying these principles to the case at hand, we conclude that consequential damages are those reasonably foreseeable by the parties at the time the harm is suffered, subject to the prevailing party's duty to mitigate damages. Cnty. of Blue Earth v. Wingen, 684 N.W.2d 919, 924-25 (Jeff. Ct. App. THIS YEAR).

Plaintiff has a duty to mitigate damages by acting reasonably in obtaining treatment for her injury. Couture v. Novotny, 211 N.W.2d 172 (Jeff. Ct. App. THIS YEAR).

Georgina

Georgina Washington

Senior Partner

Lincoln, Adams and Washington Law Firm, PLLC

952-350-1100

gwashington@lawlawfirm.com

Main Assignment File: Respondeat Superior

After doing your initial research about Pamela's legal matter involving Honey and the damages that Pamela could recover if she were to bring a claim against Andrew Weisman, you receive this email from Senior Partner Washington. She is asking you to investigate further the matter and determine whether Pamela should also (or only) name Stone Arch Construction as the defendant in a claim that the firm may bring on Pamela's behalf.

From: Georgina Washington <g.washington@lawlawfirm.com>
To: Associate Attorney <a.attorney@lawlawfirm.com>
Sent: Tuesday, December 1, THIS YEAR 10:55
Subject: Re: Client Matter: Dog Bite

Associate Attorney,

Thank you for your analysis about the damages that Pamela could recover for Honey's death. I would like you to do some additional research for this matter.

I spoke with Andrew Weisman, the Stone Arch Construction employee. Even though the dog that killed Honey belonged to Weisman and not to Stone Arch Construction, I think we still have good arguments that his employer should be held liable for Weisman's actions. Can you research this for me and give me a clear answer of whether we should name both Weisman and Stone Arch as the defendants? Or just Stone Arch Construction?

The reason that I am bringing this up is that based on my conversation with Weisman, I don't think he has the assets to satisfy any judgment that we might obtain from the court for the damages that Pamela has suffered. It makes no sense to bring a claim if there is no chance of recovery, but adding Stone Arch Construction as a defendant might help us in satisfying the judgment.

These are the notes that I jotted down from my conversation with Weisman:

- He is one of 20 employees working for Stone Arch Construction. He is a general construction worker and is not a manager or supervisor. He has been working at Stone Arch for about 3 months.
- The dog that attacked Honey is his, but Edward Ortega, one of the owners of Stone Arch Construction, was aware that Weisman was bringing his dog to work. Apparently Ortega told Weisman not to bring the dogs to work, but didn't take any specific steps to stop him when Weisman continued to do so. Weisman said it was common knowledge at Stone Arch that he brought his dogs to work. No other employees bring their dogs to work.
- Weisman started bringing his dogs to work about a month before the incident with Honey, after the truck that he uses for work was broken into. He said that tools and equipment belonging to him and to Stone Arch were stolen.
- Weisman spoke to Ortega about the theft, but Ortega thought that the crime was a random event and didn't want to take any additional measures, aside from reminding all employees to lock the trucks at all times and not to leave expensive equipment and tools inside and in plain view. The truck was in the parking lot of the Stone Arch offices when it was broken into and belongs to Stone Arch, not to Weisman.

I've attached some case summaries that the law clerk prepared and that should be helpful in preparing an initial analysis of this matter. Please prepare a memo for me about the issue of employer liability for its employee's actions and make a recommendation as to whether we should file the claim also against Stone Arch.

Thanks,

Georgina

Georgina Washington

Senior Partner

Lincoln, Adams and Washington Law Firm, PLLC

952-350-1100

gwashington@lawlawfirm.com

As you have read, you have been asked to write a predictive memo to Senior Partner Washington about whether Stone Arch Construction should be added as a party to the complaint that is filed to recover the damages that Pamela has suffered for Honey's death.

Washington has asked you to write a memo about the following:

- A summary of what has happened with Pamela and her dog Honey
- The legal issue at hand
- A summary and analysis of the law that applies (*respondeat superior*)
- Your opinion about whether you think a court would find Stone Arch Construction liable for its employee's actions and for the damages that Pamela has suffered
- Your advice as to whom should be named as a defendant: Stone Arch Construction? Andrew Weisman? Both?

You will find complete information about this assignment on the Information Page on pages 34-35.

You will use the case summaries on the following pages that were prepared by one of the law firm's law clerks.

Case Summaries: Respondeat Superior

If you study either torts or agency law during your LL.M. program, you will learn about *respondeat superior*, a Latin phrase that means "let the master answer." It is a legal doctrine that holds an employer vicariously liable[13] for the negligent acts committed by an employee while acting within the scope of employment.[14]

The law clerk at the LAW Law Firm began researching the issue to help you respond to Senior Partner Washington's email and sent to you the following rule statements from cases that he found, as well as two case summaries. However, he was unable to thoroughly research the matter as he had to focus on his final exams.

Therefore, you might want to do some additional research, using these cases and the citations included within them as a starting point. Although you will change the citations to Jefferson, all of these cases are from New York courts, with the original citations (not Jefferson). Continue to use New York sources as you do additional research.

---

[13] Vicarious liability is "[l]iability that a supervisory party (such as an employer) bears for the actionable conduct of a subordinate or associate (such as an employee) based on the relationship between the two parties." *Liability*, BLACK'S LAW DICTIONARY (10th ed. 2014).

[14] Crawford v. Westcott Steel Co. Inc., 590 N.Y.S.2d 593, 594 (N.Y. App. Div. 1992).

From: Law Clerk <law.clerk@lawlawfirm.com>
To: Associate Attorney <a.attorney@lawlawfirm.com>
Date: Thursday, December 3 THIS YEAR 16:43
Re: Respondeat Superior Matter for Georgina

Hey Associate Attorney,

I started to research the respondeat superior matter for Georgina but just haven't gotten through all of the cases. So as you'll see, I haven't put them into a proper format for you. I've pasted below summaries of two relevant cases that I found, as well as some rule statements that seem particularly good for the Park matter. I've copied the rules and rule statements from some cases.

So sorry that I can't do a proper job with the cases but I've got tons of studying to do for finals. But these cases and rules give you lots of good information and other cases that you can check out if you want to do more research.

Best,

Law Clerk

GENERAL RULES:

The doctrine of *respondeat superior* holds an employer vicariously liable for the negligent acts committed by an employee while acting in the scope of employment. See Lundberg v. State, 255 N.E.2d 177 (N.Y. 1969); Hall v. Danforth, 567 N.Y.S.2d 958 (N.Y. App. Div. 1991).

"[A]n employee acts within the scope of employment when he [or she] is acting in furtherance of the duties owed to the employer and where the employer is or could be exercising some degree of control, directly or indirectly, over the employee's activities." Swartzlander v. Forms–Rite Bus. Forms & Print. Serv., 572 N.Y.S.2d 537 (N.Y. App. Div. 1991), cited in Crawford v. Westcott Steel Co. Inc., 188 590 N.Y.S.2d 593, 594 (N.Y. 1992).

The general rule is that an employee acts within the scope of his employment when he is acting in furtherance of the duties owed to the employer and where the employer is or could be exercising some degree of control, directly or indirectly, over the employee's activities. See Lundberg, 255 N.E.2d at 179; Matos v Depalma Enters., 554 N.Y.S.2d 367 (N.Y. App. Div. 1990); Bazan v Bohne, 534 N.Y.S.2d 496 (N.Y. App. Div. 1988) , cited in Swartzlander v. Forms-Rite Bus. Forms & Printing Serv., Inc., 572 N.Y.S.2d 537 (N.Y. App. Div. 1991).

In determining whether an employee acted within the scope of his employment, consideration must be given to "the connection between the time, place and occasion for the act; the history of the relationship between employer and employee as spelled out in actual practice; whether the act is one commonly done by such an employee; the extent of departure from normal methods of performance; and whether the specific act was one that the employer could reasonably have anticipated." (Riviello v. Waldron, 391 N.E.2d 1278 (N.Y. 1979) , cited in Sports Car Ctr. of Syracuse, Ltd. v. Bombard, 672 N.Y.S.2d 201, 202-03 (N.Y. App. Div. 1998).

[T]he test [of respondeat superior] has come to be " 'whether the act was done while the servant was doing his master's work, no matter how irregularly, or with what disregard of instructions' " (Jones v. Weigand, 119 N.Y.S. 441 (N.Y. App. Div. 1909) , quoted in Baker v. Allen & Arnink Auto Renting Co., 131 N.E. 551, 552-553 (N.Y. 1921).

Thus formulated, the rule may appear deceptively simple but, because it depends largely on the facts and circumstances peculiar to each case, it is more simply said than applied. Riley v. Standard Oil Co., 132 N.E. 97, 98 (N.Y. 1921). For, while clearly intended to cover an act undertaken at the explicit direction of the employer, hardly a debatable proposition, it also encompasses the far more elastic idea of liability for "any act which can fairly and reasonably be deemed to be an ordinary and natural incident or attribute of that act." Riviello, 391 N.E.2d at 1281 (citing MECHEM ON AGENCY § 1879 (2d ed).

In Riviello, the New York Court of Appeals identified factors the court should consider in applying this test:

Among the factors to be weighed are: the connection between the time, place and occasion for the act; the history of the relationship between employer and employee as spelled out in actual practice; whether the act is one commonly done by such an employee; the extent of departure from normal methods of performance; and whether the specific act was one that the employer could reasonably have anticipated. Riviello, 391 N.E.2d at 1281

If an employee commits acts for purely personal reasons and for purposes of his own interests departs from the line of his duty, his acts constitute an abandonment of his service, the master is not liable. Judith M. v. Sisters of Charity Hosp., 75 N.E.2d 95 (N.Y. 1999) citing Jones, 119 N.Y.S. 441.

CASES:

Swierczynski v. O'Neill, 840 N.Y.S.2d 855 (N.Y. App. Div. 2007).

Procedural and Factual History: Plaintiff brought action to recover for injuries he sustained when his vehicle was struck from behind by vehicle owned and operated by county employee. The Supreme Court entered partial summary judgment in plaintiff's favor, and county appealed. The Supreme Court, Appellate Division, held that county was not liable under doctrine of respondeat superior for employee's negligence and reversed the granting of summary judgment.

Plaintiff's Arguments: The plaintiffs alleged that the defendant was liable for employee's negligence pursuant to the doctrine of respondeat superior because the accident occurred while the employee, a child protective caseworker, was en route to her home after having completed her last field appointment for the day.

Court's Reasoning: "Under the doctrine of respondeat superior, an employer will be liable for the negligence of an employee committed while the employee is acting in the scope of his [or her] employment ... As a general rule, an employee driving to and from work is not acting in the scope of his [or her] employment ... Although such activity is work motivated, the element of control is lacking. An exception to this rule is[ ] that an employee who uses his [or her] car in furtherance of his [or her] work is acting in the scope of his [or her] employment while driving home from his [or her] last business appointment, since such a person is working, and is under his [or her] employer's control, from the time he [or she] leaves the house in the morning until he [or she] returns at night."

The doctrine of respondeat superior as it relates to an employee using his or her vehicle applies only where the employee is under the control of his or her employer from the time that the employee enters his or her vehicle at the start of the workday until the employee leaves the vehicle at the end of the workday as in the case, for example, of a traveling salesperson or repairperson.

Riviello v. Waldron, 391 N.E.2d 1278 (N.Y. 1979).

Facts: Customer of a tavern brought a person injury action against tavern and its employee when that employee of the tavern, while demonstrating to customer self-defense with a pen knife, hit the customer's eye with a knife blade. Employee, who wore "several hats" at the tavern, but notably short-order cook, was talking with customer and demonstrating self-defense, but not cooking or carrying out his specific job duties. Between cooking meals for other customers, he went to the end of the bar, and while talking with the customer, flipped open a pocket knife and accidently hit the customer in the eye.

Defendant's Argument: Defendant argued that talking with customers and demonstrating self-defense was not part of employment so it could not be liable under vicarious liability.

Court's Reasoning: Court disagreed with the defendant/tavern: "For an employee to be regarded as acting within the scope of his employment, the employer need not have foreseen the precise act or the exact manner of the injury as long as the general type of conduct may have been reasonably expected."

So no longer is an employer necessarily excused merely because his employees, acting in furtherance of his interests, exhibit human failings and perform negligently or otherwise than in an authorized manner. Instead, the test has come to be whether the act was done while the servant was doing his master's work, no matter how irregularly, or with what disregard of instructions.

Additional Skills-Building Exercises

 **Ethics Dilemma**

Background for the Exercise:

The Rules of Professional Conduct regulate the actions, conduct, and behavior of lawyers in their interactions with clients, non-clients, opposing counsel, and judges and establish standards for attorney conduct and for the legal profession. Each state has promulgated its own set of Rules of Professional Conduct although the ABA Model Rules of Professional Conduct serve as a model for the rules of most states.

Being familiar with the Rules is fundamental for all attorneys. Like the law, ignorance of the rules is no defense. And while a violation of the rules can but does not always equate to legal malpractice, attorneys can end up in serious trouble for a violation. Punishment can range from a private or public admonishment to suspension of one's license to practice law and to disbarment (the removal of an attorney from the practice of law and revocation of his or her license).

Overview of the Exercise: For this exercise, you and a partner will analyze whether Senior Partner Washington violated the Jefferson Rules of Professional Conduct when she contacted and spoke with Andrew Weisman, the Stone Arch Construction employee.

Learning Objectives of the Exercise:

This exercise will build your skills to:

- Skim a reading selection (the Rules of Professional Conduct) and identify quickly which rule pertains to your facts and is relevant
- Interpret language of rules and apply the rules
- Articulate your analysis and conclusion about whether the Rules of Professional Conduct were violated

Steps for Completing the Exercise:

Use the ABA Model Rules of Professional Conduct for this exercise and assume that they are the same as the Jefferson Rules of Professional Conduct. Use a search engine like Google or Bing to locate the rules, or your professional responsibility course book if you are enrolled in the class. You can also find the rules on Westlaw, LexisNexis or Bloomberg Law. Skim over the titles to the Rules and identify which one will likely provide you with guidance to analyze this dilemma.

Don't forget to read the comments in addition to the rule itself as the comments often provide valuable insight as to how the rule should be applied.

If you like, you can also search legal ethics opinions to better determine whether Senior Partner Washington violated the rules or not. Legal ethics opinions can be found on the ABA website as well as the legal search engines.

Once you have identified the Rule that applies, read it and the accompanying comments. Discuss with your classmate or partner (depending on the instructions from your instructor) your opinion about whether the Rules were violated. Together you will analyze the language of the Rules and apply it to the fact situation and to Senior Partner Washington's conversation with Andrew Weisman. If you and your partner(s) reach different conclusions, defend your answer.

Once each of the groups has analyzed the matter, you will compare answers with your other classmates.

Grading: This exercise is not graded.

Damages Analysis Exercises

Overview of the Exercise: The following short fact patterns deal with damages. Your task is to analyze the fact patterns and answer the questions about damages that are presented with them.

Attorneys meet with potential clients, many of whom want to bring a claim against someone for a harm that the potential client has suffered. The client will likely use the more colloquial term and say that he or she wants to sue someone. An extremely important part of the attorney's work when meeting with a potential client is analyzing and evaluating the claims that the individual may bring. This analysis and evaluation will assist the attorney in deciding whether or not to accept the representation.

There are many important facts to consider when evaluating a potential client and his claims, especially when the attorney will be commencing litigation on behalf of the new client.

Many attorneys have a checklist of questions to ask:

- Does the potential client have the money to pay a retainer and pay for litigation?
- Can the potential client establish a prima facie case for the claim(s) that the attorney would bring?
- What evidence exists to support the claims?
- Do any conflicts of interest exist with other clients that the firm or attorney represents?
- What damages has the client suffered?

The last question – damages – is extremely important. Some claims, such as tort claims and personal injury, require damages, and without damages the claim will be dismissed. For other matters, low damages might be a reason not to take the case. If the client suffered only nominal damages, is it worth the time and expense of litigation? It all depends, but an evaluation of damages is essential in determining whether to accept representation of a potential client.

Learning Objectives of the Exercise:

This exercise will build your skills to:

- Analyze short fact patterns for the issue of damages
- Analyze legal issues from different perspectives, including legal, non-legal and ethical
- Articulate and effectively communicate that analysis using legal terminology

Steps for Completing the Exercise:

- Read the following fact patterns.
- By yourself, analyze each one and answer the questions presented. When you reach an answer, be sure to articulate your reasoning.
- When you are done analyzing each of the fact patterns, discuss your answers with the partner that you have been assigned. Explain to each other why you have reached the conclusion that you did.
- If you and your partner have different responses to a fact pattern, you must try to convince him or her that your answer is correct. After you both have tried to convince the other, you must choose a team answer.
- Once you have discussed each of the fact patterns, you will compare answers as a class.

Grading: This exercise is not graded. Instead, you will compare answers with your classmates.

1. Two potential clients come to the Lincoln, Adams and Washington law firm seeking advice about whether they should bring a claim. The legal issue each client is facing is defamation.

Potential client #1 is a financial advisor. She discovered Tweets and Facebook posts about her, all written by the same person, who claimed that she had stolen client money and had been arrested for fraud. The claims are false. However, the potential client has not lost any clients because of the posts nor suffered any actual damages because of them. The posts and Tweets were deleted after a week; the person who posted them is a former friend of the potential client and has about 25 followers combined on both Facebook and Twitter.

Potential client #2 is also a financial advisor who also found Facebook posts and Tweets about him; they had been posted by his ex-wife. In the posts and Tweets, she stated that he was a "womanizer" and a "gigolo" who "used and abused" women. He says that those allegations are false. His ex-wife also posted on her Facebook page a link to a newspaper article about when he was arrested for domestic violence; the article now comes up on the first page of Google when an online search of his name is conducted. As a result, it has been very hard for him to find women to date because they all see the newspaper article and his ex-wife's social media posts about him. His employer has also terminated him because of his past arrest, which his boss learned about through his ex-wife's social media activity (his boss and ex-wife are friends, both online and in real life).

Analyze whether you suggest that the LAW Law Firm accept the representation of these potential clients. In analyzing this issue, consider:

- Do the potential clients have viable claims of defamation?
- Have the potential clients suffered damages?
- Do the potential defendants have defenses that they could raise if a claim were filed?
- Should the LAW Law Firm accept representation of these clients? Why or why not?

2. Evan is a potential client who meets with you about bringing a claim under the Family Medical Leave Act, a federal law that provides employees 12 weeks of job-protected, unpaid leave for a serious medical condition of the employee or of his or her spouse.

Evan is a truck driver for a large national transportation company. He is properly classified as an independent contractor. Last week, Evan notified the company that he would need to take off 12 weeks to care for his wife, who is scheduled for open heart surgery. The day after he gave this notification, his contract was terminated, effective immediately. This is the termination provision of the contract:

> TERMINATION: Both parties retain the right to terminate the Agreement by providing two weeks' written notice to the other party. Termination need not be for a just cause or for any cause.

Evan was earning approximately $104,000 per year working as a truck driver for this company and wants to bring a claim under the FMLA, which prevents employers from interfering with employees' rights under the law (such as terminating them when they wish to take a leave or not allowing them to return to their same position after the leave).

- What claim would you bring against the trucking company (if any)?
- What damages would Evan be entitled to if you were to bring a claim? How much could he potentially recover?
- Is the claim worth taking for the law firm? Do you tell Evan that the law firm will represent him? Why or why not?

3. Jefferson statute section 491A.01 provides for the establishment of conciliation court, or small claims court. The pertinent part of the statute is copied below. The jurisdictional limit of conciliation court is $15,000; any claims worth more than that amount must be heard in district court. Conciliation court is a lot less expensive than district court (filing fees of $70 compared to $325), the time to resolve a matter is significantly less and the costs and expenses are also much less (no discovery and also parties don't need an attorney in conciliation court).

A potential client, James, comes to your office to discuss a breach of contract claim that he would like to bring against a company that hasn't paid him for work that he performed. James operates a janitorial business and cleans office buildings in Jefferson City. He is owed approximately $21,000 by the owner of several office buildings in the city. He also told you that this owner has repeatedly lied to James about paying him and even mocked him when he called to ask about payment, causing James great embarrassment and humiliation. He even told James that he was a "loser" who ran a "lousy business" and that he "stole from his clients." When James asked the owner if he had repeated these false statements to anyone else, the owner said that he had not.

- What damages could James recover in this case?
- What advice do you give him about the case? Should he file in conciliation court? District court?
- If you suggest that James file in conciliation court, he might not ask to be represented by you/the firm. If you suggest that he file in district court, he will need your representation and services. Do the fees that the firm would earn play any part in your decision?
- Do you agree to represent James? Why or why not?

Jeff. Stat. § 491A.01 ESTABLISHMENT OF CONCILIATION COURT; POWERS; JURISDICTION.[15]

Subdivision 1. Establishment.

 The district court in each county shall establish a conciliation court division with the jurisdiction and powers set forth in this chapter.

Subd. 2. Powers; issuance of process.

 The conciliation court has all powers, and may issue process as necessary or proper to carry out the purposes of this chapter. No writ of execution or garnishment summons may be issued out of conciliation court.

Subd. 3a. Jurisdiction; general.

 Except as provided in subdivision, the conciliation court has jurisdiction to hear, conciliate, try, and determine civil claims if the amount of money or property that is the subject matter of the claim does not exceed $15,000.

Subd. 4. Jurisdiction; exclusions.

 The conciliation court does not have jurisdiction over the following actions:
- involving title to real estate, including actions to determine boundary lines;
- involving claims of defamation by libel or slander;
- for specific performance;
- brought or defended on behalf of a class;
- where jurisdiction is vested exclusively in another court or division of district court;
- for eviction; and
- involving medical malpractice.

4. Valerie owns and operates a successful recycling company in the state of Jefferson. She has come to your office about a trademark matter. Her business logo is very distinct and incorporates trees into a modern graphic. Last week, Valerie saw another local company that was displaying some t-shirts with Valerie's logo on them; she had never given her permission to use the logo. Valerie spoke immediately with the other business owner, who explained that he didn't know that the logo was hers. He also explained that he had only sold one t-shirt. He immediately gave the remaining ones to Valerie and promised not to sell any others. Valerie is very upset about this since she has worked hard to build up her brand recognition.

- Can she bring a claim for trademark violation under the federal Lanham Act, even without any apparent damages?
- What do you advise Valerie to do? Do you accept her representation?

5. A personal injury client, Tracy, comes to your office. She explains to you that she was in a car accident two days ago. Her car was totaled, or completely destroyed. Fortunately, she suffered no injuries. The day

---

[15] From Minnesota Statute §491A.01.

after the crash, she went to the gym, where she ran and lifted weights. Today, she went to work in a retail store, standing all day, before coming to your office. She tells you that she would like to file a claim since "the insurance company will pay, not the other driver." From experience, you know that the insurance company will likely offer $10,000 to settle; your firm would get 40% of that amount on a contingency basis.

- Do you bring a claim on behalf of Tracy? Why or why not?
- What damages would you claim?
- Do you agree to represent Tracy? Why or why not?

6. Another potential client, Raul, comes to your office. Raul had signed a lease for a commercial space in which he planned to operate a new restaurant. Raul's business plan had estimated that he would open one month after the lease was signed and earn approximately $10,000 per month in profits once opened. Unfortunately, three days after signing the lease, the landlord told Raul that he had changed his mind and that he was going to let his daughter use the space for a restaurant that she wants to open. That was six months ago and Raul has not been able to find another space to lease. Before the landlord changed his mind, Raul had not signed any other contracts, such as with a construction firm or other service providers, that he is liable for.

- What claim could Raul bring?
- What damages could Raul claim?
- What do you advise Raul to do? Do you accept his representation?

7. Potential clients Hazel and Lee come to your office to discuss with you a claim that they would like to bring against their neighbor. Hazel and Lee discovered a short while ago that when their neighbors constructed a fence between their backyards two years ago, the fence was mistakenly built 2 inches (5 cm.) over Hazel and Lee's property line. They discovered this when they hired a surveyor because they plan to sell their home.

On their behalf, you send a demand letter to the neighbors, who then send it to their attorney. You demand that they remove the fence immediately and threatened to file a complaint in Jefferson State Court against them if they fail to do so. In his response, the neighbors' attorney told you that if you file the claim, he will successfully file a motion to dismiss since Hazel and Lee can show no damages since they didn't notice that the fence was on their property for two years and since 2 inches is so insignificant that it cannot constitute damages. He also threatened to bring a motion for sanctions since you would knowingly file a complaint that fails to state a claim since you can't prove any damages.

- You are now unsure if you should file a claim since it seems that there are no damages.
- Is the neighbors' attorney correct? Why or why not?
- What damages can Lee and Hazel show?
- Should you file a claim on their behalf? Why or why not?

Presentations: If Pamela Park Were Your Client...

Overview of the Exercise: For this exercise, you will make a professional presentation in which you answer and discuss the following question: *If Pamela Park were your client in your home country and if Pamela came to you for legal advice about her dog's death, what would you do and what advice would you give her?*

Learning Objectives of the Exercise:

This exercise will build your skills to:

- Describe a specific aspect of your country's legal system
- Compare your country's legal system with the U.S. legal system
- Listen to and understand your classmates' presentations and complete information about them

Steps for Completing the Exercise:

- Analyze the fact pattern of damages with regard to Honey's death under your country's laws.
- Determine:
  - Whether or not Andrew Weisman and/or Stone Arch Construction could be held liable for Honey's death;
  - Whether or not Pamela Park could or should bring a claim against Andrew Weisman and/or Stone Arch Construction for Honey's death;
- If she does, what damages could she recover and the legal basis for recovering such damages.
- Explain what other claims Pamela could bring against Weisman and/or Stone Arch Construction and explain how the case would be handled in your country's legal system.
- Explain what legal advice you would give Pamela if she came to you for legal advice in your home country.

Research Required for the Exercise:

The research you are required to do depends on your knowledge of these claims in your country's legal system. It is presumed that you are familiar with the law and with how you would approach this issue if she were a client of yours at home.

Grading: This presentation is not graded. You will present to a small group of your fellow classmates instead of to the entire class.

Handouts:

As part of your presentation, you must create a handout for your classmates, and the handouts must include fill-in-the-blank questions that your classmates must complete with information that you present during the presentation. Each handout must include at least five questions to complete.

For example, if U.S. law student were giving a presentation on this issue, she could include this question on her handout:

> Under American law, compensatory damages are divided into _____ and _____ losses.

> The correct answer would be economic and non-economic damages.

As you are speaking, your classmates will have to listen, follow what you are saying and fill in the blanks. If you are listening to one of your classmate's presentations and are unsure about an answer, you should ask him or her to repeat so you can fill in the blank(s).

Grammar Review:

The basis of this exercise is hypothetical or conditional verbs: *if Pamela were your client, what would you do?*

Remember the grammar when discussing hypothetical conditions.

Present: **IF + PAST SIMPLE, WOULD + BASE VERB**

*If Pamela **called** me to schedule an appointment, I **would tell** her to visit me at my office.*

NOTE: We use "were" for all tenses with the verb "to be" when using a conditional verb.

*If I **were** you, I **would not take** that class.*

*If Pamela **were** my client, I **would tell** her she could recover the cost of replacing Honey plus the medical expenses, but not punitive damages.*

Past: **IF + PAST PERFECT, WOULD + HAVE + PAST PARTICIPLE**

*If Pamela **had paid** more attention, this **would not have happened** because she would have seen Weisman's dogs.*

*If Weisman **had not brought** his dogs to the construction site, Honey **would** still **be** alive.*

Information Pages

Office Memo: Damages

Overview of the Assignment: For this assignment, you will write an office memo to the Senior Partner, summarizing your research on the damages available in the dog bite matter and providing your prediction of what damages Pamela would be able to recover if litigation were commenced. You should also give recommendations and advice to Park on what she should do.

Learning Objectives of the Assignment:

This assignment will build your skills to:

- Efficiently communicate in a written format
- Explain complex matters clearly and concisely
- Analyze and apply the rules of law regarding damages

Research for the Assignment: You are not required to do any outside research for this assignment. You should base your analysis on the Minnesota statutes and damages cases that you read:

- Soucek v. Banham, 524 N.W.2d 478 (Minn. Ct. App. 1994).
- State v. Graham, No. C1-02-887, 2003 WL 282470 (Minn. Ct. App. Feb. 11, 2003).
- State v. Weber, No. C4-94-1145, 1995 WL 238940 (Minn. Ct. App. Apr. 25, 1995).
- Jensen v. Walsh, 623 N.W.2d 247 (Minn. 2001).

If you want to practice your legal research skills, you can look for and use other cases that you find. However, if you do search on Westlaw, LexisNexis or Bloomberg Law, be sure to limit your search and the cases you use to Minnesota law and remember to change the citations and legal references to Jefferson law as indicated in the introduction.

Format of the Completed Assignment:

Your response should be in an office memo format and should include the following:

- Summary of the facts
- The relevant law
- Analysis of the law to the fact pattern
- Conclusion about how you think a court would rule if this matter were to go to court
- Your advice to the client about how to proceed

Follow the following format:

- 1 inch (2.54 cm.) margins (top/bottom and sides)
- 12 font, Times New Roman font
- Double spaced
- Maximum six pages

Notes: This memo should be predictive and not persuasive. You are not trying to persuade the senior partner or the client about the strength of your arguments or urge him to take a particular course of action; you are only trying to inform about the law, how it applies to our case, how you think a court would rule and what advice you have.

In a memo, you can also use formatting like underlining, bold font or italics. You can also create headings and subheadings to organize your answer.

For additional information about office memos and e-memos, as well as samples, refer to the online additional resources.

Grading: This assignment is worth 102 points.

Unit 1   Damages

LEGAL CONTENT	0-6 points	8 points	10 points	12 points	Points
Issue statement (IS)	Document does not include an IS or includes IS that fails to properly identify the legal issue(s) and the applicable law	Identifies the legal issue(s) and correctly states the applicable law with minor mistakes	Identifies the legal issue(s) and correctly states the applicable law	Identifies the legal issue(s) and correctly states the applicable law in an exceptionally creative and concise way	_____/12
Short Answer	Document does not include a short answer or includes a short answer with significant mistakes	Responds to IS but with key facts or applicable legal principles missing	Responds to IS with key facts and applicable legal principles with no meaningful errors	Clearly and concisely responds to IS with key facts and applicable legal principles and no irrelevancies	_____/12
Facts	Few or none of the relevant facts are included; difficult to follow or understand	Most relevant facts are included as well as non-relevant ones; at times difficult to follow	Relevant facts are included with occasional irrelevancies; easy to follow	All relevant facts are included with no irrelevancies; story is clearly and concisely told to reader in objective way	_____/12
Rule	Hard to follow and understand; does not include relevant sources or cites inappropriate sources; no rule application	Cites to some relevant sources but is incomplete in covering all relevant aspects of the rule; includes some rule application	Cite only to relevant sources and mostly clear; rule application explains but not fully how rule has been applied	Clear and concise; includes only relevant sources and includes all parts of rule necessary for analysis; clear rule application	_____/12
Analysis	Contains conclusory statements and/or no case law; facts are analyzed in a conclusory or insufficient way	Uses some case law but does not analogize or distinguish or explain its application; some conclusory statements; facts briefly analyzed	Uses case law to show how rule applies to case; case law is compared and contrasted with success; most facts are analyzed	Analyzes case law completely, comparing it fully to client matter; facts are thoroughly analyzed in an objective way	_____/12
Conclusion/ Recommendations	No conclusion or recommendations are included in document	A brief conclusion is included but without sufficient client advice	Paper includes conclusion and recommendations	Paper includes full conclusion of the legal analysis and facts and presents creative and thoughtful recommendations	_____/12
Citations	No sources are cited in document	Some sources are cited, but inconsistently; citation format is inconsistent	All citations are present; correct format is mostly used	All citations are present; correct format is used throughout document	_____/12
WRITING	**2**	**4**	**5**	**6**	**Points**
Formatting	Document does not follow format instructions or the sample provided	Document attempts to follow instructions and sample provided	Document follows the instructions and sample provided with no meaningful errors	Document exactly follows the instructions and sample provided	_____/6
Organization	No structure or organization; free flow of ideas	Structure & organization present but reorganization or headings needed for full clarity	Document is clearly organized and structured with proper use of heading and subheadings	Document is exceptionally well organized and structured with proper use of headings and subheadings	_____/6
Syntax Mechanics	Contains numerous and distracting grammatical and mechanical errors that impede understanding	Contains some grammatical and mechanical errors that impede understanding	Contains few grammatical and mechanical errors but none that impede understanding	Contains no grammatical and mechanical errors; native-like use of English	_____/6
TOTAL					_____/102

Office Memo: Respondeat Superior

Overview of the Assignment: For this assignment, you will write an office memo to the Senior Partner, summarizing your research on whether Stone Arch Construction could be held liable for Andrew Weisman's actions and providing a recommendation to the Senior Partner and Park about whom should be named as a defendant in the claim.

Learning Objectives of the Assignment:

This assignment will build your skills to:

- Efficiently communicate in a written format
- Explain complex matters clearly and concisely
- Analyze and apply the rules of law regarding *respondeat superior*

Research for the Assignment: For this assignment, you can research New York cases of *respondeat superior* using the case summaries and rule statements that are provided to you in the Main Assignment File and that the law clerk prepared for you.

You might find it necessary to do additional research to better understand the issue or to look for cases that you can use for your case analysis. You can use this research provided to you as a starting point for finding additional cases, if necessary.

Format of the Completed Assignment:

Your response should be in an office memo format and should include the following:

- Summary of the facts
- The relevant law
- Analysis of the law to the fact pattern
- Conclusion about how you think a court would rule if this matter were to go to court
- Your advice to the client about how to proceed

Follow the following format:

- 1 inch (2.54 cm.) margins (top/bottom and sides)
- 12 font, Times New Roman font
- Double spaced
- Maximum six pages

Notes: This memo should be predictive and not persuasive. You are not trying to persuade the senior partner or the client about the strength of your arguments or urge him to take a particular course of action; you are only trying to inform about the law, how it applies to our case, how you think a court would rule and what advice you have.

In a memo, you can also use formatting like underlining, bold font or italics. You can also create headings and subheadings to organize your answer.

For additional information about office memos and e-memos, as well as samples, refer to the online additional resources.

Grading: This assignment is worth 102 points.

LEGAL CONTENT	0-6 points	8 points	10 points	12 points	Points
Issue statement (IS)	Document does not include an IS or includes IS that fails to properly identify the legal issue(s) and the applicable law	Identifies the legal issue(s) and correctly states the applicable law with minor mistakes	Identifies the legal issue(s) and correctly states the applicable law	Identifies the legal issue(s) and correctly states the applicable law in an exceptionally creative and concise way	_____/12
Short Answer	Document does not include a short answer or includes a short answer with significant mistakes	Responds to IS but with key facts or applicable legal principles missing	Responds to IS with key facts and applicable legal principles with no meaningful errors	Clearly and concisely responds to IS with key facts and applicable legal principles and no irrelevancies	_____/12
Facts	Few or none of the relevant facts are included; difficult to follow or understand	Most relevant facts are included as well as non-relevant ones; at times difficult to follow	Relevant facts are included with occasional irrelevancies; easy to follow	All relevant facts are included with no irrelevancies; story is clearly and concisely told to reader in objective way	_____/12
Rule	Hard to follow and understand; does not include relevant sources or cites inappropriate sources; no rule application	Cites to some relevant sources but is incomplete in covering all relevant aspects of the rule; includes some rule application	Cite only to relevant sources and mostly clear; rule application explains but not fully how rule has been applied	Clear and concise; includes only relevant sources and includes all parts of rule necessary for analysis; clear rule application	_____/12
Analysis	Contains conclusory statements and/or no case law; facts are analyzed in a conclusory or insufficient way	Uses some case law but does not analogize or distinguish or explain its application; some conclusory statements; facts briefly analyzed	Uses case law to show how rule applies to case; case law is compared and contrasted with success; most facts are analyzed	Analyzes case law completely, comparing it fully to client matter; facts are thoroughly analyzed in an objective way	_____/12
Conclusion/ Recommendations	No conclusion or recommendations are included in document	A brief conclusion is included but without sufficient client advice	Paper includes conclusion and recommendations	Paper includes full conclusion of the legal analysis and facts and presents creative and thoughtful recommendations	_____/12
Citations	No sources are cited in document	Some sources are cited, but inconsistently; citation format is inconsistent	All citations are present; correct format is mostly used	All citations are present; correct format is used throughout document	_____/12
WRITING	**2**	**4**	**5**	**6**	**Points**
Formatting	Document does not follow format instructions or the sample provided	Document attempts to follow instructions and sample provided	Document follows the instructions and sample provided with no meaningful errors	Document exactly follows the instructions and sample provided	_____/6
Organization	No structure or organization; free flow of ideas	Structure & organization present but reorganization or headings needed for full clarity	Document is clearly organized and structured with proper use of heading and subheadings	Document is exceptionally well organized and structured with proper use of headings and subheadings	_____/6
Syntax Mechanics	Contains numerous and distracting grammatical and mechanical errors that impede understanding	Contains some grammatical and mechanical errors that impede understanding	Contains few grammatical and mechanical errors but none that impede understanding	Contains no grammatical and mechanical errors; native-like use of English	_____/6
TOTAL					_____/102

Mock Client Meeting

Overview of this Assignment: This assignment simulates a client meeting between you and your client, Pamela Park of Stray Dog Advertising, LLC. You are meeting with Park to discuss the potential claims that she may bring against Andrew Weisman and/or his employer, Stone Arch Construction.

The meeting is scheduled after you have had the opportunity to study the law of damages and *respondeat superior* and to evaluate Weisman's liability for his dog's actions, as well as his employer's for its employee's actions. You are expected to discuss both legal issues and all possible legal claims relating to the fact pattern, as well as the potential damages that Park would be entitled to.

Your instructor will indicate to you the time that you will have available for the mock client meeting.

Learning Objectives of this Assignment:

After completing this assignment, students will be able to:

- Explain and clarify the legal positions of the parties and describe potential outcomes to your client
- Respond to technical questions about litigation
- Incorporate technical legal English vocabulary that relates to damages and *respondeat superior* and use appropriate layperson explanations for your client

Steps for Completing the Assignment:

- Read and be familiar with the Main Assignment File
- Be familiar with the damages cases that you have been assigned as well as the issue of *respondeat superior*
- Recommended:
    - Anticipate the questions that you think your client might ask and prepare possible responses
    - Draft an outline of what you would like to cover in the meeting

Note: Remember that part of the grading is also based on your professional demeanor. You are expected to arrive punctually, be dressed in professional attire and act as you would with a client in real life. You should play the part from when you come into the meeting room.

Grading: This assignment worth 102 points.

Punctuality: Student-attorney arrived on time to meeting: YES _____ (10 points) NO _____ (0 points)

Professional Attire: Student-attorney was dressed in appropriate professional attire: YES _____ (10 points) NO _____ (0 points)

Professional Demeanor: Student-attorney acted in a professional manner w/ client: YES _____ (10 points) NO _____ (0 points)

GRADING CRITERIA	0- 6 points	8 points (C or 75%)	10 points (B or 85%)	12 points	Points received
Engagement I (questions)	Attorney does not ask client any questions; engages in monologue	Attorney asks few questions; questions are hard to follow or show minimal preparation or understanding of matter	Attorney asks basic questions that demonstrate understanding of matter and preparation	Attorney asks thoughtful, insightful and creative questions that demonstrate deep preparation & understanding of matter	_____/12
Engagement II (answers)	Attorney does not respond to client's questions	Attorney responds to questions, but incorrectly or with hard to follow answers	Attorney responds promptly and correctly to all of client's questions	Attorney responds promptly and correctly to all of client's questions with creative, thoughtful and insightful answers that show a deep understanding of the issues	_____/12
Knowledge of Applicable Law	Attorney provides no explanation of the applicable law	Attorney provides explanation of with serious mistakes, or hard to follow (e.g. use of legal jargon)	Attorney provides clear explanation of with some mistakes; uses some legal jargon unnecessarily or without explanations that client can understand	Attorney provides clear, concise and correct explanation of the law with legal jargon when appropriate or w/ explanations client can understand	_____/12
Ability to Analyze Applicable Law	Attorney provides does not provide an analysis of the law for the client	Attorney attempts to analyze the law but provides incomplete or incorrect analysis	Attorney provides analysis of the law with no significant mistakes or misstatements of the law or facts	Attorney provides a clear, concise and correct analysis of the law as it applies to the client matter	_____/12
Advice and Recommendations	Attorney provides no advice or poor advice for client	Attorney provides not comprehensive or inaccurate advice	Attorney provides comprehensive and accurate advice to client on his/her legal matter	Attorney provides thoughtful and creative solutions for client	_____/12
Organization	Meeting is disorganized and hard to follow or lacks any organization	Meeting has some organization but is still confusing for client for how information is presented	Meeting is clearly organized and easy to follow	Meeting is clearly organized and is easy to follow; attorney takes extra steps to ensure client's understanding	_____/12
TOTAL					_____/72
TOTAL FROM PUNCTUALITY AND PROFESSIONALISM					_____/30

Total _____/102

Client Advice Letter

Overview of the Assignment: For this assignment, you will write an advice and follow-up letter to Pamela Park, summarizing your research on damages and *respondeat superior*, as well as your meeting with her. You should also give recommendations to Park about how she should approach this matter. Be mindful that even though your client may be a sophisticated businesswoman, she is not a trained attorney. Therefore you should avoid legalese in your letter.

Under Rule 1.4(a)(3) of the Model Rules of Professional Conduct, an attorney has the duty to keep his or her client "reasonably informed about the status of the client's matter." A thorough follow-up letter after a client meeting is one of the best ways to meet this duty, as well as regular phone calls, emails or meetings.

Learning Objectives of the Assignment:

This assignment will build your skills to:

- Efficiently communicate in a written format
- Explain complex matters clearly and concisely
- Incorporate technical legal English vocabulary that relates to damages *and respondeat superior* and use appropriate layperson explanations for the client

Steps for Completing the Assignment:

- Review the predictive memos that you wrote to your senior partner about your client matter to ensure that the law and the issues are clear
- Be familiar with the case law regarding damages and *respondeat superior*, as well as the fact pattern
- Conduct your client meeting with your client, Pamela Park
- Review the Business Correspondence online resources

Research Required for the Assignment: You are not required to do any outside research for this assignment.

Format of the Completed Assignment:

Your assignment should be written as a business letter, not as an email. Even though many firms and lawyers use email for much of the correspondence carried out, formal business letters are still an essential part of the practice of law.

Your law firm has the following policy regarding business correspondence. Your client letter must follow the policy guidelines.

LAW FIRM CORRESPONDENCE POLICY

The purpose of this policy is to ensure a uniform appearance of all business correspondence that is written by the attorneys and staff of the law firm and thus to increase the professional appearance of the firm's work product. All law firm attorneys and staff are required to follow these guidelines when writing correspondence. Violation of the policy can result in disciplinary action, up to and including termination.

- The first page of all "traditional" letters must be written on law firm letterhead, which includes the firm's address and logo
- All letters must be written in a modified block letter format
- Letters must be written in Times New Roman, 12 font
- Letters must be 1.5 spaced and have 1" (2.54 cm.) margins, except for the initial page, which may have larger top margins to account for the logo, law firm address and sender's direct contact information
- Client letters must not exceed four pages

Grading: This assignment is worth 78 points.

Note: See the Online Additional Resources for examples of letters and for general information about business correspondence.

LEGAL CONTENT	0-6 points (failing)	8 points (C or 75%)	10 points (B or 85%)	12 points	Points
Introduction	Letter does not include an appropriate introduction or includes poorly constructed one	Letter includes introduction that states purpose with some irrelevancies or some relevant information missing	Introduction states purpose of letter and includes other relevant information	Introduction is engaging; states purpose of letter and includes other relevant information; written clearly and concisely	_____/12
Summary of Meeting	Letter includes no summary of the meeting	Letter includes summary but leaves out important information or states it unclearly	Letter summarizes the meeting but leaves out important information	Letter clearly and concisely summarizes the meeting, its core purpose and content	_____/12
Applicable Law	Student-attorney provides no explanation of the applicable law, or only uses legal jargon in explanation (inappropriate for audience)	Student-attorney provides explanation of with serious mistakes, or hard to follow (use of legal jargon)	Student-attorney provides clear explanation of with few mistakes; uses some legal jargon without appropriate explanations	Student-attorney provides clear, concise and correct explanation of the law with legal jargon with appropriate explanations	_____/12
Analysis	Contains conclusory statements and/ or no case law; facts are analyzed in a conclusory or insufficient way	Uses some case law but does not analogize or distinguish or explain its application; some conclusory statements; facts briefly analyzed	Uses case law to show how rule applies to case; case law is compared and contrasted with success; most facts are analyzed	Analyzes completely case law, comparing it fully to client matter; facts are thoroughly analyzed	_____/12
Conclusion/ Recommendations	No conclusion or recommendations are included in letter	A brief conclusion is included but without sufficient advice or recommendations advice or next steps	Letter includes conclusion with recommendations and next steps	Letter includes full conclusion of the legal analysis and facts, presents creative and thoughtful recommendations and includes clear next steps	_____/12
WRITING	2	4	5	6	Points
Formatting	Document does not follow format instructions or the sample provided	Document attempts to follow instructions and sample provided	Document follows the instructions and sample provided with minor errors	Document exactly follows the instructions and sample provided	_____/6
Organization	No structure or organization; free flow of ideas	Letter includes organization and structure but is still confusing	Structure and organization but some reorganization is needed for full clarity	Document is clearly organized and structured	_____/6
Syntax Mechanics	Contains numerous and distracting grammatical and mechanical errors that impede understanding	Contains some grammatical and mechanical errors that impede understanding	Contains few grammatical and mechanical errors but none that impede understanding	Contains no grammatical and mechanical errors; native-like use of English	_____/6
TOTAL					_____/78

Common Law

Unit 2 Apparent Authority
Advertising Services Contract Dispute

For this Unit, you will provide your opinion on a contract dispute involving Stray Dog Advertising and one of SDA's new clients, Canopy, Inc. The legal issue involved is apparent authority, a doctrine of agency law.

Learning Objectives of this Unit:

This Unit will build your skills to:

- Explain complex legal matters clearly and concisely
- Use appropriate technical terminology
- Identify and analyze the applicable case law and facts for the relevant legal issue
- Efficiently read and understand legal authority
- Articulate legal arguments in support of client's position
- Analyze possible outcomes for legal dispute, evaluate and articulate strengths and weaknesses of such outcomes
- Efficiently and effectively communicate in a written and oral format
- Respond to questions about the relevant law

To achieve these learning objectives, you will complete the following tasks:

- Draft an office memo to senior partner regarding apparent authority
- Draft a client advice letter regarding apparent authority and the contract dispute
- Carry out a client meeting with Pamela Park

To complete these tasks, you will use the following materials in the book:

- Assignment email from Senior Partner (page 44)
- Main Assignment File (pages 45-57)
- Apparent Authority Commented Cases:
    - Edinburg Volunteer Fire Co. v. Danko Emergency Equipment Co., 867 N.Y.S.2d 547 (N.Y. App. Div. 2008).
    - Merrell-Benco Agency, LLC v. HSBC Bank USA, 799 N.Y.S.2d 590 (N.Y. App. Div. 2005).
    - Hallock v. State of New York, 474 N.E.2d 1178 (N.Y. 1984).
    - Greene v. Hellman, 412 N.E.2d 1301 (N.Y. 1980).
    - Regency Oaks Corp. v. Norman-Spencer McKernan, 12 N.Y.S.3d 398 (N.Y. App. Div. 2015).
- ESL Workbook (pages 14-32)

Your instructor will also assign you additional skills-building exercises to bolster your understanding of the legal issues and further develop your legal reasoning and language skills. You will find an icon with each exercise that will indicate which skills the exercise will focus on.

ICON	SKILL
	Speaking — in particular about the legal issues and the law presented in the Unit
	Oral comprehension
	Legal analysis and reasoning
	Analysis of the legal issue(s) presented in the Unit
	English grammar, syntax, and vocabulary
	Legal ethics and professional responsibility
	Legal research

In this Unit, the additional skills-building exercises that accompany the Main Assignment File include:

- Apparent Authority Analysis Exercise (pages 58-61)

- Mock Negotiation Between SDA and Canopy, Inc. (page 62 plus confidential information)

- Presentation: *If SDA Were Your Client...* (pages 63-64)

Before beginning the Unit, you should read and be familiar with the Stray Dog Advertising Factual Background (pages 7-8) and the Factual Background of the Lincoln, Adams and Washington Law Firm (pages 2-3).

You will also find online at the website www.legalwritingforllms.com the following online resources that accompany this Unit. The additional online resources will help you deepen your mastery of the skills presented in the Unit and also provide additional understanding about the U.S. legal system and legal writing.

- Additional Resources:
  - Sources of American Law
  - Writing Professional Emails
  - Writing Predictive Memos
  - Writing E-memos
  - IRAC
- Additional Skills-Building Exercises:
  - Issues and Issue Statements
  - Stating the Rule
  - Analysis
  - Ethical Spotlight Exercises

Section I, Unit 2 Legal Issue
Apparent Authority

Main Assignment File	Apparent Authority Cases	ESL Workbook	Additional Exercises	Additional Online Resources
Introduction to File and Client Matter Pages 40-43	Edinburg Volunteer Fire Co. v. Danko Emergency Equip. Co., 867 N.Y.S.2d 547 (N.Y. App. Div. 2008).	Edinburg Volunteer Fire Co. v. Danko Emergency Equip. Co., 867 N.Y.S.2d 547 (N.Y. App. Div. 2008).	Apparent Authority Analysis Exercise Pages 58-61	Writing Professional Emails
Documents Related to Client Matter Pages 44-57	Merrell-Benco Agency, LLC v. HSBC Bank USA, 799 N.Y.S.2d 590 (N.Y. App. Div. 2005).	Merrell-Benco Agency, LLC v. HSBC Bank USA, 799 N.Y.S.2d 590 (N.Y. App. Div. 2005).	Mock Negotiation Page 62 (plus confidential information)	Business Correspondence (with sample letters)
Assignment Information Pages + Rubrics Pages 65-70	Hallock v. State of New York, 474 N.E.2d 1178 (N.Y. 1984).	Hallock v. State of New York, 474 N.E.2d 1178 (N.Y. 1984).	Presentation: If SDA Were Your Client... Pages 63-64	Writing Memos (office memos and e-memos)
	Greene v. Hellman, 412 N.E.2d 1301 (N.Y. 1980).	Greene v. Hellman, 412 N.E.2d 1301 (N.Y. 1980).		IRAC (including the various exercises for each element)
	Regency Oaks Corp. v. Norman-Spencer McKernan, Inc., 12 N.Y.S.3d 398 (N.Y. App. Div. 2015).	Regency Oaks Corp. v. Norman-Spencer McKernan, Inc., 12 N.Y.S.3d 398 (N.Y. App. Div. 2015).		Skills-Building Exercises for Rules, Issues and Issues Statements, Analysis and Ethical Dilemmas

Apparent Authority

Unit 2

Introduction — Apparent Authority

The Restatement (Third) of Agency defines agency as "the fiduciary relationship that arises when one person (a "principal") manifests assent to another person (an "agent") that the agent shall act on the principal's behalf and is subject to the principal's control, and when the agent manifests assent or otherwise consents so to act."[16]

To understand agency, you need to understand two key terms:

Principal – Think of the "principal" as the person in charge of the relationship who decides whether someone else can act on his or her behalf. An owner of a company can be a principal, as can a manager within the company, or the company itself.

Agent – The person who acts under the principal, answers to him or her and performs services on his or her behalf.

Agents and principals can also be "regular" people without any connection to a business or company, such as a parent acting as an agent on behalf of an adult child, or a friend acting on behalf of another friend.

> "The implication of an agency from the facts must follow from a natural and reasonable, and not a strained or distorted, construction of these facts. An agency will not be inferred because a third person assumed that it existed." 3 Am. Jur. 2d Agency § 15 (2015).

In agency law, three types of authority exist: actual authority, implied authority and apparent authority. When one of the three types of agency exists, the principal is bound by the words or actions of its agent.

Actual authority is the more straight-forward type of authority and is created when the principal tells the agent that he is authorized to act on the principal's behalf and bind him. A written or oral agreement is sufficient to create an agency relationship.[17] Implied authority arises from words, customs, or from the relations of the parties (principal and agent) and is created (thus binding the principal) if the agent is reasonable in drawing an inference that the principal intended to confer authority to him or her.[18]

Apparent authority, on the other hand, is created when the words, actions or omissions of the principal make another person (a third party) reasonably believe that the agent has the authority to act on the principal's behalf and bind the principal. So in other words, the principal never explicitly states that the agent can act on his behalf, but rather creates the reasonable belief in another person's mind that the agent is authorized to act on the principal's behalf. An agency relationship is implied from the words and conduct of the parties and whether the relationship exists will depend on the facts of each case.[19] With actual, both parties must consent to the relationship.[20] The law does not presume agency.[21]

Apparent authority is the legal issue that you will deal with in this Unit. You will analyze whether a Stray Dog Advertising employee, Charlene Thomas, had the apparent authority to modify a contract that Pamela Park signed with a client, Canopy, Inc., and whether the contract modification is binding upon the advertising agency. The Unit will also include additional skills-building exercises such as a mock negotiation between Stray Dog Advertising and Canopy, Inc. and a mock client meeting between you and Park.

---

[16] Restatement (Third) of Agency §1.01 (Am. Law Inst. 2006).
[17] 3 Am. Jur. 2d *Agency* § 15 (Westlaw database updated Sept. 2016).
[18] Koval v. Simon Telelect, Inc., 693 N.E.2d 1299, 1302 (Ind. 1998).
[19] Id.
[20] Id.
[21] Buchoz v. Klein, 184 S.W.2d 271, 271 (Tex. 1944), *cited in* Suarez v. Jordan, 35 S.W.3d 268, 272 (Tex. App. 2000).

Main Assignment File: Apparent Authority

You have received the following email from Senior Partner Georgina Washington about Stray Dog Advertising, one of the firm's main clients, and have been asked to work on this case.

> **From:** Georgina Washington <g.washington@lawlawfirm.com>
> **To:** Associate Attorney < a.attorney@lawlawfirm.com >
> **Sent:** September 2, THIS YEAR 1:02 p.m.
> **Re:** Contract Dispute Stray Dog Advertising

Associate attorney,

I will need your help with an issue that has come up with Pamela Park at Stray Dog Advertising. She has gotten a demand letter from a client's attorney about a modification of the contract that SDA signed with this client, Canopy, Inc. Canopy is owned by a local couple, Harvey and Gina McBride. The corporation owns and manages several high-profile and successful restaurants in West Rapids and Jefferson City. Pamela secured a very lucrative advertising contract for not just Canopy but for the four restaurants that the McBrides own.

As you will see in the emails that I have forwarded to you, one of Pamela's employees spoke with Gina McBride after the contract was signed, and Gina asked to modify the payment schedule. The employee agreed. Gina and Harvey now insist that this modification be binding, but Pamela didn't agree to it and doesn't want it to be part of the final contract. She says that the modified payment provision will create great hardship for SDA. Charlene, the SDA employee who agreed to modify the agreement, doesn't even have the authority at SDA to negotiate for or bind SDA in any way. Only Pamela has that authority.

I am meeting with Pamela at the end of next week. I told her that I would prepare for her a strategy of how to deal with this dispute. To develop that strategy, I need your legal research and analysis skills to help me understand the issue and the law better.

This is what I need from you before I meet with Pamela:

- A memo that states what the issue is;
- A summary of the applicable Jefferson law;
- Your analysis of the law as it applies to the facts of Pamela's case;
- Your prediction of what you think a court would decide if Pamela brings a breach of contract claim against Canopy, Inc., or if Canopy should file against SDA, as the attorney has threatened; and
- Your advice to Pamela on what she should do.

Let me know if anything isn't clear and we can call Pamela to clarify.

Georgina

As you have read, Washington has asked you to write her a memo about the following:

- A summary of what has happened between Stray Dog Advertising and Canopy, Inc.
- The legal issue at hand
- A summary and analysis of the law that applies (apparent authority)
- Your opinion about whether the contract modification agreed to by the SDA employee is binding
- Your advice to Pamela Park about how to proceed with this matter

You will find complete information about this assignment on the Information Page (pages 65-66).

You will be analyzing the client matter using the apparent authority cases that you read and review in class.

From: Pamela Park <pamela.park@straydogadvertising.com>
To: Georgina Washington <g.washington@lawlawfirm.com>
Sent: September 1, THIS YEAR 9:39 a.m.
Subject: Contract Mess with Canopy, Inc.

Hi Georgina,

I need your help on another urgent matter! Why does it seem that we can't even go a month or so without some new legal problem arising? I am lucky that I have you on my side!

Do you remember last month when we went to lunch at that new Italian restaurant in town, Il Gattone? It is owned by Canopy, Inc., the mother company that owns SunRise Bakery, La Boulangerie, and Union Circle Grill, all of which are wildly successful and have delicious food. Do you also remember that I said that I'd love to work with Canopy and develop a new marketing strategy for them and for their restaurants? Well, it's happened, and let's hope that it still will. I'll explain.

After you left, I stayed at Il Gattone and happened to see the owner, Harvey McBride (I recognized him from the article about him and his wife that was in the West Rapids Times a few months ago). I approached him, we got to talking and next thing I knew, his wife, Gina, had joined us and we were talking advertising, marketing and how Stray Dog could help them develop their brands. Gina and Harvey have great vision.

You'll see the whole story in all the documents and correspondence that I am sending you, but to make a long story short, we met the following week and then had several negotiation sessions to discuss the terms and conditions of the contract. Two of my employees, Charlene and Franco, came to the negotiations with me so that they could learn more about the dealings that go on between SDA and our clients. Franco just observed, while Charlene took a more active role and took detailed notes. I wanted a complete record of what went on and was discussed in the meetings. After three or four meetings, the McBrides signed a huge year-long contract with us for the marketing and advertising for all of their restaurants and Canopy, Inc. as well.

The following day Gina McBride called our office while I was out. David, our receptionist, put her through to Charlene. Gina had originally asked for me, but when David told her that I was in meetings and not available and asked whether she wanted to talk with Charlene instead, Gina said yes. David told me that Gina had told him that she had a question about the contract and about changing one of the contract terms. David said that since he had seen Charlene in the meeting room with me and the McBrides, he thought that she might be able to help since he thought that Gina seemed rather "anxious" to talk to someone. David put Gina through to Charlene right away. With Charlene on the phone, Gina asked whether she could change the payment terms of the contract. She no longer wanted to pay 50% at signing (our normal payment term), but asked to pay only 25% within seven days and the other 75% over the last six months of the contract. Usually, the client pays the remaining 50% in one payment six months after signing and after the initial payment.

I couldn't believe it when I found out, but Charlene agreed to Gina's modification! She modified the Word document of the contract and forwarded it to Gina, who signed the contract and immediately sent it back to Charlene.

When I arrived at the office around lunchtime, Charlene told me that she had modified the contract as Gina requested. Charlene said that she had seen another contract with those terms and thought that it was OK to change the one with Canopy. Needless to say, I was furious! We do have one client who didn't pay 50% of the contract price at signing, but that is an exception that I did as a personal favor for an old friend from college. I can't afford to offer such terms to other clients. It will really create a serious cash-flow problem for us.

I immediately called Gina and told her that the modification wasn't binding because Charlene didn't have the authority to modify the contract. Gina said that didn't matter and that it was binding. She then said that she would be sending the 25% payment, which we have received. I haven't deposited it yet because I wasn't sure if doing so would mean I couldn't claim that she still owes me the remaining 25% now and not in six months.

What do I do? Sue her? Will they sue us as their attorney has threatened? As I said, not getting the 50% now will create serious cash-flow problems with all the work we are doing these days. Can we meet next week so I can figure out what to do? I've also forwarded to you the demand letter that their attorney sent me, as well as the relevant emails, the contract and a memo that Charlene prepared.

PP

From:	Gina McBride <gina@canopyrestaurants.com>
To:	Pamela Park < pamela.park@straydogadvertising.com>
CC:	Harvey McBride <harvey@canopyrestaurants.com>
Sent:	August 1, THIS YEAR 10:39
Subject:	Follow-Up Meeting

Dear Pamela,

It was great talking with you Friday afternoon. Harvey and I really enjoyed our impromptu discussion about advertising and marketing for Canopy, Inc. and our restaurants. You've got so many creative ideas about how we can make our businesses stand out from the crowd. I think our ideas and styles fit well together, and I want to set up a more formal meeting to discuss hiring Stray Dog Advertising to take over our marketing and advertising campaigns. As we mentioned, we have been looking for a new agency to work with.

Are you free Thursday this week? We can meet at SunRise for a breakfast meeting if that works with your schedule. Our cinnamon raisin buns are to die for, and you have to try them!

Take care,

Gina

From:	Pamela Park <pamela.park@straydogadvertising.com>
To:	Gina McBride <gina@canopyrestaurants.com>
Sent:	August 1, THIS YEAR 18:07
Subject:	Re: Follow-Up Meeting

Dear Gina,

Thanks so much for your note. I would love to meet you and Harvey, and I would be thrilled to develop your branding campaigns. How about 8:30 on Thursday? Charlene Thomas, our Administrative Specialist and one of our brightest employees, will join me so you can get an idea of the talent that we have at Stray Dog Advertising.

I look forward to our meeting.

PP

From: Pamela Park <pamela.park@straydogadvertising.com>
To: Charlene Thomas <charlene.thomas@straydogadvertising.com>
Sent: August 1, THIS YEAR 18:09
Subject: Breakfast Meeting Thursday

Charlene,

You will be joining me on Thursday morning for a breakfast meeting with Gina and Harvey McBride, the owners of Canopy, Inc. The McBrides own several restaurants around town and are very interested in hiring SDA for their advertising, marketing and branding needs. On Thursday, we will be discussing what we can bring to the table if they hire us. I would like you to take notes of all the meetings with the McBrides so that we have a detailed record of what we discuss.

We are meeting at SunRise Bakery (which they own) at 8:30. I will meet you there.

PP

MEMO

To: File
From: Charlene Thomas
Re: Meeting Thursday August 4, THIS YEAR Canopy, Inc.
Date: August 5, THIS YEAR

On 8/4/THIS YEAR, Pamela and I met with Harvey and Gina McBride, owners of Canopy, Inc. to discuss how SDA can take over the marketing, advertising and branding campaigns for:

- SunRise Bakery
- La Boulangerie
- Union Circle Grill
- Il Gattone
- Canopy, Inc.

Pamela brought with her samples of SDA's work from past campaigns and current clients, and they were impressed with the quality and the creativity. The McBrides explained how their business at SunRise and Union Circle has leveled out in the past year, and they attribute that to new competition in West Rapids that offers similar products.

They want the marketing campaign to stress the quality of ingredients that they use and well as the service commitment that the McBrides and their businesses have. For example, SunRise Bakery donates the unsold bread and other products to a homeless shelter at the end of each business day. It also works with West Rapids High School to mentor young at-risk students to teach them how to bake and learn a new skill. Canopy also donates 5% of its profits to a local non-profit organization that trains service dogs, and Il Gattone hires physically challenged employees when and where it can as part of its mission to give back to the community and help those in need.

Gina said that many customers are not aware of the community work that the McBrides do, and they both think that this needs to be highlighted to bring in more business, and also to encourage other companies to do the same. We have scheduled a meeting on next Monday, August 8 at 10:00 at the SDA offices so that the McBrides can meet with Roy too.

From: Charlene Thomas <charlene.thomas@ straydogadvertising.com>
To: Pamela Park <pamela.park@straydogadvertising.com
Cc: Roy Blanco <roy.blanco@straydogadvertising.com>
Sent: August 9, THIS YEAR 12:39
Subject: Meeting Canopy, Inc.

Pamela,

Here are some of my notes from yesterday's meeting with the McBrides:

Price – the McBrides seem to agree to the price that we proposed for the contract, although I noted some body language that indicated that Gina wasn't too happy with the proposed price.

Payment terms – Harvey didn't like the requirement that we require payment in certified funds, but your explanation clarified why we require payment that way and my impression was that he was OK with that.

Campaigns – during the rest of the meeting, we discussed their ideas for their campaigns and what they would like to see communicated to the public, especially their social message.

After the meeting and after you told Gina and Harvey to contact me if they had any questions about what was discussed, Gina did call me. Twice! She wanted to verify whether her memory was correct about the payment terms and the price. I told her that I would review my notes to be sure. I reviewed my notes and then told her that her memory was correct and that the proposed price was what she had remembered. I also told her that she can call you for any more complex questions about the negotiations and about the terms you were talking about.

As you requested, I have taken one of your old contracts and modified the terms to reflect those that we discussed with the McBrides. That way, if they agree to those terms, the contract will be all ready to send them.

My impression is that they are getting ready to sign!

Charlene

From: Pamela Park <pamela.park@straydogadvertising.com>
To: Charlene Thomas <charlene.thomas@straydogadvertising.com>
Sent: August 9, THIS YEAR 19:51
Subject: Re: Meeting Canopy, Inc.

Thanks. I appreciate your hard work and the active role that you are playing in the discussions with the McBrides. It is helpful to have someone else take the notes so that I can focus on them and their needs. Having you as a secondary contact for them is also extremely useful when I am not available or at the office. I know that Gina hates calling people on their cell phones since she feels like she is disturbing, so I think she appreciates having you around as well.

I want you to take on a greater role at SDA and take on more responsibility and authority, even to negotiate with clients on your own. These negotiations with such a high-profile client are a great learning experience for you.

PP

From: Charlene Thomas <charlene.thomas@straydogadvertising.com>
To: Gina McBride <gina@canopyrestaurants.com>;
Harvey McBride <harvey@canopyrestaurants.com>
CC: Pamela Park <pamela.park@straydogadvertising.com>
Sent: August 12, THIS YEAR 16:33
Subject: Proposed Contract

Dear Mr. and Mrs. McBride,

As Pamela mentioned to you, I am forwarding to you the contract that reflects the terms that have been discussed during our meetings over the past days for the advertising, marketing and branding services that SDA will provide to Canopy, Inc.

We hope that the terms are acceptable as written.

Charlene Thomas

Administrative Specialist
Stray Dog Advertising, LLC

From: Pamela Park <pamela.park@straydogadvertising.com>
To: Gina McBride <gina@canopyrestaurants.com>;
Harvey McBride <harvey@canopyrestaurants.com>
Sent: August 12, THIS YEAR 16:37
Subject: Re: Proposed Contract

Gina and Harvey,

I am available for any questions that you have, or if you want to discuss any of the terms or have any questions about our services.

PP

Sent from my iPhone

AGREEMENT FOR ADVERTISING, MARKETING AND BRANDING SERVICES[22]

AGREEMENT between Stray Dog Advertising, LLC ("Agency"), and Canopy, Inc. ("Client").

1. Appointment

Client appoints Agency as Client's exclusive advertising agency in connection with the products and/or services of Client described in Schedule 1, attached hereto, for a term ("Term") as hereinafter provided.

2. Scope of Advertising Services

Agency will provide Client with the advertising services provided in Schedule 2, attached hereto. Should Client request Agency to perform additional services beyond what is provided in Schedule 2, Agency and Client will negotiate in good faith with respect to the terms, conditions, and compensation for such additional services. Any agreement for additional services will be set forth in writing and considered an addendum to this Agreement.

3. Ownership

All campaigns, trademarks, service marks, slogans, artwork, written materials, drawings, photographs, graphic materials, film, music, transcriptions, or other materials that are subject to copyright, trademark, patent, or similar protection (collectively, the "Work Product") produced by Agency are the property of the Client provided: (1) such Work Product is accepted in writing by the Client within twelve (12) months of being proposed by Agency; and (2) Client pays all fees and costs associated with creating and, where applicable, producing such Work Product. Work Product that does not meet the two foregoing conditions shall remain Agency's property.

Notwithstanding the foregoing, it is understood that Agency may, on occasion, license materials from third parties for inclusion in Work Product. In such circumstances, ownership of such licensed materials remains with the licensor at the conclusion of the term of the license. In such instances, Client agrees that it remains bound by the terms of such licenses. Agency will keep Client informed of any such limitations.

4. Term

The term of this Agreement shall commence on the date provided in Schedule 1 ("Commencement Date") and shall continue until terminated by either party upon ninety (90) days' prior written notice ("Notice Period"), provided that this Agreement may not be terminated effective prior to the expiration of twelve (12) months from the Commencement Date. Notice shall be deemed given on the day of mailing or, in case of notice by telegram, on the day it is deposited with the telegraph company for transmission. During the Notice Period, Agency's rights, duties, and responsibilities shall continue.

Upon termination, Agency will transfer and/or assign to Client: (1) all Work Product in Agency's possession or control belonging to Client, subject, however, to any rights of third parties; and (2) all contracts with third parties, including advertising media or others, upon being duly released by Client and any such third party from any further obligations. Client recognizes that Agency is a signatory to certain union agreements covering talent used in broadcast materials, which generally cannot be assigned except to signatories to such collective bargaining agreements governing the services rendered by such talent.

5. Compensation and Billing Procedure

Agency will be compensated and Client will be billed as provided in Schedule 3, attached hereto.

6. Confidentiality and Safeguard of Property

Client and Agency respectively agree to keep in confidence, and not to disclose or use for its own respective benefit or for the benefit of any third party (except as may be required for the performance of services under this Agreement or as may be required by law), any information, documents, or materials that are reasonably considered confidential regarding each other's products, business, customers, clients, suppliers, or methods of operation; provided, however, that such obligation of confidentiality will not extend to anything in the public domain or that was in the possession of either party prior to disclosure. Agency and Client will take

22   Agreement from ASSOCIATION OF NATIONAL ADVERTISERS, *available at* https://www.ana.net/getfile/15991 (last visited May 6, 2016). The agreement here is slightly modified from the original to suit the client matter in the Unit. The provision requiring amendments to be in writing has been deleted. The template agreement is suited to small transactions.

reasonable precautions to safeguard property of the other entrusted to it, but in the absence of negligence or willful disregard, neither Agency nor Client will be responsible for any loss or damage.

7. Indemnities

Agency agrees to indemnify and hold Client harmless with respect to any claims or actions by third parties against Client based upon material prepared by Agency, involving any claim for libel, slander, piracy, plagiarism, invasion of privacy, or infringement of copyright, except where any such claim or action arises out of material supplied by Client to Agency.

Client agrees to indemnify and hold Agency harmless with respect to any claims or actions by third parties against Agency based upon materials furnished by Client or where material created by Agency is substantially changed by Client. Information or data obtained by Agency from Client to substantiate claims made in advertising shall be deemed to be "materials furnished by Client." Client further agrees to indemnify and hold Agency harmless with respect to any death or personal injury claims or actions arising from the use of Client's products or services.

8. Commitments to Third Parties

All purchases of media, production costs, and engagement of talent will be subject to Client's prior approval. Client reserves the right to cancel any such authorization, whereupon Agency will take all appropriate steps to effect such cancellation, provided that Client will hold Agency harmless with respect to any costs incurred by Agency as a result. If at any time Agency obtains a discount or rebate from any supplier in connection with Agency's rendition of services to Client, Agency will credit Client or remit to Client such discount or rebate.

For all media purchased by Agency on Client's behalf, Client agrees that Agency shall be held solely liable for payments only to the extent proceeds have cleared from Client to Agency for such media purchase; otherwise, Client agrees to be solely liable to media ("Sequential Liability"). Agency will use its best efforts to obtain agreement by media to Sequential Liability.

9. Notices

Any notice shall be deemed given on the day of mailing or, if notice is by telegram, e-mail, or fax, on the next day following the day notice is deposited with the telegraph company for transmission, or e-mailed or faxed.

10. Governing Law

This Agreement shall be interpreted in accordance with the laws of the State of Jefferson without regard to its principles of conflicts of laws. Jurisdiction and venue shall be solely within the State of Jefferson in the County of Hemings.

IN WITNESS WHEREOF, Agency and Client have executed this Agreement.

AGENCY:

_____/s/ Pamela Park_____

By: Pamela Park for Stray Dog Advertising, LLC

Title: Owner

CLIENT:

_____/s/ Gina E. McBride_____

By: Gina E. McBride for Canopy, Inc.

Title: Owner

_____/s/ Harvey M. McBride_____

By: Harvey M. McBride for Canopy, Inc.

Title: Owner

Schedule 1: Products/Services Assigned to Agency

Canopy, Inc.

SunRise Bakery

La Boulangerie

Union Circle Grill

Il Gattone

Schedule 2: Commencement Date and Scope of Services

I.   Commencement Date: September 1, THIS YEAR

II. Scope of Services

    A.   Study Client's products or services;

    B.   Analyze Client's present and potential markets;

    C.   Create, prepare, and submit to Client for approval, advertising ideas and programs;

    D.   Employ on Client's behalf, Agency's knowledge of available media and means that can be profitably used to advertise Client's products or services;

    E.   Prepare and submit to Client for approval, estimates of costs of recommended advertising programs;

    F.   Write, design, illustrate, or otherwise prepare Client's advertisements, including commercials to be broadcast, or other appropriate forms of Client's message;

    G.   Order the space, time, or other means to be used for Client's advertising, endeavoring to secure the most advantageous rates available;

    H.   Properly incorporate the message in mechanical or other form and forward it with proper instructions for the fulfillment of the order;

    I.   Check and verify insertions, displays, broadcasts, or other means used, to such degree as is usually performed by advertising agencies; and

    J.   Audit invoices for space, time, material preparation, and services.

Schedule 3: Compensation and Billing Procedures

I.   Compensation

    A.   Client will pay a total of $1,100,000.00 in consideration of the advertising services performed by Agency. Such fee shall be deemed a nonrefundable advance against commissions to be received by Agency as follows:

        (1) On all media purchased by Agency, Agency shall bill Client at the published card rates, or negotiated rates, as may be applicable. If no agency commission, or less than five percent (5%) agency commission (the "Commission Rate"), is granted or allowed on any such purchases, Client agrees that Agency may invoice Client an amount which, after deduction of Agency's cost, will yield Agency the aforesaid Commission Rate of such amount as Agency commission. During the Notice Period following notice of termination, Agency will be entitled to commissions on all orders of advertising in print media whose published closing dates fall within the Notice Period and of broadcast media where the air dates fall within the Notice Period, regardless of who may place such orders.

        (2) With respect to the engagement of talent, Agency shall bill Client the authorized engagement rate, plus any taxes, insurance, pension and health fund contributions, etc. applicable thereto, plus an amount which, after deduction of Agency's cost, will yield Agency the Commission Rate on such amount as Agency commission.

        (3) On broadcast production, artwork, engravings, type compositions, and any and all art and mechanical expenses incurred by Agency pursuant to Client's authorization, Agency shall invoice Client an amount which, after deduction of Agency's cost, will yield Agency the Commission Rate on such amount as Agency commission.

        (4) Advances against commissions will be reconciled against commissions actually received on a (monthly, quarter-annual, or other) basis. Agency will issue the appropriate credit or debit invoices.

    B.   Client agrees to reimburse Agency for such cash outlays as Agency may incur, such as forwarding and mailing, telephoning, telegraphing, and travel, in connection with services rendered in relation to Client's account.

II.   Billing and Payment Procedures

    A.   Agency will invoice Client for all media and third-party costs sufficiently in advance of the due date to permit payment by Client to Agency in order to take advantage of all available cash discounts or rebates.

    B.   The cost of production materials and services shall be billed by Agency upon completion of the production job, or upon receipt of supplier invoice prior thereto.

    C.   On all outside purchases other than for media, Agency will attach to the invoice proof of billed charges from suppliers.

    D.   All invoices shall be rendered on or about the first day of each month and will be payable the tenth day of the month.

    E.   Invoices shall be submitted in an itemized format. Interest will be charged on overdue invoices at a rate of 8 percent (8%) per annum, or the maximum permitted by law, whichever is less.

    F.   Client agrees to pay the total $1,100,000.00 due according to the following schedule:

        50% ($550,000.00) upon signing this Agreement, to be paid by certified funds;

        50% ($550,000.00) by March 1, Year +1, to be paid by certified funds

From: Gina McBride <gina@canopyrestaurants.com>
To: Pamela Park <pamela.park@straydogadvertising.com>
CC: Harvey McBride <harvey@canopyrestaurants.com>;
Sent: August 13, THIS YEAR 05:57
Subject: Contract

Pamela,

I have attached the signed contract to this email. Harvey and I discussed at length the commitment that we will be undertaking with SDA for your services and also talked with our accountant about the payments. In the end, we decided to bite the bullet[23] and sign. We are excited to start working with you!

Right when we met at Il Gattone, I just knew that something would work out and that we would work together. I am a very perceptive person, and I just had this feeling that we would get along and that our chance meeting would turn into something more!

Harvey and I will be leaving town tomorrow evening to go visit our new grandson in Boston, so I will call you on Monday to set up a meeting at your office next week, as we discussed. Before we leave, we will drop the check in the mail for the first payment.

Best,

Gina

From: Charlene Thomas <Charlene.thomas@straydogadvertising.com>
To: Gina McBride <gina@canopyrestaurants.com>
Sent: August 14, THIS YEAR 08:52
Subject: Contract

Gina,

As per our phone conversation earlier this morning, I have attached the revised contract between Canopy, Inc. and Stray Dog Advertising. I changed only the provision that deals with the payment terms, as you requested. I changed the provision (Section II, Paragraph F on Schedule 3) as follows:

F. Client agrees to pay the total $1,100,000.00 due according to the following schedule:

    25% ($275,000.00) within seven days of signing this Agreement, to be paid by certified funds;

    25% ($275,000.00) by March 1, Year +1, to be paid by certified funds

    25% ($275,000.00) by June 1, Year +1, to be paid by certified funds

    25% ($275,000.00) by August 31, Year +1, to be paid by certified funds

I will let Pamela know about the revised term when she gets to the office. She said that she had to meet with several clients this morning so she should be here around lunchtime. Please return the signed modified agreement at your convenience.

Best,

Charlene

---

[23] To do something unpleasant or painful, such as paying a large sum of money like the McBrides are doing.

[The revised, signed contract is not included in the Main Assignment File. The entire contract, except for the above provision regarding the payment terms as included in the email on August 14 from Charlene to Gina, is the same as the contract on pages 56-60]

From:	Gina McBride <gina@canopyrestaurants.com>
To:	Charlene Thomas <charlene.thomas@straydogadvertising.com>
Sent:	August 14, THIS YEAR 08:57
Subject:	Re: Re: Contract

Charlene,

I've attached the signed modified agreement. Thank you for your cooperation. As I mentioned on the phone, we will drop in the mail the check for the initial 25% percent of the contract price. If we have time before going to the airport, we'll drop it off at the SDA office so we don't have to worry about it getting lost in the mail.

Thanks again,

Gina McBride

The Law Office of Henry Miyamoto
3200 West Broadway Avenue, Suite 2110
West Rapids, Jefferson 66535
623-509-1215

August 20, **THIS YEAR**

VIA U.S. MAIL

Stray Dog Advertising, LLC

Pamela Park

45 Sunrise Boulevard

West Rapids, Jefferson 66412

RE: Modification of Contract Signed with Canopy, Inc.

Dear Ms. Park:

This firm represents Canopy, Inc., and we write regarding the contract that Stray Dog Advertising, LLC signed with Canopy, Inc. on August 13, THIS YEAR and that was subsequently modified by your employee, Charlene Thomas on August 14, THIS YEAR. I have been informed that you have refused to abide by the modification to the payment provisions that Ms. Thomas agreed to, and claim that the modification is not binding.

As your agent, Ms. Thomas acted within her authority when she modified the contract, leading Gina McBride, owner of Canopy, Inc., to believe that the contract payment provision had been modified to reflect the terms that she agreed to with Ms. Thomas: 25% of the contract price within seven days of signing the contract, 25% by March 1, YEAR +1 25%, by June 1 YEAR +1, and the remaining 25% by August 31, YEAR +1. While your desire to have 50% of the payment upon signing may be understandable, you are bound by the legitimate modification made by your employee. Mrs. McBride has informed me that she mailed to your office the first payment of $275,000 in certified funds, as required by the contract.

Please be advised that if you continue to refuse to comply with such modification, this firm will file a breach of contract claim with the Jefferson State Court against Stray Dog Advertising. We will also move for an order of specific performance, requiring you/Stray Dog Advertising to perform under the contract. However, I am confident that we can resolve this matter promptly and amicably as my clients are eager to begin working with your agency on the advertising campaigns that you have discussed for their restaurants.

I look forward to discussing this matter with you or your attorney, and to that end, I can be reached at the above phone number or at the email miyamoto@miyamotolaw.com.

Sincerely yours,

/s/ *Henry Miyamoto*

Henry Miyamoto, Esq.

Cc: Harvey and Gina McBride

Additional Skills-Building Exercises

Apparent Authority Analysis Exercises

Overview of the Exercise: The following short fact patterns deal with apparent authority, and your task is to analyze the fact patterns and determine whether or not the principal created apparent authority in the agent and whether the agent thus bound the principal with his or her words or actions.

Learning Objectives of the Exercise:

This exercise will build your skills to:

- Articulate the legal rules regarding apparent authority
- Apply those rules to fact patterns and analyze the facts and the law
- Articulate and effectively communicate that analysis using legal terminology

Steps for Completing the Exercise:

- Read the following fact patterns.
- By yourself, analyze and decide whether or not you think apparent authority was created and why. You don't need to write out a full answer, but jot down notes about your reasoning.
- When you are done analyzing each of the fact patterns, discuss your answers with a classmate. Explain to each other why you have reached the conclusion that you did.
- If you and your partner have different responses to a fact pattern, you must try to convince him or her that your answer is correct. After you both have tried to convince the other, you must choose a team answer.
- Once you have discussed each of the fact patterns, you will compare answers as a class.

Grading: This exercise is not graded.

1. Peter lent his lawn mower to his friend, Frederica. Part of the agreement between Peter and Frederica was that Frederica would be responsible for fuel and for normal maintenance. While Frederica had the mower in her possession, she noticed that the blades were not cutting the grass well, so she decided to bring the mower to the local repair shop, Greener Lawns. While at the shop, the shop owner discovered more serious problems with the engine and discussed with Frederica the repairs, which Frederica authorized. Peter did not know that Frederica had brought the mower to the shop for the repairs.

While his mower was in the repair shop, Peter happened to bring in his snow blower to prepare for the upcoming winter. He saw his lawn mower and discussed with the mechanic the scope of the work but not the price. At that point, the repairs on the lawn mower were either completed or nearly completed. Peter asked the mechanic to fix one other thing on the lawn mower.

When the repairs were completed, the lawn mower was returned to Frederica, who used it for a short time thereafter. Greener Lawns sent the bill for $1,600 to Frederica, who failed to pay it. Unable to collect the money owed, Greener Lawns is now claiming that Peter is liable for the money owed.

- State the issue in this situation.
- Examine and analyze whether Peter is liable for Frederica's actions.
- Consult <u>Bruton v. Automatic Welding and Supply Corp.</u>, 513 P. 2d 1122 (Alaska 1973) if you want to compare your analysis to that of the court's.

2. Evelyn owns a speed boat that she enjoys using during the summer with her family. Last weekend while they were cruising down the Aster River, the engine stopped working. After being towed to shore, they called a local boat dealership, Tempo Northwest. Tempo Northwest is a local distributor for Tempo, a boat engine manufacturer. Evelyn called Tempo Northwest because one of her family's other boats had a Tempo engine, they liked the performance and wanted to replace the broken engine with a Tempo one.

When Evelyn was speaking with the Tempo Northwest representative and explaining the problems that they had with their boat, the man first told Evelyn that "Sure we can help you out," and then said that "Go to R&D, a boat repair shop in West Rapids. They can take out the old engine, take care of you and get you back on the river in no time."

Evelyn called R&D, who installed a new Tempo engine in the boat. Unfortunately, while they were using it for the first time after the repairs, the engine began shaking. Smoke began to emit from the engine and then flames. After a few minutes of smoke and flames, the engine exploded. Fortunately, no one in Evelyn's family was hurt. Because the engine and boat exploded, the investigators were unable to determine the exact cause of the explosion and whether it was because of a defective engine or because of negligent repair work.

Evelyn has now brought product liability and negligence claims against Tempo, Tempo Northwest and R&D.

- State the issue in this situation.
- Examine and analyze whether Tempo and Tempo Northwest are liable for R&D's actions.
- Consult <u>Cummins v. Nelson</u>, 115 P. 3d 536 (Alaska 2005) if you want to compare your analysis to that of the court's.

3. Laurie Lawyer is representing a wife in a divorce proceeding. The parties scheduled a negotiation at the husband's attorney's office, but Laurie's client, Wendy Wife, chose not to attend because she didn't want to be in the same room with her husband, Harry. She made herself available to her attorney by telephone and email.

After about three hours of negotiations, the husband agreed to sell the house that he and his wife owned and to split the proceedings. As a condition, however, Harry Husband stated that Wendy Wife would have to be responsible for one-half of the mortgage payments, pending sale of the house. Laurie responded, "I didn't talk to her (Wendy) about that. I'm going to have to talk to her and see if she will agree." Laurie then left the conference room to call Wendy regarding that issue, which, in Laurie's opinion, "was the only unsettled part of the negotiations, at that moment." While speaking on the phone with Wendy, Laurie became upset because she thought her client was changing her mind about issues that were already settled and raising other matters that were beyond the focus of the current negotiation. She slammed the phone down, threw a cup against the wall of the office, and left the building without returning to the negotiation.

The next day, having received an e-mail from Wendy that she believed expressly authorized and directed her to settle the case (the email said "I know that you are the attorney and know best, but I am unsure about how to settle this with my ex-husband"), Laurie drafted, signed, and transmitted to Husband's attorney the two-page final settlement agreement. Wendy did not see the agreement before Laurie signed it and sent it to Husband's attorney. Before signing and sending the agreement, Laurie had attempted to call Wendy three times to review the document she had prepared, but Wendy did not answer and did not call her back. Following transmission of the document to Husband's attorney, Laurie notified the court that the case was settled and could be removed from the trial docket.

The following day, Wendy went to Laurie's office expecting to review a draft of the "fully typed out proposed settlement agreement." Instead, she was given a copy of the agreement signed on her behalf by Laurie. That agreement, according to Wendy, did not represent what she had agreed to and was signed by Laurie without her authority or consent. Wendy claims that had she been given the opportunity to review the agreement signed by Laurie, she would not have approved or signed it.

Wendy is now asking that the court void the agreement. Laurie claims in response that an attorney, by virtue of the attorney-client relationship, has the authority to bind his or her client.

- State what the issue is.
- Examine and analyze whether the settlement agreement should be binding upon Wendy or whether the court should void it. Why or why not?
- Consult <u>Walson v. Walson</u>, 556 S.E.2d 53 (Vir. 2001) if you would like to compare your analysis to that of the court's.

4. Alvaro and his wife Alba are engaged in litigation about the boundary lines of their property. Their neighbor, Juanita, claims that Alvaro and Alba have encroached on her property by building a fence that she claims is on it. She demands that they remove the fence.

A settlement conference was scheduled. Alvaro was unable to attend the conference as he had an important business trip. Alba's English is not very fluent, so she asked their son, John, to attend in her place. Before the conference, Alvaro phoned their attorney and told her that their son would attend the settlement conference and that Alvaro was "confident that John would do the right thing."

At the conference, John signed a settlement agreement in which Alvaro and Alba agreed that their fence encroached upon Juanita's property, that they would promptly remove the fence and that they would also pay for any repairs that Juanita needed to make to restore her lawn to its original condition.

The next day, when Alvaro returned from his business trip, his attorney informed him that they had settled the case. Alvaro was extremely surprised when he saw the terms of the settlement agreement. He has now hired another attorney, who is challenging the enforceability of the settlement agreement.

- State what the issue is.
- Examine and analyze whether the settlement agreement should be binding upon Alvaro and his wife or whether the court should void it. Why or why not?
- Consult <u>Suarez v. Jordan</u>, 35 S.W.3d 268 (Tex. App. 2000) if you would like to compare your analysis to that of the court's.

5. Thomas and Alice Rosenbaum organized Rossie's, Inc., a Jefferson corporation ("Rossie's"). Rossie's entered into a franchise agreement with Red Cherry Fitness, Inc. whereby the former was authorized by the latter to use the Red Cherry Fitness trade name in connection with the operation of the gym, Rossie's Fitness Center, that the Rosenbaums operate in Jefferson City.

The Rosenbaums entered into a contract with the magazine The Jefferson Monthly which provided that the magazine would print advertisements in its magazines at specified rates for "Red Cherry Fitness" located in Jefferson City. The parties to the contract were The Jefferson Monthly, Inc. and Red Cherry Fitness, Inc. The contract was renewed by Alice Rosenbaum, the chief manager of Rossie's, Inc. in the name of "Red Cherry Fitness." The Rosenbaums also used the tradename "Red Cherry Fitness" on their front window since the franchise was expanding across the country and the Rosenbaums wanted to exploit the franchise's growth and popularity.

When the contract with The Jefferson Monthly was renewed, the magazine provided advertising services in the sum of $9,470.10 which Rossie's failed to pay. The Jefferson Monthly sued Red Cherry Fitness, Inc. on the theory of apparent authority of Rossie's representatives to bind Red Cherry Fitness.

- State what the issue is.
- Examine and analyze whether The Jefferson Monthly should be able to recover the money owed from Red Cherry Fitness, Inc. based on apparent authority. Why or why not?
- Consult <u>Duluth Herald & News Tribune v. Plymouth Optical Co.</u>, 176 N.W.2d 552 (Minn. 1970) if you would like to compare your analysis to that of the court's.

6. Donaldson's is a department store located throughout the country. Recently, it has begun to lease out space within the store to different businesses and designers to offer a greater range of products and services to its clientele.

Sherry owns and operates a high-end pet boutique called Pampered Pets Pet Boutique. Pampered Pets advertises itself as a luxury spa and salon, fitness center, theater, and hotel for the most spoiled pets in Jefferson. Pampered Pets also has a pet restaurant that serves meals to suit all the dietary needs of dogs and cats: no-gluten, diabetic, and low-calorie diets. Sherry signed a lease with Donaldson's under which she leases a space to operate her pet boutique. Donaldson's has no control over how Sherry operates her business and mandates only that she be open for business during the regular operating hours of the department store.

Brenda took her beloved dog Lilly to Pampered Pets, where Lilly was to receive the Refresh spa package, which included a massage, herbal shampoo and deep conditioner, nail treatment, blow out for her fur and a top-chef-quality gluten-free meal. Much to Brenda's dismay, the treatment to Lilly's fur (shampoo, conditioner and blow out) was done in such a negligent manner that all of Lilly's fur fell out. Brenda suffered deep mortification because of Lilly's bald appearance, and Lilly had to withdraw from a dog show that she was scheduled to compete in (and expected to win).

Sherry advertises her pet salon services in the weekly sales circular for Donaldson's. The advertisements include a coupon for a shampoo, and the circular contains other coupons for 20 or 30% discounts on other items such as clothing at Donaldson's. The name Pampered Pets Pet Boutique appears only in small print in the advertisement. Sherry's business card says "Pampered Pet Boutique in Donaldson's Department Store: A Complete High-End Pet Salon." The department store manager, George Hill, has seen Sherry's business cards and has made no comments about the language used on them.

Sherry's customers enter the pet boutique through the Donaldson's main entrance, and no separate entrance exists. To reach Pampered Pets, a customer calls the Donaldson's main number and after going through the recorded voice mail system, is told to "press 3 for Pampered Pets Pet Boutique, owned and operated by Sherry Frank."

- State what the issue is.
- Examine and analyze whether Brenda should be able to recover for the damages that she and Lilly have suffered due to Sherry's negligence but from Donaldson's based on the theory of apparent authority. Why or why not?
- Consult <u>Manning v. Leavitt Co.</u>, 5 A.2d 667 (N.H. 1939) if you would like to compare your analysis to that of the court's.

Negotiation between Stray Dog Advertising and Canopy, Inc.

Overview of the Exercise: For this exercise, you will engage in a mock negotiation between the counsel of Stray Dog Advertising, LLC and Canopy, Inc., as the parties try to avoid litigation and find a negotiated settlement to the dispute.

Your instructor will assign you the role of counsel for either SDA or Canopy, Inc.; you will also receive confidential information that you will use for the negotiations.

Learning Objectives of the Exercise:

This exercise will build your skills to:

- Use monetary and non-monetary interests of parties in negotiating a settlement agreement
- Identify primary obstacles to reaching a mutually beneficial settlement agreement
- Implement negotiation strategies and tactics

Steps for Completing the Exercise:

- Read the preparatory information that you have been assigned and that your instructor will give to you.
- In a small group with other attorneys representing your client, discuss your client's position in the negotiations, analyze your client's strengths and weaknesses and those of opposing party, and come up with possible outcomes.
- Consider both legal, business and ethical considerations while preparing for the negotiation.
- Be familiar with the case law regarding apparent authority and the fact pattern of the dispute between SDA and Canopy.
- Articulate the arguments for your client's position and anticipate opposing counsel's.

Writing Exercise:

If time allows and if directed by your instructor, you and opposing counsel will also prepare a draft of the settlement agreement that your clients will sign after you have reached a negotiated agreement.

To complete this task, you first must find a template of a settlement agreement. In real life, few attorneys start from scratch (i.e. from zero) when drafting any contract or agreement. Why recreate the wheel? Instead, attorneys use a template and then adapt it to their purposes.

Thus, using a template is part of practice. Templates can be found in a law firm's database of documents, and many attorneys will take an agreement from a past case and modify and adapt it to a new case. Bar associations have templates and forms available (often for a fee), and many are available online as well.

But using a template comes with risks too. Even though the template is prepared, you can't simply cut and paste it to a new Word document and think you are good to go. Here are some questions that you have to ask yourself as you analyze a template:

- Does it include provisions that are illegal or violate some law, either because it was written by an attorney in another state or because the law has changed?
- Is it written to be beneficial to one side? For example, is it a very landlord-friendly lease agreement? If it is and if you represent the tenant, you will need to revise it.
- Does it include all the essential provisions? Just because a template is available doesn't mean that it is complete.
- Does your client's matter have unique circumstances or agreements that must be incorporated? It isn't always possible to find a template that perfectly suits your situation, so understanding that will make it easier to find a template that works and that can be adapted.

You also want to be very careful when you use a template to ensure that you remove all references that reveal that this was a template, or that reveal that the document was used with other clients or parties.

Once you have found a template online, adapt it to suit the agreement that you reached.

Grading: This assignment is not graded.

Presentation:
If SDA Were Your Client...

Overview of the Exercise: For this exercise, you will make a professional presentation in which you answer and discuss the following question: *If Stray Dog Advertising were your client in your home country and if Pamela came to you for legal advice about the contract issue with Canopy, Inc., what would you do and what advice would you give her?*

Learning Objectives of the Exercise:

This exercise will build your skills to:

- Examine the SDA/Canopy, Inc. dispute from the perspective of your country's legal system
- Compare your country's legal system with the U.S. legal system
- Explain how the dispute would be handled in your country's legal system and the advice that you would provide Pamela Park
- Understand specific information from your classmates' presentations

Steps for Completing the Exercise:

- Analyze the Stray Dog Advertising fact pattern under your country's laws.
- Determine whether or not Pamela Park/Stray Dog Advertising would have viable claims under your country's laws.
- Explain what claims she could bring (if any) and explain how her case would be handled in your country's legal system.
- Explain what legal advice you would give Pamela if she came to you for advice in your home country.

Research Required for the Exercise: The research you are required to do depends on your knowledge of these claims in your country's legal system. It is presumed that you are familiar with the law and with how you would approach this issue if Pamela were a client of yours.

Grading: This exercise is not graded. Depending on the size of your class and your instructor's choice, you will present to your fellow classmates or to the entire class.

Handouts:

As part of your presentation, you must create a handout for your classmates, and the handouts must include fill-in-the-blank questions that your classmates must complete with information that you present during the presentation. Each handout must include at least five questions to complete.

For example, if a U.S. law student were giving a presentation on apparent authority in the United States, she could include on her handout this question:

To establish apparent authority, the plaintiff must demonstrate that:

1) _____

2) _____

3) _____

As you are speaking, your classmates will have to listen, follow what you are saying and fill in the blanks. If you are listening to one of your classmate's presentations and are unsure about an answer, you should ask him or her to repeat so you can fill in the blank(s).

Grammar Review:

The basis of this exercise is hypothetical or conditional verbs: *if SDA were your client, what would you do?*

Remember the grammar when discussing hypothetical conditions.

Present: **IF + PAST SIMPLE, WOULD + BASE VERB**

*If Pamela **called** me to schedule an appointment, I **would tell** her to visit me at my office.*

NOTE: We use "were" for all tenses with the verb "to be" when using a conditional verb.

*If I **were** you, I **would not take** that class.*

*If Pamela **were** my client, I **would tell** her that she would not have a winning claim.*

Past: **IF + PAST PERFECT, WOULD + HAVE + PAST PARTICIPLE**

*If Gina McBride **had called** back rather than spoken with Charlene, this dispute **would not have happened**.*

*If Pamela **had called** me before I left for the day, I **would have told** her to come to my office at 12:00.*

Information Pages

Office Memo: Apparent Authority

Overview of the Assignment: For this assignment, you will write a memo to the Senior Partner, summarizing your research on apparent authority and providing your prediction of what would happen if litigation were to begin. You should also give recommendations and advice on how Stray Dog Advertising, LLC should approach this matter.

Learning Objectives of the Assignment:

This assignment will build your skills to:

- Efficiently communicate in a written format
- Explain complex matters clearly and concisely
- Analyze and apply the rules of law regarding apparent authority

Research for the Assignment: You are not required to do any outside research for this assignment. You should base your analysis on the New York apparent authority cases that you read:

- Edinburg Volunteer Fire Co. v. Danko Emergency Equipment Co., 867 N.Y.S.2d 547 (N.Y. App. Div. 2008).
- Merrell-Benco Agency, LLC v. HSBC Bank USA, 799 N.Y.S.2d 590 (N.Y. App. Div. 2005).
- Hallock v. State of New York, 474 N.E.2d 1178 (N.Y. 1984).
- Ford v. Unity Hospital, 32 N.E.2d 464 (N.Y. 1973).
- Regency Oaks Corp. v. Norman-Spencer McKernan, Inc., 12 N.Y.S.3d 398 (N.Y. App. Div. 2015).
- Greene v. Hellman, 412 N.E.2d 1301 (N.Y. 1980).

If you want to practice your legal research skills, you can look for and use other cases that you find. However, if you do search on Westlaw, LexisNexis or Bloomberg Law, be sure to limit your search and the cases you use to New York law and remember to change the citations and legal references to Jefferson law as indicated in the introduction.

Format of the Completed Assignment:

Your response should be in an office memo format and should include the following:

- Summary of the facts
- The relevant law
- Analysis of the law to the fact pattern
- Conclusion about how you think a court would rule if this matter were to go to court
- Your advice to the client about how to proceed

Follow the following format:

- 1 inch (2.54 cm.) margins (top/bottom and sides)
- 12 font, Times New Roman font
- Double spaced
- Maximum six pages

Notes: This memo should be predictive and not persuasive. You are not trying to persuade the senior partner or the client about the strength of your arguments or urge her to take a particular course of action; you are only trying to inform about the law, how it applies to our case, how you think a court would rule and what advice you have.

In a memo, you can also use formatting like underlining, bold font or italics. You can also create headings and subheadings to organize your answer.

For additional information about office memos and e-memos, as well as samples, refer to the online additional resources.

Grading: This assignment is worth 102 points.

Apparent Authority

Unit 2

LEGAL CONTENT	0-6 points	8 points	10 points	12 points	Points
Issue statement (IS)	Document does not include an IS or includes IS that fails to properly identify the legal issue(s) and the applicable law	Identifies the legal issue(s) and correctly states the applicable law with minor mistakes	Identifies the legal issue(s) and correctly states the applicable law	Identifies the legal issue(s) and correctly states the applicable law in an exceptionally creative and concise way	_____/12
Short Answer	Document does not include a short answer or includes a short answer with significant mistakes	Responds to IS but with key facts or applicable legal principles missing	Responds to IS with key facts and applicable legal principles with no meaningful errors	Clearly and concisely responds to IS with key facts and applicable legal principles and no irrelevancies	_____/12
Facts	Few or none of the relevant facts are included; difficult to follow or understand	Most relevant facts are included as well as non-relevant ones; at times difficult to follow	Relevant facts are included with occasional irrelevancies; easy to follow	All relevant facts are included with no irrelevancies; story is clearly and concisely told to reader in objective way	_____/12
Rule	Hard to follow and understand; does not include relevant sources or cites inappropriate sources; no rule application	Cites to some relevant sources but is incomplete in covering all relevant aspects of the rule; includes some rule application	Cite only to relevant sources and mostly clear; rule application explains but not fully how rule has been applied	Clear and concise; includes only relevant sources and includes all parts of rule necessary for analysis; clear rule application	_____/12
Analysis	Contains conclusory statements and/or no case law; facts are analyzed in a conclusory or insufficient way	Uses some case law but does not analogize or distinguish or explain its application; some conclusory statements; facts briefly analyzed	Uses case law to show how rule applies to case; case law is compared and contrasted with success; most facts are analyzed	Analyzes case law completely, comparing it fully to client matter; facts are thoroughly analyzed in an objective way	_____/12
Conclusion/ Recommendations	No conclusion or recommendations are included in document	A brief conclusion is included but without sufficient client advice	Paper includes conclusion and recommendations	Paper includes full conclusion of the legal analysis and facts and presents creative and thoughtful recommendations	_____/12
Citations	No sources are cited in document	Some sources are cited, but inconsistently; citation format is inconsistent	All citations are present; correct format is mostly used	All citations are present; correct format is used throughout document	_____/12
WRITING	**2**	**4**	**5**	**6**	**Points**
Formatting	Document does not follow format instructions or the sample provided	Document attempts to follow instructions and sample provided	Document follows the instructions and sample provided with no meaningful errors	Document exactly follows the instructions and sample provided	_____/6
Organization	No structure or organization; free flow of ideas	Structure & organization present but reorganization or headings needed for full clarity	Document is clearly organized and structured with proper use of heading and subheadings	Document is exceptionally well organized and structured with proper use of headings and subheadings	_____/6
Syntax Mechanics	Contains numerous and distracting grammatical and mechanical errors that impede understanding	Contains some grammatical and mechanical errors that impede understanding	Contains few grammatical and mechanical errors but none that impede understanding	Contains no grammatical and mechanical errors; native-like use of English	_____/6
TOTAL					_____/102

Mock Client
Meeting with Pamela Park

Overview of this Assignment: This assignment simulates a client meeting between you and your client, Pamela Park of Stray Dog Advertising, LLC. For this assignment you will meet with your client and explain to her the status of the contract dispute with Canopy, Inc., the results of your analysis about whether the modification made by Charlene Thomas is binding on Stray Dog, and your recommendations on how to proceed.

Your instructor will indicate to you that time that you have available for the mock client meeting.

Learning Objectives of the Assignment:

This assignment will build your skills to:

- Explain and clarify the legal positions of the parties and describe potential outcomes to your client
- Respond to technical questions about litigation
- Incorporate technical legal English vocabulary that relates to apparent authority and use appropriate layperson explanations for your client

Steps for Completing the Assignment:

- Read and be familiar with the Main Assignment File
- Be familiar with the apparent authority cases that you have been assigned
- Recommended:
    - Anticipate the questions that you think your client might ask and prepare possible responses
    - Draft an outline of what you would like to cover in the meeting

Grading: This assignment is worth 102 points.

Note: Remember that part of the grading is also based on your professional demeanor. You are expected to arrive punctually, be dressed in professional attire and act as you would with a client in real life. You should play the part from when you come into the meeting room.

Punctuality: Student-attorney arrived on time to meeting: YES _____ (10 points) NO _____ (0 points)

Professional Attire: Student-attorney was dressed in appropriate professional attire: YES _____ (10 points) NO _____ (0 points)

Professional Demeanor: Student-attorney acted in a professional manner w/ client: YES _____ (10 points) NO _____ (0 points)

GRADING CRITERIA	0- 6 points	8 points (C or 75%)	10 points (B or 85%)	12 points	Points received
Engagement I (questions)	Attorney does not ask client any questions; engages in monologue	Attorney asks few questions; questions are hard to follow or show minimal preparation or understanding of matter	Attorney asks basic questions that demonstrate understanding of matter and preparation	Attorney asks thoughtful, insightful and creative questions that demonstrate deep preparation & understanding of matter	_____/12
Engagement II (answers)	Attorney does not respond to client's questions	Attorney responds to questions, but incorrectly or with hard to follow answers	Attorney responds promptly and correctly to all of client's questions	Attorney responds promptly and correctly to all of client's questions with creative, thoughtful and insightful answers that show a deep understanding of the issues	_____/12
Knowledge of Applicable Law	Attorney provides no explanation of the applicable law	Attorney provides explanation of with serious mistakes, or hard to follow (e.g. use of legal jargon)	Attorney provides clear explanation of with some mistakes; uses some legal jargon unnecessarily or without explanations that client can understand	Attorney provides clear, concise and correct explanation of the law with legal jargon when appropriate or w/ explanations client can understand	_____/12
Ability to Analyze Applicable Law	Attorney provides does not provide an analysis of the law for the client	Attorney attempts to analyze the law but provides incomplete or incorrect analysis	Attorney provides analysis of the law with no significant mistakes or misstatements of the law or facts	Attorney provides a clear, concise and correct analysis of the law as it applies to the client matter	_____/12
Advice and Recommendations	Attorney provides no advice or poor advice for client	Attorney provides not comprehensive or inaccurate advice	Attorney provides comprehensive and accurate advice to client on his/her legal matter	Attorney provides thoughtful and creative solutions for client	_____/12
Organization	Meeting is disorganized and hard to follow or lacks any organization	Meeting has some organization but is still confusing for client for how information is presented	Meeting is clearly organized and easy to follow	Meeting is clearly organized and is easy to follow; attorney takes extra steps to ensure client's understanding	_____/12
TOTAL					_____/72
TOTAL FROM PUNCTUALITY AND PROFESSIONALISM					_____/30

Total   _____/102

Client Advice Letter

Overview of the Assignment: For this assignment, you will write an advice and follow-up letter to Pamela Park, summarizing your research on apparent authority, as well as your meeting with her. You should also give recommendations on how Stray Dog Advertising, LLC should approach this matter. Be mindful that even though Park is a sophisticated businesswoman, she is not a trained attorney. Therefore you should avoid legalese in your letter.

Under Rule 1.4(a)(3) of the Model Rules of Professional Conduct, an attorney has the duty to keep his or her client "reasonably informed about the status of the client's matter." A thorough follow-up letter after a client meeting is one of the best ways to meet this duty, as well as regular phone calls, emails or meetings.

Learning Objectives of the Assignment:

This assignment will build your skills to:

- Efficiently communicate in a written format
- Explain complex matters clearly and concisely
- Incorporate technical legal English vocabulary that relates to apparent authority and use appropriate layperson explanations for the client

Steps for Completing the Assignment:

- Review the predictive memo that you wrote to your senior partner about your client matter to ensure that the law and the issues are clear
- Be familiar with the case law regarding apparent authority, as well as the fact pattern
- Conduct your client meeting with your client, Pamela Park
- Review the Business Correspondence online resources

Research Required for the Assignment: You are not required to do any outside research for this assignment.

Format of the Completed Assignment:

Your assignment should be written as a business letter, not as an email. Even though many firms and lawyers use email for much of the correspondence carried out, formal business letters are still an essential part of the practice of law.

Your law firm has the following policy regarding business correspondence. Your client letter must follow the policy guidelines.

LAW FIRM CORRESPONDENCE POLICY

The purpose of this policy is to ensure a uniform appearance of all business correspondence that is written by the attorneys and staff of the law firm and thus to increase the professional appearance of the firm's work product. All law firm attorneys and staff are required to follow these guidelines when writing correspondence. Violation of the policy can result in disciplinary action, up to and including termination.

- The first page of all "traditional" letters must be written on law firm letterhead, which includes the firm's address and logo
- All letters must be written in a modified block letter format
- Letters must be written in Times New Roman, 12 font
- Letters must be 1.5 spaced and have 1" (2.54 cm.) margins, except for the initial page, which may have larger top margins to account for the logo, law firm address and sender's direct contact information
- Client letters must not exceed four pages

Grading: This assignment is worth 78 points.

Note: See the Online Additional Resources for examples of letters and for general information about business correspondence.

Apparent Authority · **Unit 2**

LEGAL CONTENT	0-6 points (failing)	8 points (C or 75%)	10 points (B or 85%)	12 points	Points
Introduction	Letter does not include an appropriate introduction or includes poorly constructed one	Letter includes introduction that states purpose with some irrelevancies or some relevant information missing	Introduction states purpose of letter and includes other relevant information	Introduction is engaging; states purpose of letter and includes other relevant information; written clearly and concisely	____/12
Summary of Meeting	Letter includes no summary of the meeting	Letter includes summary but leaves out important information or states it unclearly	Letter summarizes the meeting but leaves out important information	Letter clearly and concisely summarizes the meeting, its core purpose and content	____/12
Applicable Law	Student-attorney provides no explanation of the applicable law, or only uses legal jargon in explanation (inappropriate for audience)	Student-attorney provides explanation of with serious mistakes, or hard to follow (use of legal jargon)	Student-attorney provides clear explanation of with few mistakes; uses some legal jargon without appropriate explanations	Student-attorney provides clear, concise and correct explanation of the law with legal jargon with appropriate explanations	____/12
Analysis	Contains conclusory statements and/or no case law; facts are analyzed in a conclusory or insufficient way	Uses some case law but does not analogize or distinguish or explain its application; some conclusory statements; facts briefly analyzed	Uses case law to show how rule applies to case; case law is compared and contrasted with success; most facts are analyzed	Analyzes completely case law, comparing it fully to client matter; facts are thoroughly analyzed	____/12
Conclusion/ Recommendations	No conclusion or recommendations are included in letter	A brief conclusion is included but without sufficient advice or recommendations advice or next steps	Letter includes conclusion with recommendations and next steps	Letter includes full conclusion of the legal analysis and facts, presents creative and thoughtful recommendations and includes clear next steps	____/12
WRITING	2	4	5	6	Points
Formatting	Document does not follow format instructions or the sample provided	Document attempts to follow instructions and sample provided	Document follows the instructions and sample provided with minor errors	Document exactly follows the instructions and sample provided	____/6
Organization	No structure or organization; free flow of ideas	Letter includes organization and structure but is still confusing	Structure and organization but some reorganization is needed for full clarity	Document is clearly organized and structured	____/6
Syntax Mechanics	Contains numerous and distracting grammatical and mechanical errors that impede understanding	Contains some grammatical and mechanical errors that impede understanding	Contains few grammatical and mechanical errors but none that impede understanding	Contains no grammatical and mechanical errors; native-like use of English	____/6
TOTAL					____/78

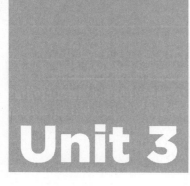

Common Law
Contract Formation and Promissory Estoppel
Unit 3
Ad Inventory Contract Dispute

For this Unit, you will provide your opinion on a contract dispute matter involving Stray Dog Advertising and a television broadcasting network, the Animal Lovers Broadcasting Company. The legal issues involved are contract formation and promissory estoppel.

Learning Objectives of this Unit:

This Unit will build your skills to:

- Explain complex legal matters clearly and concisely
- Use appropriate technical terminology
- Identify and analyze the applicable case law and relevant facts
- Efficiently read and understand legal authority
- Articulate legal arguments in support of the client's position
- Analyze possible outcomes for legal dispute, evaluate and articulate strengths and weaknesses of such outcomes
- Efficiently and effectively communicate in a written and oral format

To achieve these learning objectives, you will complete the following tasks:
- Draft a predictive office memo to senior partner regarding contract formation
- Draft a predictive office memo to senior partner regarding promissory estoppel
- Draft a client advice letter regarding the contract dispute and your client meeting
- Carry out client meeting with Pamela Park

To complete these tasks, you will use the following materials:

Contract Formation

- Assignment email from Senior Partner (page 76)
- Main Assignment File (pages 77-82)
- Contract Formation Commented Cases:
    - Cleveland Wrecking Co. v. Hercules Construction Corp., 23 F. Supp. 2d 287 (E.D.N.Y.1998).
    - International Business Machines Corp. v. Johnson, 629 F. Supp. 2d 321 (S.D.N.Y. 2009).
    - Trademark Properties Inc. v. A&E Television Networks, 422 Fed. Appx. 199 (4th Cir. 2011).
    - Kowalchuk v. Stroup, 61 A.D.3d 118 (N.Y. App. Div. (2009).
    - Bazak International Corp. v. Tarrant Apparel Group, 378 F. Supp. 2d 377 (S.D.N.Y. 2005).
- ESL Workbook (pages 33-48)

Promissory Estoppel

- Assignment email from Senior Partner (page 83)
- Main Assignment File (pages 77-82)
- Promissory Estoppel Commented Cases:
    - Goff-Hamel v. Obstetricians & Gynecologists, P.C., 588 N.W.2d 798 (Neb. 1999).
    - Maxell, Inc. v. Kenney Deans, Inc., No. A-98-930, 1999 WL 731846 (Ct. App. Neb. Sept. 21, 1999).
    - deNourie & Yost Homes, LLC v. Frost, 854 N.W.2d 298 (Neb. 2014).
    - 168th and Dodge LP v. Rave Reviews Cinemas, LLC, 501 F.3d 945 (8th Cir. 2007).
- ESL Workbook (pages 49-60)

Your instructor will also assign you additional skills-building exercises to bolster your understanding of the legal issues and further develop your legal reasoning and language skills. You will find an icon with each exercise that indicates which skills the exercise will focus on.

ICON	SKILL
	Speaking — in particular about the legal issues and the law presented in the Unit
	Oral comprehension
	Legal analysis and reasoning
	Analysis of the legal issue(s) presented in the Unit
	English grammar, syntax, and vocabulary
	Legal ethics and professional responsibility
	Legal research

In this Unit, the additional skills-building exercises that accompany the Main Assignment File include:

- Contract Formation Analysis Exercise #1 — Ambiguous Acceptance (pages 84-85)
- Contract Formation Analysis Exercise #2 — Manner of Acceptance (pages 86-90)
- Professional Presentation: *If SDA Were Your Client...* (pages 91-92)
- Ethics Dilemma (pages 93-96)

Before beginning the Unit, you should read and be familiar with the Stray Dog Advertising Factual Background (pages 7-8) and the Factual Background of the Lincoln, Adams and Washington Law Firm (pages 2-3).

You will also find online at the website www.legalwritingforllms.com the following online resources. They will help you deepen your mastery of the skills presented in the Unit and also provide additional understanding about the U.S. legal system and legal writing.

- Additional Resources:
  - Sources of American Law
  - Writing Professional Emails
  - Writing Predictive Memos
  - Writing E-memos
  - IRAC
- Additional Skills-Building Exercises:
  - Issues and Issue Statements
  - Stating the Rule
  - Analysis
  - Ethical Spotlight Exercises

Section I, Unit 3 Legal Issues
Contract Formation and Promissory Estoppel

Main Assignment File	Contract Formation Cases	ESL Workbook	Additional Exercises	Additional Online Resources
Introduction to File and Client Matter Pages 71-75	Cleveland Wrecking Co., v. Hercules Const. Corp., 23 F. Supp. 2d 287 (E.D.N.Y. 1998)).	Cleveland Wrecking Co., v. Hercules Const. Corp., 23 F. Supp. 2d 287 (E.D.N.Y. 1998)).	Contract Formation: Ambiguous Acceptance Pages 84-85	Writing Professional Emails
Documents Related to Client Matter Pages 76-83	Int'l Business Machines Corp. v. Johnson, 629 F. Supp. 2d 321 (S.D.N.Y. 2009).	Int'l Business Machines Corp. v. Johnson, 629 F. Supp. 2d 321 (S.D.N.Y. 2009).	Contract Formation: Manner of Acceptance Pages 86-90	Business Correspondence (with sample letters)
Assignment Information Pages + Rubrics Pages 97-104	Trademark Properties Inc. v. A&E Television Networks, 422 Fed. Appx. 199 (4th Cir. 2011).	Trademark Properties Inc. v. A&E Television Networks, 422 Fed. Appx. 199 (4th Cir. 2011).	Presentation: If SDA Were Your Client... Pages 91-92	Writing Memos (office memos and e-memos)
	Kowalchuk v. Stroup, 61 A.D.3d 118 (N.Y. App. Div. (2009)).	Kowalchuk v. Stroup, 61 A.D.3d 118 (N.Y. App. Div. (2009)).	Ethics Dilemma Pages 93-96	IRAC (including the various exercises for each element)
	Bazak Int'l Corp. v. Tarrant Apparel Grp., 378 F. Supp. 2d 377 (S.D.N.Y. 2005).	Bazak Int'l Corp. v. Tarrant Apparel Grp., 378 F. Supp. 2d 377 (S.D.N.Y. 2005).		Skills-Building Exercises for Rules, Issues and Issues Statements, Analysis and Ethical Dilemmas

Promissory Estoppel Cases	ESL Workbook
Goff-Hamel v. Obstetricians & Gynecologists, P.C., 588 N.W.2d 798 (Neb. 1999).	Goff-Hamel v. Obstetricians & Gynecologists, P.C., 588 N.W.2d 798 (Neb. 1999).
Maxell, Inc. v. Kenney Deans, Inc., 1999 WL 731846 (Ct. App. Neb. Sept. 21, 1999).	Maxell, Inc. v. Kenney Deans, Inc., 1999 WL 731846 (Ct. App. Neb. Sept. 21, 1999).
deNourie & Yost Homes, LLC v. Frost, 854 N.W.2d 298 (Neb. 2014).	deNourie & Yost Homes, LLC v. Frost, 854 N.W.2d 298 (Neb. 2014).
168th and Dodge LP v. Rave Reviews Cinemas, LLC, 501 F.3d 945 (8th Cir. 2007).	168th and Dodge LP v. Rave Reviews Cinemas, LLC, 501 F.3d 945 (8th Cir. 2007).

Introduction — Promissory Estoppel and Contract Formation

If you are taking contracts as part of your LL.M. program, you are probably familiar with the legal issues that you will deal with in this Unit: contract formation, breach of contract, and promissory estoppel. But for those of you who aren't, below is a brief introduction to these issues. You will likely find similarities between the laws in your country for contract formation and breach of contract while promissory estoppel may be a new concept for you.

But regardless of whether you are learning about a new issue or reviewing one you are already familiar with, part of improving your knowledge of legal English is acquiring new vocabulary. You are no doubt already familiar with two of the most common words in this Unit: contract and agreement. The question, though, is what's the difference between these two words?

> "[T]he standard merger **agreement** contains a term permitting the buyer to exit without penalty if a material adverse change occurs in the interim between signing the **contract** and concluding the merger." Alan Schwartz & Robert E. Scott, *Contract Theory and the Limits of Contract Law*, 113 YALE L.J. 541, 603 n.129 (2003) (emphasis added).

In English, we often use the terms contract and agreement interchangeably. We talk about a lease agreement, or an employment agreement. But we can also say that the parties entered into a contract. The words seem to have the same meaning, but there are actually differences between them.

A contract is a promise or a set of promises that is enforceable by law, meaning that the parties are legally obligated to perform the duties in the contract, and if one party does not, the law provides the other party remedies for the non-performance.[24] An agreement, on the other hand, is a more informal arrangement that is not enforceable by law.

But in real life, we often use the term agreement instead of contract. You might hear an attorney say that she prepared a "lease agreement" for her landlord client, or that she reviewed a "franchise agreement" for a client. But in reality, if a landlord and tenant sign a written document regarding the rental of a house or an apartment, under which the landlord allows the tenant to occupy the property and the tenant pays a certain amount of money in exchange, they have really signed a lease contract since the arrangement would be enforceable in court if the tenant failed to pay or if the landlord breached the lease in some way. But strangely enough, we usually say lease agreement instead! What you need to know is that if you see the term lease agreement, service agreement, franchise agreement, etc., you are really dealing with a contract that is enforceable by law if breached, not a more informal agreement.[25]

What needs to be present in order for a contract to be formed? In general terms, one person (the offeror) must make an offer, which another person (the offeree) must accept. Consideration must exist, and both parties must agree to the same essential terms of the contract — called mutual assent or meeting of the minds.[26]

Sometimes, no dispute exists over the existence of a valid and enforceable agreement, but whether the contract was breached. If a plaintiff brings a claim for breach of contract, he will have to show:

- the existence of a contract,
- the plaintiff's performance under the contract,
- the defendant's breach of the contract, and
- the resulting damages.[27]

---

[24] RESTATEMENT (SECOND) OF CONTRACTS § 1 (AM. LAW INST. 1981).

[25] Note too that within a contract, we can have agreements or provisions. See, e.g., Bosio v. Branigar Org., Inc., 506 N.E.2d 996, 998 (Ill. App. Ct. 1987) ("Under the [Illinois Structural Work] Act, an agreement for indemnity for one's own negligence will be enforced if it is found in a construction bond or an insurance contract,") (citing 740 ILL. COMP. STAT. 35/3 (2016)). ("This Act does not apply to construction bonds or insurance contracts or agreements.").

[26] Delcon Grp., Inc. v. N. Trust Corp., 543 N.E.2d 595, 600 (Ill. App. Ct. 1989).

[27] See Elisa Dreier Reporting Corp. v. Global Naps Networks, Inc., 921 N.Y.S.2d 329, 333 (N.Y. App. Div. 2011); Palmetto Partners, L.P. v. AJW Qualified Partners, LLC, 921 N.Y.S.2d 260, 264 (N.Y. App. Div. 2011) (citing JP Morgan Chase v. J.H. Elec. of N.Y., Inc., 893 N.Y.S.2d 237, 239 (N.Y. App. Div. 2010)); Furia v. Furia, 498 N.Y.S.2d 12, 13 (N.Y. App. Div. 1986).

Sometimes, however, a party (the promisor) might make a promise to another person (the promisee), but the promise isn't a legally enforceable contract because some element of contract formation — often consideration — is lacking. What happens if that person (the promisee) relies on the promise and takes action based on it, thinking that the promisor will carry through on his word? Is it fair to allow the promisor to just back out of the promise without any consequences for his actions?

In these situations, the claim of promissory estoppel steps in to fill the gap and enforce the promise. In such cases, courts have applied the principle of promissory estoppel in effect to form a contract, in reliance on that promise that wasn't fulfilled.[28]

The court enforces the promise out of fairness to the person to whom the promise was made, provided that he reasonably relied on the promise and that he suffered damages of some sort because of that reasonable reliance on the promise. For this reason, promissory estoppel is called a *quasi-contract* claim. Quasi is a Latin term that means "almost," and because something such as consideration is lacking, we almost (but not quite) have a contract. Even though we have only an "almost" contract (not a full, enforceable contract), recovery is still allowed under promissory estoppel.

> Promissory estoppel does not attempt to provide the plaintiff damages based upon the benefit of the bargain. This is a significant difference between contract and promissory estoppel claims. Under a breach of contract claim, a plaintiff can recover expectation damages, or in other words, the compensation that the plaintiff would have received if the contract had been performed. Under promissory estoppel, a court will look to make the plaintiff whole by awarding reliance damages and damages "as justice requires." Mary E. Becker, *Promissory Estoppel Damages*, 16 HOFSTRA L. REV. 131, 132-33 (1987).

Public policy is an important foundation of promissory estoppel. Policy arguments may play a less important role in other legal systems, so identifying and articulating them is a useful exercise. The public policy behind promissory estoppel is "an attempt by the courts to keep remedies abreast of increased moral consciousness of honesty and fair representation in all business dealings."[29] In other words, we want to encourage people to follow through on their promises, and want to provide assurances that people can rely on the promises of others, and provide a legal remedy when that does not happen.

In a complaint, an attorney can bring a claim of both breach of contract and promissory estoppel because we are allowed to argue in the alternative: my client should recover the money he is owed because a contract was formed and was breached, but if the court should determine that no contract was formed, then my client should still be allowed to recover under the theory of promissory estoppel. However, a plaintiff can never recover for both breach of contract and promissory estoppel in the same complaint and based on the same facts. You can have either a fully formed contract or promissory estoppel, but not both.

In this Unit, your focus will be on whether a valid contract was formed between Stray Dog Advertising and the Animal Lovers Broadcasting Company, and the focus will be on the acceptance and whether it was valid. You will first analyze the facts from the issue of contract formation. After determining whether or not a valid contract was formed and whether Stray Dog Advertising could successfully bring a breach of contract claim, you will then analyze whether in the alternative, the LAW Law Firm should file a claim of promissory estoppel on SDA's behalf.

The contract formation cases that you will read are from New York, while the promissory estoppel cases are from Nebraska. When writing your assignments, be sure to change the citations for our fictitious jurisdiction of Jefferson as indicated on page 9 of the Introduction.

The Nebraska rule for promissory estoppel is interesting because in most cases, a Nebraska court does not require that the promise giving rise to the cause of action be so comprehensive in scope — so "clear and definite" — as to meet the requirements of an offer that would ripen into a contract if accepted by the promisee.[30] Instead, the reliance must only be "reasonable and foreseeable."[31] The promissory estoppel rule that you study in your contracts class may be different than the rule enunciated by the Nebraska courts. Contract law is a state-law matter and legal standards, rules and laws can vary from state to state. Just because the Nebraska standard may be different than what you have learned in class does not mean that the either the Nebraska rule or the cases and rules presented in your contract law casebook are incorrect.

---

[28] 4 WILLISTON ON CONTRACTS § 8:4 (4th ed. 2016).

[29] Rosnick v. Dinsmore, 457 N.W.2d 793, 801 (Neb. 1990).

[30] Goff-Hamel v. Obstetricians & Gynecologists, P.C., 588 N.W.2d 798, 801, 804 (Neb. 1999).

[31] Id. at 801.

Main Assignment File: Contract Formation

Today, you receive the following email from Senior Partner Jack Adams. The email is about Stray Dog Advertising, one of the firm's main clients, and you have been asked to work on this case.

From: Jack Adams <j.adams@lawlawfirm.com>
To: Associate Attorney <a.attorney@lawlawfirm.com>
Sent: August 23, THIS YEAR 1:02 p.m.
Re: Contract Dispute Stray Dog Advertising

Associate attorney,

I need your help with another issue that has come up with Pamela Park over at Stray Dog Advertising. When we met with Pamela earlier this year, she mentioned that she was looking for a TV commercial to expand the national brand of SDA. She and her staff got in touch with the Animal Lovers Broadcasting Company to purchase a 30-second commercial spot in the YEAR +1 Pony Bowl show.

As you will see in the emails that I will forward to you, the purchase negotiation was a mix of email correspondence, phone calls, in-person meetings, and text messages. Eventually, ALBC made an offer to SDA of $300,000 through email, and the media buyer at SDA responded, "That would work" with a thumbs-up emoji. Pamela believed they entered into a binding contract and started preparations for the commercial. However the sales agent at ALBC claimed no contract was formed and sold the spot to someone else. Now SDA has already made a total payment of $300,000 for the commercial production. Pamela wants to be compensated for the damages as they cannot air the commercial on ALBC.

In my opinion, this is a contract formation case. I think the issue is whether a valid and enforceable contract was even formed. You might conclude differently and of course I will concede to your expertise once you research the matter. In addition to the emails, I will forward to you some cases that the law clerk found that seem to be on point.

This is what I need from you before I meet with Pamela:

- A memo that states what the issue is;
- A summary of the applicable Jefferson law;
- Your analysis of the law as it applies to the facts of Pamela's case;
- Your prediction of what you think a court would decide if Pamela sues ALBC; and
- Your advice to Pamela on what she should do.

I am meeting with Pamela at the end of next week. I will need your response a week from today. Let me know if anything isn't clear in the emails and we can call Pamela to clarify.

Jack

Adams has asked you to write him a memo about the following:

- A summary of what has happened between Stray Dog Advertising and Animal Lovers Broadcasting Company
- The legal issue at hand
- A summary and analysis of the law that applies (contract formation)
- Your opinion about whether a contract was formed between SDA and ALBC
- Your advice to Pamela Park about how to proceed with this matter

You will find complete information about this assignment on the Information Page (pages 97-98).

You will be analyzing the client matter using the contract formation cases that you read and review in class.

From:	Pamela Park <pamela.park@straydogadvertising.com>
To:	Jack Adams <j.adams@lawlawfirm.com>
Sent:	August 22, THIS YEAR 16:39
Subject:	Do I have a case?

Hi Jack,

I need your help on an urgent matter! I can't believe this is happening.

You know about this show called the Pony Bowl, right? It's on ALBC, the Animal Lovers Broadcasting Company. We get it with our cable package. I am sure you've heard of it as the channel and the Pony Bowl have become very popular.

Anyway, I met with their sales agent Richard Saucedo at an Animal Rights Conference early this year. I am very impressed by all of their shows, especially the Pony Bowl, and thought that it would be a perfect fit for us to expand our brand at the national level. Our media buyer, Emily Johnson, contacted Richard Saucedo about buying an advertising spot during the YEAR +1 Pony Bowl, and they reached an agreement pretty quickly. Most of their communication was via text messages, as Richard told Emily he was more comfortable with texting. On August 3, Richard sent Emily an offer of $300,000. Emily responded on the 7th, saying "that would work".

Believing the contract was signed, we assigned one copywriter, art director, creative director, and media analyst to work full time on this commercial, and made down payments for filming and actors and everything. However, when Emily went to make the payment yesterday morning, Richard told her she never accepted the contract and now they have sold out the entire ad inventory!! We really need this commercial; we already paid $300,000 in total! And that's excluding the price for the ad spot! What can I do? Can I enforce the contract? Or at least get our money back?

PP

From:	Emily Johnson <emily.johnson@straydogadvertising.com>
To:	Richard Saucedo <saucedo@albc.com>
Sent:	June 15, THIS YEAR 10:39
Subject:	Ad Inventory for Pony Bowl!

Dear Mr. Saucedo,

Good morning. I am the media buyer of Stray Dog Advertising. You probably remember our owner, Pamela Park, from the Media Leadership workshop at the Animal Rights Conference. We are interested in buying ad inventory for the upcoming Pony Bowl. Can I get a price quote for a 30 second ad? Please let me know if you are interested.

Take care,

Emily

From:	Richard Saucedo <saucedo@albc.com>
To:	Emily Johnson <emily.johnson@straydogadvertising.com>
Sent:	June 19, 2015 13:17
Subject:	Re: Ad Inventory for Pony Bowl!

Hi Emily,

Yes let's talk about the ad inventory. I prefer phone calls. You can reach me at 613–523–1979. I am free this afternoon.

Ricky

From: Emily Johnson <emily.johnson@straydogadvertising.com>
To: Richard Saucedo <saucedo@albc.com>
Sent: June 22, THIS YEAR 8:52
Subject: Re: Re: Ad Inventory for Pony Bowl!

Dear Ricky,

I still want to talk to you about the Pony Bowl ad inventory. I just left you a voicemail message, but wanted to follow up with an email in case you didn't hear or get it.

Would you prefer to set up a time for the phone call? I am available today or tomorrow morning. I can also talk in the evening hours if that works better for you.

Emily

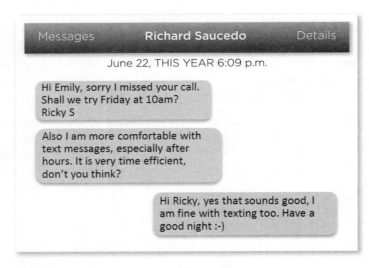

From: Emily Johnson <emily.johnson@straydogadvertising.com>
To: Pamela Park <pamela.park@straydogadvertising.com >
Sent: June 26, THIS YEAR 10:52 a.m.
Subject: Fwd: Re: Re: Ad Inventory for Pony Bowl!

Hi Pamela,

I have some updates on the Pony Bowl commercial!! I just got off the phone with Ricky at ALBC, he told me they do have a few spots left. He said the price for a 30-second ad is usually $350,000, but he is willing to hear our offer too. So far they haven't sold any ads to other advertising companies, so I think we will truly stand out if we can get this spot! We also set up a meeting on the 13th to talk about the details and negotiate the price more. He seems really nice and pretty interested in SDA. I have a good feeling about getting this. ☺

Emily

From: Pamela Park <pamela.park@straydogadvertising.com >
To: Emily Johnson <emily.johnson@straydogadvertising.com>
Sent: June 26, THIS YEAR 11:11 a.m.
Subject: Re: Fwd: Re: Re: Ad Inventory for Pony Bowl!

Hi Emily,

That sounds great! I think you are in great position to work this out with Ricky. 350K is way above our budget but I guess it is not too bad to start with. See if you can get it to 250K.

PP

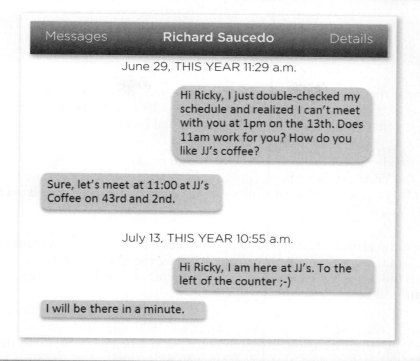

From: Emily Johnson <emily.johnson@straydogadvertising.com>
To: Pamela Park <pamela.park@straydogadvertising.com >
Sent: July 13, THIS YEAR 1:07 p.m.
Subject: Re: Re: Fwd: Re: Re: Ad Inventory for Pony Bowl!

Hi Pamela,

I just met with Ricky to discuss the Pony Bowl commercial. It went pretty well. He is so laid back and super easy to work with. We are on the same page now in terms of the general message we are sending, how it fits in with the other commercials (they are mainly social enterprises, horse boarding/training facilities, and Ag groups), the timeline, and how we can work together through the whole process. He also gave me a sample purchase agreement, which is attached to this email. The only thing we need to determine is the price. He made a second offer of 350K, I told him we can only do 250K. He said he would need to ask his boss. Is there anything else we need to nail down?

Emily

SAMPLE PURCHASE AGREEMENT OF ALBC TV ADVERTISING INVENTORY

This contract sets forth the agreement between Animal Lovers Broadcasting Company, Inc. ("ALBC"), and Stray Dog Advertising, LLC. ("Advertiser") with respect to Advertiser's purchase of certain ALBC Television Network advertising inventory. The terms and conditions shall be as follows:

1. Spot. ALBC shall provide Advertiser with the use of one 30 second advertising spot (the "Spot") to be telecast on ALBC TV during the YEAR +1 Pony Bowl (Program) halftime, and specific time frame shall be reasonably determined by ALBC in accordance with schedules and strategies reasonably requested by Advertiser following consultations with ALBC.

2. Value of Spot. The value of each of Advertiser's Spots telecast by ALBC TV pursuant to the terms hereof shall be _____ (the "Total Spot Value"). Advertiser shall pay the Total Spot Value to ALBC in cash no later than 150 days prior to the telecast. Advertiser agrees that ALBC makes no guarantee regarding what the actual rating for the Program will be.

3. Representations and Warranties. ALBC and Advertiser each represent and warrant that this Purchase Agreement has been duly authorized, executed and delivered by such party and that this Purchase Agreement constitutes the legal, valid and binding obligations of such party, enforceable against it in accordance with its terms.

4. Confidentiality. Neither party shall issue a press release or make any statement to the general public concerning this Purchase Agreement, the Spot, or the existence thereof, without the express prior written consent of the other.

5. Miscellaneous. This Purchase Agreement hereto constitutes the entire agreement and understanding of the parties relating to the subject matter hereof and supersedes all prior and contemporaneous agreements, negotiations, and understandings between the parties, both oral and written. No waiver or modification of any provision of this Purchase Agreement shall be effective unless in writing and signed by both parties. Any waiver by either party of any provision of this Purchase Agreement shall not be construed as a waiver of any other provision of this Purchase Agreement, nor shall such waiver operate as or be construed as a waiver of such provision respecting any future event or circumstance.

6. Governing Law and Jurisdiction. This Purchase Agreement shall be governed by and construed under the laws of the State of Jefferson applicable to contracts fully performed in Jefferson. The parties hereto irrevocably consent to and submit to the exclusive jurisdiction of the federal and state courts located in the State of Jefferson.

Animal Lover Broadcasting Company, Inc.

By: _____
    Richard Saucedo
    Senior Sales Agent

From: Pamela Park <pamela.park@straydogadvertising.com >
To: Emily Johnson <emily.johnson@straydogadvertising.com>
Sent: July 15, THIS YEAR 2:37 p.m.
Subject: Re: Re: Re: Fwd: Re: Re: Ad Inventory for Pony Bowl!

Hi Emily,

I am very impressed by your efficiency! Let me think about the price and maybe go over our budget again with other staff before we get back to him.

PP

From: Pamela Park <pamela.park@straydogadvertising.com >
To: Emily Johnson <emily.johnson@straydogadvertising.com>
Sent: July 15, THIS YEAR 6:12 p.m.
Subject: Re: Re: Re: Fwd: Re: Re: Ad Inventory for Pony Bowl!

Emily,

The max I am willing to pay for this commercial is $300,000 and you have authority to negotiate any price up to that amount. I'd prefer to pay around $275,000 if possible, so why don't you make that offer and see how they respond?

PP

From: Emily Johnson <emily.johnson@straydogadvertising.com>
To: Richard Saucedo <saucedo@albc.com>
Sent: July 30, THIS YEAR 3:39 p.m.
Subject: Re: Re: Re: Ad Inventory for Pony Bowl!

Hi Ricky,

After discussing it with my boss, we are willing to pay $275,000 for the ad spot. Do you still stand firm on the $350,000 😊😊😊

Emily

From: Richard Saucedo <saucedo@albc.com>
To: Emily Johnson <emily.johnson@straydogadvertising.com>
Sent: August 3, THIS YEAR 1:52 p.m.
Subject: Re: Re: Re: Re: Ad Inventory for Pony Bowl!

Hi Emily,

New deal. We will offer you a 30-second ad during the YEAR +1 Pony Bowl halftime for $300,000.

Ricky

From: Emily Johnson <emily.johnson@straydogadvertising.com>
To: Richard Saucedo <saucedo@albc.com>
Sent: August 7, THIS YEAR 10:39 a.m.
Subject: Re: Re: Re: Re: Re: Ad Inventory for Pony Bowl!

That would work.

Emily

From: Emily Johnson <emily.johnson@straydogadvertising.com>
To: Richard Saucedo <saucedo@albc.com>
Sent: August 21, THIS YEAR 10:39 a.m.
Subject: Re: Re: Re: Re: Re: Re: Ad Inventory for Pony Bowl!

Hi Ricky,

I am dropping off the check for $300,000 for the ad on the 1st. Will you be around?

Emily

From: Richard Saucedo <saucedo@albc.com>
To: Emily Johnson <emily.johnson@straydogadvertising.com>
Sent: August 22, THIS YEAR 1:52 p.m.
Subject: Re: Re: Re: Re: Re: Re: Re: Ad Inventory for Pony Bowl!

Hi Emily,

You never accepted my $300,000 offer; we sold the spot to someone else.

Ricky

Main Assignment: Promissory Estoppel

You have completed your initial research for Senior Partner Adams, which he has communicated to Pamela in the meeting that he had with her. However, Jack would like you to continue your research of the SDA matter and has sent you the following email explaining the next assignment that he would like you to do.

From: Jack Adams < j.adams@lawlawfirm.com >
To: Associate Attorney < a.attorney@lawlawfirm.com >
Sent: September 6, THIS YEAR 1:02 p.m.
Re: Contract Dispute Stray Dog Advertising

Associate attorney,

I continue to need your expertise and legal assistance with this matter involving Stray Dog Advertising and the Animal Lovers Broadcasting Company. As you know, I met with Pamela last week and we discussed the contract formation issue. However, I think that we should also consider whether to bring a promissory estoppel claim on behalf of SDA.

I have a second meeting with Pamela scheduled in two weeks. I need you to prepare for me a second memo that includes the following information:

- A brief summary of the legal issue at hand;
- A summary of the applicable Jefferson law regarding promissory estoppel;
- Your analysis of the law as it applies to the facts of Pamela's case;
- Your prediction of what you think a court would decide if Pamela sues ABLC; and
- Your advice to Pamela on what she should do.

We will be relying on the same emails that I forwarded to you before as there has been no new correspondence and no contact between anyone at SDA and ALBC.

Jack

Jack Adams
Partner
Lincoln, Adams and Washington Law Firm, PLLC

Adams has asked you to write him a memo about the following:

- A summary of what has happened between Stray Dog Advertising and Animal Lovers Broadcasting Company
- The legal issue at hand
- A summary and analysis of the law that applies (promissory estoppel)
- Your opinion about whether SDA would prevail if it were to bring a promissory estoppel claim against ALBC
- Your advice to Pamela Park about how to proceed with this matter

You will find complete information about this assignment on the Information Page (pages 99-100).

You will be analyzing the client matter using the promissory estoppel cases that you read and review in class.

Additional Skills-Building Exercises

Contract Formation Analysis Exercise #1
Ambiguous Acceptance

Overview of the Exercise: The following short fact patterns deal with ambiguous acceptance, and your task is to analyze the fact patterns and determine whether or not a contract was formed.

Learning Objectives of the Exercise:

This exercise will build your skills to:

- Understand the law of contract formation
- Analyze fact patterns and determine whether a contract was formed
- Articulate the reasoning for your conclusion, using legal terminology of contract formation

Directions for Completing the Exercise:

- Read the following fact patterns.
- By yourself, analyze and decide whether or not you think a contract was formed and why. You don't need to write out a full answer, but jot down notes about your reasoning.
- When you are done analyzing each of the fact patterns, discuss your answers with a classmate. Explain to each other why you have reached the conclusion that you did.
- If you and your partner have different responses to a fact pattern, you must try to convince him or her that your answer is correct. After you both have tried to convince the other, you must choose a team answer.
- Once you have discussed each of the fact patterns, you will compare answers as a class with your classmates.

Grading: This exercise is not graded. Instead, you will compare answers as a class.

1. Ashley texted her friend Ben: "I am selling my green 2015 Chevrolet Camaro for $20,000. Are you interested?" Ben replied, "That is a steal! Lucky me!"

2. Cara wants to have made a new set of patio seats. She offered carpenter Dale $5,000 for the job. Dale said, "Okay, if you also pay for my supplies."

3. Elizabeth is selling her house; she prefers to sell all the furniture as well to save the hassle. Frank came for a showing, and offered to buy it for $300,000 with all the furniture cleared out. Elizabeth shrugged and said, "Well, I will do a garage sale then."

4. Gina travels a lot for work and wants to find a roommate to take care of her cats when she is gone. She posted an ad on Craigslist, entitled "discount rent for pet care, $700/month OBO" and described her situation. Harrison saw the ad and emailed her saying, "I love cats and $700 sounds very reasonable". Gina replied, "Great, when can you move in?"

5. Ian asked his father, "If I score above 175 on the LSAT, would you pay for my trip to Europe?" His father laughed and said, "I guess I will pay for the trip if such a miracle can happen."

6. Jeremy offered to sublease his apartment to Kelly. He told her if she wanted to accept the offer, she had to write a check for the rent of the first month, pay the deposit in cash, and sign two copies of the sublease agreement and deliver one to Jeremy and the other to the landlady. Kelly said, "Okay, I don't do checks. I will just pay the rent in cash."

7. Laura painted a portrait of her friend Marco. Laura told Marco he could have it for $50. Marco said, "It is real art, I can't wait to have it on my wall." Laura then delivered the painting to Marco's house.

8. Natalie is a baker. When making an 8-inch birthday cake for Oliver, she messed up the order and made a 10-inch one. Usually Natalie sells the 8-inch cake for $50, and the 10-inch for $70. She called Oliver asking if he would take the cake for $60. Oliver said, "I didn't invite that many guests, but I guess the more the merrier."

Contract Formation Analysis Exercise #2
Manner of Acceptance

Overview of Exercise: For this exercise you will analyze a contract formation issue. The fact pattern will be the same one you have been studying for this Unit. However, there is a new twist. The issue is still contract formation. However, unlike the other fact pattern, this one does not involve an ambiguous acceptance, but rather whether the manner of acceptance — a text message — is sufficient to form a contract when the offeror requires acceptance in writing.

In this case, until the final emails and text messages, Ricky and Emily have had the exact same communication. After this information page, you will find one email message that is the same as the other communication string and is the last that is identical to the other emails and texts. After that email, you will find the new emails and texts exchanged between Ricky and Emily that you are to use for your analysis in this exercise only.

After you have reviewed the communications between Ricky and Emily, you will find short summaries of case law that you will review. After you have read the materials, you will discuss with a partner or in a small group the following questions:

- Was a contract formed? Why or why not?
- Is a text message a "writing" for contract formation purposes? Why or why not?
- Was the case law helpful? Why or why not? For the cases that you found helpful, explain how you would use them in your analysis. For the cases that you did not find helpful, explain why you would not use them in your analysis.
- Will you supplement your analysis with any other information, such as your personal knowledge or experience with text messages, emails or other forms of electronic communication?
- How do you think a court would rule if this case were litigated?
- Does it matter that the case law is only persuasive precedent and that there is no binding precedent on point? Why or why not?

Each member of your group must answer the above questions and state his or her opinion. Once you have discussed and answered the questions and each person has stated his or her opinion, you must come to a consensus answer for your group. If you and your partner(s) have different opinions on any of the above questions, you must try to persuade him/her/them that your answer is the correct one. Eventually, you will have to choose an answer that is representative of the group. Once all the groups have an answer, you will compare answers as a class.

Learning Objectives of the Exercise:

This exercise will build your skills to:
- Reason and analyze by analogy
- Apply persuasive precedent to a fact pattern and reach a conclusion based on law and on policy
- Articulate the reasons for your legal conclusion and defend your responses

Directions for Completing the Exercise:

- Read the variation of the fact pattern of Stray Dog Advertising and Animal Lovers Broadcasting Company
- Read and analyze the persuasive case law
- Analyze the case law as it applies to the facts to reach a conclusion to the question of whether a contract was formed
- State your conclusion and the reasons behind it to your classmates, and defend your response if it differs from other students' responses
- Come to a group consensus regarding the legal issue

Unit 3   Contract Formation and Promissory Estoppel

Grading: This exercise is not graded. Instead, you will compare your answers with those of other pairs or small groups, discuss and analyze other groups' responses and determine which response you believe is correct (i.e. a contract was or was not formed, and why).

Additional Written Exercise:

If time allows and if instructed by your instructor, write a short essay discussing the following points:
- A summary of the legal issue
- A summary of the relevant case law presented to you
- Your conclusion of whether a contract was formed
- The reasoning to support your conclusion

Like the oral exercise, the written assignment is not graded. Time permitting, you will share your paragraph with your partner and assess each other's answer for content, grammar and style.

NOTE: The first email below is the last that is identical to the email/text message string in the main assignment. Following this email, you will find the new emails and text messages exchanged between Ricky and Emily that you are to analyze for this exercise only.

From:	Pamela Park <pamela.park@straydogadvertising.com >
To:	Emily Johnson <emily.johnson@straydogadvertising.com>
Sent:	July 15, THIS YEAR 6:12 p.m.
Subject:	Re: Re: Re: Fwd: Re: Re: Ad Inventory for Pony Bowl!

Emily,

The max I am willing to pay for this commercial is $300,000 and you have authority to negotiate any price up to that amount. I'd prefer to pay around $275,000 if possible, so why don't you make that offer and see how they respond?

PP

From:	Emily Johnson <Emily.johnson@straydogadvertising.com>
To:	Richard Saucedo <saucedo@albc.com>
Sent:	July 30, THIS YEAR 3:39 p.m.
Subject:	Re: Re: Re: Ad Inventory for Pony Bowl!

Dear Ricky,

I am so glad things are moving forward this fast. After careful consideration, we are willing to pay $275,000 for a 30-second ad during the YEAR +1 Pony Bowl halftime. Do you still stand firm on the $350,000?

Emily

Contract Formation and Promissory Estoppel

Unit 3

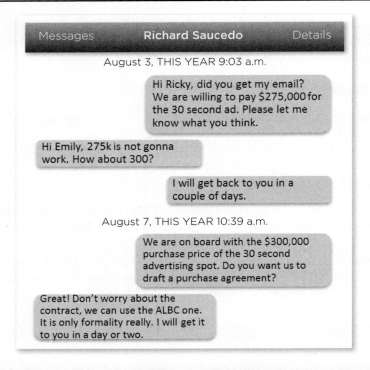

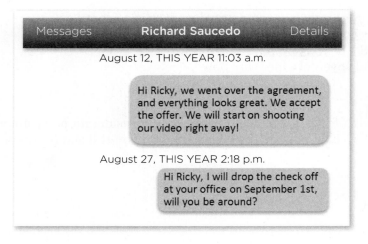

From: Richard Saucedo <saucedo@albc.com>
To: Emily Johnson <Emily.johnson@straydogadvertising.com>
Sent: August 8, THIS YEAR1:52 p.m.
Subject: Re: Re: Re: Re: Ad Inventory for Pony Bowl!

Dear Emily,

Please find attached the purchase agreement. If everything looks good to you, just respond in writing in the following week or two, then we can roll with it.

Ricky

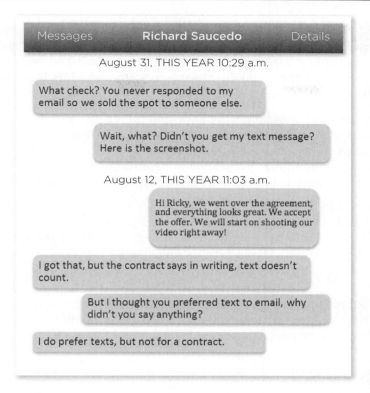

The law clerks at the LAW Law firm have researched the case law and have found the following cases, which they have also summarized. All of the cases are from jurisdictions outside of Jefferson, but as you will see, no court anywhere in the country has ruled about whether text messages are a "writing" for purposes of contract formation when the contract and offeror require a written acceptance. Therefore, you will have to reason by analogy.

An analogy is a comparison between two things, often for the sake of explanation. In legal argument, an analogy may be used when there is no precedent or prior case law close in facts and legal principle on point. Reasoning by analogy involves referring to a case that concerns unrelated subject matter but is governed by the same general principles and applying those principles to the case at hand.

After you read through the summaries of the case law, first answer the following questions:

- What is the analogy that you are trying to make?
- What are you using to make the analogy?
- Do you use reasoning by analogy in your own country's legal system?
- If you do not, how does a court decide an issue for which there is no law (article in a code, case law) on point?
- After you have answered these questions, then discuss the following:
  - What is the specific legal issue in this case?
  - How do you think a court would decide if this case were litigated? Support your answer with your legal reasoning and with references to the case law summaries.

Campbell v. General Dynamics Gov't Systems Corp., 407 F.3d 546 (1st Cir. 2005).

Plaintiff brought an employment discrimination claim against his former employer. The employer brought a motion to compel arbitration, claiming that an email announcement that was sent to all employees working at the company announcing a new dispute resolution policy, which included mandatory arbitration, was sufficient to put employee on notice that the policy was a contract that extinguished the employee's right to bring a claim in court for adjudicating an employment discrimination claim.

The court agreed with the plaintiff that although email communication was the preferred method of communication at the workplace where he was employed, email was not the usual means to handle personnel matters like a new dispute resolution policy, and thus the email did not form a binding contract.

The court noted that there was no way for the plaintiff or any employee to indicate that he or she had read the policy and accepted its terms. There was no check box or any other means normally used with online contracts to monitor acceptance; the employer could only verify whether the email had been opened. In addition, the court found that the language used in the email downplayed or diminished its importance and the fact that it contained a mandatory arbitration agreement.

The appellate court rejected the district court's statement that an email is not a proper medium for contract formation. The appellate court stated that if an email is written in a straightforward manner that explicitly delineates the terms of the agreement, it can be binding. The court relied on the E-Sign Act, a federal law which prohibits interpreting the requirement in the Federal Arbitration Act that an arbitration agreement be in writing and claiming that an acceptance is not "in writing" merely on the basis that it was in an electronic form.

Holding: The appellate court held that an email exchange can form a binding contract, provided that the language is written in a straightforward manner and that the parties know that they are entering into a binding contract. The case does not discuss text messages, although the Federal Arbitration Act does allow for arbitration agreements to be binding when an acceptance is in "electronic form."

Stevens v. Publicis, S.A., 50 A.D.3d 253 (N.Y. App. Div. 2008).

The parties entered into an employment agreement according to which any modification had to be in writing and signed by all parties. The parties then, via email, expressed an "unqualified acceptance" of a modification of the agreement. The emails in the exchange bore the typed name of the sender at the foot of the message (i.e. the signature block).

Plaintiff was then terminated and filed a breach of contract claim, arguing that the email exchange was not a "writing" for the purposes of modifying the agreement. Defendant filed for summary judgment, which was granted, and plaintiff then appealed.

The appellate court held that the emails constituted "signed writings" to properly and sufficiently modify the agreement because the plaintiff's name at the end of his email signified his intent to authenticate (validate) the contents. Likewise, the court concluded that the defendant's name at the end of his email constituted a "signed writing" and satisfied the contractual provision that any modification be signed by all parties.

Holding: An exchange of emails may constitute a binding contract provided it has sufficient indications that the parties to the contract authenticated the contents of the emails.

Rubenstein v. Clark & Green, Inc., 395 Fed. Appx. 786 (2nd Cir. 2010).

Plaintiff homebuilders brought a breach of contract claim against defendant/architecture firm, arguing that their email exchange constituted a fully binding preliminary agreement. The court dismissed their complaint, finding that no contract had been formed.

The court paid particular attention to the language that the parties used in their email exchange and found that it clearly indicated that they intended to negotiate further and enter into a formal written contract once the essential terms were agreed upon. Examples of such language include sentences that the plaintiff "would like to start working with" the defendant, but that he "had no time to get into" contract terms at that time. For the court, these statements showed an intent to negotiate and not finalize a written agreement at that point.

The court cites another case, Kowalchuk v. Stroup, which underscores the importance of analyzing the parties' language to discern their intent: "When a party gives forthright, reasonable signals that it means to be bound only by a written agreement, that intent is honored."

Holding: If the parties contemplate further negotiations and the execution of a written agreement, then an email exchange may not constitute a binding contract. Whether emails do or not depends on the content and language of the emails, which demonstrate the parties' intent.

Presentations:
If SDA Were Your Client...

Overview of the Exercise: For this exercise, you will make a professional presentation in which you answer and discuss the following question: *If Stray Dog Advertising were your client in your home country and if Pamela came to you for legal advice about the ALBC matter, what would you do and what advice would you give her?*

Learning Objectives of the Exercise:

This exercise will build your skills to:

- Examine the SDA/ALBC dispute from the perspective of your country's legal system
- Compare your country's legal system with the U.S. legal system
- Explain how the dispute would be handled in your country's legal system and the advice that you would provide Pamela Park
- Understand specific information from your classmates' presentations

Directions for Completing the Exercise:

- Analyze the Stray Dog Advertising fact pattern, for both the contract formation and promissory estoppel legal issues, under your country's laws
- Determine whether or not Pamela Park/Stray Dog Advertising would have viable claims under your country's laws
- Explain what claims she could bring (if any) and explain how her case would be handled in your country's legal system
- Explain what legal advice you would give Pamela if she came to you for legal advice in your home country

Research Required:

The research you are required to do depends on your knowledge of these claims in your country's legal system. It is presumed that you are familiar with the law and with how you would approach this issue if Pamela were a client of yours.

Grading: This presentation is not graded. Depending on the size of your class and your instructor's choice, you will present to your fellow classmates or to the entire class.

Handouts:

As part of your presentation, you must create a handout for your classmates. The handout will include fill-in-the-blank questions that your classmates must complete with information that you present during the presentation, and each handout must include at least five questions to answer.

For example, if a U.S. law student were giving a presentation on the claim of promissory estoppel in the United States, he could include on his handout this question:

The claim of promissory estoppel in the United States has three elements:

1) _____
2) _____
3) _____

As you are speaking, your classmates will have to listen, follow what you are saying and fill in the blanks. If you are listening to one of your classmate's presentations and are unsure about an answer, you should ask him or her to repeat so you can fill in the blank(s).

Grammar Review:

The basis of this exercise is hypothetical or conditional verbs: *if SDA were your client, what would you do?*

Remember the grammar of the verb tenses when discussing hypothetical conditions.

Present:　**IF + PAST SIMPLE, WOULD + BASE VERB**

*If Pamela **called** me to schedule an appointment, I **would tell** her to visit me at my office.*

NOTE: We use "were" for all tenses with the verb "to be" when using a conditional verb.

*If I **were** you, I would not take that class.*

*If Pamela **were** my client, I **would tell** her that she would not have a winning claim.*

Past:　**IF + PAST PERFECT, WOULD + HAVE + PAST PARTICIPLE**

*If Emily **had called** Ricky to tell him that she accepted, they **would have discussed** this and perhaps avoided any litigation.*

*If Pamela **had called** me before I left for the day, I **would have told** her to come to my office at 12:00.*

Ethics Dilemma

Important Note: The facts presented in this Skills-Building Exercise are for this exercise only. Do not use these facts when you analyze the Main Assignment File on contract formation and promissory estoppel.

For this exercise, presume the following facts:
- Litigation has commenced between Stray Dog Advertising and the Animal Lovers Broadcasting Company over the contract dispute for the ad spot for the YEAR +1 Pony Bowl
- Based on the advice received from the Lincoln Adams and Washington Law Firm, SDA has brought a claim of both breach of contract and promissory estoppel against ALBC. ALBC has not filed any counterclaims against SDA
- Molly Thompson of the Thompson Law Firm, PLLC is representing ALBC
- Discovery is underway

SDA served written discovery requests upon ALBC, and Thompson has produced her responses to the First Set of Requests for Production of Documents and the Interrogatories that SDA served upon her/her client. After sending her responses to the LAW Law Firm, Thompson received an additional email from her client and she now is determining whether that email must be produced to the plaintiff, SDA.

Overview of the Exercise:

In this exercise, you and a partner will analyze what attorney Molly Thompson should do with the email that she has received from her client, ALBC. As written above, the email was received by Thompson after she had already responded to the First Set of Requests for Production of Documents and sent the responses to opposing counsel.

Background:

The Rules of Professional Conduct regulate the actions, conduct and behavior of lawyers in their interactions with clients, non-clients, opposing counsel, and judges, and establish standards for attorney conduct and for the legal profession. Each state has promulgated its own set of Rules of Professional Conduct although the ABA Model Rules of Professional Conduct serve as a model for the rules of most states.

Being familiar with the Rules is fundamental for all attorneys. Like the law, ignorance of the rules is no defense. And while a violation of the rules can but does not always equate to legal malpractice, attorneys can end up in serious trouble for a violation. Punishment can range from a private or public admonishment to suspension of one's license to practice law and to disbarment (the removal of an attorney from the practice of law and revocation of his or her license).

Learning Objectives of the Exercise:

This exercise will build your skills to:
- Skim the Rules of Professional Conduct and the Federal Rules of Civil Procedure and identify quickly which rule pertains to your facts
- Interpret and apply the language of the rules
- Articulate your analysis and conclusion about whether the Rules of Professional Conduct have been violated
- Articulate your reasoning of the ethical obligations that attorneys have in litigation

Research and Steps for Completing the Exercise:

Use the ABA Model Rules of Professional Conduct for this exercise and assume that they are the same as the Jefferson Rules of Professional Conduct. Use a search engine like Google or Bing to locate the rules, or your professional responsibility course book if you are enrolled in the class. You can also find the rules on Westlaw, LexisNexis or Bloomberg Law. Skim over the titles to the Rules and identify which one will likely provide you guidance to analyze this situation. Don't forget to read the comments in addition to the rule itself as they often provide valuable insight as to how the rule should be applied.

You should also review the appropriate Federal Rules of Civil Procedure regarding discovery and the production of discovery responses.

If time permits, you and your partner should prepare a short (one paragraph) written summary, addressed to the senior partner, advising whether the email should be disclosed and the reasoning for your advice.

Grading: This exercise is not graded. Once each group has analyzed the matter, you will compare answers with your other classmates.

Molly Thompson received this discovery request from Jack Adams in the <u>Stray Dog Advertising, LLC v. Animal Lovers Broadcasting Company, Inc.</u> litigation.

STATE OF JEFFERSON   **DISTRICT COURT**

COUNTY OF HEMINGS   **FOURTH JUDICIAL DISTRICT**

                                                      CIVIL/CONTRACT

Stray Dog Advertising, LLC,
 	
          Plaintiff,
 	
vs.
 	
Animal Lovers Broadcasting Company, Inc.
 	
          Defendant
	Case No. 27-CV-15-761
	
	PLAINTIFF'S FIRST SET OF REQUESTS FOR PRODUCTION OF DOCUMENTS

TO: Defendant Animal Lovers Broadcasting Company, Inc. and its counsel of record Molly A. Thompson, Thompson Law Firm, PLLC, 1300 Gateway Center, Jefferson City, Jefferson 66451.

PLEASE TAKE NOTICE that pursuant to Rule 34 of the Jefferson Rules of Civil Procedure, Plaintiff demands Defendant Animal Lovers Broadcasting Company, Inc. produce for inspection and copying the documents described below. Production shall be made at the offices of Lincoln, Adams and Washington Law Firm, 8600 Winston Drive, Suite 1225, West Rapids, Jefferson 66435 within thirty (30) days after service on you.

REQUESTS FOR PRODUCTION OF DOCUMENTS

REQUEST NO. 1: All messages, memoranda or other electronic documents in any electronic format in Defendant's e-mail system from January 1, THIS YEAR to the present, written and exchanged between Defendant and any third parties, regarding or pertaining to the sale of the advertising spot for the Pony Bowl that is the subject of this litigation.

[*Requests continue and are omitted...*]

DATED: February 13, YEAR +1   ATTORNEYS FOR PLAINTIFF

                                      /s/ John G. Adams

                                      John G. Adams (#0559811)
                                      Lincoln, Adams and Washington Law Firm
                                      8600 Winston Drive, Suite 1225
                                      West Rapids, Jefferson 66435

After receiving the above request, Thompson produced hundreds of emails, memos and documents exchanged between ALBC and third parties that concerned and regarded the ad spot that SDA had been interested in. Given the great demand for the ad spots in the Pony Bowl, Saucedo and the other sales reps at ALBC communicated with many companies that wanted to purchase ad inventory.

In the end, a multi-national pharmaceutical company, Big Pharma, Inc., purchased the same spot that SDA wanted during the eighteen-day time period between when Emily Johnson emailed her thumbs-up emoji email to Saucedo and when she sent the email asking whether she could drop off the check. Big Pharma aired its spot during the show.

Saucedo and Daniel Van Kempt, the individual at Big Pharma responsible for purchasing advertising, exchanged many emails around the same time that Saucedo was communicating with SDA/Johnson. Thompson produced to the LAW Law Firm all of the relevant emails that she had received from her client when she first discussed the discovery requests with them and met to review their documents.

About one month after first producing the emails and memos between ALBC and the third parties, Thompson received the following email from Saucedo:

From: Ricky Saucedo <saucedo@albc.com>
To: Molly Thompson <molly@thompsonlaw.net>
Date: April 4, YEAR +1
Re: Lawsuit w/SDA

Molly, I am forwarding to you an email that I wrote to Daniel Van Kempt of Big Pharma right when they purchased the ad spot. I didn't find the email when you first contacted me about the discovery requests. I had moved it to another file on my computer and for some reason, the email didn't show up when we did the search of my computer for the discovery requests. I don't know if you need or want it since you've already given all the other emails and stuff to SDA, but I am sending it to you just in case.

Ricky Saucedo

From: Richard Saucedo <saucedo@albc.com>
To: Daniel Van Kempt <d.vankempt@bigpharma.com>
Date: August 9, THIS YEAR
Re: Last ad spot YEAR +1 Pony Bowl

Hey Dan, thanks for lunch yesterday. My boss and I discussed your offer of $450,000 for the ad spot and that's a price that we just can't turn down. The last ad spot for the YEAR +1 Pony Bowl is yours. As I mentioned, I had been negotiating with a local business for the same spot and we'd reached a deal, but we can't turn down your offer. I'll take care of things so that your ad will be aired. I gave you the purchase agreement, so if you can sign it and get it back to us with the check, that would be great. The written agreement is just a formality, though, and you have my word that the ad spot is yours.

Cheers,

Ricky

The issue you must now discuss and analyze is what Molly Thompson should do with the email that she just received from Saucedo. When analyzing this, consider the following:
- Does the email correspond to the discovery request and fit the description of documents that must be produced?
- Thompson already responded to the First Set of Requests for Production of Documents. What obligation does she have to produce additional documents?

- Does she have to wait until she receives the Second Set of Requests for Production of Documents to produce this email?
- If this email is produced, will it help or hinder ALBC? Does that matter when determining whether a document must be produced?
- How can SDA use this email in its argument and in the litigation?

For the sake of argument, Thompson doesn't produce the email because she thinks it will hurt her client and her case.

- What, if any, liability could she face for not producing the document?
- What, if any, Rules of Professional Conduct would apply to this situation?
- Are there other rules or laws that dictate what Thompson must do?

Information Pages

Office Memo: Contract Formation

Overview of the Assignment: For this assignment, you will write an office memo to the Senior Partner, summarizing your research on contract formation and providing your prediction of what would happen if litigation were to begin between Stray Dog Advertising and the Animal Lovers Broadcasting Company. You should also give recommendations as to how Stray Dog Advertising, LLC should approach this matter.

Learning Objectives of the Assignment:

This assignment will build your skills to:

- Efficiently communicate in a written format
- Explain complex matters clearly and concisely
- Analyze and apply the rules of law regarding contract formation

Research for the Assignment: You are not required to do any outside research for this assignment. You should base your analysis on the New York contract formation cases that you read:

- Cleveland Wrecking Co. v. Hercules Construction Corp., 23 F. Supp. 2d 287 (E.D.N.Y. 1998).
- International Business Machines Corp. v. Johnson, 629 F. Supp. 2d 231 (S.D.N.Y. 2009).
- Trademark Properties, Inc. v. A&E Television Networks, 422 Fed. Appx. 199 (1st Cir. 2011).
- Kowalchuk v. Stroup, 873 N.Y.S.2d 43 (N.Y. App. Div. 2009).
- Bazak International Corp. v. Tarrant Apparel Group, 378 F. Supp. 2d 377 (S.D.N.Y. 2005).

If you want to practice your legal research skills, you can look for and use other cases that you find. However, if you do search on Westlaw, LexisNexis or Bloomberg Law, be sure to limit your search and the cases you use to New York law and remember to change the citations to Jefferson law as indicated in the introduction.

Format of the Completed Assignment:

Your response should be in an office memo format and should include the following:

- Summary of the facts
- The relevant law
- Analysis of the law to the fact pattern
- Conclusion about how you think a court would rule if this matter were to go to court
- Your advice to the client about how to proceed

Follow the following format:

- 1 inch (2.54 cm.) margins (top/bottom and sides)
- 12 font, Times New Roman font
- Double spaced
- Maximum eight pages

Notes:

This memo should be predictive and not persuasive. You are not trying to persuade the senior partner or the client about the strength of your arguments or urge him or her to take a particular course of action; you are only trying to inform about the law, how it applies to the case, how you think a court would rule and what advice you have.

In a memo, you can also use formatting like underlining, bold font or italics. You can also create headings and subheadings to organize your answer.

For additional information about office memos and e-memos, as well as samples, refer to the online additional resources.

Grading: This assignment is worth 102 points.

Unit 3   Contract Formation and Promissory Estoppel

Memo: Contract Formation

Student-Attorney: _____

LEGAL CONTENT	0–6 points	8 points	10 points	12 points	Points
Issue statement (IS)	Document does not include an IS or includes IS that fails to properly identify the legal issue(s) and the applicable law	Identifies the legal issue(s) and correctly states the applicable law with minor mistakes	Identifies the legal issue(s) and correctly states the applicable law	Identifies the legal issue(s) and correctly states the applicable law in an exceptionally creative and concise way	_____/12
Short Answer	Document does not include a short answer or includes a short answer with significant mistakes	Responds to IS but with key facts or applicable legal principles missing	Responds to IS with key facts and applicable legal principles with no meaningful errors	Clearly and concisely responds to IS with key facts and applicable legal principles and no irrelevancies	_____/12
Facts	Few or none of the relevant facts are included; difficult to follow or understand	Most relevant facts are included as well as non-relevant ones; at times difficult to follow	Relevant facts are included with occasional irrelevancies; easy to follow	All relevant facts are included with no irrelevancies; story is clearly and concisely told to reader in objective way	_____/12
Rule	Hard to follow and understand; does not include relevant sources or cites inappropriate sources; no rule application	Cites to some relevant sources but is incomplete in covering all relevant aspects of the rule; includes some rule application	Cite only to relevant sources and mostly clear; rule application explains but not fully how rule has been applied	Clear and concise; includes only relevant sources and includes all parts of rule necessary for analysis; clear rule application	_____/12
Analysis	Contains conclusory statements and/or no case law; facts are analyzed in a conclusory or insufficient way	Uses some case law but does not analogize or distinguish or explain its application; some conclusory statements; facts briefly analyzed	Uses case law to show how rule applies to case; case law is compared and contrasted with success; most facts are analyzed	Analyzes case law completely, comparing it fully to client matter; facts are thoroughly analyzed in an objective way	_____/12
Conclusion/ Recommendations	No conclusion or recommendations are included in document	A brief conclusion is included but without sufficient client advice	Paper includes conclusion and recommendations	Paper includes full conclusion of the legal analysis and facts and presents creative and thoughtful recommendations	_____/12
Citations	No sources are cited in document	Some sources are cited, but inconsistently; citation format is inconsistent	All citations are present; correct format is mostly used	All citations are present; correct format is used throughout document	_____/12
WRITING	**2**	**4**	**5**	**6**	**Points**
Formatting	Document does not follow format instructions or the sample provided	Document attempts to follow instructions and sample provided	Document follows the instructions and sample provided with no meaningful errors	Document exactly follows the instructions and sample provided	_____/6
Organization	No structure or organization; free flow of ideas	Structure & organization present but reorganization or headings needed for full clarity	Document is clearly organized and structured with proper use of heading and subheadings	Document is exceptionally well organized and structured with proper use of headings and subheadings	_____/6
Syntax Mechanics	Contains numerous and distracting grammatical and mechanical errors that impede understanding	Contains some grammatical and mechanical errors that impede understanding	Contains few grammatical and mechanical errors but none that impede understanding	Contains no grammatical and mechanical errors; native-like use of English	_____/6
TOTAL					_____/**102**

Office Memo: Promissory Estoppel

Overview of the Assignment: For this assignment, you will write an office memo to the Senior Partner, summarizing your research on promissory estoppel and providing your prediction of what would happen if litigation were to begin between Stray Dog Advertising and the Animal Lovers Broadcasting Company. You should also give recommendations as to how Stray Dog Advertising, LLC should approach this matter.

Learning Objectives of the Assignment:

This assignment will build your skills to:

- Efficiently communicate in a written format
- Explain complex matters clearly and concisely
- Analyze and apply the rules of law regarding promissory estoppel

Research for the Assignment: You are not required to do any outside research for this assignment. You should base your analysis on the Nebraska promissory estoppel cases that you read:

- <u>Goff-Hamel v. Obstetricians & Gynecologists, P.C.</u>, 588 N.W.2d 798 (Neb. 1999).
- <u>Maxell, Inc. v. Kenney Deans, Inc.</u>, No. A-98-930, 1999 WL 731846 (Ct. App. Neb. Sept. 21, 1999).
- <u>deNourie & Yost Homes, LLC v. Frost</u>, 854 N.W.2d 298 (Neb. 2014).
- <u>168th and Dodge LP v. Rave Reviews Cinemas, LLC</u>, 501 F.3d 945 (8th Cir. 2007).

If you want to practice your legal research skills, you can look for and use other cases that you find. However, if you do search on Westlaw, LexisNexis or Bloomberg Law, be sure to limit your search and the cases you use to Nebraska law and don't forget to change the citations to Jefferson law as indicated in the introduction.

Format of the Completed Assignment:

Your response should be in an office memo format and should include the following:
- Summary of the facts
- The relevant law
- Analysis of the law to the fact pattern
- Conclusion about how you think a court would rule if this matter were to go to court
- Your advice to the client about how to proceed

Follow the following format:
- 1 inch (2.54 cm.) margins (top/bottom and sides)
- 12 font, Times New Roman font
- Double spaced
- Maximum eight pages

Notes:

This memo should be predictive and not persuasive. You are not trying to persuade the senior partner or the client about the strength of your arguments or urge him or her to take a particular course of action; you are only trying to inform about what the law is, how it applies to our case, how you think a court would rule and what advice you have.

In a memo, you can also use formatting like underlining, bold font or italics. You can also create headings and subheadings to organize your answer.

For additional information about office memos and e-memos, as well as samples, refer to the online additional resources.

Grading: This assignment is worth 102 points.

Memo: Promissory Estoppel

Student-Attorney: _____

LEGAL CONTENT	0–6 points	8 points	10 points	12 points	Points
Issue statement (IS)	Document does not include an IS or includes IS that fails to properly identify the legal issue(s) and the applicable law	Identifies the legal issue(s) and correctly states the applicable law with minor mistakes	Identifies the legal issue(s) and correctly states the applicable law	Identifies the legal issue(s) and correctly states the applicable law in an exceptionally creative and concise way	____/12
Short Answer	Document does not include a short answer or includes a short answer with significant mistakes	Responds to IS but with key facts or applicable legal principles missing	Responds to IS with key facts and applicable legal principles with no meaningful errors	Clearly and concisely responds to IS with key facts and applicable legal principles and no irrelevancies	____/12
Facts	Few or none of the relevant facts are included; difficult to follow or understand	Most relevant facts are included as well as non-relevant ones; at times difficult to follow	Relevant facts are included with occasional irrelevancies; easy to follow	All relevant facts are included with no irrelevancies; story is clearly and concisely told to reader in objective way	____/12
Rule	Hard to follow and understand; does not include relevant sources or cites inappropriate sources; no rule application	Cites to some relevant sources but is incomplete in covering all relevant aspects of the rule; includes some rule application	Cite only to relevant sources and mostly clear; rule application explains but not fully how rule has been applied	Clear and concise; includes only relevant sources and includes all parts of rule necessary for analysis; clear rule application	____/12
Analysis	Contains conclusory statements and/or no case law; facts are analyzed in a conclusory or insufficient way	Uses some case law but does not analogize or distinguish or explain its application; some conclusory statements; facts briefly analyzed	Uses case law to show how rule applies to case; case law is compared and contrasted with success; most facts are analyzed	Analyzes case law completely, comparing it fully to client matter; facts are thoroughly analyzed in an objective way	____/12
Conclusion/ Recommendations	No conclusion or recommendations are included in document	A brief conclusion is included but without sufficient client advice	Paper includes conclusion and recommendations	Paper includes full conclusion of the legal analysis and facts and presents creative and thoughtful recommendations	____/12
Citations	No sources are cited in document	Some sources are cited, but inconsistently; citation format is inconsistent	All citations are present; correct format is mostly used	All citations are present; correct format is used throughout document	____/12
WRITING	**2**	**4**	**5**	**6**	**Points**
Formatting	Document does not follow format instructions or the sample provided	Document attempts to follow instructions and sample provided	Document follows the instructions and sample provided with no meaningful errors	Document exactly follows the instructions and sample provided	____/6
Organization	No structure or organization; free flow of ideas	Structure & organization present but reorganization or headings needed for full clarity	Document is clearly organized and structured with proper use of heading and subheadings	Document is exceptionally well organized and structured with proper use of headings and subheadings	____/6
Syntax Mechanics	Contains numerous and distracting grammatical and mechanical errors that impede understanding	Contains some grammatical and mechanical errors that impede understanding	Contains few grammatical and mechanical errors but none that impede understanding	Contains no grammatical and mechanical errors; native-like use of English	____/6
TOTAL					____/102

Mock Client Meeting

Overview of this Assignment: This assignment simulates a client meeting between you and your client, Pamela Park of Stray Dog Advertising, LLC. You are meeting with Park to discuss the potential claims that she may bring against ALBC and to offer her advice.

The meeting is scheduled after you have had the opportunity to study both promissory estoppel and contract formation, so you are expected to discuss both legal issues, all possible legal claims relating to the fact pattern, and the likelihood of success if she were to begin litigation.

Your instructor will indicate to you the time that you will have available for the mock client meeting.

Learning Objectives of the Assignment:

This assignment will build your skills to:

- Explain and clarify the legal positions of the parties and describe potential outcomes to your client
- Respond to technical questions about litigation
- Incorporate technical legal English vocabulary that relates to promissory estoppel and contract formation and use appropriate layperson explanations for the client

Steps for Completing the Assignment:

- Read and be familiar with the Main Assignment File
- Be familiar with the contract formation and promissory estoppel cases that you have been assigned
- Recommended:
  - Anticipate the questions that you think your client might ask and prepare possible responses
  - Draft an outline of what you would like to cover in the meeting

Note: Remember that part of the grading is also based on your professional demeanor. You are expected to arrive punctually, be dressed in professional attire, and act as you would with a client in real life. You should play the part from when you come into the meeting room.

Grading: This assignment worth 102 points.

Punctuality: Student-attorney arrived on time to meeting: YES _____ (10 points) NO _____ (0 points)

Professional Attire: Student-attorney was dressed in appropriate professional attire: YES _____ (10 points) NO _____ (0 points)

Professional Demeanor: Student-attorney acted in a professional manner w/ client: YES _____ (10 points) NO _____ (0 points)

GRADING CRITERIA	0–6 points	8 points (C or 75%)	10 points (B or 85%)	12 points	Points received
Engagement I (questions)	Attorney does not ask client any questions; engages in monologue	Attorney asks few questions; questions are hard to follow or show minimal preparation or understanding of matter	Attorney asks basic questions that demonstrate understanding of matter and preparation	Attorney asks thoughtful, insightful and creative questions that demonstrate deep preparation & understanding of matter	_____ /12
Engagement II (answers)	Attorney does not respond to client's questions	Attorney responds to questions, but incorrectly or with hard to follow answers	Attorney responds promptly and correctly to all of client's questions	Attorney responds promptly and correctly to all of client's questions with creative, thoughtful and insightful answers that show a deep understanding of the issues	_____ /12
Knowledge of Applicable Law	Attorney provides no explanation of the applicable law	Attorney provides explanation of with serious mistakes, or hard to follow (e.g. use of legal jargon)	Attorney provides clear explanation of with some mistakes; uses some legal jargon unnecessarily or without explanations that client can understand	Attorney provides clear, concise and correct explanation of the law with legal jargon when appropriate or w/ explanations client can understand	_____ /12
Ability to Analyze Applicable Law	Attorney provides does not provide an analysis of the law for the client	Attorney attempts to analyze the law but provides incomplete or incorrect analysis	Attorney provides analysis of the law with no significant mistakes or misstatements of the law or facts	Attorney provides a clear, concise and correct analysis of the law as it applies to the client matter	_____ /12
Advice and Recommendations	Attorney provides no advice or poor advice for client	Attorney provides not comprehensive or inaccurate advice	Attorney provides comprehensive and accurate advice to client on his/her legal matter	Attorney provides thoughtful and creative solutions for client	_____ /12
Organization	Meeting is disorganized and hard to follow or lacks any organization	Meeting has some organization but is still confusing for client for how information is presented	Meeting is clearly organized and easy to follow	Meeting is clearly organized and is easy to follow; attorney takes extra steps to ensure client's understanding	_____ /12
TOTAL					_____ /72
TOTAL FROM PUNCTUALITY AND PROFES-SIONALISM					_____ /30

Total   _____/102

Client Advice Letter

Overview of the Assignment: For this assignment, you will write an advice and follow-up letter to Pamela Park, summarizing your research on contract formation and promissory estoppel, as well as your meeting with her. You should also give recommendations to Park on how Stray Dog Advertising, LLC should approach this matter. Be mindful that even though Park is a sophisticated businesswoman, she is not a trained attorney. Therefore you should avoid legalese in your letter.

Under Rule 1.4(a)(3) of the Rules of Professional Conduct, an attorney has the duty to keep his or her client "reasonably informed about the status of the client's matter." A thorough follow-up letter after a client meeting is one of the best ways to meet this duty, as well as regular phone calls, emails or meetings.

Learning Objectives of the Assignment:

This assignment will build your skills to:

- Efficiently communicate in a written format
- Explain complex matters clearly and concisely
- Incorporate technical legal English vocabulary that relates to contract formation and promissory estoppel and use appropriate layperson explanations for the client

Steps for Completing the Assignment:

- Review the predictive memos that you wrote to the senior partner about your client matter to ensure that the law and the issues are clear
- Be familiar with the case law regarding contract formation and promissory estoppel, as well as the fact pattern
- Conduct your client meeting with your client, Pamela Park
- Review the Business Correspondence online resources

Research Required for the Assignment: You are not required to do any outside research for this assignment.

Format of the Completed Assignment:

Your assignment should be written as a business letter, not as an email. Even though many firms and lawyers use email for much of the correspondence they write, formal business letters are still an essential part of the practice of law.

The Lincoln, Adams and Washington Law Firm has the following policy regarding business correspondence. Your client letter must follow the policy guidelines.

LAW FIRM CORRESPONDENCE POLICY

The purpose of this policy is to ensure a uniform appearance of all business correspondence that is written by the attorneys and staff of the law firm and thus to increase the professional appearance of the firm's work product. All law firm attorneys and staff are required to follow these guidelines when writing all correspondence. Violation of the policy can result in disciplinary action, up to and including termination.

- The first page of all "traditional" letters must be written on law firm letterhead, which includes the firm's address and logo
- All letters must be written in a modified block letter format
- Letters must be written in Times New Roman, 12 font
- Letters must be 1.5 spaced and have 1" (2.54 cm.) margins, except for the initial page, which may have larger top margins to account for the logo, law firm address and sender's direct contact information
- Client letters must not exceed four pages

Grading: This assignment is worth 78 points.

Unit 3   Contract Formation and Promissory Estoppel

LEGAL CONTENT	0–6 points (failing)	8 points (C or 75%)	10 points (B or 85%)	12 points	Points
Introduction	Letter does not include an appropriate introduction or includes poorly constructed one	Letter includes introduction that states purpose with some irrelevancies or some relevant information missing	Introduction states purpose of letter and includes other relevant information	Introduction is engaging; states purpose of letter and includes other relevant information; written clearly and concisely	____/12
Summary of Meeting	Letter includes no summary of the meeting	Letter includes summary but leaves out important information or states it unclearly	Letter summarizes the meeting but leaves out important information	Letter clearly and concisely summarizes the meeting, its core purpose and content	____/12
Applicable Law	Student-attorney provides no explanation of the applicable law, or only uses legal jargon in explanation (inappropriate for audience)	Student-attorney provides explanation of with serious mistakes, or hard to follow (use of legal jargon)	Student-attorney provides clear explanation of with few mistakes; uses some legal jargon without appropriate explanations	Student-attorney provides clear, concise and correct explanation of the law with legal jargon with appropriate explanations	____/12
Analysis	Contains conclusory statements and/ or no case law; facts are analyzed in a conclusory or insufficient way	Uses some case law but does not analogize or distinguish or explain its application; some conclusory statements; facts briefly analyzed	Uses case law to show how rule applies to case; case law is compared and contrasted with success; most facts are analyzed	Analyzes completely case law, comparing it fully to client matter; facts are thoroughly analyzed	____/12
Conclusion/ Recommendations	No conclusion or recommendations are included in letter	A brief conclusion is included but without sufficient advice or recommendations advice or next steps	Letter includes conclusion with recommendations and next steps	Letter includes full conclusion of the legal analysis and facts, presents creative and thoughtful recommendations and includes clear next steps	____/12
WRITING	2	4	5	6	Points
Formatting	Document does not follow format instructions or the sample provided	Document attempts to follow instructions and sample provided	Document follows the instructions and sample provided with minor errors	Document exactly follows the instructions and sample provided	____/6
Organization	No structure or organization; free flow of ideas	Letter includes organization and structure but is still confusing	Structure and organization but some reorganization is needed for full clarity	Document is clearly organized and structured	____/6
Syntax Mechanics	Contains numerous and distracting grammatical and mechanical errors that impede understanding	Contains some grammatical and mechanical errors that impede understanding	Contains few grammatical and mechanical errors but none that impede understanding	Contains no grammatical and mechanical errors; native-like use of English	____/6
TOTAL					____/78

Statutory and Common Law

Trespass and Nuisance

Liability for Dogs, Flies, and Other Disturbances

Unit 4

For this Unit, you will write a predictive memo regarding trespass, an intentional tort, and one regarding nuisance, another intentional tort. The facts involve Happy Tails Animal Rescue, a business that operates next door to Stray Dog Advertising and is disrupting SDA's business operations.

Learning Objectives of this Unit:

This unit will build your skills to:

- Explain complex legal matters clearly and concisely
- Use appropriate technical terminology
- Identify and analyze the applicable case law and facts for the relevant legal issues
- Efficiently read and understand legal authority (case law and statute)
- Articulate persuasive legal arguments in support of client's position
- Efficiently and effectively communicate in a written and oral format
- Evaluate questions about the relevant law and support your legal argument

To achieve these learning objectives, you will complete the following tasks:

- Draft two predictive memos to senior partner about the legal issues (trespass and nuisance) and your prediction of what will happen if litigation were to commence
- Carry out a mock client meeting with Pamela Park
- Draft a client letter to Pamela Park about your meeting with her and about the legal issues

To complete these tasks, you will use the following materials in the book:

Trespass

- Assignment email from Senior Partner (pages 110-111)
- Main Assignment File (pages 112-117)
- Trespass Commented Cases:
    - Public Service Co. of Colorado v. Van Wyk, 27 P.3d 377 (Colo. 2001).
    - Hoery v. United States, 64 P.3d 214 (Colo. 2003).
    - Cook v. Rockwell International Corp., 273 F. Supp. 2d 1175 (Colo. 2003).
    - Miller v. Carnation Co., 516 P. 2d 661 (Colo. Ct. App. 1973).
    - Cobai v. Young, 679 P. 2d 121 (Colo. Ct. App. 1984).
- ESL Workbook (pages 61-77)

Nuisance

- Assignment email from Senior Partner (pages 110-111)
- Main Assignment File (pages 112-117)
- Statute: Ind. Code 32-30-6-6
- Nuisance Commented Cases:
    - Wernke v. Halas, 600 N.E.2d 117 (Ind. Ct. App. 1992).
    - Owens v. Phillips, 73 Ind. 284 (Ind. 1881).
    - Bonewitz v. Parker, 912 N.E.2d 378 (Ind. 2009).
    - Davoust v. Mitchell, 257 N.E.2d 332 (Ind. Ct. App. 1970).
    - Hendricks v. Tubbs, 92 N.E.2d 561 (Ind. 1950).
- ESL Workbook (pages 78-96)

Your instructor will also assign you additional skills-building exercises to bolster your understanding of the legal issues and further develop your legal reasoning and language skills. You will find an icon with each exercise that will indicate which skills the exercise will focus on.

ICON	SKILL
	Speaking — in particular about the legal issues and the law presented in the Unit
	Oral comprehension
	Legal analysis and reasoning
	Analysis of the legal issue(s) presented in the Unit
	English grammar, syntax, and vocabulary
	Legal ethics and professional responsibility
	Legal research

In this Unit, the additional skills-building exercises that accompany the Main Assignment File include:

- Trespass and Nuisance Analysis Exercise (pages 118-119)
- Presentation: *If SDA Were Your Client...* (pages 125-126)
- Mock negotiation between SDA and Happy Tails Animal Rescue (page 120 plus confidential information)
- Research exercise: Bees, Nuisance and Trespass (pages 121-124)

Before beginning the Unit, you should read and be familiar with the Stray Dog Advertising Factual Background (pages 7-8) and the Factual Background of the Lincoln, Adams and Washington Law Firm (pages 2-3).

You will also find online at the website www.legalwritingforllms.com the following online resources that accompany this Unit. The additional online resources will help you deepen your mastery of the skills presented in the Unit and also provide additional understanding about the U.S. legal system and legal writing.

Additional Resources:

- Sources of American Law
- Writing Professional Emails
- Writing Predictive Memos
- Writing E-memos
- IRAC

Additional Skills-Building Exercises:

- Issues and Issue Statements
- Stating the Rule
- Analysis
- Ethical Spotlight Exercise

Section I, Unit 4 Legal Issues
Trespass and Nuisance

Main Assignment File

Introduction to File and Client Matter
Pages 105-109

Documents Related to Client Matter
Pages 110-117

Assignment Information Pages + Rubrics
Pages 127-134

Trespass Cases

Public Service Co. of Colorado v. Van Wyk,
27 P.3d 377
(Colo. 2001).

Hoery v. United States,
64 P.3d 214
(Colo. 2003).

Cook v. Rockwell Int'l Corp., 273 F. Supp. 1175
(Colo. 2003).

Miller v. Carnation Co.,
516 P.2d 661
(Colo. Ct. App. 1973).

Cobai v. Young,
679 P.2d 121
(Colo. Ct. App. 1984).

ESL Workbook

Public Service Co. of Colorado v. Van Wyk,
27 P.3d 377
(Colo. 2001).

Hoery v. United States,
64 P.3d 214
(Colo. 2003).

Cook v. Rockwell Int'l Corp., 273 F. Supp. 1175
(Colo. 2003).

Miller v. Carnation Co.,
516 P.2d 661
(Colo. Ct. App. 1973).

Cobai v. Young,
679 P.2d 121
(Colo. Ct. App. 1984).

Additional Exercises

Trespass and Nuisance Analysis Exercise
Pages 118-119

Presentation: If SDA Were Your Client...
Pages 125-126

Mock Negotiation
Page 120 + confidential information

Research Exercises: Bees, Nuisance and Trespass
Pages 121-124

Additional Online Resources

Writing Professional Emails

Business Correspondence (with sample letters)

Writing Memos (office memos and e-memos)

IRAC (including additional exercises for each element)

Skills-Building Exercises for Rules, Issues and Issues Statements, Analysis and Ethical Dilemmas

Nuisance Cases

Wernke v. Halas,
600 N.E.2d 117
(Ind. Ct. App. 1992).

Owens v. Phillips,
73 Ind. 284
(Ind. 1881).

Bonewitz v. Parker,
912 N.E.2d 378
(Ind. 2009).

Davoust v. Mitchell,
257 N.E.2d 332
(Ind. Ct. App. 1970).

Hendricks v. Tubbs,
92 N.E.2d 561
(Ind. 1950).

ESL Workbook

Wernke v. Halas,
600 N.E.2d 117
(Ind. Ct. App. 1992).

Owens v. Phillips,
73 Ind. 284
(Ind. 1881).

Bonewitz v. Parker,
912 N.E.2d 378
(Ind. 2009).

Davoust v. Mitchell,
257 N.E.2d 332
(Ind. Ct. App. 1970).

Hendricks v. Tubbs,
92 N.E.2d 561
(Ind. 1950).

Introduction — Trespass and Nuisance

In this Unit, you will be learning about two torts that have been defined in rather mysterious ways. They have been called "analogous," yet distinguishable.[32] The line between the torts has become "wavering and uncertain,"[33] yet the claims remain very separate and distinct. What are these torts? Trespass and nuisance.

> For liability to attach for trespass and to show intent, it is immaterial whether or not he honestly and reasonably believes that the land is his own, or that he believes he has the property owner's consent to enter, or that he is simply mistaken in believing that he can enter, just as it is immaterial whether the entry was harmless, or whether the property owner benefits from the trespass. RESTATEMENT (SECOND) OF TORTS § 163 (AM. LAW INST. 1965).

Trespass involves an intentional, physical invasion of property that interferes with the plaintiff's exclusive possessory interest in his or her land.[34] The plaintiff need not suffer any damages for the defendant to be held liable for trespass,[35] although in such a case, the plaintiff may be awarded only nominal damages. Beyond entering onto someone else's property, there are other ways in which an individual can be liable for trespass: (1) if he causes a thing or a third person to enter someone else's land, (2) if he remains on the land after being ordered to leave, or (3) if he fails to remove from the land a thing which he should have removed.[36]

Since trespass is an intentional tort,[37] the plaintiff must show only that the defendant intended to do the act that results in the unlawful invasion, not whether or not he knew that he had authorization to enter. Thus, a defendant can't defend against a claim of trespass by claiming that he didn't know the property belonged to the defendant, only that he didn't intend to enter the property by whatever means the defendant used.[38] Reasonableness on the part of the defendant is not a defense to an intentional tort like trespass.[39]

Traditionally, trespass occurred when something tangible — a person, a tree, a car or an animal — enters onto another person's property without consent and interferes with the plaintiff's exclusive possession of his or her property. However, with the evolution of science, technology, case law and litigation, creative plaintiffs have argued that trespass can occur even when non-tangible objects such as dust, noise, light, or electric and magnetic fields emitted from power lines enter onto the plaintiff's property and interfere with the plaintiff's exclusive enjoyment of the property. Many courts have rejected this argument, however, unless the plaintiff can show that the property suffered substantial damages as a result of the entry.[40] Trespass is a common-law issue and thus the rules of trespass will be found in case law and will vary from state to state.

On the other hand, nuisance, the second legal issue that you will examine in this Unit, is both a statutory and common-law issue in some jurisdictions. In other jurisdictions, it is just a common-law issue. In this Unit, you will deal with the Jefferson statute of nuisance[41] as well as case law.

---

[32] 66 C.J.S. NUISANCES § 2 (Westlaw database updated Sept. 2016).

[33] Bradley v. Am. Smelting & Ref. Co., 709 P.2d 782, 787 (Wash. 1985).

[34] RESTATEMENT (SECOND) OF TORTS § 158 (AM. LAW INST. 1965).

[35] Id.

[36] Id.

[37] As opposed to negligence, which does not require intent.

[38] RESTATEMENT (SECOND) OF TORTS § 164 (AM. LAW INST. 1965).

[39] See Johnson v. Paynesville Farmers Union Coop. Oil Co., 817 N.W.2d 693, 701 (Minn. 2012).

[40] See, e.g., id. at 700-01 (rejecting argument that trespass could occur when pesticide was sprayed onto plaintiff's land as allowing trespass with a particulate matter conflicts with the "gist of the tort," which is the "intentional interference with rights of exclusive possession."). But cf. Borland v. Sanders Lead Co., 369 So.2d 523 (Ala. 1979) (upholding a trespass claim based on defendant's emission of lead particulates and sulfoxide gases); Bradley v. Am. Smelting & Ref. Co., 709 P.2d 782 (Wash. 1985) (holding that particulate matter deposited on the plaintiff's land from the defendant's copper smelter could constitute a trespass).

[41] Taken from the Indiana nuisance statute.

Nuisance has been defined as a legal "thicket" that causes much "uncertainty and confusion."[42] Two types of nuisance exist, public and private nuisance. This Unit will deal only with private nuisance, which exists when the defendant's conduct causes substantial interference with "the private use and enjoyment of land" and that conduct is "(1) intentional and unreasonable, (2) negligent or reckless, or (3) actionable under the rules governing liability for abnormally dangerous conditions or activities."[43] There must be substantial interference with the plaintiff's use and enjoyment of his property for a claim of private nuisance to succeed.

As stated above, the claims of trespass and nuisance overlap and are seen as somewhat analogous, yet are quite distinct. The differences and distinctions between the two must be clearly understood to analyze the SDA client matter and understand which, if any, claims SDA could bring against its next-door neighbor. The New York Practice Series on the New York Law on Torts summarizes clearly the two torts:

> Although a private nuisance (and, often, a public nuisance) interferes with rights relating to land, a nuisance is distinguishable from trespass to land. Trespass involves the wrongful entry onto another's land and thus an interference, however slight or temporary, with a person's interest in the exclusive possession of land. Trespass is complete upon the wrongful entry. A private nuisance, on the other hand, does not require a wrongful entry, but only an interference with a person's right to use or enjoy the land. A tenant's harboring of a large amount of animals on his or her land could constitute a nuisance to neighbors, but is not a trespass. Also, in the case of a private nuisance, but not a trespass, the interference must be substantial, and its frequency is an important factor in this regard. Nevertheless, some types of conduct may constitute a trespass and, if continuous and substantially invasive, will also constitute a nuisance.[44]

Damages that a plaintiff can recover are fact dependent. If the trespass or nuisance has caused actual damages, the defendant will be required to compensate the plaintiff for those losses, which could be the cost of repairing the damage caused, or the diminished value of the plaintiff's property. In other cases, the damages might not actually exist. In these cases, the judge or jury could award the plaintiff nominal damages, such as a dollar, to acknowledge that the tort took place. In actuality, if there were no damages, a plaintiff would perhaps not even bring a claim due to the high costs of litigation.

In this Unit, you will learn that Stray Dog Advertising is dealing with a next-door neighbor who is disturbing and disrupting the agency's business. You will analyze whether SDA can bring a claim of trespass or nuisance against this neighbor. Your analysis will depend on what objects are entering the SDA office space and how the next-door neighbor's activities are disturbing SDA and its business.

---

[42] Copart Indus., Inc. v. Consol. Edison Co. of NY, Inc., 362 N.E.2d 968, 969-70 (N.Y. 1977).

[43] Id. at 971.

[44] 14 Lee. S. Kreindler et al., New York Practice, New York Law of Torts § 4.1, Westlaw (database updated Sept. 2016).

Main Assignment File: Trespass and Nuisance

You have received the following email from Senior Partner Lincoln about an issue facing Stray Dog Advertising at the agency's second office in the city of Sweetwater. A local animal rescue agency, located next door to Stray Dog Advertising, is disturbing and disrupting SDA's business and bothering its employees and clients. The senior partner would like you to assess the matter and advise Pamela on what she should do.

From: Amy Lincoln <a.lincoln@lawlawfirm.com>
To: Associate Attorney <a.attorney@lawlawfirm.com>
Sent: Tuesday, May 3, THIS YEAR 15:02
Subject: Nuisance or Trespass at SDA's Office?

Dear Associate Attorney,

I am forwarding to you an email from Pamela at Stray Dog Advertising. She has some issues going on at SDA's second office in Sweetwater. If you remember, we helped Pamela purchase the historic building five years ago; SDA's office are on the first floor and the second floor is leased to other businesses.

The issue, however, involves one of the next door neighbors. The street where SDA's offices are located is historic Main Street, the first street constructed when Sweetwater was founded in 1874. The buildings are from the end of the nineteenth and turn of the twentieth century, so they were built very close together and none is taller than three stories. The short distance between the two buildings compounds the issue that Pamela is facing. There are small parking lots behind the buildings, and the property owner or tenants of each building are allowed to use the lots as they see fit.

As you'll read, the building next door to SDA is leased to an animal rescue organization, Happy Tails Animal Rescue. They recently began keeping more dogs at the office, leading to barking throughout the day. Those working for Happy Tails are very animal friendly, so they have a chicken coop with two chickens in the area behind the building. This is the area that would normally be used as a parking lot, but they've converted it to a lawn and garden area. The dogs that are kept at the rescue's offices also go in this back area during the day to play or to relieve themselves. The animals at Happy Tails are in close proximity to SDA's office and have caused problems for Pamela, her employees, and clients.

I would like you to prepare a memo summarizing the facts as Pamela has presented them, outlining the legal issues as you identify them, and predicting what you think would happen if Pamela were to bring a claim against the rescue group.

I believe that we could raise potential claims of both trespass and nuisance against the rescue organization, but the trespass claim seems to be the strongest of the two. Thus, I'd like you to first prepare a memo focusing just on that claim and whether it would be successful. Then, I'd like you to look at and examine the nuisance claim. One of the law clerks has found case law that will help you in your analysis. In addition, I think the Sweetwater city dog ordinance could be helpful in your analysis. I've pasted it here, and also put the section with the relevant definitions.

SWEETWATER CITY ORDINANCE, SECTION 12.102. GENERAL DOG REGULATIONS.[45]

(a) **Restraint.** A custodian of any dog within the City shall keep the dog under restraint at all times.

(b) **Disposal of Feces.** A custodian of any dog within the City shall immediately clean from any sidewalk, street, park, school, public place, or private property of another any feces of the dog and shall dispose of such feces in a sanitary manner. Violation of this provision shall be a petty misdemeanor.

---

[45] From the Bloomington, Minnesota City Code, AMERICAN LEGAL PUBLISHING CORP., http://www.amlegal.com/codes/client/bloomington_mn/ (last visited May 6, 2016).

(c) **General Duty of Owners.** Every owner of a dog must exercise reasonable care and take all necessary steps and precautions to protect other people, property and animals from injuries or damage which might result from the dog's behavior, regardless of whether such behavior is motivated by playfulness or ferocity.

Sweetwater City Ordinance, Section 12.91. DEFINITIONS.

Under Restraint - an animal is under restraint if:

> (1) the animal is within a secure vehicle;
>
> (2) the animal is within a secure fence or building within the owner's property limits;
>
> (3) the animal is picketed in accordance with this Article of the City Code;
>
> (4) the animal is controlled by a leash, provided that when persons or other animals are within twenty (20) feet of the animal the leash is shortened to six (6) feet.

I have scheduled a meeting with Pamela and she expects not only advice and recommendations on how to proceed, but also a strategy of how to deal with these problems. I'll expect your memo before my meeting with her.

Amy

Amy Lincoln
Partner, Lincoln Adams and Washington Law Firm

As you have read, you have been asked to write two legal memoranda regarding the issues that Stray Dog Advertising is facing with its neighbor at the Sweetwater office location.

Lincoln has asked you first to write her an office memo about the following:

- A summary of what has happened between Stray Dog Advertising and Happy Tails Animal Rescue Organization
- The legal issue at hand (trespass)
- A summary and analysis of the law that applies
- Your opinion about whether Stray Dog Advertising would be successful if it brought a trespass claim against Happy Tails
- Your advice on how to proceed with this dispute

Lincoln has also asked to you prepare a second office memo about the following:

- A summary of what has happened between Stray Dog Advertising and Happy Tails Animal Rescue Organization
- The legal issue at hand (nuisance)
- A summary and analysis of the law that applies
- Your opinion about whether Stray Dog Advertising would be successful if it brought a nuisance claim against Happy Tails
- Your advice on how to proceed with this dispute

You will find complete information about these assignments on the Information Pages (pages 127-128; 129-130).

You will be analyzing the client matter using the trespass and nuisance cases that you read and review in class.

From:	Pamela Park <pamela.park@straydogadvertising.com>
To:	Amy Lincoln <a.lincoln@lawlawfirm.com>
Sent:	May 2, THIS YEAR 10:46
Subject:	FW: Neighboring Business

Hi Amy,

We need your help with an issue at our Sweetwater office. It is getting really out of hand.

The long-time tenant in the building next door to us is an animal rescue organization, Happy Tails Animal Rescue. They moved in about a year before we purchased our building and have been operating next to us without incident until recently. Last summer, they made some significant changes to the space, including converting the small parking lot behind the building into a lawn/garden area so that they have green space where the animals can go outside. They've put up a 6 foot privacy fence around the space.

Since we bought the building, Happy Tails has always kept a few dogs at their offices. But there were at most one or two dogs that stayed all the time at the office until they were adopted. Happy Tails usually finds foster homes for the animals, and the dogs stay at the foster home until they are adopted into a permanent home. But sometimes, they rescue an animal but can't find it a foster home, so it stays at the office. There has always been some barking coming from the Happy Tails office, but we've never had a real issue with the dogs until recently.

The barking has gotten worse. Over the past three or four weeks they have had up to six dogs living at their offices — all at one time. When the dogs are outside, they bark, sometimes for five to ten minutes before they quiet down. The dogs are outside at least five to six times a day, from the morning till the evening. It seems that one was adopted since this morning we saw only five dogs. But the number could increase again since dogs are admitted into the organization all the time. Some of our clients have even commented about the noise and have asked that we move our meetings to their offices.

We've also had another issue arise with regard to our clients and the rescue organization. It's spring so we keep our windows open to let in fresh air and prefer that to keeping the air conditioning on and the windows closed. In the last two to three weeks, I've noticed dog hairs all over the office. I presume that they float in through the open windows. One important potential client is very allergic to dog and cat hair, and he started sneezing and his nose started running during a meeting at our office two weeks ago. He asked to schedule our next meeting at his office to avoid the allergic reaction. Our cleaning person also commented to me that there seems to be more dust in our office space. Only one other client has complained about the dog or cat hair, and I have also noticed that our offices seem dustier.

We all have complained about the flies that have entered through the windows on several occasions. The flies are attracted to what I am sure is the dog poop that is left on the lawn, or to the two chickens kept in the chicken coop. Ebony, one of our copywriters at the Sweetwater office, has also complained to me about seeing the flies in the space. Emil and Meilin, two other employees, have kept track of the times that they have seen flies in the office, and I've forwarded to you the table that they drew up.

I wrote a letter to the director of Happy Tails and copied the landlord. I've attached the letter and their response here. I've also spoken with the city and have been told that the rescue organization has filed for the appropriate permits and variances and is complying with the local laws and ordinances. I just can't believe that we are stuck with this situation.

Can you tell me if there is anything legally that we can do? I'd like to set up a meeting with you next week to discuss our options and get some guidance from you.

PP

From: Amy Lincoln <a.lincoln@lawlawfirm.com>
To: Pamela Park <pamela.park@straydogadvertising.com>
Cc: Associate Attorney <a.attorney@lawlawfirm.com>
Sent: May 4, THIS YEAR 13:12
Subject: A Couple of Quick Questions

Pamela, I've assigned one of our associate attorneys to help you with this matter. I wanted to ask a couple of questions about the chickens and the chicken coops. You don't mention anything about the chickens. Are they noisy? And are the chicken coops well maintained, or are they dirty and unsanitary? And in general, how are the dogs kept? Are they unsanitary or unhealthy?

Amy

From: Pamela Park <pamela.park@straydogadvertising.com>
To: Amy Lincoln <a.lincoln@lawlawfirm.com>
Cc: Associate Attorney <a.attorney@lawlawfirm.com>
Sent: May 4, THIS YEAR 14:22
Subject: Re: A Couple of Quick Questions

Amy, the chickens and the dogs are kept very well at Happy Tails. Being a rescue organization, they take very good care of their animals. The cages are all clean, and the yard too. As far as the chickens go, they are actually quite quiet and we've never really had any issues with them beyond the dust and flies that enter our offices and are acerbated by them, I think.

PP

sent from my iPhone

STRAY DOG
Advertising

210 Main Street Northwest
Sweetwater, Jefferson 68910

VIA U.S. MAIL

Celeste King, Executive Director
Happy Tails Animal Rescue
218 Main Street Northwest
Sweetwater, Jefferson 68910

April 20, THIS YEAR

Re: Disturbances to Our Offices

Dear Ms. King:

I am writing about disturbances from your business, Happy Tails Animal Rescue, that have adversely affected the operations of Stray Dog Advertising. In the last month, we have noticed an increase in the barking of dogs that are housed at your office. The dogs bark throughout the day, disturbing the peace and quiet of our business. On one occasion, we have had a client complain about the noise from your dogs, and our staff members find it difficult to concentrate on their work due to the noise.

We have also noted an increase in the number of flies entering our office space now that we are keeping the windows open with the arrival of warmer spring weather. The flies are most certainly due to the dogs defecating in your back yard area and to the chicken coop that you keep. We've never before had a problem with flies since we purchased the building and began operating from it, so the problems are certainly related to your business.

Finally, we have also seen an increase in animal hair throughout our offices as well. No one at Stray Dog Advertising brings their pet to work, so the only explanation is that the hair is entering the windows from your business as well. Just the other week, a client asked not to meet at our offices because he is severely allergic to animal hair and at a previous meeting at our office, he began sneezing and his nose began running uncontrollably because of the increase in animal hair and dander in our office.

I am sure that we can resolve this matter between us and without resorting to involvement of attorneys or the courts. You can reach me at my cell phone 623-951-4950, and I look forward to speaking to you.

Sincerely yours,

Pamela Park

Pamela Park
Owner, Stray Dog Advertising
Cc: Freeman Potter Property Management

Celeste King
Happy Tails Animal Rescue
218 Main Street Northwest
Sweetwater, Jefferson 68910

Pamela Park
Stray Dog Advertising, LLC
210 Main Street Northwest
Sweetwater, Jefferson 68910

April 28, THIS YEAR

Re: Your Letter of April 20, THIS YEAR

Dear Ms. Park:

Thank you for your letter. Since Happy Tails Animal Rescue is operating legally under the laws and ordinances of the State of Jefferson and the City of Sweetwater, we won't change anything just because you are complaining.

The city and our landlord know that we have dogs at our office. The dogs are adopted to families, so if there are six dogs staying at the office at one time, it is only temporary. No dog is there on a permanent basis since we are a rescue organization and since our goal is to adopt the animals to loving, permanent families. We had only one dog at the office for the entire month of December last year, and even though she barked, it was not that bad since she was a small dog.

Our chickens are also legal under Sweetwater ordinances, and we are also operating as "agricultural activities" in raising them so the law also protects us and declares that we can't be considered a nuisance. As for the dog and cat hair and the flies, how do you know that the hair is from our animals, and that the flies aren't attracted to garbage in the garbage bins behind your building? I remember you telling me that you have pets and that most of your employees do as well. The hair could be from your animals and not ours. It seems that the obvious solution is to close your windows that look over our building and our back yard. That way, no flies can enter your office and you won't hear the noises from the different animals.

Sorry but we won't do anything to change what we're doing.

Best,

Celeste King

Cc: Freeman Potter Property Management

From: Emil Lindgren <emil.lindgren@straydogadvertising.com>
To: Pamela Park <pamela.park@straydogadvertising.com>
Sent: April 25, THIS YEAR 17:23
Subject: Barking Dogs et al.

Hi Pamela, you asked me to keep track of the dog barking over the last month or so. Here is the list that I've kept, and Meilin also kept a list too. I've added it to mine.

Emil	March 14, THIS YEAR	Counted 4 dogs in the backyard; windows closed but could still hear them. Barked up to 15 minutes before stopping
Emil	March 16, THIS YEAR	Had window open and had to go to different office to finish phone call. Client asked if I was working from home and why dogs were barking.
Meilin	March 17, THIS YEAR	Swatted away and smushed three flies during the work day! Gross!
Meilin	March 22, THIS YEAR	I counted only 1 dog outside this morning. Large Golden Retriever type who was barking non-stop at people walking by on the sidewalk throughout the day. Dog was outside all day.
Emil	March 23 – 25, THIS YEAR	Quiet! No dogs next door. We think that they were all adopted. Found a bee sitting on my desk.
Emil	April 1, THIS YEAR	Dogs are back. ☹
Emil	April 3, THIS YEAR	Noticed that one of the volunteers at Happy Tails took the dogs out one at a time instead of all together. Better, but the dogs were still barking at squirrels or at people walking by. Dogs were also outside longer since they went out one by one.
Meilin	April 6, THIS YEAR	I had my ear phones on today, so didn't hear the noise from the dogs. Saw two flies in my office.
Emil	April 11, THIS YEAR	Only three dogs at the office now. They were pretty quiet today. No issue with flies. Noticed what appears to be more dust and hair around the office.
Meilin	April 13, THIS YEAR	Office seems dirtier to me too. No problems with dogs today but noticed what seems to be dog hair and dust around the office.
Emil	April 14, THIS YEAR	The weather has gotten cold so the windows are closed. No issues with dogs or with flies. Dogs are outside less since it is raining.
Meilin	April 19, THIS YEAR	Gina McBride asked to move the meeting to her office. She says she is afraid of dogs and has heard them barking in the background when we were on the phone yesterday. When we spoke, four dogs were outside, playing and barking for about 5 min.
Emil	April 21, THIS YEAR	We opened the windows again after the cold weather spell. Noticed more dust and hair in the office after having windows closed for a week. Counted two flies in the office.
Emil	April 24, THIS YEAR	Happy Tails is back to two dogs at the office. Both seem quiet. Same issues with dust and hair as earlier this week. Saw 1 bee.
Meilin	April 25, THIS YEAR	When I got to the office this morning, found one of the dogs from Happy Tails had escaped from their building and gotten loose. He was in our parking lot under a car when I arrived. I brought him back to the HTRO building. The volunteer there thanked me for bringing him back and also said they have three dogs at the office now. In the office, I noticed the same dust and hair around. No flies today.

From: Pamela Park <pamela.park@straydogadvertising.com>
To: Amy Lincoln <a.lincoln@lawlawfirm.com>
Sent: May 7, THIS YEAR 14:22
Subject: FW: Contract

Amy, this is the last straw. We've lost a client that was about to sign a contract with us because of Happy Tails. Although it wouldn't have been a huge contract at this point (25,000), it was the beginning of what was sure to lead to more business. This is a successful growing company that will now do its advertising with someone else. We've got to do something.

PP

sent from my iPhone

From: Noah Riley <n.riley@ecogiocogames.com>
To: Pamela Park <pamela.park@straydogadvertising.com>
CC: Roy Blanco <roy.blanco@straydogadvertising.com>
Sent: May 7, THIS YEAR 14:01
Subject: Contract

Dear Pamela,

Thank you for the extensive amount of time that you've dedicated to me and my company over the past weeks while we've discussed signing a contract for your advertising and branding services. I know that in our meeting yesterday, I told you that I was "99.9%" sure that I would sign with you/Stray Dog Advertising. I am sorry to tell you that I've changed my mind.

While I appreciate that you've agreed to meet with me at my office rather than yours due to the dog hair in and around your office and my severe allergies, I realized that I just can't sign with an advertising agency whose offices I can't visit because if I do, I will have difficulty breathing, break out into a rash and start sneezing. When we talk on the phone, it sometimes sounds like I am calling the animal humane society and not an advertising agency and while I know that you can't do anything about the barking, it just isn't professional.

I hope you understand. I really do appreciate the time, energy and effort that you put into the presentations and the proposals for our toy stores.

Noah

Noah Riley

Founder and CEO, EcoGioco Children's Games

Additional Skills-Building Exercises

Trespass/Nuisance Analysis Exercises

Overview of the Exercise: For this exercise, you will analyze the following short fact patterns that deal with trespass and nuisance. Your task is to analyze the fact patterns and determine whether or not the defendant in the case could be held liable for trespass and nuisance, for just one of the claims, or for neither.

Learning Objectives of the Exercise:

This exercise will build your skills to:

- Articulate the legal rules regarding trespass and nuisance
- Apply those rules to fact patterns and analyze the facts and the law
- Articulate and effectively communicate that analysis using legal terminology

Steps for Completing the Exercise:

- Read the following fact patterns.
- By yourself, analyze each one and answer the question presented. When you reach an answer, be sure to articulate your reasoning.
- When you are done analyzing each of the fact patterns, discuss your answers with a classmate. Explain to each other why you have reached the conclusion that you did.
- If you and your partner have different responses to a fact pattern, you must try to convince him or her that your answer is correct. After you both have tried to convince the other, you must choose a team answer.
- Once you have discussed each of the fact patterns, you will compare answers as a class.

Grading: This exercise is not graded. Instead, after you and your partner have compared and discussed your answers, you will compare the answers that you reached with those of your classmates.

1. The family that lives next door to Yolanda purchased three drones as gifts for their children. During the weekends, their children are outside all afternoon playing with their drones, flying them over their backyard and over Yolanda's. Yolanda no longer likes to be outside as she is afraid that one will accidentally hit her, although they fly at least 12 to 15 feet off the ground. What claims can Yolanda bring against her neighbor, if any?

2. Yolanda's sister, Ramona, lives in another suburb of Jefferson City, very near where the airport is located and underneath a flight path leading to one of the primary runways of the busy airport. She has contacted an attorney about taking some legal action against the airport for the airplanes that travel directly overhead. What claims, if any, could Ramona bring against the airport?

3. Last week when coming home, George noticed that no one was home next door and that the water was running from the hose in the backyard, near the property line with George's property. George wanted to make sure that the water wasn't running onto his property. He was also curious to see what his neighbor's garden looked like. When he entered into the backyard, he saw that the water had been running for some time as there was a large puddle and it had started to run onto his property. George's neighbor has now contacted an attorney, who has threatened to sue George for trespass. Does the neighbor have a valid claim against George?

4. George's other next-door neighbor is a recluse, who has "no trespassing" signs on the fence surrounding his property and on his front door. Yesterday when coming home, George noticed smoke coming from the neighbor's garage. No cars were in the driveway so George was quite sure no one was home. He entered onto the neighbor's property to check that no cars were in the garage, or people in the house. He then called 911 with his cell phone. The fire department was able to extinguish the fire before the house was damaged, although the garage was a total loss. George's neighbor is now claiming that he trespassed on his property because he could have called 911 from the street without entering onto his property. If George's other neighbor also brings a claim against him, would he be successful?

5. Sara lives next door instead to a family whose children are all high school basketball players. They maintain a basketball hoop in the driveway, and the children and their friends play basketball all the time when not in school or playing games for the various teams they play for. The balls frequently enter Sara's property, as do the children when they retrieve them. The balls have damaged the shrubs, flowers and garden in Sara's front yard. Sara has sought legal advice. What advice can you give her? What claims could she bring against her neighbor?

6. In Jefferson City, Ali operates a small restaurant, located next to a movie theater. On the roof of the theater is a cooling tower, which is part of the air conditioning system. The cooling tower emits a spray that falls onto the restaurant's rear yard, which Ali wanted to use as a garden where his customers could eat during the summer months. But no one wants to sit at a table and be sprayed by the cooling tower. Ali has approached you for advice on what, if any, legal options he has.

7. Another business in Jefferson City is a bar, which has obtained all the necessary city licenses to operate. It also follows all the city ordinances. However, the music is loud until late into the night, so loud that the residents who live in apartments on the floors above the bar in the same building are unable to sleep until the bar closes at 2 a.m. The bar has been open for two months, and for these two months, the residents have been unable to sleep until the bar closes. One of the residents has approached you for legal advice. What do you tell her?

8. Frank lives down the street from a garbage recycling facility, which has recently begun recycling the garbage using a new method that is allegedly more environmentally friendly, but it is also smellier. The smells from the facility have gotten much worse and are so horrible that Frank is no longer able to keep his windows open or go outside. The facility also uses new lights to ward off trespassers, and the lights shine into Frank's home at all times of the day and night. Frank has approached you for legal advice about the claims that he could bring against the facility. What do you tell him?

Negotiation between Stray Dog Advertising and Happy Tails Animal Rescue

Overview of the Exercise: This exercise simulates a negotiation between the attorney for Stray Dog Advertising and the attorney for Happy Tails Animal Rescue. Rather than turning immediately to litigation to resolve the dispute between SDA and Happy Tails, you and opposing counsel have suggested to your clients that attempting to resolve the matter through pre-litigation negotiation would be worthwhile. Both clients have agreed.

You will be assigned the role of counsel for Stray Dog Advertising or Happy Tails Animal Rescue. The purpose of this exercise is to explain your client's position to opposing counsel, lay out the arguments for the position and explore settlement options. Before the meeting, review the confidential information that you have been provided.

Learning Objectives of the Exercise:

This exercise will build your skills to:

- Use monetary and non-monetary interests of parties in negotiating settlement agreement
- Identify primary obstacles to reaching a mutually beneficial settlement agreement
- Implement negotiation strategies and tactics

Steps for Completing the Exercise:

- Read the preparatory and confidential information that you have been given by your instructor
- Be familiar with the case law regarding nuisance and trespass and the fact pattern of Stray Dog Advertising and Happy Tails Animal Rescue
- Articulate the arguments for your client's position and anticipate opposing counsel's.

Writing Exercise:

If time allows and if directed by your instructor, you and opposing counsel will also prepare a draft of the settlement agreement that your clients will sign after you have reached a negotiated agreement.

To complete this task, you first must find a template of a settlement agreement. In real life, few attorneys start from scratch (i.e. from zero) when drafting any contract or agreement. Why recreate the wheel? Instead, attorneys will use a template and then adapt it to their purposes.

Thus, using a template is part of practice. Templates can be found in a law firm's database of documents, or many attorneys will take an agreement from a past case and modify and adapt it to a new case. Bar associations have templates and forms available (often for a fee), and many are available online as well.

But using a template comes with risks too. Even though the template is prepared, you can't simply cut and paste it to a new Word document and think you are good to go. Here are some questions that you have to ask yourself as you analyze a template:

- Does it include provisions that are illegal or violate some law, either because it was written by an attorney in another state or because the law has changed?
- Is it written to be beneficial to one side? For example, is it a very landlord-friendly lease agreement? If it is and if you represent the tenant, you will need to revise it.
- Does it include all the essential provisions? Just because a template is available doesn't mean that it is complete.
- Does your client's matter have unique circumstances or agreements that must be incorporated? It isn't always possible to find a template that perfectly suits your situation, so understanding that will make it easier to find a template that works and that can be adapted.

You also want to be very careful when you use a template to ensure that you remove all references that reveal that this was a template, or that reveal that the document was used with other clients or parties.

Once you have found a template online, adapt it to suit the agreement that you reached.

Grading: This exercise is not graded. After the meetings, the class will debrief on how the negotiations went.

Research Problem:
Bees and Owner's Liability for Them

Overview of the Exercise: For this exercise, you will conduct research on a limited and related issue stemming from the trespass and nuisance matter facing Pamela Park and the employees at Stray Dog Advertising.

You have received the following email from Pamela Park, informing you about a new problem with Happy Tails Animal Rescue Organization:

From:	Pamela Park <pamela.park@straydogadvertising.com>
To:	Associate Attorney <a.attorney@lawlawfirm.com>
Sent:	May 15, THIS YEAR 14:08
Subject:	New Problem w/Happy Tails

Associate Attorney,

I spoke on the phone with Amy, and she suggested that I write you directly for help with this new problem that has arisen with Happy Tails. Last week, they installed two bee hives in the backyard area. I was surprised to say the least. Since then, bees have been entering our offices as we continue to keep the windows open most days, despite the ongoing barking and flies. I've noticed one or two bees per day coming into the office, and two of my employees have also noticed them. No one has gotten stung, and no one is allergic to bee stings on my staff. However, I am concerned that a client may be allergic and then gets stung while at a meeting at our offices.

Can Happy Tails also be liable for any issues relating to their bees? I spoke with Celeste, and she had the same obstinate response: the bees are legal under city ordinances so they won't do anything. She still expects us to keep our windows closed.

PP

As you have read, you have been asked to research the liability that an individual may face for bees that he keeps on his property.

Learning Objectives of the Exercise:

This exercise will build your skills to:

- Conduct research about a narrow legal issue
- Identify primary and secondary sources that will help you respond to the research request
- Explain the choices of sources, their content and the research responses that you identify

Steps for Completing the Exercise:

- Begin the research problem by choosing one of the legal research websites on which you will conduct your research
- You will find on the next pages a list of initial questions to answer before you begin researching, as well as a handout that you will complete as you research the issue.

Grading: This exercise is not graded. You will work through the research exercise with your instructor as a class and compare answers as you go and also at the end of the research.

Optional Written Exercise: If time allows and if instructed, prepare a short email response to Senior Partner Lincoln about your research findings.

RESEARCH PROBLEM OF OWNER'S LIABILITY FOR BEES

Fill out this handout and answer the following questions as you research the problem of whether Happy Tails Animal Rescue could be liable for the bees that it is keeping on its property in beehives.

Initial Questions:

1. After reading the email from Pamela Park about the bees at Happy Tails, what are your initial thoughts about the potential claims that Stray Dog Advertising could bring against Happy Tails?

2. What obstacles do you think might exist to bringing the claims?

3. Has Stray Dog Advertising suffered any damages from the bees? Does that matter? Why or why not?

4. Do you know anything about the liability of an individual for animals that he/she keeps or owns? If so, summarize the law that you are familiar with.

Before You Begin Researching:

1. Before beginning to research a legal issue, one of the first questions that you should ask is whether this is a state or federal issue. Are the claims that you identified in question #1 above state or federal?

2. Another question that you ask yourself is in which database you should start your research. Look at the home page of the search engine (Westlaw Next, LexisNexis or Bloomberg Law) that you have chosen to use. Of the databases available, which seems like the best place to start? Cases? Statutes and regulations? Secondary sources? A general search of all sources? Why?

3. Another question to ask (and answer) before researching is the search terms that you will use. What do you think will be useful search terms?

4. Should you limit those search terms? If so, how can you limit them to then limit your search results?

Conducting a Search with Primary Sources:

Now that you have your search terms defined and have limited them so that you are not overwhelmed with search results, run a search with your search terms of the primary sources.

If you are doing a general search of all sources, cases are a good starting point to begin your research.

1. Review the cases in the search. If you did a search with liability /s bees on Westlaw, you should have approximately 38 results. That number is small enough that you can reasonably review the summaries provided to determine whether they are relevant.

You should be able to group the cases into several groups according to similar facts:

     1. Cases in which bees _____
     2. Cases in which bees _____
     3. Cases in which bees _____
     4. Other cases:

2. What seems to be present in the cited cases that is not present in our facts?

3. Have the cases really provided you with a good answer to the question of whether Happy Tails could be liable for the bees that have entered into the Stray Dog Advertising offices?

4. What is your initial conclusion about potential liability?

5. Do you need to continue your research? Why? Do you think that you need to do another search, or are there other sources that you can review? Why?

Conducting a Search with Secondary Sources:

1. Now conduct a search of secondary sources, using the search terms that you have identified. Review the results of the search. Which ones seem particularly promising to you? Highlight those search results. Which search results can you eliminate? Why?

2. With your partner, spend some time reviewing those search results that seem promising. Write below the claims that may be relevant here. Are they the same that you identified in the Initial Questions above?

3. What important points have you identified about potential liability of Happy Tails? Write them below.

4. After reviewing the search results and applying the law that you have read in some of the secondary sources, what conclusion can you reach about potential liability of Happy Tails Rescue for the bees that it keeps on its property?

5. What advice would you give Pamela?

Professional Presentation:
If SDA Were Your Client...

Overview of the Exercise: For this exercise, you will make a professional presentation in which you answer and discuss the following question: *If Stray Dog Advertising were your client in your home country and if Pamela came to you for legal advice about the trespass/nuisance matter, what would you do and what advice would you give her?*

Learning Objectives of the Exercise:

This exercise will build your skills to:

- Describe a specific aspect of your country's legal system
- Compare your country's legal system with the U.S. legal system
- Listen to and understand your classmates' presentations and complete information about the presentations

Steps for Completing the Exercise:

- Analyze the fact pattern of the trespass/nuisance matter under your country's laws
- Explain whether Stray Dog Advertising could successfully bring a claim of trespass or nuisance against Happy Tails Animal Rescue Organization
- Explain what other claims SDA could bring in this dispute and explain how the case would be handled in your country's legal system
- Explain what legal advice you would give Pamela if she came to you for legal advice in your home country.

Research Required for the Exercise:

The research you are required to do depends on your knowledge of these claims in your country's legal system. It is presumed that you are familiar with the law and with how you would approach this issue if SDA were a client of yours.

Grading: This presentation is not graded. You will present to a small group of your fellow classmates instead of to the entire class.

Handouts:

As part of your presentation, you must create a handout for your classmates, and the handouts must include fill-in-the-blank questions that your classmates must complete with information that you present during the presentation. Each handout must include at least five questions to complete.

For example, if a U.S. law student were giving a presentation on trespass or nuisance in the United States, he could include on his handout this question:

To successfully bring a claim of trespass in the U.S. system, a plaintiff must demonstrate:

1._____
2._____
3. _____

As you are speaking, your classmates will have to listen, follow what you are saying and fill in the blanks. If you are listening to one of your classmate's presentations and are unsure about an answer, you should ask him or her to repeat so you can fill in the blank(s).

Grammar Review:

The basis of this exercise is hypothetical or conditional verbs: *if SDA were your client, what would you do?*

Remember the grammar when discussing hypothetical conditions.

Present: **IF + PAST SIMPLE, WOULD + BASE VERB**

*If Pamela **called** me to schedule an appointment, I **would tell** her to visit me at my office.*

NOTE: We use "were" for all tenses with the verb "to be" when using a conditional verb.

*If I **were** you, I **would not take** that class.*

*If Pamela **were** my client, I **would tell** her that she should bring a claim of nuisance but not trespass against Happy Tails.*

Past: **IF + PAST PERFECT, WOULD + HAVE + PAST PARTICIPLE**

*If SDA **had not moved** to the new office, it is likely that this **would not have happened**.*

*If Happy Tails **had had** fewer dogs at its office, then Park **would not have sought out** legal advice.*

Information Pages

Office Memo: Trespass

Overview of the Assignment: For this assignment, you will write an office memo to the Senior Partner, summarizing your research on whether you think Stray Dog Advertising would be successful if it were to bring a trespass claim against Happy Tails Animal Rescue. You should also give recommendations and advice to Park on what she should do.

Learning Objectives of the Assignment:

This assignment will build your skills to:

- Efficiently communicate in a written format
- Explain complex matters clearly and concisely
- Analyze and apply the rules of law regarding trespass

Research for the Assignment: You are not required to do any outside research for this assignment. You should base your analysis on the Colorado trespass cases that you read in class:

- <u>Public Service Co. of Colorado v. Van Wyk</u>, 27 P.3d 377 (Colo. 2001).
- <u>Hoery v. United States</u>, 64 P.3d 214 (Colo. 2003).
- <u>Cook v. Rockwell International Corp.</u>, 273 F. Supp. 1175 (Colo. 2003).
- <u>Miller v. Carnation Co.</u>, 516 P.2d 661 (Colo. Ct. App. 1973).
- <u>Cobai v. Young</u>, 679 P.2d 121 (Colo. Ct. App. 1984).

If you want to practice your legal research skills, you can look for and use other cases that you find. However, if you do search on Westlaw, LexisNexis or Bloomberg Law, be sure to limit your search and the cases you use to Colorado law and remember to change the citations and legal references to Jefferson law as indicated in the introduction.

Format of the Completed Assignment:

Your response should be in an office memo format and should include the following:

- Summary of the facts
- The relevant law
- Analysis of the law to the fact pattern
- Conclusion about how you think a court would rule if this matter were to go to court
- Your advice to the client about how to proceed

Follow the following format:

- 1 inch (2.54 cm.) margins (top/bottom and sides)
- 12 font, Times New Roman font
- Double spaced
- Maximum eight pages

Notes:

This memo should be predictive and not persuasive. You are not trying to persuade the senior partner or the client about the strength of your arguments or urge him or her to take a particular course of action; you are only trying to inform about the law, how it applies to our case, how you think a court would rule and what advice you have.

In a memo, you can also use formatting like underlining, bold font or italics. You can also create headings and subheadings to organize your answer.

For additional information about office memos and e-memos, as well as samples, refer to the online additional resources.

Grading: This assignment is worth 102 points.

LEGAL CONTENT	0-6 points	8 points	10 points	12 points	Points
Issue statement (IS)	Document does not include an IS or includes IS that fails to properly identify the legal issue(s) and the applicable law	Identifies the legal issue(s) and correctly states the applicable law with minor mistakes	Identifies the legal issue(s) and correctly states the applicable law	Identifies the legal issue(s) and correctly states the applicable law in an exceptionally creative and concise way	_____/12
Short Answer	Document does not include a short answer or includes a short answer with significant mistakes	Responds to IS but with key facts or applicable legal principles missing	Responds to IS with key facts and applicable legal principles with no meaningful errors	Clearly and concisely responds to IS with key facts and applicable legal principles and no irrelevancies	_____/12
Facts	Few or none of the relevant facts are included; difficult to follow or understand	Most relevant facts are included as well as non-relevant ones; at times difficult to follow	Relevant facts are included with occasional irrelevancies; easy to follow	All relevant facts are included with no irrelevancies; story is clearly and concisely told to reader in objective way	_____/12
Rule	Hard to follow and understand; does not include relevant sources or cites inappropriate sources; no rule application	Cites to some relevant sources but is incomplete in covering all relevant aspects of the rule; includes some rule application	Cite only to relevant sources and mostly clear; rule application explains but not fully how rule has been applied	Clear and concise; includes only relevant sources and includes all parts of rule necessary for analysis; clear rule application	_____/12
Analysis	Contains conclusory statements and/or no case law; facts are analyzed in a conclusory or insufficient way	Uses some case law but does not analogize or distinguish or explain its application; some conclusory statements; facts briefly analyzed	Uses case law to show how rule applies to case; case law is compared and contrasted with success; most facts are analyzed	Analyzes case law completely, comparing it fully to client matter; facts are thoroughly analyzed in an objective way	_____/12
Conclusion/ Recommendations	No conclusion or recommendations are included in document	A brief conclusion is included but without sufficient client advice	Paper includes conclusion and recommendations	Paper includes full conclusion of the legal analysis and facts and presents creative and thoughtful recommendations	_____/12
Citations	No sources are cited in document	Some sources are cited, but inconsistently; citation format is inconsistent	All citations are present; correct format is mostly used	All citations are present; correct format is used throughout document	_____/12
WRITING	**2**	**4**	**5**	**6**	**Points**
Formatting	Document does not follow format instructions or the sample provided	Document attempts to follow instructions and sample provided	Document follows the instructions and sample provided with no meaningful errors	Document exactly follows the instructions and sample provided	_____/6
Organization	No structure or organization; free flow of ideas	Structure & organization present but reorganization or headings needed for full clarity	Document is clearly organized and structured with proper use of heading and subheadings	Document is exceptionally well organized and structured with proper use of headings and subheadings	_____/6
Syntax Mechanics	Contains numerous and distracting grammatical and mechanical errors that impede understanding	Contains some grammatical and mechanical errors that impede understanding	Contains few grammatical and mechanical errors but none that impede understanding	Contains no grammatical and mechanical errors; native-like use of English	_____/6
TOTAL					_____/102

Office Memo: Nuisance

Overview of the Assignment: For this assignment, you will write an office memo to the Senior Partner, summarizing your research on whether you think Stray Dog Advertising would be successful if it were to bring a nuisance claim against Happy Tails Animal Rescue. You should also give recommendations and advice to Park on what she should do.

Learning Objectives of the Assignment:

This assignment will build your skills to:

- Efficiently communicate in a written format
- Explain complex matters clearly and concisely
- Analyze and apply the rules of law regarding nuisance

Research for the Assignment: You are not required to do any outside research for this assignment.

You should base your analysis on the Indiana statute and nuisance cases that you read and review in class:

- Statute: IND. CODE 32-30-6-6
- Cases:
  - Wernke v. Halas, 600 N.E.2d 117 (Ind. Ct. App. 1992).
  - Owens v. Phillips, 73 Ind. 284 (Ind. 1881).
  - Bonewitz v. Parker, 912 N.E.2d 378 (Ind. 2009).
  - Davoust v. Mitchell, 257 N.E.2d 332 (Ind. Ct. App. 1970).
  - Hendricks v. Tubbs, 92 N.E.2d 561 (Ind. 1950).

If you want to practice your legal research skills, you can look for and use other cases that you find. However, if you do search on Westlaw, LexisNexis or Bloomberg Law, be sure to limit your search and the cases you use to Indiana law and remember to change the citations and legal references to Jefferson law as indicated in the introduction.

Format of the Completed Assignment:

Your response should be in an office memo format and should include the following:
- Summary of the facts
- The relevant law
- Analysis of the law to the fact pattern
- Conclusion about how you think a court would rule if this matter were to go to court
- Your advice to the client about how to proceed

Follow the following format:
- 1 inch (2.54 cm.) margins (top/bottom and sides)
- 12 font, Times New Roman font
- Double spaced
- Maximum eight pages

Notes:

This memo should be predictive and not persuasive. You are not trying to persuade the senior partner or the client about the strength of your arguments or urge him or her to take a particular course of action; you are only trying to inform about the law, how it applies to our case, how you think a court would rule and what advice you have.

In a memo, you can also use formatting like underlining, bold font or italics. You can also create headings and subheadings to organize your answer.

For additional information about office memos and e-memos, as well as samples, refer to the online additional resources.

Grading: This assignment is worth 102 points.

LEGAL CONTENT	0-6 points	8 points	10 points	12 points	Points
Issue statement (IS)	Document does not include an IS or includes IS that fails to properly identify the legal issue(s) and the applicable law	Identifies the legal issue(s) and correctly states the applicable law with minor mistakes	Identifies the legal issue(s) and correctly states the applicable law	Identifies the legal issue(s) and correctly states the applicable law in an exceptionally creative and concise way	_____/12
Short Answer	Document does not include a short answer or includes a short answer with significant mistakes	Responds to IS but with key facts or applicable legal principles missing	Responds to IS with key facts and applicable legal principles with no meaningful errors	Clearly and concisely responds to IS with key facts and applicable legal principles and no irrelevancies	_____/12
Facts	Few or none of the relevant facts are included; difficult to follow or understand	Most relevant facts are included as well as non-relevant ones; at times difficult to follow	Relevant facts are included with occasional irrelevancies; easy to follow	All relevant facts are included with no irrelevancies; story is clearly and concisely told to reader in objective way	_____/12
Rule	Hard to follow and understand; does not include relevant sources or cites inappropriate sources; no rule application	Cites to some relevant sources but is incomplete in covering all relevant aspects of the rule; includes some rule application	Cite only to relevant sources and mostly clear; rule application explains but not fully how rule has been applied	Clear and concise; includes only relevant sources and includes all parts of rule necessary for analysis; clear rule application	_____/12
Analysis	Contains conclusory statements and/or no case law; facts are analyzed in a conclusory or insufficient way	Uses some case law but does not analogize or distinguish or explain its application; some conclusory statements; facts briefly analyzed	Uses case law to show how rule applies to case; case law is compared and contrasted with success; most facts are analyzed	Analyzes case law completely, comparing it fully to client matter; facts are thoroughly analyzed in an objective way	_____/12
Conclusion/ Recommendations	No conclusion or recommendations are included in document	A brief conclusion is included but without sufficient client advice	Paper includes conclusion and recommendations	Paper includes full conclusion of the legal analysis and facts and presents creative and thoughtful recommendations	_____/12
Citations	No sources are cited in document	Some sources are cited, but inconsistently; citation format is inconsistent	All citations are present; correct format is mostly used	All citations are present; correct format is used throughout document	_____/12
WRITING	**2**	**4**	**5**	**6**	**Points**
Formatting	Document does not follow format instructions or the sample provided	Document attempts to follow instructions and sample provided	Document follows the instructions and sample provided with no meaningful errors	Document exactly follows the instructions and sample provided	_____/6
Organization	No structure or organization; free flow of ideas	Structure & organization present but reorganization or headings needed for full clarity	Document is clearly organized and structured with proper use of heading and subheadings	Document is exceptionally well organized and structured with proper use of headings and subheadings	_____/6
Syntax Mechanics	Contains numerous and distracting grammatical and mechanical errors that impede understanding	Contains some grammatical and mechanical errors that impede understanding	Contains few grammatical and mechanical errors but none that impede understanding	Contains no grammatical and mechanical errors; native-like use of English	_____/6
TOTAL					_____/102

Mock Client Meeting

Overview of the Assignment: This assignment simulates a client meeting between you and your client, Pamela Park of Stray Dog Advertising, LLC. You are meeting with Park to discuss the potential claims that she may bring against Happy Tails Animal Rescue Organization, whether you think SDA will be successful if it brings the claim(s), and your recommendations to Pamela on how she should proceed.

The meeting is scheduled after you have had the opportunity to study the law on both trespass and nuisance. You are expected to discuss both legal issues and all possible legal claims relating to the fact pattern, as well as the potential damages that Park would be entitled to.

Your instructor will indicate to you the time that you will have available for the mock client meeting.

Learning Objectives of the Assignment:

This assignment will build your skills to:

- Explain and clarify the legal positions of the parties and describe potential outcomes to your client
- Respond to technical questions about litigation
- Incorporate technical legal English vocabulary that relates to trespass and nuisance and use appropriate layperson explanations for your client

Steps for Completing the Assignment:

- Read and be familiar with the Main Assignment File
- Be familiar with the trespass and nuisance cases that you have been assigned
- Recommended:
    - Anticipate the questions that you think your client might ask and prepare possible responses;
    - Draft an outline of what you would like to cover in the meeting.

Note: Remember that part of the grading is also based on your professional demeanor. You are expected to arrive punctually, be dressed in professional attire and act as you would with a client in real life. You should play the part from when you come into the meeting room.

Grading: This assignment is worth 102 points.

Punctuality: Student-attorney arrived on time to meeting: YES _____ (10 points) NO _____ (0 points)

Professional Attire: Student-attorney was dressed in appropriate professional attire: YES _____ (10 points) NO _____ (0 points)

Professional Demeanor: Student-attorney acted in a professional manner w/ client: YES _____ (10 points) NO _____ (0 points)

GRADING CRITERIA	0- 6 points	8 points (C or 75%)	10 points (B or 85%)	12 points	Points received
Engagement I (questions)	Attorney does not ask client any questions; engages in monologue	Attorney asks few questions; questions are hard to follow or show minimal preparation or understanding of matter	Attorney asks basic questions that demonstrate understanding of matter and preparation	Attorney asks thoughtful, insightful and creative questions that demonstrate deep preparation & understanding of matter	_____/12
Engagement II (answers)	Attorney does not respond to client's questions	Attorney responds to questions, but incorrectly or with hard to follow answers	Attorney responds promptly and correctly to all of client's questions	Attorney responds promptly and correctly to all of client's questions with creative, thoughtful and insightful answers that show a deep understanding of the issues	_____/12
Knowledge of Applicable Law	Attorney provides no explanation of the applicable law	Attorney provides explanation of with serious mistakes, or hard to follow (e.g. use of legal jargon)	Attorney provides clear explanation of with some mistakes; uses some legal jargon unnecessarily or without explanations that client can understand	Attorney provides clear, concise and correct explanation of the law with legal jargon when appropriate or w/ explanations client can understand	_____/12
Ability to Analyze Applicable Law	Attorney provides does not provide an analysis of the law for the client	Attorney attempts to analyze the law but provides incomplete or incorrect analysis	Attorney provides analysis of the law with no significant mistakes or misstatements of the law or facts	Attorney provides a clear, concise and correct analysis of the law as it applies to the client matter	_____/12
Advice and Recommendations	Attorney provides no advice or poor advice for client	Attorney provides not comprehensive or inaccurate advice	Attorney provides comprehensive and accurate advice to client on his/her legal matter	Attorney provides thoughtful and creative solutions for client	_____/12
Organization	Meeting is disorganized and hard to follow or lacks any organization	Meeting has some organization but is still confusing for client for how information is presented	Meeting is clearly organized and easy to follow	Meeting is clearly organized and is easy to follow; attorney takes extra steps to ensure client's understanding	_____/12
TOTAL					_____/72
TOTAL FROM PUNCTUALITY AND PROFESSIONALISM					_____/30

Total   ____/102

Client Advice Letter

Overview of the Assignment: For this assignment, you will write an advice and follow-up letter to your client, Pamela Park, summarizing your research on trespass and nuisance, as well as your meeting with her. You should also give recommendations to Park on how she should approach this matter. Be mindful that even though Park may be a sophisticated businesswoman, she is not a trained attorney. Therefore you should avoid legalese in your letter.

Under Rule 1.4(a)(3) of the Model Rules of Professional Conduct, an attorney has the duty to keep his or her client "reasonably informed about the status of the client's matter." A thorough follow-up letter after a client meeting is one of the best ways to meet this duty, as well as regular phone calls, emails or meetings.

Learning Objectives of the Assignment:

This assignment will build your skills to:

- Efficiently communicate in a written format
- Explain complex matters clearly and concisely
- Incorporate technical legal English vocabulary that relates to trespass and nuisance and use appropriate layperson explanations for client

Steps for Completing the Assignment:

- Review the predictive memos that you wrote to your senior partner about your client matter to ensure that the law and the issues are clear
- Be familiar with the case law regarding trespass and nuisance, as well as the fact pattern
- Conduct your client meeting with your client, Pamela Park
- Review the Business Correspondence online resources

Research Required for the Assignment: You are not required to do any outside research for this assignment.

Format of the Completed Assignment

Your assignment should be written as a business letter, not as an email. Even though many firms and lawyers use email for much of the correspondence carried out, formal business letters are still an essential part of the practice of law.

Your law firm has the following policy regarding business correspondence. Your client letter must follow the policy guidelines.

LAW FIRM CORRESPONDENCE POLICY

The purpose of this policy is to ensure a uniform appearance of all business correspondence that is written by the attorneys and staff of the law firm and thus to increase the professional appearance of the firm's work product. All law firm attorneys and staff are required to employ the following guidelines when writing correspondence. Violation of the policy can result in disciplinary action, up to and including termination.

- The first page of all "traditional" letters must be written on law firm letterhead, which includes the firm's address and logo
- All letters must be written in a modified block letter format
- Letters must be written in Times New Roman, 12 font
- Letters must be 1.5 spaced and have 1" (2.54 cm.) margins, except for the initial page, which may have larger top margins to account for the logo, law firm address and sender's direct contact information
- Client letters must not exceed four pages

Grading: This assignment is worth 78 points.

Note: See the Online Additional Resources for examples of letters and for general information about business correspondence.

LEGAL CONTENT	0-6 points (failing)	8 points (C or 75%)	10 points (B or 85%)	12 points	Points
Introduction	Letter does not include an appropriate introduction or includes poorly constructed one	Letter includes introduction that states purpose with some irrelevancies or some relevant information missing	Introduction states purpose of letter and includes other relevant information	Introduction is engaging; states purpose of letter and includes other relevant information; written clearly and concisely	_____/12
Summary of Meeting	Letter includes no summary of the meeting	Letter includes summary but leaves out important information or states it unclearly	Letter summarizes the meeting but leaves out important information	Letter clearly and concisely summarizes the meeting, its core purpose and content	_____/12
Applicable Law	Student-attorney provides no explanation of the applicable law, or only uses legal jargon in explanation (inappropriate for audience)	Student-attorney provides explanation of with serious mistakes, or hard to follow (use of legal jargon)	Student-attorney provides clear explanation of with few mistakes; uses some legal jargon without appropriate explanations	Student-attorney provides clear, concise and correct explanation of the law with legal jargon with appropriate explanations	_____/12
Analysis	Contains conclusory statements and/or no case law; facts are analyzed in a conclusory or insufficient way	Uses some case law but does not analogize or distinguish or explain its application; some conclusory statements; facts briefly analyzed	Uses case law to show how rule applies to case; case law is compared and contrasted with success; most facts are analyzed	Analyzes completely case law, comparing it fully to client matter; facts are thoroughly analyzed	_____/12
Conclusion/ Recommendations	No conclusion or recommendations are included in letter	A brief conclusion is included but without sufficient advice or recommendations advice or next steps	Letter includes conclusion with recommendations and next steps	Letter includes full conclusion of the legal analysis and facts, presents creative and thoughtful recommendations and includes clear next steps	_____/12
WRITING	2	4	5	6	Points
Formatting	Document does not follow format instructions or the sample provided	Document attempts to follow instructions and sample provided	Document follows the instructions and sample provided with minor errors	Document exactly follows the instructions and sample provided	_____/6
Organization	No structure or organization; free flow of ideas	Letter includes organization and structure but is still confusing	Structure and organization but some reorganization is needed for full clarity	Document is clearly organized and structured	_____/6
Syntax Mechanics	Contains numerous and distracting grammatical and mechanical errors that impede understanding	Contains some grammatical and mechanical errors that impede understanding	Contains few grammatical and mechanical errors but none that impede understanding	Contains no grammatical and mechanical errors; native-like use of English	_____/6
TOTAL					_____/78

SECTION II

Intermediate Legal Issues

Common Law

Negligence/Duty to Warn
Property Owner's Liability for Workplace Shooting

Unit 1

For this Unit, you will write a persuasive memorandum of law in support of or in opposition to a motion to dismiss in litigation involving Stray Dog Advertising. You will represent either SDA as the defendant, or the plaintiff, the estate of Mohammed Ahmed, a former employee of Stray Dog Advertising. The legal issues involved are premises liability, negligence and duty to warn.

Learning Objectives of this Unit:

This Unit will build your skills to:

- Explain complex legal matters clearly and concisely
- Use appropriate technical terminology
- Identify and analyze the applicable case law and facts for the relevant legal issues
- Efficiently read and understand legal authority (case law)
- Articulate persuasive legal arguments in support of client's position
- Efficiently and effectively communicate in a written and oral format
- Evaluate questions about the relevant law and support your legal argument
- Respond to questions about the relevant law

To achieve these learning objectives, you will complete the following tasks:

- Draft a predictive memo to senior partner about the legal issues and your prediction of what will happen with the litigation
- Draft a persuasive memorandum of law in support of or in opposition to motion to dismiss
- Carry out a mock client meeting with either Pamela Park of SDA or the plaintiff, Maryam Ahmed
- Draft a client letter to your client about the meeting and about the legal issue
- Carry out oral argument in front of the court for the motion to dismiss

To complete these tasks, you will use the following materials in the book:

- Assignment email from Senior Partner (pages 141-143, including both plaintiff and defendant)
- Main Assignment File (pages 144-149)
- Negligence/Duty to Warn Commented Cases:
    - Lundgren v. Fultz, 354 N.W.2d 25 (Minn. 1984).
    - Bjerke v. Johnson, 742 N.W.2d 660 (Minn. 2007)
    - Patzwald v. Krey, 390 N.W.2d 920 (Minn. 1986)
    - Udofot v. Seven Eights Liquor, No. A10-431, 2010 WL 5071313 (Minn. Ct. App. March 15, 2011)
    - H.B. ex rel. v. Whittemore, 552 N.W.2d 705 (Minn. 1996)
    - Wood on Behalf of Doe v. Astleford, 412 N.W.2d 753 (Minn. Ct. App. 1987).
- ESL Workbook (pages 98-121)
- Pleadings (available online)

Your instructor will also assign you additional skills-building exercises to bolster your understanding of the legal issues and further develop your legal reasoning and language skills, whether related to legal reasoning and analysis or to English. You will find an icon with each exercise that will indicate which skills the exercise will focus upon

ICON	SKILL
	Speaking — in particular about the legal issues and the law presented in the Unit
	Oral comprehension
	Legal analysis and reasoning
	Analysis of the legal issue(s) presented in the Unit
	English grammar, syntax, and vocabulary
	Legal ethics and professional responsibility
	Legal research

In this Unit, the additional skills-building exercises that accompany the Main Assignment File include:

- Negligence/Duty to Warn Analysis Exercise (pages 150-151)

- Mock Negotiation between SDA and Maryam Ahmed (page 153 plus confidential information)

- Professional Presentation: *If SDA or Maryam Ahmed Were Your Client...* (pages 154-155)

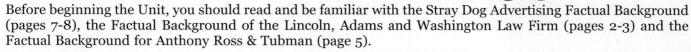
- Litigation Analysis: Does Another Plaintiff Change Liability? (page 152)

Before beginning the Unit, you should read and be familiar with the Stray Dog Advertising Factual Background (pages 7-8), the Factual Background of the Lincoln, Adams and Washington Law Firm (pages 2-3) and the Factual Background for Anthony Ross & Tubman (page 5).

You will also find online at the website www.legalwritingforllms.com the following online resources that accompany this Unit. The additional online resources will help you deepen your mastery of the skills presented in the Unit and also provide additional understanding about the U.S. legal system and legal writing.

Pleadings for Section II, Unit 1 (required)

- Additional Resources:
  - Sources of American Law
  - Writing Professional Emails
  - Writing Persuasive Memos
  - Writing E-memos
  - IRAC
- Additional Skills-Building Exercises:
  - Issues and Issue Statements
  - Stating the Rule
  - Analysis
  - Ethical Spotlight Exercise

Section II

Intermediate Legal Issues

Section II, Unit 1 Legal Issue
Premises Liability and Duty to Warn

Main Assignment File	Premises Liability Cases	ESL Workbook	Additional Exercises	Additional Online Resources
Introduction to File and Client Matter Pages 136-140	Lundgren v. Fultz, 354 N.W.2d 25 (Minn. 1984).	Lundgren v. Fultz, 354 N.W.2d 25 (Minn. 1984).	Negligence/Duty to Warn Analysis Exercise Pages 150-151	Writing Professional Emails
Documents Related to Client Matter Pages 141-149 + pleadings (available online)	Bjerke v. Johnson, 742 N.W.2d 660 (Minn. 2007).	Bjerke v. Johnson, 742 N.W.2d 660 (Minn. 2007).	Mock Negotiation Page 153 + confidential information	Business Correspondence (with sample letters)
Assignment Information Pages + Rubrics Pages 156-1651	Patzwald v. Krey, 390 N.W.2d 920 (Minn. 1986).	Patzwald v. Krey, 390 N.W.2d 920 (Minn. 1986).	Presentation: If SDA or Maryam Ahmed Were Your Client... Pages 154-155	Writing Memos (office memos and persuasive memoranda of law)
	Udofot v. Seven Eights Liquor, 2010 WL 5071313 (Minn. Ct. App. March 15, 2011).	Udofot v. Seven Eights Liquor, 2010 WL 5071313 (Minn. Ct. App. March 15, 2011).	Litigation Analysis: Another Plaintiff and Liability Page 152	IRAC (including additional exercises for each element)
	H.B. ex rel. v. Whittemore, 552 N.W.2d 705 (Minn. 1996).	H.B. ex rel. v. Whittemore, 552 N.W.2d 705 (Minn. 1996).		Skills-Building Exercises for Rules, Issues and Issues Statements, Analysis and Ethical Dilemmas
	Wood on Behalf of Doe v. Astleford, 412 N.W.2d 753 (Minn. 1987).	Wood on Behalf of Doe v. Astleford, 412 N.W.2d 753 (Minn. 1987).		

Introduction — Premises Liability

The legal issue that you will learn about and analyze in this Unit is a doctrine of tort law and of negligence: premises liability, which is the legal liability of a property owner for injuries that others suffer while on the property, whether a building (a store, office building or a house) or land.

Within the doctrine of premises liability is another doctrine called duty to warn, and this Unit deals specifically with this issue: when is a property owner required to warn those on his property about the dangers of criminal activity that might take place on the property and when is the owner liable for physical harm that a third party causes because of his or her criminal activity?

Here are two examples to better explain:

A robber enters a grocery store and during the robbery, shoots and injures an employee and a customer. Should the law hold the grocery store owner legally liable for the injuries that the employee and customer suffered?

A man, not a resident in a certain apartment building, enters the building without permission. While inside the building, he breaks into an apartment and rapes a tenant. Should the landlord be held legally liable for the injuries the tenant suffers?

As you will learn, the law imposes no duty on a property owner to warn about the danger that a third party poses and control the third party's conduct to prevent him from causing physical harm to another unless:

> "In law, we are not our brother's keeper unless a special relationship exists between the actor and the third person which imposes a duty upon the actor to control the third person's conduct." Lundgren v. Fultz, 354 N.W.2d 25, 27 (Minn. 1984) (citing Restatement (Second) of Torts § 15 (Am. Law Inst. 1965)).

a) a special relationship exists between the defendant and the third party which imposes a duty upon the actor to control the third person's conduct, or

b) a special relationship exists between the defendant and the person injured which gives to the person injured a right to protection, and

c) the harm is foreseeable.[46]

In sum, no liability will be imposed unless this special relationship exists *and* the harm is foreseeable. As you might imagine, a considerable amount of litigation has defined what a special relationship is and what circumstances must exist for the harm to be foreseeable.

As a general rule, we don't impose liability on a property owner for injuries that occur due to third-party conduct, subject to the exceptions of the above rule. Strong policy reasons exist for making liability the exception rather than the rule: we don't want to discourage people from owning property, from opening and running a business, or from buying a home for fear of litigation. We want to encourage home ownership and encourage people to open businesses and purchase real property. On the other hand, strong policy reasons also exist for compensating victims for the injuries they have suffered, especially when those injuries could have and should have been prevented. Other policy concerns depend on the facts of the case.[47]

A Texas court considered the basic principle of fairness when examining whether liability should be imposed on a property owner and posed the question in this way: Is it fair to impose liability when we can't always control third parties and even if we can, should we be held legally liable if we do not?[48]

---

[46] Lundgren v. Fultz, 354 N.W.2d 25, 27 (Minn. 1984).

[47] See, e.g., Lundgren v. Flutz, 354 N.W.2d 25, 29 (Minn. 1984) (citing Cairl v. State, 323 N.W.2d 20, 26 (Minn. 1982)) (expressing concern that extending a psychiatrist's duty to control the conduct of a patient and warn potential victims of dangers would lead to a "cacophony" of warnings that would add greatly to the stigma of mental illness while contributing little to public protection); Golden Spread Council, Inc. v. Akins, 926 S.W.2d 287, 291 (Tex. 1996) (holding Boy Scouts of America owed a duty to protect boys from sexual abuse of scoutmasters and basing ruling in part on Legislature's "strong policy to protect children from abuse.").

[48] Graff v. Beard, 858 S.W.2d 918, 920 (Tex. 1993), cited in Newsom v. B.B., 306 S.W.3d 910, 914 (Tex. App. 2010).

> "Generally, a person's duty to warn of a dangerous situation that the person did not create is a moral duty, not a legal one." <u>Newsom v. B.B.</u>, 306 S.W.3d 910, 916 (Tex. App. 2010), *cited in* 53 Tex. Jur. 3d Negligence § 43 (Westlaw database updated Sept. 2016).

These are some of the questions that you will be asking yourself as you work on the client matter presented in this Unit. You will learn that there has been a tragic workplace shooting at the Stray Dog Advertising offices, and that Pamela's partner and an SDA employee were killed. Maryam Ahmed, the widow of the deceased employee, sues SDA for negligence, claiming that SDA should have warned her husband and the other guests about the risks that the shooter posed and taken steps to protect them. Within this issue of negligence and duty to warn, you will examine whether a special relationship existed between Stray Dog Advertising and the victim, Mohammed Ahmed or the third party Wayne Lee, and whether SDA owed the victims who were injured while on its property a duty to keep them safe. You will also analyze whether that duty was breached and whether the harm was foreseeable.

As part of the Intermediate Section of the book, this Unit is part of ongoing litigation and involves motion practice, here a motion to dismiss. Your writing assignments include both predictive and persuasive writing.

Main Assignment File: Negligence/Duty to Warn

Plaintiff's File

You receive the following email from Senior Partner Anthony, asking you to work on the lawsuit that was filed against Stray Dog Advertising on behalf of your client, Maryam Ahmed, the widow of Mohammed Ahmed.

> **From:** Suzanne Anthony <suzanne.anthony@artlaw.com>
> **To:** Associate Attorney <associate@artlaw.com>
> **Sent:** August 6, THIS YEAR 07:45
> **Subject:** Stray Dog Advertising – Answer and Motion to Dismiss

Associate attorney,

I am assigning you the file of Maryam Ahmed, the widow of Mohammed Ahmed, who was killed in the shooting at Stray Dog Advertising. You met Maryam when she was here for her initial meeting. Given your experience and knowledge of the Jefferson laws on negligence and premises liability, I am confident that you will do a solid job representing this important new client. The Lincoln, Adams and Washington Law Firm is representing Stray Dog Advertising, so you will be up against very competent and aggressive lawyers.

I wasn't surprised when I saw that Georgina Washington filed a motion to dismiss with the answer. When we receive the memorandum in support of the motion, I would like you to draft our memorandum in response. I know that the law is on our side and that we can defeat the motion.

Before you write the memorandum of law in opposition to the defendant's motion to dismiss, please prepare for me a predictive memo summarizing the law, outlining our arguments and also presenting the counterarguments that the defense will make. I'd also like your prediction on what you think will happen: will the court deny their motion?

Since I want you to gain more courtroom experience, I'd like you to do the oral arguments for the motion to dismiss. I am happy to help you if you have any questions or if you'd like to practice before the actual hearing date.

SA

First, Anthony has asked you to write her a predictive office memo about the following:
- A summary of what has happened to lead to the lawsuit that has been filed against Stray Dog Advertising
- The legal issue at hand
- A summary and analysis of the law that applies
- Your opinion about what will likely happen in the litigation, both with the motion to dismiss and in the lawsuit in general (i.e. will the plaintiff succeed?)

Second, Anthony has asked you to prepare a persuasive memorandum of law in opposition to the motion to dismiss that Lincoln, Adams and Wasington has filed on behalf of SDA.

The memorandum of law will include:
- A factual background of what has led to the claim against Stray Dog Advertising
- Persuasive legal arguments that the claim should be dismissed

You will find complete information about these assignments on the Information Pages (pages 156-157 (predictive memo) and pages 162-163 (persuasive memo)).

You will be analyzing the client matter using the negligence and duty to warn cases that you read and review in class.

NOTE: The parties had engaged in a brief pre-litigation negotiation to attempt to settle the matter without commencing legal action. However, they were unsuccessful at reaching a resolution of the matter. During the pre-litigation negotiation, they exchanged some documents in informal discovery; thus both parties are in possession of the emails, documents and copies of the text messages that you will find in the Main Assignment File.

Defendant's File

You received the following email from Senior Partner Washington about a tragic event that took place at the Stray Dog Advertising office.

From: Georgina Washington <g.washington@lawlawfirm.com>
To: Associate Attorney <a.attorney@lawlawfirm.com>
Sent: July 24, THIS YEAR 07:45
Subject: Stray Dog Advertising – Answer and Motion to Dismiss

Associate attorney,

I am sure that you have been following the news of the workplace shooting that took place at Stray Dog Advertising. It is hard to believe that Pamela's partner, Jordan, was killed. She seems to be doing OK, considering the circumstances, and has told me that all of those wounded are expected to recover.

Pamela was just served with a complaint, filed by the wife and estate of her account executive, Mohammed Ahmed, who was one of the two other people killed in the shooting. It alleges that Pamela/Stray Dog was negligent in not warning about the shooter's violent tendencies. I think we have strong arguments to get this dismissed. In my opinion, Jefferson case law does not support the argument that an employer is liable when its employees are injured by the actions of a third party, at least in a situation like this.

I have drafted, filed and served the answer, as well as our notice of motion to dismiss. Now we must prepare the memorandum in support of that motion. For your reference, here is Rule 12 of the Jefferson Rules of Civil Procedure, which addresses defenses and objections. We are filing a motion for failure to state a claim upon which relief can be granted under Rule 12(b)(6). Here is the language:

(b) How to Present Defenses. Every defense to a claim for relief in any pleading must be asserted in the responsive pleading if one is required. But a party may assert the following defenses by motion:

1) lack of subject-matter jurisdiction;
2) lack of personal jurisdiction;
3) improper venue;
4) insufficient process;
5) insufficient service of process;
6) failure to state a claim upon which relief can be granted; and
7) failure to join a party under Rule 19.

We waive our right to bring a motion for failure to state a claim if we don't file it now. There is no reason why Pamela should have to be sued for something that she had no control over.

I want you to prepare the memorandum of law in support of our motion. Our argument will be that under Jefferson law, SDA had no duty to warn of the third party's actions. The law clerk has done already some research on the issue and I will send you the cases that he has found. Once you read the cases, you will see that we have good arguments on our side. The law says that an individual (or a company in this case) is liable for a third party's action, including criminal actions, only when (1) there is a "special relationship" between the parties and (2) the harm suffered was foreseeable. Although it seems that we will have to concede that there was a special relationship (you will see how it is defined by Jefferson courts), our strongest argument will be that it was not reasonably foreseeable that this individual would do what he did.

Before you write the memorandum of law in support of our motion to dismiss, please prepare for me a predictive memo summarizing the law, outlining our arguments and also presenting the counterarguments that you think the plaintiff's attorney will make. I'd also like your prediction on what you think will happen: will the court grant our motion?

I will also want you to do the oral arguments for this as I have a trial already scheduled that same week and won't be available.

I look forward to receiving your first draft of the memo and seeing the arguments that you make. Let me know if you have any questions.

Georgina

As you have read, you have been asked to write the following documents about this litigation:

First, Washington has asked you to write her a predictive office memo about the following:

- A summary of what has happened to lead to the lawsuit that has been filed against Stray Dog Advertising
- The legal issue at hand
- A summary and analysis of the law that applies
- Your opinion about what will likely happen in the litigation, both with the motion to dismiss and in the lawsuit in general (i.e. will the plaintiff succeed?)
- Your advice to Pamela Park about how to proceed with this matter

Second, Washington has asked you to prepare a persuasive memorandum of law in support of the motion to dismiss that she has filed.

The memorandum of law will include:

- A factual background of what has led to the claim against Stray Dog Advertising
- Persuasive legal arguments that the claim should be dismissed

You will find complete information about these assignments on the Information Pages (pages 156-157 (predictive memo) and pages 162-163 (persuasive memo)).

You will be analyzing the client matter using the negligence/duty to warn cases that you read and review in class.

NOTE: The parties had engaged in a brief pre-litigation negotiation to attempt to settle the matter without commencing legal action. However, they were unsuccessful at reaching a resolution of the matter. During the pre-litigation negotiation, they exchanged some documents in informal discovery; thus both parties are in possession of the same emails, documents and copies of the text messages that you will find in the Main Assignment File.

The West Rapids Times

Issue No. 132   Saturday, June 6, **THIS YEAR**

POLICE SAY THREE DEAD, SEVEN WOUNDED IN WORKPLACE SHOOTING

By Kathleen Garber

Three people are dead and seven wounded in what police are describing as the first workplace shooting to take place in Jefferson. The shooting took place at the offices of Stray Dog Advertising, a local advertising agency, located in downtown West Rapids along the Aster River.

Among those killed include Mohammed Ahmed, a sales representative for the agency; Jordan Park, the wife of Pamela Park, the owner of the company; and one other victim whose identity has still not been released pending notification of her family. Of the seven victims wounded in the shooting, all remain hospitalized in serious to critical condition at the West Rapids Medical Center. All were employees or clients of Stray Dog Advertising. The shooter, Wayne Lee, took his own life before police arrived.

According to witnesses and survivors, the agency was celebrating its 10-year anniversary with an office party.

Employees, their spouses and clients were present at the time of the shooting. The party had just started and guests were still arriving when Lee, 37 years old, entered the agency's office and began shooting.

Lee was a resident of Jefferson and according to a witness, the former fiancé of another employee of Stray Dog Advertising, Charlene Thomas. This witness, who wished to remain anonymous, told this reporter that Lee and Thomas had recently broken off their engagement due to concerns that Thomas had about Lee's violent personality. According to court records, Thomas had recently obtained an Order for Protection ("OFP") against Lee; the OFP prohibited him from contacting Thomas at her home and also at work. This witness stated that Park was aware of the OFP and her employee's concerns about Lee's violent tendencies.

Police found three high-capacity rifles in the trunk of Lee's car, parked outside the Stray Dog Advertising

offices. According to a police spokesperson, a subsequent search of the suspect's home revealed a stockpile of ammunition and dozens of handguns and rifles, all legally purchased according to state gun records.

The shooting also prompted a lockdown of all nearby businesses, including the West Rapids Cinema and the football stadium, which was hosting a high school sporting event at the time. Mitchell Jones, 18, of West Rapids, said he was outside a building down the street having his picture taken when he and his photographer heard gunfire that sounded close. "We heard lots of gunshots," Mr. Jones said. "We were shocked at what happened, and we just looked at each other. We all just took off running to our vehicles."

"Very sad situation today in West Rapids," Mayor J.R. Abbott posted on Twitter. "The victims and their families, and all affected, are in our thoughts."

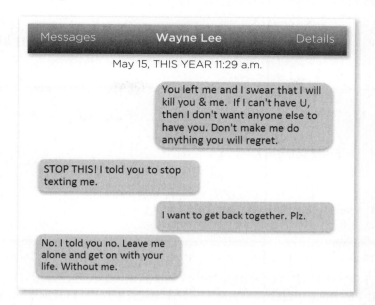

Charlene Thomas, the Administrative Specialist at Stray Dog Advertising, broke up with her fiancé two months before the shooting happened, just weeks before their wedding was scheduled. Charlene had confided in Pamela about the problems that she had been having with her fiancé, Wayne Lee, and showed her the above texts that he sent her.

Charlene also confided in Pamela that she had obtained an Order for Protection ("OFP") in Jefferson State Court against her ex-fiancé. An OFP is a document issued by a court that protects a victim of physical, sexual or psychological violence. An OFP prohibits the abuser from contacting (directly or indirectly) the victim and prohibits the abuser from approaching the victim at his or her workplace or home. Charlene provided a copy of the OFP to Pamela in case her ex-fiancé came to the SDA offices or tried to call her there. She didn't want the receptionist, David, or her boss to be unaware of the threats that Wayne had made.

On the next pages is a copy of the Order for Protection that Charlene obtained against Wayne and that she provided to Pamela.

STATE OF JEFFERSON	DISTRICT COURT
COUNTY OF TAYLOR	SIXTH JUDICIAL DISTRICT
	FAMILY COURT

Charlene Angela Thomas,

        Petitioner,

vs.

Wayne David Lee

        Respondent

Case No. 27-FM-15-9612

ORDER FOR PROTECTION

NOTICE: YOUR WILLFUL FAILURE TO OBEY THIS ORDER MAY SUBJECT YOU TO MANDATORY ARREST AND CRIMINAL PROSECUTION, WHICH MAY RESULT IN YOUR INCARCERATION FOR UP TO SEVEN YEARS FOR CRIMINAL CONTEMPT, AND/OR MAY SUBJECT YOU TO FAMILY COURT PROSECUTION AND INCARCERATION FOR UP TO SIX MONTHS FOR CONTEMPT OF COURT.

THIS ORDER OF PROTECTION WILL REMAIN IN EFFECT EVEN IF THE PROTECTED PARTY HAS, OR CONSENTS TO HAVE, CONTACT OR COMMUNICATION WITH THE PARTY AGAINST WHOM THE ORDER IS ISSUED. THIS ORDER OF PROTECTION CAN ONLY BE MODIFIED OR TERMINATED BY THE COURT. THE PROTECTED PARTY CANNOT BE HELD TO VIOLATE THIS ORDER NOR BE ARRESTED FOR VIOLATING THIS ORDER.

    A petition under Article III of the Jefferson Family Court Act, sworn to on May 26, THIS YEAR, having been filed in this Court in the above-entitled proceeding, and the Respondent having been [check applicable box]: ■ present in Court and advised of the issuance and contents of this Order ☐ not present in Court, and this Court [check applicable box]: ■ after hearing ☐ on consent , having determined that good cause has been shown for the issuance of this Order,

NOW, THEREFORE, IT IS HEREBY ORDERED that Wayne David Lee must observe the following conditions of behavior:

(Check Applicable Paragraphs and Subparagraphs):

[01] ☐ Stay away from
    [A] ■ [name(s) of protected person(s)]: <u>Charlene Angela Thomas</u> and/or from the

    [B] ☐ home of <u>Charlene Angela Thomas</u>

    [C] ☐ school of

    [D] ☐ business of

    [E] ■ place of employment of <u>Charlene Angela Thomas</u>

    [F] ☐ other [specify location]

[02] ■   Refrain from communication or any other contact or by mail, telephone, e-mail, voice-mail or other electronic or any other means with [specify protected person(s)]:___<u>Charlene Angela Thomas</u>___

[03] ■   Refrain from assault, stalking, harassment, aggravated harassment, menacing, reckless endangerment, strangulation, criminal obstruction of breathing or circulation, disorderly conduct, criminal mischief, sexual abuse, sexual misconduct, forcible touching, intimidation, threats, identity theft, grand larceny, coercion or any criminal offense against

[specify protected person(s) and/or members of protected person's family or household, and/or person(s) with custody of child(ren)]: ___Charlene Angela Thomas___

[04] ■ Refrain from intentionally injuring or killing without justification the following companion animal(s) (pet(s)) [specify type(s) and, if available, name(s)]: ___Zachary (cat)___

[05] ☐ Permit [specify individual]: _____ to enter the residence at [specify]: _____ during [specify date/time] with [specify law enforcement agency, if any]: _____ to remove personal belongings not in issue in litigation [specify items]: _____

[06] ☐ Refrain from [indicate acts]: contacting directly or indirectly Charlene Angela Thomas,

[07] ☐ Permit [specify individual]: _____, entitled by a court order or separation or other written agreement to visit with [specify child(ren)]: during the following periods of time [specify]: _____ under the following terms and conditions [specify]: _____

[08] ☐ Custody of [specify child(ren)]: _____ shall be awarded to [specify individual]: _____ under the following terms and conditions [specify]: _____

[09] ■ Surrender any and all handguns, pistols, revolvers, rifles, shotguns and other firearms owned or possessed, including, but not limited to, the following: ___all firearms in respondent's possession___ and do not obtain any further guns or other firearms. Such surrender shall take place immediately, but in no event later than [specify date/time]: June 6, THIS YEAR   at Maple View Police Station:

[10] ☐ Promptly return or transfer the following identification documents specify]: _____ to the party protected by this Order NOT LATER THAN [specify date]: in the following manner [specify manner or mode of return or transfer]: _____

[Check box(es) if applicable]:

☐ Pay or provide access to health or medical insurance for necessary medical care and treatment arising from the incident or incidents forming the basis of the order [specify beneficiary of treatment and coverage]_____
☐ Pay counsel fees (and/or) any costs associated with the order to [specify person and terms]:

■ Participate in an educational program, (and pay the costs thereof)[(specify program] Anger management program offered through Cornerstone Family Services, located in West Rapids, Jefferson

☐ Participate in a batterer's education program designed to help end violent behavior (and pay the costs thereof) [specify program]

☐ Pay to the petitioner/victim(s) restitution, as follows [specify terms and amount up to $10,000]:

☐ Observe such other condition(s) as are necessary to further the purposes of protection [specify conditions]: _____

AGGRAVATING CIRCUMSTANCES FINDING [check box and fill in if applicable]:

☐ The court has made a finding on the record of the existence of the following:

_____
_____

It is further ordered that this order of protection shall remain in force until and including [specify date]: **May 26, YEAR +1**

The Family Court Act provides that presentation of a copy of this order of protection to any police officer or peace officer acting pursuant to his or her special duties authorizes, and sometimes requires, the officer to arrest a person who is alleged to have violated its terms and to bring him or her before the Court to face penalties authorized by law.

Federal law requires that this order is effective outside, as well as inside, Jefferson State. It must be honored and enforced by state and tribal courts, including courts of a state, the District of Columbia, a commonwealth, territory or possession of the United States, if the person restrained by the order is an intimate partner of the protected party and has or will be afforded reasonable notice and opportunity to be heard in accordance with state law sufficient to protect due process will be afforded reasonable notice and opportunity to be heard in accordance with state law sufficient to protect due process rights (18 U.S.C. § 2265, 2266).

Dated: June 2, **THIS YEAR**

/s/ Agnes F. Davis

JUDGE OF THE FAMILY COURT
COUNTY OF TAYLOR

PURSUANT TO SECTION 1113 OF THE FAMILY COURT ACT, AN APPEAL FROM THIS ORDER MUST BE TAKEN WITHIN 30 DAYS OF RECEIPT OF THE ORDER BY APPELLANT IN COURT, 35 DAYS FROM THE DATE OF MAILING OF THE ORDER TO APPELLANT BY THE CLERK OF COURT, OR 30 DAYS AFTER SERVICE BY A PARTY OR THE ATTORNEY FOR THE CHILD UPON THE APPELLANT, WHICHEVER IS EARLIEST.

Check Applicable Box(es):

■ Party against whom order was issued was present in Court and advised in Court of issuance and contents of Order: Wayne Lee _____

☐ Order personally served in Court upon party against whom order was issued

☐ Service directed by other means [specify]:

☐ [Modifications or extensions only]: Order mailed on [specify date and to whom mailed]:

☐ Warrant issued for party against whom order was issued [specify date]:

☐ Additional service information [specify]:

From:	Charlene Thomas <charlene.thomas@straydogadvertising.com>
To:	Pamela Park <pamela.park@straydogadvertising.com>
Cc:	Roy Blanco <roy.blanco@straydogadvertising.com>
Sent:	June 4, THIS YEAR 10:32
Subject:	update ofp and wayne

Pamela,

I thought that I should give you an update on what's been going on with Wayne after I got the OFP. Since I've gotten it, I haven't heard anything from him. The phone calls late at night threating to kill me and then himself have stopped. Thank goodness as I was getting really scared about what he might do. I think I totally freaked out when he told me that he'd gun down me and anyone I was with unless I got back together with him. But the court ordered him to turn over all his guns by Friday. Thank goodness.

David told me that when he was leaving the office yesterday, he saw someone in the parking lot, just hanging around. David told me that he couldn't tell who it was, but knew it was a man from his height and build. He said it might have been Wayne since this person was quite tall and David knows how tall Wayne is. David also said that it was suspicious how this guy was hanging out in the parking lot. He also said that this person was looking towards our offices and watching the main door. I called the cops, and they told me that they couldn't do anything since I wasn't sure it was Wayne.

With my family living out of state, I don't know how I could have handled it without you and everyone here. You are really like a family to me, and I appreciate it so much. I think everyone here is so tired of hearing my story and all the drama that's been happening lately, but the support that you, Roy and Mohammed have given me has been invaluable. David has been great as an extra set of eyes to keep me safe.

I'm really looking forward to the office party on Friday. It will help me keep my mind off of things.

Thanks again,

Charlene

Additional Skills-Building Exercises

Premises Liability/Duty to Warn Analysis Exercise

Overview of the Exercise: The following short fact patterns deal with negligence/duty to warn and your task is to analyze the fact patterns and determine whether or not the defendant in the case could be held liable for negligence/duty to warn.

Learning Objectives of the Exercise:

This exercise will build your skills to:

- Articulate the legal rules regarding negligence and duty to warn
- Apply those rules to fact patterns and analyze the facts and the law
- Articulate and effectively communicate that analysis using legal terminology

Steps for Completing the Exercise:

- Read the following fact patterns.
- By yourself, analyze each one and decide whether or not you think the property owner could be liable for a breach of the duty to warn and why. You don't need to write out a full answer, but jot down notes about your reasoning.
- When you are done analyzing each of the fact patterns, discuss your answers with the partner that you have been assigned. Explain to each other why you have reached the conclusion that you did.
- If you and your partner have different responses to a fact pattern, you must try to convince him or her that your answer is correct. After you both have tried to convince the other, you must choose a team answer.
- Once you have discussed each of the fact patterns, you will compare answers as a class.

Remember that for some of these short fact patterns, you do not have all of the facts. Part of analyzing completely a fact pattern or a situation is to hypothesize about whether liability could be imposed if a certain fact were present or happened.

You must analyze all parts of the issue and the law:

- Did D owe P a duty to warn him or her of the danger present in the fact pattern? This involves analyzing whether there was a special relationship between the parties.
- If D did owe P a duty, was that duty breached?
- Was the harm foreseeable?

1. Plaintiff is an adult who was a guest at a pool party held at defendant's house. Defendant ("D") is a work colleague of Plaintiff ("P"). P dove into the pool and hit his head on the bottom, breaking his neck. P remained a quadriplegic. P sues D, claiming that he should have warned P about the dangers of diving into a pool. Should P be allowed to recover from D for his damages?

2. Defendant owns a convenience store in a part of the city where crime is rampant. In the past three months, five victims have been mugged on the block where D's store is located, and another victim was car-jacked while leaving the parking lot of the store. Two days ago, two young men entered the store and robbed it. While doing so, they shot one of the customers who happened to be buying a soda. The doctors say that she will suffer permanent brain damage as a result of the injuries. Should the store owner be liable for the injuries that the customer suffered?

3.　Plaintiff is a 15-year-old high school student who is spending the summer at a camp for teenagers who are having problems with their parents, with school and with the law. P was ordered to attend the camp as part of a disposition through juvenile court after she was caught truant (not attending school) for several months. While at the camp, one of the camp counselors, an 18-year-old senior in high school, sexually assaulted P. Her parents are now suing the county and the owner of the camp, claiming that they should have warned them about the camp counselor's criminal behavior and that they should have taken steps to protect the campers. Should the court impose liability upon the camp and the county? Why or why not?

4.　P and her husband were visiting a friend who lives in northern Jefferson, where the weather becomes extremely cold during the winter. P and her husband are from Florida and had never been in the snow before. Their friend knew this. While they were having dinner, a bad snow storm moved into the area, with record-breaking winds. Despite the weather, P and her husband left after dinner to return to the hotel where they were staying. Unfortunately on the way to the hotel, their car broke down. Their cell phone was not working due to the storm so P's husband got out of the car and tried to return to their friend's home for assistance. He was overtaken by the cold, wind and snow, collapsed into a snowbank and died. His wife, who remained in the car, suffered serious injuries from the cold. She has now sued the friend, claiming that she should have warned them about the dangers of going out in the snowstorm. Should Plaintiff be liable for the injuries her friends suffered? Why or why not?

5.　D owns an apartment building. At the front and back doors, he has installed an intercom system so that visitors must be let into the building by a resident. No security cameras are installed at either the front or the back door. The apartment building is on an isolated road near a lake and a park. Last month, a new resident was moving into the building and propped open the back door for the delivery people who were delivering his new living room furniture. While the door was propped open, a man entered. While in the building, he broke into an apartment and raped one of the residents. She now claims that the landlord is liable for the injuries that she has suffered from being raped. Should the court hold the landlord liable?

6.　Harry owns a clothing store in a shopping mall in Jefferson City. The neighborhood where the shopping mall is located is in a part of town with a low crime rate, except for some occasional shoplifting. Because of the neighborhood's and the shopping mall's reputation for being safe, Harry was surprised when he heard on the news that there was an attempted kidnapping last month. A woman returning to her car was grabbed as she was walking through the parking lot, and the assailant tried to force her into his car. Fortunately, she escaped. Last week, another customer of a near-by store was shot in an armed robbery as he was walking back to his car. Yesterday, another robber entered Harry's store. When Harry refused to give the robber the money in the cash register, the robber shot at Harry and his employee. Harry was not hit, but his employee was shot and seriously injured. Is Harry liable for the injuries?

7.　Linda owns a day care for young children and babies. She knows that a sex offender lives about ½ a mile away from her home, where she operates the day care. He was incarcerated for nearly 15 years for molesting teenage girls. Linda knows that he lives there because the neighborhood newspaper includes updates on crime and also on whether any former criminals (felons) have moved into the area. Linda takes no extra steps at her day care when she learns this information. One afternoon, Linda takes the young children in her care to a nearby park. While there, the sex offender lures away a 5-year-old girl and molests her. Linda had turned her back on the little girl for just a few minutes while she was changing the diaper of another child when this happened. Linda had 6 children in her charge but no assistant with her. Is Linda liable for the injuries suffered?

Another Plaintiff: Does it Change Potential Liability?

Overview of the Exercise: This exercise will develop your ability to analyze the law of negligence and duty to warn when one important fact is changed: the plaintiff that has filed the negligence claim against Stray Dog Advertising.

Learning Objectives of the Exercise:

This exercise will build your skills to:

- Articulate the legal rules regarding negligence and duty to warn
- Apply those rules to the facts of the workplace shooting but with one important difference: the plaintiff is not the estate of Mohammed Ahmed, a former employee of Stray Dog Advertising, but another victim — James Kelly — who was a guest at the office party but not an SDA employee
- Analyze whether the potential liability would change by simply changing the plaintiff
- Articulate and effectively communicate that analysis using legal terminology

Steps for Completing this Assignment:

- Be familiar with the facts of this Unit and the law regarding negligence and duty to warn
- Before beginning this exercise, discuss with your partner(s) whether you have concluded that SDA will likely be held liable for the wrongful death of Mohammed Ahmed. Explain the reason for your conclusion and be prepared to defend your answer if you and your partner(s) have reached different conclusions.
- Apply the rules of duty to warn when the plaintiff is *not* a former employee of Stray Dog Advertising but is rather a guest at the office party
    - Is there a special relationship between SDA and a guest of the party? Why or why not?
    - If you determine that there is no special relationship, can SDA be held liable for failure to warn? Why or why not?
    - If you determine that there is a special relationship, what is the next step of the analysis?
    - Based on that next step, what conclusion will you reach about whether SDA would be held liable?

Did you come to a different conclusion than the one that you have reached in the Estate of Ahmed v. Stray Dog Advertising, LLC case? If you did, can you articulate any policy reasons that would explain those different conclusions?

If you were the judge in the case of Kelly v. Stray Dog Advertising, LLC and a motion to dismiss were filed by SDA, how would you rule? Why?

Grading: This exercise is not graded. Instead, you will compare your answer with those your classmates reached.

Mock Negotiation

Overview of the Exercise: This exercise simulates a negotiation between the attorney for Stray Dog Advertising and the attorney for the plaintiff, the widow of Mohammed Ahmed. As part of the litigation process, the parties have been instructed by the court to attempt to resolve the matter through an alternative dispute resolution method. Before hiring a mediator to help resolve the matter, counsel have suggested to their clients that they try to negotiate a settlement instead. Both clients have agreed.

You will be assigned the role of counsel for Stray Dog Advertising or the estate of Mohammed Ahmed. The purpose of this assignment is to explain your client's position to opposing counsel, lay out the arguments for the position and to explore settlement options. Before the meeting, review the confidential information that you have been provided.

Learning Objectives of the Exercise:

This exercise will build your skills to:

- Use monetary and non-monetary interests of parties in negotiating settlement agreement
- Identify primary obstacles to reaching a mutually beneficial settlement agreement
- Implement negotiation strategies and tactics

Steps for Completing the Exercise:

- Read the preparatory information that you have been assigned and that your instructor will give to you
- Be familiar with the case law regarding premises liability and duty to warn and the fact pattern of Estate of Ahmed v. Stray Dog Advertising, LLC
- Articulate the arguments for your client's position and anticipate opposing counsel's

Writing Exercise:

If time allows and if directed by your instructor, you and opposing counsel will also prepare a draft of the settlement agreement that your clients will sign once you have reached a negotiated agreement.

To complete this task, you first must find a template of a settlement agreement. In real life, few attorneys start from scratch (i.e. from zero) when drafting any contract or agreement. Why recreate the wheel? Instead, attorneys will use a template and then adapt it to their purposes.

Thus, using a template is part of practice. Templates can be found in a law firm's database of documents, or many attorneys will take an agreement from a past case and modify and adapt it to a new case. Bar associations have templates and forms available (often for a fee) and many are available online as well.

But using a template comes with risks too. Even though the template is prepared, you can't simply cut and paste it to a new Word document and think you are good to go. Here are some questions that you have to ask yourself as you analyze a template:

- Does it include provisions that are illegal or violate some law, either because it was written by an attorney in another state or because the law has changed?
- Is it written to be beneficial to one side? For example, is it a very landlord-friendly lease agreement? If it is and if you represent the tenant, you will need to revise it.
- Does it include all the essential provisions? Just because a template is available doesn't mean that it is complete.
- Does your client's matter have unique circumstances or agreements that must be incorporated? It isn't always possible to find a template that perfectly suits your situation, so understanding that will make it easier to find a template that works and that can be adapted.

You also want to be very careful when you use a template to ensure that you remove all references that reveal that this was a template, or that reveal that the document was used with other clients or parties.

Once you have found a template online, adapt it to suit the agreement that you reached.

Grading: This exercise is not graded. After the meetings, the class will debrief on how the negotiations went.

Presentations:
If SDA or Maryam Ahmed Were Your Client...

Negligence/Duty to Warn

Unit 1

Overview of the Exercise: For this exercise, you will make a professional presentation in which you answer and discuss the following question:

If Stray Dog Advertising were your client in your home country and if Pamela came to you for legal advice about the negligence complaint filed against her, what would you do and what advice would you give her?

OR

If Mohammed Ahmed's widow were your client in your home country and came to you for advice about the shooting that killed her husband and about bringing a claim against Stray Dog Advertising for his death and the losses she has suffered, what advice would you give her?

You will do the presentation based on the client whom you represent.

Learning Objectives of the Exercise:

This exercise will build your skills to:

- Describe a specific aspect of your country's legal system
- Compare your country's legal system with the U.S. legal system
- Listen to and understand your classmates' presentations and complete information about them

Steps for Completing the Exercise:

- Analyze the <u>Estate of Ahmed v. Stray Dog Advertising, LLC</u> fact pattern under your country's laws.
- Determine whether or not Mohammed Ahmed's widow would have a viable claim under your country's laws, and whether Stray Dog Advertising could raise any viable defenses against the negligence/failure to warn claim.
- Explain what other claims Ahmed's widow could bring (if any) or SDA could bring against her (if any) and explain how the case would be handled in your country's legal system.
- Explain what legal advice you would give Pamela or Ahmed's widow if they came to you for legal advice in your home country.

Research Required: The research you are required to do depends on your knowledge of these claims in your country's legal system. It is presumed that you are familiar with the law and with how you would approach this issue if these were clients of yours at home.

Grading: This presentation is not graded. You will present to a small group of your fellow classmates instead of to the entire class.

Handouts:

As part of your presentation, you must create a handout for your classmates, and the handouts must include fill-in-the-blank questions that your classmates must complete with information that you present during the presentation. Each handout must include at least five questions to complete.

For example, if a U.S. law student were giving a presentation on negligence/duty to warn in the United States, she could include on her handout this question:

To successfully bring a negligence claim for failure to warn, a plaintiff must establish that a special relationship exists. A special relationship is defined as:

As you are speaking, your classmates will have to listen, follow what you are saying and fill in the blanks. If you are listening to one of your classmate's presentations and are unsure about an answer, you should ask him or her to repeat so you can fill in the blank(s).

Grammar Review:

The basis of this exercise is hypothetical or conditional verbs: ***if SDA or Maryam Ahmed were your client, what would you do?***

Remember the grammar when discussing hypothetical conditions.

Present: **IF + PAST SIMPLE, WOULD + BASE VERB**

*If Pamela **called** me to schedule an appointment, I **would tell** her to visit me at my office.*

NOTE: We use "were" for all tenses with the verb "to be" when using a conditional verb.

*If I **were** you, I **would not take** that class.*

*If Pamela **were** my client, I **would tell** her that Ahmed's widow would probably be unsuccessful in bringing her claim.*

Past: **IF + PAST PERFECT, WOULD + HAVE + PAST PARTICIPLE**

*If SDA **had hired** a security guard, it is likely that this **would not have happened** and SDA would not be facing this lawsuit.*

*If the defendant **had taken** steps to protect the guests at the party, then none of the guests **would have gotten** hurt.*

Information Pages

Office Memo: Negligence/Duty to Warn

Overview of the Assignment: For this assignment, you will write an office memo to your respective Senior Partner, summarizing your research on whether you think the court will grant or deny the motion to dismiss that the LAW Law Firm has filed on behalf of SDA.

Learning Objectives of the Assignment:

This assignment will build your skills to:

- Efficiently communicate in a written format
- Explain complex matters clearly and concisely
- Analyze and apply the rules of law regarding negligence/duty to warn

Research for the Assignment: You are not required to do any outside research for this assignment. You should base your analysis on the Minnesota negligence/duty to warn cases that you have read:

- Lundgren v. Fultz, 354 N.W.2d 25 (Minn. 1984).
- Bjerke v. Johnson, 742 N.W.2d 660 (Minn. 2007).
- Patzwald v. Krey, 390 N.W.2d 920 (Minn. 1986).
- Udofot v. Seven Eights Liquor, No. A10-431, 2010 WL 5071313 (Minn. Ct. App. March 15, 2011).
- H.B. ex rel. v. Whittemore, 552 N.W.2d 705 (Minn. 1996).
- Wood on Behalf of Doe v. Astleford, 412 N.W.2d 753 (Minn. Ct. App. 1987).

If you want to practice your legal research skills, you can look for and use other cases that you find. However, if you do search on Westlaw, LexisNexis or Bloomberg Law, be sure to limit your search and the cases you use to Minnesota law and remember to change the citations to Jefferson law as indicated in the introduction.

Format of the Completed Assignment:

Your response should be in an office memo format and should include the following:

- Summary of the facts
- The relevant law
- Analysis of the law to the fact pattern
- Conclusion about how you think a court would rule if this matter were to go to court
- Your advice to the client about how to proceed

Follow the following format:

- 1 inch (2.54 cm.) margins (top/bottom and sides)
- 12 font, Times New Roman font
- Double spaced
- Maximum eight pages

Notes:

This memo should be predictive and not persuasive. You are not trying to persuade the senior partner or the client about the strength of your arguments or urge him or her to take a particular course of action; you are only trying to inform him about the law, how it applies to our case, how you think a court would rule and what advice you have.

In a memo, you can also use formatting like underlining, bold font or italics. You can also create headings and subheadings to organize your answer.

For additional information about office memos and e-memos, as well as samples, refer to the online additional resources.

Grading: This assignment is worth 102 points.

LEGAL CONTENT	0-6 points	8 points	10 points	12 points	Points
Issue statement (IS)	Document does not include an IS or includes IS that fails to properly identify the legal issue(s) and the applicable law	Identifies the legal issue(s) and correctly states the applicable law with minor mistakes	Identifies the legal issue(s) and correctly states the applicable law	Identifies the legal issue(s) and correctly states the applicable law in an exceptionally creative and concise way	_____/12
Short Answer	Document does not include a short answer or includes a short answer with significant mistakes	Responds to IS but with key facts or applicable legal principles missing	Responds to IS with key facts and applicable legal principles with no meaningful errors	Clearly and concisely responds to IS with key facts and applicable legal principles and no irrelevancies	_____/12
Facts	Few or none of the relevant facts are included; difficult to follow or understand	Most relevant facts are included as well as non-relevant ones; at times difficult to follow	Relevant facts are included with occasional irrelevancies; easy to follow	All relevant facts are included with no irrelevancies; story is clearly and concisely told to reader in objective way	_____/12
Rule	Hard to follow and understand; does not include relevant sources or cites inappropriate sources; no rule application	Cites to some relevant sources but is incomplete in covering all relevant aspects of the rule; includes some rule application	Cite only to relevant sources and mostly clear; rule application explains but not fully how rule has been applied	Clear and concise; includes only relevant sources and includes all parts of rule necessary for analysis; clear rule application	_____/12
Analysis	Contains conclusory statements and/or no case law; facts are analyzed in a conclusory or insufficient way	Uses some case law but does not analogize or distinguish or explain its application; some conclusory statements; facts briefly analyzed	Uses case law to show how rule applies to case; case law is compared and contrasted with success; most facts are analyzed	Analyzes case law completely, comparing it fully to client matter; facts are thoroughly analyzed in an objective way	_____/12
Conclusion/ Recommendations	No conclusion or recommendations are included in document	A brief conclusion is included but without sufficient client advice	Paper includes conclusion and recommendations	Paper includes full conclusion of the legal analysis and facts and presents creative and thoughtful recommendations	_____/12
Citations	No sources are cited in document	Some sources are cited, but inconsistently; citation format is inconsistent	All citations are present; correct format is mostly used	All citations are present; correct format is used throughout document	_____/12
WRITING	2	4	5	6	Points
Formatting	Document does not follow format instructions or the sample provided	Document attempts to follow instructions and sample provided	Document follows the instructions and sample provided with no meaningful errors	Document exactly follows the instructions and sample provided	_____/6
Organization	No structure or organization; free flow of ideas	Structure & organization present but reorganization or headings needed for full clarity	Document is clearly organized and structured with proper use of heading and subheadings	Document is exceptionally well organized and structured with proper use of headings and subheadings	_____/6
Syntax Mechanics	Contains numerous and distracting grammatical and mechanical errors that impede understanding	Contains some grammatical and mechanical errors that impede understanding	Contains few grammatical and mechanical errors but none that impede understanding	Contains no grammatical and mechanical errors; native-like use of English	_____/6
TOTAL					_____/102

Mock Client Meeting

Overview of this Assignment: This assignment simulates a client meeting between you and your client, Pamela Park of Stray Dog Advertising, LLC or Maryam Ahmed, representing the estate of her deceased husband.

The meeting is scheduled to provide your client with an update about the status of the litigation, the likelihood of success with regard to the motion to dismiss, and your advice and recommendations on how your client should proceed.

Your instructor will indicate to you the time that you will have available for the mock client meeting.

Learning Objectives of the Assignment:

This assignment will build your skills to:

- Explain and clarify the legal positions of the parties and describe potential outcomes to your client
- Respond to technical questions about litigation
- Incorporate technical legal English vocabulary that relates to negligence, premises liability and duty to warn and use appropriate layperson explanations for your client

Steps for Completing the Assignment:

- Read and be familiar with the Main Assignment File
- Be familiar with the negligence/duty to warn cases that you have been assigned
- Recommended:
    - Anticipate the questions that you think your client might ask and prepare possible responses
    - Draft an outline of what you would like to cover in the meeting

Note: Remember that part of the grading is also based on your professional demeanor. You are expected to arrive punctually, be dressed in professional attire and act as you would with a client in real life. You should play the part from when you come into the meeting room.

Grading: This assignment worth 102 points.

Punctuality: Student-attorney arrived on time to meeting: YES _____ (10 points) NO _____ (0 points)

Professional Attire: Student-attorney was dressed in appropriate professional attire: YES _____ (10 points) NO _____ (0 points)

Professional Demeanor: Student-attorney acted in a professional manner w/ client: YES _____ (10 points) NO _____ (0 points)

GRADING CRITERIA	0- 6 points	8 points (C or 75%)	10 points (B or 85%)	12 points	Points received
Engagement I (questions)	Attorney does not ask client any questions; engages in monologue	Attorney asks few questions; questions are hard to follow or show minimal preparation or understanding of matter	Attorney asks basic questions that demonstrate understanding of matter and preparation	Attorney asks thoughtful, insightful and creative questions that demonstrate deep preparation & understanding of matter	_____/12
Engagement II (answers)	Attorney does not respond to client's questions	Attorney responds to questions, but incorrectly or with hard to follow answers	Attorney responds promptly and correctly to all of client's questions	Attorney responds promptly and correctly to all of client's questions with creative, thoughtful and insightful answers that show a deep understanding of the issues	_____/12
Knowledge of Applicable Law	Attorney provides no explanation of the applicable law	Attorney provides explanation of with serious mistakes, or hard to follow (e.g. use of legal jargon)	Attorney provides clear explanation of with some mistakes; uses some legal jargon unnecessarily or without explanations that client can understand	Attorney provides clear, concise and correct explanation of the law with legal jargon when appropriate or w/ explanations client can understand	_____/12
Ability to Analyze Applicable Law	Attorney provides does not provide an analysis of the law for the client	Attorney attempts to analyze the law but provides incomplete or incorrect analysis	Attorney provides analysis of the law with no significant mistakes or misstatements of the law or facts	Attorney provides a clear, concise and correct analysis of the law as it applies to the client matter	_____/12
Advice and Recommendations	Attorney provides no advice or poor advice for client	Attorney provides not comprehensive or inaccurate advice	Attorney provides comprehensive and accurate advice to client on his/her legal matter	Attorney provides thoughtful and creative solutions for client	_____/12
Organization	Meeting is disorganized and hard to follow or lacks any organization	Meeting has some organization but is still confusing for client for how information is presented	Meeting is clearly organized and easy to follow	Meeting is clearly organized and is easy to follow; attorney takes extra steps to ensure client's understanding	_____/12
TOTAL					_____/72
TOTAL FROM PUNCTUALITY AND PROFESSIONALISM					_____/30

Section II

Intermediate Legal Issues

Total _____/102

Client Advice Letter

Overview of the Assignment: For this assignment, you will write an advice and follow-up letter to your client (Pamela Park or Maryam Ahmed), summarizing your research on negligence/duty to warn, as well as your meeting with her. You should also give recommendations to your client on how she should approach this matter. Be mindful that your client is not a trained attorney. Therefore you should avoid legalese in your letter.

Under Rule 1.4(a)(3) of the Model Rules of Professional Conduct(a)(3), an attorney has the duty to keep his or her client "reasonably informed about the status of the client's matter." A thorough follow-up letter after a client meeting is one of the best ways to meet this duty, as well as regular phone calls, emails or meetings.

Learning Objectives of the Assignment:

This assignment will build your skills to:

- Efficiently communicate in a written format
- Explain complex matters clearly and concisely
- Use appropriate technical terminology

Steps for Completing the Assignment:

- Review the predictive memo that you wrote to the senior partner about the law regarding negligence/duty to warn and the fact pattern
- Review the Business Correspondence resources
- Be familiar with the case law regarding negligence/duty to warn, as well as the fact pattern.

Research for the Assignment: You are not required to do any outside research for this assignment.

Format of the Completed Assignment:

Your assignment should be written as a business letter, not as an email. Even though many firms and lawyers use email for much of the correspondence carried out, formal business letters are still an essential part of the practice of law.

Your law firm has the following policy regarding business correspondence. Your client letter must follow the policy guidelines.

LAW FIRM CORRESPONDENCE POLICY

The purpose of this policy is to ensure a uniform appearance of all business correspondence that is written by the attorneys and staff of the law firm and thus to increase the professional appearance of the firm's work product. All law firm attorneys and staff are required to employ the following guidelines when writing correspondence. Violation of the policy can result in disciplinary action, up to and including termination.

- The first page of all "traditional" letters must be written on law firm letterhead, which includes the firm's address and logo
- All letters must be written in a modified block letter format
- Letters must be written in Times New Roman, 12 font
- Letters must be 1.5 spaced and have 1" (2.54 cm.) margins, except for the initial page, which may have larger top margins to account for the logo, law firm address and sender's direct contact information
- Client letters must not exceed four pages

Grading: This assignment is worth 78 points.

Note: See the Online Additional Resources for examples of letters and for general information about business correspondence.

LEGAL CONTENT	0-6 points (failing)	8 points (C or 75%)	10 points (B or 85%)	12 points	Points
Introduction	Letter does not include an appropriate introduction or includes poorly constructed one	Letter includes introduction that states purpose with some irrelevancies or some relevant information missing	Introduction states purpose of letter and includes other relevant information	Introduction is engaging; states purpose of letter and includes other relevant information; written clearly and concisely	_____/12
Summary of Meeting	Letter includes no summary of the meeting	Letter includes summary but leaves out important information or states it unclearly	Letter summarizes the meeting but leaves out important information	Letter clearly and concisely summarizes the meeting, its core purpose and content	_____/12
Applicable Law	Student-attorney provides no explanation of the applicable law, or only uses legal jargon in explanation (inappropriate for audience)	Student-attorney provides explanation of with serious mistakes, or hard to follow (use of legal jargon)	Student-attorney provides clear explanation of with few mistakes; uses some legal jargon without appropriate explanations	Student-attorney provides clear, concise and correct explanation of the law with legal jargon with appropriate explanations	_____/12
Analysis	Contains conclusory statements and/or no case law; facts are analyzed in a conclusory or insufficient way	Uses some case law but does not analogize or distinguish or explain its application; some conclusory statements; facts briefly analyzed	Uses case law to show how rule applies to case; case law is compared and contrasted with success; most facts are analyzed	Analyzes completely case law, comparing it fully to client matter; facts are thoroughly analyzed	_____/12
Conclusion/ Recommendations	No conclusion or recommendations are included in letter	A brief conclusion is included but without sufficient advice or recommendations advice or next steps	Letter includes conclusion with recommendations and next steps	Letter includes full conclusion of the legal analysis and facts, presents creative and thoughtful recommendations and includes clear next steps	_____/12
WRITING	**2**	**4**	**5**	**6**	**Points**
Formatting	Document does not follow format instructions or the sample provided	Document attempts to follow instructions and sample provided	Document follows the instructions and sample provided with minor errors	Document exactly follows the instructions and sample provided	_____/6
Organization	No structure or organization; free flow of ideas	Letter includes organization and structure but is still confusing	Structure and organization but some reorganization is needed for full clarity	Document is clearly organized and structured	_____/6
Syntax Mechanics	Contains numerous and distracting grammatical and mechanical errors that impede understanding	Contains some grammatical and mechanical errors that impede understanding	Contains few grammatical and mechanical errors but none that impede understanding	Contains no grammatical and mechanical errors; native-like use of English	_____/6
TOTAL					_____/78

Memorandum of Law in Support of or in Opposition to Motion to Dismiss

Negligence/Duty to Warn

Unit 1

Overview of the Assignment: Stray Dog Advertising is being sued by the estate of its former employee, Mohammed Ahmed, who was tragically killed in the workplace shooting at the SDA offices. You have been assigned to represent either Stray Dog Advertising or Ahmed's estate.

In the Main Assignment File, you have also received your assignment from the senior partner of your respective law firm and have been asked to write the memorandum of law in support of or in opposition to the motion to dismiss that the defendant, Stray Dog Advertising, has filed, and also to conduct the oral argument.

Learning Objectives of the Assignment:

This assignment will build your skills to:

- Efficiently read and understand legal authority
- Analyze the fact pattern by applying the relevant case law
- Adapt the IRAC organization and the formal memorandum of law structure
- Communicate effectively and in a persuasive manner to convince the court and the reader of the merits of your client's position and of the relief that you seek

Research for the Assignment: You are not required to do any outside research for this assignment.

You should base your analysis on the negligence/duty to warn cases that you have read in class:

- Lundregn v. Fultz, 354 N.W.2d 25 (Minn. 1984).
- Bjerke v. Johnson, 742 N.W.2d 660 (Minn. 2007).
- Patzwald v. Krey, 390 N.W.2d 920 (Minn. 1986).
- Udofot v. Seven Eights Liquor, No. A10-431, 2010 WL 5071313 (Minn. Ct. App. March 15, 2011).
- H.B. ex rel. v. Whittemore, 552 N.W.2d 705 (Minn. 1996).
- Wood on Behalf of Doe v. Astleford, 412 N.W.2d 753 (Minn. Ct. App. 1987).

If you want to practice your legal research skills, you can look for and use other cases that you find. However, if you do search on Westlaw, LexisNexis or Bloomberg Law, be sure to limit your search and the cases you use to Minnesota law and remember to change the citations to Jefferson law as indicated in the introduction.

Format of the Completed Assignment:

For your completed assignment, you must follow Local Rule 5.2 of the Courts of Jefferson.

Local Rule 5.2 GENERAL FORMAT OF DOCUMENTS TO BE FILED

Format: All documents filed must be typewritten, printed, or prepared by a clearly legible duplication process. Document text must be double-spaced, except for quoted material and footnotes, and pages must be numbered consecutively at the bottom. Documents filed after the case-initiating document must contain—on the front page and above the document's title—the case number and the name or initials of the assigned district judge and magistrate judge.

Represented Parties. A memorandum of law filed by a represented party must be typewritten. All text in the memorandum, including footnotes, must be set in at least font size 12 (i.e., a 12-point font) as font sizes are designated in the word-processing software used to prepare the memorandum. Text must be double-spaced, with these exceptions: headings and footnotes may be single-spaced, and quotations more than two lines long may be indented and single-spaced. Pages must be 8 ½ by 11 inches in size, and no text — except for page numbers — may appear outside an area measuring 6 ½ by 9 inches.

Length: No memorandum filed with the court shall exceed the length of twelve pages, excluding caption and table of contents.

Grading: This assignment is worth 90 points.

Note: See the online resources for additional information about memoranda of law and persuasive writing.

LEGAL CONTENT	0-6 points	8 points	10 points	12 points	Points
Introduction	Document does not include an Introduction or includes issue statement instead	Introduction is not persuasive or does not include persuasive or relevant facts or the law	Student attempts to make introduction persuasive, to "put the spin" but does not include all facts or something...	Introduction is persuasive, clear and concise and clearly introduces reader to the client's story and position and identifies the relief sought	_____/12
Facts	Few or none of the relevant facts are included; difficult to follow or understand	Relevant facts are included as well as non-relevant ones; mostly clear	Relevant facts are included; factual background is mostly clear and easy to follow with few irrelevancies	Relevant facts are included with no irrelevant facts; story is clearly and concisely told to reader in persuasive way	_____/12
Rule	Hard to follow and understand; does not include relevant sources or cites inappropriate sources; no rule application	Cites to some relevant sources but is incomplete in covering all relevant aspects of the rule	Cite only to relevant sources; rule application explains but not fully how rule has been applied	Clear and concise; includes only relevant sources and includes all parts of rule necessary for analysis; clear rule application	_____/12
Argument	Contains conclusory statements and/or no case law; facts are analyzed in a conclusory or insufficient way	Uses some case law but does not analogize or distinguish or explain its application; some conclusory statements; facts briefly analyzed; student attempts to make persuasive arguments	Uses case law to show how rule applies to case; case law is compared and contrasted with success; facts are analyzed and argued in a persuasive way	Analyzes completely case law, comparing it fully to client matter; all facts are thoroughly analyzed and argued in a very persuasive way	_____/12
Conclusion	No conclusion is included in document	A brief conclusion is included but unclear relief sought	Paper includes conclusion with relief sought	Paper includes full conclusion of the legal analysis and facts and persuasively argues for relief sought	_____/12
Citations	No sources are cited in document or citation formats are incorrect and inconsistent	Sources are cited, but inconsistently; citation format has meaningful mistakes in format	Citations are complete; few meaningful mistakes in format	No mistakes in citations; correct format is used throughout document	_____/12
WRITING	**2**	**4**	**5**	**6**	**Points**
Formatting	Document does not follow format instructions or the sample provided	Document attempts to follow instructions and sample provided	Document follows the instructions and sample provided with minor errors	Document exactly follows the instructions and sample provided	_____/6
Organization	No structure or organization; free flow of ideas	Document includes some organization and structure but is still confusing; no use of headings or subheadings	Structure & organization present but reorganization needed full clarity; subheadings included but not effectively persuasive	Document is clearly organized and structured with proper use of persuasive heading and subheadings	_____/6
Syntax Mechanics	Contains numerous and distracting grammatical and mechanical errors that impede understanding	Contains some grammatical and mechanical errors that impede understanding	Contains few grammatical and mechanical errors but none that impede understanding	Contains no grammatical and mechanical errors; native-like use of English	_____/6
TOTAL					_____/90

Section II

Intermediate Legal Issues

Mock Oral Argument

Overview of the Assignment: For this assignment, you will carry out the oral argument for the motion to dismiss in the <u>Estate of Ahmed v. Stray Dog Advertising, LLC</u> case, currently docketed in the Hemings County District Court.

You will represent the party that your instructor has assigned to you.

Learning Objectives of the Assignment:

This assignment will build your skills to:

- Effectively and persuasively communicate legal rules and argument
- Conduct yourself orally in a professional courtroom setting
- Respond to questions about the relevant law

Steps for Completing the Assignment:

Before the oral arguments, review and be familiar with the following:

- Pleadings
- Notice of Motion and Motion to Dismiss
- Your Memorandum of Law, as well as that of your opposing counsel
- Cases cited in your memo and opposing counsel's
- Facts of the client matter

Research for the Assignment: Although no additional research is required for the assignment, you should review the memorandum of your opposing counsel and review the cases that he/she includes, consider how you can rebut the cases or explain how they are inapposite to the matter at hand and address those cases in your oral argument.

Format of the Assignment:

Each side has 20 minutes for his or her argument. The moving party first presents his/her arguments and may reserve time for rebuttal. It is the moving party's decision to reserve time for rebuttal. After the moving party has presented his/her arguments, it is the non-moving party's turn. The non-moving party does not receive time for rebuttal since he/she can listen to opposing counsel and respond directly to any arguments made. After the non-moving party finishes, the moving party responds with rebuttal, if he/she previously asked the court to reserve time for it.

Be prepared to answer questions from the court, and part of your preparation should be anticipating the questions that the judge might ask and preparing answers. But in the event that the judge doesn't ask questions or asks few, be prepared to fill the time allotted with your argument.

Grading: This assignment is worth 90 points.

Punctuality: Attorney arrived on time to oral argument: YES _____ (10 points) NO _____ (0 points)

Professional Attire: Attorney was dressed in appropriate professional attire: YES _____ (10 points) NO _____ (0 points)

Professional Demeanor: Attorney acted in a professional manner w/court and opposing counsel: YES _____ (10 points) NO _____ (0 points)

GRADING CRITERIA	0-6 points (failing)	8 points (C or 75%)	10 points (B or 85%)	12 points	Points received
Engagement	Attorney does not respond to the court's questions	Attorney responds to questions, but incorrectly or with hard to follow answers	Attorney responds promptly and correctly to all of the court's questions	Attorney responds promptly and correctly to all of court's questions with creative, thoughtful and insightful answers that show a deep understanding of the issues	_____/12
Knowledge of Applicable Law	Attorney provides no explanation of the applicable law	Attorney provides explanation of with few meaningful mistakes or with explanation that is hard to follow	Attorney provides clear explanation of the law with no meaningful mistakes	Attorney provides clear, concise and correct explanation of the law	_____/12
Analysis of Applicable Law	Attorney provides no analysis of the law or provides analysis that is incorrect or incomplete	Attorney provides analysis of the law but has some mistakes or misstatements of the law or facts	Attorney provides a clear, concise and correct analysis of the law as it applies to the client matter	Attorney present unimpeachable case for the client, analyzing persuasively, concisely and clearly the law as it applies to client matter	_____/12
Conclusion and Relief	Attorney does not identify relief sought or conclude argument	Attorney provides advice, but	Attorney provides advice but	Attorney clearly identifies the relief sought and summarizes the client's position	_____/12
Organization	Argument is disorganized and has serious faults of organization	Argument has minor faults of organization	Argument is clearly organized and easy to follow	Argument is exceptionally well organized and presents arguments in novel way	_____/12
TOTAL					_____/60
TOTAL FROM PUNCTUALITY AND PROFESSIONALISM					_____/30

TOTAL   _____/90

Common Law

Unit 2 Defamation
Qualified Privilege as a Defense

For this Unit, you will write a persuasive memorandum of law in support of or in opposition to a motion to dismiss in litigation involving Pamela Park (personally, not her company, Stray Dog Advertising, LLC) and another individual, Fran Beaumont. The legal issue involved is defamation.

You will be assigned to represent either the plaintiff, Fran Beaumont, or the defendant, Pamela Park. Both sides have the same documents available to them, and no information is confidential or available to only one side.

Learning Objectives of this Unit:

This Unit will build your skills to:

- Explain complex legal matters clearly and concisely
- Use appropriate technical terminology
- Identify and analyze the applicable case law and facts for the relevant legal issues
- Efficiently read and understand legal authority
- Articulate persuasive legal arguments in support of client's position
- Analyze possible outcomes for legal dispute, evaluate and articulate strengths and weaknesses of such outcomes
- Efficiently and effectively communicate in a written and oral format
- Respond to questions about the relevant law

To achieve these learning objectives, you will complete the following tasks:

- Draft a predictive memo to senior partner about the legal issues and your prediction of what will happen with the litigation
- Draft a persuasive memorandum of law in support of or in opposition to motion to dismiss
- Carry out a mock client meeting with either Pamela Park or Frances Beaumont
- Draft a client letter to your client about your meeting and about the legal issue
- Carry out oral argument in front of the court for the motion to dismiss

To complete these tasks, you will use the following materials in the book:

- Assignment email from Senior Partner (pages 171-172; 176-177)
- Main Assignment File (pages 173-175)
- Defamation/Qualified Privilege Commented Cases:
    - Herlihy v. The Metropolitan Museum of Art, 633 N.Y.S.2d 106 (N.Y. App. Div. 1995).
    - Baldwin v. Shell Oil Co., 419 N.Y.S.2d 752 (N.Y. App. Div. 1979).
    - Buckley v. Litman, 443 N.E.2d 469 (N.Y. 1982).
    - Byam v. Collins, 19 N.E. 75 (N.Y. 1888).
    - Van Wyck v. Aspinwall, 17 N.E. 190 (N.Y. 1858).
- ESL Workbook (pages 122-141)
- Pleadings (online)

Your instructor will also assign you additional skills-building exercises to bolster your understanding of the legal issues and further develop your legal reasoning and language skills, whether related to legal reasoning and analysis or to English. You will find an icon with each exercise that will indicate which skills the exercise will focus upon.

ICON	SKILL
![icon]	Speaking — in particular about the legal issues and the law presented in the Unit
![icon]	Oral comprehension
![icon]	Legal analysis and reasoning
![icon]	Analysis of the legal issue(s) presented in the Unit
![icon]	English grammar, syntax, and vocabulary
![icon]	Legal ethics and professional responsibility
![icon]	Legal research

In this Unit, the additional skills-building exercises that accompany the Main Assignment File include:

- Ethics Dilemma: Conflict of Interest (page 178)
- Defamation Analysis Exercise (pages 179-180)
- Third-Party Practice (pages 181-182)
- Professional Presentation: *If Pamela Park or Fran Beaumont Were Your Client...*(pages 188-184)

Before beginning the Unit, you should read and be familiar with the Stray Dog Advertising Factual Background (pages 7-8) and the Factual Background of the Lincoln, Adams and Washington Law Firm (pages 2-3) and the Anthony, Ross and Tubman Law Office (page 5).

You will also find online at the website www.legalwritingforllms.com the following online resources that accompany this Unit. The additional online resources will help you deepen your mastery of the skills presented in the Unit and also provide additional understanding about the U.S. legal system and legal writing.

Pleadings for Seciton II, Unit 2 (required)

- Additional Resources:
  - Sources of American Law
  - Writing Professional Emails
  - Writing Persuasive Memos
  - Writing E-memos
  - IRAC
- Additional Skills-Building Exercises:
  - Issues and Issue Statements
  - Stating the Rule
  - Analysis
  - Ethical Spotlight Exercise

Section II, Unit 2 Legal Issue
Defamation

Main Assignment File	Defamation Cases	ESL Workbook	Additional Exercises	Additional Online Resources
Introduction to File and Client Matter Pages 166-170	Herlihy v. The Metro. Museum of Art, 214 A.D.2d 250 (N.Y. App. Div. 1995).	Herlihy v. The Metro. Museum of Art, 214 A.D.2d 250 (N.Y. App. Div. 1995).	Ethics Dilemma: Conflict of Interests Page 178	Writing Professional Emails
Documents Related to Client Matter Pages 171-177 + pleadings (available online)	Baldwin v. Shell Oil Co., 71 A.D.2d 907 (N.Y. App. Div. 1979).	Baldwin v. Shell Oil Co., 71 A.D.2d 907 (N.Y. App. Div. 1979).	Defamation Analysis Exercise Pages 179-180	Business Correspondence (with sample letters)
Assignment Information Pages + Rubrics Pages 185-194	Buckley v. Litman, 57 N.Y.2d 516 (Ct. App. N.Y. 1982).	Buckley v. Litman, 57 N.Y.2d 516 (Ct. App. N.Y. 1982).	Third-Party Practice Pages 181-182	Writing Memos (office memos and persuasive memoranda of law)
	Byam v. Collins, 66 Sickels 143 (Ct. App. N.Y. 1888).	Byam v. Collins, 66 Sickels 143 (Ct. App. N.Y. 1888).	Presentation: If SDA or Fran Beaumont Were Your Client... Pages 183-184	IRAC (including additional exercises for each element)
	Van Wyck v. Aspinwall, 3 E.P. Smith 190 (N.Y. 1858).	Van Wyck v. Aspinwall, 3 E.P. Smith 190 (N.Y. 1858).		Skills-Building Exercises for Rules, Issues and Issues Statements, Analysis and Ethical Dilemmas

Defamation

Unit 2

Introduction — Defamation

The First Amendment provides, in pertinent part, that *"Congress shall make no law . . . abridging freedom of speech."* Like all constitutional rights, however, this right is not absolute, and courts have defined certain types of speech that are not constitutionally protected. Those types of speech are

Obscenity[49]

Fighting words[50]

Child pornography

Perjury[51]

Blackmail[52]

Solicitations to commit crimes

Incitement[53] to imminent lawless action

True threats

Defamation (including libel and slander)

The legal issue you will be dealing with in this Unit is the last in the above list of the types of speech not protected under the constitution: defamation. A dictionary definition of defamation is "[t]he publication of material injurious to a person's good name and reputation," and it "[i]ncludes both libel and slander."[54] Two types of defamation exist: slander, defined as a "[o]ral defamation; spoken words that defame a person in front of others and that cause harm or some damage,"[55] and libel, "[a]ny false and malicious written publication printed for the purpose of defaming another's character or reputation . . . . "[56] We speak in general about defamation.

A type of defamation is defamation *per se*, which is a "statement that is defamatory in and of itself . . . ."[57] Defamation *per se* imputes to the plaintiff any one of the following: (1) a crime involving moral turpitude, (2) a loathsome disease (such as a sexually transmitted disease), (3) conduct that would adversely affect one's business or profession, or (4) unchastity (especially of a woman).[58] When the statements made are *per se* defamatory, a plaintiff does not need to prove special damages as they are presumed.

Truth is a defense to a claim of defamation, and another defense that a defendant may raise is that the communication was privileged. The First Amendment gives the press a privilege to report and comment upon the official actions of public servants in full detail,[59] while employers also have a privilege to communicate information about current and former employees.[60] However, a privilege is not absolute and can be abused and lost.

---

[49] Speech that (1) the average person, when applying contemporary community standards, would find appeals to the prurient interest; (2) depicts or describes, in a patently offensive way, sexual conduct specifically defined by the applicable state law; and (3) lacks serious literary, artistic, political, or scientific value. Miller v. California, 413 U.S. 15, 24 (1973).

[50] Fighting words are "those [words] which by their very utterance inflict injury or tend to incite an immediate breach of the peace." Chaplinsky v. New Hampshire, 315 U.S. 568, 572 (1942).

[51] The criminal offense of making a false statement under oath in a legal proceeding with no sincere belief in its truth, when it is relevant to a material issue in the proceeding. *Perjury*, GILBERT'S POCKET SIZE LAW DICTIONARY (3rd ed. 2014).

[52] Extortion of money by threat to do bodily harm, expose a wrong-doing, or disgrace the character of another. *Blackmail*, GILBERT'S POCKET SIZE LAW DICTIONARY (3rd ed. 2014).

[53] "The act or an instance of provoking, urging on, or stirring up." *Incitement*, BLACK'S LAW DICTIONARY (10th ed. 2014).

[54] *Defamation*, GILBERT'S POCKET SIZE LAW DICTIONARY (3rd ed. 2014).

[55] *Slander,* GILBERT'S POCKET SIZE LAW DICTIONARY (3rd ed. 2014).

[56] *Libel,* GILBERT'S POCKET SIZE LAW DICTIONARY (3rd ed. 2014).

[57] *Defamation*, BLACK'S LAW DICTIONARY (10th ed. 2014).

[58] Holtzscheiter v. Thompson Newspapers, Inc., 505 N.E.2d 497 (S.C. 1998).

[59] New York Times Co. v. Sullivan, 376 U.S. 254 (1964).

[60] See, e.g., Zinda v. Louisiana Pac. Corp., 440 N.W.2d 548, 552 (Wis. 1989) (stating that employers enjoy a "common interest" privilege, which is "particularly germane" to the employer-employee relationship).

"A communication made *bona fide* upon any subject-matter in which the party communicating has an interest, or in reference to which he has a duty, is privileged, if made to a person having a corresponding interest or duty, although it contains criminating matter which, without this privilege, would be slanderous and actionable; and this though the duty be not a legal one, but only a moral or social duty of imperfect obligation." Byam v. Collins, 19 N.E. 75, 75 (N.Y. 1888).

For the media, its constitutional privilege, when reporting about public figures like politicians, can be lost if the plaintiff can show that the defamatory statement was made with actual malice, that is knowledge that it was false or with reckless disregard of whether it was false or not.[61]

As for employers, their qualified privilege can be lost when it is abused under a similar standard: the employer communicates the statement with malice.[62] This same privilege applies not just to an employer but to any person facing a defamation claim.[63]

In our fact pattern, the plaintiff, Frances Beaumont, claims that Pamela has defamed her. One of the issues that you will analyze is whether Pamela's statements were privileged, or whether they were made or communicated with malice. In particular, you will examine whether Pamela is a person of interest in this case, which would provide her a defense to the defamation claim, whether she communicated the statements to another person of interest, and whether the statements were defamatory *per se*. The procedural issue that you will deal with is a motion to dismiss; the defendant, Pamela Park, has filed this motion, asking the court to dismiss Beaumont's claim against her.

---

[61] New York Times v. Sullivan, 376 U.S. 254, 279-289 (1964).

[62] Sanderson v. Bellevue Maternity Hosp. Inc., 686 N.Y.S.2d 535, 537 (N.Y. App. Div. 1999) (citing Grier v. Johnson, 648 N.Y.S.2d 764, 767 (N.Y. App. Div. 1996).

[63] Id. (stating that this privilege applies "when a person makes a good-faith, bona fide communication upon a subject in which he or she has an interest, or a legal, moral or societal interest to speak, and the communication is made to a person with a corresponding interest.").

Main Assignment File — Defamation

Plaintiff's File

You have received this email from Suzanne Anthony, who has recently been hired by Fran Beaumont to bring the defamation claim against Pamela Park.

From:	Suzanne Anthony <anthony@artlawoffice.com >
To:	Associate Attorney <associate@artlawoffice.com >
Sent:	Jan 8, THIS YEAR 09:38 a.m.
Re:	Defamation Matter New Client Beaumont

Good morning,

I am writing to enlist your assistance with a new client, Fran Beaumont. Fran is the daughter of one of the senior partners at the law firm where I first worked after graduating from law school. Fran is an important new client.

The case is an interesting one involving a name you are probably familiar with, given your involvement with the West Rapids Chamber of Commerce: Pamela Park of the advertising agency Stray Dog Advertising. I've met Pamela at a few Chamber events and have tried to lure her away from her long-time relationship with Lincoln, Adams and Washington, but Pamela is too loyal, even to her attorneys!

I have drafted and filed a complaint on Fran's behalf against Pamela individually, not against the LLC, for defamation. Fran was dating Pamela's nephew, and Pamela told her nephew some facts about Fran that were false, upon encouragement from her nephew's parents (Pamela's sister and brother-in-law). It seems that they wanted to break up the engagement between Fran and their son. When I met with Fran last week, she brought with her the emails that were exchanged between her ex-fiancée's parents and his aunt, Pamela, as well as the report that the PI drafted about Fran. It seems that Tim's parents gave him copies of the emails and the PI report which he then gave to Fran.

Amy Lincoln and I spoke, and she informed me that she will file a motion to dismiss along with the answer. Even though we haven't gotten the answer or the memo yet, let's start work on it so we are ready when they do serve it on us.

I need you to prepare the memo in opposition to the motion to dismiss. But before that, I want you to prepare a memo for me so that I can understand the law better. I also want your prediction as to how you think a court will rule in this case and on the motion.

I want you to do the oral argument since I will be on vacation in Italy that week. One of the new law clerks has researched the law already and will be sending you some relevant cases.

Thanks,

Suzanne

As you have read, you have been asked to write the following documents about this litigation:

Anthony has asked you to write her a predictive office memo about the following:

- A summary of what has happened between Pamela Park and Fran Beaumont.
- The legal issue at hand
- A summary and analysis of the law that applies (defamation and qualified privilege)
- Your opinion about whether the communications that Pamela made about Fran were privileged
- Your advice about how to proceed with this matter

You will find complete information about this assignment on the Information Page (pages 185-186).

Second, Anthony has asked you to prepare a persuasive memorandum of law in opposition to the motion to dismiss that Amy Lincoln has filed.

The memorandum of law will include:

- A factual background of what has led to the claim against Stray Dog Advertising
- Persuasive legal arguments that the claim should not be dismissed

You will find complete information about this assignment on the Information Page (pages 191-192).

Below are the emails that were exchanged between Pamela Park, her sister and her brother-in-law and that Senior Partner Lincoln forwarded to you.

Section II

Intermediate Legal Issues

From:	Emma Park-Matheson <e.matheson1967@gmail.com>
To:	Pamela Park <pamela.park@straydogadvertising.com>
CC:	Ian Matheson <ian_matheson@aol.com>
Sent:	November 19, YEAR -1 21:04
Subject:	Re: Re: Help with Tim

THANK YOU!!! We really owe you big time.

I only have a hard copy of the report that the PI sent us (he is old-fashioned and concerned about hacking so doesn't send anything as attachments or through email) so I will scan and send it to you, but here is what you have to let Tim know:

Fran was arrested and convicted of forgery and theft by swindle in the Miami-Dade county court in August YEAR -4. According to what the PI found out, she served nine months in the county jail.

In YEAR -2, she declared bankruptcy when she was still in Florida and right before she moved here to Jefferson.

Emma

From:	Pamela Park <pamela.park@straydogadvertising.com>
To:	Emma Park-Matheson <e.matheson1967@gmail.com>
CC:	Ian Matheson <ian_matheson@aol.com>
Sent:	November 19, YEAR -1 16:45
Subject:	Re: Help with Tim

Are you guys crazy? Tim is 26...a grown man. Don't you think that he can (and should) make his own decisions about who he marries and dates? I wasn't too keen on Fran either when I met her (as I told you after the party), but I just don't think that it is any of my business.

But I owe you after all the help you gave me last year. Why don't you tell me exactly what you want me to tell him. Or is there something that I need to show him, like what the PI found out?

PP

From: Emma-Park Matheson <e.matheson1967@gmail.com>
To: Pamela Park <pamela.park@straydogadvertising.com>
CC: Ian Matheson <ian_matheson@aol.com>
Sent: November 19, YEAR -1 10:39
Subject: Help with Tim

Hi Pammy,

Ian and I need your help. We are really worried about Tim and this new girl that he is dating, Fran. You remember meeting her at my birthday party last month, don't you? I was floored when Tim told us last night, but he's proposed to her! After dating only two months! What is he thinking?

I still just don't have a good vibe about her. I think she is a gold-digger and just after Tim's money. She knows that he is successful, has earned a lot and is only going to earn more as he continues his success. I think he takes after his Auntie Pam!

With this feeling that something was amiss with her, I contacted a private investigator. I saw his ad on Craigslist and the price was cheap, so I emailed him and asked him to look for information about Frances Beaumont. I knew that she was born in Miami so it wasn't hard to find her, the PI told me.

And I knew it! She's been convicted of two crimes and has even declared bankruptcy! She apparently has no money to her name, so I am even more sure that she just wants Tim's.

Can you talk to him and try to get some sense in his mind? Tell him what we found out and get him to break off the engagement? We think that he is more likely to listen to you rather than his mom and dad. Please?

Love, Emma

PRIVATE INVESTIGATOR REPORT
CONFIDENTIAL

PREPARED FOR: EMMA MATHESON

PREPARED BY: THOMAS GLENDALE (Jefferson State P.I. License # 09-1487)

RE: INVESTIGATIVE SEARCH FOR FRANCES BEAUMONT

DATE: November 13, YEAR -1

Private Investigator Thomas Glendale ("Glendale") was contacted by client Emma Matheson ("Matheson") upon concerns regarding her son, Timothy Matheson, and his relationship with a certain Frances Beaumont ("Beaumont").

According to Matheson, the aforesaid concerns were in regard to Beaumont's financial situation and whether her financial affairs were sound. Matheson requested that all information regarding Beaumont be searched, but that only information relevant to her financial situation, her criminal background and her mental health be divulged.

According to Matheson, Beaumont was born on July 23, YEAR -23 in Miami, Florida. Matheson was not in possession of any other information regarding Beaumont other than her address in Sweetwater, Jefferson.

P.I. Glendale conducted an online search using the websites of all fifty state bureaus of criminal apprehension (or similar departments or bureaus), as well as the website database of the federal government. P.I. Glendale also conducted an online search of all search engines using a proprietary Internet search device that is able to disclose all online information regarding a person.

Upon completing the above-referenced searches, P.I. Glendale located the following information regarding Beaumont:

- Beaumont declared bankruptcy in YEAR -2 in Florida Bankruptcy Court. The bankruptcy was granted and no creditors objected. Beaumont's debts discharged in the bankruptcy amounted to $155,973.58 (one hundred fifty five thousand nine hundred seventy three dollars and fifty eight cents).

- Beaumont was convicted of forgery and theft by swindle in YEAR -4. She served nine months in the Pine County Jail for said crimes. The court records were closed thus preventing P.I. Glendale from accessing specific information about the crime such as the victim and the circumstances surrounding it.

- Beaumont moved to Jefferson in MONTHS -18 and has had no interactions with any law enforcement in Jefferson since moving here. It appears that she is still on probation for the offenses in Florida, although P.I. Glendale was unable to verify.

P.I. Glendale took all reasonable steps as required by licensed private investigators to verify that the information regarded the same Frances Beaumont and ascertains to the best of his professional knowledge that the individual is the same.

The investigation of Beaumont revealed no information regarding her mental health and no other information beyond what is stated above.

Defendant's File

You represent the defendant, Stray Dog Advertising, in this litigation matter and have received the following email from Senior Partner Amy Lincoln about pending litigation facing Pamela Park of Stray Dog Advertising.

From:	Amy Lincoln < a.lincoln@lawlawfirm.com >
To:	Associate Attorney < a.attorney@lawlawfirm.com >
Sent:	Jan. 13, THIS YEAR 1:02 p.m.
Re:	Defamation Matter/Pamela Park

Associate attorney,

Pamela Park of Stray Dog Advertising has come to me with a personal problem that she has encountered. Much to her surprise, she has been personally served with a complaint, filed by the ex-girlfriend of Pamela's nephew, Tim. I plan on filing a motion to dismiss with the answer, so we need to research and draft the memorandum of law in support of our motion.

I spoke on the phone with Pamela yesterday, and she shared with me the facts that I've included in this email. She also forwarded to me several emails that pertain to this matter, and I have copied them for you. It is my understanding that these emails have also been shared with Pamela's nephew's ex-girlfriend, the plaintiff. Pamela told me that her sister gave all the emails to her son, Tim, and that Tim later gave copies of them to his fiancée.

Here is what's happened: Pamela's sister and brother-in-law (Tim's parents) contacted Pamela and asked her to talk to their son, Tim, about his new girlfriend, to whom he had proposed marriage even though they had known each other only two months. Tim's parents were concerned that this woman, Fran Beaumont, was only after Tim's money (he is a successful entrepreneur with several successful bars in West Rapids) and didn't have good intentions towards their son.

Tim's parents contacted a private investigator, who did an online search about Fran and found that she had been convicted in another state for forgery and theft by swindle and had served nine months in prison for those crimes. She had also declared bankruptcy. I've also copied for you the report that this PI put together after his investigation.

Tim's parents asked Pamela to reveal this information to Tim so that he would reconsider and hopefully rescind his marriage proposal once he could see that Fran was likely just after his money. Pamela and Tim met at Union Circle Grill, a local restaurant owned by one of Stray Dog Advertising's clients, and Pamela shared with Tim the information that the private investigator had discovered about Fran and tried to dissuade him from marrying her, as her sister and brother-in-law had asked her to do.

As luck would have it, the private investigator wasn't very good at his job, and he found information about another Fran Beaumont. The Fran Beaumont that Tim was engaged to had never been in prison and never even received a speeding ticket, let alone a conviction for forgery or theft by swindle. She had also never declared bankruptcy and is in fact very thrifty.

Note the use of the past tense — "was engaged." After Pamela's meeting with her nephew, Tim confronted Fran about this information, asking her whether it was true and what her true intentions were. Fran was enraged that her boyfriend's parents would be so suspicious of her. She declared that she could never marry someone whose parents were so distrustful. She broke off the engagement and she and Tim have not spoken since.

Pamela is distraught and very upset. She says that she was only trying to help her sister and do what she thought was best for her beloved nephew. She feels like she has been caught in the middle. And now to make matters worse, she has been served with this complaint for defamation. I've attached it here for your review.

I am meeting with Pamela at the end of next week. I told her that I would prepare a litigation strategy for her. To develop that strategy, I first need your legal research and analysis skills to help me understand the issue and the law better.

Before my meeting with Pamela, I need you to prepare a legal memo for me. I would like:

- A memo that states what the issue is;
- A summary of the applicable Jefferson law;
- Your analysis of the law as it applies to the facts of Pamela's case;
- Your prediction of what you think a court will rule on the motion to dismiss; and
- Your advice to Pamela on what she should do in this litigation.

I also want you to prepare the memorandum of law in support of our motion to dismiss. Our argument will be that the communication that Pamela made to Tim about Fran was privileged and thus non-defamatory. We can also argue that she has not suffered any actual damages. I think we have good arguments and the law is in our favor.

I will also want you to do the oral arguments for this as I have depositions scheduled that same week and won't be available.

I look forward to receiving your first draft of the memo and seeing the arguments that you make. Let me know if you have any questions.

Amy

Amy Lincoln

Partner

p.s. You will see that Pamela's sister and brother-in-law have not been served and that Pamela is the sole defendant. I think that Fran served only Pamela thinking that she has deep pockets.

As you have read, you have been asked to write a summary of the client matter and prepare a memorandum of law in support of the motion to dismiss.

Lincoln has asked you to write her a predictive office memo about the following:

- A summary of what has happened between Pamela Park and Fran Beaumont
- The legal issue at hand
- A summary and analysis of the law that applies (defamation and qualified privilege)
- Your opinion about whether the communications that Pamela made about Fran were privileged
- Your advice about how to proceed with this matter

You will find complete information about this assignment on the Information Page (pages 185-186).

Second, Lincoln has asked you to prepare a persuasive memorandum of law in support of the motion to dismiss that she has filed.

The memorandum of law will include:

- A factual background of what has led to the claim against Pamela Park
- Persuasive legal arguments that the claim should be dismissed

You will find complete information about this assignment on the Information Page (pages 191-192).

Additional Skills-Building Exercises

 **Ethics Dilemma**

Overview of the Exercise: For purposes of this exercise, assume that you work for the Lincoln, Adams and Washington Law Firm and represent the defendant, Pamela Park, regardless of whether you represent the plaintiff or the defendant in this matter.

This exercise will require you to analyze whether representing Pamela individually is a conflict of interest because the LAW Law Firm already represents the corporate entity, Stray Dog Advertising, LLC, of which Pamela is the sole owner and member.

Learning Objectives of the Exercise:

This exercise will build your skills to:

- Articulate the legal rules regarding conflicts of interests with current clients and dual representation
- Apply those rules to the litigation involving Pamela Park
- Articulate and effectively communicate that analysis using appropriate legal terminology

Steps for Completing the Exercise:

- Read the following short summary of the Model Rules of Professional Conduct
- Find online the Model Rules of Professional Conduct
- By yourself, analyze whether you think the LAW Law Firm can ethically represent both Pamela and Stray Dog Advertising, LLC
- When you are done analyzing this matter, discuss your answer with a classmate. Explain to each other why you have reached the conclusion that you did
- If you and your partner have different responses, you must try to convince him or her that your answer is correct. After you both have tried to convince the other, you must choose a team answer
- Once you have discussed with your partner, you will compare answers as a class

Be sure to support your conclusion with adequate reasoning and analysis and that you avoid conclusory statements (i.e. conclusions without any analysis to explain why or how you reached that conclusion).

Research and Background for the Exercise:

Rule 1.13 of the Model Rules of Professional Conduct regulates the conduct of attorneys whose clients are corporations or other legal entities and/or organizations. Since a corporate attorney deals with the individuals that work within the company, it is often easy to forget that the organization itself, and not the individuals, is the real client whose interests the attorney must protect and serve.

As has happened in this Unit, attorneys representing corporations or organizations are often called on to represent individuals working within the entity. The question that then arises is whether the Rules of Professional Conduct permit this dual representation. To begin analyzing this matter, you will need to find Rule 1.13 of the Model Rules of Professional Conduct. As you will learn when you find the Rule, dual representation of a corporate client is permitted, subject to the provisions of Rule 1.7, which deals with conflicts of interests for current clients. Thus, you will need to find both Rules to complete this ethics dilemma exercise.

Be sure that you also review the comments that accompany the Rules as the comments provide useful insight into the Rules and their application.

Grading: This exercise is not graded. Instead, you will discuss the matter with a partner or in a small group and then share your conclusions with the rest of the class.

Defamation Analysis Exercise

Overview of the Exercise: The following short fact patterns deal with defamation, and your task is to analyze the fact patterns to determine whether or not the speech in question would be considered defamatory.

Learning Objectives of the Exercise:

This exercise will build your skills to:

- Articulate the legal rules regarding defamation and freedom of speech
- Apply those rules to fact patterns and analyze the facts and the law
- Articulate and effectively communicate that analysis using legal terminology

Steps for Completing the Exercise:

- Read the following fact patterns.
- By yourself, analyze each one and decide whether or not you think the statements are defamatory and why. You don't need to write out a full answer, but jot down notes about your reasoning.
- When have finished analyzing each of the fact patterns, discuss your answers with the partner that you have been assigned. Explain to each other why you have reached the conclusion that you did.
- If you and your partner have different responses to a fact pattern, you must try to convince him or her that your answer is correct. After you both have tried to convince the other, you must choose a team answer.
- Once you have discussed each of the fact patterns, you will compare answers as a class.

Research for the Exercise:
You are not required to do any research for this exercise. However, doing research of cases and secondary sources on the legal research websites is always good practice. Some helpful search terms have been included for you after each short fact pattern so that you can improve your research skills.

If you search for case law, it is suggested that you limit your search to one jurisdiction. To narrow your results and not be overwhelmed with the number of cases in the search results, choose a state. Since the cases included with this Unit are from New York, you might choose to continue researching New York law. Your results will also be more uniform than if you conduct a 50-state search since there can be variations and differences between how states analyze defamation matters.

Grading:
This exercise is not graded. Instead you will compare answers with your classmates once you have finished analyzing the fact patterns.

1.   After a night out at a local restaurant, you decide to write a review on a website that publishes reviews about businesses and service providers. You were not satisfied with the food, the service or the restaurant in general, and you want other people to know this before they waste their hard-earned money at this restaurant.

This is your review:

Save your money and don't go to Tom's Burger Joint! The hamburgers are the worst I've ever eaten. My cheeseburger had a strange smell to it and I think the meat was rancid and the cheese moldy! I am sure that there were mice or some other rodents in the kitchen. I looked over and was sure I saw something running across the kitchen floor! Our server was rude and left us waiting for the check for 30 minutes after we asked for it. Save your time, money and health and avoid Tom's!

Tom's Burger Joint's attorney has sent you a cease and desist letter, demanding that you remove the review immediately. If you refuse, she has threatened to file a defamation claim against you. You really did think (but weren't sure) that you saw a mouse run across the floor, and although the cheeseburger tasted bad and was way overcooked, you don't know for sure that the meat was rancid or the cheese moldy.

- Is your review protected, or is it defamation? Explain your answer.
- Suggested search terms: defamation /s opinion[64]

2.   Polly is the manager at Tom's Burger Joint. One of her servers, Ron, walked off the job (i.e. quit during the middle of a shift). Polly wasn't surprised since he was a poor worker, often late and slow. Polly received a phone call from a prospective employer, asking for a reference for Ron. Polly told the individual that Ron was "lazy," "unreliable" and "dishonest." Ron had never stolen from Polly or the restaurant, but Polly believes that a person who doesn't take seriously his job responsibilities is simply unethical. Polly has a very strong work ethic. Because of Polly's reference, Ron was not hired for the new job.

Tom's Burger Joint has now been served with a defamation claim, alleging that Polly's statements about Ron were defamatory and that Ron has suffered damages from the lost wages that he would have earned if he were hired for the position. He was qualified for the job and wasn't hired because of Polly's reference.

- Are Polly's statements protected under an employer's privilege? Why or why not?
- Suggested search terms: defamation /s employe! /p privilege[65]

3.   Tom's Burger Joint has been served with another defamation complaint, this time because of statements that a customer claims another server, Andrea, made about him. According to the complaint, Andrea made racist comments about the customer and his wife, calling them "damn immigrants" and telling them to "speak in English (they were speaking in their mother tongue), return to their home country and get the heck out of the US."

- Are Andrea's statements defamatory?
- If they are, are they protected under the employer privilege?

4.   Juan has recently gone on a diet and begun working out and as a result of his efforts, has lost nearly 80 pounds. He posted on his Facebook profile a recent picture of him showing off his new physique. One of his elementary school "friends" responded to the picture, writing "Hey, Juan, man you've gotten skinny. What'd you do, get AIDS or something? Gain some weight back, man!" Many friends and acquaintances read the post before Juan was able to delete it.

Juan plans to speak to an attorney this week to see whether he should file a defamation complaint against this "friend," whom he has now defriended.

- What would you advise Juan to do?
- Was the statement defamatory? Why or why not?
- Suggested search terms: "defamation per se"

5.   Steve Saunders is a political cartoonist who works for the Jefferson City Times, the daily newspaper in Jefferson City. His cartoons are satirical and poke fun at politicians and other public figures in Jefferson. Last week, he drew a cartoon of Mary Ellen De Soto, one of the justices of the Jefferson Supreme Court, depicting her in a bikini at the beach in front of a polluted lake. The cartoon was in response to a decision the court had recently issued, holding unconstitutional a certain environmental law, and Saunders wanted to underscore what he believed was a poor judicial decision and the hypocrisy of her decision.

De Soto has approached you about filing a defamation claim against the Jefferson City Times and against Saunders individually because she has felt extreme embarrassment over the cartoon, which she feels has damaged her professional reputation as a supreme court justice.

- Can Saunders be held liable for defamation for his satirical cartoon? Why or why not?
- Suggested search terms: "public figure" /s defamation. Be sure to include in your search US Supreme Court cases.

---

[64]   Writing search terms in this way will limit your search results. The "/s" means that you want to locate cases that have the words *defamation* and *opinion* within the same sentence. If you put "/p" instead, you will locate cases that have those two words within the same paragraph. Limiting your search results can be helpful, but you also don't want to limit the search terms so much that relevant cases aren't included in the search results.

[65]   Using an exclamation point is another tip for doing searches. When you put an exclamation point at the end of the word allows you to search for the root word and terms that can be created by adding a letter (or letters) to the end of the root (here for example, the exclamation point is in place of the "r" for employer or the "e" for employee). By using the search terms "employe!/s defamation," you are telling the search engine to locate cases or sources with both employer *and* employee in the same sentence as defamation, and within the same paragraph as privilege. Using the exclamation point saves you from doing one search with "employer" and another with "employee."

Third-Party Defendant

Overview of the Exercise: The exercise will require you to analyze Rule 14 of the Federal Rules of Civil Procedure, which deals with third-party practice. Third-party practice is when the defendant in a lawsuit files a separate claim against a third party who to that point, is not involved in the litigation. The defendant believes that this person is liable for the losses that the plaintiff claims to have suffered and brings him into the action to assess liability on him.[66]

The defendant becomes the third-party plaintiff (because he is suing another person) and the new defendant becomes the third-party defendant. In turn the third-party defendant can file a claim against another individual if he believes that person is liable for the losses. The third-party defendant is now also the fourth-party plaintiff, and the person that he sues is the fourth-party defendant, who can also file a claim against another individual who becomes the fifth-party defendant, and the fourth-party defendant is also the fifth-party plaintiff....and so on and so on.[67] It can become confusing and drawing a graphic can help to keep it all straight:

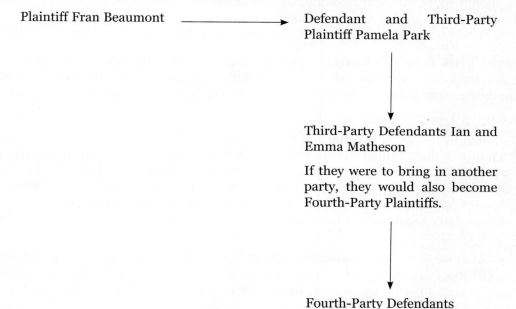

Plaintiff Fran Beaumont → Defendant and Third-Party Plaintiff Pamela Park

Third-Party Defendants Ian and Emma Matheson

If they were to bring in another party, they would also become Fourth-Party Plaintiffs.

Fourth-Party Defendants

For this exercise, you will analyze:

1. Whether the Rules of Civil Procedure allow Pamela to bring a third-party complaint against her sister and brother-in-law,
2. Whether you would advise Pamela to bring the third-party claim against them,
3. If you would so advise her, what claims would you bring, and
4. What steps you should take to bring the claim.

Presume that you are making this assessment and deciding whether to file a third-party complaint against Ian and Emma twenty-nine days after you served and filed the answer on Fran Beaumont.

---

[66] Don't confuse third-party practice with *counterclaims*, which are those that the defendant brings against the plaintiff, or with *crossclaims*, which are those that one defendant brings against another defendant in the same matter. Rule 13 of the Federal Rules of Civil Procedure deals with counter and crossclaims.

[67] In federal and state court decisions (at least those on Westlaw), the case with the most named third-parties is <u>Ceiling Specialties Co. v. Reginald Wong & Wong & Co.</u>, No. 42077, 1980 WL 355376 (Ohio Ct. App. Nov. 20, 1980). The court notes that during the litigation, the plaintiff filed a complaint against an eleventh-party defendant.

In addition, do not consider whether you represent Fran Beaumont or Pamela Park for the Unit. All student-attorneys should complete this exercise regardless of who their client is.

Learning Objectives of the Exercise:

This exercise will build your skills to:

- Articulate the legal rules regarding third-party practice under the Federal Rules of Civil Procedure
- Apply those rules to our fact pattern and analyze the facts and the law, as well as non-legal reasons for taking action in litigation
- Articulate and effectively communicate that analysis using appropriate legal terminology

Steps for Completing the Exercise:

- Read Rule 14 (below) of the Federal Rules of Civil Procedure.
- By yourself, analyze the rule and make an initial assessment of the above questions 1–4.
- When you are done analyzing, discuss your answers with the partner that you have been assigned. Explain to each other why you have reached the conclusion that you did.
- If you and your partner have different responses to any of the above questions or to what you think Pamela should do, you must try to convince him or her that your answer is correct. After you both have tried to convince the other, you must choose a team answer.
- Once you have discussed each of the fact patterns, you will compare answers as a class.

Research For This Assignment: You are not required to do any outside research for this assignment, but you must first read and review the relevant part of Rule 14 of the Federal Rules of Civil Procedure. While you are reading the rule, pay particular attention to what the parties must do, as compared to what they may do.

Federal Rules of Civil Procedure, Rule 14

(a) When a Defending Party May Bring in a Third Party.

    (1) Timing of the Summons and Complaint. A defending party may, as third-party plaintiff, serve a summons and complaint on a nonparty who is or may be liable to it for all or part of the claim against it. But the third-party plaintiff must, by motion, obtain the court's leave if it files the third-party complaint more than 14 days after serving its original answer.

    (2) Third-Party Defendant's Claims and Defenses. The person served with the summons and third-party complaint—the "third-party defendant":

        (A) must assert any defense against the third-party plaintiff's claim under Rule 12;

        (B) must assert any counterclaim against the third-party plaintiff under Rule 13a, and may assert any counterclaim against the third-party plaintiff under Rule 13(b) or any crossclaim against another third-party defendant under Rule 13(g);

        (C) may assert against the plaintiff any defense that the third-party plaintiff has to the plaintiff's claim; and

        (D) may also assert against the plaintiff any claim arising out of the transaction or occurrence that is the subject matter of the plaintiff's claim against the third-party plaintiff.

    (3) Plaintiff's Claims Against a Third-Party Defendant. The plaintiff may assert against the third-party defendant any claim arising out of the transaction or occurrence that is the subject matter of the plaintiff's claim against the third-party plaintiff. The third-party defendant must then assert any defense under Rule 12 and any counterclaim under Rule 13(a), and may assert any counterclaim under Rule 13(b) or any crossclaim under Rule 13(g).

Grading: This assignment is not graded. Instead, you will compare your answers to those of your classmates.

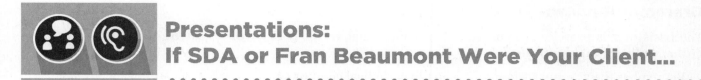

Presentations:
If SDA or Fran Beaumont Were Your Client...

Overview of the Exercise: For this exercise, you will make a professional presentation in which you answer and discuss the following question:

If Stray Dog Advertising were your client in your home country and if Pamela came to you for legal advice about the defamation complaint, what would you do and what advice would you give her?

OR

If Fran Beaumont were your client in your home country and came to you for advice about the statements that Pamela Park made about her, what would you do and what advice would you give her?

You will do the presentation based on the client whom you represent.

Learning Objectives of the Exercise:

This exercise will build your skills to:

- Describe a specific aspect of your country's legal system
- Compare and contrast your country's legal system with the U.S. legal system
- Understand your classmates' presentations and extrapolate information from the presentations

Steps for Completing the Exercise:

- Analyze the <u>Beaumont v. Park</u> fact pattern under your country's laws.
- Determine whether or not Fran Beaumont would have a viable claim under your country's laws, and whether Pamela Park could raise any viable defenses against the defamation claim.
- Explain what other claims Fran could bring (if any) or Pamela could bring against Fran (if any) and explain how her case would be handled in your country's legal system.
- Explain what legal advice you would give Pamela or Fran if she came to you for legal advice in your home country.

Research Required: The research you are required to do depends on your knowledge of these claims in your country's legal system. It is presumed that you are familiar with the law and with how you would approach this issue if Pamela were a client of yours.

Grading: This presentation is not graded. You will present to a small group of your fellow classmates instead of to the entire class.

Handouts:

As part of your presentation, you must create a handout for your classmates, and the handouts must include fill-in-the-blank questions that your classmates must complete with information that you present during the presentation. Each handout must include at least five questions to complete.

For example, if a U.S. law student were giving a presentation on defamation in the United States he could include on his handout this question:

To successfully bring a defamation claim, a plaintiff must establish three elements:

1._____

2._____

3. _____

As you are speaking, your classmates will have to listen, follow what you are saying and fill in the blanks. If you are listening to a classmate's presentations and are unsure about an answer, you should ask him or her to repeat so you can fill in the blank(s).

Grammar Review:

The basis of this exercise is hypothetical or conditional verbs: *if SDA or Fran Beaumont were your client, what would you do?*

Remember the grammar when discussing hypothetical conditions.

Present: **IF + PAST SIMPLE, WOULD + BASE VERB**

*If Pamela **called** me to schedule an appointment, I **would tell** her to visit me at my office.*

NOTE: We use "were" for all tenses with the verb "to be" when using a conditional verb.

*If I **were** you, I **would not take** that class.*

*If Pamela **were** my client, I **would tell** her that Fran Beaumont would probably be unsuccessful in bringing her claim.*

Past: **IF + PAST PERFECT, WOULD + HAVE + PAST PARTICIPLE**

*If Emma and Tim **had discussed** this matter with Fran rather than involving Pamela, they **would have saved** Pamela a lot of headaches.*

*If Fran **had** really **been convicted** of a crime, she probably **would not have been able** to leave Florida because of the terms of her probation.*

Information Pages

Office Memo: Defamation

• •

Overview of the Assignment: For this assignment, you will write an office memo to the Senior Partner, summarizing your research on defamation and providing your prediction of what will happen in the litigation.

Learning Objectives of the Assignment:

This assignment will build your skills to:

- Efficiently communicate in a written format
- Explain complex matters clearly and concisely
- Analyze and apply the rules of law regarding defamation

Research for the Assignment: You are not required to do any outside research for this assignment. You should base your analysis on the New York defamation cases that you have read in class:

- <u>Herlihy v. The Metropolitan Museum of Art</u>, 633 N.Y.S.2d 106 (N.Y. App. Div. 1995).
- <u>Baldwin v. Shell Oil Co.</u>, 419 N.Y.S.2d 752 (N.Y. App. Div. 1979).
- <u>Buckley v. Litman</u>, 443 N.E.2d 469 (N.Y. 1982).
- <u>Byam v. Collins</u>, 19 N.E. 75 (N.Y. 1888).
- <u>Van Wyck v. Aspinwall</u>, 17 N.E. 190 (N.Y. 1858).

If you want to practice your legal research skills, you can look for and use other cases that you find. However, if you do search on Westlaw, LexisNexis or Bloomberg Law, be sure to limit your search and the cases you use to New York law and remember to change the citations to Jefferson.

Format of the Completed Assignment:

Your response should be in an office memo format and should include the following:

- Summary of the facts
- The relevant law
- Analysis of the law to the fact pattern
- Conclusion about how you think a court would rule if this matter were to go to court
- Your advice to the client about how to proceed

Follow the following format:

- 1 inch (2.54 cm.) margins (top/bottom and sides)
- 12 font, Times New Roman font
- Double spaced
- Maximum eight pages

Notes:

This memo should be predictive and not persuasive. You are not trying to persuade the senior partner or the client about the strength of your arguments or urge him or her to take a particular course of action; you are only trying to inform about the law, how it applies to our case, how you think a court would rule and what advice you have.

In a memo, you can also use formatting like underlining, bold font or italics. You can also create headings and subheadings to organize your answer.

For additional information about office memos and e-memos, as well as samples, refer to the online additional resources.

Grading: This assignment is worth 102 points.

Defamation

Unit 2

LEGAL CONTENT	0-6 points	8 points	10 points	12 points	Points
Issue statement (IS)	Document does not include an IS or includes IS that fails to properly identify the legal issue(s) and the applicable law	Identifies the legal issue(s) and correctly states the applicable law with minor mistakes	Identifies the legal issue(s) and correctly states the applicable law	Identifies the legal issue(s) and correctly states the applicable law in an exceptionally creative and concise way	_____/12
Short Answer	Document does not include a short answer or includes a short answer with significant mistakes	Responds to IS but with key facts or applicable legal principles missing	Responds to IS with key facts and applicable legal principles with no meaningful errors	Clearly and concisely responds to IS with key facts and applicable legal principles and no irrelevancies	_____/12
Facts	Few or none of the relevant facts are included; difficult to follow or understand	Most relevant facts are included as well as non-relevant ones; at times difficult to follow	Relevant facts are included with occasional irrelevancies; easy to follow	All relevant facts are included with no irrelevancies; story is clearly and concisely told to reader in objective way	_____/12
Rule	Hard to follow and understand; does not include relevant sources or cites inappropriate sources; no rule application	Cites to some relevant sources but is incomplete in covering all relevant aspects of the rule; includes some rule application	Cite only to relevant sources and mostly clear; rule application explains but not fully how rule has been applied	Clear and concise; includes only relevant sources and includes all parts of rule necessary for analysis; clear rule application	_____/12
Analysis	Contains conclusory statements and/or no case law; facts are analyzed in a conclusory or insufficient way	Uses some case law but does not analogize or distinguish or explain its application; some conclusory statements; facts briefly analyzed	Uses case law to show how rule applies to case; case law is compared and contrasted with success; most facts are analyzed	Analyzes case law completely, comparing it fully to client matter; facts are thoroughly analyzed in an objective way	_____/12
Conclusion/ Recommendations	No conclusion or recommendations are included in document	A brief conclusion is included but without sufficient client advice	Paper includes conclusion and recommendations	Paper includes full conclusion of the legal analysis and facts and presents creative and thoughtful recommendations	_____/12
Citations	No sources are cited in document	Some sources are cited, but inconsistently; citation format is inconsistent	All citations are present; correct format is mostly used	All citations are present; correct format is used throughout document	_____/12
WRITING	**2**	**4**	**5**	**6**	**Points**
Formatting	Document does not follow format instructions or the sample provided	Document attempts to follow instructions and sample provided	Document follows the instructions and sample provided with no meaningful errors	Document exactly follows the instructions and sample provided	_____/6
Organization	No structure or organization; free flow of ideas	Structure & organization present but reorganization or headings needed for full clarity	Document is clearly organized and structured with proper use of heading and subheadings	Document is exceptionally well organized and structured with proper use of headings and subheadings	_____/6
Syntax Mechanics	Contains numerous and distracting grammatical and mechanical errors that impede understanding	Contains some grammatical and mechanical errors that impede understanding	Contains few grammatical and mechanical errors but none that impede understanding	Contains no grammatical and mechanical errors; native-like use of English	_____/6
TOTAL					_____/102

Mock Client Meeting
with Pamela Park or Fran Beaumont

Overview of the Assignment: This assignment simulates a client meeting between you and your client, Pamela Park of Stray Dog Advertising, LLC or Fran Beaumont.

For this exercise, you will meet with your client and explain to her the status of the litigation <u>Beaumont v. Park</u>, the results of your analysis about how a court might rule on the motion to dismiss and your recommendations on how to proceed.

Learning Objectives of the Assignment:

This assignment will build your skills to:

- Explain and clarify the legal positions of the parties and describe potential outcomes to your client
- Respond to technical questions about litigation and defamation
- Incorporate technical legal English vocabulary that relates to defamation and use appropriate layperson explanations for your client

Steps for Completing the Assignment:

- Read and be familiar with the Main Assignment File
- Be familiar with the defamation cases that you have been assigned
- Recommended:
    - Anticipate the questions that you think your client might ask and prepare possible responses
    - Draft an outline of what you would like to cover in the meeting

Note: Remember that part of the grading is also based on your professional demeanor. You are expected to arrive punctually, be dressed in professional attire and act as you would with a client in real life. You should play the part from when you come into the meeting room.

Grading: This assignment worth 102 points.

Punctuality: Student-attorney arrived on time to meeting: YES _____ (10 points) NO _____ (0 points)

Professional Attire: Student-attorney was dressed in appropriate professional attire: YES _____ (10 points) NO _____ (0 points)

Professional Demeanor: Student-attorney acted in a professional manner w/ client: YES _____ (10 points) NO _____ (0 points)

GRADING CRITERIA	0- 6 points	8 points (C or 75%)	10 points (B or 85%)	12 points	Points received
Engagement I (questions)	Attorney does not ask client any questions; engages in monologue	Attorney asks few questions; questions are hard to follow or show minimal preparation or understanding of matter	Attorney asks basic questions that demonstrate understanding of matter and preparation	Attorney asks thoughtful, insightful and creative questions that demonstrate deep preparation & understanding of matter	_____/12
Engagement II (answers)	Attorney does not respond to client's questions	Attorney responds to questions, but incorrectly or with hard to follow answers	Attorney responds promptly and correctly to all of client's questions	Attorney responds promptly and correctly to all of client's questions with creative, thoughtful and insightful answers that show a deep understanding of the issues	_____/12
Knowledge of Applicable Law	Attorney provides no explanation of the applicable law	Attorney provides explanation of with serious mistakes, or hard to follow (e.g. use of legal jargon)	Attorney provides clear explanation of with some mistakes; uses some legal jargon unnecessarily or without explanations that client can understand	Attorney provides clear, concise and correct explanation of the law with legal jargon when appropriate or w/ explanations client can understand	_____/12
Ability to Analyze Applicable Law	Attorney provides does not provide an analysis of the law for the client	Attorney attempts to analyze the law but provides incomplete or incorrect analysis	Attorney provides analysis of the law with no significant mistakes or misstatements of the law or facts	Attorney provides a clear, concise and correct analysis of the law as it applies to the client matter	_____/12
Advice and Recommendations	Attorney provides no advice or poor advice for client	Attorney provides not comprehensive or inaccurate advice	Attorney provides comprehensive and accurate advice to client on his/her legal matter	Attorney provides thoughtful and creative solutions for client	_____/12
Organization	Meeting is disorganized and hard to follow or lacks any organization	Meeting has some organization but is still confusing for client for how information is presented	Meeting is clearly organized and easy to follow	Meeting is clearly organized and is easy to follow; attorney takes extra steps to ensure client's understanding	_____/12
TOTAL					_____/72
TOTAL FROM PUNCTUALITY AND PROFESSIONALISM					_____/30

Total   _____/102

Client Advice Letter

Overview of the Assignment: For this assignment, you will write an advice and follow-up letter to your client (Pamela Park or Fran Beaumont), summarizing your research on defamation, as well as your meeting with her. You should also give recommendations to Park or Beaumont on how she should approach this matter. Be mindful that even though your client may be a sophisticated and experienced professional, she is not a trained attorney. Therefore you should avoid legalese in your letter.

Under Rule 1.4(a)(3) of the Model Rules of Professional Conduct, an attorney has the duty to keep his or her client "reasonably informed about the status of the client's matter." A thorough follow-up letter after a client meeting is one of the best ways to meet this duty, as well as regular phone calls, emails or meetings.

Learning Objectives of the Assignment:

This assignment will build your skills to:

- Efficiently communicate in a written format
- Explain complex matters clearly and concisely
- Incorporate technical legal English vocabulary that relates to defamation and use appropriate layperson explanations for client

Steps for Completing the Assignment:

- Review the predictive memo that you wrote to your senior partner about your client matter to ensure that the law and the issues are clear
- Be familiar with the case law regarding defamation and motions to dismiss, as well as the fact pattern
- Conduct your client meeting with your client, Pamela Park or Frances Beaumont
- Review the Business Correspondence online resources

Research Required for the Assignment: You are not required to do any outside research for this assignment.

Format of the Completed Assignment:

Your assignment should be written as a business letter, not as an email. Even though many firms and lawyers use email for much of the correspondence carried out, formal business letters are still an essential part of the practice of law.

Your law firm has the following policy regarding business correspondence. Your client letter must follow the policy guidelines.

LAW FIRM CORRESPONDENCE POLICY

The purpose of this policy is to ensure a uniform appearance of all business correspondence that is written by the attorneys and staff of the law firm and thus to increase the professional appearance of the firm's work product. All law firm attorneys and staff are required to follow these guidelines when writing correspondence. Violation of the policy can result in disciplinary action, up to and including termination.

- The first page of all "traditional" letters must be written on law firm letterhead, which includes the firm's address and logo
- All letters must be written in a modified block letter format
- Letters must be written in Times New Roman, 12 font
- Letters must be 1.5 spaced and have 1" (2.54 cm.) margins, except for the initial page, which may have larger top margins to account for the logo, law firm address and sender's direct contact information
- Client letters must not exceed four pages

Grading: This assignment is worth 78 points.

Note: See the Online Additional Resources for examples of letters and for general information about business correspondence.

Unit 2 Defamation

LEGAL CONTENT	0-6 points (failing)	8 points (C or 75%)	10 points (B or 85%)	12 points	Points
Introduction	Letter does not include an appropriate introduction or includes poorly constructed one	Letter includes introduction that states purpose with some irrelevancies or some relevant information missing	Introduction states purpose of letter and includes other relevant information	Introduction is engaging; states purpose of letter and includes other relevant information; written clearly and concisely	____/12
Summary of Meeting	Letter includes no summary of the meeting	Letter includes summary but leaves out important information or states it unclearly	Letter summarizes the meeting but leaves out important information	Letter clearly and concisely summarizes the meeting, its core purpose and content	____/12
Applicable Law	Student-attorney provides no explanation of the applicable law, or only uses legal jargon in explanation (inappropriate for audience)	Student-attorney provides explanation of with serious mistakes, or hard to follow (use of legal jargon)	Student-attorney provides clear explanation of with few mistakes; uses some legal jargon without appropriate explanations	Student-attorney provides clear, concise and correct explanation of the law with legal jargon with appropriate explanations	____/12
Analysis	Contains conclusory statements and/or no case law; facts are analyzed in a conclusory or insufficient way	Uses some case law but does not analogize or distinguish or explain its application; some conclusory statements; facts briefly analyzed	Uses case law to show how rule applies to case; case law is compared and contrasted with success; most facts are analyzed	Analyzes completely case law, comparing it fully to client matter; facts are thoroughly analyzed	____/12
Conclusion/ Recommendations	No conclusion or recommendations are included in letter	A brief conclusion is included but without sufficient advice or recommendations advice or next steps	Letter includes conclusion with recommendations and next steps	Letter includes full conclusion of the legal analysis and facts, presents creative and thoughtful recommendations and includes clear next steps	____/12
WRITING	**2**	**4**	**5**	**6**	**Points**
Formatting	Document does not follow format instructions or the sample provided	Document attempts to follow instructions and sample provided	Document follows the instructions and sample provided with minor errors	Document exactly follows the instructions and sample provided	____/6
Organization	No structure or organization; free flow of ideas	Letter includes organization and structure but is still confusing	Structure and organization but some reorganization is needed for full clarity	Document is clearly organized and structured	____/6
Syntax Mechanics	Contains numerous and distracting grammatical and mechanical errors that impede understanding	Contains some grammatical and mechanical errors that impede understanding	Contains few grammatical and mechanical errors but none that impede understanding	Contains no grammatical and mechanical errors; native-like use of English	____/6
TOTAL					____/78

Memorandum of Law for Motion to Dismiss

Overview of the Assignment: You have been asked to prepare the memorandum of law in opposition to or in support of the motion to dismiss in the litigation that Fran Beaumont has commenced against Pamela Park.

Learning Objectives of the Assignment:

This assignment will build your skills to:

- Efficiently read and understand legal authority
- Analyze the fact pattern by applying the relevant case law
- Adapt the IRAC organization and the formal memorandum of law structure
- Communicate effectively and in a persuasive manner to convince the court and the reader that your client's position and argument is the one to follow

Research for the Assignment: You are not required to do any outside research for this assignment. You should base your analysis on the New York defamation cases that you have read in class:

- Herlihy v. The Metropolitan Museum of Art, 633 N.Y.S.2d 106 (N.Y. App. Div. 1995).
- Baldwin v. Shell Oil Co., 419 N.Y.S.2d 752 (N.Y. App. Div. 1979).
- Buckley v. Litman, 443 N.E.2d 469 (N.Y. 1982).
- Byam v. Collins, 19 N.E. 75 (N.Y. 1888).
- Van Wyck v. Aspinwall, 17 N.E. 190 (N.Y. 1858).

If you want to practice your legal research skills, you can look for and use other cases that you find. However, if you do search on Westlaw, LexisNexis or Bloomberg Law, be sure to limit your search and the cases you use to New York law and remember to change the citations to Jefferson law as indicated in the introduction.

Format of the Completed Assignment:

For your completed assignment, you must follow Local Rule 5.2 of the Courts of Jefferson.

Local Rule 5.2 GENERAL FORMAT OF DOCUMENTS TO BE FILED

Format: All documents filed must be typewritten, printed, or prepared by a clearly legible duplication process. Document text must be double-spaced, except for quoted material and footnotes, and pages must be numbered consecutively at the bottom. Documents filed after the case-initiating document must contain—on the front page and above the document's title—the case number and the name or initials of the assigned district judge and magistrate judge.

Represented Parties. A memorandum of law filed by a represented party must be typewritten. All text in the memorandum, including footnotes, must be set in at least font size 12 (i.e., a 12-point font) as font sizes are designated in the word-processing software used to prepare the memorandum. Text must be double-spaced, with these exceptions: headings and footnotes may be single-spaced, and quotations more than two lines long may be indented and single-spaced. Pages must be 8 ½ by 11 inches in size, and no text — except for page numbers — may appear outside an area measuring 6 ½ by 9 inches.

Length: No memorandum filed with the court shall exceed the length of twelve pages, excluding caption and table of contents.

Grading: This assignment is worth 90 points.

Note: See the online resources for additional information about memoranda of law and persuasive writing.

Section II

Intermediate Legal Issues

Unit 2   Defamation

LEGAL CONTENT	0-6 points	8 points	10 points	12 points	Points
Introduction	Document does not include an Introduction or includes issue statement instead	Introduction is not persuasive or does not include persuasive or relevant facts or the law	Student attempts to make introduction persuasive, to "put the spin" but does not include all facts or something...	Introduction is persuasive, clear and concise and clearly introduces reader to the client's story and position and identifies the relief sought	____/12
Facts	Few or none of the relevant facts are included; difficult to follow or understand	Relevant facts are included as well as non-relevant ones; mostly clear	Relevant facts are included; factual background is mostly clear and easy to follow with few irrelevancies	Relevant facts are included with no irrelevant facts; story is clearly and concisely told to reader in persuasive way	____/12
Rule	Hard to follow and understand; does not include relevant sources or cites inappropriate sources; no rule application	Cites to some relevant sources but is incomplete in covering all relevant aspects of the rule	Cite only to relevant sources; rule application explains but not fully how rule has been applied	Clear and concise; includes only relevant sources and includes all parts of rule necessary for analysis; clear rule application	____/12
Argument	Contains conclusory statements and/ or no case law; facts are analyzed in a conclusory or insufficient way	Uses some case law but does not analogize or distinguish or explain its application; some conclusory statements; facts briefly analyzed; student attempts to make persuasive arguments	Uses case law to show how rule applies to case; case law is compared and contrasted with success; facts are analyzed and argued in a persuasive way	Analyzes completely case law, comparing it fully to client matter; all facts are thoroughly analyzed and argued in a very persuasive way	____/12
Conclusion	No conclusion is included in document	A brief conclusion is included but unclear relief sought	Paper includes conclusion with relief sought	Paper includes full conclusion of the legal analysis and facts and persuasively argues for relief sought	____/12
Citations	No sources are cited in document or citation formats are incorrect and inconsistent	Sources are cited, but inconsistently; citation format has meaningful mistakes in format	Citations are complete; few meaningful mistakes in format	No mistakes in citations; correct format is used throughout document	____/12
WRITING	2	4	5	6	Points
Formatting	Document does not follow format instructions or the sample provided	Document attempts to follow instructions and sample provided	Document follows the instructions and sample provided with minor errors	Document exactly follows the instructions and sample provided	____/6
Organization	No structure or organization; free flow of ideas	Document includes some organization and structure but is still confusing; no use of headings or subheadings	Structure & organization present but reorganization needed full clarity; subheadings included but not effectively persuasive	Document is clearly organized and structured with proper use of persuasive heading and subheadings	____/6
Syntax Mechanics	Contains numerous and distracting grammatical and mechanical errors that impede understanding	Contains some grammatical and mechanical errors that impede understanding	Contains few grammatical and mechanical errors but none that impede understanding	Contains no grammatical and mechanical errors; native-like use of English	____/6
TOTAL					____/90

Mock Oral Argument

Overview of the Assignment: For this assignment, you will present oral arguments to the court on behalf of your client and persuade the court that the motion to dismiss filed by Pamela Park should be granted or dismissed, depending on which party you represent.

You will represent the party that your instructor has assigned to you.

Learning Objectives of the Assignment:

This assignment will build your skills to:

- Effectively and persuasively communicate legal rules and argument
- Conduct yourself orally in a professional courtroom setting
- Respond to questions about the relevant law

Steps for Completing the Assignment:

Before the oral arguments, review the following:

- Pleadings
- Notice of Motion and Motion to Dismiss
- Your Memorandum of Law, as well as that of your opposing counsel
- Cases cited in your memo and opposing counsel's
- Facts of the client matter

Research for the Assignment: Although no additional research is required for the assignment, you should review the memorandum of your opposing counsel and review the cases that he/she includes, consider how you can rebut the cases, or explain how they are inapposite to the matter at hand and address those cases in your oral argument.

Format of the Assignment:

Each side has 20 minutes for his or her argument. The moving party first presents his/her arguments and may reserve time for rebuttal. It is the moving party's decision to reserve time for rebuttal. After the moving party has presented his/her arguments, it is the non-moving party's turn. The non-moving party does not receive time for rebuttal since he/she can listen to opposing counsel and respond directly to any arguments made. After the non-moving party finishes, the moving party responds with rebuttal, if he/she previously asked the court to reserve time for it.

Be prepared to answer questions from the court, and part of your preparation should be anticipating the questions that the judge might ask and preparing answers. But in the event that the judge doesn't ask questions or asks few, be prepared to fill the time allotted with your argument.

Grading: This assignment is worth 90 points.

Punctuality: Attorney arrived on time to oral argument: YES _____ (10 points) NO _____ (0 points)

Professional Attire: Attorney was dressed in appropriate professional attire: YES _____ (10 points) NO _____ (0 points)

Professional Demeanor: Attorney acted in a professional manner w/court and opposing counsel: YES _____ (10 points) NO _____ (0 points)

GRADING CRITERIA	0-6 points (failing)	8 points (C or 75%)	10 points (B or 85%)	12 points	Points received
Engagement	Attorney does not respond to the court's questions	Attorney responds to questions, but incorrectly or with hard to follow answers	Attorney responds promptly and correctly to all of the court's questions	Attorney responds promptly and correctly to all of court's questions with creative, thoughtful and insightful answers that show a deep understanding of the issues	_____/12
Knowledge of Applicable Law	Attorney provides no explanation of the applicable law	Attorney provides explanation of with few meaningful mistakes or with explanation that is hard to follow	Attorney provides clear explanation of the law with no meaningful mistakes	Attorney provides clear, concise and correct explanation of the law	_____/12
Analysis of Applicable Law	Attorney provides no analysis of the law or provides analysis that is incorrect or incomplete	Attorney provides analysis of the law but has some mistakes or misstatements of the law or facts	Attorney provides a clear, concise and correct analysis of the law as it applies to the client matter	Attorney present unimpeachable case for the client, analyzing persuasively, concisely and clearly the law as it applies to client matter	_____/12
Conclusion and Relief	Attorney does not identify relief sought or conclude argument	Attorney provides advice, but	Attorney provides advice but	Attorney clearly identifies the relief sought and summarizes the client's position	_____/12
Organization	Argument is disorganized and has serious faults of organization	Argument has minor faults of organization	Argument is clearly organized and easy to follow	Argument is exceptionally well organized and presents arguments in novel way	_____/12
TOTAL					_____/60
TOTAL FROM PUNCTUALITY AND PROFESSIONALISM					_____/30

TOTAL _____/90

Statutory Law
State Constitutional Right to Privacy

For this Unit, you will write a persuasive memorandum of law in support of or in opposition to a motion for a preliminary injunction in litigation involving the City of Longworth, which the Lincoln, Adams and Washington Law Firm represents, and a group of residents from that same city who are represented by the Anthony Ross Tubman law firm. The lawsuit challenges the constitutionality of an ordinance that the City recently passed. You will represent either the City as the defendant, or the plaintiff-residents. The legal issue involved is right to privacy under the Jefferson state constitution.

Regardless of whether you represent the plaintiff or the defendant, both sides have the same documents available to them, and no information is confidential or available to only one side.

Learning Objectives of this Unit:

This Unit will build your skills to:

- Explain complex legal matters clearly and concisely
- Use appropriate technical terminology
- Identify and analyze the applicable case law and facts for the relevant legal issues
- Efficiently read and understand legal authority
- Articulate persuasive legal arguments in support of client's position
- Analyze possible outcomes for legal dispute, evaluate and articulate strengths and weaknesses of such outcomes
- Efficiently and effectively communicate in a written and oral format
- Respond to questions about the relevant law

To achieve these learning objectives, you will complete the following tasks:

- Draft a predictive memo to senior partner about legal issues and your prediction of what will happen with the litigation
- Draft a persuasive memorandum of law in support of or in opposition to motion for preliminary injunction
- Carry out a mock client meeting with either Pamela Park of SDA or one of the plaintiffs, Roger Mudd or Hillary Vonn
- Draft a client letter to your client about your meeting and about the legal issues
- Carry out oral argument in front of the court for the motion for preliminary injunction

To complete these tasks, you will use the following materials in the book:

- Assignment email from Senior Partner (pages 200-201; 201-203)
- Main Assignment File (pages 204-207)
- Right to Privacy Commented Cases:
    - State v. Boland, 800 P.2d 1112 (Wash. 1990).
    - State v. Sweeney, 107 P.3d 110 (Wash. Ct. App. 2005).
    - State v. Graffius, 871 P.2d 1115 (Wash. Ct. App. 1994).
    - State v. Rodriguez, 828 P.2d 636 (Wash. Ct. App. 1992).
- ESL Workbook (pages 142-154)
- Pleadings (online)

Your instructor will also assign you additional skills-building exercises to bolster your understanding of the legal issues and further develop your legal reasoning and language skills, whether related to legal reasoning and analysis or to English. You will find an icon with each exercise that will indicate which skills the exercise will focus upon.

ICON	SKILL
	Speaking — in particular about the legal issues and the law presented in the Unit
	Oral comprehension
	Legal analysis and reasoning
	Analysis of the legal issue(s) presented in the Unit
	English grammar, syntax, and vocabulary
	Legal ethics and professional responsibility
	Legal research

In this Unit, the additional skills-building exercises that accompany the Main Assignment File include:

- Constitutional Privacy Analysis Exercises (pages 208-210)

- Professional Presentation: *If the City of Longworth or the residents were your clients...* (pages 215-216)

- Injunction Analysis Exercise (pages 211-214)

Before beginning the Unit, you should read and be familiar with the Factual Background of the Lincoln, Adams and Washington Law Firm (pages 2-3) and Anthony, Ross and Tubman (page 5).

You will also find online at the website www.legalwritingforllms.com the following online resources that accompany this Unit. The additional online resources will help you deepen your mastery of the skills presented in the Unit and also provide additional understanding about the U.S. legal system and legal writing.

Pleadings for Section II, Unit 3 (required)

- Additional Resources:
  - Sources of American Law
  - Writing Professional Emails
  - Writing Persuasive Memos
  - Writing E-memos
  - IRAC
- Additional Skills-Building Exercises:
  - Issues and Issue Statements
  - Stating the Rule
  - Analysis
  - Ethical Spotlight Exercise

Section II, Unit 3 Legal Issue
State Constitutional Right to Privacy

Main Assignment File	Right to Privacy Cases	ESL Workbook	Additional Exercises	Additional Online Resources
Introduction to File and Client Matter Pages 195-199	State v. Boland, 800 P.2d 1112 (Wash. 1990).	State v. Boland, 800 P.2d 1112 (Wash. 1990).	Constitutional Privacy Analysis Exercise Pages 208-210	Writing Professional Emails
Documents Related to Client Matter Pages 200-207 + pleadings (available online)	State v. Sweeney, 107 P.3d 110 (Wash. Ct. App. 2005).	State v. Sweeney, 107 P.3d 110 (Wash. Ct. App. 2005).	Presentation: If SDA or the City of Longworth Were Your Client... Pages 215-216	Business Correspondence (with sample letters)
Assignment Information Pages + Rubrics Pages 217-226	State v. Graffius, 871 P.2d 1115 (Wash. Ct. App. 1994).	State v. Graffius, 871 P.2d 1115 (Wash. Ct. App. 1994).	Injunction Analysis Exercise Pages 211-214	Writing Memos (office memos and persuasive memoranda of law)
	State v. Rodriguez, 828 P.2d 636 (Wash. Ct. App. 1992).	State v. Rodriguez, 828 P.2d 636 (Wash. Ct. App. 1992).		IRAC (including additional exercises for each element)
				Skills-Building Exercises for Rules, Issues and Issues Statements, Analysis and Ethical Dilemmas

Introduction — State Constitutional Right to Privacy

The right to privacy is one of the fundamental rights guaranteed under the U.S. Constitution,[68] yet the right is never explicitly stated or granted in the text of the Constitution itself. Instead, the right to privacy has been crafted through Supreme Court jurisprudence and implied from the other rights guaranteed through the Bill of Rights — the right to be free from unreasonable searches and seizures under the Fourth Amendment as well as rights guaranteed under the First Amendment such as freedom of assembly and of speech.[69] It is found in the "penumbra of rights" guaranteed under our Constitution and first described in the landmark 1965 Supreme Court case Griswold v. Connecticut:

> [S]pecific guarantees in the Bill of Rights have penumbras, formed by emanations from those guarantees that help give them life and substance . . . . Various guarantees create zones of privacy. The right of association contained in the penumbra of the First Amendment is one . . . . The Third Amendment in its prohibition against the quartering of soldiers 'in any house' in time of peace without the consent of the owner is another facet of that privacy. The Fourth Amendment explicitly affirms the 'right of the people to be secure in their persons, houses, papers, and effects, against unreasonable searches and seizures.' The Fifth Amendment in its Self-Incrimination Clause enables the citizen to create a zone of privacy which government may not force him to surrender to his detriment . . . . The Fourth and Fifth Amendments [are] . . . as protection against all governmental invasions 'of the sanctity of a man's home and the privacies of life [and] . . . the Fourth Amendment [creates] a 'right to privacy, no less important than any other right carefully and particularly reserved to the people.'[70]

An unusual characteristic of the federal system in the United States is that each state, in addition to having its own branches of government, laws and court system, also has its own constitution. The original thirteen colonies had all ratified their own state constitutions by 1780, before the end of the Revolutionary War.

State constitutions can and do vary greatly from the Federal Constitution. Like state laws, a state constitution can always provide additional protections that the U.S. Constitution does not, but can never provide fewer protections, take away those guaranteed in the Federal Constitution, or violate it. For example, women were granted the right to vote with the passage of the 19th Amendment of the U.S. Constitution in 1919, so a state could never deprive women of that vote, even for local or state elections. But a state could have granted (and did grant) women the vote under its own constitution earlier than when the U.S. constitutional amendment was ratified. In 1889, thirty years before women were granted the right to vote under the U.S. Constitution, Wyoming had already granted women the right under its state constitution.[71]

Even though the U.S. Constitution does not explicitly provide the right to privacy, some states have taken a different approach and have deemed the right important enough to be enumerated as one of the fundamental rights that people within the state enjoy.

---

[68] See Roe v. Wade, 410 U.S. 113, 152-53 (1973).
[69] Griswold v. Connecticut, 381 U.S. 479, 484 (1965) .
[70] Id. at 484-85 (1965).
[71] *This Day In History: Wyoming Legislators Write the First State Constitution to Grant Women the Vote*, HISTORY.COM, http://www.history.com/this-day-in-history/wyoming-legislators-write-the-first-state-constitution-to-grant-women-the-vote (last visited Oct. 12, 2016).

Section 1 of the California Constitution, for example, includes the right to privacy. Its inclusion in the first section of the entire constitution, with other rights such as those to "life, liberty and the pursuit of happiness,"[72] underscores the importance that the California legislature has placed on this right.

Nine other states — Alaska, Arizona, Florida, Hawaii, Illinois, Louisiana, Montana, South Carolina and Washington — also include a specific right to privacy in their state constitutions.[73] This is the issue that you will deal with in this Unit.

> "All people are by nature free and independent and have inalienable rights. Among these are enjoying and defending life and liberty, acquiring, possessing, and protecting property, and pursuing and obtaining safety, happiness, and privacy." CAL. CONST. art. I § 1 (amended 1972).

Here, you will deal with the right to privacy in the Jefferson state constitution, and specifically whether the state constitution gives individuals the right to privacy in the trash or garbage that they leave on the street or at the end of their driveway for pickup by the city trash collectors. The U.S. Supreme Court has refused to recognize this right.[74] But as explained above, state constitutions can and do provide additional protections.

The specific issue you will face is whether a local ordinance, which gives Longworth, a city in the state of Jefferson, the right to search residents' garbage to ensure that they are not disposing of recyclable materials, violates the Jefferson state constitution. A group of residents has filed a claim against the city, asking the court to issue an injunction to prevent the ordinance from being enforced. Half of the class will represent the City of Longworth, arguing for the constitutionality and enforceability of the ordinance and against the issuance of the injunction, while the other half will represent the plaintiff-residents, arguing against the ordinance and in favor of the issuance of the injunction.

Section II

Intermediate Legal Issues

---

[72] These rights instead are included in the preamble of the Declaration of Independence, which states: "We hold these truths to be self-evident that all men are created equal and that they are endowed by their Creator with certain unalienable Rights that among these are Life, Liberty and the pursuit of Happiness." THE DECLARATION OF INDEPENDENCE para. 2 (U.S. 1776).

[73] For the constitutional provisions in each state's constitution, see *Privacy Protections in State Constitutions*, NAT'L CONF. ST. LEGISLATURES http://www.ncsl.org/research/telecommunications-and-information-technology/privacy-protections-in-state-constitutions.aspx (last visited Oct. 12, 2016).

[74] California v. Greenwood, 486 U.S. 35, 43-44 (1988) ("[S]ociety as a whole possesses no such understanding [that] ... garbage left for collection at the side of a public street [is deserving of] scrupulous protection from government invasion.").

Main Assignment File:
State Constitutional Right to Privacy

Plaintiff's File

You are an associate attorney at the law firm of Anthony Ross and Tubman. Today, you receive the following email from Senior Partner Brittany Ross, who has asked for your assistance on an important case that the firm has commenced on behalf of a group of residents of the city of Longworth.

Longworth, like many cities across the country, is searching for ways to become greener and more environmentally friendly. Some of these attempts have been met with resistance by the community, such as converting many car lanes on city streets to bike lanes, while others have been quite well received, such as tax incentives for residents who install solar panels on their homes. The latest attempt is an ordinance that requires residents to recycle a certain percentage of their garbage or face a fine. The ordinance also allows garbage collectors to look into garbage cans to determine if a household is recycling enough of its garbage or if the household should receive the fine. Critics of the ordinance have been outspoken and numerous.

Anthony Ross and Tubman has a reputation for being a firm that takes on tough cases against defendants like multinational corporations and the government, whether federal, state or local. When a group of residents approached Senior Partner Ross soon after the ordinance was passed, Ross immediately recognized the importance of this case and agreed to represent the group. Like most cases of this nature, the firm has taken the case on a contingency basis, meaning that the clients are not paying for the lawyers' time nor paying for costs and expenses. Instead, the firm will receive compensation only if it prevails.

The ordinance and the lawsuit have received considerable attention from the media, both local and national, and Ross has underscored the importance of winning this case so that the firm can continue to attract high-profile cases and clients, and increase its national exposure.

From:	Brittany Ross <brittany.ross@artlaw.com>
To:	Associate Attorney <associate@artlaw.com>
Sent:	April 2, THIS YEAR 1:02 p.m.
Re:	Case Against City/Right to Privacy

Associate attorney,

Even though you've been with the firm just a short while, I want you to take on the case that we just filed against the City of Longworth. Your experience in constitutional law will be an asset.

As we discussed in the case-update meeting this week, we've filed and served the complaint on the City, and the answer's been filed too. We now need to focus on the motion for the preliminary injunction. The motion and notice of motion have been filed, and I need you to take care of preparing the memo in support of the motion.

I had done some research of the issue when I first met with Mr. Mudd and the other plaintiffs, and you will find those cases in the client file. It seems to me that the Jefferson Supreme Court case law is very much in our favor for the constitutional violation. We wouldn't have much argument if we were bringing this as a 4th Amendment violation, but fortunately we have our state constitution that protects Jefferson citizens more broadly.

I also expect you to handle the oral arguments that have been scheduled in front of Judge Hines on April 25, THIS YEAR. I am confident that we will prevail and the court will grant the motion. Once that is taken care of, we can focus on preparing discovery.

Before you start drafting the persuasive memorandum of law, I'd like you to prepare for me a predictive memo that lays out your argument and the law and predicts what you think will happen once Judge Hines takes the matter under advisement.

Let one of the law clerks know if you need any other research or if they can help you in any other way with the memo.

Thanks,

Brittany
Brittany Ross
Partner, Anthony, Ross and Tubman Law Firm

As you have read, you have been asked by Senior Partner Ross to prepare a memorandum of law in support of the motion for a preliminary injunction that the law firm has filed on behalf of its clients, asking the court to stop the enforcement of the city ordinance for the duration of the lawsuit until its constitutionality can be determined. No discovery has been exchanged and no documents were attached to the complaint or the answer. Thus, the entire file that both sides will work with is included in this Assignment File.

First, you will draft a predictive office memo to your senior partner that includes:

- A summary of what has happened to give rise to the litigation involving the City of Longworth and the garbage ordinance
- A summary and analysis of the law that applies (constitutional right to privacy)
- The arguments that you will make in support of the motion for a preliminary injunction
- Counterarguments that you anticipate that opposing party will make
- Your opinion about whether you think the court will grant the motion for the preliminary injunction

Second, you will draft a persuasive memorandum of law in support of the motion for a preliminary injunction in the litigation that includes:

- Persuasive statements of the facts in a light that best represents your client
- Summary of the legal issue and the relevant law
- Persuasive arguments for which the injunction should be granted, including why your client will likely prevail on the underlying claim (violation of the right to privacy)

You will find complete information about these assignments on the Information Pages (pages 217-218; 223-224).

You will be analyzing the client matter using the right to privacy cases that you read and review in class.

Defendant's File

You are an associate attorney at the law firm of Lincoln, Adams and Washington. Today, you receive the following email from Senior Partner Georgina Washington. The email is about the City of Longworth, a new client that the firm is representing. Longworth is located about 90 miles to the southeast of the Jefferson City/ West Rapids metropolitan area and has a population of about 45,000 people.

Like many smaller cities, Longworth does not employ full-time city attorneys to handle its legal matters. With regard to criminal matters, felonies are prosecuted by the Hemings County Attorney's Office, and misdemeanor and gross misdemeanors are instead prosecuted by a private law firm that contracts with the city to serve as city prosecutors. The same private law firm also represents the city in any civil matters, whether as a plaintiff or defendant. Just last year, a group of local business owners filed a claim against the city, alleging that the city had violated their constitutional rights by taking private property without just compensation.[75] More recently, the city was the plaintiff in a high-profile claim brought against a multi-national corporation that the city accused of polluting the city's lakes, streams and waters in violation of the Clean Waters Act.

Until last month, the private law firm that had been awarded the contract to represent the City of Longworth was the Schmidt Law Firm. However, after repeated complaints from other attorneys about the firm and the attorneys' professional conduct, Mayor Jason Lange decided that it would be in the city's best interests to announce that it was accepting proposals from other firms to take over the job of representing the City. After a grueling application and interview process, Lincoln, Adams and Washington, PLLC was awarded the contract.

The matter you will deal with involves the City of Longworth and a recently-passed city ordinance that regards garbage, recycling and composting. A group of citizens has filed a lawsuit against the City, claiming that the ordinance is unconstitutional and requesting that the court issue an injunction prohibiting the ordinance from being enforced.

---

[75] The Fifth Amendment of the U.S. Constitution provides in pertinent part that ""[P]rivate property [shall not] be taken for public use, without just compensation." U.S. Const. amend. X. Called the Just Compensation Clause, it requires that the government (federal, state or local) pay private property owners just compensation for their property when it is taken for a public use, which could include a freeway, interstate or other road and even private commercial development. See Kelo v. City of New London, 545 U.S. 469 (2005).

From: Georgina Washington <g. washington@lawlawfirm.com>
To: Associate Attorney <a.attorney@lawlawfirm.com>
Sent: April 2, THIS YEAR 4:17 p.m.
Re: FW: City of Longworth Violation of Right to Privacy

Associate attorney,

I am writing about a new issue involving our new client, the City of Longworth. I need your assistance with this matter. I have forwarded to you an email that I just received from Mayor Lange, as well as the complaint that was served on the city. As you will see, the plaintiffs, a group of residents of Longworth, are also seeking an injunction. Our new attorney, Helen, is drafting the answer to the complaint. Your job will be to prepare our memorandum of law in opposition to the plaintiffs' request for an injunction. We have not yet received the plaintiffs' memo in support of their motion.

A hearing is scheduled on April 25, THIS YEAR in front of Judge Randolph Hines. The issue, as you will see in the attached documents, is whether a new ordinance that the City passed at the end of last year violates the Jefferson State Constitution. The ordinance requires residents to separate recyclable garbage, which now includes food scraps. The controversial part is that the City garbage collectors can now look through the garbage that they pick up, and if they determine that more than 10% of a container or can is made up of recyclable materials, the resident will be fined $50.00. You will find a copy of the entire ordinance with the client file that should already be on your desk.

As you will also see, the specific issue is a violation of the right to privacy under the Jefferson state constitution. The plaintiffs allege that by allowing the garbage collectors to look through the garbage to determine whether it meets that 10% limit of recyclable materials, the city is conducting a "search," and since no warrant is obtained, that search is unconstitutional. While it is true that our state constitution's right to privacy is broader than that in the U.S. constitution, I find it hard to fathom that a judge would agree with the plaintiffs. But you will have to make your determinations based on the relevant Jefferson case law.

Unfortunately, there is not a lot of binding precedent out there. You will also find in the client file four cases that deal with the right to privacy and garbage. While the U.S. Supreme Court cases will certainly be important, remember that this is a state constitutional issue.

I don't think I need to underscore the importance of this matter. The City of Longworth is a new and extremely important client. The revenue that the contract brings to the firm is considerable, and we want to put forth our best effort in defending the City against this frivolous claim.

Mayor Lange has stated that he is available if you should have any questions, and I am as well. Please begin as soon as you receive this email; I would like an outline of your argument and a summary of the cases as soon as possible, as well as a predictive memo of your arguments and the law before you begin drafting the memorandum of law. I want to be sure that we have strong arguments and that you are on the right path.

Georgina

From: Mayor Jason Lange <mayorlange@city.longworth.state.jf>
To: Georgina Washington <g.washington@lawlawfirm.com>
Sent: April 2, THIS YEAR 1:02 p.m.
Re: City of Longworth Violation of Right to Privacy

Georgina,

We are certainly making use of your firm's services since you won the contract. We have a new lawsuit that a group of residents just filed against the city. I have attached the complaint and the other legal documents that we received when we were served.

The case involves the new garbage and recycling ordinance. I am not surprised, to be honest, given the controversy that the ordinance provoked and the opposition that was brewing. One of the plaintiffs, Roger Mudd, is known to the city. He is always complaining about something and frequently writes letters to the city paper, as well as emails to me, expressing his displeasure about something happening in the city, or a new measure that we have decided to take.

Fight this case tooth and nail. This ordinance is important to the city, not only environmentally but also for our reputation as a green city. We also need the extra revenue that the fines will bring in so that we can successfully build the compost facility and further our goals of achieving the #1 spot of the list of Greenest Cities in the States.

Thanks,

Jason Lange

Mayor, City of Longworth

As you have read, you have been asked by Senior Partner Washington to prepare a memorandum of law in opposition to the motion for a preliminary injunction that the plaintiffs have filed, asking the court to stop the enforcement of the city ordinance. No discovery has been exchanged and no documents were attached to the complaint or the answer. Thus, the entire file that both sides will work with is included in this Assignment File.

First, you will draft a predictive office memo to your senior partner that includes:

- A summary of what has happened to give rise to the litigation involving the City of Longworth and the garbage ordinance
- A summary and analysis of the law that applies (constitutional right to privacy)
- The arguments that you will make in opposition to the motion for preliminary injunction
- Counterarguments that you anticipate that opposing party will make
- Your opinion about whether you think the court will grant the motion for the preliminary injunction

Second, you will draft a persuasive memorandum of law in opposition to the motion for a preliminary injunction in the litigation that includes:

- Persuasive statements of the facts in a light that best represents your client
- Summary of the legal issue and the relevant law
- Persuasive arguments for which the injunction should not be granted, including why opposing party client will likely *not* prevail on the underlying claim (violation of the right to privacy)

You will find complete information about these assignments on the Information Pages (pages 217-218; 223-224).

You will be analyzing the client matter using the right to privacy cases that you read and review in class.

LONGWORTH TIMES

December 24, (YEAR -1)   longworthtimes.com

$1.00   -5° | 15°

Trash Talk: Longworth Gets Serious About Recycling

By Heather Williams – Longworth

In many other cities across Jefferson, residents can turn a blind eye as they toss in their garbage cans their left-over breakfast muffins, lunchtime sandwiches and the pizza or hamburgers that they had for dinner. Not so in Longworth as of January 1.

The city has decided to get serious about recycling, after more than a decade of successful single-sort recycling that requires residents to place recyclable materials such as recyclable paper, recyclable cardboard, glass or plastic bottles and jars, aluminum or tin cans in a specific recycling container and all other waste in another.

Starting next year, residents will also have to sort out food waste and put it in the recycling container, no longer in the "regular" trash cans. "We'd like Longworth to be a pioneer in recycling," stated Jason Lange, mayor of Longworth since **YEAR -3**, "and requiring recycling of food scraps is a step in that direction. The city will begin composting, or converting the food waste into fertilizer that will be made available for a nominal fee to residents starting next June."

Under the new ordinance, Longworth residents will face a hefty fine if they do not comply with the requirements to separate their recyclable and compostable garbage. The ordinance grants city garbage collectors the authority to monitor residents' garbage and assess whether recyclable materials, which should be placed in the separate container, make up more than 10% of a garbage can or container. If the trash bins of a resident or a building are made up of more than 10% of recyclable or compostable materials, the garbage collectors will leave a warning notice at the first offense.

Following the first warning notice, if the garbage collectors note that the same home, apartment building or commercial building continues to place more than 10% of its recyclable or compostable garbage in the regular garbage bins, the $50 fine will be imposed. It will be mailed to the resident or the owner of the building, who will have 30 days to pay.

At a City Council meeting last week, Michael Taylor, operations supervisor for Longworth City Garbage Collections, said the ordinance won't turn his drivers into the "garbage police." According to Taylor, they will just "take note" of the garbage can's contents as they dispose of it in the garbage truck. Taylor also happened to mention at the meeting that the city garbage collectors have undergone special training so that they are able to measure by eye whether the can exceeds the 10% threshold established by the ordinance.

Ongoing Efforts to Be Greener

The City is attempting to reduce the amount of waste that is sent to landfills, especially organic waste such as food scraps. Unlike what many people think, leftover food does not decompose once dumped at a landfill but rather adds to greenhouse gases and global warming.

Will the $50 fine change people's habits? Helen Ramos, a spokeswoman for Longworth Public Utilities, acknowledged in a telephone interview with this reporter that the revenue could be "significant" if residents do not comply. Ramos also expressed her "confidence" that all Longworth residents will see the "wisdom" and "utility" of the ordinance and will welcome the environmental benefits.

Not All in Longworth Are Happy

Not all Longworth residents are happy about the new ordinance, however. A telephone survey of 1,000 Longworth residents conducted by the Jefferson Times and the television station WJEF indicated that 80% of those surveyed approve of the plan, while 13% are opposed to it. The remaining 7% were unsure or unaware of the ordinance.

Guillermo Diaz, an accountant who lives in the Hyde Park neighborhood, has become one of the most outspoken voices against the ordinance: "What's happened to our sense of privacy? Where does the line get drawn for what the City can and can't do? Today, they go through our garbage and charge us 50 bucks if we aren't green enough. Tomorrow? Who knows?"

Diaz informed this reporter that a small group of residents who are equally disgruntled with the ordinance have spoken with a prominent local law firm and plan to file a lawsuit in Jefferson State Court, alleging that the ordinance violates citizens' right to privacy under the Jefferson State Constitution.[76]

---

[76] Jack Broom, *Seattle talks trash: New garbage rules, potential fines start Jan 1,* SEATTLE TIMES, Dec. 23, 2014, http://www.seattletimes.com/seattle-news/seattle-talks-trash-new-garbage-rules-potential-fines-start-jan-1/.

CITY OF LONGWORTH
PUBLIC UTILITIES ORDINANCE NUMBER LW-402.1[77]
EFFECTIVE JANUARY 1, THIS YEAR
TITLE: PROHIBITION OF RECYCLABLES IN GARBAGE

1. Purpose

Longworth Municipal Code (LMC) 21.36.082 and 21.36.083 prohibit the disposal of certain recyclable materials in the garbage by businesses and residents with penalties to be imposed for noncompliance. LMC 21.36.05 also prohibits the disposal of yard waste in the garbage by residents.

Both residents and commercial businesses have been required to recycle paper, cardboard, glass bottles and jars, aluminum and tin cans, as well as yard waste. LMC 21.36.082 and

21.36.083 expand the list of materials that must be recycled by all residential customers and commercial establishments, including those hauling their own waste. These new items will include food waste and compostable paper.

Longworth Public Utilities (LPU) will begin a program of educational outreach regarding the food waste and compostable paper recycling requirements.

2. Rule

Commercial Establishments

Significant amounts of recyclables in the garbage for commercial establishments mean that any of the following, alone or in combination, make up more than 10 percent by volume of the contents of a garbage can, detachable container or drop box, as determined by an inspection by an LPU inspector or contractor: recyclable paper (including paper cups), recyclable cardboard, glass bottles and jars, plastic bottles and cups, aluminum and tin cans, yard waste, food waste and compostable paper.

All commercial establishments that generate food waste or compostable paper will subscribe to a composting service, process their food waste on-site or self-haul their food waste for processing. All building owners will provide composting service for their tenants or provide space for the tenant's own food waste containers.

LPU will monitor commercial containers and provide educational notices or tags for commercial garbage cans, detachable containers, and drop boxes with food waste and compostable paper as of January 1, **THIS YEAR**.

As of January **THIS YEAR**, the presence of significant amounts of recyclables, including food waste and compostable paper, in a commercial garbage can, detachable container, and drop box will be subject to an additional collection fee of $50 per collection after one warning notice has been mailed to the garbage account customer at the address in LPU's customer records.

Residential—Can Customers

Significant amounts of recyclables in the garbage for residential cans mean that any of the following, alone or in combination, make up more than 10 percent by volume of the contents of a garbage can, as determined by an inspection by an LPU inspector or contractor: recyclable paper, recyclable cardboard, glass or plastic bottles and jars, aluminum or tin cans, yard waste, food waste and compostable paper.

LPU will place educational notices or tags on garbage containers with recyclables, including food waste and compostable paper as of January 1, **THIS YEAR**.

As of January **THIS YEAR**, the presence of significant amounts of recyclables, including food waste and compostable paper, in a commercial garbage can, detachable container, and drop box will be subject to an additional collection fee of $50 per collection after one warning notice has been mailed to the garbage account of the customer at the address in LPU's customer records.

---

[77] From the Seattle city ordinance of the same number.

Residential—Detachable Container and Drop Box Accounts

Significant amounts of recyclables in the garbage for detachable containers and drop boxes mean that any of the following, alone or in combination, make up more than 10 percent by volume of the contents of a garbage can, as determined by visual inspection by an LPU inspector or contractor: recyclable paper, recyclable cardboard, glass or plastic bottles and jars, aluminum or tin cans yard waste, food waste and compostable paper.

As of January 1, **THIS YEAR**, the presence of significant amounts of recyclables, including food waste and compostable paper, in a residential detachable container or drop box will be subject to an additional collection fee of $50 per collection after a warning notice has been mailed to the garbage account customer at the address in LPU's customer records.

City Transfer Stations

Significant amounts of recyclables mean that any of the following, alone or in combination, make up more than 10 percent by volume of a self-haul vehicle's load to be deposited as garbage, as determined by visual inspection by a scale house operator or transfer station floor monitor: recyclable paper, recyclable cardboard, glass or plastic bottles and jars, aluminum or tin cans, yard waste, food waste and compostable paper.

Customers whose garbage taken to a City transfer station contains a significant amount of recyclables, including food waste and compostable paper, will be informed that they will need to separate these materials.

As of January 1, **THIS YEAR**, if self-haul customers have loads of garbage with significant amounts of recyclables, including food waste and compostable paper, they will be instructed to separate the designated recyclables at or away from the City transfer station. Loads containing significant amounts of recyclables, including food waste and compostable paper, will not be accepted in the garbage disposal areas of City transfer stations.

3. Determination of Garbage Account Customer Responsibility

Space Limitations—Existing and New Structures

Commercial and multifamily customers in existing structures may be exempted by the Director from all or portions of this rule, in writing, if the Director or designee determines through a site visit requested by the customer that there is not adequate storage space for recyclable and compostable materials, including food waste and compostable paper, on-site and that it is infeasible for the customer to share containers for recycling and compostable materials with a customer on the adjoining property. If the Director or designee determines that it is feasible for recycling and compostable material containers to be placed on site or shared with an adjoining customer at no additional cost, then that customer will be responsible for compliance with the rule.

New or expanded structures permitted in commercial zones and expanded multifamily structures may be exempted by the Director from all or portions of this rule if the Director or designee determines compliance is not feasible due to demonstrated difficulty in meeting the solid-waste and recyclable-materials storage space specifications required under LMC 23.54.040.

Placement of Recyclables and Compostable Material in Garbage Containers by the Public

Commercial establishments will not be responsible for recyclable and compostable materials deposited in commercial garbage containers made available to members of the general public. This includes any garbage can made available to the general public or the customers of a business for bussing their own food waste and compostable paper. Such containers are exempt from the enforcement of these requirements.

Upon request a LPU inspector will meet with operations personnel of educational and health institutions, public-transportation and entertainment facilities, and hotels and mixed use buildings to determine which garbage containers receive substantial waste from the general public in the public-access areas of the property. Garbage containers the Director determines are expected to receive waste exclusively from employees, residents, or guests (subject to the self-bussing of food waste and compostable paper exemption under section E.2.a) will be subject to enforcement of the recycling requirements.

On a case-by-case basis, a garbage customer will not be held responsible for recyclables, including food waste and compostable paper, deposited by the public in curb/alley containers located outside a premise on a public street or alley if the customer demonstrates to the Director that (1) the public was the source of the recyclables, including food waste and compostable paper, (2) the customer has collection services for those types of recyclables and compostables that are prohibited in that customer's garbage, or (3) a free lock for the garbage container was either not offered by the City or, if offered and accepted, was not received by the customer.

A hotel, inn, or similar facility will not be held responsible for recyclables including food waste and compostable paper deposited in individual room garbage containers by its guests if the facility has a method and system for guests to recycle paper (including paper cups), cardboard, cans and bottles, as well as plastic cups. This system will include instructions for the guests on the means of recycling as well as the fact that the paper, cardboard, cans, and bottle recycling is a requirement of the City of Longworth.

<u>Multiple-Building Situations</u>

The Director of LPU may reach a tailored agreement with a housing authority, large institution, or private business with multiple buildings and operations on how to apply the definition of significant amounts of recyclables in the garbage across multiple buildings while preserving the spirit and intention of this rule.

4. Appeals

Customer disputes or appeals of any notice or charge imposed under this rule are governed by Longworth Public Utilities – Policy & Procedure, LPU-CS-104.

Section II

Intermediate Legal Issues

Additional Skills-Building Exercises

Analysis Exercise: Constitutional Right to Privacy

Overview of the Exercise: The following short fact patterns deal with the constitutional right to privacy and injunctions, the legal issues presented in this Unit. You will analyze the fact patterns to determine whether or not the constitutional right to privacy was violated and whether an injunction should be issued.

Learning Objectives of the Exercise:

This exercise will build your skills to:

- Articulate the legal rules regarding the right to privacy and injunctions
- Apply those rules to fact patterns and analyze the facts and the law
- Articulate and effectively communicate that analysis using legal terminology

Steps for Completing the Exercise:

- Read the following fact patterns.
- By yourself, analyze each one and decide whether or not you think the right to privacy was violated and whether an injunction should be issued. You don't need to write out a full answer, but jot down notes about your reasoning.
- When you are done analyzing each of the fact patterns, discuss your answers with the partner that you have been assigned. Explain to each other why you have reached the conclusion that you did.
- If you and your partner have different responses to a fact pattern, you must try to convince him or her that your answer is correct. After you both have tried to convince the other, you must choose a team answer.
- Once you have discussed each of the fact patterns, you will compare answers as a class.

Research Required for the Assignment: You are not required to do any outside research for this assignment. You can refer to the cases that you read for class for the standard for the constitutional right to privacy. Remember, however, that violation of the right to privacy is also a tort claim, and the section of the Restatement (Second) of Torts that deals with invasion of privacy is included below for your review and for your analysis.

Grading: This assignment is not graded. Instead, you will compare your answers with those of your classmates once you have finished.

The Restatement (Second) of Torts § 652D (1977) provides the general rule for invasion of privacy. It states:

One who gives publicity to a matter concerning the private life of another is subject to liability to the other for invasion of his privacy, if the matter publicized is of a kind that

1. would be highly offensive to a reasonable person, and
2. is not of legitimate concern to the public.[78]

1.   Yolanda works for the City of Longworth as an animal control officer. As part of her job, she investigates allegations of animal abuse, helps control abandoned or unattended animals, and helps remove dangerous animals. The City has recently announced new policies that will affect all city employees and that will allow the City to use technology to monitor its employees. The provision has been included in the updated Employee Handbook, which has been distributed to all employees. This is the provision:

---

[78] Reid v. Pierce Cty., 961 P.2d 333, 338 (Wash. 1998) (citing Restatement (Second) of Torts § 652D (1977)).

Employee Monitoring

Employees of the City of Longworth have no expectation and no right of personal privacy in any matter stored in, created, received, or sent over the City's email system and in any communications carried out using the City's communications systems (telephone, computer, wireless, etc). The City monitors all communications done by its employees, whether on land-line telephones, cellular phones, text messages or messages exchanged online.

In an effort to control budget costs and to ensure that its employees are engaged in productive and safe activities throughout the work day, the City requires all employees to wear security badges at all times. When they enter and leave the building, enter and leave a bathroom or enter and leave a breakroom, employees are required to swipe their security badge and record their movements.

All employees who drive a City car, truck or other motorized vehicle as part of their job duties are also monitored via a GPS device attached to the vehicle that will record the vehicle's movements, speed and location.

The City also takes all measures to protect its reputation, employees and its intellectual property. As part of these ongoing efforts, the City monitors all employees' social media pages and profiles to ensure that no harassing or discriminatory messages are posted and that no confidential or proprietary information is shared.

Yolanda has approached you about whether this policy is legal and would like your advice. Should a claim be filed against the City alleging violations of the Constitution (state and federal) and an injunction sought? What do you think a court would decide if a claim were filed and if an injunction sought? What do you advise Yolanda? Support your answer.

2.   Yolanda's brother, Leonard, works for a private employer in Jefferson City. He has discovered that his employer has installed security cameras throughout the office. He has seen cameras in the lobby, in all employees' offices, in closets and storage rooms, and in the common-area breakroom where all employees eat their lunch and take their breaks. He even noted cameras in the men's restrooms and was told by a colleague that she saw them in the women's restroom as well.

Leonard has also approached you about whether you think that a claim should be brought against his employer. His employer is a private company, as opposed to his sister's employer, which is a public employer (the City). Does your analysis change with regard to whether a claim should be brought? Do the claims change? If an injunction were filed to prevent the employer from using the cameras, what do you think a court would decide? What advice do you give Leonard? Support your answer.

3.   Wendy is a drug dealer who routinely sells cocaine and ecstasy to customers of a popular bar and night club in the city of West Rapids. To avoid detection and to not arouse the suspicions of the staff, Wendy usually makes her deals in the bar's bathroom. Many of the regular customers know her and follow her to the bathroom when they see her arrive.

On one occasion, Wendy went into the bathroom and into a toilet stall. The door was left ajar about 4-5 inches so that her clients would know she was available and not actually using the toilet. After she entered the stall, another woman, who was an undercover West Rapids police officer, walked towards the stall next to Wendy's, pretending to go into it. While walking pass the stall where Wendy was, the officer looked into the space where the door was left ajar and while doing so, saw Wendy take out of her purse a bag of cocaine. To see what Wendy was doing and record her actions, the officer put a small camera on a wire under the wall of the stall as soon as she entered it. Wendy did not notice the camera because moments later, a client entered Wendy's stall and purchased the cocaine. When the client exited the stall, the officer immediately arrested Wendy.

Wendy's defense attorney has now filed a motion to dismiss, alleging that the officer's actions violated Wendy's right to privacy. You are the judge in the case. What do you decide? Support your answer. You can check the case State v. Berber, 740 P. 2d 863 (Wash. 1987) to compare your answer to the court's reasoning.

4.   Sam's wife and daughter were killed in a tragic car accident six years ago. The accident was investigated by the Jefferson City police, and the Hemings County Medical Examiner Charles Tyson also took part in the investigation (as he does for all investigations of accidental deaths that occur in the county). As part of the investigations, Tyson took pictures of the corpses of Sam's wife and daughter.

Taking pictures of accident victims is standard procedure in the Medical Examiner's Office. The pictures were placed in the file of the accident.

In addition to acting as the Hemings County medical examiner, Tyson also teaches a class in safe driving to individuals who have been convicted of DUI (driving under the influence). Attendance at the class is mandated as part of their sentencing. While preparing for class, Tyson decides that using some shocking pictures of car accident victims will be an effective way of persuading the individuals in the class not to drink and drive. Before class, Tyson grabs the pictures of Sam's wife and daughter, as well as pictures of other victims, and shows them during his lecture.

Since the tragic death of his wife and daughter, Sam has struggled to cope and has developed a drinking habit. He was arrested and convicted for drunk driving, and was attending the class in which Tyson showed the pictures of his wife and daughter.

Sam has since contacted you about suing Tyson and the county for showing the pictures of his wife's and his daughter's corpses. What advice do you give Sam? Could he successfully bring a claim of violation of privacy? Why or why not? You can check the case <u>Reid v. Pierce Cty.</u>, 961 P.2d 333 (Wash. 1998) to compare your answer to the court's reasoning.

5. Frank was arrested after he broke into and robbed a local convenience store. He was brought to the Jefferson City jail, booked and detained until his court hearing the next morning. As part of the routine booking process, the law enforcement officers require all detainees to wear an orange jumpsuit that identifies them as inmates. The clothing that the individual is wearing at the time of the arrest is inventoried and kept in storage at the jail.

The officer that booked Frank and inventoried his clothing had a suspicion that Frank was responsible for another robbery that had just taken place in Jefferson City, days before Frank's arrest. At that robbery, the victim had been brutally assaulted. While investigating the crime scene, the officers took a photograph of a shoe print that the criminal was wearing.

Based on his suspicion, the officer compared the shoe that had been inventoried and stored upon Frank's arrest with the photograph of the shoe print at the other crime scene. The prints and the shoe size matched. Based on that evidence, Frank was also charged with aggravated armed robbery and now faces charges for both crimes.

Frank's defense attorney has filed a motion to suppress the evidence of the matching shoe print, claiming that it was obtained in violation of Frank's right to privacy. You are the judge in this matter. What do you decide? Support your answer. You can check the case <u>State v. Cheatam</u>, 81 P.3d 830 (Wash. 2003) to compare your answer to the court's reasoning.

6. The State of Jefferson has recently enacted a new law whose purpose is to protect children given up for adoption by their parents and then adopted by new families and to ensure that the children have adequate information about their birth family's medical history.

The law requires adoption agencies to report to the state when a child is brought to the agency for adoption, or when a child is adopted to a new family. When a child is given up for adoption, the agency must also fill out a four-page form with all the medical information that it can obtain about the child and its birth family. The forms must then be transmitted to the state, where the information is stored until (and if) a child or his or her family requests it.

The law was passed following and in response to a tragic situation in which a child died after given a certain medication that she was allergic to. The child was adopted and the adoptive family was not aware of the child's allergy, which she was genetically predisposed to as both her parents had the same allergy and passed the gene to their child.

Barbara is a young single mother who has decided to give her newborn son up for adoption. She objects to completing the long form required by the state and feels that it is an invasion of her right to privacy. Barbara has approached you, requesting your opinion on whether a claim should be brought against the state and whether an injunction should be sought, asking the court to stop enforcement of the statute. What advice do you give Barbara? What do you think that the court will rule for the violation of privacy claim and for the injunction? Support your answer.

Injunction Analysis Exercise

Overview of the Exercise: The following short fact patterns deal with injunctions and the issuance of injunctions, and your task is to analyze the fact patterns and determine whether or not you think a court should issue an injunction.

Learning Objectives of the Exercise:

This exercise will build your skills to:

- Articulate the legal rules regarding injunctions
- Apply those rules to brief fact patterns and analyze the facts and the law
- Articulate and effectively communicate that analysis using legal terminology

Steps for Completing the Exercise:

- Read the following fact patterns.
- By yourself, analyze each one and decide whether or not you think the court should issue an injunction. You don't need to write out a full answer, but jot down notes about your reasoning.
- When doing your analysis, be sure to follow the test as articulated in the Washington cases that you have read for this Unit.
- When you are done analyzing each of the fact patterns, discuss your answers with the partner that you have been assigned. Explain to each other why you have reached the conclusion that you did.
- If you and your partner have different responses to a fact pattern, you must try to convince him or her that your answer is correct. After you both have tried to convince the other, you must choose a team answer.
- Once you have discussed each of the fact patterns, you will compare answers as a class.

Research Required for the Exercise: You are not required to do any outside research for this exercise.

Grading: This assignment is not graded. Instead, you will compare your answers with those of your classmates.

1. Nuisance:

Rule

Jeff. Stat. Ann. § 657.1 defines nuisance as "whatever is injurious to health, indecent, or unreasonably offensive to the senses, or an obstruction to the free use of property, so as essentially to interfere unreasonably with the comfortable enjoyment of life or property." The statute also states that an individual can commence a civil action "to enjoin and abate the nuisance and to recover damages sustained on account of the nuisance."

Case Law

A discomfort which is purely mental, unaccompanied by anything else, may not be alleviated by injunctive relief. Delaney v. Fitzgerald, 13 S.W.2d 767, 768 (Jeff. 1929).

An injunction should be refused when it was sought to prevent soot and cinders from the smokestack of a factory being carried into the dwelling house of the complainant. The court held that the smoke and soot from the particular factory would not be regarded as a greater nuisance than the other manufacturing establishments in the city. The court stated that one living in a city necessarily must submit to the annoyances incidental to city life. It was also held that manufacturing establishments were necessary and indispensable to the growth and prosperity of every city, and they were entitled to protection in the proper conduct of their business, although some inconvenience might result to others. <u>Louisville Coffin Co. v. Warren</u>, 78 Ky. 400 (Jeff. 1880).

A thing is not a nuisance merely because it is calculated to create fear and apprehension, and an injunction should be refused where the thing sought to be restrained is not unavoidable and not in itself noxious, but only something which may, according to circumstances, prove so. <u>Delaney</u>, 13 S.W.2d at 768.

Facts

Jose and Veronica recently purchased a home on the outskirts of New Mesa, Jefferson. The neighborhood is mostly rural and their home is located on a road where three other families also live. At the end of the road, about ¼ mile (approximately 400 meters) from their home, is a large empty field. Before purchasing the house, they didn't ask the real estate agent if the field was used for anything.

About a month after they moved in, a traveling carnival was set up in this field. The advertisements that Jose and Veronica saw in the paper and around town said that the circus was going to be there for the next five months. The first days that the circus was operating, Jose and Veronica heard the yells of vendors, the singing and shouting of the performers, and noises of the audience, rendering it impossible for them to get proper rest or sleep. Although the circus operates only during the day, both Jose and Veronica work the night shift and sleep during the day. Jose and Veronica have also complained that the odors of the cooking of foods are offensive. The carnival operators are careful that the audience members do not litter and if there is any trash left behind, management quickly cleans it so that there is no garbage on the road. However, Jose and Veronica have found on a few occasions some soda cans and beverage cups, as well as food wrappers, on the street in front of their home.

This is the tenth year that the carnival has traveled to New Mesa and it is always well attended by the residents of the city and the surrounding area.

You represent Jose and Veronica and have filed on their behalf a complaint in Jefferson state court against the carnival, claiming that the carnival is a nuisance. You have also filed a motion for a temporary injunction, asking the court to enjoin the carnival from operating. What do you think the court will decide? Why?

2. Trademark Infringement

Rule

In order to obtain relief in an action for trademark infringement, plaintiff has the burden of proof in establishing three requisites, namely:

1) That plaintiff's name has a special significance or secondary meaning in the trade;

2) That plaintiff has an exclusive right to, or a protectable interest in, the trademark with reference to his goods, service, or business and with reference to the territorial or special group market in which his trademark is used; and

3) That defendant has unfairly used plaintiff's trademark, or a confusing simulation thereof (although not necessarily with a fraudulent intent), whereby the ordinary purchaser, to plaintiff's or the public's detriment, has been, or is reasonably likely to be, deceived as to the true identity of the goods, services, or business, and is misled into believing that he is getting plaintiff's product when he is in fact getting that of defendant. <u>Howard Clothes, Inc. v. Howard Clothes Corp.</u>, 52 N.W.2d 753, 757-58 (Jeff. 1952).

Courts have developed four categories of terms for trademark purposes. In ascending order of strength they are: (1) generic, (2) descriptive, (3) suggestive, and (4) arbitrary or fanciful. <u>Scott v. Mego Int'l Inc.</u>, 519 F. Supp. 1118, 1126 (D. Jeff. 1981).

A generic term is one which is commonly used as the name or description of a kind of goods and is afforded no trademark protection. <u>Id.</u> A descriptive term is one which conveys an immediate idea of the ingredients, qualities, or characteristics of goods and is only entitled to protection if it has acquired secondary meaning. <u>Imported Auto Parts Corp. v. R.B. Shaller & Sons, Inc.</u>, 258 N.W.2d 797, 800 (Jeff. 1977).

A suggestive term is one which falls between the descriptive category and the arbitrary and fanciful category. An arbitrary or fanciful term is one which has no relation to the nature of the product and is entitled to trademark protection without proof of secondary meaning. Id. at 799. Arbitrary terms are afforded the strongest trademark protection. If the business selects a name which is "arbitrary with respect to its trade or merely suggestive of it, the business' first use of the mark will establish common law rights, if another has not yet appropriated it." Id.

Likelihood of confusion can be created when products have functionally identical uses and share numerous similarities in package design. Aurora World, Inc. v. Ty Inc., 719 F. Supp. 2d 1115, 1142 (C.D. Jeff. 2009).

Rearden LLC v. Rearden Commerce, Inc. iterates eight factors that contribute to "likelihood of confusion." They are strength of the mark; proximity of the goods; similarity of the marks; evidence of actual confusion; marketing channels used; type of goods and degree of care likely to be exercised by the purchaser; defendant's intent in selecting the mark; and likelihood of expansion of the product lines. 683 F.3d 1190, 1209 (9th Cir. 2012).

Similarity between retail outlets where products are sold and customers to whom products are aimed can also contribute to the possibility of confusion. Amstar Corp. v. Domino's Pizza, Inc., 615 F.2d 252, 262 (5th Cir. 1980). This factor takes into consideration where, how, and to whom the parties' products are sold and direct competition between the parties is not required for this factor to weigh in favor of a likelihood of confusion. See Jaguar Cars Ltd. v. Skandrani, 771 F.Supp. 1178, 1184 (S.D.Jeff.1991).

Facts

Lynn is the owner of a company called CHECKPOINT. It operates in the industry of "corporate security," in which it sells electronic-security equipment and systems to help retailers protect against the physical theft of merchandise from stores. Raymond also operates a company called Check Point; it operates solely online at the domain "checkpoint.com" to sell and promote its products, computer software that protects the electronic flow of information. Lynn's domain is "checkpointsecurity.com." Lynn began operating in 2005, while Raymond started operations in 2009. Lynn's company has a website, but she does not sell her products through it but rather promotes her company and its products. Raymond sells his products throughout the United States, while Lynn operates in Jefferson and the surrounding states. Raymond has been significantly more successful than Lynn, with nearly two times the annual revenue.

Lynn's attorney has recently filed a claim in Jefferson federal court for trademark infringement and unfair competition, alleging that the name of Raymond's company creates the likelihood of confusion in the minds of consumers and thus infringes upon Lynn's intellectual property rights. The attorney has also filed a motion for a preliminary injunction, asking the court to order Raymond to stop selling his products.

Raymond has come to you for advice about whether you think the court will decide in Lynn's favor. What do you tell him?

3. Conversion

Rule

The elements of common law conversion are (1) the plaintiff has a property interest and (2) the defendant deprives the plaintiff of that interest." Lassen v. First Bank Eden Prairie, 514 N.W.2d 831, 838 (Jeff. Ct. App. 1994) ; see also Larson v. Archer–Daniels–Midland Co., 32 N.W.2d 649, 650 (Jeff. 1948) ; Mertes v. Estate of King, 501 N.W.2d 660, 665 (Jeff. Ct. App. 1993).

Case Law

Jefferson state and federal courts have yet to rule on the issue of whether the law of conversion protects electronic data or information.

The court of the nearby state of Franklin has concluded that the law of conversion may protect electronic data or information. See Kremen v. Cohen, 337 F.3d 1024, 1034 (9th Cir. 2002) (concluding that plaintiff had an intangible property right in his domain name, and a jury could find that defendant had wrongfully disposed him of that right by giving the domain name to a third party).

The Franklin federal district court has also decided the issue when it recently granted default judgment against a defendant that had broadcast without authorization and license a boxing match to which plaintiff offered sublicensing agreements to publicly exhibit the program. The court found that plaintiff alleged its ownership over the commercial distribution rights to the boxing match and that Defendant broadcast it at his establishment in contravention of Plaintiff's exclusive commercial distribution rights and alleged damages. J & J Sports Prods., Inc. v. Leger, No. 13-cv-02071-SC, WL 6492114 (N.D. Fran. Dec 10, 2013).

District courts within the Third Circuit (which Jefferson is not a part of) have instead found that the Copyright Act preempts state law conversion claims regarding copyrighted property. In Apparel Business Systems, LLC v. Tom James Co., No. 06-1092, 2008 U.S. Dist. LEXIS 26313, (E.D. Pa. Mar. 28, 2008), the district court determined that because the plaintiff's conversion claim arose from copying and misuse of its work, it was functionally equivalent to a copyright claim. The court also noted that because it is intangible property, software is generally not subject to a conversion claim. Id.

In Gemel Precision Tool Co. v. Pharma Tool Corp., No. 94-5305, 1995 WL 71243(E.D. Pa. Feb. 13, 1995), the district court found that an act of conversion regarding plaintiff's copyrighted blueprints and computer databases was substantively similar to a copyright claim. Likewise, the district court in Sullivan Associates v. Dellots, Inc., Civ. A. 97-5457, 1997 WL 778976 (E.D. Pa. Dec. 17, 1997), utilized a very similar analysis holding that plaintiff's conversion claim involving its software, databases, and computer files was functionally equivalent to a copyright claim.

Finally, courts in the states of West Virginia and Virginia have concluded that while the tort of conversion usually applies only to tangible property, "courts have recognized the tort of conversion in cases where intangible rights arise from or are merged with a document." Combined Ins. Co. of Am. v. Wiest, 578 F. Supp. 2d 822, 835 (W.D. Va. 2008) (quoting United Leasing Corp. v. Thrift Ins. Corp., 440 S.E.2d 902, 906 (Va. 1994)).

Facts

Murat is a website developer who writes and develops code for his clients' websites. He is very innovative and creative and has developed a code that no one else has. It allows his clients' website to appear first on Google, even though the sites violate many of Google's rules. Murat is one step ahead of Google with his coding. With his special skills, Murat has been able to grow his business considerably over the past year.

Lesley is a competitor of Murat and has her own, not very successful website developing business. Last month, Lesley hacked into Murat's wireless system and computers and was able to download onto her own computer Murat's codes. In the past month, Lesley has used Murat's code and already moved her clients' websites up to the top of the Google rankings.

Using his superior computer skills, Murat was able to discover that Lesley was the hacker who broke into his computer and stole his code. Murat has now come to your law firm for advice. He wants to know if he can sue Lesley, on what grounds and whether the court can order Lesley to stop using Murat's computer code.

What do you tell Murat? Will he be able to obtain an injunction? Why or why not?

Presentation:
If The City or the Resident-Plaintiffs
Were Your Client...

Overview of the Exercise: For this exercise, you will make a professional presentation in which you answer and discuss the following question:

If the plaintiffs were your client in your home country and if they came to you for legal advice about the garbage ordinance and the privacy issue, what would you do and what advice would you give them?

OR

If the City of Longworth were your client in your home country and if Mayor Lange came to you for legal advice about the ordinance and the lawsuit filed against the city, what would you do and what advice would you give him?

You will do the presentation for the client that you have been assigned and that you represent for the Unit.

Learning Objectives of the Exercise:

This exercise will build your skills to:

- Examine the dispute over the right to privacy in garbage from the perspective of your country's legal system
- Compare your country's legal system with the U.S. legal system
- Explain how the dispute would be handled in your country's legal system and the advice that you would provide to your client
- Understand specific information from your classmates' presentations

Steps for Completing the Exercise:

- Analyze the right to privacy fact pattern under your country's laws or constitution.
- Determine whether or not your client would have viable claims or defenses if the case were brought in your country's legal system.
- Explain how the case would be handled in your country's legal system and what the probable outcome would be.
- Explain what legal advice you would give your client if they came to you for legal advice in your home country.

Research Required: The research you are required to do depends on your knowledge of these claims in your country's legal system. It is presumed that you are familiar with the law and with how you would approach this issue if your client in this matter were a client of yours in your home country.

Grading: This presentation is not graded. Depending on the size of your class and your instructor's choice, you will present to your fellow classmates or to the entire class.

Handouts:

As part of your presentation, you must create a handout for your classmates, and the handouts must include fill-in-the-blank questions that your classmates must complete with information that you present during the presentation. Each handout must include at least five questions to complete.

For example, if a U.S. law student were giving a presentation on constitutional rights and the right to privacy in the United States, she could include on her handout this question:

> The U.S. Supreme Court has held that the right to privacy can be found in what is called the _____ of rights.

As you are speaking, your classmates will have to listen, follow what you are saying and fill in the blanks. If you are listening to one of your classmate's presentations and are unsure about an answer, you should ask him or her to repeat so you can fill in the blank(s).

Grammar Review:

The basis of this exercise is hypothetical or conditional verbs: *if the City of Longworth or the plaintiff-residents were your client, what would you do?*

Remember the grammar when discussing hypothetical conditions.

Present: **IF + PAST SIMPLE, WOULD + BASE VERB**

*If Mayor Lange **called** me to schedule an appointment, I **would tell** him to visit me at my office.*

NOTE: We use "were" for all tenses with the verb "to be" when using a conditional verb.

*If I **were** you, I **would not take** that class.*

*If the City **were** my client, I would tell Mayor Lange that they **would** likely **win** the case.*

Past: **IF + PAST PERFECT, WOULD + HAVE + PAST PARTICIPLE**

*If Mayor Lange **had called** me before the city council enacted the legislation, I **would have advised** him about not including the provision that allows the garbage collectors to look through the residents' garbage.*

*If the plaintiffs **had called** my office earlier in the day, I **would have told** them to come to my office at 12:00.*

Information Pages

Office Memo:
State Constitutional Right to Privacy

Overview of the Assignment: For this assignment, you will write an office memo to the Senior Partner, summarizing your research on the right to privacy under the Jefferson constitution and the ordinance passed by the City of Longworth, and providing your prediction of what will happen in the litigation.

Learning Objectives of the Assignment:

This assignment will build your skills to:

- Efficiently communicate in a written format
- Explain complex matters clearly and concisely
- Analyze and apply the rules of law regarding the constitutional right to privacy

Research Required for the Assignment: You are not required to do any outside research for this assignment. You should base your analysis on the Washington right to privacy cases that you have read:

- <u>State v. Boland</u>, 800 P.2d 1112 (Wash. 1990).
- <u>State v. Sweeney</u>, 107 P.3d 110 (Wash. Ct. App. 2005).
- <u>State v. Graffius</u>, 871 P.2d 1115 (Wash. Ct. App. 1994).
- <u>State v. Rodriguez</u>, 828 P.2d 636 (Wash. Ct. App. 1992).

If you want to practice your legal research skills, you can look for and use other cases that you find. However, if you do search on Westlaw, LexisNexis or Bloomberg Law, be sure to limit your search and the cases you use to Washington law, or use other jurisdictions as persuasive precedent. Be sure to change the citations to Jefferson if using cases from Washington. For persuasive precedent from other states, keep the state identifiers the same.

Format of the Completed Assignment:

Your response should be in an office memo format and should include the following:

- Summary of the facts
- The relevant law
- Analysis of the law to the fact pattern
- Conclusion about how you think a court would rule if this matter were to go to court
- Your advice to the client about how to proceed

Follow the following format:

- 1 inch (2.54 cm.) margins (top/bottom and sides)
- 12 font, Times New Roman font
- Double spaced
- Maximum eight pages

Notes:

This memo should be predictive and not persuasive. You are not trying to persuade the senior partner or the client about the strength of your arguments or urge him or her to take a particular course of action; you are only trying to inform about the law, how it applies to our case, how you think a court would rule and what advice you have.

In a memo, you can also use formatting like underlining, bold font or italics. You can also create headings and subheadings to organize your answer.

For additional information about office memos and e-memos, as well as samples, refer to the online additional resources.

Grading: This assignment is worth 102 points.

LEGAL CONTENT	0-6 points	8 points	10 points	12 points	Points
Issue statement (IS)	Document does not include an IS or includes IS that fails to properly identify the legal issue(s) and the applicable law	Identifies the legal issue(s) and correctly states the applicable law with minor mistakes	Identifies the legal issue(s) and correctly states the applicable law	Identifies the legal issue(s) and correctly states the applicable law in an exceptionally creative and concise way	_____/12
Short Answer	Document does not include a short answer or includes a short answer with significant mistakes	Responds to IS but with key facts or applicable legal principles missing	Responds to IS with key facts and applicable legal principles with no meaningful errors	Clearly and concisely responds to IS with key facts and applicable legal principles and no irrelevancies	_____/12
Facts	Few or none of the relevant facts are included; difficult to follow or understand	Most relevant facts are included as well as non-relevant ones; at times difficult to follow	Relevant facts are included with occasional irrelevancies; easy to follow	All relevant facts are included with no irrelevancies; story is clearly and concisely told to reader in objective way	_____/12
Rule	Hard to follow and understand; does not include relevant sources or cites inappropriate sources; no rule application	Cites to some relevant sources but is incomplete in covering all relevant aspects of the rule; includes some rule application	Cite only to relevant sources and mostly clear; rule application explains but not fully how rule has been applied	Clear and concise; includes only relevant sources and includes all parts of rule necessary for analysis; clear rule application	_____/12
Analysis	Contains conclusory statements and/or no case law; facts are analyzed in a conclusory or insufficient way	Uses some case law but does not analogize or distinguish or explain its application; some conclusory statements; facts briefly analyzed	Uses case law to show how rule applies to case; case law is compared and contrasted with success; most facts are analyzed	Analyzes case law completely, comparing it fully to client matter; facts are thoroughly analyzed in an objective way	_____/12
Conclusion/ Recommendations	No conclusion or recommendations are included in document	A brief conclusion is included but without sufficient client advice	Paper includes conclusion and recommendations	Paper includes full conclusion of the legal analysis and facts and presents creative and thoughtful recommendations	_____/12
Citations	No sources are cited in document	Some sources are cited, but inconsistently; citation format is inconsistent	All citations are present; correct format is mostly used	All citations are present; correct format is used throughout document	_____/12
WRITING	2	4	5	6	Points
Formatting	Document does not follow format instructions or the sample provided	Document attempts to follow instructions and sample provided	Document follows the instructions and sample provided with no meaningful errors	Document exactly follows the instructions and sample provided	_____/6
Organization	No structure or organization; free flow of ideas	Structure & organization present but reorganization or headings needed for full clarity	Document is clearly organized and structured with proper use of heading and subheadings	Document is exceptionally well organized and structured with proper use of headings and subheadings	_____/6
Syntax Mechanics	Contains numerous and distracting grammatical and mechanical errors that impede understanding	Contains some grammatical and mechanical errors that impede understanding	Contains few grammatical and mechanical errors but none that impede understanding	Contains no grammatical and mechanical errors; native-like use of English	_____/6
TOTAL					_____/102

Mock Client Meeting

Overview of the Assignment: This assignment simulates a client meeting between you and your client. If you represent the plaintiffs, you will be meeting with Roger Mudd or Hillary Vonn, and if you represent the defendant, you will be meeting with Mayor Jason Lange.

The purpose of the meeting is to explain to your client the status of the litigation <u>Mudd et al. v. City of Longworth</u>, the results of your analysis about how a court might rule on the motion for the preliminary injunction, and your recommendations on how to proceed.

Learning Objectives of the Assignment:

This assignment will build your skills to:

- Explain and clarify the legal positions of the parties and describe potential outcomes to your client
- Respond to technical questions about litigation
- Incorporate technical legal English vocabulary that relates to the constitutional right to privacy and use appropriate layperson explanations for your client

Steps for Completing the Assignment:

- Read and be familiar with the Main Assignment File
- Be familiar with the right to privacy cases that you have been assigned
- Recommended:
  - Anticipate the questions that you think your client might ask and prepare possible responses
  - Draft an outline of what you would like to cover in the meeting

Note: Remember that part of the grading is also based on your professional demeanor. You are expected to arrive punctually, be dressed in professional attire and act as you would with a client in real life. You should play the part from when you come into the meeting room.

Grading: This assignment is worth 102 points.

Punctuality: Student-attorney arrived on time to meeting: YES _____ (10 points) NO _____ (0 points)

Professional Attire: Student-attorney was dressed in appropriate professional attire: YES _____ (10 points) NO _____ (0 points)

Professional Demeanor: Student-attorney acted in a professional manner w/client: YES _____ (10 points) NO _____ (0 points)

GRADING CRITERIA	0- 6 points	8 points (C or 75%)	10 points (B or 85%)	12 points	Points received
Engagement I (questions)	Attorney does not ask client any questions; engages in monologue	Attorney asks few questions; questions are hard to follow or show minimal preparation or understanding of matter	Attorney asks basic questions that demonstrate understanding of matter and preparation	Attorney asks thoughtful, insightful and creative questions that demonstrate deep preparation & understanding of matter	_____/12
Engagement II (answers)	Attorney does not respond to client's questions	Attorney responds to questions, but incorrectly or with hard to follow answers	Attorney responds promptly and correctly to all of client's questions	Attorney responds promptly and correctly to all of client's questions with creative, thoughtful and insightful answers that show a deep understanding of the issues	_____/12
Knowledge of Applicable Law	Attorney provides no explanation of the applicable law	Attorney provides explanation of with serious mistakes, or hard to follow (e.g. use of legal jargon)	Attorney provides clear explanation of with some mistakes; uses some legal jargon unnecessarily or without explanations that client can understand	Attorney provides clear, concise and correct explanation of the law with legal jargon when appropriate or w/ explanations client can understand	_____/12
Ability to Analyze Applicable Law	Attorney provides does not provide an analysis of the law for the client	Attorney attempts to analyze the law but provides incomplete or incorrect analysis	Attorney provides analysis of the law with no significant mistakes or misstatements of the law or facts	Attorney provides a clear, concise and correct analysis of the law as it applies to the client matter	_____/12
Advice and Recommendations	Attorney provides no advice or poor advice for client	Attorney provides not comprehensive or inaccurate advice	Attorney provides comprehensive and accurate advice to client on his/her legal matter	Attorney provides thoughtful and creative solutions for client	_____/12
Organization	Meeting is disorganized and hard to follow or lacks any organization	Meeting has some organization but is still confusing for client for how information is presented	Meeting is clearly organized and easy to follow	Meeting is clearly organized and is easy to follow; attorney takes extra steps to ensure client's understanding	_____/12
TOTAL					_____/72
TOTAL FROM PUNCTUALITY AND PROFESSIONALISM					_____/30

Total _____/102

Client Advice Letter

Overview of the Assignment: For this assignment, you will write an advice and follow-up letter to your client, summarizing your research on the right to privacy, as well as your client meeting. You should include any recommendations that you made to your client in the meeting and any predictions about how you think the court will rule on the motion for a preliminary injunction. Be mindful that neither the plaintiffs nor the City/defendant are trained attorneys; therefore you should avoid legalese in your letter.

Under Rule 1.4(a)(3) of the Model Rules of Professional Conduct, an attorney has the duty to keep his or her client "reasonably informed about the status of the client's matter." A thorough follow-up letter after a client meeting is one of the best ways to meet this duty, as well as regular phone calls, emails or meetings.

Learning Objectives of the Assignment:

This assignment will build your skills to:

- Efficiently communicate in a written format
- Explain complex matters clearly and concisely
- Incorporate technical legal English vocabulary that relates to the right to privacy and injunctions and use appropriate layperson explanations for client

Steps for Completing the Assignment:

- Review the predictive memo that you wrote to your senior partner about your client matter to ensure that the law and the issues are clear
- Be familiar with the case law regarding the right to privacy and motions for preliminary injunctions, as well as the fact pattern
- Conduct your client meeting with your client, Mayor Jason Lange for the defendant or Roger Mudd or Hillary Vonn for the plaintiffs
- Review the Business Correspondence online resources

Research Required for the Assignment: You are not required to do any outside research for this assignment.

Format of the Completed Assignment:

Your assignment should be written as a business letter, not as an email. Even though many firms and lawyers use email for much of the correspondence carried out, formal business letters are still an essential part of the practice of law.

Your law firm has the following policy regarding business correspondence. Your client letter must follow the policy guidelines.

LAW FIRM CORRESPONDENCE POLICY

The purpose of this policy is to ensure a uniform appearance of all business correspondence that is written by the attorneys and staff of the law firm and thus to increase the professional appearance of the firm's work product. All law firm attorneys and staff are required to employ the following guidelines when writing correspondence. Violation of the policy can result in disciplinary action, up to and including termination.

- The first page of all "traditional" letters must be written on law firm letterhead, which includes the firm's address and logo
- All letters must be written in a modified block letter format
- Letters must be written in Times New Roman, 12 font
- Letters must be 1.5 spaced and have 1" (2.54 cm.) margins, except for the initial page, which may have larger top margins to account for the logo, law firm address and sender's direct contact information
- Client letters must not exceed four pages

Grading: This assignment is worth 78 points.

Note: See the Online Additional Resources for examples of letters and for general information about business correspondence.

LEGAL CONTENT	0-6 points (failing)	8 points (C or 75%)	10 points (B or 85%)	12 points	Points
Introduction	Letter does not include an appropriate introduction or includes poorly constructed one	Letter includes introduction that states purpose with some irrelevancies or some relevant information missing	Introduction states purpose of letter and includes other relevant information	Introduction is engaging; states purpose of letter and includes other relevant information; written clearly and concisely	_____/12
Summary of Meeting	Letter includes no summary of the meeting	Letter includes summary but leaves out important information or states it unclearly	Letter summarizes the meeting but leaves out important information	Letter clearly and concisely summarizes the meeting, its core purpose and content	_____/12
Applicable Law	Student-attorney provides no explanation of the applicable law, or only uses legal jargon in explanation (inappropriate for audience)	Student-attorney provides explanation of with serious mistakes, or hard to follow (use of legal jargon)	Student-attorney provides clear explanation of with few mistakes; uses some legal jargon without appropriate explanations	Student-attorney provides clear, concise and correct explanation of the law with legal jargon with appropriate explanations	_____/12
Analysis	Contains conclusory statements and/or no case law; facts are analyzed in a conclusory or insufficient way	Uses some case law but does not analogize or distinguish or explain its application; some conclusory statements; facts briefly analyzed	Uses case law to show how rule applies to case; case law is compared and contrasted with success; most facts are analyzed	Analyzes completely case law, comparing it fully to client matter; facts are thoroughly analyzed	_____/12
Conclusion/ Recommendations	No conclusion or recommendations are included in letter	A brief conclusion is included but without sufficient advice or recommendations advice or next steps	Letter includes conclusion with recommendations and next steps	Letter includes full conclusion of the legal analysis and facts, presents creative and thoughtful recommendations and includes clear next steps	_____/12
WRITING	**2**	**4**	**5**	**6**	**Points**
Formatting	Document does not follow format instructions or the sample provided	Document attempts to follow instructions and sample provided	Document follows the instructions and sample provided with minor errors	Document exactly follows the instructions and sample provided	_____/6
Organization	No structure or organization; free flow of ideas	Letter includes organization and structure but is still confusing	Structure and organization but some reorganization is needed for full clarity	Document is clearly organized and structured	_____/6
Syntax Mechanics	Contains numerous and distracting grammatical and mechanical errors that impede understanding	Contains some grammatical and mechanical errors that impede understanding	Contains few grammatical and mechanical errors but none that impede understanding	Contains no grammatical and mechanical errors; native-like use of English	_____/6
TOTAL					_____/78

Memorandum of Law
for Motion for Preliminary Injunction

Overview of the Assignment: For this assignment, you will draft the memorandum of law in support of or in opposition to the motion for a preliminary injunction filed by the plaintiffs in the case <u>Mudd et al. v. City of Longworth</u>, currently docketed in the Hemings County District Court.

Learning Objectives of the Assignment:

This assignment will build your skills to:

- Efficiently read and understand legal authority
- Analyze the fact pattern by applying the relevant case law
- Adapt the IRAC organization and the formal memorandum of law structure
- Communicate effectively and in a persuasive manner to convince the court and the reader that your client's position and argument is the one to follow

Research for the Assignment: You are not required to do any outside research for this assignment. You should base your analysis on the right to privacy cases that you have read in class:

- <u>State v. Boland</u>, 800 P.2d 1112 (Wash. 1990).
- <u>State v. Sweeney</u>, 107 P.3d 110 (Wash. Ct. App. 2005).
- <u>State v. Graffius</u>, 871 P.2d 1115 (Wash. Ct. App. 1994).
- <u>State v. Rodriguez</u>, 828 P.2d 636 (Wash. Ct. App. 1992).

If you want to practice your legal research skills, you can look for and use other cases that you find. However, if you do search on Westlaw, LexisNexis or Bloomberg Law, use Washington law for binding precedent. Be sure to change the citations to Jefferson if using cases from Washington. For persuasive precedent from other states, keep the state identifiers the same.

Format of the Completed Assignment:

For your completed assignment, you must follow Local Rule 5.2 of the Courts of Jefferson.

Local Rule 5.2 GENERAL FORMAT OF DOCUMENTS TO BE FILED

<u>Format</u>: All documents filed must be typewritten, printed, or prepared by a clearly legible duplication process. Document text must be double-spaced, except for quoted material and footnotes, and pages must be numbered consecutively at the bottom. Documents filed after the case-initiating document must contain—on the front page and above the document's title—the case number and the name or initials of the assigned district judge and magistrate judge.

<u>Represented Parties</u>. A memorandum of law filed by a represented party must be typewritten. All text in the memorandum, including footnotes, must be set in at least font size 12 (i.e., a 12-point font) as font sizes are designated in the word-processing software used to prepare the memorandum. Text must be double-spaced, with these exceptions: headings and footnotes may be single-spaced, and quotations more than two lines long may be indented and single-spaced. Pages must be 8 ½ by 11 inches in size, and no text — except for page numbers — may appear outside an area measuring 6 ½ by 9 inches.

<u>Length</u>: No memorandum filed with the court shall exceed the length of twelve pages, excluding caption and table of contents.

Grading: This assignment is worth 90 points.

Note: See the online resources for additional information about memoranda of law and persuasive writing.

Unit 3   State Constitutional Right to Privacy

LEGAL CONTENT	0-6 points	8 points	10 points	12 points	Points
Introduction	Document does not include an Introduction or includes issue statement instead	Introduction is not persuasive or does not include persuasive or relevant facts or the law	Student attempts to make introduction persuasive, to "put the spin" but does not include all facts or something...	Introduction is persuasive, clear and concise and clearly introduces reader to the client's story and position and identifies the relief sought	_____/12
Facts	Few or none of the relevant facts are included; difficult to follow or understand	Relevant facts are included as well as non-relevant ones; mostly clear	Relevant facts are included; factual background is mostly clear and easy to follow with few irrelevancies	Relevant facts are included with no irrelevant facts; story is clearly and concisely told to reader in persuasive way	_____/12
Rule	Hard to follow and understand; does not include relevant sources or cites inappropriate sources; no rule application	Cites to some relevant sources but is incomplete in covering all relevant aspects of the rule	Cite only to relevant sources; rule application explains but not fully how rule has been applied	Clear and concise; includes only relevant sources and includes all parts of rule necessary for analysis; clear rule application	_____/12
Argument	Contains conclusory statements and/or no case law; facts are analyzed in a conclusory or insufficient way	Uses some case law but does not analogize or distinguish or explain its application; some conclusory statements; facts briefly analyzed; student attempts to make persuasive arguments	Uses case law to show how rule applies to case; case law is compared and contrasted with success; facts are analyzed and argued in a persuasive way	Analyzes completely case law, comparing it fully to client matter; all facts are thoroughly analyzed and argued in a very persuasive way	_____/12
Conclusion	No conclusion is included in document	A brief conclusion is included but unclear relief sought	Paper includes conclusion with relief sought	Paper includes full conclusion of the legal analysis and facts and persuasively argues for relief sought	_____/12
Citations	No sources are cited in document or citation formats are incorrect and inconsistent	Sources are cited, but inconsistently; citation format has meaningful mistakes in format	Citations are complete; few meaningful mistakes in format	No mistakes in citations; correct format is used throughout document	_____/12
WRITING	**2**	**4**	**5**	**6**	**Points**
Formatting	Document does not follow format instructions or the sample provided	Document attempts to follow instructions and sample provided	Document follows the instructions and sample provided with minor errors	Document exactly follows the instructions and sample provided	_____/6
Organization	No structure or organization; free flow of ideas	Document includes some organization and structure but is still confusing; no use of headings or subheadings	Structure & organization present but reorganization needed full clarity; subheadings included but not effectively persuasive	Document is clearly organized and structured with proper use of persuasive heading and subheadings	_____/6
Syntax Mechanics	Contains numerous and distracting grammatical and mechanical errors that impede understanding	Contains some grammatical and mechanical errors that impede understanding	Contains few grammatical and mechanical errors but none that impede understanding	Contains no grammatical and mechanical errors; native-like use of English	_____/6
TOTAL					_____/90

Mock Oral Argument

Overview of the Assignment: For this assignment, you will carry out the oral argument for the motion for a preliminary injunction in the <u>Mudd et al. v. City of Longworth</u> case, currently docketed in the Hemings County District Court. Oral arguments are scheduled for the motion filed by the plaintiffs, asking the court to issue an injunction enjoining the enforcement of the garbage ordinance.

You will represent the party that your instructor has assigned to you.

Learning Objectives of the Assignment:

This assignment will build your skills to:

- Effectively and persuasively communicate legal rules and argument
- Conduct yourself orally in a professional courtroom setting
- Respond to questions about the relevant law

Steps for Completing the Assignment:

Before the oral arguments, review the following:

- Pleadings
- Notice of Motion and Motion for a Preliminary Injunction
- Your Memorandum of Law, as well as that of your opposing counsel
- Cases cited in your memo and opposing counsel's
- Facts of the client matter

Research for the Assignment: Although no additional research is required for the assignment, you should review the memorandum of your opposing counsel and review the cases that he/she includes, consider how you can rebut the cases, or explain how they are inapposite to the matter at hand and address those cases in your oral argument.

Format of the Assignment:

Each side has 20 minutes for his or her argument. The moving party first presents his/her arguments and may reserve time for rebuttal. It is the moving party's decision to reserve time for rebuttal. After the moving party has presented his/her arguments, it is the non-moving party's turn. The non-moving party does not receive time for rebuttal since he/she can listen to opposing counsel and respond directly to any arguments made. After the non-moving party finishes, the moving party responds with rebuttal, if he/she previously asked the court to reserve time for it.

Be prepared to answer questions from the court, and part of your preparation should be anticipating the questions that the judge might ask and preparing answers. But in the event that the judge doesn't ask questions or asks few, be prepared to fill the time allotted with your argument.

Grading: This assignment is worth 90 points.

Punctuality: Attorney arrived on time to oral argument: YES _____ (10 points) NO _____ (0 points)

Professional Attire: Attorney was dressed in appropriate professional attire: YES _____ (10 points) NO _____ (0 points)

Professional Demeanor: Attorney acted in a professional manner w/court and opposing counsel: YES _____ (10 points) NO _____ (0 points)

GRADING CRITERIA	0-6 points (failing)	8 points (C or 75%)	10 points (B or 85%)	12 points	Points received
Engagement	Attorney does not respond to the court's questions	Attorney responds to questions, but incorrectly or with hard to follow answers	Attorney responds promptly and correctly to all of the court's questions	Attorney responds promptly and correctly to all of court's questions with creative, thoughtful and insightful answers that show a deep understanding of the issues	_____/12
Knowledge of Applicable Law	Attorney provides no explanation of the applicable law	Attorney provides explanation of with few meaningful mistakes or with explanation that is hard to follow	Attorney provides clear explanation of the law with no meaningful mistakes	Attorney provides clear, concise and correct explanation of the law	_____/12
Analysis of Applicable Law	Attorney provides no analysis of the law or provides analysis that is incorrect or incomplete	Attorney provides analysis of the law but has some mistakes or misstatements of the law or facts	Attorney provides a clear, concise and correct analysis of the law as it applies to the client matter	Attorney present unimpeachable case for the client, analyzing persuasively, concisely and clearly the law as it applies to client matter	_____/12
Conclusion and Relief	Attorney does not identify relief sought or conclude argument	Attorney provides advice, but	Attorney provides advice but	Attorney clearly identifies the relief sought and summarizes the client's position	_____/12
Organization	Argument is disorganized and has serious faults of organization	Argument has minor faults of organization	Argument is clearly organized and easy to follow	Argument is exceptionally well organized and presents arguments in novel way	_____/12
TOTAL					_____/60
TOTAL FROM PUNCTUALITY AND PROFESSIONALISM					_____/30

TOTAL   _____/90

Statutory Law

LLC/Partnership Dispute
Termination of a Membership Interest in LLC

For this Unit, you will provide your opinion about a dispute involving a new client of the law firm and his business partner. The client, Anthony Becerra, has approached the firm for advice on how he can remove his business partner from the limited liability company (LLC) that the two operate together. The issues you will consider and analyze are both legal and non-legal (business) issues, as is often the case when attorneys advise corporate or business clients.

Learning Objectives of this Unit:

This Unit will build your skills to:

- Efficiently and effectively analyze a client matter to identify the legal and non-legal issues at hand
- Effectively research statutes and case law to determine what recommendations you will make to the client
- Contemplate ethical considerations when advising a client
- Articulate legal arguments in support of client's position
- Analyze possible outcomes for legal dispute, evaluate and articulate strengths and weaknesses of such outcomes
- Efficiently and effectively communicate in a written and oral format
- Respond to questions about the relevant law

To achieve these learning objectives, you will complete the following tasks:

- Draft a predictive memo to senior partner about legal issues and your prediction of what will happen if the case were litigated
- Carry out a mock client meeting with Anthony Becerra about the legal issues
- Draft a client advice letter to Anthony Becerra with your recommendations on how he should proceed
- Draft a provision of the Operating Agreement for Desert Suites Salon, LLC in accordance with the goals of the client and the ethical analysis that you conduct

To complete these tasks, you will use the following materials in the book:

- Assignment email from Senior Partner (pages 232-235)
- Main Assignment File (email from senior partner plus online documents (leases, LLC certificate))
- Illinois LLC Act, 805 ILL. COMP. STAT. ANN. 180/*et seq.* (West 2016) (selected sections are included in the Commented Cases and Legal Authorities book. To review all the sections of the Act, you can find it online at the Illinois General Assembly website or on a legal research website).
- Limited Liability Company Commented Cases:
  - Anest v. Audino, 773 N.E.2d 202 (Ill. App. Ct. 2002).
  - Gifford v. Gallano Farms, LLC, Nos. 2–10–0055, 2–10–0355, 2011 WL 10109462 (Ill. App. Ct. May 18, 2011).
  - Azulay, Horn and Seiden LLC, v. Horn, 2013 Il App. (1st) 1120625 (Ill. App. Ct. Aug. 1, 2013).
  - Shrock v. Meier, 2012 Il App (1st) 111408-U (Ill. App. Ct. Mar. 19, 2012).
  - Tully v. McLean, 948 N.E.2d 714 (Ill. App. Ct. 2011).
- ESL Workbook (pages 155-172)

Your instructor will also assign you additional skills-building exercises to bolster your understanding of the legal issues and further develop your legal reasoning and language skills, whether related to legal reasoning and analysis or to English. You will find an icon with each exercise that will indicate which skills the exercise will focus upon.

ICON	SKILL
	Speaking — in particular about the legal issues and the law presented in the Unit
	Oral comprehension
	Legal analysis and reasoning
	Analysis of the legal issue(s) presented in the Unit
	English grammar, syntax, and vocabulary
	Legal ethics and professional responsibility
	Legal research

In this Unit, the additional skills-building exercises that accompany the Main Assignment File include:

- Ethics Dilemma (pages 236-237)
- Presentation: *If Becerra Were Your Client...* (pages 238-239)
- Drafting Provision of Operating Agreement (pages 240-242)
- Analysis of English in Legal Documents (pages 243-247)

Before beginning the Unit, you should read and be familiar with the Factual Background of the Lincoln, Adams and Washington Law Firm (pages 2-3).

You will also find online at the website www.legalwritingforllms.com the following online resources that accompany this Unit. The additional online resources will help you deepen your mastery of the skills presented in the Unit and also provide additional understanding about the U.S. legal system and legal writing.

- Additional documents (leases, LLC certificate)
- Additional Resources:
  - Sources of American Law
  - Writing Professional Emails
  - Writing Predictive Memos
  - Writing E-memos
  - Writing Business Correspondence
  - IRAC
- Additional Skills-Building Exercises:
  - Issues and Issue Statements
  - Stating the Rule
  - Analysis
  - Ethical Spotlight Exercise

Section II, Unit 4 Legal Issue
LLC/Partnership Dispute

Main Assignment File	LLC Cases	ESL Workbook	Additional Exercises	Additional Online Resources

Introduction to File and Client Matter
Pages 227-231

Anest v. Audino, 773 N.E.2d 202 (Ill. App. Ct. 2002).

Anest v. Audino, 773 N.E.2d 202 (Ill. App. Ct. 2002).

Ethics Dilemma: Pages 236-237

Writing Professional Emails

Documents Related to Client Matter
Pages 232-235
+ online documents

Gifford v. Gallano Farms, LLC, 2011 WL 10109462 (Ill. App. Ct. May 18, 2011).

Gifford v. Gallano Farms, LLC, 2011 WL 10109462 (Ill. App. Ct. May 18, 2011).

Presentation: If Becerra Were Your Client... Pages 238-239

Business Correspondence (with sample letters)

Assignment Information Pages + Rubrics
Pages 248-253

Azulay, Horn and Seiden LLC, v. Horn, 2013 Il App. 1120625 (Ill. App. Ct. Aug. 1, 2013).

Azulay, Horn and Seiden LLC, v. Horn, 2013 Il App. 1120625 (Ill. App. Ct. Aug. 1, 2013).

Drafting Provision of an Operating Agreement Pages 240-242

Writing Memos (office memos and e-memos)

Shrock v. Meier, 2012 IL App (1st) 111408-U (Ill. App: Ct. Mar. 19, 2012).

Shrock v. Meier, 2012 IL App (1st) 111408-U (Ill. App. Ct. Mar. 19, 2012).

Analysis of English in Legal Documents Pages 243-247

IRAC (including additional exercises for each element)

Tully v. McLean, 948 N.E.2d 714 (Ill. App. Ct. 2011).

Tully v. McLean, 948 N.E.2d 714 (Ill. App. Ct. 2011).

Skills-Building Exercises for Rules, Issues and Issues Statements, Analysis and Ethical Dilemmas

Section II

Intermediate Legal Issues

Introduction — Limited Liability Companies

In this Unit, you will be dealing with issues that a new client of the Lincoln, Adams and Washington Law Firm is facing with his business partner. This new client, Anthony Becerra, and his business partner, Greg Iijima, have formed an LLC, or limited liability company. Thus, the legal issues that you will analyze revolve around limited liability companies. This introduction will provide you some background on this form of corporate entities.

In 1977, Wyoming was the first state to pass a limited liability company statute.[79] By 1996, all fifty states and the District of Columbia had enacted such statutes, satisfying the need for a corporate form that combined the most useful characteristics of partnerships and corporations: limited liability, partnership default rules and flexibility, and flow-through taxation.[80]

> "A limited liability company may be organized under this chapter for any lawful purpose or purposes, unless some other statute of this state requires organization for any of those purposes under a different law. Unless otherwise provided in its articles of organization, a limited liability company has general business purposes." MINN. STAT. § 322B.10 (2008).

Like corporations and limited partnerships, a limited liability company is a creature of statute. These corporate entities stand in contrast to general partnerships, for which no statutory requirements need to be followed to be created and for which no documents such as articles of organization need to be submitted to a state office such as the Secretary of State. A general partnership can be created by a contract, whether oral, written, express or implied.[81] Likewise, no statutory formalities need to be followed for an individual to establish a sole proprietorship.

Why are limited liability companies seen as a combination of the best features of corporations and partnerships? First, members of a limited liability company enjoy a "corporate-styled" liability shield.[82] Second, they also enjoy the "informality of organization and operation" that characterizes partnerships, internal governance via contracts or corporate documents such as operating agreements or member control agreements, "direct participation by members in the company, and no taxation at the entity level."[83] Instead, a limited liability company is seen as a "flow-through" entity for tax purposes, and an LLC with two or more members is taxed as a partnership unless it elects to be taxed as a corporation.[84] An LLC with one member is taxed as a sole proprietorship.[85]

Because an LLC is a creature of statute, an individual must follow the state laws to establish one, and state laws can and do vary. Some similarities exist as many are modeled after the Uniform Limited Liability Company Act. Generally, these are the steps that must be followed to establish a limited liability company:

- Choose a business name
- File the articles of organization with the Secretary of State of the state in which the LLC is incorporated
- Pay the appropriate filing fee[86]
- Best practices: Create an operating agreement and/or member control agreement

---

[79] Dale W. Cotton et al., *The 2010 Wyoming Limited Liability Company Act: A Uniform Recipe with Wyoming "Home Cooking,"* 11 WYO. L. REV. 49, 51 (2011) (citation omitted).

[80] 54 C.J.S. *Limited Liability Companies* § 3 (Westlaw database updated Sept. 2016).

[81] Arnold v. De Booy, 201 N.W. 437, 438 (Minn. 1924) (holding that there can be no partnership or joint venture without a contract, whether express or implied).

[82] 54 C.J.S. *Limited Liability Companies* § 3 (Westlaw database updated Sept. 2016).

[83] Id.

[84] Historic Boardwalk Hall, LLC v. C.I.R., 694 F.3d 425, 429 n.1 (3rd Cir. 2012).

[85] 26 C.F.R. § 301.7701-3(a) (2006) ("An [LLC] with at least two members can elect to be classified as either an association (and thus a corporation). . . or a partnership, and an [LLC] with a single owner can elect to be classified as an association or to be disregarded as an entity separate from its owner.").

[86] This varies too. For example, the filing fee for an LLC in Illinois is $500, 805 ILL. COMP. STAT. 180/50-10 (2016), while in New York it is $200. N.Y. LTD. LIAB. CO. LAW § 1101(f) (McKinney 2016). The fee is only $100 in Georgia. GA. CODE. § 14-11-1101(a)(1) (2016).

No minimum of capital is required to operate, and LLCs must pay an annual renewal fee. Nothing beyond the initial articles of organization is filed with the state. Since no internal corporate documents are submitted to the state or any state entity or agency, no state office, absent an audit or other investigatory activity, has the right to demand that an LLC or its members produce any such documents such as profit and loss, balance sheets or bank account documents.

> "A limited liability company may, but need not, have bylaws, which may, but need not, be known as an operating agreement. The bylaws may contain any provision relating to the management of the business or the regulation of the affairs of the limited liability company not inconsistent with law or the articles of organization." MINN. STAT. § 322B.603 (1999).

While once upon a time limited liability companies were required to have at least two members who own membership interests, most states now allow for single-member LLCs. Regardless of whether there is one member or six members, though, the company has a legal existence separate from its members and managers and the acts of the company are independent and separate from the acts of its members.[87]

Members in a limited liability company owe one another fiduciary duties, just as partners do in a partnership.[88] These duties include the duty of good faith, utmost trust and loyalty.[89] However, there are jurisdictions that view members of a limited liability company more like shareholders in a corporation than partners in a partnership and hold that LLC members do not owe one another a fiduciary duty.[90]

Furthermore, the operating agreement that the LLC members draft and sign can "define, limit, modify or eliminate the scope of the fiduciary duty imposed upon its members."[91] In the absence of a written agreement, the state's LLC statute and its provisions will prevail. The state's LLC statute may place restrictions on what the LLC members can agree to or waive in the operating agreement, so it is important for an attorney practicing business law in a certain state to be familiar with the state's LLC statute.

As you will learn, the new client of the Lincoln, Adams and Washington Law Firm, although a 50/50 member in an LLC with his business partner, has no written internal documents such as an operating agreement. Nevertheless, he would like advice on how to remove, or "dissociate" his business partner from the LLC due to various actions that the business partner has taken. Part of your analysis and work will be to advise him on how to proceed in this matter without a written agreement and the provisions of the written agreement that he should sign with his business partner, if you determine that it is in his best interests to draft and sign one. You will also be faced with non-legal issues, both business and ethical, which are often as important in advising a client, especially a business one, and can impact the advice and suggestions that you give.

Your written assignments will also include drafting a provision of an operating agreement that the firm's client could potentially sign with his business partner, as well as an office memo to the senior partner and a client advice letter. In addition, you will hold a mock client meeting in which you will advise your client on how he should proceed.

---

[87] 51 AM. JUR. 20 *Limited Liability Companies* § 1 (Westlaw database updated Sept. 2016).
[88] 54 C.J.S. *Limited Liability Companies* § 31 (Westlaw database updated Sept. 2016).
[89] Id.
[90] Id.
[91] Id.

Main Assignment File: LLC/Partnership Dispute

You received the following email from Senior Partner Jack Adams, who has asked you to work with a new client, Anthony Becerra, who has many questions regarding some problems with his business partner and has turned to the firm for advice.

From:	Jack Adams <j.adams@lawlawfirm.com>
To:	Associate Attorney <a.attorney@lawlawfirm.com>
Date:	February 4, THIS YEAR 11:03
Re:	FW: Advice Needed

Associate attorney,

You are going to have to deal with this for me. I am in trial all week and next week too. It seems to me that there are a lot of different issues here. Please analyze the situation and determine all possible outcomes, solutions and approaches for Mr. Becerra. I'd like you to research the issues, draft a memo for me and meet with me about the situation before Mr. Becerra returns to the States and you then meet with him.

JA

Sent from my iPhone

From:	Anthony Becerra <anthony@desertsalonsuites.com>
To:	Jack Adams <j.adams@lawlawfirm.com>
Date:	February 4, THIS YEAR 09:25
Re:	Advice Needed
🔗	|3 Attachments (78.2 KB total)

Dear Mr. Adams,

I am writing you upon the recommendation of Pamela Park. Pamela and Stray Dog Advertising provide my company, Desert Salon Suites, with our marketing and advertising services. When I realized that I needed to speak with an attorney about some on-going issues with my business partner, I asked Pamela if she knew of any experienced business attorneys that I could talk to. Pamela had only flattering things to say about you and your firm, so I hope that you can help me and provide me with some solid advice and guidance.

I am the co-owner of a new business, Desert Salon Suites. My business partner, Greg Iijima, and I started the company last year. We incorporated Desert Salon Suites, LLC with the Jefferson Secretary of State (I've attached the certificate of incorporation to this email), but we haven't signed any written corporate documents like an operating agreement or member control agreement. We both graduated from the MBA program at the University of Jefferson and have known each other for several years, so we've done everything with a handshake. I know that we need something written between us to better protect my interests, but we've been so busy that we just haven't gotten around to it.

The business is divided 50-50 between Greg and me. However, Greg made an initial contribution to the LLC of $60,000 for our start-up expenses; I provided my labor and services instead since I didn't (and don't) have money to contribute or loan to the LLC. Like everything else, we didn't put anything in writing about this initial contribution.

Desert Salon Suites is a salon suite concept. We lease a 4,300 square foot space from a landlord, Riverview Property Management, Inc. In turn, we have built out that space into 40 smaller spaces, which we rent to professionals who operate their business — hair stylists, massage therapists, nails, waxing, chiropractors and other alternative medicine professionals (acupuncturists, Reiki, craniosacral therapy). They sublease the space from us and in exchange for their rent, receive their own private space that they can personalize. We provide marketing assistance, a receptionist, some equipment, cleaning services and a high-end salon environment.

In the 12 months that we've been opened, we have been very successful. 90% of our spaces have been leased out to these professionals, and we have gotten good word of mouth from our tenants. In turn, their clients have commented that they are happy with the services that we provide. My business partner, Greg, is also a professional who uses one of the spaces. He is a massage therapist. When we first began discussing our business, we agreed that he would have a space within Desert Salon Suites where he could operate his massage therapy business, and that he would pay no rent. Unlike the other subtenants, Greg has no written lease with Desert Salon Suites. For your information, I've attached the sublease that all of our tenants have signed (except Greg, of course).

The lease that Greg and I signed with Riverview Property Management is also attached to the email. As you will see, the lease is in the name of the LLC, and we both signed it as co-owners of the LLC, but we were both required to sign a personal guaranty. Because we are a new business, the landlord insisted. I didn't want to, but had no choice so that we could get the space and start operating.

To be blunt, Greg has turned out to be a lousy business partner and I want to get rid of him. One of the pieces of advice that I hope you can give me is how I can accomplish that. He had the available capital to build out the space and get the business up and running, which is really why I agreed to partner with him. I'd prefer to be on my own. Let me tell you some of the things that he has done.

First, Greg is a distraction to the other tenants. Since he runs his massage business more as a hobby (I think he inherited a lot of money so really doesn't need to work), he doesn't have that many clients, unlike the other tenants. He is always wandering the halls, talking with them, interrupting their work and just being a nuisance. He also isn't very business-like. With the other tenants, he criticizes and talks badly about me and my wife, Heather, who also has a space within the Salon where she operates her acupuncture business (she doesn't pay rent either). He doesn't do anything for Desert Salon Suites. I do all the rent collections, meet with prospective tenants, deal with any current tenant issues (which fortunately have been few) and also promote the business to find new tenants.

Two weeks ago, Heather told me that one of the tenants, Emma, a hair stylist, told her that one of her clients, who also sees Greg for massages on a weekly basis, was sexually assaulted by Greg during a massage! He touched her inappropriately. She was very upset, as you can imagine, and told her husband, who insisted that she file a police report. Emma told Heather that this client has indeed filed a police report. Nothing has taken place because of it, as far as I know, but Emma's client supposedly was told that the police will investigate.

After learning about this, I did some online searching about Greg. And I found a Facebook profile under the name Greg Desert (instead of his real name, as he also has a profile under that name), and on the profile, there were pictures of...well....his private parts...if you know what I mean. I knew it was the same Greg because there was one picture taken at the Salon, and I could recognize the furnishings in the picture. After some further searching, I found other profiles on some dating sites, with other pictures of him half-naked. These profiles were even under his real name. He is married, and I doubt that his wife is aware of these profiles and pictures. When reviewing the security tapes one evening after we had an attempted break-in, I saw Greg walking through the Salon after hours in just his underwear! I couldn't tell if anyone else was in the space with him at the time (no tenants were there with their clients since they are limited to using the space during our hours from 9:00 a.m. to 9:30 p.m.), but it bothers me that he is doing such inappropriate things even when the Salon is closed.

We originally talked about making Desert Salon Suites a franchise, and this is still my ultimate goal. So far, though, we have barely broken even in the first year of operations given the initial expenses that we've had with construction. If all goes according to projections, we will have a profit next year.

Greg and I have discussed selling the business too, but Greg has an unrealistic expectation of what we could get for the business now. He set a price of $350,000 when we first talked about selling! I am confident that the business will be worth that much in a few years, but not yet. As I mentioned, I'd like to get rid of Greg, and I even brought up with him one day how much I would have to pay to buy him out, and the price he quoted me was $175,000, exactly 50% of what he believes the business is worth. Even if I wanted to, there is no way that I could pay him that amount of money. I wish I could, but am not independently wealthy like Greg.

Here are some questions that I have for you:

- How can I get rid of Greg as a partner in Desert Salon Suites, LLC?
- Can we sign an operating agreement or a member control agreement that has a provision that I could then use to get rid of him? I know that he will sign anything and not read it before signing since I've seen him do this on numerous occasions, so could we put in the agreement a provision that I could then use to my advantage to get him out of the business?
- Can we use his sexual assault as a reason to get rid of him?
- Basically, what should I do?

I am out of the country starting tomorrow and without phone or internet access for the next two weeks, so I hope all of the information that I've provided you is sufficient. I would like to set up a meeting with you upon my return so that you can provide me with some guidance about how to proceed.

Thank you in advance for your help.

Best regards,

Anthony Becerra

Owner, Salon Desert Suites

Based on his initial reading of the email from Becerra, Senior Partner Adams identified two legal issues — unconscionability in contract formation and tenancies — that he thought seemed relevant. To help you with the task he's assigned, he asked the firm's paralegal to research these two issues for you and write a short memo summarizing his research. The memo the paralegal prepared is below, and you can use the case law that he included to help you as you work through Becerra's email and prepare your memo in response.

You are to use these short summaries of case law in addition to the cases included in the Commented Cases book, and the LLC statutes, for your analysis of this client matter.

LEGAL RESEARCH MEMO

To:	Associate Attorney <a.attorney@lawlawfirm.com>
From:	Paralegal <paralegal@lawlawfirm.com>
Date:	February 5, THIS YEAR
Re:	Desert Salon Suits, LLC

Associate attorney,

Jack asked me to search the law of Jefferson on unconscionability of a contract and tenancy at will as he thought that those issues might be relevant to the Desert Salon Suites, LLC matter. Here is the summary of cases I found helpful.

Unconscionability: Adams mentioned to me that he thinks the issue of unconscionability might apply if an operating agreement were drafted to prejudice Iijima, as Becerra asked.

Kinkel deals with the unconscionability of a mandatory arbitration clause. Kinkel v. Cingular Wireless LLC, 857 N.E.2d 250 (2006). In this case, the Supreme Court of Jefferson held that the class action waiver contained in the mandatory arbitration clause was substantially unconscionable and thus unenforceable because the clause was contained in an adhesion contract that failed to inform the customer of the costs of arbitrating a dispute and did not provide a cost-effective mechanism for individual customers to obtain a remedy — in either a judicial or an arbitral forum — for the specific injury alleged. Id. at 278. To determine whether a provision is unconscionable or not, the court viewed the provision in the context of the contract as a whole. Id. at 264. A finding of unconscionability may be based on either procedural or substantive unconscionability, or a combination of both. Id. at 263.

Procedural unconscionability refers to a situation where a term is so difficult to find, read, or understand that the plaintiff cannot fairly be said to have been aware that he was agreeing to it. Sanchez v. CleanNet USA, Inc., 78 F. Supp. 3d 747, 755 (2015); Kinkel, 857 N.E.2d at 264. This analysis also takes into account the disparity of bargaining power between the drafter of the contract and the party claiming unconscionability. Sanchez, at 755; Kinkel, 857 N.E.2d at 264. According to the Jefferson Supreme Court, procedural unconscionability boils down to "impropriety during the process of forming the contract depriving a party of a meaningful choice." Sanchez, 78 F. Supp. 3d at 755. To determine whether a meaningful choice existed, Illinois courts consider (1) the manner in which the contract was formed, (2) whether each party had a reasonable chance to understand the contract, and (3) whether key terms were "hidden in a maze of fine print." Id.

The court found a degree of procedural unconscionability in the mandatory arbitration provision because it did not inform the client that she would have to pay towards the cost of arbitration. The court did not conclude this degree of procedural unconscionability to be sufficient to render the class action waiver unenforceable, but it is a factor to be considered in combination with our findings on the question of substantive unconscionability.

Substantive unconscionability concerns the actual terms of the contract and examines the relative fairness of the obligations assumed. Sanchez, 78 F. Supp. 3d at 755. Indicative of substantive unconscionability are contract terms so one-sided as to oppress or unfairly surprise an innocent party, an overall imbalance in the obligations and rights imposed by the bargain, and significant cost-price disparity. Id. After a very thorough research, the court concluded a class action waiver will not be found unconscionable if the plaintiff had a meaningful opportunity to reject the contract term or if the agreement containing the waiver is not burdened by other features limiting the ability of the plaintiff to obtain a remedy for the particular claim being asserted in a cost-effective manner. Kinkel, 857 N.E.2d at 274.

Tenant's Rights:

Adams also said that he thought the issue of Iijima's rights as a tenant might be worth exploring even though he isn't paying rent.

As for the issue of tenancy, Jefferson courts have consistently held that people living in a house by the owner's consent while they have no lease nor pay rent, are mere tenants at will. See Zilch v. Young, 184 Jeff. 333, 337 (Jeff. 1900); Herrell v. Sizeland 81 Jeff. 457, 459 (1876) (both quoting 4 Kent, Comm. 114, "if the tenant be placed on the land without any terms prescribed or rent reserved, and as a mere occupier, he is strictly a tenant at will"). Tenancy at will can be terminated at any instant at the will of the lessor. Evans v. Evans, 163 Jeff. App. 203, 209 (1911). There must be a demand of possession before bringing an action to the court. Zilch v. Young, 184 Jeff. 333, 337 (1900). Even when a tenant does not pay rent, the landlord may not use self-help methods such as a lock-out to evict the tenant and must follow the same statutory procedures that apply to paying tenants (i.e. filing an eviction action if the tenant does not vacate).

Additional Skills-Building Exercises

Ethics Dilemma

The Rules of Professional Conduct regulate the actions, conduct, and behavior of lawyers in their interactions with clients, non-clients, opposing counsel, and judges and establish standards for attorney conduct and for the legal profession. Each state has promulgated its own set of Rules of Professional Conduct although the ABA Model Rules of Professional Conduct serve as a model for the rules of most states.

Being familiar with the Rules and their requirements is fundamental for all attorneys. Like the law, ignorance of the rules is no defense. And while a violation of the rules can but does not always equate to legal malpractice, attorneys can end up in serious trouble for a violation. Punishment can range from a private admonishment to suspension of one's license to practice law and to disbarment (the removal of an attorney from the practice of law and revocation of his or her license).

However, attorneys may oftentimes face situations that aren't addressed by the Rules of Professional Conduct, but still implicate ethical considerations. Other times, corporate or business attorneys may be required to provide advice or make decisions that raise business concerns and interests, which can be as important for a corporate client as the legal considerations.

With all of these independent, yet overlapping concerns, attorneys must make difficult yet important decisions on a regular if not daily basis and must evaluate and balance all of these considerations.

Overview of the Exercise: For this exercise, you and a partner will analyze your choices of action in the LLC/partnership matter involving Anthony Becerra. In particular, you will analyze the requests that Becerra has made to you in the initial email he sent to the LAW Law Firm and consider the advice that you have considered providing Becerra regarding the many issues that he faces. You must then determine whether the requests made by Becerra or your advice would violate the Rules of Professional Conduct or are ethically questionable for other reasons. Always support your conclusion with analysis and reasoning such as references to the Rules or other statutes, rules or regulations.

As stated, corporate and business attorneys often face decisions that have not only legal implications, but also business and personal implications for their clients. Thus, you should also consider whether Becerra's requests and your advice would be disadvantageous for his business based on his concerns, interests, and ultimate goals of franchising his business concept and of operating a successful and profitable business.

Learning Objectives of the Exercise:

This exercise will build your skills to:

- Skim a reading selection (the Rules of Professional Conduct) and identify quickly which rule pertains to your facts and is relevant

- Interpret language of rules and apply those rules of professional conduct

- Evaluate other ethical and/or business concerns when providing advice to a client, or when considering the requests made by a client

- Articulate your analysis and conclusion about whether the Rules of Professional Conduct could be violated or whether other important ethical or business considerations should be taken into account when advising the client

Research for the Exercise: Use the ABA Model Rules of Professional Conduct for this exercise as they are the same as the Jefferson Rules of Professional Conduct. Use a search engine like Google or Bing to locate the rules, or your professional responsibility course book if you are enrolled in the class. You can also find the rules on Westlaw, LexisNexis or Bloomberg Law.

Don't forget to read the comments in addition to the rule itself as the comments often provide valuable insight as to how the rule should be applied.

Grading: This exercise is not graded. Instead, once you and your partner have completed your analysis, you will compare your answer with your other classmates.

Presentations:
If Anthony Becerra Were Your Client...

Overview of the Exercise: For this exercise, you will make a professional presentation in which you answer and discuss the following question: *If Anthony Becerra were your client in your home country and if he came to you for legal advice about the matters involving his business partner, what would you do and what advice would you give him?*

Learning Objectives of the Exercise:

This assignment will build your skills to:

- Describe a specific aspect of your country's legal system
- Compare your country's legal system with the U.S. legal system
- Understand your classmates' presentations and complete information about them

Steps for Completing the Exercise:

- Analyze the fact pattern dealing with Anthony Becerra, his business and his business partner under your country's laws.
- Determine whether or not Becerra would have a viable claim (or claims) under your country's laws, and define what those claims would be.
- Explain if Iijima, Becerra's business partner, could raise any viable defenses if Becerra were to bring a claim against him and what those defenses might be.
- Explain what other advice you would give Becerra.

Research Required for the Exercise: The research you are required to do depends on your knowledge of these claims in your country's legal system. It is presumed that you are familiar with the law and with how you would approach this issue if Becerra were a client of yours.

Grading: This presentation is not graded. You will present to a small group of your fellow classmates instead of to the entire class.

Handouts:

As part of your presentation, you must create a handout for your classmates, and the handouts must include fill-in-the-blank questions that your classmates must complete with information that you present during the presentation. Each handout must include at least five questions to complete.

For example, if a U.S. law student were giving a presentation on LLCs in the United States, she could include on her handout this question:

> LLCs are a statutory creation that combine characteristics of _____ and _____.

As you are speaking, your classmates will have to listen, follow what you are saying and fill in the blanks. If you are listening to one of your classmate's presentations and are unsure about an answer, you should ask him or her to repeat so you can fill in the blank(s).

Grammar Review:

The basis of this exercise is hypothetical or conditional verbs: *if Anthony Becerra were your client, what would you do?*

Remember the grammar when discussing hypothetical conditions.

Present: **IF + PAST SIMPLE, WOULD + BASE VERB**

*If Becerra **called** me to schedule an appointment, I **would tell** him to visit me at my office.*

NOTE: We use "were" for all tenses with the verb "to be" when using a conditional verb.

*If I **were** you, I **would not take** that class.*

*If Becerra **were** my client, I **would tell** him that he should immediately sign an operating agreement with his business partner since it is illegal in my country for an LLC to operate without a written one, filed with the state office.*

Past: **IF + PAST PERFECT, WOULD + HAVE + PAST PARTICIPLE**

*If Becerra **had discussed** this matter with me before starting the business, I **would have advised** him not to allow Greg Iijima to rent a space in the salon and operate his other business.*

*If Becerra **had planned** better, it is possible that he **would not have had** these same problems with his business partner.*

Drafting of an Operating Agreement

Overview of Exercise: For this exercise, you will draft a provision of the operating agreement[92] that you suggest Becerra sign with his business partner, Iijima. The provision that you will draft regards the termination of a membership interest and the removal of a member since one of Becerra's main objectives is to remove Iijima from the LLC.

Learning Objectives of the Exercise:

This exercise will build your skills to:

- Evaluate the ethical considerations of how to assist Becerra in achieving his objectives
- Incorporate those considerations into a provision of the operating agreement
- Draft the provision of the agreement to suit legal and ethical needs as well as your client's interests

Research Required for the Exercise: You are not required to do any outside research for this assignment. Online, at websites such as those of the New York Bar Association or of other state bar associations, you can find complete sample operating agreements and member control agreements. If you choose to draft additional provisions or if your instructor should assign other provisions for you to draft, you can use the complete operating agreement to find provisions to revise and draft.

Steps for Completing the Exercise:

As you have discussed and analyzed, the main issue facing Becerra is how he can remove his business partner, Greg Iijima, from the LLC, and whether Iijima's actions outside of the LLC would provide grounds for removal, or whether he can be forced to withdraw from the LLC.

The Jefferson LLC statutes provide some guidance. You have learned that a membership in an LLC is personal property. As such, it cannot be simply taken away from a member, just as you can't take a car or other piece of personal property from someone. You have also learned that the statutes allow a member to withdraw from an LLC, if the operating agreement provides for such an occurrence, and allow a member to withdraw before the dissolution and winding up of the LLC. Nothing in the Jefferson LLC Act prohibits an operating agreement from including a provision for the removal of a member, and the Act also provides examples of the types of occurrences that can lead to a member's disassociation.

Thus, to help Becerra achieve his goals, he needs a written operating agreement. Before you begin examining the following provisions and revising them to suit your client's needs, discuss with your partner the following:

- Which of the two provisions on the next pages best suits your situation? Should you include just one in the operating agreement? Both? Should the two provisions be combined into one? Or should you draft an entirely new provision?
- What is the best way to accomplish your client's objectives?
- What about the ethical considerations of drafting an agreement that heavily favors your client? Is that ethical? Is it a good business practice? Is an attorney prevented from doing so? What reasons are there not to draft such an agreement? To draft it?

Once you have discussed what you would like to draft, work with your partner on drafting the provision. After you have finished, you will be instructed by your instructor on how you will compare and correct your completed provisions.

---

[92] The sample provisions are from an operating agreement from the New York Bar Association website and the agreement is based on New York law. New York State Bar Association, https://www.nysba.org/WorkArea/DownloadAsset.aspx?id=21867 (last visited May 7, 2016).

Removal Of Member.

A Member may be involuntarily removed from the LLC only under either of the following circumstances: (1) the Member is required to provide services to the LLC (as reflected in this agreement), said Member is not substantially performing the promised services, and a Supermajority in interest of LLC Members vote for removal or (2) the Member has defaulted upon its obligations under this agreement to make capital contributions (or loans) to the LLC.

In the case of a removal for failure to preform required services, 60 days prior to any vote to remove, the other LLC Members shall cause a notice to be issued to the Member in question stating that they shall bring to a vote of the LLC Members a motion to remove said Member within 60 days for unsatisfactory performance of required services and detail specific instances or tasks that were allegedly not satisfactorily performed. The other LLC Members shall then give the Member in question a good faith opportunity to cure the deficiencies in performance of services prior to the vote of removal. The period of this good faith opportunity to cure need not extend beyond 60 days. If the Member in question completes a cure within 60 days of receiving the aforementioned notice, then the motion pending before the LLC Members for removal shall be withdrawn.

In the case of a removal for failure to make required capital contributions, 30 days prior to any vote to remove, the other LLC Members shall cause a notice to be issued to the Member in question stating that they shall bring to a vote of the LLC Members a motion to remove said Member within 30 days for non-payment of required capital contributions. The Member in question shall then have 30 days within which to cure the default which shall consist of making all required capital contributions plus 7% per annum interest (compounded annually) upon the amount of any deficiency computed from the date said contribution was due to be made to the LLC. If the Member in question completes this cure within 30 days of receiving the aforementioned notice, then the motion pending before the LLC Members for removal shall be withdrawn and the Member in question shall, henceforth, be consider in good standing. If, however, the 30 day cure period expires and the Member in question fails to make the required capital contribution plus interest on the deficiency, then this Member shall be barred from voting on the motion for removal.

If, after complying with the above notice and cure provisions, an affirmative vote of Supermajority vote in interest of LLC Members is made to remove the Member in question, then, as of that moment, this person shall no longer be entitled to exercise any rights, powers or privileges of a Member and his or her LLC Units shall be considered redeemed by the LLC. In the case of removal for failure to make require capital contributions, the Supermajority in interest shall be determined without regard to the LLC interest of the member to be removed. For example, if the member to be removed holds a 20% interest, only a Supermajority percentage of the remaining 80% LLC interest is required to effect removal.

Upon the affirmative Supermajority vote in interest of LLC Members to remove a Member, the remaining LLC members shall cause a prompt preparation of financial statements for the LLC as of the end of the month in which the resolution was passed by the LLC Members removing said Member and this shall be the effective date of removal for the Member for accounting purposes only under this agreement.

Should the LLC fail to perform upon its obligation under this section to make payments when due, in addition to any other remedies possessed, the LLC shall be liable to the removed Member for interest upon the amount of any deficiency at the rate of 7% per annum (compounded annually) computed from the date that said deficient payment was due under this agreement.

(note that in this sample, suggestions are provided in brackets { }, and you can choose one of the suggested terms or provide your own langauge):

Resignation or Removal

Any Manager may resign at any time by giving notice to the Members, effective upon receipt thereof or at such later time specified therein. Unless otherwise specified in the notice, acceptance of a resignation shall not be necessary to make it effective. The resignation of a Member-Manager shall not affect its rights as a Member and shall not constitute a Withdrawal Event.

At a meeting of Members called expressly for that purpose, any or all Managers may be removed at any time {, with or without cause,) by vote of {Two-thirds in Interest of} the Members entitled to vote for the election of such Manager{s}. The removal of a Member-Manager shall not affect its rights as a Member {and shall not constitute a Withdrawal Event}. {In no event shall any Member-Manager be removed, other than for good cause.} {All Managers shall be automatically removed, without any required vote of the Members, as of the end of {specify Fiscal Year} if distributions to the Members since the date hereof have not, in the aggregate, exceeded {${}} {specify formula}.}

Language Focus:
Analysis of English in Legal Documents

Overview of Exercise: Language and words are a lawyer's tools, just as a hammer is for a carpenter and a sewing machine for a tailor. Whether writing a contract, an appellate brief or a client letter, an attorney has to carefully choose the words that he uses and verify that the grammar and punctuation are correct. Mistakes in grammar, word choice and language in general can lead to ambiguity, misinterpretation and even malpractice.

In this exercise, you will review contracts, pleadings, statutes, and correspondence and analyze the English. All of the writing samples provided in the assignment have mistakes of some sort — grammar, ambiguity, punctuation, word choice — and your task is to identify the mistake and correct it to improve the writing and thus improve your own command of English.

Learning Objectives of the Exercise:

This exercise will build your skills to:

- Analyze different writings in English for grammar, syntax, punctuation and word choice mistakes
- Identify how the writings can be improved
- Redraft the original writings in an improved format

Research Required for the Exercise: No research is required for this assignment.

Grading: This exercise is not graded. Instead, you will compare answers with your classmates when you have completed the assignment.

1. Ambiguity

The property manager at an apartment complex wrote the following email to the landlord's attorney, requesting that she put in writing what the landlord and a tenant agreed to.

> **From:** Property Manager <manager@freemanpropertymanagement.com>
> **To:** Laurie Lawyer <laurie@laurieslawfirm.com>
> **Date:** September 2, THIS YEAR
> **Re:** Agreement to Vacate

Hi Laurie,

The landlord, Bill, instructed the tenant, Jim, to vacate on September 29. Jim agreed. Would you draft a short written agreement so we have something in writing that shows what Jim agreed to?

Thanks,

Pam

Property Manager

Your task is to now draft a short statement that memorializes the agreement that Bill and Jim reached.

What problems do you identify when trying to draft the agreement? What can be done to correct the problem?

2. Punctuation

Over several months, you negotiated an important purchase agreement for your client. Under the five-year agreement, your client agreed to purchase a set amount of lumber from the other party at a specific price that was locked in place for the duration of the contract. You and opposing party also discussed renewal and termination terms.

The duration and termination provision of the contract provides as follows:

> *The agreement shall continue in force for a period of five years from the date it is made, and thereafter for successive five year terms, unless and until terminated by one year prior notice in writing by either party.*

Two years after the contract was signed, opposing party — the party supplying the lumber — notified your client in writing that the contract would terminate next year and that thereafter, the price of the lumber would increase by 25% if the parties chose to sign a new contract.

Your client is incredulous and has come to you, furious, for advice. You were convinced that you negotiated a five-year agreement with a set price for that time period. Opposing party claims that the provision as written allows them to terminate with one-year prior written notice.

Which party is correct? What in the above provision supports your answer? How can you change the above provision so that it conforms to what you thought and want it to state?

3. The "grammatical monstrosity"[93]

Potential client, Ruby, came to your office today with a question about a will under which she was named a beneficiary, at least she thinks. She would like your advice and analysis.

The will was written by Ruby's uncle, Michael, who died last month. Michael was not married and had no other close relatives except Ruby and her sister, Amber. Michael's will includes this provision:

Article II – Money and Personal Property

> *I give all my tangible personal property and all policies and proceeds of insurance covering such property to my niece, Ruby J. Glatz and/or my niece, Amber F. Glatz. If they do not survive me, I give that property to be donated to the Animal Humane Society of the United States. My executors may pay out of my estate the expenses of delivering tangible personal property to my beneficiaries.*

What problems can you identify with this provision of the will? What advice do you give to Ruby? If you were writing (or rewriting) the will, what would you change?

4. Contract: Personal Liability?

You are disputing whether personal liability should attach to members of a limited liability company for debt owed by the LLC. Your client, Natalie, is one of the three members (the other two are named Nathan and Raymond), and your position is that the LLC was properly established, no fraudulent activity occurred, your client should be protected under the corporate shield and that the debt should attach only to the LLC. However, an issue has arisen regarding the language used in one of the documents that the members signed when taking out the loan. Opposing party is arguing that the judgment note demonstrates that your client agreed to be personally liable for the debt.

The judgment note evidenced the obligation of the LLC to pay the creditor the sum of $25,000 at ten percent (10%) interest per annum. A final payment of the balance of $15,549.07 was due on the last day of the five-year loan. It also contained a provision for judgment by confession, which reads as follows:

> *The New G & G LLC ("Obligor" or "New G&G"), hereby authorizes any attorney at law to appear in any Court of record in the State of Jefferson or any other State in the United States, on default in the payment of any installment due on the above obligation, and waives the*

---

[93] <u>Boggs v. Commonwealth</u>, 148 S.W.2d 703, 704 (Ky. 1941), cited in <u>In The Matter Of the Estate of Massey</u>, 721 A.2d 1033, 1034 (N.J. Super. Ct. Ch. Div. 1998).

issuance and service of process, and confesses a judgment against me in favor of the Creditor, Inc. for the amount of the note, together with costs of suit and attorney's commission of five percent (5%) for collection and release of all errors, and without stay of execution, and inquisition and extension upon any levy on real estate is hereby waived by me, and condemnation agreed to, and the exemption of personal property from levy and sale on any execution herein is also hereby expressly waived, and no benefit of exemption be claimed under and by virtue of any exception law now in force or which may be hereafter passed.

This agreement shall be binding upon the heirs, executors, administrators, successors and assigns of the undersigned and if there are more than one undersigned, each of them agrees that they and their respective heirs, executors, administrators, successors and assigns are jointly and severally liable hereunder and that wherever the undersigned of the heirs, executors, administrators, successors and assigns of the undersigned are referred to herein in the singular the same shall include the plural.

Obligor hereby recognized she is executing a judgment note with a judgment by confession clause and Obligor hereby specifically waives any rights to notice and an opportunity to be heard prior to entry of judgment on this note against Obligor.

Each of the three members of the LLC signed the judgment note (and the other relevant documents) in their official capacity as members and managers of the LLC. The above language from the judgment note is the only part of the documents that opposing counsel is using to argue that your client is personally liable for the debt. The other documents executed as part of the transaction clearly show that the agreement was between the LLC and the Creditor.

What mistakes, if any, can you identify in the above judgment note? What arguments can be made that your client should be held personally liable? What arguments can be made that she should not? If you were the judge and based on this language, what would you decide?

5. More Punctuation

You are a labor attorney and represent a union, which has recently begun negotiations with management to revise the collective bargaining agreement that was originally signed with the employer in YEAR -7.

The employer is seeking to include an arbitration agreement into the collective bargaining agreement and suggests that the collective bargaining agreement be defined so that it is clear which agreement(s) will be covered by arbitration.

It has been proposed that the collective bargaining agreement be defined as "a contract between an employer and employees or between their respective representatives." Another proposal was that it be defined as a "contract between an employer and employees, or their respective representatives."

What is the difference? If you represent the employees and the union, which version would be better? Why? Conversely, if you represent the employer, which version would you want? Why?

6. Pleadings Written by Another Attorney[94]

You are involved in litigation involving sexual harassment claims filed against your client, a local school. A new attorney at the firm, who is your subordinate, submits to you a draft of the pleadings to submit in the litigation. The pleadings include the following two statements:

Monday Police Chief Clark in person told Helen Tourtillotte and Charles Keegan that despite his claims in November and December YEAR -5 that there was a July 2001 police report of inappropriate sexual conduct by the principle of the school Fred Lewis with a former student he had been incorrect; Fred Lewis was not the individual under investigation for inappropriate advances on a former student it was a different Lewis who worked for the school district.

---

[94] Language from pleadings filed in the case <u>Lewis v. Town of Boothbay</u>. See Order on Motions, <u>Lewis v. Town of Boothbay</u>, Docket No. CV-03-027, at 7 (Me. Dec. 20, 2004).

An incident he investigated himself involving a student E. Hodgdon and after speaking with students in the class found no substantiating evidence that Mr. Lewis looked at her breasts as she claimed and that Mr. Lewis does not make dirty jokes other students in the shop class do.

What do you tell the new attorney about the statements? Do you correct them? If so, how? If you do not, what, if any, ethical concerns should you have about your subordinate's work product?

7. Ambiguous Regulations

You have recently been hired by the Jefferson Department of Natural Resources. Your supervisor, the head of the DNR, has asked you to analyze and if necessary revise the following regulation:

> *This rule proposes the Spring/Summer subsistence harvest regulations in Jefferson for migratory birds that expire on August 31, YEAR +3.*[95]

First analyze the language and determine whether or not it is written well or poorly. If it is written poorly, what is wrong with it? How can it be improved? If you determine that the regulation needs to be revised, revise it.

Your supervisor was so impressed with your revision of that regulation that she bragged about you to a colleague of hers, the head of the Jefferson Department of Emergency Relief. The head of that department would also like you to analyze and if necessary revise a regulation of that agency:

> *This regulation governs disaster assistance for services to prevent hardship caused by fire, flood, or acts of nature that are not provided by Jefferson Emergency Relief Services or the Red Cross.*

First analyze the language and determine whether or not it is written well or poorly. If it is written poorly, what is wrong with it? How can it be improved? If you determine that the regulation needs to be revised, revise it.

8. Contract Drafting:

You are working at a firm that represents clients in personal injury claims, such as car accidents and slip and falls. One of the firm's clients was injured while on vacation in Colorado at a ski resort. While snowboarding, he collided with a snowmobile being driven by an employee of the ski resort, who was attempting to reach a skier who had been injured. The defendant claims that because your client signed a waiver, or release of liability, she is barred from bringing any personal injury claim against the resort. This is the release that your client signed:

RELEASE OF LIABILITY: I understand and accept the fact that skiing/snowboarding in its various forms is a hazardous sport that has many inherent dangers and risks. I realize that injuries are a common and ordinary occurrence of these sports. In consideration of the right to purchase a season pass, I freely accept and voluntarily assume all risk of personal injury or death or property damage, and HEREBY RELEASE AND FOREVER DISCHARGE GRANITE PEAK CORPORATION and the State of Wisconsin, and their agents, employees, owners, directors, officers and shareholders from any and all liability which results in any way from any NEGLIGENCE of GRANITE PEAK CORPORATION or the State of Wisconsin, or their owners, agents, employees, directors, officers, and shareholders with respect to the design, construction, inspection, maintenance, or repair of the conditions on or about the premises or facilities, including equipment or the operation of the ski area, including but not limited to grooming, snow making, trail design, ski lift operations, including loading and unloading, conditions on or about the premises, and conditions in or about the terrain park including man made features, or my participation in skiing, snow boarding, or other activities in the area, accepting for myself the full responsibility for any and all such damage or injury of any kind which may result. The performance of inverted ariel maneuvers is strongly discouraged by Granite Peak Corporation. These activities are extremely dangerous and can result in severe debilitating injuries, paralysis, or even death. I, the undersigned, have carefully read and understand the terms of the season pass and the RELEASE OF LIABILITY, which is an essential part of the season pass terms. I am signing this season pass and RELEASE OF LIABILITY freely and of my own accord. I understand that by signing this RELEASE OF LIABILITY I am waiving certain legal rights, including the right to sue. I realize this season pass and RELEASE OF LIABILITY is binding upon myself, my heirs and assigns, and in the event that I am signing it on behalf of any minors (ages 17 & under), I have full authority to do so, realizing its binding effect on them as well as myself.

---

[95] Examples from www.plainlanguage.gov.

CAUTION! READ BEFORE SIGNING. THIS DOCUMENT AFFECTS YOUR LEGAL RIGHTS AND WILL BAR YOUR RIGHT TO SUE.

What, if any, arguments can you make to the court that the above release of liability should not be enforceable? When considering the arguments, focus in particular on the language of the release. Also consider whether the circumstances of the accident, as explained above, would fall under the definitions included in the release.

9. Provision of LLC Operating Agreement:

ARTICLE III

You represent an LLC. As part of your representation, you drafted, and the four members of the LLC, signed an Operating Agreement, which included the following provision regarding capital contributions and capital accounts:

Capital Contributions and Capital Accounts

3.1   Initial Capital Contributions. On the date hereof, each Member shall contribute to the Company as its Initial Capital Contribution cash in the amount of $15,000. Each Member contributing property as a Capital Contribution represents and warrants, as of the date of such Capital Contribution, that it has good and marketable title to such property, free and clear of all liens, claims, encumbrances, restrictions and other interests whatsoever. Each such Member shall bear all costs and expenses in connection with the Transfer of property to the Company.

One of the members has failed to pay any of the agreed-upon capital contributions, and the chief manager has approached you about what to do. This member claims that the agreement as written does not require him to make the capital contribution, only that he may make it, and he has decided not to because he no longer has the $15,000 available.

You are confused because the language of the operating agreement that you drafted seems quite clear that the members are required to make the contribution. Who is correct? The member who refuses to make the contribution? You and the LLC? Why?

When analyzing the language of the provision, consult the following secondary and primary sources:

- *Shall*, BLACK'S LAW DICTIONARY (10th ed. 2014).
- Gutierrez de Martinez v. Lamagno, 515 U.S. 417 (1995).

Information Pages

Office Memo: LLC/Partnership Matter

Overview of the Assignment: For this assignment, you will write an office memo to the Senior Partner, summarizing your research on the LLC and partnership issues facing Anthony Becerra in his business, Desert Salon Suites, LLC. You should also provide your advice and recommendations for him, as well as your predictions on how the matter would be resolved if litigation were commenced.

Learning Objectives of the Assignment:

This assignment will build your skills to:

- Efficiently communicate in a written format
- Explain complex matters clearly and concisely
- Analyze and apply the rules of law regarding limited liability companies

Research for the Assignment: You are not required to do any outside research for this assignment. You should base your analysis on the limited liability company statutes and cases that you have read:

- Anest v. Audino, 773 N.E.2d 202 (Ill. App. Ct. 2002).
- Gifford v. Gallano Farms, LLC, Nos. 2–10–0055, 2–10–0355, 2011 WL 10109462 (Ill. App. Ct. May 18, 2011).
- Azulay, Horn and Seiden, LLC v. Horn, 2013 Il App. (1st) 1120625 (Ill. App. Ct. Aug. 1, 2013).
- Shrock v. Meier, 2012 IL App (1st) 111408-U (Ill. App. Ct. Mar. 19, 2012).
- Tully v. McLean, 948 N.E.2d 714 (Ill. App. Ct. 2011).

If you want to practice your legal research skills, you can look for and use other cases that you find. However, if you do search on Westlaw, LexisNexis or Bloomberg Law, be sure to limit your search and the cases you use to Illinois law and remember to change the state identifiers in the citations to Jefferson as indicated in the introduction.

Format of the Completed Assignment:

Your response should be in an office memo format and should include the following:

- Summary of the facts
- The relevant law
- Analysis of the law to the fact pattern
- Conclusion about how you think a court would rule if this matter were to go to court
- Your advice to the client about how to proceed

Follow the following format:

- 1 inch (2.54 cm.) margins (top/bottom and sides)
- 12 font, Times New Roman font
- Double spaced
- Maximum eight pages

Notes:

This memo should be predictive and not persuasive. You are not trying to persuade the senior partner or the client about the strength of your arguments or urge him or her to take a particular course of action; you are only trying to inform about the law, how it applies to our case, how you think a court would rule and what advice you have.

In a memo, you can also use formatting like underlining, bold font or italics. You can also create headings and subheadings to organize your answer.

For additional information about office memos and e-memos, as well as samples, refer to the online additional resources.

Grading: This assignment is worth 102 points.

LEGAL CONTENT	0-6 points	8 points	10 points	12 points	Points
Issue statement (IS)	Document does not include an IS or includes IS that fails to properly identify the legal issue(s) and the applicable law	Identifies the legal issue(s) and correctly states the applicable law with minor mistakes	Identifies the legal issue(s) and correctly states the applicable law	Identifies the legal issue(s) and correctly states the applicable law in an exceptionally creative and concise way	_____/12
Short Answer	Document does not include a short answer or includes a short answer with significant mistakes	Responds to IS but with key facts or applicable legal principles missing	Responds to IS with key facts and applicable legal principles with no meaningful errors	Clearly and concisely responds to IS with key facts and applicable legal principles and no irrelevancies	_____/12
Facts	Few or none of the relevant facts are included; difficult to follow or understand	Most relevant facts are included as well as non-relevant ones; at times difficult to follow	Relevant facts are included with occasional irrelevancies; easy to follow	All relevant facts are included with no irrelevancies; story is clearly and concisely told to reader in objective way	_____/12
Rule	Hard to follow and understand; does not include relevant sources or cites inappropriate sources; no rule application	Cites to some relevant sources but is incomplete in covering all relevant aspects of the rule; includes some rule application	Cite only to relevant sources and mostly clear; rule application explains but not fully how rule has been applied	Clear and concise; includes only relevant sources and includes all parts of rule necessary for analysis; clear rule application	_____/12
Analysis	Contains conclusory statements and/or no case law; facts are analyzed in a conclusory or insufficient way	Uses some case law but does not analogize or distinguish or explain its application; some conclusory statements; facts briefly analyzed	Uses case law to show how rule applies to case; case law is compared and contrasted with success; most facts are analyzed	Analyzes case law completely, comparing it fully to client matter; facts are thoroughly analyzed in an objective way	_____/12
Conclusion/ Recommendations	No conclusion or recommendations are included in document	A brief conclusion is included but without sufficient client advice	Paper includes conclusion and recommendations	Paper includes full conclusion of the legal analysis and facts and presents creative and thoughtful recommendations	_____/12
Citations	No sources are cited in document	Some sources are cited, but inconsistently; citation format is inconsistent	All citations are present; correct format is mostly used	All citations are present; correct format is used throughout document	_____/12
WRITING	**2**	**4**	**5**	**6**	**Points**
Formatting	Document does not follow format instructions or the sample provided	Document attempts to follow instructions and sample provided	Document follows the instructions and sample provided with no meaningful errors	Document exactly follows the instructions and sample provided	_____/6
Organization	No structure or organization; free flow of ideas	Structure & organization present but reorganization or headings needed for full clarity	Document is clearly organized and structured with proper use of heading and subheadings	Document is exceptionally well organized and structured with proper use of headings and subheadings	_____/6
Syntax Mechanics	Contains numerous and distracting grammatical and mechanical errors that impede understanding	Contains some grammatical and mechanical errors that impede understanding	Contains few grammatical and mechanical errors but none that impede understanding	Contains no grammatical and mechanical errors; native-like use of English	_____/6
TOTAL					_____/102

Section II

Intermediate Legal Issues

Mock Client Meeting

Overview of the Assignment: This assignment simulates a client meeting between you and your client, Anthony Becerra of Desert Salon Suites, LLC. During the meeting, you will discuss with Becerra the results of your research and your analysis of his business matter, and your predictions on what would happen if he were to commence litigation or take other steps to resolve the disputes with his business partner. You should also provide him your advice and recommendations on how to proceed.

Learning Objectives of the Assignment:

This assignment will build your skills to:

- Explain and clarify the legal positions of the parties and describe potential outcomes to your client
- Respond to technical questions about litigation
- Incorporate technical legal English vocabulary that relates to LLCs and use appropriate layperson explanations for your client

Steps for Completing the Assignment:

- Read and be familiar with the Main Assignment File
- Be familiar with the limited liability company statutes and cases that you have been assigned
- Recommended:
  - Anticipate the questions that you think your client might ask and prepare possible responses;
  - Draft an outline of what you would like to cover in the meeting.

Note: Remember that part of the grading is also based on your professional demeanor. You are expected to arrive punctually, be dressed in professional attire and act as you would with a client in real life. You should play the part from when you come into the meeting room.

Grading: This assignment is worth 102 points.

Punctuality: Student-attorney arrived on time to meeting: YES _____ (10 points) NO _____ (0 points)

Professional Attire: Student-attorney was dressed in appropriate professional attire: YES _____ (10 points) NO _____ (0 points)

Professional Demeanor: Student-attorney acted in a professional manner w/client: YES _____ (10 points) NO _____ (0 points)

GRADING CRITERIA	0- 6 points	8 points (C or 75%)	10 points (B or 85%)	12 points	Points received
Engagement I (questions)	Attorney does not ask client any questions; engages in monologue	Attorney asks few questions; questions are hard to follow or show minimal preparation or understanding of matter	Attorney asks basic questions that demonstrate understanding of matter and preparation	Attorney asks thoughtful, insightful and creative questions that demonstrate deep preparation & understanding of matter	_____/12
Engagement II (answers)	Attorney does not respond to client's questions	Attorney responds to questions, but incorrectly or with hard to follow answers	Attorney responds promptly and correctly to all of client's questions	Attorney responds promptly and correctly to all of client's questions with creative, thoughtful and insightful answers that show a deep understanding of the issues	_____/12
Knowledge of Applicable Law	Attorney provides no explanation of the applicable law	Attorney provides explanation of with serious mistakes, or hard to follow (e.g. use of legal jargon)	Attorney provides clear explanation of with some mistakes; uses some legal jargon unnecessarily or without explanations that client can understand	Attorney provides clear, concise and correct explanation of the law with legal jargon when appropriate or w/explanations client can understand	_____/12
Ability to Analyze Applicable Law	Attorney provides does not provide an analysis of the law for the client	Attorney attempts to analyze the law but provides incomplete or incorrect analysis	Attorney provides analysis of the law with no significant mistakes or misstatements of the law or facts	Attorney provides a clear, concise and correct analysis of the law as it applies to the client matter	_____/12
Advice and Recommendations	Attorney provides no advice or poor advice for client	Attorney provides not comprehensive or inaccurate advice	Attorney provides comprehensive and accurate advice to client on his/her legal matter	Attorney provides thoughtful and creative solutions for client	_____/12
Organization	Meeting is disorganized and hard to follow or lacks any organization	Meeting has some organization but is still confusing for client for how information is presented	Meeting is clearly organized and easy to follow	Meeting is clearly organized and is easy to follow; attorney takes extra steps to ensure client's understanding	_____/12
TOTAL					_____/72
TOTAL FROM PUNCTUALITY AND PROFESSIONALISM					_____/30

Total   ____/102

Section II

Intermediate Legal Issues

Client Advice Letter

Overview of the Assignment: For this assignment, you will write an advice and follow-up letter to Anthony Becerra after your meeting with him in which you discussed the business issues that he is facing. The letter should summarize your research on limited liability companies and explain to your client what his options are, which you recommend and why. Be mindful that even though Becerra is a sophisticated businessman, he is not a trained attorney. Therefore you should avoid legalese in your letter.

Under Rule 1.4(a)(3) of the Model Rules of Professional Conduct, an attorney has the duty to keep his or her client "reasonably informed about the status of the client's matter." A thorough follow-up letter after a client meeting is one of the best ways to meet this duty, as well as regular phone calls, emails or meetings.

Learning Objectives of the Assignment:

This assignment will build your skills to:

- Efficiently communicate in a written format
- Explain complex matters clearly and concisely
- Incorporate technical legal English vocabulary that relates to limited liability companies and use appropriate layperson explanations for client

Steps for Completing the Assignment:

- Review the predictive memo that you wrote to your senior partner about your client matter to ensure that the law and the issues are clear
- Be familiar with the statutes and case law regarding limited liability companies, as well as the fact pattern
- Conduct your client meeting with your client, Anthony Becerra
- Review the Business Correspondence online resources

Research Required for the Assignment: You are not required to do any outside research for this assignment.

Format of the Completed Assignment:

Your assignment should be written as a business letter, not as an email. Even though many firms and lawyers use email for much of the correspondence carried out, formal business letters are still an essential part of the practice of law.

Your law firm has the following policy regarding business correspondence. Your client letter must follow the policy guidelines.

LAW FIRM CORRESPONDENCE POLICY

The purpose of this policy is to ensure a uniform appearance of all business correspondence that is written by the attorneys and staff of the law firm and thus to increase the professional appearance of the firm's work product. All law firm attorneys and staff are required to follow these guidelines when writing correspondence. Violation of the policy can result in disciplinary action, up to and including termination.

- The first page of all "traditional" letters must be written on law firm letterhead, which includes the firm's address and logo
- All letters must be written in a modified block letter format
- Letters must be written in Times New Roman, 12 font
- Letters must be 1.5 spaced and have 1" (2.54 cm.) margins, except for the initial page, which may have larger top margins to account for the logo, law firm address and sender's direct contact information
- Client letters must not exceed four pages

Grading: This assignment is worth 78 points.

Note: See the Online Additional Resources for examples of letters and for general information about business correspondence.

LEGAL CONTENT	0-6 points (failing)	8 points (C or 75%)	10 points (B or 85%)	12 points	Points
Introduction	Letter does not include an appropriate introduction or includes poorly constructed one	Letter includes introduction that states purpose with some irrelevancies or some relevant information missing	Introduction states purpose of letter and includes other relevant information	Introduction is engaging; states purpose of letter and includes other relevant information; written clearly and concisely	_____/12
Summary of Meeting	Letter includes no summary of the meeting	Letter includes summary but leaves out important information or states it unclearly	Letter summarizes the meeting but leaves out important information	Letter clearly and concisely summarizes the meeting, its core purpose and content	_____/12
Applicable Law	Student-attorney provides no explanation of the applicable law, or only uses legal jargon in explanation (inappropriate for audience)	Student-attorney provides explanation of with serious mistakes, or hard to follow (use of legal jargon)	Student-attorney provides clear explanation of with few mistakes; uses some legal jargon without appropriate explanations	Student-attorney provides clear, concise and correct explanation of the law with legal jargon with appropriate explanations	_____/12
Analysis	Contains conclusory statements and/or no case law; facts are analyzed in a conclusory or insufficient way	Uses some case law but does not analogize or distinguish or explain its application; some conclusory statements; facts briefly analyzed	Uses case law to show how rule applies to case; case law is compared and contrasted with success; most facts are analyzed	Analyzes completely case law, comparing it fully to client matter; facts are thoroughly analyzed	_____/12
Conclusion/ Recommendations	No conclusion or recommendations are included in letter	A brief conclusion is included but without sufficient advice or recommendations advice or next steps	Letter includes conclusion with recommendations and next steps	Letter includes full conclusion of the legal analysis and facts, presents creative and thoughtful recommendations and includes clear next steps	_____/12
WRITING	2	4	5	6	Points
Formatting	Document does not follow format instructions or the sample provided	Document attempts to follow instructions and sample provided	Document follows the instructions and sample provided with minor errors	Document exactly follows the instructions and sample provided	_____/6
Organization	No structure or organization; free flow of ideas	Letter includes organization and structure but is still confusing	Structure and organization but some reorganization is needed for full clarity	Document is clearly organized and structured	_____/6
Syntax Mechanics	Contains numerous and distracting grammatical and mechanical errors that impede understanding	Contains some grammatical and mechanical errors that impede understanding	Contains few grammatical and mechanical errors but none that impede understanding	Contains no grammatical and mechanical errors; native-like use of English	_____/6
TOTAL					_____/78

Section II

Intermediate Legal Issues

SECTION III

Advanced Legal Issues

Unit 1 Restrictive Covenants and Preliminary Injunctions

For this Unit, you will write a persuasive memorandum of law in support of or in opposition to a motion for a preliminary injunction in litigation involving Stray Dog Advertising and Rachael Winsted, a former employee who signed a non-competition and non-solicitation agreement while working at SDA and has now violated it by starting her own company and allegedly soliciting a client from SDA. As a result, SDA has filed a breach of contract claim against Winsted and is also asking the court to issue a preliminary injunction to prevent Winsted from continuing to operate her business for the duration of the litigation.

The legal issue involved is breach of contract and the procedural issue is the preliminary injunction. You will represent either SDA as the plaintiff, or the defendant, Rachael Winsted. Both sides have the same documents available to them, and no information is confidential or available to only one side.

Learning Objectives of this Unit:

This Unit will build your skills to:

- Explain complex legal matters clearly and concisely
- Use appropriate technical terminology
- Identify and analyze the applicable case law and facts for the relevant legal issues
- Efficiently read and understand legal authority
- Articulate persuasive legal arguments in support of client's position
- Analyze possible outcomes for legal dispute, evaluate and articulate strengths and weaknesses of such outcomes
- Efficiently and effectively communicate in a written and oral format
- Respond to questions about the relevant law

To achieve these learning objectives, you will complete the following tasks:

- Draft a predictive memo to senior partner about the legal issues and your prediction of what will happen with the litigation
- Draft a persuasive memorandum of law in support of or in opposition to motion for preliminary injunction
- Carry out a mock client meeting with either Pamela Park of SDA or Rachael Winsted
- Draft a client letter to your client about your meeting and about the legal issues
- Carry out oral argument in front of the court for the motion for preliminary injunction

To complete these tasks, you will use the following materials in the book:

- Assignment email from Senior Partner (pages 261-262; 262-263)
- Main Assignment File (pages 264-277)
- Restrictive Covenant Commented Cases:
  - <u>Reed, Roberts Associates, Inc. v. Strauman</u>, 353 N.E.2d 590 (N.Y. 1976)
  - <u>BDO Seidman v. Hirshberg</u>, 712 N.E.2d 1220 (N.Y. 1999).
  - <u>Kanan, Corbin, Schupak, Aronow, Inc. v. FD International, Ltd.</u>, 797 N.Y.S.2d 883 (N.Y. Sup. Ct. 2005).
  - <u>Veramark Technologies, Inc. v. Bouk</u>, 10 F. Supp. 3d 395 (W.D.N.Y. 2014).
  - <u>Scott, Stackrow & Co. v. Skavina</u>, 780 N.Y.S.2d 675 (N.Y. App. Div. 2004).
  - <u>Merrill Lynch, Pierce, Fenner & Smith v. Dunn</u>, 191 F. Supp. 2d 1346 (M.D. Fla. 2002).
  - <u>Lucente v. International Business Machines Corp.</u>, 310 F.3d 243 (2nd Cir. 2002).
  - <u>Zellner v. Conrad</u>, 589 N.Y.S.2d 903 (N.Y. App. Div. 1992).
  - <u>Ashland Management Incorporated v. Altair Investments NA, LLC</u>, 869 N.Y.S.2d 465 (N.Y. App. Div. 2008).
- ESL Workbook (pages 174-209)
- Pleadings (online)

Your instructor will also assign you additional skills-building exercises to bolster your understanding of the legal issues and further develop your legal reasoning and language skills, whether related to legal reasoning and analysis or to English. You will find an icon with each exercise that will indicate which skills the exercise will focus upon.

ICON	SKILL
	Speaking — in particular about the legal issues and the law presented in the Unit
	Oral comprehension
	Legal analysis and reasoning
	Analysis of the legal issue(s) presented in the Unit
	English grammar, syntax, and vocabulary
	Legal ethics and professional responsibility
	Legal research

In this Unit, the additional skills-building exercises that accompany the Main Assignment File include:

- Injunction Analysis Exercise (pages 278-281)
- Restrictive Covenant and Social Media Analysis Exercise (pages 284-287)
- Mock Meeting of Restrictive Covenant and Social Media Analysis (page 288)
- Presentation: *If SDA or Winsted Were Your Client...* (pages 282-283)

Before beginning the Unit, you should read and be familiar with the Factual Background of Stray Dog Advertising (pages 7-8), of the Lincoln, Adams and Washington Law Firm (pages 2-3) and of the Law Office of Bennett, Elliot and Darcy (page 4).

You will also find online at the website www.legalwritingforllms.com the following online resources that accompany this Unit. The additional online resources will help you deepen your mastery of the skills presented in the Unit and also provide additional understanding about the U.S. legal system and legal writing.

Pleadings: Section III, Unit 1 (required)

- Additional Resources:
    - Sources of American Law
    - Writing Professional Emails
    - Writing Persuasive Memos
    - Writing E-memos
    - IRAC
- Additional Skills-Building Exercises:
    - Issues and Issue Statements
    - Stating the Rule
    - Analysis
    - Ethical Spotlight Exercise

Section III, Unit 1 Legal Issue
Restrictive Covenants and Preliminary Injunctions

Main Assignment File	Restrictive Covenant Cases	ESL Workbook	Additional Exercises	Additional Online Resources
Introduction to File and Client Matter Pages 256-260	Reed, Roberts Associates, Inc. v. Strauman, 353 N.E.2d 590 (N.Y. 1976)	Reed, Roberts Associates, Inc. v. Strauman, 353 N.E.2d 590 (N.Y. 1976)	Injunction Analysis Exercise Pages 278-281	Writing Professional Emails
Documents Related to Client Matter Pages 261-277 + pleadings online	BDO Seidman v. Hirshberg, 712 N.E.2d 1220 (N.Y. 1999).	BDO Seidman v. Hirshberg, 712 N.E.2d 1220 (N.Y. 1999).	Restrictive Covenant and Social Media Analysis Exercise Pages 284-287	Business Correspondence (with sample letters)
Assignment Information Pages + Rubrics Pages 289-298	Kanan, Corbin, Schupak, Aronow, Inc. v. FD Int'l, Ltd., 797 N.Y.S.2d 883 (N.Y. Sup. Ct. 2005).	Kanan, Corbin, Schupak, Aronow, Inc. v. FD Int'l, Ltd., 797 N.Y.S.2d 883 (N.Y. Sup. Ct. 2005).	Mock Meeting of Restrictive Covenant and Social Media Exercise Page 288 + confidential information	Writing Memos (office memos and persuasive memoranda of law)
	Veramark Technologies, Inc. v. Bouk, 10 F. Supp. 395 (W.D.N.Y. 2014).	Veramark Technologies, Inc. v. Bouk, 10 F. Supp. 395 (W.D.N.Y. 2014).	Presentation: If SDA or Winsted Were Your Client... Pages 282-283	IRAC (including additional exercises for each element)
	Scott, Stackrow & Co. v. Skavina, 780 N.Y.S.2d 675 (N.Y. App. Div. 2004).	Scott, Stackrow & Co. v. Skavina, 780 N.Y.S.2d 675 (N.Y. App. Div. 2004).		Skills-Building Exercises for Rules, Issues and Issues Statements, Analysis and Ethical Dilemmas
	Merrill Lynch, Pierce, Fenner & Smith v. Dunn, 191 F. Supp. 2d 1346 (M.D. Fla. 2002).	Merrill Lynch, Pierce, Fenner & Smith v. Dunn, 191 F. Supp. 2d 1346 (M.D. Fla. 2002).		
	Lucente v. Int'l Bus. Machines Corp., 310 F.3d 243 (2nd Cir. 2002).	Lucente v. Int'l Bus. Machines Corp., 310 F.3d 243 (2nd Cir. 2002).		
	Zellner v. Conrad, 183 A.D.2d 250 (NY. App. Div. 1992).	Zellner v. Conrad, 183 A.D.2d 250 (NY. App. Div. 1992).		
	Ashland Management Incorporated v. Altair Investments NA, LLC, 869 N.Y.S.2d 465 (N.Y. App. Div. 2008).	Ashland Management Incorporated v. Altair Investments NA, LLC, 869 N.Y.S.2d 465 (N.Y. App. Div. 2008).		

Introduction — Restrictive Covenants and Preliminary Injunctions

In general, a restrictive covenant[96] is a contractual promise not to do something. We see restrictive covenants usually in the following contexts:

- A sale of a business
- Sale or dissolution of a partnership, or
- An employment contract[97]

If a business owner sells his business or if a partner sells his share of a partnership, the purchase agreement will typically include a restrictive covenant according to which the owner or partner agrees not to engage in the same type of business (usually by starting a new business) for a certain period of time in the same market as his old business. These agreements are enforceable and valid as they help to protect the goodwill of the business. The buyer is protected against the seller starting a new, competing business just down the street, or in the same neighborhood and thus siphoning off customers from his new business under the belief that customers would likely follow the former owner to his new business.

This Unit will deal with restrictive covenants in the other context – in an employment contract or agreement. Restrictive covenants can be divided into three types: a non-disclosure agreement, which prohibits an employee from disclosing confidential information or trade secrets; a non-competition agreement, which prohibits the employee from competing with his former employer by working for a competitor or by starting his own competing business; and a non-solicitation agreement, which prohibits an employee from soliciting business from his former employer's clients or customers. A non-solicitation agreement will often also prohibit an employee from soliciting the former employer's employees by enticing them to come work with him at his new business.

In an employer-employee situation, restrictive covenants are more carefully scrutinized than in the context of a sale of a business or a partnership, and less often enforced because they are seen as an unfair restraint of trade since they prevent an individual from earning a living.[98] In fact, for policy reasons, California refuses to enforce restrictive covenants unless for the sale of a business or the dissolution of a partnership.[99] Non-solicitation agreements are less carefully scrutinized and more often enforced than non-competition agreements as they don't prevent an employee from working, or force her to travel great distances to do so, or start working in a new industry or learn a new trade. A non-solicitation agreement says that an employee can start a new business or work for a competitor, but just can't grow her business with the former employer's clients. The competing public policy considerations – protection of a business and its goodwill versus encouraging competition and the growth of the marketplace – are thus balanced.

But in most other states, restrictive covenants in an employment agreement are enforceable, provided that they are reasonable in terms of scope of the restriction for both time and territory (known as the temporal and geographic restrictions) and that they protect legitimate business interests. In many states, restrictive

---

[96] Also called a non-competition or non-compete agreement, a covenant not to compete, a non-compete covenant, a covenant in restraint of trade, a promise not to compete or a contract not to compete. *Covenant*, BLACK'S LAW DICTIONARY (10th ed. 2014).

[97] Id.

[98] See, e.g., Johnstone v. Tom's Amusement Co., 491 S.E.2d 394, 398 (Ga. Ct. App. 1977) ("The rationale behind the distinction in analyzing covenants not to compete [in an employment context differently than those in the sale of a business or other business context] is that a contract of employment inherently involves parties of unequal bargaining power to the extent that the result is often a contract of adhesion. On the other hand, a contract for the sale of a business interest is far more likely to be one entered into by parties on equal footing. An employee negotiating with his employer regarding the employer's assets has little bargaining clout . . . He [is] nothing more than an employee, albeit an important one, and as an employee [he] could reasonably have assumed that if he did not do as [the employer] wished he would be stigmatized as not being a team player, thereby jeopardizing his career prospects with [the employer].") (citing Watson v. Waffle House, 324 S.E.2d 175, 177 (Ga. 1985); White v. Fletcher/Mayo/Assocs. Inc., 303 S.E.2d 746, 750 (Ga. 1983).

[99] "[C]ovenants not to compete in contracts other than for sale of goodwill or dissolution of partnership are void." Kolani v. Gluska, 75 Cal. Rptr. 2d 257, 259-60 (Cal. Ct. App. 1998) (citing CAL. BUS. & PROF. CODE § 16600 (West 2016)).

covenants will be enforced only if the employee or his skills are unique or he has knowledge of the former employer's trade secrets.[100] Whether a restrictive covenant will be enforced in a particular situation is thus very fact specific and is determined on a case-by-case basis.

> The "reasonableness [of a restrictive covenant] must be measured by the circumstances and context in which enforcement is sought." Gelder Med. Grp. v. Webber, 363 N.E.2d 573, 577 (N.Y. 1977).

If an employer believes that a former employee who signed a restrictive covenant has violated it, the employer can then bring a breach of contract claim against the employee (i.e. for breaching the restrictive covenant). Often the employer will also file at the same time a motion for a preliminary or temporary injunction, which is an injunction (a court order ordering a party to do or not do something) issued during litigation to prevent an irreparable injury from occurring before the court has a chance to decide the merits of the underlining case (here, the breach of contract claim).[101] A preliminary injunction lasts for the duration of the litigation, and can be modified into a permanent injunction after the litigation has ended.

Courts use different tests to determine whether an injunction should be issued; the test will likely have from three to five prongs, depending on the state. For example, in Massachusetts, a party seeking a preliminary injunction must establish three prongs:

(1) a likelihood of success on the merits;

(2) that irreparable harm will result from denial of the injunction; and

(3) that, in light of the moving party's likelihood of success on the merits, the risk of irreparable harm to the moving party outweighs the potential harm to the nonmoving party in granting the injunction.[102]

A litigant in Virginia, in contrast, has to establish four elements: (1) the likelihood that the plaintiff will suffer irreparable harm without a preliminary injunction; (2) the likelihood of harm to the defendant with an injunction; (3) the likelihood that the plaintiff will prevail on the merits of the claim; and (4) the impact of an injunction on the public interest.[103] An attorney seeking an injunction for a client, whether in litigation for the enforcement of a restrictive covenant or another situation, must thus be familiar with the state law in which she is practicing. As the cases that you are reading for this Unit are from New York, you will learn what New York courts require to grant a preliminary injunction.

In this Unit, you will deal with the following issues: the violation of a restrictive covenant by Rachael Winsted, a former employee of Stray Dog Advertising, litigation to enforce the covenant she signed, and motion practice seeking a preliminary injunction to prevent her from operating her own competing business for the duration of the litigation. You will be dealing both with the substantive issue of the restrictive covenant and its alleged breach, and also with the procedural issue of the preliminary injunction.

---

[100] See, e.g., Reed, Roberts Assocs., Inc. v. Strauman, 353 N.E.2d 590, 593 (N.Y. 1976) (holding that injunctive relief was unavailable where the employees' services were not extraordinary or unique and trade secrets were not involved); Columbia Ribbon & Carbon Mfg. Co. v. A-1-A Corp., 369 N.E.2d 4, 6 (N.Y. 1977) ("if the employee's services are truly special, unique or extraordinary and not merely of high value to his employer, injunctive relief may be available though trade secrets are not involved"); Greenwich Mills Co. v. Barrie House Coffee Co., 459 N.Y.S.2d 454, 457-58 (N.Y. App. Div. 1983) (where former employees do not possess any unique or extraordinary skill, trade secrets are necessary for the enforcement of a restrictive covenant), cited in 13 KENNETH W. TABER ET AL., NEW YORK PRACTICE, EMPLOYMENT LITIGATION IN NEW YORK § 3:97 (Westlaw database updated Sept. 2016).

[101] Id.

[102] Tri–Nel Mgmt., Inc. v. Bd. of Health of Barnstable, 741 N.E.2d 37, 40 (Mass. 2001).

[103] Midgette v. Arlington Props., Inc., 83 Va. Cir. 26 (Va. Cir. Ct. 2011) (stating that the Supreme Court of the Commonwealth of Virginia has not described the pleading elements necessary for a temporary injunction to issue but applying the four elements as articulated by the Fourth Circuit, "alongside other circuit courts in the Commonwealth.").

Main Assignment File: Restrictive Covenants and Preliminary Injunctions

Plaintiff's File

Today, you receive the following email from Senior Partner Lincoln. She is asking for your help with a legal matter that Pamela Park at Stray Dog Advertising is facing. A former employee has violated the restrictive covenant that she signed with the agency, and Pamela has asked the law firm to file a complaint against this employee.

From: Amy Lincoln < a.lincoln@lawlawfirm.com >
To: Associate Attorney < a.attorney@lawlawfirm.com >
Sent: August 2, THIS YEAR 1:02 p.m.
Re: Stray Dog Advertising/Non-Compete Violation

Associate Attorney,

Hi—I need your help with a new matter involving Pamela Park and Stray Dog Advertising. A few months ago, Pamela had her employees sign a non-competition and non-solicitation agreement. I've attached a copy of the agreement and other relevant documentation to this email.

Since then, one of the employees (Rachael Winsted) has violated the agreement. She's started her own company and also taken one of Stray Dog's biggest clients, the craft brewery Zenith.

Pamela instructed me to file a complaint against Winsted for breach of contract. That has been filed and served, and we have also received an answer from the defendant.

You will find a copy of the summons and complaint and the answer attached to the email as well. Our paralegal, Tim, drafted the complaint.

I suggested to Pamela that we now ask the court to grant her a temporary injunction against this employee so that she doesn't cause any more damage to Pamela and her agency during the course of the litigation. We don't want her taking away any other clients from SDA.

Please review all of the documentation. I want you to draft the memorandum of law that we will submit with the motion, but before that prepare for me a straight-forward predictive memo about the matter. We already have the motion hearing scheduled with the court and you will find the motion and notice of motion attached here. Finally, I have also forwarded to you some case law that one of the law clerks found and thought was relevant and useful. In sum, you will find everything that you need.

You know how important Pamela and Stray Dog Advertising are as clients of the firm. I need you to do a top-notch job with this motion.

Amy

As you have read, you have been asked to write the following documents about this litigation:

First, you will draft a predictive office memo to the senior partner that includes:

- A summary of what has happened between Stray Dog Advertising and Rachael Winsted
- The legal issue at hand

- ˙ A summary and analysis of the law that applies (restrictive covenants and preliminary injunctions)
- The arguments that you will make about the motion for preliminary injunction
- Counterarguments that you anticipate the defendant, Rachael Winsted, will make
- Your opinion about whether you think the court will grant the motion

Second, you will draft a persuasive memorandum of law in support of the motion for a preliminary injunction that includes:

- Persuasive statements of the facts in a light that best represents your client
- Summary of the legal issue and the relevant law
- Persuasive arguments for which the injunction should be granted, including why your client will likely prevail on the underlying claim (breach of contract)

You will find complete information about these assignments on the Information Pages (pages 289-290; 295-296).

You will be analyzing the client matter using the restrictive covenant and preliminary injunction cases that you read and review in class.

Defendant's File

You have received the following email from Senior Partner Graham Darcy. He is asking you to help with a matter involving a new client of the firm, Rachael Winsted. She has been sued by her former employer, Stray Dog Advertising, for breach of contract and needs the firm's assistance in defending against the claims.

From:	Graham Darcy <darcy@bennettlaw.com>
To:	Associate Attorney <a.attorney@bennettlaw.com>
Sent:	August 4, THIS YEAR 11:22 p.m.
Re:	Rachael Winsted Defense

Associate Attorney,

I am assigning you to the Winsted matter. She is the new client, being sued by Stray Dog Advertising for breach of the non-competition and non-solicitation agreement. Amy Lincoln has filed for a preliminary injunction so in addition to defending against these ludicrous claims, we now have to persuade the court to do what is obvious: deny the motion for the preliminary injunction and allow Rachael to continue to operate her social media agency.

I've spoken with Lincoln about the claims, and she continues to insist that Winsted was the caliber of employee who deserves a non-compete. I know that you will make strong arguments that she wasn't and that the purpose of the non-compete is not to protect legitimate business interests but to punish our client.

I am confident that we can defeat the motion for the preliminary injunction so that Rachael can continue to earn a living during the course of the litigation. But there are no slam dunks in litigation, so we need to be completely prepared and make our best arguments.

This is what I need from you:

- A predictive memo that explains the law for restrictive covenants and preliminary injunctions.
- Your analysis of the law as it applies to the facts.
- Your prediction of whether you think the court will grant the motion or not.

Once that is done and we have the law straight in our minds, prepare the memo in opposition to the motion. I also want you to take care of the oral arguments as I have another trial scheduled that same day. We might settle, but just in case I want you to handle the hearing.

We will also set up a meeting with Rachael in the coming weeks so we can keep her informed about her case.

Thanks,

Graham

As you have read, you have been asked to write the following documents about this litigation:

First, you will draft a predictive office memo to the senior partner that includes:

- A summary of what has happened between Stray Dog Advertising and Rachael Winsted
- The legal issue at hand
- A summary and analysis of the law that applies (restrictive covenants and preliminary injunctions)
- The arguments that you will make about the motion for preliminary injunction
- Counterarguments that you anticipate that Stray Dog Advertising will make
- Your opinion about whether you think the court will grant the motion

Second, you will draft a persuasive memorandum of law in opposition to the motion for a preliminary injunction that includes:

- Persuasive statements of the facts in a light that best represents your client
- Summary of the legal issue and the relevant law
- Persuasive arguments for which the injunction should not be granted, including why the plaintiff will likely not prevail on the underlying claim (breach of contract)

You will find complete information about these assignments on the Information Pages (pages 289-290; 295-296).

You will be analyzing the client matter using the restrictive covenant and preliminary injunction cases that you read and review in class.

JOB DESCRIPTION

Organization

In **YEAR -10**, Stray Dog Advertising began as a small advertising agency in West Rapids, Jefferson. Since then, it has grown to be one of the most dynamic and fast-growing ad agencies in the state and in the country. We are known for our innovative advertising across all media that catches consumers' attention and creates buzz and excitement.

The Social Media Specialist is responsible for the ongoing management and growth of the social media needs of Stray Dog Advertising and of its clients.

Key Accountabilities

- Collaborate with cross-functional teams to develop marketing and communications plans that leverage the social media space.
- Responsible for developing content across owned and earned social channels. This could include blog posts, tweets, status updates, pins, photos and videos.
- Creates, manages and grows business presence across social media channels, including, but not limited to blogs, Twitter, Facebook, Snap Chat, Vine, G+, Pinterest, LinkedIn, YouTube and Instagram.
- Leverages measurement tools to provide progress reports and mine insights, while continually finding ways to improve on those metrics through testing and new initiatives.

Job Requirements

Qualifications/Requirements:

- Working knowledge and real-world experience in planning, managing and executing social media initiatives.
- Real-word experience planning social media programs that span owned (e.g. Blogs), earned (e.g. Facebook) and paid (sponsored tweets).
- Knowledge of digital marketing, current best practices and understanding of the digital production processes.
- Knowledge of social media legal guidelines, including, but not limited to, "pay-per-post."
- Knowledge of strategic planning and processes for brand management and creative development, including research tools and evaluation of results, especially as related to "Integrated Communication Planning."
- Knowledge of media strategy and planning options and the media role in integrated communication.

Experience/Education:

- 2+ years' experience or equivalent exposure to a corporate environment.
- BA or BS with focus on communication and/or Advertising/Marketing.
- Experience with social media platforms, including, but not limited to Facebook, Snap Chat, Foursquare, Pinterest, Twitter, YouTube, Google+, Instagram and Vine.
- Experience with leveraging social media management and analytics tools, including, HootSuite, and Google Analytics.
- Experience writing, editing and crafting content for the social media space.

Compensation

Compensation will be in accordance with the ideal candidate's experience, skills and qualifications. We offer a competitive salary and superb benefits including medical/dental/vision, life/disability insurance, paid holidays, and a 401(k) plan with a significant company match.

Stray Dog Advertising is an Equal Opportunity employer. Personnel are chosen on the basis of ability without regard to race, color, sex, religion, national origin, age, disability, marital status or any other protected class, in accordance with federal, state and local law.

To apply for this position, send a cover letter, CV and three references to Pamela Park at pamela.park@straydogadvertising.com

Rachael Winsted
4100 East 23rd Avenue, Apt. 6A
West Rapids, Jefferson 66424

Pamela Park
Stray Dog Advertising
45 Sunrise Boulevard
West Rapids, Jefferson 66412

January 10, YEAR -1

Re: Submission of Resume for Social Media Specialist Position

Dear Ms. Park:

I am sending you my resume to be considered for the position of the Social Media Specialist that is open at your agency. Roy Blanco, your senior creative director, taught the online communications strategies course that I took during the spring YEAR -3 semester at Jefferson State College and told me about the job. I graduated in YEAR -2 with a major in advertising and a minor in communications.

My qualifications and social media skills have no rivals in Jefferson. I send out at least 1,000 tweets per day and have more than 500 friends on Facebook. I even maintain a MySpace page, as well as Facebook, Snap Chat, Instagram, Pinterest, Google+ and Vine accounts, all of which I use a lot. I will bring that same connectivity to your agency and your clients.

In addition, I have been named one of the 10 most connected individuals in Jefferson by the West Rapids Hipster Magazine. I also developed one of the hottest social media campaigns while I was an intern at the Hawthorne Advertising Agency. The campaign was so hot that it was named one of the top 10 campaigns for the entire country. And I was only an intern. Just think of what I can do for you and your agency if you hire me.

I would welcome the chance to meet with you and to learn more about Stray Dog Advertising and the position. I thank you in advance for your consideration.

Sincerely yours,

Rachael A. Winsted

Rachael A. Winsted

RACHAEL WINSTED

4100 East 23rd Avenue, Apt. 6A
West Rapids, Jefferson 66424

Telephone: 744-555-1212
rachael.a.winsted@msn.com

WORK EXPERIENCE

Jefferson State College   *September YEAR -2 to present*
Social Media Coordinator

- Increased traffic to website of Jefferson State College by 158% within 12 month period

Twitter Marketing Coordinator Intern   *June – August YEAR -2*
San Francisco, California

- Provided support for Head of Marketing in executing marketing plan for U.S. market
- Organized best in class events for advertisers and agencies

Hawthorne Advertising   *June 2012 – August YEAR -3*
Agency Social Media Intern,
Sweetwater, Jefferson

- Social media campaign developed for The Daily Grind Coffeehouse rated in top 10 of hippest social media campaigns by West Rapids Hipster Magazine
- Worked closely with agency's clients to develop campaigns that suited their needs and matched their brand

EDUCATION

Jefferson State College   *YEAR -6 to YEAR -2*
Sweetwater, Jefferson

B.A. in Advertising
Minor in Communications
GPA: 3.6/4.0

Honors:
- Henry A. McNabb Communication Major Scholarship
- Sara Lee Scholar (GPA of 3.5 and above)

Activities:
- Jefferson State College Air Frisbee Team, captain
- President, Student Association of Jefferson State College
- Volunteer National Environment Fund

Fairhills High School   *YEAR -10 to YEAR -6*
Fairhills, Chickasaw

GPA 3.75/4.0

OTHER INTERESTS

Gardening, cinema, horseback riding, and woodworking

45 Sunrise Boulevard
West Rapids, Jefferson 66412

Rachael Winsted

4100 East 23rd Avenue, Apt. 6A

West Rapids, Jefferson 66424

February 13, YEAR -1

RE: Offer of Employment

Dear Ms. Winsted:

We are pleased to submit the following Offer of Employment for you to join Stray Dog Advertising. We believe that you have the attributes needed for a successful career with our company.

Set forth below are the specifics of the employment offer we have discussed with you:

Title, Start Date and Responsibilities

Your title will be Social Media Specialist. You will be an employee of Stray Dog Advertising and will report directly to Pamela Park. Your starting date of employment will be February 25, YEAR -1.

As the Social Media Specialist, you will be responsible for formulating social media strategies for the agency's clients, as well as for Stray Dog Advertising itself. You may also be assigned other job duties by Pamela Park or other individuals within the firm and are expected to complete these duties, regardless of whether they fall within the job duties as outlined in this Offer of Employment.

Compensation

Your salary is $60,000 per year (gross). You position is exempt, meaning that you are not entitled to overtime for any hours worked over 40 in a workweek.

Benefits

You are eligible for the full benefits plan that Stray Dog Advertising offers its employees. For further information, including how to sign up for the benefits, please refer to our Benefits Plan Document.

Employment At-Will

Stray Dog Advertising strives to maintain long-term successful relationships with its employees; however, this offer of employment is not for a definite period of time and is employment at-will, meaning that we, the employer, or you, the employee, have the right to terminate the employment at any time and for any reason, expect one prohibited by law.

Please note that this offer is contingent upon verification of the information you provided on your employment application and the findings of our background investigations. Stray Dog Advertising may rescind this offer based on the results of the background check or any finding of falsified information.

Rachael, we are very excited to have you join our team. We believe that you will fit in exceptionally well at Stray Dog Advertising and that you will make an outstanding contribution here. Please acknowledge your acceptance of this offer by signing below, returning the original to me and keeping a copy of this letter for your records.

Sincerely yours,

Pamela Park

Pamela Park
Owner, Stray Dog Advertising

I accept the above offer of employment.

Accepted By: *Rachael A. Winsted*

Date: February 15, YEAR -1

From: Pamela Park <pamela.park@straydogadvertising.com>
To: Stray Dog Employees rachael.winsted@straydogadvertising.com + 20 others
CC: Roy Blanco <roy.blanco@straydogadvertising.com>
Sent: January 17, THIS YEAR 07:29
Subject: Important Employment Documents + Meeting

Everyone,

We will be having an important meeting this Thursday at 10:00 a.m. in the main conference room. In addition to discussing the recent changes to your health care plans, we will also ask you to sign a non-competition and non-solicitation agreement. You will have plenty of time during the meeting to ask questions about the agreement and review it, but in a nutshell the agreement means that you can't work for a competitor of Stray Dog Advertising or open a competing agency for 18 months after your leave your position at Stray Dog and you can't solicit business from any client of Stray Dog either.

The agreement is pretty standard in the advertising agency industry and something that has been suggested that we do with all of our employees.

See you Thursday and thanks for all your hard work, as always!

PP

Sent from my iPad

Pamela and all the employees of Stray Dog Advertising met the following Thursday. All employees but Roy Blanco were given the following Non-Competition and Non-Solicitation Agreement, which they all signed. All employees signed the same agreement.

Non-Solicitation and Non-Competition Agreements

In consideration of the continued employment of Rachael Winsted ("Winsted" or "Employee") with Stray Dog Advertising ("SDA" or "Employer"), the parties mutually agree that to best protect the Employer's business interests, confidential information and trade secrets, Employee has agreed to sign the following Non-Solicitation and Non-Competition Agreement.

During your employment with Stray Dog Advertising, you will not provide professional services outside the scope of your relationship with Stray Dog Advertising on behalf of or to any person or organization in competition with Stray Dog Advertising, except with the prior written approval of Pamela Park, president of Stray Dog Advertising.

Non-Solicitation Agreement

For a period of eighteen (18) months after the termination (for any reason) of your employment by Stray Dog Advertising, you will not personally engage in, nor will you support or assist any third party in,

- the contact of any Stray Dog Advertising client or representative thereof or the performance of any review of an existing Stray Dog Advertising engagement,

- offering services which are the same or similar to that offered by Stray Dog Advertising, discussing a future engagement with, consulting to, or submitting a proposal to any then current client of Stray Dog Advertising or any organization to which Stray Dog Advertising is or has been in the proposal process with during the twenty-four (24) months prior to the termination of your employment from Stray Dog Advertising ("Stray Dog Advertising Clients and Prospects"), or

- recruiting the staff of any then current client of Stray Dog Advertising. In the event, following your termination, you have any questions with respect to Stray Dog Advertising Clients and Prospects, you may contact the Stray Dog Advertising legal counsel or Stray Dog Advertising's president who will confirm the existence of any potential conflicts.

Furthermore, for a period of eighteen (18) months after the termination for any reason of your employment from Stray Dog Advertising, you will not contact or cause to be contacted any employee or contractor of Stray Dog Advertising for the purpose of recruiting such for employment or engagement by yourself or any third party. If you violate the foregoing sentence and such violation results in the recruitment by yourself or any third party of a then current Stray Dog Advertising employee or contract, you will cause Stray Dog Advertising irreparable harm, and because damages in such event would in all likelihood be impossible or unreasonably difficult to assess, you agree to pay Stray Dog Advertising, as liquidated damages and not as a penalty, an amount equal to the annual billing of such individual based on Stray Dog Advertising's standard billing rate for such individual.

Non-Competition Agreement

Furthermore, you agree that, for a period of eighteen (18) months following the date of the termination of your employment with Stray Dog Advertising, for any reason, you shall not, without the express prior written consent of Stray Dog Advertising, perform any services for any person or business entity which competes with the business of Stray Dog Advertising, whether such services are performed as an employee, consultant, independent contractor, principal, officer, director, shareholder, member or otherwise.

Signed

Pamela Park

Pamela Park, Owner Stray Dog Advertising

Date: January 23, THIS YEAR

Rachael A. Winsted

Rachael Winsted

Date: January 20, THIS YEAR

From: Pamela Park <pamela.park@straydogadvertising.com>
To: Rachael Winsted < rachael.winsted@straydogadvertising.com >
Sent: February 19, THIS YEAR 07:43
Subject: Annual Review

Rachael, we need to set up a time for your annual review. I would like to meet next Wednesday from 1:30 – 2:30 in my office. Please mark the time on your calendar. In preparation for the review, I would like you to fill out the employee self-evaluation report, which is available on the Intranet. Juan can show you where to find it if you don't know. Send me the evaluation report at least 2 days before our meeting.

PP

From: Rachael Winsted < rachael.winsted@straydogadvertising.com >
To: Pamela Park <pamela.park@straydogadvertising.com>
Sent: February 19, THIS YEAR 16:23
Subject: Re: Annual Review

Pamela,

I will fill out the self-evaluation form before our meeting. Just to give you a heads up, I will want to talk about some of the on-going issues that I have already brought to your attention and that I think need to be addressed so that I can do my job as the social media specialist better.

I still don't have the most up-to-date iPhone. Nor is my computer the newest and fastest one on the market. I really need a tablet too so I can do my job wherever I am. I'd prefer an iPad, of course. A Mini would be best. I don't know how you think I can do my job without the newest computer, cell and tablet.

Also, I'd like more feedback. You know that I am used to getting feedback all the time from my 500+ friends on Facebook. They "like" my posts all the time, so I know I am great. I need that feedback and feel that it is essential so that I can get my job done to the best of my abilities.

Finally, I work best at home. I am on my computer all the time, so I don't think that I should have to come into the office. I can do my job from my bedroom, my living room or any coffee shop around. I know that you've told me before that I need to come into the office, but the commute is killing me! I really hope that you will change your mind so that I can continue to be the best in social media for Stray Dog and our clients. Otherwise, I don't know how you can expect me to continue to do my job so well.

Rachael

Employee:	Rachael Winsted
Title:	Social Media Specialist
Supervisor:	Pamela Park
Review Period:	February 26, THIS YEAR

PERFORMANCE REVIEW PLAN

1. <u>CURRENT RESPONSIBILITIES:</u> Attach a copy of your current job descriptions. If applicable, make note of any significant changes since last year's performance review.

2. <u>PERFORMANCE ASSESSMENT:</u> Evaluate and discuss the employee's job performance. Base your evaluation on the position requirements, achievement of the goals established last year, and your assessment of the employee's performance.

    1. Rachael continues to produce high quality and creative social media campaigns for SDA's clients. Her campaigns for Big Bold Bacon and the Jefferson Diabetes Association led to an increase of 212% and 150%, respectively, in traffic to the clients' websites. JDA saw a 75% increase in donations.

    2. But, Rachael struggles at times with organization. Her work would improve if she were to make more weekly 'to-do' lists, prioritizing her projects. She seems to work in a more haphazard way, which is fine when working alone, but not when she is part of a team and other people rely on her work and on it being done in a consistent manner and on time.

    3. We have received positive feedback from clients about their interactions with Rachael. They are very pleased with the quality of her work and its creativity. She is engaging and engaged with SDA's clients and we receive nothing but good feedback from all clients she works with, who are impressed with her ability to forge and foster relationships and build trust so that they are confident in what she, and SDA, can deliver.

    4. Are there areas of performance that need attention or improvement? Provide concrete examples.

        Time management – work for Big Bold Bacon was turned in nearly 48 hours late, despite telling client that the initial campaign draft would be done.

        Communication can improve with other team members when working on the same campaign. Realize that others rely on you.

    5. State and discuss the expectations and goals for the upcoming review period. Give examples of how these goals can be met.

        Rachael is a star when it comes to engaging people on social media. She has expanded our clients' brands and gotten them well known in Jefferson and around the country. In this way, she has exceeded expectations. She needs to continue to improve her strategic assessment skills and time management and stay abreast on new social media platforms. Rachael will be given a 3% increase in salary, effective immediately.

3. <u>PROFESSIONAL DEVELOPMENT PLAN:</u> List specific activities the employee will engage in as part of his/her professional goals. How will you support him/her in these activities?

    Training and continued education for strategic planning

4. <u>EMPLOYEE COMMENTS (OPTIONAL)</u>: The employee may comment on the performance review in the space below.

> Although I agree that sometimes, I am not the most prompt person in the world, I also think that I would be better able to do my job if I had the newest computer and cell phone, as I have told Pamela. I have also told her about other issues (feedback, working from home) that she is not willing to compromise on and that make it very hard for me to carry out my job.

> These issues were discussed during the meeting. I (Pamela Park) reiterated to Rachael that we do our best to make her job as comfortable as possible. We have budgeted to buy new computers in the YEAR +1 fiscal year. Working from home is not an option because it is important for her to be in the office to build team spirit.

This annual performance review will be part of your SDA's personnel file. Please sign below to acknowledge that you have received this document.

Employee's Signature: _Rachael A. Winsted_ Date_ February 26, THIS YEAR_

Supervisor's Signature: _Pamela Park_   Date: _February 26, THIS YEAR_

From: Rachael Winsted <rachael.a.winsted@msn.com>
To: Pamela Park <pamela.park@straydogadvertising.com>
Sent: April 27, THIS YEAR 13:04
Subject: Resignation

Dear Pamela,

I am writing to tell you that I have decided to resign from my position here at Stray Dog. Today will be my last day. You have continued to make it impossible for me to do my job, as I have told you already. I need a faster computer and really work better from home. I am sorry that you can't accommodate my reasonable needs.

I have also decided that I want to try my hand at being my own boss and want to open up my own social media agency. I think I will name it Sugar Snap.

Best regards,

Rachael Winsted

From: Pamela Park <pamela.park@straydogadvertising.com>
To: Rachael Winsted <rachael.a.winsted@msn.com>
Sent: April 27, THIS YEAR 14:34
Subject: Re: Resignation

Rachael,

While I am not surprised to receive notice of your resignation, I am disappointed that we will no longer have your creative drive working for us. I wasn't expecting you to leave Stray Dog after being here for only 14 months, but understand that you want to move on to other challenges in the world of social media. It is always an exciting endeavor to build a new company from zero.

I have notified Juan of your resignation. He will come to your desk as soon as he returns from an outside meeting to get your computer, cell phone and office keys. You do not need to stay until the end of the day and will be paid for a full day's work.

You will receive information about continuing your health care benefits under COBRA and can contact Juan with any questions.

PP

Shortly after Winsted left Stray Dog Advertising, Park was online checking her ConnectUp account. Park is connected to Winsted on ConnectUp and noticed the following updates to her profile:

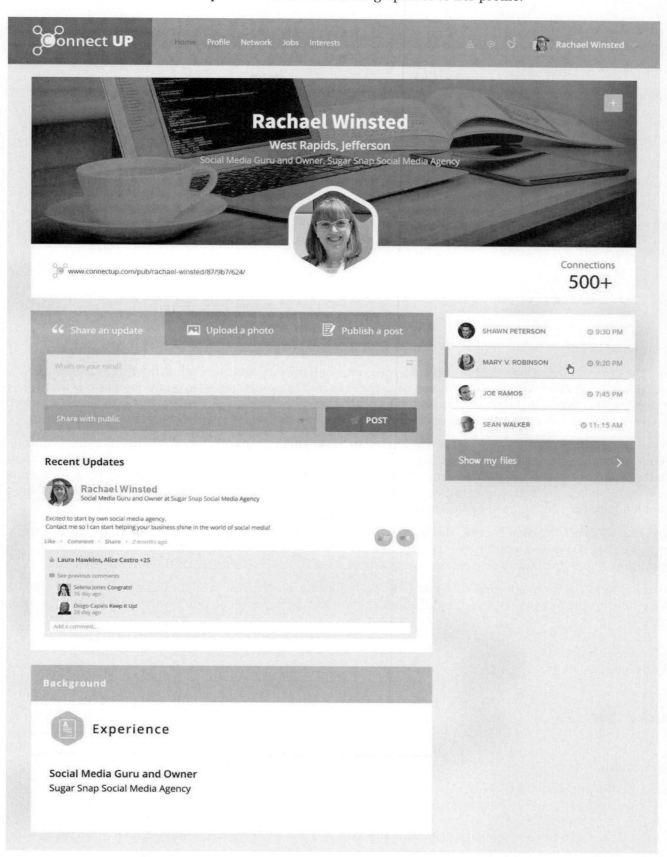

Zenith Brewery, LLC

6790 Freedom Drive

Appleton, Jefferson 65325

Pamela Park

Stray Dog Advertising

45 Sunrise Boulevard

West Rapids, Jefferson 66412

DATE June 20, THIS YEAR

Re: Termination of Contract

Dear Pamela:

I am writing to inform you that we have decided not to renew our contract with Stray Dog Advertising for our social media services. When we last negotiated the contract 12 months ago, we mentioned to you that cost was a significant concern for us. It continues to be. With the new expansion of our brewery and the new pubs that we have opened, our expenses have risen dramatically.

We have decided that it is more cost effective to hire someone part time as an independent contractor. We contacted Rachael Winsted, your former employee, when we saw on her ConnectUp page that she had just started her own social media company, Sugar Snap, after leaving Stray Dog. We worked with Rachael only a few times while we were still working with you, but trust you and your judgment about employees. If she was good enough for you, she will be good enough for us too.

Because Rachael's agency is new, she is offering super competitive prices. She is experienced after working at Stray Dog for over a year so we feel that our needs will be taken care of. But it will also be nice to have continuity since Rachael already understands our needs and goals having worked for you.

Thank you again for everything that you have done for us over the last year for our social media campaigns. We will continue to work with you for all of our other advertising needs, so don't worry that we are abandoning you!

Best regards,

Jake Smith

Jake Smith

CEO, Zenith Brewery, LLC

From: Pamela Park <pamela.park@straydogadvertising.com>
To: Rachael Winsted <rachael.a.winsted@msn.com>
Sent: June 20, THIS YEAR 10:32
Subject: Zenith Brewery

Rachael,

I just received a letter from one of our best clients, Zenith Brewery. As you are well aware, they represent nearly 15% of our annual revenue. Jake Smith, the CEO, told me that he is not renewing his contract with Stray Dog and instead is signing a contract with your new business!

It is clear that you used our confidential information to steal this client. I know that you contacted Jake when you left Stray Dog and stole this account! What a betrayal!

And don't forget that you signed a non-compete agreement with us! That agreement is perfectly valid since you signed it. You can't work with Zenith or any of our clients or for any competitor 18 months from when you left Stray Dog. You can't open your own agency either! So if you keep working with Zenith and operating your new social media agency, be aware that I will contact our lawyer right away and we will sue you.

PP
Sent from my iPhone

From: Rachael Winsted <rachael.a.winsted@msn.com>
To: Pamela Park <pamela.park@straydogadvertising.com>
Sent: June 21, THIS YEAR 09:44
Subject: Re: Zenith Brewery

Pamela,

The non-compete? What are you talking about? You aren't saying that you will actually try to enforce it against me? Come on. I thought we were all like a family. And when you had all of us sign the non-competes that day, you told us that it was "no big deal" and just something that your attorneys wanted all your employees to sign. We all had work to do that day and didn't even have time to look it over before signing. We also thought that we couldn't keep working at Stray Dog if we didn't sign. It was like we had no choice!

My new agency will be a small fish in the water compared to Stray Dog. Besides, there are lots of clients out there for everyone, so don't be so concerned!

Rachael

Additional Skills-Building Exercises

Injunction
Analysis Exercise

Overview of the Exercise: The following short fact patterns deal with injunctions and the issuance of injunctions, and your task is to analyze the fact patterns and determine whether or not you think a court should issue an injunction.

Learning Objectives of the Exercise:

This exercise will build your skills to:

- Articulate the legal rules regarding injunctions
- Apply those rules to brief fact patterns and analyze the facts and the law
- Articulate and effectively communicate that analysis using legal terminology

Steps for Completing the Exercise:

- Read the following fact patterns.
- By yourself, analyze each one and decide whether or not you think the court should issue an injunction and why (or why not). You don't need to write out a full answer, but jot down notes about your reasoning.
- When doing your analysis, be sure to follow the test as articulated in the cases that you have read for this Unit.
- When you are done analyzing each of the fact patterns, discuss your answers with the partner that you have been assigned. Explain to each other why you have reached the conclusion that you did.
- If you and your partner have different responses to a fact pattern, you must try to convince him or her that your answer is correct. After you both have tried to convince the other, you must choose a team answer.
- Once you have discussed each of the fact patterns, you will compare answers as a class.

Research Required for the Exercise: You are not required to do any outside research for this exercise.

Grading: This exercise is not graded.

---

1. Nuisance:

<u>Rule</u>

Jeff. Stat. Ann. § 657.1 defines nuisance as "whatever is injurious to health, indecent, or unreasonably offensive to the senses, or an obstruction to the free use of property, so as essentially to interfere unreasonably with the comfortable enjoyment of life or property." The statute also states that an individual can commence a civil action "to enjoin and abate the nuisance and to recover damages sustained on account of the nuisance."

<u>Case Law</u>

A discomfort which is purely mental, unaccompanied by anything else, may not be alleviated by injunctive relief. <u>Delaney v. Fitzgerald</u>, 13 S.W.2d 767, 768 (Jeff. 1929).

An injunction should be refused when it was sought to prevent soot and cinders from the smokestack of a factory being carried into the dwelling house of the complainant. The court held that the smoke and soot from the particular factory would not be regarded as a greater nuisance than the other manufacturing establishments in the city. The court stated that one living in a city necessarily must submit to the annoyances incidental to city life. It was also held that manufacturing establishments were necessary and indispensable to the growth and prosperity of every city, and they were entitled to protection in the proper conduct of their business, although some inconvenience might result to others. Louisville Coffin Co. v. Warren, 78 N.W.2d 400 (Jeff. 1880).

A thing is not a nuisance merely because it is calculated to create fear and apprehension, and an injunction should be refused where the thing sought to be restrained is not unavoidable and not in itself noxious, but only something which may, according to circumstances, prove so. Delaney, 13 S.W.2d at 768.

Facts

Jose and Veronica recently purchased a home on the outskirts of New Mesa, Jefferson. The neighborhood is mostly rural and their home is located on a road where three other families also live. At the end of the road, about ¼ mile (approximately 400 meters) from their home, is a large empty field. Before purchasing the house, they didn't ask the real estate agent if the field was used for anything.

About a month after they moved in, a traveling carnival was set up in this field. The advertisements that Jose and Veronica saw in the paper and around town said that the circus was going to be there for the next five months. The first days that the circus was operating, Jose and Veronica heard the yells of vendors, the singing and shouting of the performers, and noises of the audience, rendering it impossible for them to get proper rest or sleep. Although the circus operates only during the day, both Jose and Veronica work the night shift and sleep during the day. Jose and Veronica have also complained that the odors of the cooking of foods are offensive. The carnival operators are careful that the audience members do not litter and if there is any trash left behind, management quickly cleans it so that there is no garbage on the road. However, Jose and Veronica have found on a few occasions some soda cans and beverage cups, as well as food wrappers, on the street in front of their home.

This is the tenth year that the carnival has traveled to New Mesa and it is always well attended by the residents of the city and the surrounding area.

You represent Jose and Veronica and have filed on their behalf a complaint in Jefferson state court against the carnival, claiming that the carnival is a nuisance. You have also filed a motion for a temporary injunction, asking the court to enjoin the carnival from operating. What do you think the court will decide? Why?

2. Trademark Infringement

Rule

In order to obtain relief in an action for trademark infringement, plaintiff has the burden of proof in establishing three requisites, namely:

1) That plaintiff's name has a special significance or secondary meaning in the trade;
2) That plaintiff has an exclusive right to, or a protectable interest in, the trademark with reference to his goods, service, or business and with reference to the territorial or special group market in which his trademark is used; and
3) That defendant has unfairly used plaintiff's trademark, or a confusing simulation thereof (although not necessarily with a fraudulent intent), whereby the ordinary purchaser, to plaintiff's or the public's detriment, has been, or is reasonably likely to be, deceived as to the true identity of the goods, services, or business, and is misled into believing that he is getting plaintiff's product when he is in fact getting that of defendant. Howard Clothes, Inc. v. Howard Clothes, Corp., 52 N.W.2d 753, 757-58 (Jeff. 1952).

Courts have developed four categories of terms for trademark purposes. In ascending order of strength they are: (1) generic, (2) descriptive, (3) suggestive, and (4) arbitrary or fanciful. Scott v. Mego Int'l Inc., 519 F. Supp. 1118, 1126 (D. Jeff. 1981).

A generic term is one which is commonly used as the name or description of a kind of goods and is afforded no trademark protection. Id. A descriptive term is one which conveys an immediate idea of the ingredients, qualities, or characteristics of goods and is only entitled to protection if it has acquired secondary meaning. Imported Auto Parts Corp. v. R.B. Schaller & Sons, Inc., 258 N.W.2d 797, 800 (Jeff. 1977).

A suggestive term is one which falls between the descriptive category and the arbitrary and fanciful category. An arbitrary or fanciful term is one which has no relation to the nature of the product and is entitled to trademark protection without proof of secondary meaning. Id. at 799. Arbitrary terms are afforded the strongest trademark protection. If the business selects a name which is "arbitrary with respect to its trade or merely suggestive of it, the business' first use of the mark will establish common law rights, if another has not yet appropriated it." Id.

Likelihood of confusion can be created when products have functionally identical uses and share numerous similarities in package design. Aurora World, Inc. v. Ty Inc., 719 F. Supp. 2d 1115 (C.D. Jeff. 2009).

Rearden LLC v. Rearden Commerce, Inc. iterates eight factors that contribute to "likelihood of confusion." They are strength of the mark; proximity of the goods; similarity of the marks; evidence of actual confusion; marketing channels used; type of goods and degree of care likely to be exercised by the purchaser; defendant's intent in selecting the mark; and likelihood of expansion of the product lines. 683 F.3d 1190, 1209 (9th Cir. 2012).

Similarity between retail outlets where products are sold and customers to whom products are aimed can also contribute to the possibility of confusion. Amstar Corp. v. Domino's Pizza, Inc., 615 F.2d 252, 262 (5th Cir. 1980). This factor takes into consideration where, how, and to whom the parties' products are sold and direct competition between the parties is not required for this factor to weigh in favor of a likelihood of confusion. See Jaguar Cars Ltd. v. Skandrani, 771 F.Supp. 1178, 1184 (S.D.Jeff.1991).

Facts

Lynn is the owner of a company called CHECKPOINT. It operates in the industry of "corporate security," in which it sells electronic-security equipment and systems to help retailers protect against the physical theft of merchandise from stores. Raymond also operates a company called Check Point; it operates solely online at the domain "checkpoint.com" to sell and promote its products, computer software that protects the electronic flow of information. Lynn's domain is "checkpointsecurity.com." Lynn began operating in 2005, while Raymond started operations in 2009. Lynn's company has a website, but she does not sell her products through it but rather promotes her company and its products. Raymond sells his products throughout the United States, while Lynn operates in Jefferson and the surrounding states. Raymond has been significantly more successful than Lynn, with nearly two times the annual revenue.

Lynn's attorney has recently filed a claim in Jefferson federal court for trademark infringement and unfair competition, alleging that the name of Raymond's company creates the likelihood of confusion in the minds of consumers and thus infringes upon Lynn's intellectual property rights. The attorney has also filed a motion for a preliminary injunction, asking the court to order Raymond to stop selling his products.

Raymond has come to you for advice about whether you think the court will decide in Lynn's favor. What do you tell him?

3. Conversion

Rule

The elements of common law conversion are (1) the plaintiff has a property interest and (2) the defendant deprives the plaintiff of that interest." Lassen v. First Bank Eden Prairie, 514 N.W.2d 831, 838 (Jeff. Ct. App. 1994) ; see also Larson v. Archer–Daniels–Midland Co., 32 N.W.2d 649, 650 (Jeff. 1948) ; Mertes v. Estate of E.L. King, 501 N.W.2d 660, 665 (Jeff. Ct. App.1993).

Case Law

Jefferson state and federal courts have yet to rule on the issue of whether the law of conversion protects electronic data or information.

The court of the nearby state of Franklin has concluded that the law of conversion may protect electronic data or information. See Kremen v. Cohen, 337 F.3d 1024, 1034 (9th Cir. 2002) (concluding that plaintiff had an intangible property right in his domain name, and a jury could find that defendant had wrongfully disposed him of that right by giving the domain name to a third party).

The Franklin federal district court has also decided the issue when it recently granted default judgment against a defendant that had broadcast without authorization and license a boxing match to which plaintiff offered sublicensing agreements to publicly exhibit the program. The court found that plaintiff alleged its ownership over the commercial distribution rights to the boxing match and that Defendant broadcast it at his establishment in contravention of Plaintiff's exclusive commercial distribution rights and alleged damages. J & J Sports Prods., Inc. v. Leger, No. 13-cv-02071-SC, Wl 6492114 (N.D. Fran. Dec 10, 2013).

District courts within the Third Circuit (which Jefferson is not a part of) have instead found that the Copyright Act preempts state law conversion claims regarding copyrighted property. In Apparel Business Systems, LLC v. Tom James Co., No. 06-1092, 2008 U.S. Dist. LEXIS 26313 (E.D. Pa. Mar. 28, 2008) , the district court determined that because the plaintiff's conversion claim arose from copying and misuse of its work, it was functionally equivalent to a copyright claim. The court also noted that because it is intangible property, software is generally not subject to a conversion claim. Id.

In Gemel Precision Tool Co., v. Pharma Tool Corp., No. 94-5305, 1995 WL 71243(E.D. Pa. Feb. 13, 1995) , the district court found that an act of conversion regarding plaintiff's copyrighted blueprints and computer databases was substantively similar to a copyright claim. Likewise, the district court in Sullivan Assocs v. Dellots, Inc., CIV. A. 97-5457, 1997 WL 778976 (E.D. Pa. Dec. 17, 1997), utilized a very similar analysis holding that plaintiff's conversion claim involving its software, databases, and computer files was functionally equivalent to a copyright claim.

Finally, courts in the states of West Virginia and Virginia have concluded that while the tort of conversion usually applies only to tangible property, "courts have recognized the tort of conversion in cases where intangible rights arise from or are merged with a document." Combined Ins. Co. of Am. v. Wiest, 578 F. Supp. 2d 822, 835 (W.D. Va. 2008) (quoting United Leasing Corp. v. Thrift Ins. Corp., 440 S.E.2d 902, 906 (Va. 1994)).

Facts

Murat is a website developer who writes and develops code for his clients' websites. He is very innovative and creative and has developed a code that no one else has. It allows his clients' website to appear first on Google, even though the sites violate many of Google's rules. Murat is one step ahead of Google with his coding. With his special skills, Murat has been able to grow his business considerably over the past year.

Lesley is a competitor of Murat and has her own, not very successful website developing business. Last month, Lesley hacked into Murat's wireless system and computers and was able to download onto her own computer Murat's codes. In the past month, Lesley has used Murat's code and already moved her clients' websites up to the top of the Google rankings.

Using his superior computer skills, Murat was able to discover that Lesley was the hacker who broke into his computer and stole his code. Murat has now come to your law firm for advice. He wants to know if he can sue Lesley, on what grounds and whether the court can order Lesley to stop using Murat's computer code.

What do you tell Murat? Will he be able to obtain an injunction? Why or why not?

Presentations:
If SDA or Rachael Winsted Were Your Client...

Overview of the Exericse: For this exercise, you will make a professional presentation in which you answer and discuss the following question:

If Stray Dog Advertising were your client in your home country and if Park came to you for legal advice about the restrictive covenant issue, what would you do and what advice would you give her?

OR

If Rachael Winsted were your client in your home country and if she came to you for legal advice about the restrictive covenant issue, what would you do and what advice would you give her?

You will give the presentation based on the client that you have been assigned to represent.

Learning Objectives of the Exercise:

This exercise will build your skills to:

- Examine the <u>Stray Dog Advertising, LLC v. Winsted</u> litigation from the perspective of your country's legal system
- Compare your country's legal system with the U.S. legal system
- Explain how the dispute would be handled in your country's legal system and the advice that you would provide to your client
- Understand specific information from your classmates' presentations

Steps for Completing the Exericse:

- Analyze the Stray Dog Advertising fact pattern under your country's laws
- Determine whether or not Pamela Park/Stray Dog Advertising would have viable claims under your country's laws, and whether Winsted would have strong defenses against the claims
- Explain what claims SDA could bring (if any) and explain how the case would be handled in your country's legal system.
- Explain what legal advice you would give Pamela or Rachael if she came to you for legal advice in your home country.

Research Required for the Exercise: The research you are required to do depends on your knowledge of these claims in your country's legal system. It is presumed that you are familiar with the law and with how you would approach this issue if Pamela or Rachael were a client of yours.

Grading: This presentation is not graded. Depending on the size of your class and your instructor's choice, you will present to your fellow classmates or to the entire class.

Handouts:

As part of your presentation, you must create a handout for your classmates, and the handouts must include fill-in-the-blank questions that your classmates must complete with information that you present during the presentation. Each handout must include at least five questions to complete.

For example, if a U.S. law student were giving a presentation on non-competition agreements in the United States, he could include on his handout this question:

To be enforceable, a non-competition agreement in an employment context must be:

Supported by _____ consideration in many but not all states,

Reasonable in _____ and _____ scope, and

Protect _____ business interests.

As you are speaking, your classmates will have to listen, follow what you are saying and fill in the blanks. If you are listening to one of your classmate's presentations and are unsure about an answer, you should ask him or her to repeat so you can fill in the blank(s).

Grammar Review:

The basis of this exercise is hypothetical or conditional verbs: *if SDA or Rachael Winsted were your client, what would you do?*

Remember the grammar when discussing hypothetical conditions.

Present: **IF + PAST SIMPLE, WOULD + BASE VERB**

*If Pamela **called** me to schedule an appointment, I **would tell** her to visit me at my office.*

NOTE: We use "were" for all tenses with the verb "to be" when using a conditional verb.

*If I **were** you, I **would not take** that class.*

*If Pamela **were** my client, I **would tell** her that she would not have a winning claim.*

Past: **IF + PAST PERFECT, WOULD + HAVE + PAST PARTICIPLE**

*If Rachael **had called** Zenith to offer her services, that **would have been** a very clear violation of the non-solicitation agreement.*

*If Pamela **had called** me before I left for the day, I **would have told** her to come to my office at 12:00.*

Restrictive Covenant in Social Media Analysis Exercise

Overview of the Exercise: This exercise requires you to analyze a fact pattern that involves another employee, working for different companies. The facts are similar to those involving SDA and Rachael Winsted, but the facts in this exercise deal solely with the issue of whether a social media posting can constitute a violation of a non-solicitation agreement.

Learning Objectives of the Exercise:

This exercise will build your skills to:

- Analyze a set of facts and a settled area of law (restrictive covenants) in relation to changes in today's society via technology
- Articulate arguments and counterarguments for your position
- Defend your position with well-reasoned support
- Draft a written explanation of your position

Steps for Completing the Exercise:

- Review the following fact pattern, which asks whether a ConnectUp (similar to LinkedIn) posting can be a solicitation to violate an enforceable non-solicitation agreement.
- Review the persuasive case law provided.
- By yourself, analyze the fact pattern and decide whether or not you think Rosa Morales violated the non-solicitation agreement that she signed with her former employer. You don't need to write out a full answer, but jot down notes about your reasoning.
- When you are done analyzing, discuss your answers with the partner that you have been assigned. Explain to each other why you have reached the conclusion that you did.
- If you and your partner have different responses, you must try to convince him or her that your answer is correct. After you both have tried to convince the other, you must choose a team answer.
- Once you have discussed each of the fact patterns, you will compare answers as a class.

Research Required for the Exercise: No outside research is required for this assignment.

Grading: This exercise is not graded. Instead, you will compare the conclusion that you and your partner reached with that of your classmates.

CAN A LINKEDIN POSTING BE A CLIENT SOLICITATION?

Rosa Morales was hired in YEAR -5 to work in sales for Hartwell Technologies, Inc. Her job took her across the country, selling the company's top-of-the line Internet security systems. When she was hired, she was asked to sign a non- solicitation agreement:

> Employee agrees that for 24 months after Employee is no longer employed by the Company, Employee will not directly or indirectly solicit services of any type that the Company can render ("Services") for any person or entity who paid or engaged the Company for Services, or who received the benefit of the Company's Services, or with whom Employee had any substantial dealing while employed by the Company. However, this restriction with respect to Services applies only to those Services rendered by Employee or an office or unit of the Company in which Employee worked or over which Employee had supervisory authority. This restriction also applies to assisting any employer or other third party.

Eighteen months ago, Rosa left her job with Hartwell Technologies, Inc. to work for SecureBest, Inc., a main competitor of Hartwell's. Her new position involves selling products that directly compete with Hartwell's security software products, which are aimed at medium to large-sized companies.

On her first day at SecureBest, Rosa posted an update on her ConnectUp profile page. On the following page you will see her profile, as well as the update. Rosa has over 500 contacts on ConnectUp and is very active on the site. A good number of her contacts are individuals that Rosa met while working for Hartwell, including many individuals who work for companies that are clients of Hartwell and who are the decision-makers when it comes to purchasing products such as the Internet security systems that Hartwell and SecureBest sell.

After posting the update, several of Rosa's connections made comments on her update, "liked" it and shared it with others. Everyone was happy for her, as SecureBest is an exciting new start-up company that has everyone talking for its innovative approach to Internet security.

Four months ago, Rosa went through her contacts and asked about 25 potential clients – those who she thought would be most likely to sign with SecureBest -- to "join her professional network" on ConnectUp. Included in this group was the purchasing manager at one of Hartwell's top clients, Big Corporation, Inc. After accepting the request, the manager noticed her status update and called Rosa to set up a meeting so that he could learn more about the SecureBest systems. After the meeting and Rosa's presentation, the manager decided to switch to SecureBest. The company's contract with Hartwell was up for renewal anyway, and he felt more comfortable signing a contract with SecureBest since Rosa was now working there.

Rosa's former manager is also connected with Rosa on ConnectUp. When she learned that Big Corporation, Inc. was not renewing its contract with Hartwell and when the purchasing manager told her that the company would be working with SecureBest, she decided to do some research. She did a company search of SecureBest on ConnectUp and learned that Rosa was now working there. Upon looking at Rosa's profile, she saw the update that Rosa had posted announcing her new position. Rosa's manager then confirmed with the purchasing manager at Big Corporation, Inc. that he had indeed contacted Rosa when he learned via ConnectUp that she was now working there.

The manager brought all of this information, plus copies of Rosa's ConnectUp profile and update, to the corporate counsel. Upon reviewing the non-solicitation agreement that Rosa had signed and the facts as explained above, the company decided to file a breach of contract claim against Rosa in Jefferson state court and also petition the court for a preliminary injunction to enjoin Rosa from continuing to work for SecureBest for the duration of the litigation.

Jefferson state courts follow New York courts in their approach to restrictive covenants in employment agreements. Neither state has issued a decision regarding the breach of a non-solicitation provision via ConnectUp or social media. Based on the cases that we have read about restrictive covenants and the persuasive case summaries below about solicitation in social media, do you think that Rosa has violated the non-solicitation agreement that she signed? Should the court issue the preliminary injunction? Support your answer and provide arguments for both sides.

Restrictive Covenants and Preliminary Injunctions

Unit 1

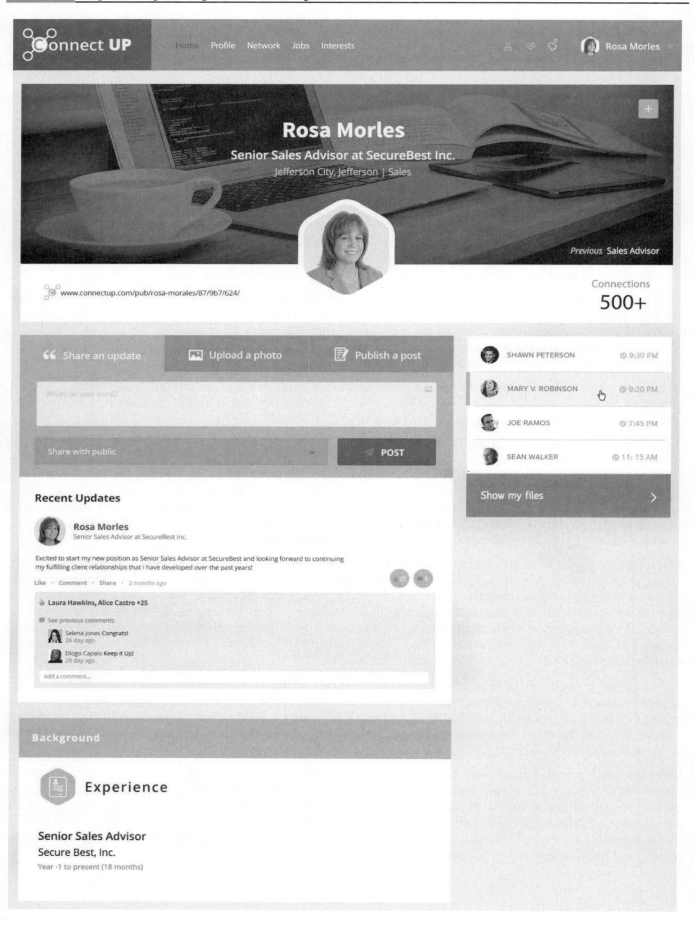

Case Law (persuasive precedent):

Enhanced Network Solutions Group, Inc. v. Hypersonic Technologies Corp., 951 N.E.2d 265 (Ind. Ct. App. 2011).

Synopsis: Software engineering company (ENS) brought suit against a networking company (Hypersonic) arguing that they violated the terms of a sub-contractor agreement. Issue is whether the trial court erred when it found that Hypersonic did not violate the terms of the agreement by inducing an ENS employee to terminate his employment. Court of Appeals affirmed the trial court's decision.

LinkedIn Connection: Hypersonic posted on its LinkedIn account that it was hiring an outside sales specialist. Seeing the posting, an ENS employee contacted the president of Hypersonic inquiring about the position, after which Hypersonic made an offer of employment that the employee accepted.

Because it was the employee who contacted Hypersonic, and not the other way around, there was no breach of the non-solicitation clause of the sub-contractor agreement between ENS and Hypersonic.

All major steps were taken by the employee:

- Commencing conversations with Hypersonic
- Conveying the terms of the agreement to Hypersonic

Graziano v. Nesco Service Co., No. 1:09 CV 2661, 2011 WL 1219259, (N.D. Ohio March 4th, 2011).

Synopsis: Graziano was terminated due to the economic downturn. His severance agreement contained a non-compete clause. When Graziano joined LinkedIn, Nesco (former employer) refused to continue its performance under the severance agreement.

Problem with using this case: the court doesn't acknowledge who actually breached the agreement.

Invidia, LLC v. DiFonzo, 30 Mass. L. Reptr. 390 (Mass. Sup. Ct. 2012).

Synopsis: DiFonzo signed a two-year non-solicitation agreement as part of beginning her employment at Invidia (a salon). She also agreed not to disclose or discuss trade secrets. Invidia argued that DiFonzo solicited clients via facebook by "friending" them and announcing her employment at a different salon.

Held: Invidia was not able to prove a violation of the non-solicitation agreement sufficient to sustain its preliminary injunction. Evidence of "friending" is too thin.

NDSL, Inc. v. Patnoude, 914 F. Supp. 2d 885 (W.D. Mich. 2012).

Synopsis: Patnoude signed a 12-month noncompetition and nonsolicitation agreement with NDSL while under its employment. After his resignation from the company, Patnoude joined a new company called IntelliBatt, at which he acted in a sales role. Patnoude asked a former coworker to join his professional network on LinkedIn as part of a mass, 500-person invite. They did not have any additional communication.

Conclusion: a *generic* LinkedIn invitation, on its own, is insufficient to establish a solicitation.

Mock Meeting

Overview of the Exercise: This exercise simulates a meeting between the general counsel of Hartwell Technologies, Inc. and SecureBest, Inc. regarding Rosa Morales's alleged breach of the non-solicitation agreement that she signed with Hartwell Technologies, Inc. Hartwell Technologies, Inc. has filed a breach of contract claim against Rosa in Jefferson state court and also asked the court to issue a preliminary injunction to enjoin her from working for SecureBest, Inc. during the course of the litigation. Hartwell Technologies, Inc. alleges that Rosa violated the non-solicitation agreement when she posted on ConnectUp that she was now working for SecureBest, Inc. As a result of this posting, one of Hartwell's top clients chose not to renew its contract with Hartwell and to contract with SecureBest, Inc. instead for its Internet security needs.

In addition to filing the claim against Rosa, Hartwell is asking the court to enforce the agreement. In return, SecureBest has brought a complaint challenging the agreement. Because Rosa is a valued employee, SecureBest has agreed to defend her in the litigation.

General counsel for the two companies have arranged a meeting to discuss the case. You will be assigned the role of counsel for Hartwell Technologies, Inc. or SecureBest, Inc. The purpose of the meeting is to explain your client's position to opposing counsel, lay out the arguments for the position and to explore settlement options. Before the meeting, review the information that you have been provided.

Learning Objectives of the Exercise:

This exercise will build your skills to:

- Organize information from case summaries to identify both helpful and unhelpful legal precedent
- Use monetary and non-monetary interests of parties in negotiating an agreement
- Identify primary obstacles to reaching a mutually beneficial settlement agreement
- Implement negotiation strategies and tactics

Steps for Completing the Exercise:

- Read the preparatory information that you have been assigned
- Read the case summaries that have been provided to you
- Be familiar with the case law regarding restrictive covenants and the fact pattern of Rosa Morales and her ConnectUp posting
- Articulate the arguments for your client's position and anticipate opposing counsel's

Grading: This exercise is not graded. After the meetings, the class will debrief on how the meetings went.

Information Pages

Office Memo: Restrictive Covenants and Preliminary Injunction

. . . .

Overview of the Assignment: For this assignment, you will write an office memo to the Senior Partner, summarizing your research on restrictive covenants and injunctions and providing your prediction of what will happen in the litigation (i.e. whether the injunction would be issued and whether the underlying claim of breach of contract would be successful).

Learning Objectives of the Assignment:

This assignment will build your skills to:

- Efficiently communicate in a written format
- Explain complex matters clearly and concisely
- Analyze and apply the rules of law regarding restrictive covenants and preliminary injunctions

Research Required for the Assignment: You are not required to do any outside research for this assignment. You should base your analysis on the New York restrictive covenants cases that you have read:

- Reed, Roberts Associates, Inc. v. Strauman, 353 N.E.2d 590 (N.Y. 1976)
- BDO Seidman v. Hirshberg, 712 N.E.2d 1220 (N.Y. 1999).
- Kanan, Corbin, Schupak, Aronow, Inc. v. FD International, Ltd., 797 N.Y.S.2d 883 (N.Y. Sup. Ct. 2005).
- Veramark Technologies, Inc. v. Bouk, 10 F. Supp. 3d 395 (W.D.N.Y. 2014).
- Scott, Stackrow & Co. v. Skavina, 780 N.Y.S.2d 675 (N.Y. App. Div. 2004).
- Merrill Lynch, Pierce, Fenner & Smith v. Dunn, 191 F. Supp. 2d 1346 (M.D. Fla. 2002).
- Lucente v. International Business Machines Corp., 310 F.3d 243 (2nd Cir. 2002).
- Zellner v. Conrad, 589 N.Y.S.2d 903 (N.Y. App. Div. 1992).
- Ashland Management Incorporated v. Altair Investments NA, LLC, 869 N.Y.S.2d 465 (N.Y. App. Div. 2008).

If you want to practice your legal research skills, you can look for and use other cases that you find. However, if you do search on Westlaw, LexisNexis or Bloomberg Law, be sure to limit your search and the cases you use to New York law and remember to change the citations to Jefferson as indicated in the introduction.

Format of the Completed Assignment:

Your response should be in an office memo format and should include the following:

- Summary of the facts
- The relevant law
- Analysis of the law to the fact pattern
- Conclusion about how you think a court would rule if this matter were to go to court
- Your advice to the client about how to proceed

Follow the following format:

- 1 inch (2.54 cm.) margins (top/bottom and sides)
- 12 font, Times New Roman font
- Double spaced
- Maximum eight pages

Notes:

This memo should be predictive and not persuasive. You are not trying to persuade the senior partner or the client about the strength of your arguments or urge him or her to take a particular course of action; you are only trying to inform about the law, how it applies to our case, how you think a court would rule and what advice you have.

In a memo, you can also use formatting like underlining, bold font or italics. You can also create headings and subheadings to organize your answer.

For additional information about office memos and e-memos, as well as samples, refer to the online additional resources.

Grading: This assignment is worth 102 points.

Unit 1   Restrictive Covenants and Preliminary Injunctions

LEGAL CONTENT	0-6 points	8 points	10 points	12 points	Points
Issue statement (IS)	Document does not include an IS or includes IS that fails to properly identify the legal issue(s) and the applicable law	Identifies the legal issue(s) and correctly states the applicable law with minor mistakes	Identifies the legal issue(s) and correctly states the applicable law	Identifies the legal issue(s) and correctly states the applicable law in an exceptionally creative and concise way	_____/12
Short Answer	Document does not include a short answer or includes a short answer with significant mistakes	Responds to IS but with key facts or applicable legal principles missing	Responds to IS with key facts and applicable legal principles with no meaningful errors	Clearly and concisely responds to IS with key facts and applicable legal principles and no irrelevancies	_____/12
Facts	Few or none of the relevant facts are included; difficult to follow or understand	Most relevant facts are included as well as non-relevant ones; at times difficult to follow	Relevant facts are included with occasional irrelevancies; easy to follow	All relevant facts are included with no irrelevancies; story is clearly and concisely told to reader in objective way	_____/12
Rule	Hard to follow and understand; does not include relevant sources or cites inappropriate sources; no rule application	Cites to some relevant sources but is incomplete in covering all relevant aspects of the rule; includes some rule application	Cite only to relevant sources and mostly clear; rule application explains but not fully how rule has been applied	Clear and concise; includes only relevant sources and includes all parts of rule necessary for analysis; clear rule application	_____/12
Analysis	Contains conclusory statements and/or no case law; facts are analyzed in a conclusory or insufficient way	Uses some case law but does not analogize or distinguish or explain its application; some conclusory statements; facts briefly analyzed	Uses case law to show how rule applies to case; case law is compared and contrasted with success; most facts are analyzed	Analyzes case law completely, comparing it fully to client matter; facts are thoroughly analyzed in an objective way	_____/12
Conclusion/ Recommendations	No conclusion or recommendations are included in document	A brief conclusion is included but without sufficient client advice	Paper includes conclusion and recommendations	Paper includes full conclusion of the legal analysis and facts and presents creative and thoughtful recommendations	_____/12
Citations	No sources are cited in document	Some sources are cited, but inconsistently; citation format is inconsistent	All citations are present; correct format is mostly used	All citations are present; correct format is used throughout document	_____/12
WRITING	**2**	**4**	**5**	**6**	**Points**
Formatting	Document does not follow format instructions or the sample provided	Document attempts to follow instructions and sample provided	Document follows the instructions and sample provided with no meaningful errors	Document exactly follows the instructions and sample provided	_____/6
Organization	No structure or organization; free flow of ideas	Structure & organization present but reorganization or headings needed for full clarity	Document is clearly organized and structured with proper use of heading and subheadings	Document is exceptionally well organized and structured with proper use of headings and subheadings	_____/6
Syntax Mechanics	Contains numerous and distracting grammatical and mechanical errors that impede understanding	Contains some grammatical and mechanical errors that impede understanding	Contains few grammatical and mechanical errors but none that impede understanding	Contains no grammatical and mechanical errors; native-like use of English	_____/6
TOTAL					_____/102

Mock Client Meeting

Overview of the Assignment: This assignment simulates a client meeting between you and your client, Pamela Park of Stray Dog Advertising, LLC or Rachael Winsted.

You will meet with your client and explain to her the status of the litigation <u>Stray Dog Advertising, LLC v. Winsted</u>, the results of your analysis about how a court might rule on the motion for a preliminary injunction and your recommendations on how to proceed.

Learning Objectives of the Exercise:

This assignment will build your skills to:

- Explain and clarify the legal positions of the parties and describe potential outcomes to your client
- Respond to technical questions about litigation
- Incorporate technical legal English vocabulary that relates to restrictive covenants and preliminary injunctions and use appropriate layperson explanations for your client

Steps for Completing the Exercise:

- Read and be familiar with the Main Assignment File
- Be familiar with the restrictive covenant cases that you have been assigned
- Recommended:
  - Anticipate the questions that you think your client might ask and prepare possible responses;
  - Draft an outline of what you would like to cover in the meeting.

Note: Remember that part of the grading is also based on your professional demeanor. You are expected to arrive punctually, be dressed in professional attire and act as you would with a client in real life. You should play the part from when you come into the meeting room.

Grading: This assignment worth 102 points.

Punctuality: Student-attorney arrived on time to meeting: YES _____ (10 points) NO _____ (0 points)

Professional Attire: Student-attorney was dressed in appropriate professional attire: YES _____ (10 points) NO _____ (0 points)

Professional Demeanor: Student-attorney acted in a professional manner w/ client: YES _____ (10 points) NO _____ (0 points)

GRADING CRITERIA	0- 6 points	8 points (C or 75%)	10 points (B or 85%)	12 points	Points received
Engagement I (questions)	Attorney does not ask client any questions; engages in monologue	Attorney asks few questions; questions are hard to follow or show minimal preparation or understanding of matter	Attorney asks basic questions that demonstrate understanding of matter and preparation	Attorney asks thoughtful, insightful and creative questions that demonstrate deep preparation & understanding of matter	____/12
Engagement II (answers)	Attorney does not respond to client's questions	Attorney responds to questions, but incorrectly or with hard to follow answers	Attorney responds promptly and correctly to all of client's questions	Attorney responds promptly and correctly to all of client's questions with creative, thoughtful and insightful answers that show a deep understanding of the issues	____/12
Knowledge of Applicable Law	Attorney provides no explanation of the applicable law	Attorney provides explanation of with serious mistakes, or hard to follow (e.g. use of legal jargon)	Attorney provides clear explanation of with some mistakes; uses some legal jargon unnecessarily or without explanations that client can understand	Attorney provides clear, concise and correct explanation of the law with legal jargon when appropriate or w/ explanations client can understand	____/12
Ability to Analyze Applicable Law	Attorney provides does not provide an analysis of the law for the client	Attorney attempts to analyze the law but provides incomplete or incorrect analysis	Attorney provides analysis of the law with no significant mistakes or misstatements of the law or facts	Attorney provides a clear, concise and correct analysis of the law as it applies to the client matter	____/12
Advice and Recommendations	Attorney provides no advice or poor advice for client	Attorney provides not comprehensive or inaccurate advice	Attorney provides comprehensive and accurate advice to client on his/her legal matter	Attorney provides thoughtful and creative solutions for client	____/12
Organization	Meeting is disorganized and hard to follow or lacks any organization	Meeting has some organization but is still confusing for client for how information is presented	Meeting is clearly organized and easy to follow	Meeting is clearly organized and is easy to follow; attorney takes extra steps to ensure client's understanding	____/12
TOTAL					____/72
TOTAL FROM PUNCTUALITY AND PROFESSIONALISM					____/30

Total ____/102

Client Advice Letter

Overview of the Assignment: For this assignment, you will write an advice and follow-up letter to your client, Pamela Park or Rachael Winsted, following your client meeting. You should include a summary of the legal issues and the law that you discussed, respond to any pending questions or matters, include your predictions on what you think will happen in the litigation and state any recommendations that you may have for your client. Be mindful that even though your client may be a sophisticated businesswoman, neither Park nor Winsted is a trained attorney. Therefore you should avoid legalese in your letter.

Under Rule 1.4(a)(3) of the Model Rules of Professional Conduct, an attorney has the duty to keep his or her client "reasonably informed about the status of the client's matter." A thorough follow-up letter after a client meeting is one of the best ways to meet this duty, as well as regular phone calls, emails or meetings.

Learning Objectives of the Assignment:

This assignment will build your skills to:

- Efficiently communicate in a written format
- Explain complex matters clearly and concisely
- Incorporate technical legal English vocabulary that relates to restrictive covenants and injunctions and use appropriate layperson explanations for client

Steps for Completing the Assignment:

- Review the predictive memo that you wrote to your senior partner about your client matter to ensure that the law and the issues are clear
- Be familiar with the case law regarding restrictive covenants and injunctions, as well as the fact pattern
- Conduct your client meeting with your client, Pamela Park or Rachael Winsted
- Review the Business Correspondence online resources

Research Required for the Assignment: You are not required to do any outside research for this assignment.

Format of the Completed Assignment:

Your assignment should be written as a business letter, not as an email. Even though many firms and lawyers use email for much of the correspondence carried out, formal business letters are still an essential part of the practice of law.

Your law firm has the following policy regarding business correspondence. Your client letter must follow the policy guidelines.

LAW FIRM CORRESPONDENCE POLICY

The purpose of this policy is to ensure a uniform appearance of all business correspondence that is written by the attorneys and staff of the law firm and thus to increase the professional appearance of the firm's work product. All law firm attorneys and staff are required to follow these guidelines when writing correspondence. Violation of the policy can result in disciplinary action, up to and including termination.

- The first page of all "traditional" letters must be written on law firm letterhead, which includes the firm's address and logo
- All letters must be written in a modified block letter format
- Letters must be written in Times New Roman, 12 font
- Letters must be 1.5 spaced and have 1" (2.54 cm.) margins, except for the initial page, which may have larger top margins to account for the logo, law firm address and sender's direct contact information
- Client letters must not exceed four pages

Grading: This assignment is worth 78 points.

Note: See the Online Additional Resources for examples of letters and for general information about business correspondence.

LEGAL CONTENT	0-6 points (failing)	8 points (C or 75%)	10 points (B or 85%)	12 points	Points
Introduction	Letter does not include an appropriate introduction or includes poorly constructed one	Letter includes introduction that states purpose with some irrelevancies or some relevant information missing	Introduction states purpose of letter and includes other relevant information	Introduction is engaging; states purpose of letter and includes other relevant information; written clearly and concisely	____/12
Summary of Meeting	Letter includes no summary of the meeting	Letter includes summary but leaves out important information or states it unclearly	Letter summarizes the meeting but leaves out important information	Letter clearly and concisely summarizes the meeting, its core purpose and content	____/12
Applicable Law	Student-attorney provides no explanation of the applicable law, or only uses legal jargon in explanation (inappropriate for audience)	Student-attorney provides explanation of with serious mistakes, or hard to follow (use of legal jargon)	Student-attorney provides clear explanation of with few mistakes; uses some legal jargon without appropriate explanations	Student-attorney provides clear, concise and correct explanation of the law with legal jargon with appropriate explanations	____/12
Analysis	Contains conclusory statements and/ or no case law; facts are analyzed in a conclusory or insufficient way	Uses some case law but does not analogize or distinguish or explain its application; some conclusory statements; facts briefly analyzed	Uses case law to show how rule applies to case; case law is compared and contrasted with success; most facts are analyzed	Analyzes completely case law, comparing it fully to client matter; facts are thoroughly analyzed	____/12
Conclusion/ Recommendations	No conclusion or recommendations are included in letter	A brief conclusion is included but without sufficient advice or recommendations advice or next steps	Letter includes conclusion with recommendations and next steps	Letter includes full conclusion of the legal analysis and facts, presents creative and thoughtful recommendations and includes clear next steps	____/12
WRITING	**2**	**4**	**5**	**6**	**Points**
Formatting	Document does not follow format instructions or the sample provided	Document attempts to follow instructions and sample provided	Document follows the instructions and sample provided with minor errors	Document exactly follows the instructions and sample provided	____/6
Organization	No structure or organization; free flow of ideas	Letter includes organization and structure but is still confusing	Structure and organization but some reorganization is needed for full clarity	Document is clearly organized and structured	____/6
Syntax Mechanics	Contains numerous and distracting grammatical and mechanical errors that impede understanding	Contains some grammatical and mechanical errors that impede understanding	Contains few grammatical and mechanical errors but none that impede understanding	Contains no grammatical and mechanical errors; native-like use of English	____/6
TOTAL					____/78

Memorandum of Law
for Preliminary Injunction

Overview of the Assignment: For this assignment, you will draft the memorandum of law in support of or in opposition to the motion for a preliminary injunction filed in the litigation of <u>Stray Dog Advertising, LLC v. Winsted</u>.

Learning Objectives of the Assignment:

This assignment will build your skills to:

- Efficiently read and understand legal authority
- Analyze the fact pattern by applying the relevant case law
- Adapt the IRAC organization and the formal memorandum of law structure
- Communicate effectively and in a persuasive manner to convince the court and the reader that your client's position and argument is the one to follow

Research for the Assignment: You are not required to do any outside research for this assignment. You should base your analysis on the New York restrictive covenant cases that you have read in class:

- <u>Reed, Roberts Associates, Inc. v. Strauman</u>, 353 N.E.2d 590 (N.Y. 1976)
- <u>BDO Seidman v. Hirshberg</u>, 712 N.E.2d 1220 (N.Y. 1999).
- <u>Kanan, Corbin, Schupak, Aronow, Inc. v. FD International, Ltd.</u>, 797 N.Y.S.2d 883 (N.Y. Sup. Ct. 2005).
- <u>Veramark Technologies, Inc. v. Bouk</u>, 10 F. Supp. 3d 395 (W.D.N.Y. 2014).
- <u>Scott, Stackrow & Co. v. Skavina</u>, 780 N.Y.S.2d 675 (N.Y. App. Div. 2004).
- <u>Merrill Lynch, Pierce, Fenner & Smith v. Dunn</u>, 191 F. Supp. 2d 1346 (M.D. Fla. 2002).
- <u>Lucente v. International Business Machines Corp.</u>, 310 F.3d 243 (2nd Cir. 2002).
- <u>Zellner v. Conrad</u>, 589 N.Y.S.2d 903 (N.Y. App. Div. 1992).
- <u>Ashland Management Incorporated v. Altair Investments NA, LLC</u>, 869 N.Y.S.2d 465 (N.Y. App. Div. 2008).

If you want to practice your legal research skills, you can look for and use other cases that you find. However, if you do search on Westlaw, LexisNexis or Bloomberg Law, be sure to limit your search and the cases you use to New York law and remember to change the citations to Jefferson as indicated in the introduction.

Format of the Completed Assignment:

For your completed assignment, you must follow Local Rule 5.2 of the Courts of Jefferson.

Local Rule 5.2 GENERAL FORMAT OF DOCUMENTS TO BE FILED

<u>Format</u>: All documents filed must be typewritten, printed, or prepared by a clearly legible duplication process. Document text must be double-spaced, except for quoted material and footnotes, and pages must be numbered consecutively at the bottom. Documents filed after the case-initiating document must contain—on the front page and above the document's title—the case number and the name or initials of the assigned district judge and magistrate judge.

<u>Represented Parties</u>. A memorandum of law filed by a represented party must be typewritten. All text in the memorandum, including footnotes, must be set in at least font size 12 (i.e., a 12-point font) as font sizes are designated in the word-processing software used to prepare the memorandum. Text must be double-spaced, with these exceptions: headings and footnotes may be single-spaced, and quotations more than two lines long may be indented and single-spaced. Pages must be 8 ½ by 11 inches in size, and no text — except for page numbers — may appear outside an area measuring 6 ½ by 9 inches.

<u>Length</u>: No memorandum filed with the court shall exceed the length of twelve pages, excluding caption and table of contents.

Grading: This assignment is worth 90 points.

Note: See the online resources for additional information about memoranda of law and persuasive writing.

Unit 1 · Restrictive Covenants and Preliminary Injunctions

LEGAL CONTENT	0-6 points	8 points	10 points	12 points	Points
Introduction	Document does not include an Introduction or includes issue statement instead	Introduction is not persuasive or does not include persuasive or relevant facts or the law	Student attempts to make introduction persuasive, to "put the spin" but does not include all facts or something…	Introduction is persuasive, clear and concise and clearly introduces reader to the client's story and position and identifies the relief sought	___/12
Facts	Few or none of the relevant facts are included; difficult to follow or understand	Relevant facts are included as well as non-relevant ones; mostly clear	Relevant facts are included; factual background is mostly clear and easy to follow with few irrelevancies	Relevant facts are included with no irrelevant facts; story is clearly and concisely told to reader in persuasive way	___/12
Rule	Hard to follow and understand; does not include relevant sources or cites inappropriate sources; no rule application	Cites to some relevant sources but is incomplete in covering all relevant aspects of the rule	Cite only to relevant sources; rule application explains but not fully how rule has been applied	Clear and concise; includes only relevant sources and includes all parts of rule necessary for analysis; clear rule application	___/12
Argument	Contains conclusory statements and/or no case law; facts are analyzed in a conclusory or insufficient way	Uses some case law but does not analogize or distinguish or explain its application; some conclusory statements; facts briefly analyzed; student attempts to make persuasive arguments	Uses case law to show how rule applies to case; case law is compared and contrasted with success; facts are analyzed and argued in a persuasive way	Analyzes completely case law, comparing it fully to client matter; all facts are thoroughly analyzed and argued in a very persuasive way	___/12
Conclusion	No conclusion is included in document	A brief conclusion is included but unclear relief sought	Paper includes conclusion with relief sought	Paper includes full conclusion of the legal analysis and facts and persuasively argues for relief sought	___/12
Citations	No sources are cited in document or citation formats are incorrect and inconsistent	Sources are cited, but inconsistently; citation format has meaningful mistakes in format	Citations are complete; few meaningful mistakes in format	No mistakes in citations; correct format is used throughout document	___/12
WRITING	**2**	**4**	**5**	**6**	**Points**
Formatting	Document does not follow format instructions or the sample provided	Document attempts to follow instructions and sample provided	Document follows the instructions and sample provided with minor errors	Document exactly follows the instructions and sample provided	___/6
Organization	No structure or organization; free flow of ideas	Document includes some organization and structure but is still confusing; no use of headings or subheadings	Structure & organization present but reorganization needed full clarity; subheadings included but not effectively persuasive	Document is clearly organized and structured with proper use of persuasive heading and subheadings	___/6
Syntax Mechanics	Contains numerous and distracting grammatical and mechanical errors that impede understanding	Contains some grammatical and mechanical errors that impede understanding	Contains few grammatical and mechanical errors but none that impede understanding	Contains no grammatical and mechanical errors; native-like use of English	___/6
TOTAL					___/90

Mock Oral Argument

Overview of the Assignment: For this assignment, you will carry out the oral argument for the motion for a preliminary injunction in the <u>Stray Dog Advertising, LLC v. Winsted</u> case, currently docketed in the Hemings County District Court. Oral arguments are scheduled for the motion filed by Stray Dog Advertising, LLC, asking the court to stop Winsted from competing with SDA for the duration of the litigation.

You will represent the party that your instructor has assigned to you.

Learning Objectives of the Assignment:

This assignment will build your skills to:

- Effectively and persuasively communicate legal rules and argument
- Conduct yourself orally in a professional courtroom setting
- Respond to questions about the relevant law

Steps for Completing the Assignment:

Before the oral arguments, review the following:

- Pleadings
- Notice of Motion and Motion for a Preliminary Injunction
- Your Memorandum of Law, as well as that of your opposing counsel
- Cases cited in your memo and opposing counsel's
- Facts of the client matter

Research for the Assignment: Although no additional research is required for the assignment, you should review the memorandum of your opposing counsel and review the cases that he/she includes, consider how you can rebut the cases, or explain how they are inapposite to the matter at hand and address those cases in your oral argument.

Format of the Assignment:

Each side has 20 minutes for his or her argument. The moving party first presents his/her arguments and may reserve time for rebuttal. It is the moving party's decision to reserve time for rebuttal. After the moving party has presented his/her arguments, it is the non-moving party's turn. The non-moving party does not receive time for rebuttal since he/she can listen to opposing counsel and respond directly to any arguments made. After the non-moving party finishes, the moving party responds with rebuttal, if he/she previously asked the court to reserve time for it.

Be prepared to answer questions from the court, and part of your preparation should be anticipating the questions that the judge might ask and preparing answers. But in the event that the judge doesn't ask questions or asks few, be prepared to fill the time allotted with your argument.

Grading: This assignment is worth 90 points.

Punctuality: Attorney arrived on time to oral argument: YES _____ (10 points) NO _____ (0 points)

Professional Attire: Attorney was dressed in appropriate professional attire: YES _____ (10 points) NO _____ (0 points)

Professional Demeanor: Attorney acted in a professional manner w/court and opposing counsel: YES _____ (10 points) NO _____ (0 points)

GRADING CRITERIA	0-6 points (failing)	8 points (C or 75%)	10 points (B or 85%)	12 points	Points received
Engagement	Attorney does not respond to the court's questions	Attorney responds to questions, but incorrectly or with hard to follow answers	Attorney responds promptly and correctly to all of the court's questions	Attorney responds promptly and correctly to all of court's questions with creative, thoughtful and insightful answers that show a deep understanding of the issues	_____/12
Knowledge of Applicable Law	Attorney provides no explanation of the applicable law	Attorney provides explanation of with few meaningful mistakes or with explanation that is hard to follow	Attorney provides clear explanation of the law with no meaningful mistakes	Attorney provides clear, concise and correct explanation of the law	_____/12
Analysis of Applicable Law	Attorney provides no analysis of the law or provides analysis that is incorrect or incomplete	Attorney provides analysis of the law but has some mistakes or misstatements of the law or facts	Attorney provides a clear, concise and correct analysis of the law as it applies to the client matter	Attorney present unimpeachable case for the client, analyzing persuasively, concisely and clearly the law as it applies to client matter	_____/12
Conclusion and Relief	Attorney does not identify relief sought or conclude argument	Attorney provides advice, but	Attorney provides advice but	Attorney clearly identifies the relief sought and summarizes the client's position	_____/12
Organization	Argument is disorganized and has serious faults of organization	Argument has minor faults of organization	Argument is clearly organized and easy to follow	Argument is exceptionally well organized and presents arguments in novel way	_____/12
TOTAL					_____/60
TOTAL FROM PUNCTUALITY AND PROFESSIONALISM					_____/30

TOTAL   _____/90

Personal Jurisdiction and the Internet

Unit 2

Motion to Dismiss for Lack of Personal Jurisdiction

For this Unit, you will write a persuasive memorandum of law in support of or in opposition to a motion to dismiss in litigation that has been brought against Stray Dog Advertising in another state: Franklin. You will represent either SDA as the defendant, or the plaintiff, Groovia, Inc. The legal issue involved is personal jurisdiction. You will analyze whether the Franklin court would have personal jurisdiction over the out-of-state defendant SDA and make persuasive arguments on behalf of your client that the court should or should not exercise personal jurisdiction over Stray Dog Advertising.

Learning Objectives of this Unit:

This Unit will build your skills to:

- Explain complex legal matters clearly and concisely
- Use appropriate technical terminology
- Identify and analyze the applicable case law and facts for the relevant legal issues
- Efficiently read and understand legal authority
- Articulate persuasive legal arguments in support of client's position
- Efficiently and effectively communicate in a written and oral format
- Respond to questions about the relevant law

To achieve these learning objectives, you will complete the following tasks:

- Draft a predictive memo to senior partner about the legal issues and your prediction of what will happen with the litigation
- Draft a persuasive memorandum of law in support of or in opposition to motion to dismiss
- Carry out a mock client meeting with either Pamela Park of SDA or Peter Dorfman of Groovia, Inc.
- Draft a client letter to your client about your meeting and about the legal issues
- Carry out oral argument in front of the court for the motion to dismiss

To complete these tasks, you will use the following materials in the book:

- Assignment email from Senior Partner (pages 304-305; 305-306)
- Main Assignment File (pages 306-311)
- Statutes:
  - TEX. CIV. PRAC. & REM. CODE ANN. § 17.041 (West 2015).
  - TEX. CIV. PRAC. & REM. CODE ANN. § 17.042 (West 2015).
- Personal Jurisdiction Commented Cases:
  - <u>Atkinson v. McLaughlin</u>, 343 F. Supp. 2d 868 (D.N.D. 2004).
  - <u>Mink v. AAAA Development, Inc.</u> 190 F.3d 333 (5th Cir. 1999).
  - <u>Carrot Bunch Co., v. Computer Friends, Inc.</u>, 218 F. Supp. 2d 820 (N.D. Tex. 2002).
  - <u>Ford v. Mentor Worldwide, LLC</u>, 2F. Supp. 3d 898 (E.D. La. 2014).
  - <u>Gatte v. Ready 4 A Change, LLC</u>, 2013 WL 123613 (W.D. La. Jan. 13, 2013).
  - <u>The Kelly Law Firm, P.C. v. An Attorney For You</u>, 679 F. Supp. 2d 755 (S.D. Tex. 2009).
  - <u>Percle v. SFGL Foods, Inc.</u>, 356 F. Supp. 2d 629 (M.D. La. 2004).
  - <u>Tempur-Pedic International, Inc. v. Go Satellite, Inc.</u>, 758 F. Supp. 2d 366 (N.D. Tex. 2010).
- ESL Workbook (pages 210-237)
- Pleadings (online)

NOTE: For our purposes, of the above cases, the decisions of the courts in the state of Franklin are those issued by Texas courts. The Franklin abbreviation for citations is Fran. Franklin is part of the 5th Circuit, which includes the state of Louisiana.

Your instructor will also assign you additional skills-building exercises to bolster your understanding of the legal issues and further develop your legal reasoning and language skills, whether related to legal reasoning and analysis or to English. You will find an icon with each exercise that will indicate which skills the exercise will focus upon.

Personal Jurisdiction and the Internet

Unit 2

ICON	SKILL
	Speaking — in particular about the legal issues and the law presented in the Unit
	Oral comprehension
	Legal analysis and reasoning
	Analysis of the legal issue(s) presented in the Unit
	English grammar, syntax, and vocabulary
	Legal ethics and professional responsibility
	Legal research

In this Unit, the additional skills-building exercises that accompany the Main Assignment File include:

- Personal Jurisdiction Analysis Exercise (pages 312-314)

- Presentations: *If SDA or Groovia Were Your Client...* (pages 315-316)

- Ethics Dilemma: Revealing Information to Opposing Party (pages 317-318)

Before beginning the Unit, you should read and be familiar with the Factual Background of Stray Dog Advertising (pages 7-8), of the Lincoln, Adams and Washington Law Firm (pages 2-3) and of the Baldwin & Bell Law Firm (page 6).

You will also find online at the website www.legalwritingforllms.com the following online resources that accompany this Unit. The additional online resources will help you deepen your mastery of the skills presented in the Unit and also provide additional understanding about the U.S. legal system and legal writing.

Pleadings: Section III, Unit 2 (required)

- Additional Resources:
  - Sources of American Law
  - Writing Professional Emails
  - Writing Persuasive Memos
  - Writing E-memos
  - IRAC

- Additional Skills-Building Exercises:
  - Issues and Issue Statements
  - Stating the Rule
  - Analysis
  - Ethical Spotlight Exercise

Section III, Unit 2 Legal Issue
Personal Jurisdiction and Motion to Dismiss

Main Assignment File	Personal Jurisdiction Cases	ESL Workbook	Additional Exercises	Additional Online Resources
Introduction to File and Client Matter Pages 299-303	Atkinson v. McLaughlin, 343 F. Supp. 2d 868 (D.N.D. 2004).	Atkinson v. McLaughlin, 343 F. Supp. 2d 868 (D.N.D. 2004).	Personal Jurisdiction Analysis Exercise Pages 312-314	Writing Professional Emails
Documents Related to Client Matter Pages 304-311 + pleadings online	Mink v. AAAA Development, Inc., 190 F.3d 333 (5th Cir. 1999).	Mink v. AAAA Development, Inc., 190 F.3d 333 (5th Cir. 1999).	Presentation: If ISDA or Groovia Were Your Client... Pages 315-316	Business Correspondence (with sample letters)
Assignment Information Pages + Rubrics Pages 319-329	Carrot Bunch Co., v. Computer Friends, Inc., 218 F. Supp. 2d 820 (N.D. Tex. 2002).	Carrot Bunch Co., v. Computer Friends, Inc., 218 F. Supp. 2d 820 (N.D. Tex. 2002).	Ethical Dilemma: Revealing Information to Opposing Party Pages 317-318	Writing Memos (office memos and persuasive memoranda of law)
	Ford v. Mentor Worldwide, LLC, 2 F. Supp. 3d 898 (E.D. La. 2014).	Ford v. Mentor Worldwide, LLC, 2 F. Supp. 3d 898 (E.D. La. 2014).		IRAC (including additional exercises for each element)
	Gatte v. Ready 4 A Change, LLC, 2013 WL 123613 (W.D. La. Jan. 13, 2013).	Gatte v. Ready 4 A Change, LLC, 2013 WL 123613 (W.D. La. Jan. 13, 2013).		Skills-Building Exercises for Rules, Issues and Issues Statements, Analysis and Ethical Dilemmas
	The Kelly Law Firm, P.C. v. An Attorney For You, 679 F. Supp. 2d 755 (S.D. Tex. 2009).	The Kelly Law Firm, P.C. v. An Attorney For You, 679 F. Supp. 2d 755 (S.D. Tex. 2009).		
	Percle v. SFGL Foods, Inc., 356 F. Supp. 2d 629 (M.D. La. 2004).	Percle v. SFGL Foods, Inc., 356 F. Supp. 2d 629 (M.D. La. 2004).		
	Tempur-Pedic Int'l, Inc., v. Go Satellite, Inc., 758 F. Supp. 2d 366 (N.D. Tex. 2010).	Tempur-Pedic Int'l, Inc., v. Go Satellite, Inc., 758 F. Supp. 2d 366 (N.D. Tex. 2010).		

Section III

Advanced Legal Issues

Introduction – Personal Jurisdiction and the Internet

Black's Law Dictionary defines jurisdiction as "[a] court's power to decide a case or issue a decree."[104]   Many types of jurisdiction exist; if you look up the term *jurisdiction* in Black's, you will find seventy five separate entries! This Unit deals with personal jurisdiction, which is "[a] court's power to bring a person into its adjudicative process" and render decisions "over a defendant's personal rights, rather than property interests."[105] It is also known as *in personam* jurisdiction.

> "[D]ue process requires only that in order to subject a defendant to a judgment *in personam*, if he be not present within the territory of the forum, he have certain minimum contacts with it such that the maintenance of the suit does not offend traditional notions of fair play and substantial justice." Int'l Shoe Co. v. Washington, 326 U.S. 310, 316 (1945).

Whether a court can exercise personal jurisdiction over a defendant can become a disputed issue when the defendant resides in a state that is different from the state in which the plaintiff filed the lawsuit. If a lawsuit is filed in New York and the defendant lives in Iowa, is it fair for the New York court to exercise jurisdiction over the Iowa resident defendant (whether an individual or a business)?[106] The answer to that question is the same as many answers in law: it depends.

Actually, the answer is not quite that slippery and we have statutory and constitutional guidelines about when a court can exercise its jurisdiction over a non-resident. The inquiry is a two-step process.

The first step involves examining the long-arm statute of the state that is attempting to exercise jurisdiction over the non-resident (in the example above about our Iowa non-resident defendant, we would analyze the New York long-arm statute). These statutes accomplish exactly what their name implies: they allow a court in one state to reach into another state (with a very long arm if a court is reaching from New York to Iowa!) and grab a resident who lives in that state and bring him into the other state's court (or hale him into court, we often say) and make him the subject of a lawsuit.

A long-arm statute confers upon the courts within the state the authority to exercise jurisdiction over non-residents only in certain circumstances. As a general rule, an out-of-state defendant must have "sufficient minimum contacts" with the state for the court to exercise jurisdiction over him. The exercise of personal jurisdiction also must not offend the "traditional notions of fair play and substantial justice," since constitutional considerations of due process, guaranteed under the 5th and 14th Amendments, come into play as well.

For example, the New York long-arm statute, which is similar to those in other states, allows a New York court to exercise jurisdiction over a non-resident when the non-resident:

- transacts any business within the state or contracts anywhere (not just in New York) to supply goods or services within New York;

- commits any tort (except defamation, which can have its own rules) within the state;

- commits a tort outside of New York that causes injury to someone or something within the state of the defendant; and

  - regularly solicits business or derives substantial revenue from good used or consumed or services rendered in the state; or

  - should reasonably expect his acts to have consequences within New York and derives substantial income from interstate or international commerce; or

- owns, uses or possesses any real property within New York.[107]

---

[104] *Jurisdiction*, BLACK'S LAW DICTIONARY (10th ed. 2014).

[105] *Personal Jurisdiction*, BLACK'S LAW DICTIONARY (10th ed. 2014).

[106] An out-of-state defendant is also referred to as "non-domiciliary." See, e.g., Brandt v. Toraby, 710 N.Y.S.2d 115, 117 (N.Y. App. Div. 2000); N.Y. C.P.L.R. 302 (MCKINNEY 2008).

[107] See N.Y. C.P.L.R. 302 (MCKINNEY 2008) for a complete list of when a court can exercise personal jurisdiction over a non-

The second step of the inquiry is determining whether the exercise of jurisdiction conforms with the traditional and constitutional notions of fairness of due process.[108]

In the age of the Internet, the issue of personal jurisdiction has become even more complicated. Let's say that you purchase a coffee maker from an online company located in Georgia. You live in California. While using the coffee maker, it explodes. Glass and boiling coffee are hurled in the air and in your direction. You suffer second-degree burns and serious cuts on your face; the doctor tells you some scars will likely be permanent. You consult with an attorney about bringing a personal injury claim in California over the Georgia company for the injuries you suffered. Whether the court will hear the claim depends on the state's long-arm statute and the state court's caselaw regarding personal jurisdiction and the Internet.

Generally, the type of website that the defendant operates will determine whether the court can exercise personal jurisdiction over the non-resident in an online setting.[109] Websites are categorized into passive or interactive websites, dependent on the degree of interactivity that the user has with the website and what can be done on it. A passive website, that only transmits information to the user, will likely be insufficient to grant personal jurisdiction over an out-of-state defendant, while an interactive website, where the user is exchanging and transmitting files and entering into contracts, will sometimes be sufficient to grant jurisdiction over an out-of-state defendant.

This is the issue that you will examine, analyze and argue in this Unit. As you will learn, Stray Dog Advertising has been named the defendant in a lawsuit filed in the state of Franklin, based on a business relationship with a new client, Groovia, Inc., that has gone sour. Groovia and its CEO, Peter Dorfman, discovered SDA through the Internet and SDA's website and communicated with Pamela and carried out all the business online. You will represent either SDA or Groovia, Inc. and try to convince the court with your persuasive writing and argument that the claim filed against SDA should or should not be dismissed for lack of personal jurisdiction.

---

domiciliary.

[108] See Int'l Shoe Co. v. Washington, 326 U.S. 310, 316 (1945) (establishing the standard for long-arm jurisdiction over non-residents and that it must not offend the "traditional notions of fair play and substantial justice.").

[109] See, e.g., Grimaldi v. Guinn, 895 N.Y.S.2d 156, 165-67 (N.Y. App. Div. 2010).

Main Assignment File:
Personal Jurisdiction and the Internet

Plaintiff's File

Today you receive the following email from Senior Partner Baldwin about a legal dispute between the firm's client, Groovia, Inc., and Stray Dog Advertising, a company located in the state of Jefferson and with which Groovia entered into a contract for advertising services. Groovia has brought a claim against Stray Dog Advertising, and you have been asked to help with the dispute and to draft the memorandum of law in opposition to the motion to dismiss that SDA's attorney has filed.

From:	Rose Baldwin <rose.baldwin@baldwinbell.com>
To:	Associate Attorney <associateattorney@baldwinbell.com>
Sent:	January 19, THIS YEAR 09:43
Subject:	Groovia Dispute vs. Stray Dog Advertising/Motion Dismiss

Associate attorney,

I would like you to take over this matter involving Groovia and Peter Dorfman. As we discussed last week in the firm's client update meeting, we've brought a claim on behalf of Groovia against this advertising agency in Jefferson, Stray Dog Advertising, for breach of the UCC. Groovia signed a contract for advertising and social media services, and Stray Dog didn't live up to its promises. I have attached for you a memo that Laurie Lawclerk wrote about this matter after she met with Peter the other day, as well as other correspondence that is relevant to the dispute.

I will not be available to continue with this matter. I've got too many other client files going on right now that need my attention, including that defamation claim that is scheduled for trial in less than a month.

I want you to draft the memo in opposition to the motion to dismiss and also take care of the oral arguments. Cheryl can tell you when they are scheduled. Before you begin working on the memo, please prepare for me a predictive office memo summarizing the dispute, outlining the law and providing me with your predictions of how you think this matter will be resolved. I believe we have strong arguments that this matter should be heard in a Franklin court, not in Jefferson.

Please have the predictive office memo on my desk next Monday so I can review it to make sure you are on the right track before you begin working on the brief.

Thanks,

Rose

As you have read, you have been asked to write the following documents about this litigation:

First, you will draft a predictive office memo that includes:

- A summary of what has happened between Groovia and Stray Dog Advertising
- The legal issue at hand (personal jurisdiction)
- A summary and analysis of the law that applies
- Your opinion about whether the motion to dismiss filed by SDA will be granted

You will find complete information about this assignment on the Information Page (pages 319-320).

Second, you will draft a persuasive memorandum of law in opposition to the motion to dismiss that Stray Dog Advertising has filed in the litigation commenced by Groovia that includes:

- A persuasive summary of the facts
- The legal issue at hand and a summary of the applicable law
- Persuasive arguments and analysis why the motion should be denied

You will find complete information about this assignment on the Information Page (pages 325-326).

NOTE: The Memo included on pages 306-307 is general background information available to both parties. Other documents, such as the memo from Stray Dog Advertising, are also available to both parties. No documents are considered confidential and are available to only one side.

Defendant's File

Today you receive the following email from Senior Partner Lincoln about a legal dispute between Stray Dog Advertising and one of its clients located in the state of Franklin. You are asked to help with the dispute and to draft the memorandum of law in support of a motion to dismiss.

From:	Amy Lincoln <a.lincoln@lawlawfirm.com>
To:	Associate Attorney <a.attorney@lawlawfirm.com>
Sent:	January 22, THIS YEAR 14:58
Subject:	Fwd: Follow-Up Website/Logo Development

Associate Attorney,

Please see below the email that Pamela Park at Stray Dog Advertising wrote to me about a dispute that SDA is involved in with a client, Groovia, Inc., located in Franklin. Pamela also forwarded to me an email from this client regarding the litigation.

I have also attached for you a memo that Laurie Lawclerk wrote about this matter after she met with Pamela the other day, as well as other correspondence that is relevant to the dispute. Interestingly enough, this client (Peter Dorfman) accidentally sent an email to Pamela that was intended for someone within his company; Pamela sent me a copy of the email that I've provided to you.

We need to move to have this complaint dismissed for lack of personal jurisdiction. There is no way that a Franklin court should have jurisdiction over Pamela when her business is here in Jefferson.

I would like you to do the following:

- Deliver to me a memo about whether you think the Franklin court can exercise personal jurisdiction over SDA
- Draft the memorandum of law that we will file with the Franklin court, asking it to dismiss the claim for lack of personal jurisdiction
- Meet with Pamela and inform her about your legal opinion regarding the lawsuit and whether you think the court will dismiss it
- Travel to Franklin for the hearing to make your arguments to the court

Please ask your assistant to schedule the hearing with the court in Amelia County. If I remember the Rules of Civil Procedure correctly, we must file the motion to dismiss with the answer, otherwise we waive the right to object to the court's jurisdiction. Can you verify for me?

Thanks,

Amy

As you have read, you have been asked to write the following documents about this litigation:

First, you will draft a predictive office memo that includes:

- A summary of what has happened between Groovia and Stray Dog Advertising
- The legal issue at hand (personal jurisdiction)
- A summary and analysis of the law that applies
- Your opinion about whether the motion to dismiss filed by SDA will be granted

You will find complete information about this assignment on the Information Page (pages 319-320).

Second, you will draft a persuasive memorandum of law in support of the motion to dismiss that Stray Dog Advertising has filed in the litigation commenced by Groovia that includes:

- A persuasive summary of the facts
- The legal issue at hand and a summary of the applicable law
- Persuasive arguments and analysis why the motion should be granted

You will find complete information about this assignment on the Information Page (pages 325-326).

NOTE: The Memo included on pages 306-307 is general background information available to both parties. Other documents, such as the memo from Stray Dog Advertising, are also available to both parties. No documents are considered confidential and are available to only one side.

OFFICE MEMO

To:	File
From:	Laurie Lawclerk
Date:	April 19, THIS YEAR
Re:	SDA/Groovia dispute

Stray Dog Advertising recently began working with a business client in Franklin. The client, Groovia, Inc., sells healthy beverages and energy drinks. The company's president, Peter Dorfman, contacted Stray Dog after reading about the agency and its work on the Jefferson Daily News website. Dorfman is originally from Jefferson, although he has been living in Franklin for the past ten years. He still keeps up with the local news of his home state by reading the Daily News website and subscribing to local magazines.

After reading the article, Dorfman did some online research on Stray Dog. Dorman first found the company's listing on a website, www.findapro.com, on which individuals and companies can place postings of their qualifications for skills such as graphic arts and website design and then bid on projects that people from all over the world post. Stray Dog's listing showed that it had worked with many clients in different states, including Franklin.

He then visited Stray Dog's website, which includes a local number that potential clients can call, as well as a toll-free number for those outside of Jefferson. There is also a "contact us" form on the website.

While reading through the Stray Dog Advertising website, Dorfman came across the "About Us" page, which includes the following information:

> Stray Dog Advertising is an advertising agency that combines the best of the big and the small. Like small agencies, we provide our clients with one-on-one, personalized services so that all of our clients feel like they are the only client we are working for. But at the same time, we provide a breadth of services and a wide range of creative talents and technologies that you can only find at large agencies. Our clients range from local businesses in the state of Jefferson to companies in all fifty states and around the world, from small mom-and-pop businesses to some of the largest corporations around. Contact us today to see how we can help your business stand out in today's rough and tumble marketplace.

> Stray Dog Advertising. Local Touch. International Reach.

Dorfman was particularly interested in some of the information that Stray Dog included on its website, as well as some of the services it provides for its clients.

First, the website included a map of the United States that indicated how many clients Stray Dog had worked for in each of the fifty states. Dorfman was impressed when he saw that Stray Dog had worked with six clients from Franklin over the past few years. In some other states outside of Jefferson, in contrast, Stray Dog had worked with nearly thirty clients. Notwithstanding the smaller number of past clients in Franklin, Dorfman felt that the agency would have a good feel for the Franklin market based on its experiences with clients from other states and countries.

Second, he saw that Stray Dog offered overnight delivery of mock-ups and drafts of products, when it wasn't possible to use email with clients. Stray Dog mails overnight delivery the drafts or mock-ups to the clients, wherever they were located, and then the client would simply drop the item off at a post-office or UPS office, postage pre-paid, to return it to Stray Dog with revisions and suggestions. Most agencies don't make it so easy for the client or insist on doing everything via email, which just doesn't work all the time, in Dorfman's opinion.

On October 3, YEAR -1, Dorfman completed the "contact us" form on the Stray Dog Advertising website. The form was directly sent to the email of David McClellan, the agency's receptionist, who then called Dorfman the next day to learn more about his needs. In the case file are the notes of his phone call with Dorfman. David is the first contact of potential clients contacting SDA through the website, and he then connects the potential client with the appropriate person within the agency for additional help and information.

Over the next few weeks, Park and Dorfman negotiated an agreement according to which Stray Dog Advertising would complete the following:

- Design a new logo for the Groovia Energy Drinks
- Develop an online, social media marketing campaign for the new flavors of the Groovia drinks
- Develop a website for Groovia and all of its products, including Groovia Energy Drinks

The Groovia All-Natural Energy Drinks were a new product in the Groovia line and Dorfman was particularly concerned about them doing well in a competitive marketplace. The contract was signed via email as PDF attachments, with first Pamela signing and sending that copy to Peter, who then signed and sent it back to Pamela so that she had a version signed by both parties as well. The contract had no forum selection clause.

After the contract was signed, Park visited the Groovia offices, and she and Peter met in person for the first time. Park had already planned a trip out east to Washington D.C. to visit family who had just moved out there and decided to combine business and pleasure while on the east coast. Even though Stray Dog had worked with other clients from Franklin in the past, this was Park's first time visiting the state.

In November YEAR -1, Stray Dog completed the project for logo design and website development. Dorfman was initially thrilled with the work that Stray Dog did because the logo was original and creative, the website interactive and eye-catching, and the social media campaign hip and popular.

Unfortunately, however, Dorfman's satisfaction over the agency's work was short-lived. Three months after the launch of the new site, Dorfman was contacting Park on a regular basis, demanding to know why his company's business had not already "taken off," as he claims she promised him it would. He claims that during the contract negotiations between Park and Dorfman, Park also promised Dorfman that the coding in their websites was superior to that of other website developers and that because of this special coding, their clients were "guaranteed" to jump to first position on Google search results within a month and to at least double their revenue within the first six months from the site's launch. According to Dorfman, not only had they seen no "dramatic" increase in revenue, but the site was nowhere to be found on the first page of Google results.

Being an impatient man, Dorfman grew frustrated with Park's explanations about Google rankings and the fickleness of the market and contacted his attorney, who immediately filed a claim against Stray Dog Advertising in Franklin state court for breach of express warranty and warranty for a particular purpose under sections 2-313 and 2-315, respectively, of the U.C.C.

- Notes phone call P. Dorfman – he had found us through Jefferson Daily News article (says he is from here originally), found our website and also www.findapro.com profile

- Founder/CEO of company Groovia, soft drinks and energy drinks

- Needs new logo for energy drinks (all natural, healthy), social media campaign and new website for entire company (different divisions and products)

- Find out if Pamela is familiar with them

- He asked about our experience outside of Jefferson – concerned because Groovia is regional product expanding to other markets

- I told him about our other clients in Franklin

- Also explained how we work – lots via email, online but we do send to clients some materials if they can't be done online – also client portal where they can log in to see color pantones, fonts, and products developed

- Wayne McCormick will follow up with him to find out more details of what he needs

- Dorfman said that he will call back tomorrow since he will be traveling (I gave him Wayne's number so he can call)

- I also asked Wayne to send him a follow-up email. This seems like a good account that we should try to get to continue to grow in other states.

From: Wayne McCormick <wayne.mccormick@straydogadvertising.com>
  To: Peter Dorfman <peterdorfman@groovia.com>
Sent: October 3, YEAR -1 13:15
Subject: Follow-Up Website/Logo Development

Dear Mr. Dorfman,

Thank you for your inquiry about Stray Dog Advertising. I would be pleased to provide you with additional information about our agency and our business.

As you read on our website, SDA was founded by Pamela Park in YEAR -10; under her tutelage, SDA has grown to be the most successful advertising agency in the State of Jefferson. We boast numerous clients within the state, including Zenith Brewery, the fastest-growing craft brewery in Jefferson; Canopy, Inc., owner of several high-profile restaurants in Jefferson; and Florentine Holdings, an international corporation that owns several well-known brands, including Marco's Frozen Italian Pizza, Marco's Italian Coffee Makers and Marco's

Italian-Style Barley Coffee. These clients, as well as many others, have seen their business expand due to SDA's creative and unique marketing and advertising strategies.

In addition to these clients within Jefferson, we have also continued our growth outside of the state. As you saw on the map on our website, we have clients throughout the United States and in Franklin. Our experience with the clients in Franklin has given us a keen understanding of the state's market and an advantage at meeting their needs.

We've continued to pursue business outside of Jefferson and are certain that our presence will expand. Our website and client portal allow us to meet the needs of clients all around the country and even around the globe. We are available whenever our clients need us and can travel to our clients' offices if it is more convenient for them.

Please let me know if I can be of additional service to you or if I can answer any other questions that you may have. You can also submit any questions through our website; those email inquiries will then be forwarded to me or one of the other account executives at the office.

Best regards,

Wayne McCormick

Senior Account Executive

Stray Dog Advertising

From: Peter Dorfman <peterdorfman@groovia.com>
To: Pamela Park <pamela.park@straydogadvertising.com>
Sent: October 8, YEAR -1 15:23
Subject: Meetings w/Stray Dog

Hi Hannah,

I wanted to fill you in on what's been going on with the advertising agency, Stray Dog Advertising, and the work that they will be doing for us on the website and for our logo and social media campaign. As Groovia's CFO, you need to know where the money is going!

Pamela Park, the owner of Stray Dog Advertising, was here just last week. She said that she had planned a trip to Franklin to visit some friends and decided to take advantage of being on the east coast to come to our facilities. I showed her around (she seemed very impressed and liked the products too) and we discussed even more the work that they are doing for us.

I expressed to her my concerns about the website helping us make an impact on the energy drink market, which you know is quite saturated. She repeated to me some of the success stories of other clients of theirs who have seen a "dramatic" increase in sales once the website that Stray Dog developed was launched. She said something about some secret code that they use when developing the clients' websites. She also told me again about some other social media campaigns that they've done and also talked about the success they had, at times doubling or tripling the revenue for some clients.

She also told me more about the work that they've done with clients outside of Jefferson and also abroad. It seems like she wants people to know that they are not just a local agency but have experience, and want more experience, with clients in other states.

We made a good choice!

Peter

From: Pamela Park <pamela.park@straydogadvertising.com>
To: Peter Dorfman <peterdorfman@groovia.com>
Sent: October 8, YEAR -1 17:11
Subject: Re: Meetings w/Stray Dog

Peter, I think you copied me on this email by mistake. It is addressed to "Hannah" not to me, and must be for someone within your company.

PP

From: Peter Dorfman <peterdorfman@groovia.com>
To: Pamela Park <pamela.park@straydogadvertising.com>
Sent: October 9, YEAR -1 06:46
Subject: Re: Re: Meetings w/Stray Dog

Thanks, Pamela. My assistant is Hannah Parker. My email program must have filled in your name when I was typing Parker and I didn't realize that I was sending it to you by mistake. I should pay more attention when typing my emails so I don't send them to the wrong person.

We are looking forward to seeing your magical touch with our website traffic and our sales!

Peter Dorfman

From: Peter Dorfman <peterdorfman@groovia.com>
To: Wayne McCormick <wayne.mccormick@straydogadvertising.com>
CC: Pamela Park <pamela.park@straydogadvertising.com>
Sent: December 13, YEAR -1 12:39
Subject: WTH???

WHAT IS GOING ON?? WHERE ARE OUR SALES??? WHERE IS OUR INCREASE IN REVENUE??? WHERE IS THE INCREASE IN TRAFFIC TO OUR WEBSITE???

WHY AREN'T WE #1 ON GOOGLE!?!?!?!?!

I WANT MY MONEY BACK!!!!! IF YOU DON'T END THE CONTRACT WE WILL SUE YOU!!!!

P. DORFMAN

From: Wayne McCormick <wayne.mccormick@straydogadvertising.com>
To: Peter Dorfman <peterdorfman@groovia.com>
CC: Pamela Park <pamela.park@straydogadvertising.com>
Sent: December 13, YEAR -1 14:27
Subject: Website Performance

Dear Peter,

We are sorry to hear that you are not satisfied yet with the performance of your website and the growth of your business due to the Stray Dog social media campaigns and marketing services. As we mentioned in one of our phone calls, the results are not immediate but with perseverance and patience, we guarantee that they will be seen.

Let's plan a phone conference for tomorrow afternoon – does 2:00 your time work – to discuss. We will share with you the growth of traffic to your site that we have observed with our analytics software. I am sure that you will feel reassured that we are moving in the right direction after you see these numbers.

Wayne

STRAYDOG
Advertising

WHILE YOU WERE OUT...

TO: Pamela Park

DATE: December 14, YEAR -1

MESSAGE

Sorry to tell you this yet again, but Peter Dorfman of Groovia called this afternoon. I didn't tell him when you would be back. He repeated what he told you the other day:

- He has seen no increase in sales

- No increase in visitors to the company's website

- The social media campaign is "garbage"

His last words: "Tell Park I will see her in court!"

Additional Skills-Building Exercises

Personal Jurisdiction Analysis Exercise

Overview of the Exercise: The following short fact patterns deal with personal jurisdiction, and your task is to analyze the fact patterns to determine whether or not the court would have personal jurisdiction over the out-of-state defendant.

Learning Objectives of the Exercise:

This assignment will build your skills to:

- Articulate the legal rules regarding personal jurisdiction
- Apply those rules to brief fact patterns and analyze the facts and the law
- Articulate and effectively communicate that analysis using legal terminology

Steps for Completing the Exercise:

- Read the following fact patterns.
- By yourself, analyze each one and decide whether or not you think the court would have personal jurisdiction over the defendant and why. If the court in the fact pattern doesn't have personal jurisdiction over the defendant, where should the plaintiff sue? You don't need to write out a full answer, but jot down notes about your reasoning.
- When analyzing the fact patterns, remember to first analyze whether the state long-arm statute would provide personal jurisdiction over the defendant, and then analyze as well whether personal jurisdiction would comport with the constitutional requirements.
- When have finished analyzing each of the fact patterns, discuss your answers with the partner that you have been assigned. Explain to each other why you have reached the conclusion that you did.
- If you and your partner have different responses to a fact pattern, you must try to convince him or her that your answer is correct. After you both have tried to convince the other, you must choose a team answer.
- Once you have discussed each of the fact patterns, you will compare answers as a class.

Research Required for the Exercise: You are not required to do any outside research for this exercise. Instead, use the personal jurisdiction cases that you have read for class and this Unit.

Grading: This exercise is not graded. Instead, when you and your partner have finished comparing answers, you will compare your answers with your class and review the results you obtained.

---

1.   Motley Music sells vinyl records from its brick and mortar store in Jefferson City, Jefferson. It also maintains an Internet website, through which it sold a record to Brenda, who lives in the state of Wisconsin and also owns a music store named Motley Music. The Wisconsin Motley Music operates two retail stores in the state and also sells CDs and vinyl records through its website.

In addition to the sale of the record to Brenda, the Jefferson Motley Music store also purchased a cash register from a company located in Wisconsin. Aside from the sale to Brenda and the purchase of the cash register, the Jefferson store has no contacts with Wisconsin.

Brenda has now filed a trademark infringement claim against the Jefferson store in Wisconsin federal court. The attorney representing the store has filed a motion to dismiss for lack of personal jurisdiction. Should the court grant the motion, or should it exercise personal jurisdiction over the out-of-state defendant? You can consult <u>Millennium Enterprises, Inc. v. Millennium Music, LP</u>, 33 F. Supp. 2d 907 (D. Or. 1999) to compare your reasoning to that of the court.

2. A potential client, a financial institution named Countryside Bank, has approached the Lincoln, Adams and Washington law firm about bringing a trademark infringement claim against another financial institution, Countrywide Banks, alleging that the name of the bank infringes upon Countryside Bank's trademark. Countrywide is located in the state of Franklin and has no physical locations in the state of Jefferson. However, Countrywide maintains two Web sites pertaining to their mortgage origination business where customers in any state can apply for loans on-line as well as print out an application for submission by facsimile and can click on a "hyper link" to "chat" on-line with a representative of Countrywide. Customers in Jefferson and other states can e-mail the bank with home loan questions and receive a response from an online representative in less than an hour. The attorney representing Countrywide has filed a motion to dismiss for lack of personal jurisdiction. Should the court grant the motion, or should it exercise personal jurisdiction over the out-of-state defendant? You can consult Citigroup Inc. v. City Holding Co., 97 F. Supp. 2d 549 (S.D.N.Y. 2000) to compare your reasoning to that of the court.

3. Jillian operates a travel agency in the state of Jefferson. She was approached by a sales representative of a company, headquartered in New York, that operates a computerized airline reservation system, hosted on servers located in the state of Florida. Jillian signed a two-year contract for the company's services. The contract was signed at her office in Jefferson. Shortly after signing the contract, Jillian began having malfunctions and service problems, which the company refused to repair. After two months, the system stopped working entirely. She refused to pay what remained under the contract since she could no longer use the company's services. The company has now brought a breach of contract claim against Jillian in Florida state court, alleging that she owes the entire amount due under the contract. Jillian's attorney has filed a motion to dismiss for lack of personal jurisdiction. Should the court grant the motion, or should it exercise personal jurisdiction over the out-of-state defendant? You can consult Pres-Kap, Inc. v. System One, Direct Access, Inc., 636 So. 2d 1351 (Fla. Dist. Ct. 1994) to compare your reasoning to that of the court.

4. Giovanni now lives in Jefferson, but when he was still living in Rome, he entered into a contract with an Italian company under which he would provide virtual accounting services to the company's clients, who are located around the world, including in Italy and in Jefferson. It seemed like the perfect arrangement now that Giovanni has moved to Jefferson to pursue his dream of opening a real Italian pizzeria. Since signing the contract, Giovanni has rendered nearly 250 hours of services to the company, but they have not paid him one dollar (or one Euro, as the case may be). The services were rendered entirely while he was in Jefferson. The company owes Giovanni more than $6,000. Giovanni has filed a claim against the company in Darrow County Conciliation Court and also properly served the company in Rome. The attorney representing the Italian company has filed a motion to dismiss for lack of personal jurisdiction. Should the court grant the motion, or should it exercise personal jurisdiction over the out-of-state defendant?

5. Nan lives in Jefferson and received in the mail a letter from an ex-boyfriend, who now lives in the state of Georgia. The letter accused Nan of embezzling more than $1,000,000 from her employer, a bank. This is false. Nan saw that her supervisor was copied on the letter. She has brought a claim of defamation against this ex-boyfriend in Jefferson state court. His attorney has filed a motion to dismiss for lack of personal jurisdiction, arguing that the tortious act (the writing of the defamatory letter) was committed in Georgia, not in Jefferson, so the court should not and cannot exercise jurisdiction over the out-of-state defendant. Should the court grant or deny the motion?

6. Naima went on vacation to a lake resort in northern Jefferson. Naima is a resident of the neighboring state of Franklin and had never been to Jefferson before this vacation. While at the resort, she tripped and fell over a rug that was not secured to the floor, injuring her knee. Since returning home, she has been told that she tore a ligament in her knee when she fell and that she will have to have surgery to repair it. Naima has approached a law firm in Franklin about bringing a personal injury claim against the resort, but the attorney is unsure whether Franklin is the proper forum. Where should the attorney bring the claim? In Franklin or in Jefferson state court? If the attorney files the claim in Franklin state court and if the attorney representing the defendant files a motion to dismiss for lack of personal jurisdiction, how do you think the court will rule? Will it grant or dismiss the motion?

7.   Adam owns a food processing company that makes processed soups and that has recently developed a new recipe for cabbage soup. Although Adam's company is located in Jefferson, it sells its soup across the country. One of the grocery stores that purchases Adam's soups is located in Florida. The grocery store orders the soup on a monthly basis from Adam, who conducts all of his business via email and over the phone. He does not take any orders through his website and does no advertising outside of his website. Adam first contacted the grocery store owner when he did a massive email campaign last year, sending out thousands of emails to grocery stores around the country hoping to increase the market of his soups and other products. The grocery store owner contacted Adam because of this email.

The grocery store owner is now claiming that the soups he just purchased from Adam contained rotten cabbage and he cannot sell them. He has brought a breach of contract claim against Adam in Florida state court, demanding that the contract be rescinded and that the money he paid on the last order be reimbursed. Adam's attorney has filed a motion to dismiss for lack of personal jurisdiction. Should the court grant or deny the motion?

8.   Jack's company is located in the state of Franklin and manufacturers pressure tanks. One of the tanks was sold to a company in Jefferson, which purchased the tank after seeing it on Jack's website. The website doesn't allow for online purchases so the Jefferson company phoned Jack and ordered over the phone the pressure tank. It was delivered via FedEx to Jefferson. Two days after it arrived, it exploded, seriously injuring two employees of the Jefferson company. The employees have brought personal injury claims in Jefferson state court against Jack's company. Jack's attorney has filed a motion to dismiss for lack of personal jurisdiction. Should the court grant or deny the motion? You can consult Feathers v. McLucas, 209 N.E.2d 68 (N.Y. 1965) to compare your reasoning to that of the court.

9.   Alfredo is a limited partner in a partnership that produces movies. He is an investor and is not involved in the daily production activities. The movie production company is located in New York, and all the movies are produced there. Alfredo lives and works in the state of Jefferson. A New York resident has filed a claim in New York courts against Alfredo's partnership and against each of the partners individually, claiming that she was defamed by the latest documentary that the partnership produced. Alfredo's attorney has filed a motion to dismiss for lack of personal jurisdiction, arguing that since Alfredo is a limited partner who only invested in the partnership, he should not be subject to New York jurisdiction. Should the court grant or deny the motion? You can consult Lynn v. Cohen, 359 F. Supp. 565 (S.D. N.Y. 1973) to compare your reasoning to that of the court.

Presentations:
If SDA or Groovia Were Your Client...

Overview of the Exercise: For this exercise, you will make a professional presentation in which you answer and discuss the following question:

If Stray Dog Advertising were your client in your home country and if Pamela came to you for legal advice about the complaint filed against SDA by Groovia, what would you do and what advice would you give her?

OR

If Groovia, Inc. were your client in your home country and Peter Dorfman came to you for advice about filing a claim against SDA, what would you do and what advice would you give him?

You will do the presentation based on the client whom you represent.

Learning Objectives of the Exercise:

This exercise will build your skills to:

- Describe a specific aspect of your country's legal system
- Compare and contrast your country's legal system with the U.S. legal system
- Listen to and understand your classmates' presentations and extrapolate information from those presentations

Steps for Completing the Exercise:

- Analyze the <u>Groovia, Inc. v. Stray Dog Advertising, LLC</u> fact pattern under your country's laws.
- Determine whether or not a court could exercise personal jurisdiction over Stray Dog Advertising based on the facts presented.
- Explain how the case would be handled in your country's legal system.
- Explain what legal advice you would give Pamela or Peter if he/she came to you for advice in your home country.

Research Required:

The research you are required to do depends on your knowledge of these claims in your country's legal system. It is presumed that you are familiar with the law and with how you would approach this issue if SDA or Groovia, Inc. were a client of yours.

Grading: This presentation is not graded. You will present to a small group of your fellow classmates instead of to the entire class.

Handouts:

As part of your presentation, you must create a handout for your classmates, and the handouts must include fill-in-the-blank questions that your classmates must complete with information that you present during the presentation. Each handout must include at least five questions to complete.

For example, if a U.S. law student were giving a presentation on jurisdiction in the United States, she could include on her handout this question:

> To exercise personal jurisdiction over an out-of-state defendant, a court must first analyze whether jurisdiction is allowed under the state's _____ statute.

As you are speaking, your classmates will have to listen, follow what you are saying and fill in the blanks. If you are listening to one of your classmate's presentations and are unsure about an answer, you should ask him or her to repeat so you can fill in the blank(s).

Grammar Review:

The basis of this exercise is hypothetical or conditional verbs: *if SDA or Groovia were your client, what would you do?*

Remember the grammar when discussing hypothetical conditions.

Present: **IF + PAST SIMPLE, WOULD + BASE VERB**

*If Pamela **called** me to schedule an appointment, I **would tell** her to visit me at my office.*

NOTE: We use "were" for all tenses with the verb "to be" when using a conditional verb.

*If I **were** you, I **would not take** that class.*

*If Pamela **were** my client, I **would tell** her that the claim Groovia, Inc. filed against SDA would likely be dismissed.*

Past: **IF + PAST PERFECT, WOULD + HAVE + PAST PARTICIPLE**

*If Groovia **had discussed** this matter with Pamela rather than just filing the claim, the litigation likely **would not have been commenced.***

*If Peter **had** really **wanted** to resolve the matter, he **would have called** Pamela to talk with her rather than just filing the complaint.*

Ethics Dilemma: Revealing Information to Opposing Party

Overview of the Exercise: For purposes of this exercise, assume that you work for the Lincoln, Adams and Washington Law Firm and represent the defendant, Stray Dog Advertising, regardless of whether you represent the plaintiff or the defendant in this Unit.

As you read in the Main Assignment File, Peter Dorfman mistakenly sent an email to Pamela Park, believing that the email was addressed to his assistant, Hannah Parker. The email was innocuous and contained no information that would have hurt Dorfman or his case against SDA.

Now, however, Dorfman has sent another email by mistake to Park. Park immediately forwarded it to you upon her receipt of it, and did not inform Dorfman that he had mistakenly sent it to her instead of his assistant, Hannah Parker. The email is on page 318. As you will see, this email is not quite as innocuous and in fact contains damaging information for Dorfman and his claim against SDA. This exercise will require you to analyze what you should ethically do with this email.

NOTE: The email that is the object of this Ethics Dilemma exercise is only for this exercise. When you are analyzing the motion to dismiss and making your arguments in opposition to and in support of it, do not consider this email.

Learning Objectives of the Exercise:

This assignment will build your skills to:

- Articulate the ethical rules regarding communications and revealing information
- Apply those rules to the litigation involving Stray Dog Advertising and Groovia
- Articulate and effectively communicate that analysis using legal terminology

Steps for Completing the Exercise:

- Review the Model Rules of Professional Conduct and identify which rule(s) apply to this situation.
- Analyze the rules to determine what guidance they provide about what should be done with the email and the information contained in it.
- You can also do online searches to find ethics opinions or information online on other sites regarding the dilemma.
- By yourself, analyze whether you think the LAW Law Firm should reveal to opposing counsel that the email and the information contained therein were accidentally sent to Pamela Park. Analyze also whether you can ethically use the information, such as in the answer or in asserting defenses, or whether you should pretend that you haven't seen it. Are there other courses of action that you can take?
- When you are done analyzing this matter, discuss your answer with the partner(s) that you have been assigned. Explain to each other why you have reached your conclusion.
- If you and your partner have different responses, you must try to convince him or her that your answer is correct. After you both have tried to convince the other, you must choose a team answer.
- Once you have discussed the ethics dilemma, you will compare answers as a class.

Background:

The Rules of Professional Conduct regulate the actions, conduct, and behavior of lawyers in their interactions with clients, non-clients, opposing counsel, and judges and establish standards for attorney conduct and for the legal profession. Each state has promulgated its own set of Rules of Professional Conduct although the ABA Model Rules of Professional Conduct serve as a model for the rules of most states.

Being familiar with the Rules is fundamental for all attorneys. Like the law, ignorance of the rules is no defense. And while a violation of the rules can but does not always equate to legal malpractice, attorneys can end up in serious trouble for a violation. Punishment can range from a private or public admonishment to suspension of one's license to practice law and to disbarment (the removal of an attorney from the practice of law and revocation of his or her license).

Research for the Assignment:

Use the ABA Model Rules of Professional Conduct for this exercise as they are the same as the Jefferson Rules of Professional Conduct. Use a search engine like Google or Bing to locate the rules, or your professional responsibility course book if you are enrolled in the class. You can also find the rules on Westlaw, LexisNexis or Bloomberg Law. Skim over the titles to the Rules and identify which one will likely provide you with guidance to analyze this dilemma. Don't forget to read the comments in addition to the rule itself as the comments often provide valuable insight as to how the rule should be applied.

Written Assignment:

If time permits, you and your partner should prepare a short written summary, addressed to the senior partner, advising him or her on whether the email should be disclosed and the reasoning for your advice.

Grading: This assignment is not graded. Instead, you will discuss the matter with a partner or in a small group and then share your conclusions with the rest of the class.

From:	Peter Dorfman <peterdorfman@groovia.com>
To:	Pamela Park <pamela.park@straydogadvertising.com>
Sent:	December 12, THIS YEAR 09:15
Subject:	Meetings w/Stray Dog

Hannah,

I want to get out of the contract with Stray Dog. I met with someone yesterday at the Amelia County Chamber of Commerce; his name is Thomas Gardenshire and he owns a website development company here in town. I want to go local rather than continue to work with an out-of-state company. Our numbers haven't risen as dramatically as Pamela claimed that they would. I feel like we were duped. Sure, we've seen an increase in traffic, but not that much.

Let's tell them that our numbers haven't increased at all and that we've seen zero increase in revenue. I know it isn't the truth, but how many business people tell the truth all the time? Isn't the saying "all's fair in love, war and business?" LOL

We'll get them to terminate the contract if we threaten them enough. When I met Pamela, I had a feeling that she would be a pushover. She thinks she's tough, but I can tell that she'd give in to some demand letter from our lawyer, or even threats from me.

Gardenshire told me that he can provide us the same services but at half the cost. You know how much I like to save as much money as I can!

I'll send Pamela an email tomorrow.

Peter

Information Pages

Office Memo:
Personal Jurisdiction and the Internet

Overview of the Assignment: For this assignment, you will write an office memo to the Senior Partner, summarizing your research on personal jurisdiction and providing your prediction of what will happen in the litigation.

Learning Objectives of the Assignment:
This assignment will build your skills to:

- Efficiently communicate in a written format
- Explain complex matters clearly and concisely
- Analyze and apply the rules of law regarding personal jurisdiction

Research for the Assignment: You are not required to do any outside research for this assignment. You should base your analysis on the personal jurisdiction cases that you have read:

- Atkinson v. McLaughlin, 343 F. Supp. 2d 868 (D.N.D. 2004).
- Mink v. AAAA Development, Inc. 190 F.3d 333 (5th Cir. 1999).
- Carrot Bunch Co., v. Computer Friends, Inc., 218 F. Supp. 2d 820 (N.D. Tex. 2002).
- Ford v. Mentor Worldwide, LLC, 2 F. Supp. 3d 898 (E.D. La. 2014).
- Gatte v. Ready 4 A Change, LLC, 2013 WL 123613 (W.D. La. Jan. 13, 2013).
- The Kelly Law Firm, P.C. v. An Attorney For You, 679 F. Supp. 2d 755 (S.D. Tex. 2009).
- Percle v. SFGL Foods, Inc., 356 F. Supp. 2d 629 (M.D. La. 2004).
- Tempur-Pedic International, Inc. v. Go Satellite, Inc., 758 F. Supp. 2d 366 (N.D. Tex. 2010).

If you want to practice your legal research skills, you can look for and use other cases that you find. However, if you do search on Westlaw, LexisNexis or Bloomberg Law, be sure to limit your search and the cases you use to Texas or 5th Circuit law.

Format of the Completed Assignment:

Your response should be in an office memo format and should include the following:

- Summary of the facts
- The relevant law
- Analysis of the law to the fact pattern
- Conclusion about how you think a court would rule if this matter were to go to court
- Your advice to the client about how to proceed

Follow the following format:

- 1 inch (2.54 cm.) margins (top/bottom and sides)
- 12 font, Times New Roman font
- Double spaced
- Maximum eight pages

Notes:

This memo should be predictive and not persuasive. You are not trying to persuade the senior partner or the client about the strength of your arguments or urge him or her to take a particular course of action; you are only trying to inform about the law, how it applies to our case, how you think a court would rule and what advice you have.

In a memo, you can also use formatting like underlining, bold font or italics. You can also create headings and subheadings to organize your answer.

For additional information about office memos and e-memos, as well as samples, refer to the online additional resources.

Grading: This assignment is worth 102 points.

Personal Jurisdiction and the Internet

Unit 2

LEGAL CONTENT	0-6 points	8 points	10 points	12 points	Points
Issue statement (IS)	Document does not include an IS or includes IS that fails to properly identify the legal issue(s) and the applicable law	Identifies the legal issue(s) and correctly states the applicable law with minor mistakes	Identifies the legal issue(s) and correctly states the applicable law	Identifies the legal issue(s) and correctly states the applicable law in an exceptionally creative and concise way	_____/12
Short Answer	Document does not include a short answer or includes a short answer with significant mistakes	Responds to IS but with key facts or applicable legal principles missing	Responds to IS with key facts and applicable legal principles with no meaningful errors	Clearly and concisely responds to IS with key facts and applicable legal principles and no irrelevancies	_____/12
Facts	Few or none of the relevant facts are included; difficult to follow or understand	Most relevant facts are included as well as non-relevant ones; at times difficult to follow	Relevant facts are included with occasional irrelevancies; easy to follow	All relevant facts are included with no irrelevancies; story is clearly and concisely told to reader in objective way	_____/12
Rule	Hard to follow and understand; does not include relevant sources or cites inappropriate sources; no rule application	Cites to some relevant sources but is incomplete in covering all relevant aspects of the rule; includes some rule application	Cite only to relevant sources and mostly clear; rule application explains but not fully how rule has been applied	Clear and concise; includes only relevant sources and includes all parts of rule necessary for analysis; clear rule application	_____/12
Analysis	Contains conclusory statements and/or no case law; facts are analyzed in a conclusory or insufficient way	Uses some case law but does not analogize or distinguish or explain its application; some conclusory statements; facts briefly analyzed	Uses case law to show how rule applies to case; case law is compared and contrasted with success; most facts are analyzed	Analyzes case law completely, comparing it fully to client matter; facts are thoroughly analyzed in an objective way	_____/12
Conclusion/ Recommendations	No conclusion or recommendations are included in document	A brief conclusion is included but without sufficient client advice	Paper includes conclusion and recommendations	Paper includes full conclusion of the legal analysis and facts and presents creative and thoughtful recommendations	_____/12
Citations	No sources are cited in document	Some sources are cited, but inconsistently; citation format is inconsistent	All citations are present; correct format is mostly used	All citations are present; correct format is used throughout document	_____/12
WRITING	**2**	**4**	**5**	**6**	**Points**
Formatting	Document does not follow format instructions or the sample provided	Document attempts to follow instructions and sample provided	Document follows the instructions and sample provided with no meaningful errors	Document exactly follows the instructions and sample provided	_____/6
Organization	No structure or organization; free flow of ideas	Structure & organization present but reorganization or headings needed for full clarity	Document is clearly organized and structured with proper use of heading and subheadings	Document is exceptionally well organized and structured with proper use of headings and subheadings	_____/6
Syntax Mechanics	Contains numerous and distracting grammatical and mechanical errors that impede understanding	Contains some grammatical and mechanical errors that impede understanding	Contains few grammatical and mechanical errors but none that impede understanding	Contains no grammatical and mechanical errors; native-like use of English	_____/6
TOTAL					_____/102

Mock Client Meeting

Overview of the Assignment: This assignment simulates a client meeting between you and your client, Pamela Park of Stray Dog Advertising, LLC or Peter Dorfman of Groovia, Inc. For this exercise, you will meet with your client and explain to him or her the status of the litigation <u>Groovia Inc. v. Stray Dog Advertising, LLC</u>, the results of your analysis about how a court might rule on the motion to dismiss and your recommendations on how to proceed.

Learning Objectives of the Assignment:

This assignment will build your skills to:

- Explain and clarify the legal positions of the parties and describe potential outcomes to your client
- Respond to technical questions about litigation
- Incorporate technical legal English vocabulary that relates to personal jurisdiction and use appropriate layperson explanations for your client

Steps for Completing the Assignment:

- Read and be familiar with the Main Assignment File
- Be familiar with the personal jurisdiction cases that you have been assigned
- Recommended:
    - Anticipate the questions that you think your client might ask and prepare possible responses;
    - Draft an outline of what you would like to cover in the meeting.

Note: Remember that part of the grading is also based on your professional demeanor. You are expected to arrive punctually, be dressed in professional attire and act as you would with a client in real life. You should play the part from when you come into the meeting room.

Grading: This assignment is worth 102 points.

Punctuality: Student-attorney arrived on time to meeting: YES _____ (10 points) NO _____ (0 points)

Professional Attire: Student-attorney was dressed in appropriate professional attire: YES _____ (10 points) NO _____ (0 points)

Professional Demeanor: Student-attorney acted in a professional manner w/client: YES _____ (10 points) NO _____ (0 points)

GRADING CRITERIA	0- 6 points	8 points (C or 75%)	10 points (B or 85%)	12 points	Points received
Engagement I (questions)	Attorney does not ask client any questions; engages in monologue	Attorney asks few questions; questions are hard to follow or show minimal preparation or understanding of matter	Attorney asks basic questions that demonstrate understanding of matter and preparation	Attorney asks thoughtful, insightful and creative questions that demonstrate deep preparation & understanding of matter	_____/12
Engagement II (answers)	Attorney does not respond to client's questions	Attorney responds to questions, but incorrectly or with hard to follow answers	Attorney responds promptly and correctly to all of client's questions	Attorney responds promptly and correctly to all of client's questions with creative, thoughtful and insightful answers that show a deep understanding of the issues	_____/12
Knowledge of Applicable Law	Attorney provides no explanation of the applicable law	Attorney provides explanation of with serious mistakes, or hard to follow (e.g. use of legal jargon)	Attorney provides clear explanation of with some mistakes; uses some legal jargon unnecessarily or without explanations that client can understand	Attorney provides clear, concise and correct explanation of the law with legal jargon when appropriate or w/ explanations client can understand	_____/12
Ability to Analyze Applicable Law	Attorney provides does not provide an analysis of the law for the client	Attorney attempts to analyze the law but provides incomplete or incorrect analysis	Attorney provides analysis of the law with no significant mistakes or misstatements of the law or facts	Attorney provides a clear, concise and correct analysis of the law as it applies to the client matter	_____/12
Advice and Recommendations	Attorney provides no advice or poor advice for client	Attorney provides not comprehensive or inaccurate advice	Attorney provides comprehensive and accurate advice to client on his/her legal matter	Attorney provides thoughtful and creative solutions for client	_____/12
Organization	Meeting is disorganized and hard to follow or lacks any organization	Meeting has some organization but is still confusing for client for how information is presented	Meeting is clearly organized and easy to follow	Meeting is clearly organized and is easy to follow; attorney takes extra steps to ensure client's understanding	_____/12
TOTAL					_____/72
TOTAL FROM PUNCTUALITY AND PROFESSIONALISM					_____/30

Total   _____/102

Client Advice Letter

Overview of the Assignment: For this assignment, you will write an advice and follow-up letter to Pamela Park or to Peter Dorfman after your client meeting with him/her. The letter should summarize the legal issues and the law you discussed, include your prediction on what you think will happen with the litigation and state any recommendations that you may have for your client. Be mindful that even though Park and Dorfman are sophisticated and experienced professionals, they are not trained attorneys. Therefore you should avoid legalese in your letter.

Under Rule 1.4(a)(3) of the Model Rules of Professional Conduct, an attorney has the duty to keep his or her client "reasonably informed about the status of the client's matter." A thorough follow-up letter after a client meeting is one of the best ways to meet this duty, as well as regular phone calls, emails or meetings.

Learning Objectives of the Assignment:

This assignment will build your skills to:

- Efficiently communicate in a written format
- Explain complex matters clearly and concisely
- Incorporate technical legal English vocabulary that relates to personal jurisdiction and motions to dismiss and use appropriate layperson explanations for client

Steps for Completing the Assignment:

- Review the predictive memo that you wrote to your senior partner about your client matter to ensure that the law and the issues are clear
- Be familiar with the case law regarding to personal jurisdiction and motions to dismiss, as well as the fact pattern
- Conduct your client meeting with your client, Pamela Park or Peter Dorfman
- Review the Business Correspondence online resources

Research Required for the Assignment: You are not required to do any outside research for this assignment.

Format of the Completed Assignment:

Your assignment should be written as a business letter, not as an email. Even though many firms and lawyers use email for much of the correspondence carried out, formal business letters are still an essential part of the practice of law.

Your law firm has the following policy regarding business correspondence. Your client letter must follow the policy guidelines.

LAW FIRM CORRESPONDENCE POLICY

The purpose of this policy is to ensure a uniform appearance of all business correspondence that is written by the attorneys and staff of the law firm and thus to increase the professional appearance of the firm's work product. All law firm attorneys and staff are required to follow these guidelines when writing correspondence. Violation of the policy can result in disciplinary action, up to and including termination.

- The first page of all "traditional" letters must be written on law firm letterhead, which includes the firm's address and logo
- All letters must be written in a modified block letter format
- Letters must be written in Times New Roman, 12 font
- Letters must be 1.5 spaced and have 1" (2.54 cm.) margins, except for the initial page, which may have larger top margins to account for the logo, law firm address and sender's direct contact information
- Client letters must not exceed four pages

Grading: This assignment is worth 78 points.

Note: See the Online Additional Resources for examples of letters and for general information about business correspondence.

Unit 2   Personal Jurisdiction and the Internet

LEGAL CONTENT	0-6 points (failing)	8 points (C or 75%)	10 points (B or 85%)	12 points	Points
Introduction	Letter does not include an appropriate introduction or includes poorly constructed one	Letter includes introduction that states purpose with some irrelevancies or some relevant information missing	Introduction states purpose of letter and includes other relevant information	Introduction is engaging; states purpose of letter and includes other relevant information; written clearly and concisely	_____/12
Summary of Meeting	Letter includes no summary of the meeting	Letter includes summary but leaves out important information or states it unclearly	Letter summarizes the meeting but leaves out important information	Letter clearly and concisely summarizes the meeting, its core purpose and content	_____/12
Applicable Law	Student-attorney provides no explanation of the applicable law, or only uses legal jargon in explanation (inappropriate for audience)	Student-attorney provides explanation of with serious mistakes, or hard to follow (use of legal jargon)	Student-attorney provides clear explanation of with few mistakes; uses some legal jargon without appropriate explanations	Student-attorney provides clear, concise and correct explanation of the law with legal jargon with appropriate explanations	_____/12
Analysis	Contains conclusory statements and/or no case law; facts are analyzed in a conclusory or insufficient way	Uses some case law but does not analogize or distinguish or explain its application; some conclusory statements; facts briefly analyzed	Uses case law to show how rule applies to case; case law is compared and contrasted with success; most facts are analyzed	Analyzes completely case law, comparing it fully to client matter; facts are thoroughly analyzed	_____/12
Conclusion/ Recommendations	No conclusion or recommendations are included in letter	A brief conclusion is included but without sufficient advice or recommendations advice or next steps	Letter includes conclusion with recommendations and next steps	Letter includes full conclusion of the legal analysis and facts, presents creative and thoughtful recommendations and includes clear next steps	_____/12
WRITING	2	4	5	6	Points
Formatting	Document does not follow format instructions or the sample provided	Document attempts to follow instructions and sample provided	Document follows the instructions and sample provided with minor errors	Document exactly follows the instructions and sample provided	_____/6
Organization	No structure or organization; free flow of ideas	Letter includes organization and structure but is still confusing	Structure and organization but some reorganization is needed for full clarity	Document is clearly organized and structured	_____/6
Syntax Mechanics	Contains numerous and distracting grammatical and mechanical errors that impede understanding	Contains some grammatical and mechanical errors that impede understanding	Contains few grammatical and mechanical errors but none that impede understanding	Contains no grammatical and mechanical errors; native-like use of English	_____/6
TOTAL					_____/78

Memorandum of Law for Motion to Dismiss

Overview of Assignment: For this assignment, you will draft a memorandum of law in opposition to or in support of the motion to dismiss that Stray Dog Advertising has filed in the litigation with Groovia, Inc.

You have been assigned to represent either Stray Dog Advertising or Groovia. In the Main Assignment File, you have also received your assignment from the senior partner of your respective law firm and have been asked to write the memorandum of law and also to conduct the oral argument.

Learning Objectives of the Assignment:

This assignment will build your skills to:

- Efficiently read and understand legal authority
- Analyze the fact pattern by applying the relevant case law
- Adapt the IRAC organization and the formal memorandum of law structure
- Communicate effectively and in a persuasive manner to convince the court and the reader that your client's position and argument is the one to follow (in both an oral and written format)

Research for the Assignment: You are not required to do any outside research for this assignment. You should base your analysis on the personal jurisdiction cases that you read and review in class:

- Atkinson v. McLaughlin, 343 F. Supp. 2d 868 (D.N.D. 2004).
- Mink v. AAAA Development, Inc. 190 F.3d 333 (5th Cir. 1999).
- Carrot Bunch Co., v. Computer Friends, Inc., 218 F. Supp. 2d 820 (N.D. Tex. 2002).
- Ford v. Mentor Worldwide, LLC, 2F. Supp. 3d 898 (E.D. La. 2014).
- Gatte v. Ready 4 A Change, LLC, 2013 WL 123613 (W.D. La. Jan. 13, 2013).
- The Kelly Law Firm, P.C. v. An Attorney For You, 679 F. Supp. 2d 755 (S.D. Tex. 2009).
- Percle v. SFGL Foods, Inc., 356 F. Supp. 2d 629 (M.D. La. 2004).
- Tempur-Pedic International, Inc. v. Go Satellite, Inc., 758 F. Supp. 2d 366 (N.D. Tex. 2010).

If you want to practice your legal research skills, you can look for and use other cases that you find. However, if you do search on Westlaw, LexisNexis or Bloomberg Law, be sure to limit your search and the cases you use to Texas or 5th Circuit law.

Format of the Completed Assignment:

For your completed assignment, you must follow Local Rule 5.2 of the Courts of Jefferson.

Local Rule 5.2 GENERAL FORMAT OF DOCUMENTS TO BE FILED

Format: All documents filed must be typewritten, printed, or prepared by a clearly legible duplication process. Document text must be double-spaced, except for quoted material and footnotes, and pages must be numbered consecutively at the bottom. Documents filed after the case-initiating document must contain—on the front page and above the document's title—the case number and the name or initials of the assigned district judge and magistrate judge.

Represented Parties. A memorandum of law filed by a represented party must be typewritten. All text in the memorandum, including footnotes, must be set in at least font size 12 (i.e., a 12-point font) as font sizes are designated in the word-processing software used to prepare the memorandum. Text must be double-spaced, with these exceptions: headings and footnotes may be single-spaced, and quotations more than two lines long may be indented and single-spaced. Pages must be 8 ½ by 11 inches in size, and no text — except for page numbers — may appear outside an area measuring 6 ½ by 9 inches.

<u>Length</u>: No memorandum filed with the court shall exceed the length of twelve pages, excluding caption and table of contents.

Grading: This assignment is worth 90 points.

Note: See the online resources for additional information about memoranda of law and persuasive writing.

LEGAL CONTENT	0-6 points	8 points	10 points	12 points	Points
Introduction	Document does not include an Introduction or includes issue statement instead	Introduction is not persuasive or does not include persuasive or relevant facts or the law	Student attempts to make introduction persuasive, to "put the spin" but does not include all facts or something...	Introduction is persuasive, clear and concise and clearly introduces reader to the client's story and position and identifies the relief sought	____/12
Facts	Few or none of the relevant facts are included; difficult to follow or understand	Relevant facts are included as well as non-relevant ones; mostly clear	Relevant facts are included; factual background is mostly clear and easy to follow with few irrelevancies	Relevant facts are included with no irrelevant facts; story is clearly and concisely told to reader in persuasive way	____/12
Rule	Hard to follow and understand; does not include relevant sources or cites inappropriate sources; no rule application	Cites to some relevant sources but is incomplete in covering all relevant aspects of the rule	Cite only to relevant sources; rule application explains but not fully how rule has been applied	Clear and concise; includes only relevant sources and includes all parts of rule necessary for analysis; clear rule application	____/12
Argument	Contains conclusory statements and/or no case law; facts are analyzed in a conclusory or insufficient way	Uses some case law but does not analogize or distinguish or explain its application; some conclusory statements; facts briefly analyzed; student attempts to make persuasive arguments	Uses case law to show how rule applies to case; case law is compared and contrasted with success; facts are analyzed and argued in a persuasive way	Analyzes completely case law, comparing it fully to client matter; all facts are thoroughly analyzed and argued in a very persuasive way	____/12
Conclusion	No conclusion is included in document	A brief conclusion is included but unclear relief sought	Paper includes conclusion with relief sought	Paper includes full conclusion of the legal analysis and facts and persuasively argues for relief sought	____/12
Citations	No sources are cited in document or citation formats are incorrect and inconsistent	Sources are cited, but inconsistently; citation format has meaningful mistakes in format	Citations are complete; few meaningful mistakes in format	No mistakes in citations; correct format is used throughout document	____/12
WRITING	2	4	5	6	Points
Formatting	Document does not follow format instructions or the sample provided	Document attempts to follow instructions and sample provided	Document follows the instructions and sample provided with minor errors	Document exactly follows the instructions and sample provided	____/6
Organization	No structure or organization; free flow of ideas	Document includes some organization and structure but is still confusing; no use of headings or subheadings	Structure & organization present but reorganization needed full clarity; subheadings included but not effectively persuasive	Document is clearly organized and structured with proper use of persuasive heading and subheadings	____/6
Syntax Mechanics	Contains numerous and distracting grammatical and mechanical errors that impede understanding	Contains some grammatical and mechanical errors that impede understanding	Contains few grammatical and mechanical errors but none that impede understanding	Contains no grammatical and mechanical errors; native-like use of English	____/6
TOTAL					____/90

Mock Oral Argument

• •

Overview of the Assignment: For this assignment, you will present oral arguments to the court on behalf of your client and persuade the court that the motion to dismiss filed by Stray Dog Advertising should be granted or dismissed, depending on which party you represent. You will represent the party that your instructor has assigned to you.

Learning Objectives of the Assignment:

This assignment will build your skills to:

- Effectively and persuasively communicate legal rules and argument
- Conduct yourself orally in a professional courtroom setting
- Respond to questions about the relevant law

Steps for Completing the Assignment:

Before the oral arguments, review the following:

- Pleadings
- Notice of Motion and Motion to Dismiss
- Your Memorandum of Law, as well as that of your opposing counsel
- Cases cited in your memo and opposing counsel's
- Facts of the client matter

Research for the Assignment: Although no additional research is required for the assignment, you should review the memorandum of your opposing counsel and review the cases that he/she includes, consider how you can rebut the cases, or explain how they are inapposite to the matter at hand and address those cases in your oral argument.

Format of the Assignment:

Each side has 20 minutes for his or her argument. The moving party first presents his/her arguments and may reserve time for rebuttal. It is the moving party's decision to reserve time for rebuttal. After the moving party has presented his/her arguments, it is the non-moving party's turn. The non-moving party does not receive time for rebuttal since he/she can listen to opposing counsel and respond directly to any arguments made. After the non-moving party finishes, the moving party responds with rebuttal, if he/she previously asked the court to reserve time for it.

Be prepared to answer questions from the court, and part of your preparation should be anticipating the questions that the judge might ask and preparing answers. But in the event that the judge doesn't ask questions or asks few, be prepared to fill the time allotted with your argument.

Grading: This assignment is worth 90 points.

Punctuality: Attorney arrived on time to oral argument: YES _____ (10 points) NO _____ (0 points)

Professional Attire: Attorney was dressed in appropriate professional attire: YES _____ (10 points) NO _____ (0 points)

Professional Demeanor: Attorney acted in a professional manner w/court and opposing counsel: YES _____ (10 points) NO _____ (0 points)

GRADING CRITERIA	0-6 points (failing)	8 points (C or 75%)	10 points (B or 85%)	12 points	Points received
Engagement	Attorney does not respond to the court's questions	Attorney responds to questions, but incorrectly or with hard to follow answers	Attorney responds promptly and correctly to all of the court's questions	Attorney responds promptly and correctly to all of court's questions with creative, thoughtful and insightful answers that show a deep understanding of the issues	_____/12
Knowledge of Applicable Law	Attorney provides no explanation of the applicable law	Attorney provides explanation of with few meaningful mistakes or with explanation that is hard to follow	Attorney provides clear explanation of the law with no meaningful mistakes	Attorney provides clear, concise and correct explanation of the law	_____/12
Analysis of Applicable Law	Attorney provides no analysis of the law or provides analysis that is incorrect or incomplete	Attorney provides analysis of the law but has some mistakes or misstatements of the law or facts	Attorney provides a clear, concise and correct analysis of the law as it applies to the client matter	Attorney present unimpeachable case for the client, analyzing persuasively, concisely and clearly the law as it applies to client matter	_____/12
Conclusion and Relief	Attorney does not identify relief sought or conclude argument	Attorney provides advice, but	Attorney provides advice but	Attorney clearly identifies the relief sought and summarizes the client's position	_____/12
Organization	Argument is disorganized and has serious faults of organization	Argument has minor faults of organization	Argument is clearly organized and easy to follow	Argument is exceptionally well organized and presents arguments in novel way	_____/12
TOTAL					_____/60
TOTAL FROM PUNCTUALITY AND PROFESSIONALISM					_____/30

TOTAL   ____/90

Section III

Advanced Legal Issues

Unit 3

Title VII of the Civil Rights Act of 1964 and Religious Accommodations

For this Unit, you will write a persuasive memorandum of law in support of or in opposition to a motion for summary judgment in litigation involving Stray Dog Advertising and a former employee, Jasmine Singh, who has sued Stray Dog Advertising for religious discrimination under a federal law, Title VII of the Civil Rights Act of 1964. You will represent either SDA as the defendant, or the plaintiff, Jasmine Singh. The legal issue involved is religious discrimination and specifically whether Stray Dog Advertising should have accommodated Singh's religious practices in the workplace.

Both sides have the same documents available to them, and no information is confidential or available to only one side.

Learning Objectives of the Unit:

This Unit will build your skills to:

- Explain complex legal matters clearly and concisely
- Use appropriate technical terminology
- Identify and analyze the applicable case law and facts for the relevant legal issues
- Efficiently read and understand legal authority
- Articulate persuasive legal arguments in support of client's position
- Analyze possible outcomes for legal dispute, evaluate and articulate strengths and weaknesses of such outcomes
- Efficiently and effectively communicate in a written and oral format
- Respond to questions about the relevant law

To achieve these learning objectives, you will complete the following tasks:

- Draft a predictive memo to senior partner about the legal issues and your prediction of what will happen with the litigation
- Draft a persuasive memorandum of law in support of or in opposition to motion for summary judgment
- Carry out a mock client meeting with either Pamela Park of SDA or Jasmine Singh
- Draft a client letter to your client about your meeting and about the legal issues
- Carry out oral argument in front of the court for the motion for summary judgment

To complete these tasks, you will use the following materials in the book:

- Assignment email from Senior Partner (pages 336-338; 339-341)
- Main Assignment File (pages 335-341 + pleadings, written discovery and deposition transcripts (online))
- Title VII/Religious Accommodations Commented Cases:
    - American Postal Workers Union v. Postmaster General, 781 F.2d 772 (9th Cir. 1986).
    - Anderson v. General Dynamics Convair Aerospace Division, 589 F.2d 397 (9th Cir. 1978).
    - Bhatia v. Chevron U.S.A., Inc., 734 F.2d 1382 (9th Cir. 1984).
    - Burns v. Southern Pacific Transportation Co., 589 F.2d 403 (9th Cir. 1978).
    - EEOC v. AutoNation USA Corp., 52 Fed. Appx. 327 (9th Cir. 2002).
    - EEOC v. Townley Engineering & Manufacturing Co., 859 F.2d 610 (9th Cir. 1988).
    - International Association of Machinists & Aerospace Workers v. Boeing Co., 833 F.2d 165 (9th Cir. 1987).
    - Proctor v. Consolidated Freightways Corp. of Delaware, 795 F.2d 1472 (9th Cir. 1986).
    - Slater v. Douglas County, 743 F. Supp. 2d 1188 (D. Or. 2010).
    - Tiano v. Dillard Department Stores, Inc., 139 F.3d 679 (9th Cir. 1998).
    - EEOC Consent Decree EEOC v. Razzoo's, L.P., No. 3:05-cv-00562 (N.D. Tex. June 16, 2006).
- ESL Workbook (pages 238-269)

Your instructor will also assign you additional skills-building exercises to bolster your understanding of the legal issues and further develop your legal reasoning and language skills, whether related to legal reasoning and analysis or to English. You will find an icon with each exercise that will indicate which skills the exercise will focus upon.

ICON	SKILL
	Speaking — in particular about the legal issues and the law presented in the Unit
	Oral comprehension
	Legal analysis and reasoning
	Analysis of the legal issue(s) presented in the Unit
	English grammar, syntax, and vocabulary
	Legal ethics and professional responsibility
	Legal research

Section III

Advanced Legal Issues

In this Unit, the additional skills-building exercises that accompany the Main Assignment File include:

- Title VII/Religious Accommodations Analysis Exercise (pages 342-344)

- Summary Judgment Analysis Exercise (pages 345-351)

- Professional Presentation: *If SDA or Singh Were Your Client...* (pages 352-353)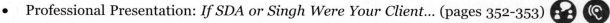

- Mock Negotiation between SDA and Singh (page 354 plus confidential information)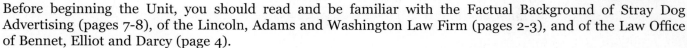

Before beginning the Unit, you should read and be familiar with the Factual Background of Stray Dog Advertising (pages 7-8), of the Lincoln, Adams and Washington Law Firm (pages 2-3), and of the Law Office of Bennet, Elliot and Darcy (page 4).

You will also find online at the website www.legalwritingforllms.com the following online resources that accompany this Unit. The additional online resources will help you deepen your mastery of the skills presented in the Unit and also provide additional understanding about the U.S. legal system and legal writing.

Pleadings: Section III, Unit 3 (required)

- Additional Resources:
  - Sources of American Law
  - Writing Professional Emails
  - Writing Persuasive Memos
  - Writing E-memos
  - IRAC

- Additional Skills-Building Exercises:
  - Issues and Issue Statements
  - Stating the Rule
  - Analysis
  - Ethical Spotlight Exercise

Section III, Unit 3 Legal Issue
Title VII of the Civil Rights Act of 1964 and Religious Accommodations

Main Assignment File	Religious Accommodation Cases	ESL Workbook	Additional Exercises	Additional Online Resources
Introduction to File and Client Matter Pages 330-334	Am. Postal Workers Union v. Postmaster General, 781 F.2d 772 (9th Cir. 1986).	Am. Postal Workers Union v. Postmaster General, 781 F.2d 772 (9th Cir. 1986).	Title VII/Religious Accommodation Analysis Exercise Pages 342-344	Writing Professional Emails
Documents Related to Client Matter Pages 335-341 + pleadings and discovery documents online	Anderson v. General Dynamics Convair Aerospace Div., 589 F.2d 397 (9th Cir. 1978).	Anderson v. General Dynamics Convair Aerospace Div., 589 F.2d 397 (9th Cir. 1978).	Summary Judgment Analysis Exercise Pages 345-351	Business Correspondence (with sample letters)
Assignment Information Pages + Rubrics Pages 355-365	Bhatia v. Chevron U.S.A., Inc., 734 F.2d 1382 (9th Cir. 1984).	Bhatia v. Chevron U.S.A., Inc., 734 F.2d 1382 (9th Cir. 1984).	Presentation: If ISDA or Singh Were Your Client... Pages 352-353	Writing Memos (office memos and persuasive memoranda of law)
	Burns v. Southern Pac. Transp. Co., 589 F.2d 403 (9th Cir. 1978).	Burns v. Southern Pac. Transp. Co., 589 F.2d 403 (9th Cir. 1978).	Mock Negotiation Page 354 + confidential information	IRAC (including exercises for each element)
	EEOC v. AutoNation USA Corp., 52 Fed. Appx. 327 (9th Cir. 2002).	EEOC v. AutoNation USA Corp., 52 Fed. Appx. 327 (9th Cir. 2002).		Skills-Building Exercises for Rules, Issues and Issues Statements, Analysis and Ethical Dilemmas
	EEOC v. Townley Eng'g & Mfg. Co., 859 F.2d 610 (9th Cir. 1988).	EEOC v. Townley Eng'g & Mfg. Co., 859 F.2d 610 (9th Cir. 1988).		
	Int'l. Assoc. of Machinists & Aerospace Workers v. Boeing Co., 833 F.2d 165 (9th Cir. 1987).	Int'l. Assoc. of Machinists & Aerospace Workers v. Boeing Co., 833 F.2d 165 (9th Cir. 1987).		
	Proctor v. Consolidated Freightways Corp. of Delaware, 795 F.2d 1472 (9th Cir. 1986).	Proctor v. Consolidated Freightways Corp. of Delaware, 795 F.2d 1472 (9th Cir. 1986).		
	Slater v. Douglas Cty., 743 F. Supp. 2d 1188 (D. Or. 2010).	Slater v. Douglas Cty., 743 F. Supp. 2d 1188 (D. Or. 2010).		
	Tiano v. Dillard Department Stores, Inc., 139 F.3d 679 (9th Cir. 1998).	Tiano v. Dillard Department Stores, Inc., 139 F.3d 679 (9th Cir. 1998).		
	EEOC Consent Decree EEOC v. Razzoo's, L.P., No. 3:05-cv-00562 (N.D. Tex. June 16, 2006).	EEOC Consent Decree EEOC v. Razzoo's, L.P., No. 3:05-cv-00562 (N.D. Tex. June 16, 2006).		

Introduction — Title VII of the Civil Rights Act of 1964 and Religious Accommodations

The Civil Rights Act of 1964 is a landmark piece of legislation, arguably the most important of modern legislative history after the Voting Rights Act of 1965. Signed into law by President Lyndon Baines Johnson on July 2, 1964, the Civil Rights Act prohibits discrimination based on race, color, national origin, sex and religion in many areas of life such as employment, public accommodations, voting, and education.

Like other federal laws, the Civil Rights Act of 1964 is divided into titles, or sections. Title VII, which you will deal with in this Unit, prohibits discrimination in employment. With regard to religious discrimination under Title VII, an employer can violate the law in two ways:

- By treating an employee or candidate differently and less favorably based on his or her religion than another individual outside of the protected class;

- By failing to grant an employee's request for a reasonable accommodation to his or her religious observances or practices unless the accommodation would impose an undue hardship on the employer.[110]

This Unit deals with the second type of discrimination, failure to accommodate by refusing to grant a reasonable accommodation. What is a "reasonable accommodation" turns on the facts of each case. A reasonable accommodation for one employer may be unreasonable for another and cause an "undue hardship" depending on the size of the business (both number of employees and revenue) or the nature or cost of the request. Although fact-dependent, courts have held that as a general rule, an "undue hardship" is found when there is more than a *de minimis* burden on the employer or on other employees, and the request can thus be denied without potential legal liability.[111]

As you will learn in the cases that you will read, there are many rules and factors that are taken into consideration when determining whether an accommodation is reasonable or whether it would impose an undue hardship. Because these issues are so fact-dependent, they have frequently been litigated.

In this Unit, the accommodation you will be analyzing is a change of job assignments when Jasmine Singh, a copywriter at Stray Dog Advertising, begins to ask her co-worker and fellow copywriter, Tony DiGennaro, to complete the copywriting assignments that she believes conflict with her religion. As you will learn, Singh recently converted to the religion of Jainism and decides that she can no longer write copy for clients who mistreat or harm animals as her religion espouses non-violence towards animals and other living beings.

Thus the substantive issue that you will deal with is religious discrimination and namely failure to accommodate under Title VII. Procedurally, you will deal with summary judgment as Stray Dog Advertising has moved for it, asking the court to grant judgment as a matter of law in its favor as it alleges that there are no genuine issues of material fact in dispute as to whether the proposed accommodation would impose an undue hardship.

---

[110] 42 U.S.C. § 2000e-2 (2012); 42 U.S.C. § 2000e(j) (2012).

[111] Trans World Airlines, Inc. v. Hardison, 432 U.S. 63, 84 (1977). A Latin term, *de minimis* means "trifling" or "negligible." *De Minimis*, BLACK'S LAW DICTIONARY (10th ed. 2014).

Litigation has been underway for nearly a year in this case, and you have been brought on near the end of the matter. You will find written discovery and deposition transcripts that you will use for your arguments, as well as 9th Circuit case law regarding religious accommodations.

Main Assignment File: Title VII of the Civil Rights Act of 1964 and Religious Accommodations

TIMELINE

EVENT	DATE
Singh was hired at Stray Dog Advertising, LLC	September YEAR -8
Singh met her husband, Jack	May YEAR -4
Singh converted to Jainism	February YEAR -2
Singh spoke to Pamela Park for the first time regarding her conversion and the conflict between her work and religious beliefs	June 20, YEAR -2
Singh sent email to Park explaining that she could no longer work on Herbal Spirit campaign	July 8, YEAR -2
Singh sent email to Park explaining that she could no longer write copy for Jefferson Diabetes Association	July 17, YEAR -2
Singh was terminated	July 21, YEAR -2
Charge of discrimination was filed	August 13, YEAR -2
Right-to-sue letter sent	February 20, YEAR -1
Complaint was served and filed	April 9 (served) April 10 (filed), YEAR -1
Answer was filed and served	April 26, YEAR -1
Scheduling order was issued	June 5, YEAR -1
Depositions scheduled	January THIS YEAR
Discovery complete	February 1, THIS YEAR
Non-dispositive motion deadline	March 15, THIS YEAR
Dispositive motion deadline	April 15, THIS YEAR
Trial scheduled	July 24, THIS YEAR

Section III

Advanced Legal Issues

Plaintiff's File

You will represent the plaintiff, Jasmine Singh, in the <u>Singh v. Stray Dog Advertising, LLC</u> case, and you have received the following email from Senior Partner Bennett about the case.

From: Jim Bennett <jim.bennett@bennettlaw.com>
To: Associate Attorney <associate.attorney@bennetlaw.com>
Date: February 4, THIS YEAR 09:25
Re: Jasmine Singh matter

Associate attorney,

I believe you know that we represent Jasmine Singh in the claim that she's brought against Stray Dog Advertising. I am the attorney of record on the case and want you to help me with it.

Since you are new to the firm, let me give you a run-down on what's happened:

- We met with Jasmine right after she was terminated and filed the charge of discrimination with the EEOC on her behalf.
- We requested the right to sue and then shortly thereafter, filed a complaint in state court. It wasn't removed to federal court.
- We've gone through written discovery as well as depositions. You will find in the files the transcripts of the depositions and the recordings, as well the answers to the interrogatories and documents produced.
- Stray Dog Advertising has filed a motion for summary judgment (no surprise there) and oral argument is scheduled in front of Judge Hines on April 21.

I have a trial scheduled for that same week. While we could likely settle the case (we have a mediation set for mid-March), I can't take that chance and be double-scheduled for the same date. I want you to do the oral argument in my place.

Since you will be doing the oral argument, you will also need to prepare the memo of law in opposition to SDA's motion.

The law clerk Rosemary has researched the issue and found some cases that you can use. You will find them on the firm intranet in the folder for Jasmine's case.

As you will learn, the issue in the case is one of religious accommodations and whether it would have been an undue hardship for Stray Dog to accommodate Jasmine. We have a lot of good arguments to make and I am confident that the court will deny the motion.

I will need a first draft of your complete memo as soon as possible so that I can give you my feedback. It will be then up to you to prepare the final version.

Opposing counsel is Amy Lincoln. You worked for her so know what a good advocate she is. But she is no match for us and our skills!

Let me know if you have any questions.

Jim

As you have read, you have been asked to write the following documents about this litigation:

First, you will draft a predictive office memo to the senior partner that includes:

- A summary of what has happened between Stray Dog Advertising and Jasmine Singh
- The legal issue at hand
- A summary and analysis of the law that applies (Title VII of the Civil Rights Act and religious accommodations)
- The arguments that you will make about the motion for summary judgment
- Counterarguments that you anticipate that the defendant, SDA, will make
- Your opinion about whether you think the court will grant the motion

Second, you will draft a persuasive memorandum of law in opposition to the motion for summary judgment that includes:

- Persuasive statements of the facts in a light that best represents your client
- Summary of the legal issue and the relevant law
- Persuasive arguments stating why the court should deny the motion for summary judgment that Stray Dog Advertising has filed

You will find complete information about these assignments on the Information Pages (pages 355-356; 362-363).

You will be analyzing the client matter using the Title VII/religious accommodations cases that you read and review in class.

125 South 5th Street, Suite 1450
West Rapids, Jefferson 66402

James J. Bennett
Jim.bennett@bennettlaw.com
612-555-1212

<u>VIA U.S. MAIL</u>

August 10, YEAR -2

Ms. Amy Lincoln
Lincoln, Adams and Washington Law Firm, PLLC
8600 Winston Boulevard, Suite 1450
West Rapids, Jefferson 66412

RE: Singh v. Stray Dog Advertising, LLC

Dear Ms. Lincoln:

Please be advised that I represent Jasmine Singh in the above-referenced matter. Any communications with Ms. Singh should be directed through me or one of the other attorneys at our firm.

To keep you abreast of the matter, we have filed a charge of discrimination with the local EEOC office. Once the 180-day statutory period has ended, we will request the right to sue and plan on filing the complaint against your client shortly thereafter.

I look forward to collaborating with you again on another client matter and feel free to call me at any time to discuss any aspect of the case.

Sincerely yours,

/s/ Jim Bennett

James J. Bennett

Partner
Law Office of Bennett, Elliot and Darcy, PLLC

Cc: Jasmine Singh (via email)

Defendant's File

You have received the following email from Senior Partner Lincoln about a legal matter involving Stray Dog Advertising, which has been involved in ongoing litigation involving a former employee of SDA, Jasmine Singh. You will represent the defendant, Stray Dog Advertising.

Jasmine Singh is a copywriter at Stray Dog Advertising. She was hired at the agency nearly six years ago and for the period of her employment, was a productive, successful and positive addition to the Stray Dog staff. She always worked with a range of clients, from shoe companies to accounting firms and restaurants.

In February YEAR -2, Jasmine converted to a new religion: Jainism. Jainism upholds nonviolence as the supreme religion and believes in equality of souls, irrespective of differing physical forms, ranging from human beings to animals.

Shortly after her conversion, Jasmine became a vegan, which means that she does not use or eat animal products. She believes that the religion's philosophy of nonviolence and equality of all living beings means that she is prohibited from eating animals or using any animal products.

Because of her new religion and its beliefs, Jasmine began to have difficulties working on certain clients' projects. She asked Pamela if she could not work on advertising campaigns for clients that she believed mistreated animals since in her opinion, writing copy for these clients conflicted with her religious beliefs. Over a period of about six weeks, Jasmine found additional clients that she could not work with because of the conflict with her religion. However, instead of simply refusing to do the client work, Jasmine asked her coworker, Tony DiGennaro, to complete the work for him, which he did.

On July 21, YEAR -2, Pamela terminated Jasmine because she felt that she was not producing sufficient copy and not doing her job because there were too many clients that she was unable to work for. Believing that the termination was in violation of Title VII of the Civil Rights Act of 1964, Jasmine filed a charge of discrimination against Stray Dog Advertising in August YEAR -2. Jasmine's attorney requested a right-to-sue letter and then filed a complaint on her behalf in Jefferson State Court. Litigation is now underway.

Lincoln, Adams and Washington
LAW FIRM

OFFICE MEMO

From: Amy Lincoln
To: Associate Attorney
Date: February 2, THIS YEAR 3:54 p.m.
Re: Stray Dog Advertising/Jasmine Singh Matter

I am assigning you a matter involving Pamela Park and Stray Dog Advertising.

Although I have been dealing with Pamela on this case, I need you to take over for me. I just have too much going on these days to really dedicate the time that Pamela needs.

We've discussed the case in our weekly client update meetings, but here is a summary so that you are reminded of the facts and save yourself a bit of time going through the file:

Pamela fired a copywriter, Jasmine Singh, about a year and a half ago. Pamela says that the termination was because Singh wasn't doing her job and wasn't producing copy (which she wasn't), but Singh claims that Pamela should have tried to accommodate her religion before terminating her.

Singh filed a charge of discrimination against Stray Dog, got the right to sue and then filed the complaint in state court. We chose not to remove to federal court. The case is in front of Judge Hines, who is always very defendant-friendly. We've had a lot of decisions in our favor from him and didn't want to risk the assignment in federal court if we removed.

We've gone through discovery already. We deposed Jasmine Singh as well as another employee. Pamela was deposed as well. You'll find all the transcripts in the file. Written discovery is there as well.

I filed a motion for summary judgment last week. The oral arguments are scheduled for the end of April. I don't remember the exact date, so you will have to check my calendar. You will be responsible for the oral arguments.

I also need you to draft the brief in support of the summary judgment motion. The case law is without a doubt in our favor, so we should get the motion granted. It is up to you to show that there is nothing in dispute and that Pamela didn't discriminate and did what she had to do under Title VII to accommodate Jasmine and her religion. Before you draft the brief, however, I would like you to prepare a predictive memo about the case.

I will need a first draft of the brief as soon as possible. Feel free to contact Pamela too if you have any questions, and I am available as well, of course.

Amy

As you have read, you have been asked to write the following documents about this litigation:

First, you will write a predictive office memo to the senior partner that includes:

- A summary of what has happened between Stray Dog Advertising and Jasmine Singh
- The legal issue at hand
- A summary and analysis of the law that applies (Title VII of the Civil Rights Act and religious accommodations)
- The arguments that you will make about the motion for summary judgment
- Counterarguments that you anticipate that the plaintiff, Jasmine Singh, will make
- Your opinion about whether you think the court will grant the motion

Second, you will draft a persuasive memorandum of law in support of the motion for summary judgment that includes:

- Persuasive statements of the facts in a light that best represents your client
- Summary of the legal issue and the relevant law
- Persuasive arguments stating why the court should grant the motion for summary judgment that Stray Dog Advertising has filed

You will find complete information about these assignments on the Information Pages (pages 355-356; 362-363).

You will be analyzing the client matter using the Title VII/religious accommodations cases that you read and review in class.

Additional Skills-Building Exercises

Title VII/Religious Accommodations Analysis Exercise

Overview of the Exercise: For this exercise, you will read the following fact patterns, all of which deal with religious accommodations in the workplace. Your task will be to determine whether the accommodation should be granted under Title VII. When you conclude whether an accommodation should or should not be granted, be sure to articulate your analysis, or the why behind that conclusion.

Learning Objectives of the Exercise:

This exercise will build your skills to:

- Articulate the legal rules regarding Title VII and religious accommodations
- Apply those rules to brief fact patterns and analyze the facts and the law
- Articulate and effectively communicate that analysis using legal terminology

Steps for Completing the Exercise:

- Read the following fact patterns.
- By yourself, analyze each one and decide whether or not you think the employer should grant the religious accommodation or whether doing so would impose an undue hardship. You don't need to write out a full answer, but jot down notes about your reasoning.
- When you are done analyzing each of the fact patterns, discuss your answers with the partner that you have been assigned. Explain to each other why you have reached the conclusion that you did.
- If you and your partner have different responses to a fact pattern, you must try to convince him or her that your answer is correct. After you both have tried to convince the other, you must choose a team answer.
- Once you have discussed each of the fact patterns, you will compare answers as a class.

Grading: This exercise is not graded.

1. Isaac works as a cashier at Bull's Eye, a local discount store. The store has the following dress code policy:

   Appearance and perception play a key role in member service. Our goal is to be dressed in professional attire that is appropriate to our business at all times. All Bull's Eye employees must practice good grooming and personal hygiene to convey a neat, clean and professional image. No visible body piercings or tattoos are allowed including but not limited to nose rings, eyebrow rings, tongue studs and earlobe spacers. If on the arm, tattoos must be covered by a long-sleeve shirt.

Isaac is a member of an ancient Egyptian religion that requires all members to have a tattoo on their wrist. Isaac's tattoos is about 2" wide (5 cm.) and has a floral theme. Bull's Eye has received no complaints about Isaac's tattoo. However, Isaac's manager has asked him to cover it by wearing a wrist band, citing the Bull's Eye dress code policy and telling him that Bull's Eye public image is of a family-friendly store and tattoos do not match that image. Isaac has refused and says that it violates his religious beliefs to cover it. Isaac and his manager are at an impasse.

Should the accommodation be granted? Why or why not?

2. Dupak applied for a position as a server at a local restaurant, The Cat's Eye. Dupak is a member of the Sikh religion, which requires men to wear a turban and prohibits them from cutting their hair (on their head and facial hear) since they see hair as a sign of respect towards God.

The Cat's Eye has this appearance policy for its male employees:

> *Hair must be cut above the back of your collar, be neat in style and appropriate for the food service industry. Kitchen team members may have hair longer than the collar as long as it is in a ponytail and either tucked underneath a hat or hair net. Hair color must be natural and root growth maintained to match the color/style of your hair.*

> *Facial hair must be clean-shaven when you arrive at work. Moustaches and goatees must (a) be fully grown-in (no stubble), i.e., must be grown during time off work, (b) consist of a traditional moustache only, neatly trimmed and not extending below the corner of your mouth, or (c) consist of a traditional goatee only, Van Dyke style, neatly trimmed, "full" around chin with no shaved gaps. All other styles of beards are not permitted.*

During the interview, the manager informed Dupak about the restaurant's appearance policy and then inquired as to whether he would have difficulty complying with it. Dupak said that he could not shave his beard but mentioned that his hair was covered in the turban that he wears.

The manager told Dupak that he could not be hired if he didn't shave his beard to comply with the policy. Dupak has now filed a claim of discrimination against The Cat's Eye.

Should the manager have hired Dupak and provided an accommodation? Why or why not?

3. Harry has been working for three months at The Cat's Eye restaurant. He is a server. Last week, he came to work unshaven with new growth. His manager reminded Harry of the restaurant's appearance policy, which requires men to be clean-shaven, and told him that his "5:00-shadow" beard was unacceptable. Harry was told to shave or go home for the day. Harry told his manager that his beard was a religious requirement and that shaving his beard would violate his religion. Harry had never mentioned his religion before to his manager and never indicated that his religion had any specific requirements for his appearance. The manager refused his request to not shave and terminated Harry because he refused to shave.

Should the manager grant Harry's requested accommodation and allow him to not shave? Why or why not? Did The Cat's Eye violate Title VII when it terminated Harry? Why or why not?

4. Diana is a member of a white supremacy group called the Aryan Nation. She has various tattoos on her that show burning crosses and swastikas, but she covers them while at work in compliance with her employer's dress-code policy. However, part of her beliefs as a white supremacist is that she cannot work with or associate with anyone of any minority group.

Diana works as customer service representative at an insurance company. In her work group, there is one Hispanic co-worker and one black co-worker. Diana knows that in another work group, there are no minorities. Employees have sometimes moved from one work group to another. The work group determines where employees sit in the building. If Diana were to move to this other work group, she would not have to sit near any black or Hispanic co-workers.

Diana has approached her manager and explained her beliefs to him. Diana's manager is unsure of how to proceed. Should her manager grant her requested accommodation? Why or why not?

5. Patrick has just been hired to work at a manufacturing plant. Patrick is a member of the Rastafarian faith, a religious movement of Jamaican origin. As part of their religious beliefs, Rastas wear dreadlocks and smoke marijuana. Under Jefferson law, possession of marijuana is a crime, and Patrick's employer has a no-drug policy.

Last Thursday was a holy day for Rastafarianism and as part of the religious celebrations, believers are required to smoke marijuana. During his lunch break, Patrick went to his car and smoked some marijuana. Patrick's manager smelled the marijuana and confronted Patrick about it. Patrick confessed to smoking and explained that he did so for religious reasons. Citing the company's no-drug policy, Patrick's manger terminated him.

Patrick has now filed a claim of religious discrimination with the state human rights department. Should Patrick's employer have granted him an accommodation to smoke marijuana as part of his religious practices? Why or why not?

6. William is employed as a correctional officer at a state prison. He has sought permission from his employer to wear a fez as an act of faith on a particular holy day as part of his religious expression. Patrick's employer has denied the request, citing a uniformly applied workplace policy that prohibits employees from wearing any type of head covering.

You are counsel for the prison. After denying the request and a threat from William that he planned to file a charge of discrimination against the prison for failure to accommodate, the operational manager has contacted you for advice. What do you suggest the prison do? Support your answer.

7. Edith is a taxi driver. As part of her religious beliefs, she believes that alcohol is sinful and the product of the devil. Her employer has recently assigned to her a new route and she is required to pick up customers from the West Rapids International Airport. On more than one occasion, when Edith could tell that a customer was carrying alcohol (some passengers coming from European countries like Italy or France have bottles of wine in clear plastic bags, for example), she refused to take them to their destination. The customers have filed complaints with the Better Business Bureau and with the taxi company.

Edith's manager has asked her to come to the headquarters today to talk about the situation. Edith plans on asking her employer for an accommodation for her religious beliefs that would allow her to refuse to transport passengers whom she knows or has reason to know are carrying alcohol. Should Edith's manager refuse or grant the request? Why or why not?

Summary Judgment Analysis Exercise

Overview of the Exercise: This exercise will provide you the opportunity to deepen your understanding of how summary judgment works by analyzing the following short fact patterns and determining whether or not summary judgment should be granted.

Learning Objectives of the Exercise:

This exercise will build your skills to:

- Analyze the elements of summary judgment
- Identify and analyze the applicable case law, facts and standards for summary judgment
- Articulate the factors that courts analyze when deciding motions for summary judgment, the arguments that the parties make and the reasoning behind the granting or denial of a motion

Steps for Completing the Exercise:

- Read the following fact patterns and the accompanying case law.
- With a partner, answer the following questions for each fact pattern.
    - What are the claims that the plaintiff would bring against the defendant? Would the defendant raise any defenses?
    - What are the material facts of the issue(s)? Are they in dispute? Are there some material facts that would not be in dispute? If so, which?
    - If this case were being litigated, who would likely file for summary judgment? Why?
    - What arguments would each party make with regard to the motion for summary judgment?
    - If you were the judge, would you grant or deny the motion? Why?

Research Required for the Exercise:

Before analyzing the fact patterns, review the law of summary judgment.

Summary judgment is "a procedural device used during civil litigation to promptly and expeditiously dispose of a case without a trial."[112] It is used when there is no dispute as to the material facts of the case and a party is entitled to judgment as a matter of law. In legal actions, the term matter of law is used to define a particular area that is the responsibility of the court. Matter of law is distinguished from matter of fact, which is the responsibility of the jury.

Rule 56 of the Federal Rules of Civil Procedure states that "[a] party may move for summary judgment, identifying each claim or defense — or the part of each claim or defense — on which summary judgment is sought. The court shall grant summary judgment if the movant shows that there is no genuine dispute as to any material fact and the movant is entitled to judgment as a matter of law. The court should state on the record the reasons for granting or denying the motion."[113]

The following is a rule statement of the Minnesota rules of summary judgment, which is for all essential purposes the same as the federal rule.[114]

> Summary judgment is appropriate where there are no genuine issues of material fact and where the moving party is entitled to judgment as a matter of law. MINN. R. CIV. P. 56.03; DLH, Inc. v. Russ, 566 N.W. 2d 60, 68 (Minn. 1997). When faced with a motion for summary judgment under Rule 56, the Court is to first determine whether a genuine issue of material fact exists. The moving party has the burden of proof, and the evidence must be viewed in the light most favorable to the nonmoving party. Grondahl v. Bulluck, 318 N.W.2d 240, 242 (Minn. 1982).

---

[112] SUDHANSHU JOSHI, DICTIONARY OF LEGAL TERMS 117 (2011).

[113] Fed. R. Civ. P. 56.

[114] Rule 56 of the Minnesota Rule of Civil Procedure would regulate matters in state court, while the federal rule would apply to those matters in federal court, even if the federal court is adjudicating a substantive matter of state law. See MINN. R. CIV. PRO. 56.01–03 (West 2016) for the exact language.

The mere existence of a factual dispute does not, by itself, make summary judgment inappropriate. Rather, the fact in dispute must be material. Pischke v. Kellen, 384 N.W.2d 201, 205 (Minn. Ct. App. 1986). A material fact is one that will affect the result or outcome of the case, depending upon its resolution. Zappa v. Fahey, 245 N.W.2d 258, 259-60 (Minn. 1976). Any doubt regarding the existence of a genuine fact issue will be resolved in favor of its existence. Rathbun v. W.T. Grant Co., 219 N.W.2d 641, 646 (Minn. 1974). The non-moving party may not rely on general statements of fact to oppose a motion for summary judgment; rather, it must identify specific facts that establish the existence of a triable issue. Hunt v. IBM Mid Am. Employees Fed. Credit Union, 384 N.W.2d 853, 855 (Minn. 1986).

For comparison's sake, here is a rule statement from New York. You can see that the standards and the rules between the two states are similar.

"[T]he proponent of a summary judgment motion must make a prima facie showing of entitlement to judgment as a matter of law, tendering sufficient evidence to demonstrate the absence of any material issues of fact.' "Jacobson v. New York City Health and Hospitals Corp., 22 N.Y.3d 824, 833 (N.Y. 2014) (quoting Alvarez v. Prospect Hosp., 324, 501 N.E.2d 572 (N.Y. 1986)). "This burden is a heavy one and on a motion for summary judgment, facts must be viewed in the light most favorable to the non-moving party.' " Id. (quoting William J. Jenack Estate Appraisers and Auctioneers, Inc. v. Rabizadeh, 22 N.Y.3d 470, 475 (N.Y. 2013)). "If the moving party meets this burden, the burden then shifts to the non-moving party to establish the existence of material issues of fact which require a trial of the action." Id. (quoting Vega v. Restani Constr. Corp., 965 N.E.2d 240 (N.Y. 2012)), cited in Lease Fin. Grp. LLC v. Indries, 49 Misc. 3d 1219(A) (N.Y. Civ. Ct. 2015).

The following are the main points to remember about summary judgment:

- Either party can move for summary judgment at any time, but a court can deny a motion if it is brought too early. See, e.g., Lewis v. Agency Rent-A-Car, 562 N.Y.S.2d 558, 559 (N.Y. App. Div. 1990) (denying plaintiff's motion for summary judgment in personal injury matter because motion was brought before any discovery was conducted, revealing that the "most basic of facts remain unanswered.").
- Summary judgment is issued when there are no genuine issues of material facts, so nothing for a jury to decide.
- The material facts are those that go to the elements of the claim or defense and that affect the result or outcome of a case.
- Court examines the facts in favor of the non-moving party because examining them in favor of the moving party would be unfair.
- The burden rests with the moving party.
- Just because one party thinks that a factual dispute exists doesn't mean that it does – the factual dispute must be material.
- Could a reasonable jury decide the case in favor of the non-moving party, based on the facts and the case law? If the answer is yes, then the motion should be denied.
- Parties rely on admissible evidence such as written discovery responses, deposition testimony, memoranda of law and affidavits in support of or in opposition to the motion.
- If the motion is denied, then the case will move forward to the jury.
- Summary judgment is a procedural device to save time and resources by resolving claims that have no disputes for the jury to decide.

1   Breach of Contract

Under Jefferson law, a claim of breach of contract requires proof of three elements: (1) the formation of a contract, (2) the performance of conditions precedent by the plaintiff, and (3) the breach of the contract by the defendant. Briggs Transp. Co. v. Ranzenberger, 217 N.W.2d 198, 200 (Jeff. 1974). When a party to a contract commits a "material breach," the other party may rescind. Liebsch v. Abbott, 122 N.W.2d 578, 581 (Jeff. 1963). This "annihilates the contract and [returns] ... each party ... to his previously existing rights." Marso v. Mankato Clinic, Ltd., 153 N.W.2d 281, 290 (Jeff. 1967).

Whether a contract exists generally is a question for the fact-finder. Morrisette v. Harrison Int'l Corp., 486 N.W.2d 424, 427 (Jeff.1992). "The formation of a contract requires communication of a specific and definite offer, acceptance, and consideration." Commercial Assocs. Inc., v. Work Connection, 712 N.W.2d 772, 782 (Jeff. Ct. App. 2006) (citing Pine River State Bank v. Mettille, 333 N.W.2d 622, 626–27 (Jeff.1983)). Formation of a contract is judged by the objective conduct of the parties rather than their subjective intent. Commercial Assocs. Inc., 712 N.W.2d at 782 (citing Cederstrand v. Lutheran Bhd., 117 N.W.2d 213, 221 (Jeff. 1962)).

Rose Gomez entered into a contract with Stone Arch Construction, LLC according to which Stone Arch would build an addition to Gomez's house. The contract was in writing and stated the specifications of the addition, the date that Stone Arch would begin construction, and the date by which they would finish (January 20, THIS YEAR). The start date of the construction was set at November 12, YEAR -1. Gomez also made a down payment of $20,000.

On November 12, YEAR -1, no one from Stone Arch Construction arrived at Gomez's home to begin the construction. No one answered the phone when Gomez called the company's office. One day passed, and then two days, and soon two weeks had gone by and Gomez had heard nothing from anyone at Stone Arch Construction. It was as though everyone from the company had disappeared.

Gomez's attorney has filed a complaint against Stone Arch Construction in Jefferson State court.

Discuss the questions above regarding summary judgment for the case. Should the court grant the motion? Why or why not?

2. Breach of Contract

Around the same time that Gomez entered into a contract with Stone Arch Construction, another individual, Ahmed Nassar, also contracted with Stone Arch, which agreed to remodel Nassar's kitchen and two bathrooms. Nassar is planning on selling his house and has decided to put it on the market as soon as the remodeling is complete. The terms of the agreement that Nassar entered into with Stone Arch were similar to those of Gomez's agreement: the specifications of the remodeling, the start date and the date by which the construction would be finished (January 15, THIS YEAR), as well as the price and down payment.

Strangely enough, Stone Arch did not disappear like it did with Gomez's project. The workers showed up on the stipulated date and began construction. The project went according to plan, except that the construction was completed at 10:00 in the morning on January 17, THIS YEAR. Nassar now refuses to pay Stone Arch because he claims that they finished past the stipulated date and that their breach relived him of his obligation to pay them for their work.

Nassar has hired an attorney who has filed a claim against Stone Arch Construction, LLC.

Discuss the questions above regarding summary judgment for the case. Should the court grant the motion? Why or why not?

3. UCC Defective Goods

This case involves a business owner named Keith Moore, who operates a snowmobile dealership in northern Jefferson. In May YEAR -1, Moore bought a large number of snowmobiles from the regional distributor. With the meteorologists forecasting cold temperatures and above-average snowfall this winter, Moore was hoping to have a successful winter season at his dealership. Moore purchased the snowmobiles during the summer because the prices were slightly lower and because it was easier to transport the vehicles to Moore's dealership without the snow and ice on the roads.

When the first snow arrived in November, Moore took some of the new snowmobiles out for a test ride before his customers came to purchase them. While riding, he immediately noticed that the snowmobile he was riding would not shift gears and would not drive faster than 20 mph. Moore began to test-drive each of the snowmobiles. Much to his dismay, he discovered that of the fifty-five snowmobiles that he had purchased, twenty were defective. All had the same problem that they failed to shift gears and would not drive faster than 20 mph. Moore promptly notified the distributor and manufacturer of the snowmobiles of the defects and told them that he was revoking his acceptance of those defective ones. Both the distributor and the manufacturer told Moore that his revocation was too late since he had purchased the snowmobiles in May of last year.

Moore has now filed a claim in Jefferson state court against the distributor and manufacturer. This section of the Jefferson Uniform Commercial Code (UCC) is at issue.

336.2-608 REVOCATION OF ACCEPTANCE IN WHOLE OR IN PART.

1) The buyer may revoke an acceptance of a lot or commercial unit whose nonconformity substantially impairs its value to the buyer if it was accepted
   a) on the reasonable assumption that its nonconformity would be cured and it has not been seasonably cured; or
   b) without discovery of such nonconformity if the acceptance was reasonably induced either by the difficulty of discovery before acceptance or by the seller's assurances.
2) Revocation of acceptance must occur within a reasonable time after the buyer discovers or should have discovered the ground for it and before any substantial change in condition of the goods which is not caused by their own defects. It is not effective until the buyer notifies the seller of it.
3) A buyer who so revokes has the same rights and duties with regard to the goods involved as if the buyer had rejected them.

In January THIS YEAR, later in the season and while the litigation was underway in the Jefferson state court, Moore discovered that ten of the remaining thirty-five snowmobiles that did not have the initial defect could drive no faster than 40 mph. The specifications of the model of snowmobiles that Moore had purchased stated that the vehicles could travel at speeds "up to 45 mph." Moore has now contacted again the distributor and the manufacturer, told them that these ten snowmobiles are defective and that he wants to return them. As before, both the distributor and the manufacturer refused, telling Moore that it was too late to return them.

Moore's attorney has asked the court for permission to amend the complaint to include the facts of these additional ten snowmobiles. The court has granted permission and the complaint includes allegations about the first twenty defective snowmobiles as well as the other ten.

Discuss the questions above regarding summary judgment for the case. Should the court grant the motion? Why or why not?

4. Duty to Warn

This matter involves negligence and whether a property owner can be held liable for failing to warn an individual about a danger on his or her property.

In this case, a young woman, Rebecca Wu, was accidently shot by a friend, Evan Simmons. The incident happened at a cabin owned by Mark Francisco, who was the boyfriend of the mother of a young man named Jeff Warner. Warner had invited Wu, Simmons and another friend (all of whom are of legal age) to the cabin for the weekend; Francisco was unaware that the four friends were at the cabin for the weekend and had told Warner on several occasions that he was not to go to or use the cabin without his permission.

One month before the accident, Francisco had placed a loaded hunting rifle near the door to the cabin to protect against bears. When the four friends entered the cabin, Warner told his friends not to play with it. He did not know if it was loaded or not. Despite Warner's warning, Simmons picked up the gun. Warner told him to put it down. Several hours later, Simmons again picked up the gun. This time, the gun discharged, hitting Wu in the face and causing severe injuries.

Wu filed a negligence claim against Simmons, Warner and Francisco. She settled in pre-litigation negotiations with Simmons for an undisclosed amount. Wu now claims that Warner should have warned her about the gun and about the dangers that is posed, and that Francisco was negligent in keeping the loaded gun in the cabin (Francisco has a valid hunting license and legally purchased the gun). Wu claims that since Warner did not warn her of the danger of the gun and since she was injured, Warner should be held liable for her injuries. Warner has filed a motion for summary judgment. Should the court grant it?

Negligence is generally defined as the failure "to exercise such care as persons of ordinary prudence usually exercise under such circumstances." Flom v. Flom, 291 N.W.2d 914, 916 (Jeff.1980). To recover for a claim of negligence, a plaintiff must prove (1) the existence of a duty of care, (2) a breach of that duty, (3) an injury, and (4) that the breach of the duty of care was a proximate cause of the injury. See Funchess v. Cecil Newman Corp., 632 N.W.2d 666, 672 (Jeff.2001) (citing Lubbers v. Anderson, 539 N.W.2d 398, 401 (Jeff.1995)).

Generally, a defendant's duty to a plaintiff is a threshold question because "[i]n the absence of a legal duty, the negligence claim fails." Gilbertson v. Leininger, 599 N.W.2d 127, 130 (Jeff.1999) (citation omitted); see also State Farm Fire & Cas. v. Aquila Inc., 718 N.W.2d 879, 887 (Jeff.2006) (stating that plaintiffs failed to present a prima facie case for negligence when they could not establish that defendants owed a duty of reasonable care).

Under Jefferson law, a property owner has a reasonable duty to protect persons on the property from injury, unless the risk of injury is open and obvious. Peterson v. W.T. Rawleigh Co., 144 N.W.2d 555, 557-58 (Jeff. 1966) ; Restatement (Second) of Torts § 343A (1965). The test for whether a condition is "open and obvious" is not whether the condition was actually seen, "but whether it was in fact visible." Bundy v. Holmquist, 669 N.W. 2d 627, 633 (Jeff. Ct. App. 2003) (citing Martinez v. MN Zoological Gardens, 526 N.W. 2d 416, 418 (Jeff. Ct. App. 1995).

"When a brief inspection would have revealed the condition, [then] it is not concealed", it is visible, and as such is an open and obvious hazard of which a property owner need not give notice. Johnson v. State, 478 N.W.2d 769, 773 (Jeff. 1991) ; see also Sowles v. Urschel Laboratories, Inc., 595 F.2d 1361, 1365 (8th Cir. 1979) ("no one needs notice of what he knows or reasonably may be expected to know."); Sperr v. Ramsey County, 429 N.W.2d 315, 317-318 (Jeff. Ct. App. 1998) (no duty exists to warn pedestrian of low-hanging branch that is clearly visible); Lawrence v. Hollerich, 394 N.W.2d 853, 856 (Jeff. Ct. App. 1986) (steep grade of hill so apparent that no warning was necessary); Bisher v. Homart Dev. Co., 328 N.W.2d 731, 733-734 (Jeff. 1983) (obvious danger presented by large planter in shopping center precluded necessity to warn customers of its presence); Hammerlind v. Clear Lake Star Factory Skydiver's Club, 258 N.W.2d 590, 593-94 (Jeff. 1977) (lake was obvious danger to parachutists); Munoz v. Applebaum's Food Market., Inc., 196 N.W.2d 921,921-922, (Minn. 1972) (20-foot-square pool of water was an obvious hazard and no warning was required). The Munoz Court reaffirmed the general rule accepted by Jefferson courts that recovery is barred when the danger to the injured is open and obvious. Munoz, 196 N.W.2d at 922.

Discuss the questions above regarding summary judgment for the case. Should the court grant the motion? Why or why not?

5. Duty to Protect

Negligence is generally defined as the failure "to exercise such care as persons of ordinary prudence usually exercise under such circumstances." Flom v. Flom, 291 N.W.2d 914, 916 (Jeff.1980) (citations omitted). To recover for a claim of negligence, a plaintiff must prove (1) the existence of a duty of care, (2) a breach of that duty, (3) an injury, and (4) that the breach of the duty of care was a proximate cause of the injury. See Funchess v. Cecil Newman Corp., 632 N.W.2d 666, 672 (Jeff.2001) (citing Lubbers v. Anderson, 539 N.W.2d 398, 401 (Jeff.1995)).

Generally, a defendant's duty to a plaintiff is a threshold question because "[i]n the absence of a legal duty, the negligence claim fails." Gilbertson v. Leininger, 599 N.W.2d 127, 130 (Jeff.1999) (citation omitted); see also State Farm Fire & Cas. v. Aquila Inc., 718 N.W.2d 879, 887 (Jeff.2006) (stating that plaintiffs failed to present a prima facie case for negligence when they could not establish that defendants owed a duty of reasonable care). But we have continued to recognize that generally "[i]n law, we are not our brother's keeper." Lundgren v. Fultz, 354 N.W.2d 25, 27 (Jeff.1984). Inaction by a defendant — such as a failure to warn — constitutes negligence only when the defendant has a duty to act for the protection of others. See Ruberg v. Skelly Oil Co., 297 N.W.2d 746, 750 (Jeff.1980).

An affirmative duty to control the conduct of a third party or to protect another can be established when a special relationship exists between either the actor and the third person ("duty to control") or the actor and the other person ("duty of who has a 'right to protect'"). Delgado v. Lohmar, 289 N.W.2d 479, 483 (Jeff. 1979). "[S]pecial relationship[s] giving rise to a duty to warn . . . [are generally] only found on the part of common carriers, innkeepers, possessors of land who hold it open to the public, and persons who have custody of another under circumstances in which that other person is deprived of normal opportunities of self-protection and that other person is in a vulnerable or dependent position." Harper v. Herman, 499 N.W.2d 472, 474 (Jeff. 1993) (special relationship not found between "social host" of private boat and guest on that boat) (citing Restatement of Torts § 315 (1965)).

The case in litigation involves a college-aged young man, Sam Pierce, who was left outside on a cold winter night last January. He had been out drinking with some friends, all of whom were quite drunk at the end of the evening. Rather than drive home, they took at taxi. At about 1:30 a.m., they arrived on the street where Pierce lived. One of Pierce's friends told the taxi driver to stop when they were in front of Pierce's house. Pierce got out of the taxi, said goodbye to his friends and made his way up the front path to the house. The taxi drove away.

Unfortunately, in his drunken state, Pierce was unable to find his house key in his pocket. He decided to sit down on the chair on the front porch, but soon passed out. The temperature plummeted to minus 25° F (-31° C) that night. Early the next morning, at about 6:00 a.m., Pierce's neighbor happened to notice Pierce slumped over on the porch chair in the cold. He called an ambulance because Pierce was unresponsive. The ambulance arrived and took Pierce to the emergency room. There, the doctors were able to bring Pierce's body temperature back to normal and to revive him. However, both of Pierce's hands had to be amputated because they had frozen in the extreme cold. He had to have six of his toes amputated as well.

Pierce has sued the taxi company and his friends who let him get out of the taxi, claiming that all of them had a duty to protect him from the cold and failed to do so when they let him get out of the taxi and didn't ensure that he was safely in the house before driving away. The taxi company and Pierce's friends have filed motions for summary judgment. Should the court grant them?

Discuss the questions above regarding summary judgment for the case. Should the court grant the motion? Why or why not?

6. Battery

A battery is a harmful or offensive contact with a person resulting from an act intended to cause the person such contact. <u>Saba v. Darling</u>, 575 A.2d 1240, 1242 (Jeff. 1990) (citing RESTATEMENT (SECOND) OF TORTS, § 13). The act in question must be some positive or affirmative action on the part of the defendant. <u>Id.</u> (citing PROSSER & KEETON, THE LAW OF TORTS, § 9 (5th ed.1984)). A battery may occur through a defendant's direct or indirect contact with the plaintiff. <u>Nelson v. Carroll</u>, 735 A.2d 1096, 1100 (Jeff. 1999). Therefore, indirect contact, such as when a bullet strikes a victim, may constitute a battery. <u>See Nelson</u>, 735 A.2d at 1101 ("It is enough that the defendant sets a force in motion which ultimately produces the result . . . ." (citing PROSSER & KEETON, THE LAW OF TORTS § 9, at 40 (5th ed.1984))). Some form of intent is required for battery. <u>Nelson</u>, 735 A.2d at 1100.

For purposes of liability for battery, a defendant satisfies the intent required for the tort if his or her intent is directed at causing the relevant tortious consequence to a third party, rather than to the plaintiff, but the defendant's conduct causes harm or injury to the plaintiff. <u>Id.</u> Moreover, a purely accidental touching is not sufficient to establish the intent requirement for battery. <u>Id.</u>

You represent two plaintiffs in separate battery cases. The first involves an elderly woman who was walking at a local park one afternoon. She was on the walking path when suddenly, a large dog came running towards her without warning. The dog jumped up against her and violently threw its large paws on her shoulders, causing her to lose her balance and fall to the ground. Your client was bruised and shaken, but fortunately did not break any bones.

You have filed a claim of battery against the owner of the dog. During litigation, it has been revealed that several witnesses heard the dog's owner tell the dog "go get 'em" before unleashing the dog and pointing in the general direction of your client. There were several other people on the walking path near your client when the incident occurred. The defendant admits that he wanted his dog to knock down someone, but claims that the intended target was a friend of his that he was mad at who was walking near your client.

The second case involves a woman, Sara, who was standing in line at a movie theater one evening, waiting to buy tickets. Suddenly, she was pushed from behind by a man. Falling forward from the strength of the push, she fell into another patron who was in line in front of her. The man who pushed Sara claims that he lost his balance when he bent over to tie his shoe, put out his arm to break his fall and accidently fell into Sara, pushing her. A witness standing nearby claims that he saw the man put out his arm before he collided with Sara. He said he was "pretty sure" the man was tying his shoe when this happened as he didn't see anything before Sara was pushed.

You represent Sara. The other patron who was pushed by Sara has also filed a claim of battery, naming Sara as the defendant.

Discuss the questions above regarding summary judgment for each of the cases. Should the court grant the motion? Why or why not?

7. IIED

In order to sustain a claim for intentional infliction of emotional distress, a defendant must show: (1) there was extreme and outrageous conduct, (2) the conduct was intentional or reckless, (3) it caused emotional distress, and (4) the distress was severe. Hubbard v. United Press Int'l, Inc., 330 N.W.2d 428, 438–39 (Jeff.1983). The conduct must be "so atrocious that it passes the boundaries of decency and is utterly intolerable to the civilized community." Haagenson v. National Farmers Union Property & Casualty Co., 277 N.W.2d 648, 652 n. 3 (Jeff.1979). The distress must be so severe that no reasonable person can be expected to endure it. Hubbard, 330 N.W.2d at 439 (citing Restatement (Second) of Torts § 46 cmt. (1965)). Summary judgment is proper where a person does not meet the high standard of proof needed for an intentional infliction of emotional distress claim. Strauss v. Thorne, 490 N.W.2d 908, 913 (Jeff. Ct. App. 1992).

This case involves a man named Henry Rodriquez, who was a server at a restaurant in West Rapids, Jefferson for more than fifteen years. The offer letter and employee handbook stated that he was an at-will employee. Henry was always a model employee.

To save costs, the business owner decided to change the service model of his restaurant, which is now the type where the customers order for themselves at the counter and are then assigned a number, which is called when the food is ready. The customer then goes to pick the food up. Because of this new service model, the owner does not need the same number of servers working for him. On December 23, he notified Rodriquez that he was being laid off.

Because he was laid off only two days before Christmas, Rodriquez became very anxious and worried about the presents that he had bought for his children. He didn't know how he would pay for the presents and the bills that were piling up. Rodriquez wasn't able to sleep for nearly two weeks. He lost a significant amount of weight and began to see a therapist to help him with his severe anxiety and depression. He has even developed an ulcer as a result of being laid off.

Rodriquez has contacted an attorney, who filed a claim of intentional infliction of emotional distress against the restaurant owner, asking for more than $500,000 in emotional damages due to the "outrageous" actions of the restaurant owner.

Discuss the questions above regarding summary judgment for the case. Should the court grant the motion? Why or why not?

8. Fit or Unfit Leased Premises

Jefferson statute section 504B.161, Subd. 1 states that in every residential lease, the landlord covenants that the "premises and all common areas are fit for the use intended by the parties."

Jack and Diane rent a house in Sweetwater, Jefferson from a landlord named Claire Barnes. Jack and Diane have two children and a cat. Barnes has not changed the carpeting in the house for more than ten years. There are stains on it, many of which were there before Jack and Diane moved in two years ago, and it is dirty.

Diane has recently applied for a license to run a small day-care center from the house. Barnes is aware of this and has given her approval for the business to operate from her property. However, Jack and Diane now claim that because the carpet is stained and quite old, the leased premises are no longer "fit for the use intended by the parties." Because Diane will be operating a business in the home, they claim that the premises are even less fit because the image of her new business will be harmed when clients and potential clients see the stained carpet. The carpet could also be harmful for the toddlers who crawl on the floor.

Jack and Diane have filed a rent escrow claim with the court, asking that their monthly rent ($1,200) be reduced because of the stained carpet.

Discuss the questions above regarding summary judgment for the case. Should the court grant the motion if Barnes filed it? If Jack and Diane filed it? Why or why not?

Section III

Advanced Legal Issues

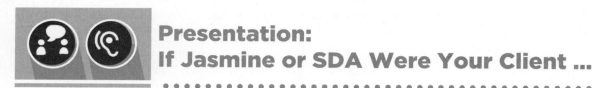

Presentation:
If Jasmine or SDA Were Your Client ...

Overview of the Exercise: For this exercise, you will make a professional presentation in which you answer and discuss the following question:

If you were representing SDA in your home country and if your client came to you for legal advice about the religious discrimination issue, what would you do and what advice would you give her?

OR

If you were representing Jasmine Singh in your home country and if your client came to you for legal advice about the religious discrimination issue, what would you do and what advice would you give her?

You will make the presentation about the client that you are representing for this Unit.

Learning Objectives of the Exercise:

This exercise will build your skills to:

- To examine religious discrimination and religious accommodations from the perspective of your country's legal system
- To compare your country's legal system with the U.S. legal system
- To explain how the dispute would be handled in your country's legal system and the advice that you would provide to your client
- To understand specific information from your classmates' presentations

Steps for Completing the Exercise:

- Analyze the <u>Singh v. Stray Dog Advertising, LLC</u> matter under your country's laws.
- Determine whether or not your client would have viable claims or defenses if the case were brought in your country's legal system.
- Explain how her case would be handled in your country's legal system and what the probable outcome would be.
- Explain what legal advice you would give your client if she came to you for legal advice in your home country.

Research Required: The research you are required to do depends on your knowledge of these claims in your country's legal system. It is presumed that you are familiar with the law and with how you would approach this issue if SDA or Singh were a client of yours.

Grading: This presentation is not graded. Depending on the size of your class and your instructor's choice, you will present to your fellow classmates or to the entire class.

Handouts:

As part of your presentation, you must create a handout for your classmates, and the handouts must include fill-in-the-blank questions that your classmates must complete with information that you present during the presentation. Each handout must include at least five questions to complete.

For example, if a U.S. law student were giving a presentation on Title VII and religious accommodations in the United States, he could include on his handout this question:

To make a prima facie case of failure to accommodate under Title VII of the Civil Rights Act, a plaintiff must demonstrate that:

1._____

2._____

3._____

As you are speaking, your classmates will have to listen, follow what you are saying and fill in the blanks. If you are listening to one of your classmate's presentations and are unsure about an answer, you should ask him or her to repeat so you can fill in the blank(s).

Grammar Review:

The basis of this exercise is hypothetical or conditional verbs: *if SDA or Singh were your client, what would you do?*

Remember the grammar when discussing hypothetical conditions.

Present: **IF + PAST SIMPLE, WOULD + BASE VERB**

If Pamela **called** me to schedule an appointment, I **would tell** her to visit me at my office.

NOTE: We use "were" for all tenses with the verb "to be" when using a conditional verb.

If I **were** you, I **would not take** that class.

If Pamela **were** my client, I would tell her that she **should have done** more to accommodate Jasmine.

Past: **IF + PAST PERFECT, WOULD + HAVE + PAST PARTICIPLE**

If Jasmine **had asked** Pamela if she could swap clients with Tony, this dispute **would** likely **not have happened**.

If Jasmine **had called** me before I left for the day, I **would have told** her to come to my office at 12:00.

Mock Negotiation between Stray Dog Advertising and Jasmine Singh

Overview of the Exercise: This exercise simulates a negotiation between the attorney for Stray Dog Advertising and for Jasmine Singh in the litigation of <u>Singh v. Stray Dog Advertising, LLC</u>. As part of the litigation process, the court has instructed the parties to attempt to resolve the matter through an alternative dispute resolution method. Before hiring a mediator, counsel have suggested to their clients that they try to negotiate a settlement instead. Both clients have agreed.

You have been assigned the role of counsel for Stray Dog Advertising or Jasmine Singh. Before the meeting, review the preparatory and confidential information that you have been provided.

Learning Objectives of the Exercise:

This exercise will build your skills to:

- Use monetary and non-monetary interests of parties in negotiating settlement agreement
- Identify primary obstacles to reaching a mutually beneficial settlement agreement
- Implement negotiation strategies and tactics

Steps for Completing the Exercise:

- Read the preparatory and confidential information that you have been assigned
- Be familiar with the case law regarding religious discrimination and reasonable accommodations and the fact pattern of <u>Singh vs. Stray Dog Advertising, LLC</u>
- Articulate the arguments for your client's position and anticipate opposing counsel's

Writing Exercise:

If time allows and if directed by your instructor, you and opposing counsel will also prepare a draft of the settlement agreement that your clients will sign after you have reached a negotiated agreement.

To complete this task, you first must find a template of a settlement agreement. In real life, few attorneys start from scratch (i.e. from zero) when drafting any contract or agreement. Why recreate the wheel? Instead, attorneys will use a template and then adapt it to their purposes.

Thus, using a template is part of practice. Templates can be found in a law firm's database of documents, or many attorneys will take an agreement from a past case and modify and adapt it to a new case. Bar associations have templates and forms available (often for a fee) and many are available online as well.

But using a template comes with risks too. Even though the template is prepared, you can't simply cut and paste it to a new Word document and think you are good to go. Here are some questions that you have to ask yourself as you analyze a template:

- Does it include provisions at are illegal or violate some law, either because it was written by an attorney in another state or because the law has changed?
- Is it written to be beneficial to one side? For example, is it a very landlord-friendly lease agreement? If it is and if you represent the tenant, you will need to revise it.
- Does it include all the essential provisions? Just because a template is available doesn't mean that it is complete?
- Does your client's matter have unique circumstances or agreements that must be incorporated? It isn't always possible to find a template that perfectly suits your situation, so understanding that will make it easier to find a template that works and that can be adapted.

You also want to be very careful when you use a template to ensure that you remove all references that reveal that this was a template, or that reveal that the document was used with other clients or parties.

Once you have found a template online, adapt it to suit the agreement that you reached.

Grading: This exercise is not graded. After the meetings, the class will debrief on how the negotiations went.

Information Pages

Office Memo:
Title VII of the Civil Rights Act of 1964 and Religious Accommodations

Overview of the Assignment: For this assignment, you will write an office memo to the Senior Partner, summarizing your research on religious accommodations under Title VII and providing your prediction of what will happen with the motion for summary judgment that has been filed.

Learning Objectives of the Assignment:

This assignment will build your skills to:

- Efficiently communicate in a written format
- Explain complex matters clearly and concisely
- Analyze and apply the rules of law regarding Title VII and religious accommodations

Research Required for the Assignment: You are not required to do any outside research for this assignment. You should base your analysis on the 9th Circuit religious accommodations cases that you have read:

- American Postal Workers Union v. Postmaster General, 781 F.2d 772 (9th Cir. 1986).
- Anderson v. General Dynamics Convair Aerospace Division, 589 F.2d 397 (9th Cir. 1978).
- Bhatia v. Chevron U.S.A., Inc., 734 F.2d 1382 (9th Cir. 1984).
- Burns v. Southern Pacific Transportation Co., 589 F.2d 403 (9th Cir. 1978).
- EEOC v. AutoNation USA Corp., 52 Fed. Appx. 327 (9th Cir. 2002).
- EEOC v. Townley Engineering & Manufacturing Co., 859 F.2d 610 (9th Cir. 1988).
- International Association of Machinists & Aerospace Workers v. Boeing Co., 833 F.2d 165 (9th Cir. 1987).
- Proctor v. Consolidated Freightways Corp. of Delaware, 795 F.2d 1472 (9th Cir. 1986).
- Slater v. Douglas County, 743 F. Supp. 2d 1188 (D. Or. 2010).
- Tiano v. Dillard Department Stores, Inc., 139 F.3d 679 (9th Cir. 1998).
- EEOC Consent Decree EEOC v. Razzoo's, L.P., No. 3:05-cv-00562 (N.D. Tex. June 16, 2006).

If you want to practice your legal research skills, you can look for and use other cases that you find. However, if you do search on Westlaw, LexisNexis or Bloomberg Law, be sure to limit your search and the cases you use to 9th Circuit law.

Format of the Completed Assignment:

Your response should be in an office memo format and should include the following:

- Summary of the facts
- The relevant law
- Analysis of the law to the fact pattern
- Conclusion about how you think a court would rule if this matter were to go to court
- Your advice to the client about how to proceed

Follow the following format:

- 1 inch (2.54 cm.) margins (top/bottom and sides)
- 12 font, Times New Roman font
- Double spaced
- Maximum eight pages

Notes: This memo should be predictive and not persuasive. You are not trying to persuade the senior partner or the client about the strength of your arguments or urge him or her to take a particular course of action; you are only trying to inform about the law, how it applies to our case, how you think a court would rule and what advice you have.

In a memo, you can also use formatting like underlining, bold font or italics. You can also create headings and subheadings to organize your answer.

For additional information about office memos and e-memos, as well as samples, refer to the online additional resources.

Grading: This assignment is worth 102 points.

Title VII of the Civil Rights Act of 1964 and Religious Accommodations

Unit 3

LEGAL CONTENT	0-6 points	8 points	10 points	12 points	Points
Issue statement (IS)	Document does not include an IS or includes IS that fails to properly identify the legal issue(s) and the applicable law	Identifies the legal issue(s) and correctly states the applicable law with minor mistakes	Identifies the legal issue(s) and correctly states the applicable law	Identifies the legal issue(s) and correctly states the applicable law in an exceptionally creative and concise way	_____/12
Short Answer	Document does not include a short answer or includes a short answer with significant mistakes	Responds to IS but with key facts or applicable legal principles missing	Responds to IS with key facts and applicable legal principles with no meaningful errors	Clearly and concisely responds to IS with key facts and applicable legal principles and no irrelevancies	_____/12
Facts	Few or none of the relevant facts are included; difficult to follow or understand	Most relevant facts are included as well as non-relevant ones; at times difficult to follow	Relevant facts are included with occasional irrelevancies; easy to follow	All relevant facts are included with no irrelevancies; story is clearly and concisely told to reader in objective way	_____/12
Rule	Hard to follow and understand; does not include relevant sources or cites inappropriate sources; no rule application	Cites to some relevant sources but is incomplete in covering all relevant aspects of the rule; includes some rule application	Cite only to relevant sources and mostly clear; rule application explains but not fully how rule has been applied	Clear and concise; includes only relevant sources and includes all parts of rule necessary for analysis; clear rule application	_____/12
Analysis	Contains conclusory statements and/or no case law; facts are analyzed in a conclusory or insufficient way	Uses some case law but does not analogize or distinguish or explain its application; some conclusory statements; facts briefly analyzed	Uses case law to show how rule applies to case; case law is compared and contrasted with success; most facts are analyzed	Analyzes case law completely, comparing it fully to client matter; facts are thoroughly analyzed in an objective way	_____/12
Conclusion/ Recommendations	No conclusion or recommendations are included in document	A brief conclusion is included but without sufficient client advice	Paper includes conclusion and recommendations	Paper includes full conclusion of the legal analysis and facts and presents creative and thoughtful recommendations	_____/12
Citations	No sources are cited in document	Some sources are cited, but inconsistently; citation format is inconsistent	All citations are present; correct format is mostly used	All citations are present; correct format is used throughout document	_____/12
WRITING	2	4	5	6	Points
Formatting	Document does not follow format instructions or the sample provided	Document attempts to follow instructions and sample provided	Document follows the instructions and sample provided with no meaningful errors	Document exactly follows the instructions and sample provided	_____/6
Organization	No structure or organization; free flow of ideas	Structure & organization present but reorganization or headings needed for full clarity	Document is clearly organized and structured with proper use of heading and subheadings	Document is exceptionally well organized and structured with proper use of headings and subheadings	_____/6
Syntax Mechanics	Contains numerous and distracting grammatical and mechanical errors that impede understanding	Contains some grammatical and mechanical errors that impede understanding	Contains few grammatical and mechanical errors but none that impede understanding	Contains no grammatical and mechanical errors; native-like use of English	_____/6
TOTAL					_____/102

Mock Client Meeting

Overview of the Assignment: This assignment simulates a client meeting between you and your client, Pamela Park of Stray Dog Advertising, LLC or Jasmine Singh. For this exercise, you will meet with your client and explain to her the status of the litigation <u>Singh v. Stray Dog Advertising, LLC</u>, the results of your analysis about how a court might rule on the motion for summary judgment, and your recommendations on how to proceed.

Learning Objectives of the Assignment:

This assignment will build your skills to:

- Explain and clarify the legal positions of the parties and describe potential outcomes to your client
- Respond to technical questions about litigation
- Incorporate technical legal English vocabulary that relates to Title VII of the Civil Rights Act and religious accommodations and use appropriate layperson explanations for your client

Steps for Completing the Assignment:

- Read and be familiar with the Main Assignment File
- Be familiar with the Title VII cases that you have been assigned
- Recommended:
    - Anticipate the questions that you think your client might ask and prepare possible responses;
    - Draft an outline of what you would like to cover in the meeting.

Note: Remember that part of the grading is also based on your professional demeanor. You are expected to arrive punctually, be dressed in professional attire and act as you would with a client in real life. You should play the part from when you come into the meeting room.

Grading: This assignment is worth 102 points.

Punctuality: Student-attorney arrived on time to meeting: YES _____ (10 points) NO _____ (0 points)

Professional Attire: Student-attorney was dressed in appropriate professional attire: YES _____ (10 points) NO _____ (0 points)

Professional Demeanor: Student-attorney acted in a professional manner w/client: YES _____ (10 points) NO _____ (0 points)

GRADING CRITERIA	0- 6 points	8 points (C or 75%)	10 points (B or 85%)	12 points	Points received
Engagement I (questions)	Attorney does not ask client any questions; engages in monologue	Attorney asks few questions; questions are hard to follow or show minimal preparation or understanding of matter	Attorney asks basic questions that demonstrate understanding of matter and preparation	Attorney asks thoughtful, insightful and creative questions that demonstrate deep preparation & understanding of matter	_____/12
Engagement II (answers)	Attorney does not respond to client's questions	Attorney responds to questions, but incorrectly or with hard to follow answers	Attorney responds promptly and correctly to all of client's questions	Attorney responds promptly and correctly to all of client's questions with creative, thoughtful and insightful answers that show a deep understanding of the issues	_____/12
Knowledge of Applicable Law	Attorney provides no explanation of the applicable law	Attorney provides explanation of with serious mistakes, or hard to follow (e.g. use of legal jargon)	Attorney provides clear explanation of with some mistakes; uses some legal jargon unnecessarily or without explanations that client can understand	Attorney provides clear, concise and correct explanation of the law with legal jargon when appropriate or w/ explanations client can understand	_____/12
Ability to Analyze Applicable Law	Attorney provides does not provide an analysis of the law for the client	Attorney attempts to analyze the law but provides incomplete or incorrect analysis	Attorney provides analysis of the law with no significant mistakes or misstatements of the law or facts	Attorney provides a clear, concise and correct analysis of the law as it applies to the client matter	_____/12
Advice and Recommendations	Attorney provides no advice or poor advice for client	Attorney provides not comprehensive or inaccurate advice	Attorney provides comprehensive and accurate advice to client on his/her legal matter	Attorney provides thoughtful and creative solutions for client	_____/12
Organization	Meeting is disorganized and hard to follow or lacks any organization	Meeting has some organization but is still confusing for client for how information is presented	Meeting is clearly organized and easy to follow	Meeting is clearly organized and is easy to follow; attorney takes extra steps to ensure client's understanding	_____/12
TOTAL					_____/72
TOTAL FROM PUNCTUALITY AND PROFESSIONALISM					_____/30

Total   _____/102

Client Advice Letter

Overview of the Assignment: For this assignment, you will write an advice and follow-up letter to your client (Pamela Park or Jasmine Singh) after your client meeting. In addition to including a summary of your meeting, you should also include any advice that you gave your client at the meeting as well as any summaries of the law so that your client is informed about the matter. Be mindful that even though your client may be a sophisticated and experienced professional, she is not a trained attorney. Therefore you should avoid legalese in your letter.

Under Rule 1.4(a)(3) of the Model Rules of Professional Conduct, an attorney has the duty to keep his or her client "reasonably informed about the status of the client's matter." A thorough follow-up letter after a client meeting is one of the best ways to meet this duty, as well as regular phone calls, emails or meetings.

Learning Objectives of the Assignment:

This assignment will build your skills to:

- Efficiently communicate in a written format
- Explain complex matters clearly and concisely
- Incorporate technical legal English vocabulary that relates to religious discrimination and religious accommodations and use appropriate layperson explanations for client

Steps for Completing the Assignment:

- Review the predictive memo that you wrote to your senior partner about your client matter to ensure that the law and the issues are clear
- Be familiar with the case law regarding religious discrimination and religious accommodations, as well as the fact pattern
- Conduct your client meeting with your client, Pamela Park or Jasmine Singh
- Review the Business Correspondence online resources

Research Required for the Assignment: You are not required to do any outside research for this assignment.

Format of the Completed Assignment:

Your assignment should be written as a business letter, not as an email. Even though many firms and lawyers use email for much of the correspondence carried out, formal business letters are still an essential part of the practice of law.

Your law firm has the following policy regarding business correspondence. Your client letter must follow the policy guidelines.

LAW FIRM CORRESPONDENCE POLICY

The purpose of this policy is to ensure a uniform appearance of all business correspondence that is written by the attorneys and staff of the law firm and thus to increase the professional appearance of the firm's work product. All law firm attorneys and staff are required to follow these guidelines when writing correspondence. Violation of the policy can result in disciplinary action, up to and including termination.

- The first page of all "traditional" letters must be written on law firm letterhead, which includes the firm's address and logo
- All emails must include the standard firm signature block with the following information:
  - Full name of sender
  - Position within firm (associate attorney, partner, paralegal, etc.)
  - Full firm address
  - Sender's direct dial
  - Confidentiality policy
- All letters must be written in a modified block letter format
- Letters must be written in Times New Roman, 12 font
- Letters must be 1.5 spaced and have 1" (2.54 cm.) margins, except for the initial page, which may have larger top margins to account for the logo, law firm address and sender's direct contact information
- Client letters must not exceed four pages

Grading: This assignment is worth 78 points.

Note: See the Online Additional Resources for examples of letters and for general information about business correspondence.

LEGAL CONTENT	0-6 points (failing)	8 points (C or 75%)	10 points (B or 85%)	12 points	Points
Introduction	Letter does not include an appropriate introduction or includes poorly constructed one	Letter includes introduction that states purpose with some irrelevancies or some relevant information missing	Introduction states purpose of letter and includes other relevant information	Introduction is engaging; states purpose of letter and includes other relevant information; written clearly and concisely	_____/12
Summary of Meeting	Letter includes no summary of the meeting	Letter includes summary but leaves out important information or states it unclearly	Letter summarizes the meeting but leaves out important information	Letter clearly and concisely summarizes the meeting, its core purpose and content	_____/12
Applicable Law	Student-attorney provides no explanation of the applicable law, or only uses legal jargon in explanation (inappropriate for audience)	Student-attorney provides explanation of with serious mistakes, or hard to follow (use of legal jargon)	Student-attorney provides clear explanation of with few mistakes; uses some legal jargon without appropriate explanations	Student-attorney provides clear, concise and correct explanation of the law with legal jargon with appropriate explanations	_____/12
Analysis	Contains conclusory statements and/or no case law; facts are analyzed in a conclusory or insufficient way	Uses some case law but does not analogize or distinguish or explain its application; some conclusory statements; facts briefly analyzed	Uses case law to show how rule applies to case; case law is compared and contrasted with success; most facts are analyzed	Analyzes completely case law, comparing it fully to client matter; facts are thoroughly analyzed	_____/12
Conclusion/ Recommendations	No conclusion or recommendations are included in letter	A brief conclusion is included but without sufficient advice or recommendations advice or next steps	Letter includes conclusion with recommendations and next steps	Letter includes full conclusion of the legal analysis and facts, presents creative and thoughtful recommendations and includes clear next steps	_____/12
WRITING	**2**	**4**	**5**	**6**	**Points**
Formatting	Document does not follow format instructions or the sample provided	Document attempts to follow instructions and sample provided	Document follows the instructions and sample provided with minor errors	Document exactly follows the instructions and sample provided	_____/6
Organization	No structure or organization; free flow of ideas	Letter includes organization and structure but is still confusing	Structure and organization but some reorganization is needed for full clarity	Document is clearly organized and structured	_____/6
Syntax Mechanics	Contains numerous and distracting grammatical and mechanical errors that impede understanding	Contains some grammatical and mechanical errors that impede understanding	Contains few grammatical and mechanical errors but none that impede understanding	Contains no grammatical and mechanical errors; native-like use of English	_____/6
TOTAL					_____/78

Section III

Advanced Legal Issues

Memorandum of Law
for Motion for Summary Judgment

Overview of the Assignment: For this assignment, you will draft a memorandum of law in support of or in opposition to the motion for summary judgment that Stray Dog Advertising has filed in the litigation with Jasmine Singh.

You have been assigned to represent either Stray Dog Advertising or Singh. In the Main Assignment File, you have also received your assignment from the senior partner of your respective law firm and have been asked to write the memorandum of law and also to conduct the oral argument.

Learning Objectives of the Assignment:

This assignment will build your skills to:

- Efficiently read and understand legal authority (statute and case law)
- Analyze the fact pattern by applying the relevant case law
- Adapt the IRAC organization and the formal memorandum of law structure
- Communicate effectively and in a persuasive manner to convince the court and the reader that your client's position and argument is the one to follow

Research for the Assignment: You are not required to do any outside research for this assignment. You should base your analysis on the Title VII/religious accommodations cases that you read in class:

- American Postal Workers Union v. Postmaster General, 781 F.2d 772 (9th Cir. 1986).
- Anderson v. General Dynamics Convair Aerospace Division, 589 F.2d 397 (9th Cir. 1978).
- Bhatia v. Chevron U.S.A., Inc., 734 F.2d 1382 (9th Cir. 1984).
- Burns v. Southern Pacific Transportation Co., 589 F.2d 403 (9th Cir. 1978).
- EEOC v. AutoNation USA Corp., 52 Fed. Appx. 327 (9th Cir. 2002).
- EEOC v. Townley Engineering & Manufacturing Co., 859 F.2d 610 (9th Cir. 1988).
- International Association of Machinists & Aerospace Workers v. Boeing Co., 833 F.2d 165 (9th Cir. 1987).
- Proctor v. Consolidated Freightways Corp. of Delaware, 795 F.2d 1472 (9th Cir. 1986).
- Slater v. Douglas County, 743 F. Supp. 2d 1188 (D. Or. 2010).
- Tiano v. Dillard Department Stores, Inc., 139 F.3d 679 (9th Cir. 1998).
- EEOC Consent Decree EEOC v. Razzoo's, L.P., No. 3:05-cv-00562 (N.D. Tex. June 16, 2006).

If you want to practice your legal research skills, you can look for and use other cases that you find. However, if you do search on Westlaw, LexisNexis or Bloomberg Law, be sure to limit your search and the cases you use to 9th Circuit law.

Format of the Completed Assignment:

For your completed assignment, you must follow Local Rule 5.2 of the Courts of Jefferson.

Local Rule 5.2 GENERAL FORMAT OF DOCUMENTS TO BE FILED

Format: All documents filed must be typewritten, printed, or prepared by a clearly legible duplication process. Document text must be double-spaced, except for quoted material and footnotes, and pages must be numbered consecutively at the bottom. Documents filed after the case-initiating document must contain—on the front page and above the document's title—the case number and the name or initials of the assigned district judge and magistrate judge.

Represented Parties. A memorandum of law filed by a represented party must be typewritten. All text in the memorandum, including footnotes, must be set in at least font size 12 (i.e., a 12-point font) as font sizes are designated in the word-processing software used to prepare the memorandum. Text must be double-spaced, with these exceptions: headings and footnotes may be single-spaced, and quotations more than two lines long may be indented and single-spaced. Pages must be 8 ½ by 11 inches in size, and no text — except for page numbers — may appear outside an area measuring 6 ½ by 9 inches.

Length: No memorandum filed with the court shall exceed the length of twelve pages, excluding caption and table of contents.

Grading: This assignment is worth 90 points.

Note: See the online resources for additional information about memoranda of law and persuasive writing.

LEGAL CONTENT	0-6 points	8 points	10 points	12 points	Points
Introduction	Document does not include an Introduction or includes issue statement instead	Introduction is not persuasive or does not include persuasive or relevant facts or the law	Student attempts to make introduction persuasive, to "put the spin" but does not include all facts or something…	Introduction is persuasive, clear and concise and clearly introduces reader to the client's story and position and identifies the relief sought	_____/12
Facts	Few or none of the relevant facts are included; difficult to follow or understand	Relevant facts are included as well as non-relevant ones; mostly clear	Relevant facts are included; factual background is mostly clear and easy to follow with few irrelevancies	Relevant facts are included with no irrelevant facts; story is clearly and concisely told to reader in persuasive way	_____/12
Rule	Hard to follow and understand; does not include relevant sources or cites inappropriate sources; no rule application	Cites to some relevant sources but is incomplete in covering all relevant aspects of the rule	Cite only to relevant sources; rule application explains but not fully how rule has been applied	Clear and concise; includes only relevant sources and includes all parts of rule necessary for analysis; clear rule application	_____/12
Argument	Contains conclusory statements and/or no case law; facts are analyzed in a conclusory or insufficient way	Uses some case law but does not analogize or distinguish or explain its application; some conclusory statements; facts briefly analyzed; student attempts to make persuasive arguments	Uses case law to show how rule applies to case; case law is compared and contrasted with success; facts are analyzed and argued in a persuasive way	Analyzes completely case law, comparing it fully to client matter; all facts are thoroughly analyzed and argued in a very persuasive way	_____/12
Conclusion	No conclusion is included in document	A brief conclusion is included but unclear relief sought	Paper includes conclusion with relief sought	Paper includes full conclusion of the legal analysis and facts and persuasively argues for relief sought	_____/12
Citations	No sources are cited in document or citation formats are incorrect and inconsistent	Sources are cited, but inconsistently; citation format has meaningful mistakes in format	Citations are complete; few meaningful mistakes in format	No mistakes in citations; correct format is used throughout document	_____/12
WRITING	2	4	5	6	Points
Formatting	Document does not follow format instructions or the sample provided	Document attempts to follow instructions and sample provided	Document follows the instructions and sample provided with minor errors	Document exactly follows the instructions and sample provided	_____/6
Organization	No structure or organization; free flow of ideas	Document includes some organization and structure but is still confusing; no use of headings or subheadings	Structure & organization present but reorganization needed full clarity; subheadings included but not effectively persuasive	Document is clearly organized and structured with proper use of persuasive heading and subheadings	_____/6
Syntax Mechanics	Contains numerous and distracting grammatical and mechanical errors that impede understanding	Contains some grammatical and mechanical errors that impede understanding	Contains few grammatical and mechanical errors but none that impede understanding	Contains no grammatical and mechanical errors; native-like use of English	_____/6
TOTAL					_____/90

Mock Oral Argument

Overview of the Assignment: For this assignment, you will carry out the oral argument for the motion for summary judgment in the <u>Singh v. Stray Dog Advertising, LLC</u> case, currently docketed in the Hemings County District Court. Oral arguments are scheduled for the motion filed by Stray Dog Advertising, LLC, asking the court to enter judgment in its favor and dismiss the plaintiff's claim of religious discrimination.

You will represent the party that your instructor has assigned to you.

Learning Objectives of the Assignment:

This assignment will build your skills to:

- Effectively and persuasively communicate legal rules and argument
- Conduct yourself orally in a professional courtroom setting
- Respond to questions about the relevant law

Steps for Completing the Assignment:

Before the oral arguments, review the following:

- Pleadings
- Notice of Motion and Motion for Summary Judgment
- Your Memorandum of Law, as well as that of your opposing counsel
- Cases cited in your memo and opposing counsel's
- Facts of the client matter

Research for the Assignment: Although no additional research is required for the assignment, you should review the draft memorandum of your opposing counsel and review the cases that he/she includes, consider how you can rebut the cases, or explain how they are inapposite to the matter at hand and address those cases in your oral argument.

Format of the Assignment:

Each side has 20 minutes for his or her argument. The moving party first presents his/her arguments and may reserve time for rebuttal. It is the moving party's decision to reserve time for rebuttal. After the moving party has presented his/her arguments, it is the non-moving party's turn. The non-moving party does not receive time for rebuttal since he/she can listen to opposing counsel and respond directly to any arguments made. After the non-moving party finishes, the moving party responds with rebuttal, if he/she previously asked the court to reserve time for it.

Be prepared to answer questions from the court, and part of your preparation should be anticipating the questions that the judge might ask and preparing answers. But in the event that the judge doesn't ask questions or asks few, be prepared to fill the time allotted with your argument.

Grading: This assignment is worth 90 points.

Punctuality: Attorney arrived on time to oral argument: YES _____ (10 points) NO _____ (0 points)

Professional Attire: Attorney was dressed in appropriate professional attire: YES _____ (10 points) NO _____ (0 points)

Professional Demeanor: Attorney acted in a professional manner w/court and opposing counsel: YES _____ (10 points) NO _____ (0 points)

GRADING CRITERIA	0-6 points (failing)	8 points (C or 75%)	10 points (B or 85%)	12 points	Points received
Engagement	Attorney does not respond to the court's questions	Attorney responds to questions, but incorrectly or with hard to follow answers	Attorney responds promptly and correctly to all of the court's questions	Attorney responds promptly and correctly to all of court's questions with creative, thoughtful and insightful answers that show a deep understanding of the issues	_____/12
Knowledge of Applicable Law	Attorney provides no explanation of the applicable law	Attorney provides explanation of with few meaningful mistakes or with explanation that is hard to follow	Attorney provides clear explanation of the law with no meaningful mistakes	Attorney provides clear, concise and correct explanation of the law	_____/12
Analysis of Applicable Law	Attorney provides no analysis of the law or provides analysis that is incorrect or incomplete	Attorney provides analysis of the law but has some mistakes or misstatements of the law or facts	Attorney provides a clear, concise and correct analysis of the law as it applies to the client matter	Attorney present unimpeachable case for the client, analyzing persuasively, concisely and clearly the law as it applies to client matter	_____/12
Conclusion and Relief	Attorney does not identify relief sought or conclude argument	Attorney provides advice, but	Attorney provides advice but	Attorney clearly identifies the relief sought and summarizes the client's position	_____/12
Organization	Argument is disorganized and has serious faults of organization	Argument has minor faults of organization	Argument is clearly organized and easy to follow	Argument is exceptionally well organized and presents arguments in novel way	_____/12
TOTAL					_____/60
TOTAL FROM PUNCTUALITY AND PROFESSIONALISM					_____/30

TOTAL _____/90

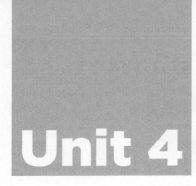

Unit 4

Premises Liability
Liability between Commercial Landlord and Tenant

For this Unit, you will write a persuasive memorandum of law in support of or in opposition to a motion for summary judgment in litigation involving Stray Dog Advertising. As you will read, SDA has been brought into a lawsuit between its landlord, Gateway West Development, Inc. (the defendant), and Julianna Diaz (the plaintiff), a friend of Roy Blanco's, the creative director at SDA. Diaz was injured while visiting Blanco at the SDA offices and has sued Gateway West for the injuries she has suffered. Gateway West has brought SDA into the litigation as a third-party defendant, claiming that SDA, not Gateway West, is liable for her injuries.

The legal issue involved is negligence and premises liability and specifically the liability of a commercial landlord for injuries that occur on its property.

Learning Objectives of this Unit:

This Unit will build your skills to:

- Explain complex legal matters clearly and concisely
- Use appropriate technical terminology
- Identify and analyze the applicable case law and facts for the relevant legal issues
- Articulate persuasive legal arguments in support of client's position
- Efficiently and effectively communicate in a written and oral format
- Respond to questions about the relevant law

To achieve these learning objectives, you will complete the following tasks:

- Draft a predictive memo to senior partner about the legal issues and your prediction of what will happen with the litigation
- Draft a persuasive memorandum of law in support of or in opposition to motion for summary judgment
- Carry out a mock client meeting with either Pamela Park of SDA or Greg Blackman, the CEO of Gateway West
- Draft a client letter to your client about your meeting and about the legal issues
- Carry out oral argument in front of the court for the motion for summary judgment

To complete these tasks, you will use the following materials in the book:

- Assignment email from Senior Partner (pages 372 and 373)
- Main Assignment File (online, including pleadings, lease agreement, written discovery responses and deposition transcripts)
- Premises Liability Statutes:
    - MASS. GEN. LAWS ANN. 186 §15 (West 2012).
    - MASS. GEN. LAWS ANN. 186 §19 (West 2012).
- Premises Liability Commented Cases:
    - Young v. Garawcki, 402 N.E.2d 1045 (Mass. 1980).
    - Humphrey v. Byron, 850 N.E.2d 1044 (Mass. 2006).
    - Monterosso v. Gaudette, 391 N.E.2d 948 (Mass. App. Ct. 1979).
    - Bishop v. TES Realty Trust, 942 N.E.2d 173 (Mass. 2011).
    - Chausse v. Coz, 540 N.E.2d 667 (Mass. 1989).
    - The Great Atlantic and Pacific Tea Co. v. Yanofsky, 403 N.E.2d 370 (Mass. 1980).
- ESL Workbook (pages 270-295)

Your instructor will also assign you additional skills-building exercises to bolster your understanding of the legal issues and further develop your legal reasoning and language skills, whether related to legal reasoning and analysis or to English. You will find an icon with each exercise that will indicate which skills the exercise will focus upon.

ICON	SKILL
	Speaking — in particular about the legal issues and the law presented in the Unit
	Oral comprehension
	Legal analysis and reasoning
	Analysis of the legal issue(s) presented in the Unit
	English grammar, syntax, and vocabulary
	Legal ethics and professional responsibility
	Legal research

In this Unit, the additional skills-building exercises that accompany the Main Assignment File include:

- Analysis of Contract Language (pages 374-381)
- Mock Negotiation Between SDA and Gateway West Development (pages 390-391 plus confidential information)
- Summary Judgment Analysis Exercise (pages 382-389)
- Presentation: *If SDA or Gateway West Were Your Client...* (pages 392-393)

Before beginning the Unit, you should read and be familiar with the Factual Background of Stray Dog Advertising (pages 7-8), of the Lincoln, Adams and Washington Law Firm (pages 2-3) and the law firm of Anthony Ross and Tubman (page 5).

You will also find online at the website www.legalwritingforllms.com the following online resources that accompany this Unit. The additional online resources will help you deepen your mastery of the skills presented in the Unit and also provide additional understanding about the U.S. legal system and legal writing.

Pleadings: Section III, Unit 4 (required)

- Additional Resources:
    - Sources of American Law
    - Writing Professional Emails
    - Writing Persuasive Memos
    - Writing E-memos
    - IRAC
- Additional Skills-Building Exercises:
    - Issues and Issue Statements
    - Stating the Rule
    - Analysis
    - Ethical Spotlight Exercise

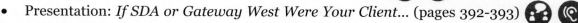

Section III, Unit 4 Legal Issue
Premises Liability and Commercial Landlord and Tenant

Main Assignment File	Premises Liability Cases and Applicable Statutes	ESL Workbook	Additional Exercises	Additional Online Resources
Introduction to File and Client Matter Pages 366-370	Young v. Garawcki, 402 N.E.2d 1045 (Mass. 1980).	Young v. Garawcki, 402 N.E.2d 1045 (Mass. 1980).	Analysis of Contract Language Pages 374-381	Writing Professional Emails
Documents Related to Client Matter Pages 371-373 + pleadings and discovery documents online	Humphrey v. Byron, 850 N.E.2d 1044 (Mass. 2006).	Humphrey v. Byron, 850 N.E.2d 1044 (Mass. 2006).	Mock Negotiation Pages 390-391 + confidential information	Business Correspondence (with sample letters)
Assignment Information Pages + Rubrics Pages 394-403	Monterosso v. Gaudette, 391 N.E.2d 948 (Mass. App. Ct. 1979).	Monterosso v. Gaudette, 391 N.E.2d 948 (Mass. App. Ct. 1979).	Summary Judgment Analysis Exercise Pages 382-389	Writing Memos (office memos and persuasive memoranda of law)
	Bishop v. TES Realty Trust, 942 N.E.2d 173 (Mass. 2011).	Bishop v. TES Realty Trust, 942 N.E.2d 173 (Mass. 2011).	Presentation: If SDA or Gateway West Were Your Client... Pages 392-393	IRAC (including additional exercises for each element)
	Chausse v. Coz, 540 N.E.2d 667 (Mass. 1989).	Chausse v. Coz, 540 N.E.2d 667 (Mass. 1989).		Skills-Building Exercises for Rules, Issues and Issues Statements, Analysis and Ethical Dilemmas
	The Great Atlantic and Pacific Tea Co. v. Yanofsky, 403 N.E.2d 370 (Mass. 1980).	The Great Atlantic and Pacific Tea Co. v. Yanofsky, 403 N.E.2d 370 (Mass. 1980).		
	M.G.L.A. 186 §15 and §19	M.G.L.A. 186 §15 and §19		

Premises Liability

Unit 4

Introduction – Premises Liability

The legal issue that you will learn about and analyze in this Unit is a doctrine of tort law and of negligence: premises liability, which is the legal liability of a property owner for injuries that others suffer while on the property, whether in a building (a store, office building or a house) or on land.

Historically under common law, the duty that a property owner owed to an individual who entered onto his property depended on the status of that individual, which in turn depended on why that person entered or remained on the land.[115] The three categories of status for purposes of premises liability are trespasser, invitee and licensee.

Since a trespasser enters onto the property owner's land without permission, the landowner traditionally owed a duty simply to "refrain from engaging in intentional, malicious, or willful misconduct, such as setting up spring guns or other anti-trespasser traps."[116] This was quite a low standard for the property owner not to be held liable for injuries that the trespasser suffered while on his property.

In contrast, if the person entering the property did so for the economic benefit of the owner, like a customer or client entering a shop or a restaurant, the person's status was an "invitee," and the property owner owed him or her a duty to use reasonable care to make the land safe and to warn of any hidden dangers that the invitee would not or could not see on his or her own.[117] "Invitees" were owed the highest duty under the traditional common law.

Everyone else — neither trespasser nor invitee — was known as "licensees" or "social guests." These individuals had the express or implied permission to be on the land, but were not there for the property owner's economic benefit.[118] Thus, if you were a guest at a friend's house for dinner or a party, you were a "licensee" under the traditional common law approach. As such, your friend would have owed you the same "minimal" duty he or she owed to a trespasser.[119] It hardly seems fair that the common law standard of care for you as a dinner guest was the same duty that your friend owed towards a trespasser just because you didn't confer any economic benefits to your friend, but just good company.

> Liability for injuries sustained on the real estate generally depends upon who has control of the premises. Thus the liability of a tenant for the personal injuries of his guests, invitees and other persons lawfully in the premises is determined by the possession and control of the premises. Nunan v. Dudley Props., 91 N.E.2d 840, 841 (Mass. 1950).

But courts began to see these distinctions as too rigid to fit modern society and "unnecessary" in an increasingly urban and complex world; as a result they disregarded them and imposed on owners and occupiers of property "a single duty of care in all the circumstances," regardless of why an individual was on his or her land.[120]

Thus in this Unit, the first issue that you will face is what duty was owed to the individual, Julianna Diaz, who was injured while visiting the Stray Dog Advertising offices within the building owned by the landlord, Gateway West Development, but not within the space that Stray Dog Advertising leases. Was that duty of reasonable care breached? You will also examine and analyze which party is to blame when both parties could potentially be liable for the injuries that Diaz suffered. Should blame fall on the landlord who owns the property, or the tenant who leases it and uses it on a daily basis?

You will learn that an out-of-possession landlord is generally not liable for a third party's injuries when that person is injured while on his or her premises unless the landlord has notice of the defect and has consented to

---

[115] 15 Lee. S. Kreindler et al., New York Practice, New York Law of Torts § 12:4 (Westlaw database updated Sept. 2016).

[116] Id.

[117] Id.

[118] Id.

[119] Id.

[120] See, e.g., Basso v. Miller, 352 N.E.2d 868, 872 (N.Y. 1976) (rejecting the traditional distinctions between invitee, licensee and trespasser while referring to them as a "semantic morass" and citing persuasive precedent of many "sister States" that had already rejected the rigid, old-fashioned distinctions between status to determine the duty owed).

be responsible for maintenance or repair or the injury occurs in a common area under the landlord's control.[121] But of course that general rule has exceptions, which you will learn about in the cases that you will read. The cases for this Unit are from Massachusetts, and in Massachusetts the rule regarding landlord liability is both common law and statutory.

As a Unit in the Advanced Section of the book, the litigation you will deal with involves third-party litigation, which occurs when the defendant in the "main" cause of action brings into the lawsuit another party that the defendant claims is responsible for the damages that the plaintiff has suffered. The defendant might claim that this other party is either partially or wholly responsible for the damages, but is in some way pointing the finger at someone else for the blame.

When this happens, the defendant becomes the third-party plaintiff (because he is suing another person) and the new defendant becomes the third-party defendant. In turn the third-party defendant can file a claim against another individual if he believes that person is liable for the losses. The third-party defendant is now also the fourth-party plaintiff, and the person that he sues is the fourth-party defendant, who can also file a claim against another individual who becomes the fifth-party defendant, and the fourth-party defendant is also the fifth-party plaintiff....and so on and so on.[122] It can become confusing and drawing a graphic can help to keep it all straight.

In our case, the plaintiff, Julianna Diaz, brought the negligence claim against the landlord, Gateway West Development, which in turn filed the third-party claim against Stray Dog Advertising, alleging that SDA was in fact liable for the injuries suffered. The motion that you will draft and argue for this Unit is a motion for summary judgment between the third-party plaintiff, Gateway West Development, and the third-party defendant, Stray Dog Advertising, which has filed the motion on the grounds that no genuine issue of material fact exists as to whether Gateway West is liable for the injuries that Diaz suffered, not Stray Dog Advertising. You will not analyze the litigation between Diaz and Gateway West Development.

To keep the complex litigation straight in your mind, here is a graphic of the cases Diaz v. Gateway West Development, Inc. and Gateway West Development, Inc. v. Stray Dog Advertising, LLC.

Plaintiff Julianna Diaz ⟶ Defendant and Third-Party Plaintiff

Gateway West Development, Inc.

↓

Third-Party Defendant

Stray Dog Advertising, LLC

---

[121] Lopez v. 1372 Shakespeare Ave. Hous. Dev. Fund Corp., 750 N.Y.S.2d 44, 46 (N.Y. App. Div. 2002) (citing Manning v. N.Y. Tel. Co., 555 N.Y.S.2d 720, 721 (N.Y. App. Div. 2002); Velazquez v. Tyler Graphics, Ltd., 625 N.Y.S.2d 537, 538 (N.Y. App. Div. 1995)).

[122] In federal and state court decisions (at least those on Westlaw), the case with the most named third-parties is Ceiling Specialties Co. v. Reginald Wong & Wong & Co., No. 42077, 1980 WL 355376 (Ohio Ct. App. Nov. 20, 1980). The court notes that during the litigation, the plaintiff filed a complaint against an eleventh-party defendant.

Main Assignment File: Premises Liability

TIMELINE IN LITIGATION OF
DIAZ V. GATEWAY WEST DEVELOPMENT, INC. AND GATEWAY WEST DEVELOPMENT, INC. V. STRAY DOG ADVERTISING, LLC.

EVENT	DATE
Stray Dog Advertising and Gateway West Development, Inc. signed lease for SDA's office space	May 5, YEAR -5
Julianna Diaz was injured in water heater storage room	May 15, YEAR -2
Diaz filed her complaint for negligence/personal injury against Gateway West in Jefferson State Court	July 10, YEAR -1
Gateway West filed third-party complaint against Stray Dog Advertising, LLC	July 23, YEAR -1
Stray Dog Advertising filed answer against third-party complaint	August 7, YEAR -1
Depositions of Pamela Park, Dwayne Harvey and Greg Blackman conducted	January 9–12 THIS YEAR
Lincoln, Adams and Washington Law Firm filed motion for summary judgment on third-party complaint	March 5, THIS YEAR
Oral argument for motion for summary judgment to be held	April 26, THIS YEAR

Third-Party Plaintiff's File

You received the following email from Senior Partner Ross about the litigation involving the firm's client, Gateway West Development, Inc. and Stray Dog Advertising and Julianna Diaz.

From: Elizabeth Ross <liz.ross@anthonyrosstubmanlaw.com>
To: Associate Attorney <associate@anthonyrosstubmanlaw.com>
Sent: March 8, THIS YEAR 10:23
Subject: SJ Motion/Gateway West

Associate Attorney,

Thank you for all your hard work on the Gateway West file. Your decision to bring in Stray Dog Advertising was a smart one; after reviewing the law it seems clear to me that this is a case where SDA should be liable for Diaz's injuries, not Blackman.

You are responsible for continuing with the file through the summary judgment motion that SDA has filed. I just spoke with Georgina Washington earlier this morning and she told me that they are filing the motion today. I am sure that we can survive SJ. If we do, I think settlement will be the best option but that of course will be our client's decision.

Before you begin working on the memo in opposition to SDA's motion, please prepare for me an office memo with your arguments that we will make, as well as a summary and analysis of the law. I'd also like your predictions about what you think SDA will argue based on Jefferson law.

When you are done with that, please prepare the memo to submit to the court. One of the law clerks will help you with the research. By the way, do not discuss whether the plaintiff in the original claim, Julianna Diaz, is partially negligent for her injuries. That is not the issue for this motion of summary judgment; we only need to argue that SDA, not Gateway West, would be liable and that there are facts in dispute as to the liability.

Blackman has been very satisfied with your work on the case and has had nothing but good things to say.

Best,
Liz

As you have read, you have been asked to write the following documents about this litigation:

First, you will draft a predictive office memo to the senior partner that includes:

- A summary of what has happened between Stray Dog Advertising and Gateway West
- The legal issue at hand
- A summary and analysis of the law that applies (premises liability and commercial landlord and tenants)
- The arguments that you will make about the motion for summary judgment
- Counterarguments that you anticipate that the third-party defendant, SDA, will make
- Your opinion about whether you think the court will grant the motion

Second, you will draft a persuasive memorandum of law in opposition to the motion for summary judgment that includes:

- Persuasive statements of the facts in a light that best represents your client
- Summary of the legal issue and the relevant law
- Persuasive arguments stating why the court should deny the motion for summary judgment that Stray Dog Advertising has filed

You will find complete information about these assignments on the Information Pages (pages 394-395; 400-401).

You will be analyzing the client matter using the premises liability cases that you read and review in class.

Third-Party Defendant's File

You received the following email from Senior Partner Washington about ongoing litigation that Stray Dog Advertising has been involved in.

From:	Georgina Washington <g.washington@lawlawfirm.com>
To:	Associate Attorney <a.attorney@lawlawfirm.com>
Sent:	March 8, THIS YEAR 07:45
Subject:	Stray Dog Advertising – Motion for Summary Judgment

Associate attorney,

I need your help with one of the legal matters involving Stray Dog Advertising and the case that SDA is a third-party defendant in. If you remember, SDA was brought into the litigation by its landlord, Gateway West, after the landlord was sued by an individual injured while at SDA's office, or rather in the space within the building. The woman who was injured, Juliana Diaz, is a friend of Roy Blanco, Pamela's creative director. The personal relationships in this case have made things even more complicated. I am sure that because Diaz is a friend of Pamela and Roy, she decided not to sue SDA and brought the lawsuit against the landlord instead.

I have too many other cases going on right now and need you to take over for me. Discovery has been completed. We've deposed Greg Blackman, the CEO of Gateway West, and Dwayne Harvey, the property manager, and Pamela has been deposed as well. The deposition transcripts are in the client file. We've also completed the written discovery and you will find the pertinent responses in the file as well.

I've scheduled and noticed a motion for summary judgment. We need to get the case against Pamela dismissed and SJ is the only way to accomplish that goal at this point since our motion to dismiss was denied. I think that the court will see that this is a case where the landlord is liable for the injuries this woman suffered, not SDA as the tenant. Please do not discuss whether the plaintiff in the original claim, Julianna Diaz, is partially negligent for her injuries. We are focusing only on the liability between Stray Dog and Gateway West.

I want you to draft the brief in support of our motion for summary judgment and also be responsible for the oral arguments scheduled in front of Judge Noble. Before you draft the memo, I would like a predictive memo that summarizes the facts and explains the law and the arguments that you will make, as well as the counterarguments that you anticipate Gateway West will make.

Thanks for your help, and I look forward to receiving your work. Let me know if you have any questions.

Georgina

As you have read, you have been asked to write the following documents about this litigation:

First, you will draft a predictive office memo to the senior partner that includes:

- A summary of what has happened between Stray Dog Advertising and Gateway West
- The legal issue at hand
- A summary and analysis of the law that applies (premises liability and commercial landlord and tenants)
- The arguments that you will make about the motion for summary judgment
- Counterarguments that you anticipate that the third-party plaintiff, Gateway West, will make
- Your opinion about whether you think the court will grant the motion

Second, you will draft a persuasive memorandum of law in support of the motion for summary judgment that includes:

- Persuasive statements of the facts in a light that best represents your client
- Summary of the legal issue and the relevant law
- Persuasive arguments stating why the court should grant the motion for summary judgment that Stray Dog Advertising has filed

You will find complete information about these assignments on the Information Pages (pages 394-395; 400-401).

You will be analyzing the client matter using the premises liability cases that you read and review in class.

Additional Skills-Building Exercises

 Contract Language Analysis Exercise

Overview of the Exercise: The dispute between Stray Dog Advertising and Gateway West hinges in part upon the language of the lease agreement that the parties signed. The language of a contract can be determinative as to whether your client's interests and rights are protected in case of a dispute, and drafting a contract that meets that goal can be challenging.

In this exercise, you will analyze contract provisions from the perspective of one of the contracting parties and determine whether the language as written helps that party achieve its goals. You will then if necessary rewrite the contractual language to better serve that party's interests.

Learning Objectives of the Exercise:

This exercise will build your skills to:

- Analyze contract provisions and determine whether the language suits the needs of a party
- Articulate what words or phrases in the contractual provision can and should be revised to better meet the party's needs
- Revise the contractual provision to meet those needs

Steps for Completing the Exercise:

- Read the following fact patterns, which include a short summary of the contract, the parties, the needs of one of the parties, and a contract provision
- With a partner, analyze whether the contractual provision is written in a way that meets the needs of one of the parties
- Determine whether the contract language should be revised to better meet the party's needs and how it should be revised
- Revise the contract provision
- Once you have finished, you will compare your answers with the rest of the class

Research Required for the Exercise: You are not required to do any outside research to complete this assignment.

Grading: This exercise is not graded. Instead, you will compare your answers with those of your classmates.

Note: When you are revising the agreement, also keep in mind the realities of contract negotiations. An agreement that is 100% in favor of one party, to the detriment of the other party, is unlikely to be signed or enforced. So when you revise the contract provisions, be reasonable and realistic while still keeping in mind your client's interests.

1. Wedding Photography Agreement

You represent a woman whose wedding is scheduled in six months. The woman and her fiancé have been searching for a wedding photographer to take their wedding pictures. However, your client has confided in you that she and her fiancé have already cancelled one wedding at the last minute (five days before the date), and they have broken off their engagement several times over the past two years. She is afraid that if they cancel the wedding at the last minute this time, they will lose money.

She has come to you with the Portrait Photography Agreement that the photographer has given her. She would like you to draft the agreement in a way that best protects her and her fiancé and provides them the most flexibility in terminating the agreement, without fees or expenses, if they should cancel the agreement — and their wedding — at the last minute.

When revising the agreement, you cannot eliminate completely any of the provisions. Instead, you must revise the provisions as provided, but make them better serve and protect your client's interests. Your client wants:

- as much flexibility as possible for cancelling the agreement without incurring fees or expenses
- terms that favor her for changing the date of the event or any other details of the wedding
- provisions that do not penalize her in case she and her fiancé cancel the wedding or have something else come up that requires them to reschedule

WEDDING PHOTOGRAPHY AGREEMENT

Overview

This agreement contains the entire understanding between the Photographer and the Client. It supersedes all prior and simultaneous agreements between the Parties. The only way to add or change this agreement is to do so in writing, signed by all the Parties. If the Parties waive one provision of this agreement, they do not waive the enforcement of any other provision. The party against whom a waiver is sought to be effective must have signed a waiver in writing.

Coverage

Coverage will begin at 6:00 p.m. on June 13, THIS YEAR and end at 2:00 a.m. on June 14, THIS YEAR.

Change of Date or Venue

The Photographer must be notified immediately of any changes in schedule or location, at least one week prior to the scheduled date of event. Notification of any changes can be made by phone along with written notice sent via email for documentation. If an email is sent, a confirmation of receipt must be sent back by the Photographer in writing or via email. It is the client's responsibility to confirm all arrangements at least 7-10 days prior to the event. In the event of change of address or contact information (time, etc.) as listed, you must notify the Photographer.

The Photographer kindly asks that the Client get in touch with the Photographer two weeks prior to the date of the event in order to touch base and go over last minute details. The Photographer will make every effort to get in touch with the Client, but it is the Client's responsibility to contact the Photographer to confirm all events and times.

Retainer

A retainer fee of $1,000 is required for all portrait sessions. This is a non-refundable retainer. In the event of cancellation, the retainer paid is non-refundable. It shall be liquidated for damages to the Photographer in the event of a cancellation, or breach of contract by the Client. No date is reserved until a retainer is received. The retainer shall be applied towards the total cost of the service to be rendered. The balance of the complete package price must be paid before or on the day of event. If final payment is not received, the Photographer will not be expected to attend said event. Additional custom orders (reprints, enlargements, albums) must be paid in full at the time of order.

Cancellation

There shall be no refund of retainer after the signing of the Agreement and the reservation of the photography date. If the event is cancelled within two weeks of the date, the client shall pay the balance of the contract due to the high probability that the Photographer will not be able to further book that date. Once a balance is paid, it is non-refundable. Any other arrangements shall be discussed between the Clients and the Photographer. All arrangements will be put in writing. Cancellation must be in writing even if a phone call was made to inform the Photographer of the cancellation.

Failure to Perform

The parties agree to cheerful cooperation and communication for the best possible result within the definition of this assignment. Due to the limited and subjective nature of the event, the Photographer cannot be held responsible for requested photographs not taken or missed, lack of coverage resulting from weather conditions, or schedule complications caused by but not limited to, anyone in or at the event, or by church or location restrictions. The Photographer is not responsible for lost photo opportunities due to other cameras or flashes, the lateness of the clients or other principles. The Photographer is not responsible for the lack of coverage due to weather conditions, scheduling complications due to lateness of individuals, rules and restrictions of venue, or the rendering of decorations of the location. It is acknowledged that any lists submitted to the Photographer will be used for organizational purposes only and in no way represent photography that will actually be produced. The Photographer will do its best to fulfill all requests but can make no guarantees all images will be delivered. The Photographer recommends that the Client point out important individuals for informal or candid photographs to the photographer during portrait shooting that they wish to have photographed. The Photographer will not be held accountable for not photographing desired people if there is no one to assist in identifying people or gathering people for photographs. The Photographer is not responsible if key individuals fail to appear or cooperate during photography sessions or for missed images due to details not revealed to the Photographer.

2. Consultancy Agreement

Your client is an independent wellness consultant. She works with large and small companies to help them establish wellness programs for their employees. She is negotiating a contract with a Fortune 500 company, which has presented her with the corporation's standard independent consultancy agreement. She would like your advice on whether the agreement should be modified to better suit her needs, or whether she should sign it as is. In particular, she is concerned about intellectual property and the programs that she prepares for the clients. She creates a unique program for each of her clients, and these programs are her "brainchild" and what set her apart from other consultants. Thus, she wants advice about these two IP provisions and how they can be drafted to better protect her and her work creations.

Your client wants:

- To retain as much ownership as she can in the programs that she prepares
- To grant a limited license to her clients to use the programs while retaining ownership
- To receive a fee if possible for the use of the programs (if you think this is advisable)
- To retain as much of the intellectual property created during the consultancy as possible

WELLNESS CONSULTANCY AGREEMENT

On October 28, THIS YEAR ("Effective Date"), Maggie Glenn ("Consultant") and Corporation Grande, Inc. ("Company"), a Delaware corporation, agree (this "Agreement") as follows:

1. **Services and Payment.** Consultant agrees to undertake and complete the Services (as defined in Exhibit A) in accordance with and on the schedule specified in Exhibit A. As the only consideration due Consultant regarding the subject matter of this Agreement, Company will pay Consultant in accordance with Exhibit A.

2. **Ownership; Rights; Proprietary Information; Publicity.**

2.1. Company shall own all right, title and interest (including patent rights, copyrights, trade secret rights, mask work rights, trademark rights, *sui generis* database rights and all other rights of any sort throughout the world) relating to any and all inventions (whether or not patentable), works of authorship, mask works, designations, designs, know-how, ideas and information made or conceived or reduced to practice, in whole or in part, by Consultant in connection with Services or any Proprietary Information (as defined below) (collectively, "Inventions") and Consultant will promptly disclose and provide all Inventions to Company. All Inventions are works made for hire to the extent allowed by law. In addition, if any Invention does not qualify as a work made for hire, Consultant hereby makes all assignments necessary to accomplish the foregoing ownership. Consultant shall further assist Company, at Company's expense, to further evidence, record and perfect such assignments, and to perfect, obtain, maintain, enforce, and defend any rights assigned. Consultant hereby irrevocably designates and appoints Company and its agents as attorneys in fact to act for and in Consultant's behalf to execute and file any document and to do all other lawfully permitted acts to further the foregoing with the same legal force and effect as if executed by Consultant.

2.2. Consultant agrees that all Inventions and all other business, technical and financial information (including, without limitation, the identity of and information relating to customers or employees) Consultant develops, learns or obtains in connection with Services or that are received by or for Company in confidence, constitute "Proprietary Information." Consultant will hold in confidence and not disclose or, except in performing the Services, use any Proprietary Information. However, Consultant shall not be obligated under this paragraph with respect to information Consultant can document is available or becomes readily publicly available without restriction through no fault of Consultant. Upon termination and as otherwise requested by Company, Consultant will promptly return to Company all items and copies containing or embodying Proprietary Information, except that Consultant may keep its personal copies of its compensation records and this Agreement. Consultant also recognizes and agrees that Consultant has no expectation of privacy with respect to Company's telecommunications, networking or information processing systems (including, without limitation, stored computer files, e-mail messages and voice messages) and that Consultant's activity, and any files or messages, on or using any of those systems may be monitored at any time without notice. Consultant further agrees that any property situated on the Company's premises and owned, leased or otherwise possessed by the Company, including computers, computer files, email, voicemail, storage media, filing cabinets or other work areas, is subject to inspection by Company personnel at any time with or without notice.

3. Collective Bargaining Agreement

You are corporate counsel for Totum Factum, a corporation that specializes in the manufacture of widgets, which have become extremely popular throughout the world due to a strong social media campaign by the advertising agency, Stray Dog Advertising. Your workforce is unionized, meaning that you have collective bargaining agreements with the different unions within the company. Each union represents a group of employees who carry out the same job and are similarly situated.

Although business has been strong and sales of your widgets have increased tenfold over the past two years, you want the employees at the company to give up some of the benefits that they have been granted over the years. You are prudent and always anticipating when sales might go down, and with the current contract set to expire in three months, now is the perfect time to renegotiate some of the generous benefits given to your employees as those benefits are quite costly.

The provisions below are those that you and your assistant corporate counsel have identified as being most appropriate for renegotiation with the union representatives. The CEO of Totum Factum would like advice on how the provisions can be written to better serve the corporate's interests before sitting down at the bargaining table. For the CEO, better serving the corporation's interests can be accomplished by keeping down costs of salaries and wages (in any way) and limiting the rights of employees (to the extent allowed by law).

NOTE: Under federal law, employees are entitled to overtime for all hours over forty worked during a workweek.

COLLECTIVE BARGAINING AGREEMENT

Article I: Wages

Effective DATE, all employees shall receive a 4 percent increase in their weekly pay; no such increase shall be less than $25 or exceed $50 per week.

Article II: Hours of Work

Section 1. The normal work day for full-time Employees shall be seven and one-half (7.5) hours and the normal work week shall consist of five (5) days or thirty-seven and one-half (37.5) hours, which need not be worked consecutively, being the normal times worked at straight time rates. A part-time Employee is one who works less than thirty-seven and one-half (37.5) hours per week. The normal workweek shall commence on a Sunday or any other day which shall be selected at the option of the Employer. This section is intended only to provide a basis for the calculation of overtime and it should not be construed as a guarantee of work per day or per week.

Section 2. All regular full-time Employees asked to report for work shall be guaranteed seven and one-half (7.5) hours per day and all part-time Employees asked to report for work shall be guaranteed four (4) hours per day, except those voluntarily agreeing to work less hours.

Section 4. All hours worked in excess of seven and one half (7.5) hours in any one day and/or thirty-seven and one-half (37.5) hours per week, shall be compensated at the rate of time and one-half the straight time hourly classification rate.

Section 5. Time and one-half the straight time hourly classification rate shall be paid for all hours worked on the sixth (6th) day and double time on the seventh (7th) consecutive day of any one (1) work week. For the purposes of this section the day is defined as no less than seven and one half (7.5) hours worked, with the exception of those voluntarily agreeing to work less hours.

Section 6. Overtime is to be calculated on either the daily or weekly basis, whichever is greater, but not on both.

Section 7. Except in the event of an emergency, no Employee may be required to work more than ten (10) hours in any one (1) day. As far as possible the distribution of available overtime shall be equally divided among all Employees, subject, however, to the qualifications of such Employee to do the required work. For the purpose of this Agreement, emergency shall be defined as a malfunction in the production line or plant support, an unavoidable absence with regard to which the Employer was not notified within a reasonable time or an injury occurring during the work day with regard to whose station no replacement can be reasonably found.

Article III: Night Premium

A night premium of twenty cents ($.20) per hour will be paid to employees regularly assigned to second or third shifts. Night premium will be included in the overtime computation for the assigned second and third shift employees.

4. Commercial Lease Agreement

You represent the landlord of a commercial development in downtown West Rapids. Your client has been in contact with a local hair salon that would like to rent one of the available spaces in the commercial development. Your client would now like you to negotiate with the potential tenant to finalize the terms of the lease.

After initial discussions with the potential tenant, your client has told you that these are some important considerations for both the tenant and for him:

- The tenant would like to sign a five-year lease and the maximum amount that she can pay is $1,500 per month, which is less than what your client normally rents the space for. But because the potential tenant is the daughter of a friend of his, he is willing to make this concession.
- The potential tenant is new to the hair salon business. She would like to have the option to operate another business in the space if her hair salon is not successful. Your property is zoned for commercial, although limitations apply to what type of business can operate within the development.
- The potential tenant would also like to have the option to terminate the lease early if her business ventures are not successful. Your client is willing to agree to that, provided that she pays a fee of some sort.
- Your client would also like the tenant responsible for more of the maintenance of the leased space since she is getting a bargain on the rent.
- Your client discussed only the above with the potential tenant; all other provisions can be drafted to best protect your client.

COMMERCIAL LEASE AGREEMENT

This Lease is made between _____ ("Lessor"), and _____, ("Tenant"). Tenant hereby offers to lease from Lessor the real property located in the City of West Rapids, State of Jefferson, with a common address of _____ _____, (the "Real Property"), upon the following terms and conditions. (This document shall hereafter be referred to as the "Lease").

TERMS AND CONDITIONS

A. **Term and Rent.**

Lessor leases to Lessee the above Real Property for a term of _____ years, commencing _____, and terminating on _____, or sooner as provided herein at the annual rental of _____Dollars ($), payable in equal installments of _____ in advance on the first day of each month for that month's rental, during the term of this Lease. All rental payments shall be made to Lessor at the address specified below.

B. **Option to Renew.**

Provided that Tenant is not in default in the performance of this Lease, Tenant shall have the option to renew the Lease for one (or, if more than one option period given, insert number here _____) additional term(s) of _____ months commencing at the expiration of the initial Lease term. All of the terms and conditions of the Lease shall apply during the renewal term except that the monthly rent shall be the sum of $_____. The option shall be exercised by written notice given to Lessor not less than _____ days prior to the expiration of the prior Lease term. (If no other time is inserted, notice shall be given ninety (90) days prior to the expiration of the prior lease term). If notice is not given in the manner provided herein within the time specified, this option shall lapse and expire.

C. **Use.**

Tenant shall use and occupy the Real Property for the commercial purpose of _____. The Real Property shall be used for no other purpose.

D. **Care and Maintenance of Real Property.**

Tenant acknowledges that the Real Property is in good order and repair unless otherwise indicated herein. Tenant shall, at his own expense and at all times, maintain the Real Property in good and safe condition, including plate glass, electrical wiring, plumbing and heating installations and any other system or equipment upon the Real Property and shall surrender the same, at termination hereof, in as good condition as received, normal wear and tear excepted.

5. Airplane Purchase Agreement

You represent the seller of a private airplane who has listed the airplane for sale and has begun negotiations with a buyer. He has contacted you about drafting a purchase agreement for him. He has brought you the agreement that he signed when he bought the aircraft ten years ago, and wonders if this agreement would be suitable for the purposes of this sale.

Because he is selling the airplane for a good price, he wants the buyer to accept more of the risk and the costs of the transaction than what a buyer would normally, or what parties might otherwise negotiate. The buyer is also not represented by an attorney and in fact said that he would rather "rot in hell" than have to pay an attorney. Knowing that, your client would also like to know if you can make this agreement as seller-friendly as possible. The parties have not finalized the price, and your client would like you to leave that blank for now while you revise the other provisions.

For your client, a "seller-friendly" agreement is one that:

- Limits the buyer's rights, such as the time to inspect, to return or to object to any conditions
- Limits the buyer's right to a refund of any deposit made, whether by including a non-refundable deposit or a fee if the deposit is refunded

- Limits the time after the purchase for the buyer to object to any conditions that he identifies and objects to
- Protects the seller's interests in any other way that you can identify

AIRCRAFT PURCHASE AGREEMENT

THIS AGREEMENT, is entered into this _____ day of _____, _____, by and between _____, (the "Buyer"), a(n) _____ (individual(s), corporation, partnership, or LLC) whose principal address is _____ ; and _____ (the "Seller"), a(n) _____ (individual(s), corporation, partnership, or LLC) whose principal address is _____:

IN WITNESS WHEREOF, in consideration of the premises, the mutual covenants contained herein, and other good and valuable consideration, the sufficiency of which is hereby acknowledged, the parties do hereby agree as follows:

1. Sale of Aircraft. Seller agrees to sell to Buyer and Buyer agrees to purchase from Seller the following Aircraft (the "Aircraft"):

Aircraft Make: _____

Aircraft Model:_____ Aircraft Year: _____

Aircraft Registration Number:_____

Aircraft Serial Number:_____

Seller warrants that Seller holds legal title to the Aircraft and that title will be transferred to Buyer free and clear of any liens, claims, charges, or encumbrances. Upon delivery of the Aircraft and payment of the balance of the purchase price, in accordance with this Agreement, Seller shall execute a bill of sale granting good and marketable title to the Aircraft.

2. Consideration. It is agreed that the price of the Aircraft is _____ Dollars ($_____) and is due on delivery of the Aircraft. All monies paid in accordance with this Agreement will be made by cash, cashier's check, certified check, wire transfer, or equivalent.

3. Escrow. It is agreed that within _____(_____) business days after execution of this agreement an escrow account will be established with escrow agent agreeable to both parties. All funds, including the deposit, and the following documents pertaining to this transaction, shall be transmitted through the escrow account: (a) Bill of sale for the Aircraft from Seller to Buyer; and (b) Application for Registration of the Aircraft to Buyer. The fees for the escrow service shall be split evenly between Buyer and Seller.

4. Deposit. The Buyer shall pay a deposit of _____Dollars ($_____) in to the escrow account immediately upon the establishment of that account. The deposit is fully refundable to Buyer except as otherwise stipulated herein. The deposit shall be credited to the purchase price of the Aircraft.

5. Pre-purchase Inspection. After the signing of this Agreement and the payment of the deposit into escrow, the Buyer shall have the right to perform a pre-purchase inspection of the Aircraft. Such inspection shall be at the Buyer's expense and may be performed by an individual(s) of Buyer's choice, so long as he/she/they hold current mechanic certificates issued by the Federal Aviation Administration.

The inspection shall be performed at the Jefferson City Airport. If the Buyer does not perform or have this inspection performed within 15 days of the signing of this Agreement, then Buyer shall be deemed to have waived his right to such inspection. Upon completion of this inspection, Buyer shall have 21 days to notify Seller that he will not purchase the Aircraft. If Buyer elects not to purchase the Aircraft, the Buyer shall notify Seller in writing of this decision. Upon receipt of such notice, Seller shall return, or have returned, within 3 days, to Buyer all payments made by Buyer, except for the deposit.

6. Aircraft Delivery.

It is agreed that the Aircraft and its logbooks shall be delivered on _____(date) at _____ Airport. Payment in full, as described above, is a condition of delivery. Title and risk of loss or damage to the Aircraft shall pass to Buyer at the time of delivery. The Aircraft will be delivered to Buyer in its present condition, normal wear and tear excepted, with a valid FAA Certificate of Airworthiness.

7. Warranties.

Seller warrants that: (a) the Aircraft is in airworthy condition; (b) the Aircraft has a current annual inspection; (c) the Aircraft has a currently effective Standard Category airworthiness certificate issued by the Federal Aviation Administration; (d) all of the Aircraft's logbooks are accurate and current; (e) all applicable Airworthiness Directives have been complied with.

8. Seller's Inability to Perform.

(a) If the Aircraft is destroyed or in Seller's opinion damaged beyond repair, or is seized by the United States Government, Seller shall promptly notify Buyer. On receipt of such notification, this Agreement will be terminated and the Seller shall return to Buyer all payments made in accordance with this Agreement, and Seller will be relieved of any obligation to replace or repair the Aircraft.

(b) Seller will not be responsible or deemed to be in default for delays in performance of this Agreement due to causes beyond Seller's control and not caused by Seller's fault or negligence.

Summary Judgment Analysis Exercise

Overview of the Exercise: This exercise will provide you the opportunity to deepen your understanding of how summary judgment works by analyzing the following short fact patterns and determining whether or not summary judgment should be granted.

Learning Objectives of the Exercise:

This exercise will build your skills to:
- Analyze the elements of summary judgment
- Identify and analyze the applicable case law, facts and standards for summary judgment
- Articulate the factors that courts analyze when deciding motions for summary judgment, the arguments that the parties make and the reasoning behind the granting or denial of a motion

Steps for Completing the Exercise:

- Read the following fact patterns and the accompanying case law.
- With a partner, answer the following questions for each fact pattern.
    - What are the claims that the plaintiff would bring against the defendant? Would the defendant raise any defenses?
    - What are the material facts of the issue(s)? Are they in dispute? Are there some material facts that would not be in dispute? If so, which?
    - If this case were being litigated, who would likely file for summary judgment? Why?
    - What arguments would each party make with regard to the motion for summary judgment?
    - If you were the judge, would you grant or deny the motion? Why?

Research Required for the Exercise:

Before analyzing the fact patterns, review the law of summary judgment.

Summary judgment is a "procedural device used during civil litigation to promptly and expeditiously dispose of a case without a trial."[123] It is used when there is no dispute as to the material facts of the case and a party is entitled to judgment as a matter of law. In legal actions, the term matter of law is used to define a particular area that is the responsibility of the court. Matter of law is distinguished from matter of fact, which is the responsibility of the jury.

Rule 56 of the Federal Rules of Civil Procedure states that "[a] party may move for summary judgment, identifying each claim or defense — or the part of each claim or defense — on which summary judgment is sought. The court shall grant summary judgment if the movant shows that there is no genuine dispute as to any material fact and the movant is entitled to judgment as a matter of law. The court should state on the record the reasons for granting or denying the motion."[124]

The following is a rule statement of the Minnesota rules of summary judgment, which is for all essential purposes the same as the federal rule.[125]

> Summary judgment is appropriate where there are no genuine issues of material fact and where the moving party is entitled to judgment as a matter of law. Minn. R. Civ. P. 56.03; DLH, Inc. v. Russ, 566 N.W.2d 60, 68 (Minn. 1997). When faced with a motion for summary judgment under Rule 56, the Court is to first determine whether a genuine issue of material fact exists. The moving party has the burden of proof, and the evidence must be viewed in the light most favorable to the nonmoving party. Grondahl v. Bulluck, 318 N.W.2d 240, 242 (Minn. 1982).

---

[123] Sudhanshu Joshi, Dictionary of Legal Terms 117 (2011).

[124] Fed. R. Civ. P. 56.

[125] Rule 56 of the Minnesota Rule of Civil Procedure would regulate matters in state court, while the federal rule would apply to those matters in federal court, even if the federal court is adjudicating a substantive matter of state law. See Minn. R. Civ. Pro. 56.01–03 (West 2016) for the exact language.

The mere existence of a factual dispute does not, by itself, make summary judgment inappropriate. Rather, the fact in dispute must be material. Pischke v. Kellen, 384 N.W.2d 201, 205 (Minn. Ct. App. 1986). A material fact is one that will affect the result or outcome of the case, depending upon its resolution. Zappa v. Fahey, 245 N.W.2d 258, 259-60 (Minn. 1976). Any doubt regarding the existence of a genuine fact issue will be resolved in favor of its existence. Rathbun v. W.T. Grant Co., 219 N.W.2d 641, 646 (Minn. 1974). The non-moving party may not rely on general statements of fact to oppose a motion for summary judgment; rather, it must identify specific facts that establish the existence of a triable issue. Hunt v. IBM Mid Am. Employees Fed. Credit Union, 384 N.W.2d 853, 855 (Minn. 1986).

For comparison's sake, here is a rule statement from New York. You can see that the standards and the rules between the two states are similar.

"[T]he proponent of a summary judgment motion must make a prima facie showing of entitlement to judgment as a matter of law, tendering sufficient evidence to demonstrate the absence of any material issues of fact.' "Jacobson v. New York City Health and Hospitals Corp., 22 N.Y.3d 824, 833 (N.Y. 2014) (quoting Alvarez v. Prospect Hosp., 68 N.Y.2d 320, 324, 501 N.E.2d 572 (N.Y. 1986)). "This burden is a heavy one and on a motion for summary judgment, facts must be viewed in the light most favorable to the non-moving party.' " Id. (quoting William J. Jenack Estate Appraisers and Auctioneers, Inc. v. Rabizadeh, 22 N.Y.3d 470, 475, (N.Y. 2013)). "If the moving party meets this burden, the burden then shifts to the non-moving party to establish the existence of material issues of fact which require a trial of the action." Id. (quoting Vega v. Restani Constr. Corp., 965 N.E.2d 240 (N.Y. 2012)), *cited in* Lease Fin. Grp. LLC v. Indries, 49 Misc. 3d 1219(A) (N.Y. Civ. Ct. 2015).

The following are the main points to remember about summary judgment:

- Either party can move for summary judgment at any time, but a court can deny a motion if it is brought too early. See, e.g., Lewis v. Agency Rent-A-Car, 562 N.Y.S.2d 558, 559 (N.Y. App. Div. 1990) (denying plaintiff's motion for summary judgment in personal injury matter because motion was brought before any discovery was conducted, revealing that the "most basic of facts remain unanswered.").
- Summary judgment is issued when there are no genuine issues of material facts, so nothing for a jury to decide.
- The material facts are those that go to the elements of the claim or defense and that affect the result or outcome of a case.
- Court examines the facts in favor of the non-moving party because examining them in favor of the moving party would be unfair.
- The burden rests with the moving party.
- Just because one party thinks that a factual dispute exists doesn't mean that it does – the factual dispute must be material.
- Could a reasonable jury decide the case in favor of the non-moving party, based on the facts and the case law? If the answer is yes, then the motion should be denied.
- Parties rely on admissible evidence such as written discovery responses, deposition testimony, memoranda of law and affidavits in support of or in opposition to the motion.
- If the motion is denied, then the case will move forward to the jury.
- Summary judgment is a procedural device to save time and resources by resolving claims that have no disputes for the jury to decide.

1   Breach of Contract

Under Jefferson law, a claim of breach of contract requires proof of three elements: (1) the formation of a contract, (2) the performance of conditions precedent by the plaintiff, and (3) the breach of the contract by the defendant. Briggs Transp. Co. v. Ranzenberger, 217 N.W.2d 198, 200 (Jeff. 1974). When a party to a contract commits a "material breach," the other party may rescind. Liebsch v. Abbott, 122 N.W.2d 578, 581 (Jeff. 1963). This "annihilates the contract and [returns] ... each party ... to his previously existing rights." Marso v. Mankato Clinic, Ltd., 153 N.W.2d 281, 290 (Jeff. 1967).

Whether a contract exists generally is a question for the fact-finder. <u>Morrisette v. Harrison Int'l Corp.</u>, 486 N.W.2d 424, 427 (Jeff.1992). "The formation of a contract requires communication of a specific and definite offer, acceptance, and consideration." <u>Commercial Assocs. Inc., v. Work Connection Inc.</u>, 712 N.W.2d 772 (Jeff. Ct. App. 2006) (citing <u>Pine River State Bank v. Mettille</u>, 333 N.W.2d 622, 626–27 (Jeff.1983)). Formation of a contract is judged by the objective conduct of the parties rather than their subjective intent. <u>Commercial Assocs. Inc.</u>, 712 N.W.2d at <u>782</u> (citing <u>Cederstrand v. Lutheran Bhd.</u>, 117 N.W.2d 213, 221 (Jeff. 1962)).

Rose Gomez entered into a contract with Stone Arch Construction, LLC according to which Stone Arch would build an addition to Gomez's house. The contract was in writing and stated the specifications of the addition, the date that Stone Arch would begin construction, and the date by which they would finish (January 20, THIS YEAR). The start date of the construction was set at November 12, YEAR -1. Gomez also made a down payment of $20,000.

On November 12, YEAR -1, no one from Stone Arch Construction arrived at Gomez's home to begin the construction. No one answered the phone when Gomez called the company's office. One day passed, and then two days, and soon two weeks had gone by and Gomez had heard nothing from anyone at Stone Arch Construction. It was as though everyone from the company had disappeared.

Gomez's attorney has filed a complaint against Stone Arch Construction in Jefferson State court.

Discuss the questions above regarding summary judgment for the case. Should the court grant the motion? Why or why not?

2. Breach of Contract

Around the same time that Gomez entered into a contract with Stone Arch Construction, another individual, Ahmed Nassar, also contracted with Stone Arch, which agreed to remodel Nassar's kitchen and two bathrooms. Nassar is planning on selling his house and has decided to put it on the market as soon as the remodeling is complete. The terms of the agreement that Nassar entered into with Stone Arch were similar to those of Gomez's agreement: the specifications of the remodeling, the start date and the date by which the construction would be finished (January 15, THIS YEAR), as well as the price and down payment.

Strangely enough, Stone Arch did not disappear like it did with Gomez's project. The workers showed up on the stipulated date and began construction. The project went according to plan, except that the construction was completed at 10:00 in the morning on January 17, THIS YEAR. Nassar now refuses to pay Stone Arch because he claims that they finished past the stipulated date and that their breach relived him of his obligation to pay them for their work.

Nassar has hired an attorney who has filed a claim against Stone Arch Construction, LLC.

Discuss the questions above regarding summary judgment for the case. Should the court grant the motion? Why or why not?

3. UCC Defective Goods

This case involves a business owner named Keith Moore, who operates a snowmobile dealership in northern Jefferson. In May YEAR -1, Moore bought a large number of snowmobiles from the regional distributor. With the meteorologists forecasting cold temperatures and above-average snowfall this winter, Moore was hoping to have a successful winter season at his dealership. Moore purchased the snowmobiles during the summer because the prices were slightly lower and because it was easier to transport the vehicles to Moore's dealership without the snow and ice on the roads.

When the first snow arrived in November, Moore took some of the new snowmobiles out for a test ride before his customers came to purchase them. While riding, he immediately noticed that the snowmobile he was riding would not shift gears and would not drive faster than 20 mph. Moore began to test-drive each of the snowmobiles. Much to his dismay, he discovered that of the fifty-five snowmobiles that he had purchased, twenty were defective. All had the same problem that they failed to shift gears and would not drive faster than 20 mph. Moore promptly notified the distributor and manufacturer of the snowmobiles of the defects and told them that he was revoking his acceptance of those defective ones. Both the distributor and the manufacturer told Moore that his revocation was too late since he had purchased the snowmobiles in May of last year.

Moore has now filed a claim in Jefferson state court against the distributor and manufacturer. This section of the Jefferson Uniform Commercial Code (UCC) is at issue.

> 336.2-608 REVOCATION OF ACCEPTANCE
>
> IN WHOLE OR IN PART.
>
> 1) The buyer may revoke an acceptance of a lot or commercial unit whose nonconformity substantially impairs its value to the buyer if it was accepted
>   a) on the reasonable assumption that its nonconformity would be cured and it has not been seasonably cured; or
>   b) without discovery of such nonconformity if the acceptance was reasonably induced either by the difficulty of discovery before acceptance or by the seller's assurances.
> 2) Revocation of acceptance must occur within a reasonable time after the buyer discovers or should have discovered the ground for it and before any substantial change in condition of the goods which is not caused by their own defects. It is not effective until the buyer notifies the seller of it.
> 3) A buyer who so revokes has the same rights and duties with regard to the goods involved as if the buyer had rejected them.

In January THIS YEAR, later in the season and while the litigation was underway in the Jefferson state court, Moore discovered that ten of the remaining thirty-five snowmobiles that did not have the initial defect could drive no faster than 40 mph. The specifications of the model of snowmobiles that Moore had purchased stated that the vehicles could travel at speeds "up to 45 mph." Moore has now contacted again the distributor and the manufacturer, told them that these ten snowmobiles are defective and that he wants to return them. As before, both the distributor and the manufacturer refused, telling Moore that it was too late to return them.

Moore's attorney has asked the court for permission to amend the complaint to include the facts of these additional ten snowmobiles. The court has granted permission and the complaint includes allegations about the first twenty defective snowmobiles as well as the other ten.

Discuss the questions above regarding summary judgment for the case. Should the court grant the motion? Why or why not?

4. Duty to Warn

This matter involves negligence and whether a property owner can be held liable for failing to warn an individual about a danger on his or her property.

In this case, a young woman, Rebecca Wu, was accidently shot by a friend, Evan Simmons. The incident happened at a cabin owned by Mark Francisco, who was the boyfriend of the mother of a young man named Jeff Warner. Warner had invited Wu, Simmons and another friend (all of whom are of legal age) to the cabin for the weekend; Francisco was unaware that the four friends were at the cabin for the weekend and had told Warner on several occasions that he was not to go to or use the cabin without his permission.

One month before the accident, Francisco had placed a loaded hunting rifle near the door to the cabin to protect against bears. When the four friends entered the cabin, Warner told his friends not to play with it. He did not know if it was loaded or not. Despite Warner's warning, Simmons picked up the gun. Warner told him to put it down. Several hours later, Simmons again picked up the gun. This time, the gun discharged, hitting Wu in the face and causing severe injuries.

Wu filed a negligence claim against Simmons, Warner and Francisco. She settled in pre-litigation negotiations with Simmons for an undisclosed amount. Wu now claims that Warner should have warned her about the gun and about the dangers that is posed, and that Francisco was negligent in keeping the loaded gun in the cabin (Francisco has a valid hunting license and legally purchased the gun). Wu claims that since Warner did not warn her of the danger of the gun and since she was injured, Warner should be held liable for her injuries.

Negligence is generally defined as the failure "to exercise such care as persons of ordinary prudence usually exercise under such circumstances." Flom v. Flom, 291 N.W.2d 914, 916 (Jeff. 1980) (citations omitted). To recover for a claim of negligence, a plaintiff must prove (1) the existence of a duty of care, (2) a breach of that duty, (3) an injury, and (4) that the breach of the duty of care was a proximate cause of the injury. See Funchess v. Cecil Newman Corp., 632 N.W.2d 666, 672 (Jeff.2001) (citing Lubbers v. Anderson, 539 N.W.2d 398, 401 (Jeff.1995)).

Generally, a defendant's duty to a plaintiff is a threshold question because "[i]n the absence of a legal duty, the negligence claim fails." Gilbertson v. Leininger, 599 N.W.2d 127, 130 (Jeff.1999) (citation omitted); see also State Farm Fire & Cas. v. Aquila Inc., 718 N.W.2d 879, 887 (Jeff.2006) (stating that plaintiffs failed to present a prima facie case for negligence when they could not establish that defendants owed a duty of reasonable care). But we have continued to recognize that generally "[i]n law, we are not our brother's keeper." Lundgren v. Fultz, 354 N.W.2d 25, 27 (Jeff.1984). Inaction by a defendant — such as a failure to warn — constitutes negligence only when the defendant has a duty to act for the protection of others. See Ruberg v. Skelly Oil Co., 297 N.W.2d 746, 750 (Jeff.1980).

Under Jefferson law, a property owner has a reasonable duty to protect persons on the property from injury, unless the risk of injury is open and obvious. Peterson v. W.T. Rawleigh Co., 144 N.W.2d 555, 557-58 (Jeff. 1966) ; RESTATEMENT (SECOND) OF TORTS § 343A (1965). The test for whether a condition is "open and obvious" is not whether the condition was actually seen, "but whether it was in fact visible." Bundy v. Holmquist, 669 N.W. 2d 627, 633 (Jeff. Ct. App. 2003) (citing Martinez v. MN Zoological Gardens, 526 N.W. 2d 416, 418 (Jeff. Ct. App. 1995).

"When a brief inspection would have revealed the condition, [then] it is not concealed", it is visible, and as such is an open and obvious hazard of which a property owner need not give notice. Johnson v. State, 478 N.W.2d 769, 773 (Jeff. 1991) ; see also Sowles v. Urschel Laboratories, Inc., 595 F.2d 1361, 1365 (8th Cir. 1979) ("[N]o one needs notice of what he knows or reasonably may be expected to know."); Sperr v. Ramsey Cty., 429 N.W.2d 315, 317-318 (Jeff. Ct. App. 1998) (no duty exists to warn pedestrian of low-hanging branch that is clearly visible); Lawrence v. Hollerich, 394 N.W.2d 853, 856 (Jeff. Ct. App. 1986) (steep grade of hill so apparent that no warning was necessary); Bisher v. Homart Dev. Co., 328 N.W.2d 731, 733-734 (Jeff. 1983) (obvious danger presented by large planter in shopping center precluded necessity to warn customers of its presence); Hammerlind v. Clear Lake Star Factory Skydiver's Club, 258 N.W.2d 590, 593-94 (Jeff. 1977) (lake was obvious danger to parachutists); Munoz v. Applebaum's Food Market., Inc., 196 N.W.2d 921,921-922, (Jeff. 1972) (20-foot-square pool of water was an obvious hazard and no warning was required). The Munoz Court reaffirmed the general rule accepted by Jefferson courts that recovery is barred when the danger to the injured is open and obvious. Munoz, 196 N.W.2d at 922.

Discuss the questions above regarding summary judgment for the case. Should the court grant the motion? Why or why not?

5. Duty to Protect

Negligence is generally defined as the failure "to exercise such care as persons of ordinary prudence usually exercise under such circumstances." Flom v. Flom, 291 N.W.2d 914, 916 (Jeff. 1980) (citations omitted). To recover for a claim of negligence, a plaintiff must prove (1) the existence of a duty of care, (2) a breach of that duty, (3) an injury, and (4) that the breach of the duty of care was a proximate cause of the injury. See Funchess v. Cecil Newman Corp., 632 N.W.2d 666, 672 (Jeff.2001) (citing Lubbers v. Anderson, 539 N.W.2d 398, 401 (Jeff.1995)).

Generally, a defendant's duty to a plaintiff is a threshold question because "[i]n the absence of a legal duty, the negligence claim fails." Gilbertson v. Leininger, 599 N.W.2d 127, 130 (Jeff.1999) (citation omitted); see also State Farm Fire & Cas. v. Aquila Inc., 718 N.W.2d 879, 887 (Jeff.2006) (stating that plaintiffs failed to present a prima facie case for negligence when they could not establish that defendants owed a duty of reasonable care). But we have continued to recognize that generally "[i]n law, we are not our brother's keeper." Lundgren v. Fultz, 354 N.W.2d 25, 27 (Jeff.1984). Inaction by a defendant — such as a failure to warn — constitutes negligence only when the defendant has a duty to act for the protection of others. See Ruberg v. Skelly Oil Co., 297 N.W.2d 746, 750 (Jeff.1980).

An affirmative duty to control the conduct of a third party or to protect another can be established when a special relationship exists between either the actor and the third person ("duty to control") or the actor and the other person ("duty of who has a 'right to protect'"). Delgado v. Lohmar, 289 N.W.2d 479, 483 (Jeff. 1979). "[S]pecial relationship[s] giving rise to a duty to warn . . . [are generally] only found on the part of common carriers, innkeepers, possessors of land who hold it open to the public, and persons who have custody of another under circumstances in which that other person is deprived of normal opportunities of self-protection and that other person is in a vulnerable or dependent position." Harper v. Herman, 499 N.W.2d 472, 474 (Jeff. 1993) (special relationship not found between "social host" of private boat and guest on that boat) (citing RESTATEMENT (SECOND) OF TORTS § 315 (1965)).

The case in litigation involves a college-aged young man, Sam Pierce, who was left outside on a cold winter night last January. He had been out drinking with some friends, all of whom were quite drunk at the end of the evening. Rather than drive home, they took at taxi. At about 1:30 a.m., they arrived on the street where Pierce lived. One of Pierce's friends told the taxi driver to stop when they were in front of Pierce's house. Pierce got out of the taxi, said goodbye to his friends and made his way up the front path to the house. The taxi drove away.

Unfortunately, in his drunken state, Pierce was unable to find his house key in his pocket. He decided to sit down on the chair on the front porch, but soon passed out. The temperature plummeted to minus 25° F (-31° C) that night. Early the next morning, at about 6:00 a.m., Pierce's neighbor happened to notice Pierce slumped over on the porch chair in the cold. He called an ambulance because Pierce was unresponsive. The ambulance arrived and took Pierce to the emergency room. There, the doctors were able to bring Pierce's body temperature back to normal and to revive him. However, both of Pierce's hands had to be amputated because they had frozen in the extreme cold. He had to have six of his toes amputated as well.

Pierce has sued the taxi company and his friends who let him get out of the taxi, claiming that all of them had a duty to protect him from the cold and failed to do so when they let him get out of the taxi and didn't ensure that he was safely in the house before driving away.

Discuss the questions above regarding summary judgment for the case. Should the court grant the motion? Why or why not?

6. Battery

A battery is a harmful or offensive contact with a person resulting from an act intended to cause the person such contact. Saba v. Darling, 575 A.2d 1240, 1242 (Jeff. 1990) (citing RESTATEMENT (SECOND) OF TORTS, § 13 (1965)). The act in question must be some positive or affirmative action on the part of the defendant. Id. (citing PROSSER & KEETON, THE LAW OF TORTS, § 9 (5th ed.1984)). A battery may occur through a defendant's direct or indirect contact with the plaintiff. Nelson v. Carroll, 735 A.2d 1096, 1100 (Jeff. 1999). Therefore, indirect contact, such as when a bullet strikes a victim, may constitute a battery. See Nelson, 735 A.2d at 1101 ("It is enough that the defendant sets a force in motion which ultimately produces the result . . . ." (citing PROSSER & KEETON, THE LAW OF TORTS § 9, at 40 (5th ed.1984))). Some form of intent is required for battery. Nelson, 735 A.2d at 1100.

For purposes of liability for battery, a defendant satisfies the intent required for the tort if his or her intent is directed at causing the relevant tortious consequence to a third party, rather than to the plaintiff, but the defendant's conduct causes harm or injury to the plaintiff. Nelson, 735 A.2d at 1100 (citing PROSSER & KEETON, THE LAW OF TORTS § 9, at 40 (5th ed. 1984)). Moreover, a purely accidental touching is not sufficient to establish the intent requirement for battery. Nelson, 735 A.2d at 1100 (citation omitted).

You represent two plaintiffs in separate battery cases. The first involves an elderly woman who was walking at a local park one afternoon. She was on the walking path when suddenly, a large dog came running towards her without warning. The dog jumped up against her and violently threw its large paws on her shoulders, causing her to lose her balance and fall to the ground. Your client was bruised and shaken, but fortunately did not break any bones.

You have filed a claim of battery against the owner of the dog. During litigation, it has been revealed that several witnesses heard the dog's owner tell the dog "go get 'em" before unleashing the dog and pointing in the general direction of your client. There were several other people on the walking path near your client when the incident occurred. The defendant admits that he wanted his dog to knock down someone, but claims that the intended target was a friend of his that he was mad at who was walking near your client.

The second case involves a woman, Sara, who was standing in line at a movie theater one evening, waiting to buy tickets. Suddenly, she was pushed from behind by a man. Falling forward from the strength of the push, she fell into another patron who was in line in front of her. The man who pushed Sara claims that he lost his balance when he bent over to tie his shoe, put out his arm to break his fall and accidently fell into Sara, pushing her. A witness standing nearby claims that he saw the man put out his arm before pushing Sara. He is unsure if the man was tying his shoe when this happened as he didn't see anything before Sara was pushed.

You represent Sara. The other patron who was pushed by Sara has also filed a claim of battery, naming Sara as the defendant.

Discuss the questions above regarding summary judgment for each of the cases. Should the court grant the motion? Why or why not?

7. IIED

In order to sustain a claim for intentional infliction of emotional distress, a defendant must show: (1) there was extreme and outrageous conduct, (2) the conduct was intentional or reckless, (3) it caused emotional distress, and (4) the distress was severe. Hubbard v. United Press Int'l, Inc., 330 N.W.2d 428, 438–39 (Jeff.1983). The conduct must be "so atrocious that it passes the boundaries of decency and is utterly intolerable to the civilized community." Haagenson v. Nat'l Farmers Union Prop. & Casualty Co., 277 N.W.2d 648, 652 n. 3 (Jeff.1979). The distress must be so severe that no reasonable person can be expected to endure it. Hubbard, 330 N.W.2d at 439 (citing RESTATEMENT (SECOND) OF TORTS § 46 cmt. (1965)). Summary judgment is proper where a person does not meet the high standard of proof needed for an intentional infliction of emotional distress claim. Lee v. Metro Airport Comm'n, 428 N.W.2d 815, 823, cited in Strauss v. Thorne, 490 N.W.2d 908, 913 (Jeff. Ct. App. 1992).

This case involves a man named Henry Rodriquez, who was a server at a restaurant in West Rapids, Jefferson for more than fifteen years. The offer letter and employee handbook stated that he was an at-will employee. Henry was always a model employee.

To save costs, the business owner decided to change the service model of his restaurant, which is now the type where the customers order for themselves at the counter and are then assigned a number, which is called when the food is ready. The customer then goes to pick the food up. Because of this new service model, the owner does not need the same number of servers working for him. On December 23, he notified Rodriquez that he was being laid off.

Because he was laid off only two days before Christmas, Rodriquez became very anxious and worried about the presents that he had bought for his children. He didn't know how he would pay for the presents and the bills that were piling up. Rodriquez wasn't able to sleep for nearly two weeks. He lost a significant amount of weight and began to see a therapist to help him with his severe anxiety and depression. He has even developed an ulcer as a result of being laid off.

Rodriquez has contacted an attorney, who filed a claim of intentional infliction of emotional distress against the restaurant owner, asking for more than $500,000 in emotional damages due to the "outrageous" actions of the restaurant owner.

Discuss the questions above regarding summary judgment for the case. Should the court grant the motion? Why or why not?

8. Fit or Unfit Leased Premises

Jeff. Stat. § 504B.161, Subd. 1 states that in every residential lease, the landlord covenants that the "premises and all common areas are fit for the use intended by the parties."

Jack and Diane rent a house in Sweetwater, Jefferson from a landlord named Claire Barnes. Jack and Diane have two children and a cat. Barnes has not changed the carpeting in the house for more than ten years. There are stains on it, many of which were there before Jack and Diane moved in two years ago, and it is dirty.

Diane has recently applied for a license to run a small day-care center from the house. Barnes is aware of this and has given her approval for the business to operate from her property. However, Jack and Diane now claim that because the carpet is stained and quite old, the leased premises are no longer "fit for the use intended by the parties." Because Diane will be operating a business in the home, they claim that the premises are even less fit because the image of her new business will be harmed when clients and potential clients see the stained carpet. The carpet could also be harmful for the toddlers who crawl on the floor.

Jack and Diane have filed a rent escrow claim with the court, asking that their monthly rent ($1,200) be reduced because of the stained carpet.

Discuss the questions above regarding summary judgment for the case. Should the court grant the motion? Why or why not?

Mock Negotiation

Overview of the Exercise: This exercise simulates a negotiation between the attorney for the third-party plaintiff, Gateway West Development, Inc. and the third-party defendant, Stray Dog Advertising. The parties are preparing their memoranda of law for the motion for summary judgment that SDA has filed. On the advice of their attorneys, both Greg Blackman and Pamela Park have agreed to attempt to negotiate a settlement to the dispute for strategic reasons.

You will be assigned the role of counsel for Stray Dog Advertising or Gateway West Development, depending on the client that you are representing. Before the meeting, review the preparatory and confidential information that you have been provided.

Strategy in Litigation: Attorneys engaged in litigation, or considering commencing litigation on behalf of a client, face numerous strategic decisions that will affect the potential outcome of the case.[126]

One of the most important initial strategic decisions that an attorney faces at the beginning of a lawsuit is which claims she will bring. Some attorneys decide to bring all possible claims and see what "sticks," or is successful, while others prefer to choose to bring only those that are likely to be successful, rather than those that are likely to be dismissed.

Another important decision to make at the beginning of litigation is which defendant (or defendants) will be brought into the case. In this Unit, Julianna Diaz's attorney made an initial decision to only name Gateway West as a defendant. Why do you think he made that decision? If you were her attorney, who would you have named as a defendant? Why?

As litigation proceeds, more important strategic decisions must be made: Should the defendant file a motion to dismiss? Which witnesses will be deposed? Will the parties attempt to settle the matter through mediation, negotiation or another alternative dispute resolution method? What other strategic decisions do you think an attorney would make during litigation and after litigation is over? What considerations come into play when making strategic decisions in litigation?

When a case involves third-party litigation, such as the <u>Gateway West Development, Inc. v. Stray Dog Advertising, LLC</u> matter, different strategies are taken into consideration, often before a third-party complaint is even filed.

When a defendant files a third-party complaint against another party, alleging that the third-party defendant is either completely or partially responsible for the plaintiff's damages, the plaintiff now has two parties at whom it can point its fingers of blame. In essence, the plaintiff can tell the jury, "It doesn't matter which defendant is liable, you choose, but one of the two is responsible for the damages I suffered." From the plaintiff's perspective, it is better to have two parties to blame rather than one.

To avoid such a scenario, third-party litigants will often negotiate a type of truce before a complaint is filed. They'll agree to first let the "main" complaint be decided between the plaintiff and the defendant. Or if litigation has commenced, the parties will ask the court to issue a stay of the proceedings until the main matter is finalized. Only if the defendant is found liable for any or all of the plaintiff's damages will the third-party action then be commenced so that those two parties can determine how and if the liability will be apportioned between them, without the distraction of the plaintiff and his claims. Strategically, it makes sense.

In the <u>Gateway West Development, Inc. v. Stray Dog Advertising, LLC</u> matter, this strategic conversation and decision-making didn't happen. Instead, with summary judgment around the corner, counsel for the two parties will meet to try to negotiate a settlement to the case.

---

[126] See Rule 1.2 of the Rules of Professional Conduct and its comments for guidance on who is responsible for making decisions in litigation, the attorney or the client, and how the decision-making authority is shared between them. See also Arnold R. Rosenfeld, *In Lawyer-Client Relationship Who Makes the Decisions?* New England In House (July 12, 2012) http://newenglandinhouse.com/2012/07/16/in-lawyer-client-relationship-who-makes-the-decisions/ (last visited May 7, 2016).

Learning Objectives of the Exercise:

This assignment will build your skills to:

- Use monetary and non-monetary interests of parties in negotiating settlement agreement
- Identify primary obstacles to reaching a mutually beneficial settlement agreement
- Implement negotiation strategies and tactics

Steps for Completing the Exercise:

- Read the preparatory information that your instructor has given you
- Be familiar with the case law regarding premises liability and the fact pattern of <u>Gateway West Development, Inc. v. Stray Dog Advertising, LLC</u>
- Articulate the arguments for your client's position and anticipate opposing counsel's.

Writing Exercise:

If time allows and if directed by your instructor, you and opposing counsel will also prepare a draft of the settlement agreement that your clients will sign after you have reached a negotiated agreement.

To complete this task, you first must find a template of a settlement agreement. In real life, few attorneys start from scratch (i.e. from zero) when drafting any contract or agreement. Why recreate the wheel? Instead, attorneys will use a template and then adapt it to their purposes.

Thus, using a template is part of practice. Templates can be found in a law firm's database of documents, or many attorneys will take an agreement from a past case and modify and adapt it to a new case. Bar associations have templates and forms available (often for a fee) and many are available online as well.

But using a template comes with risks too. Even though the template is prepared, you can't simply cut and paste it to a new Word document and think you are good to go. Here are some questions that you have to ask yourself as you analyze a template:

- Does it include provisions that are illegal or violate some law, either because it was written by an attorney in another state or because the law has changed?
- Is it written to be beneficial to one side? For example, is it a very landlord-friendly lease agreement? If it is and if you represent the tenant, you will need to revise it.
- Does it include all the essential provisions? Just because a template is available doesn't mean that it is complete.
- Does your client's matter have unique circumstances or agreements that must be incorporated? It isn't always possible to find a template that perfectly suits your situation, so understanding that will make it easier to find a template that works and that can be adapted.

You also want to be very careful when you use a template to ensure that you remove all references that reveal that this was a template, or that reveal that the document was used with other clients or parties.

Once you have found a template online, adapt it to suit the agreement that you reached.

Grading: This exercise is not graded. After the meetings, the class will debrief on how the negotiations went.

Presentation:
If SDA or Gateway West Were Your Client ...

Overview of the Exercise: For this exercise, you will make a professional presentation in which you discuss the following question:

If Stray Dog Advertising were your client in your home country and if Pamela came to you for legal advice about the litigation between SDA and Gateway West, what would you do and what advice would you give her?

OR

If Gateway West were your client in your home country and if Greg came to you for legal advice about the litigation between SDA and Gateway West, what would you do and what advice would you give him?

You will make the presentation about the client that you are representing.

Learning Objectives of the Exercise:

This exercise will build your skills to:

- Examine the dispute over premises liability from the perspective of your country's legal system
- Compare your country's legal system with the U.S. legal system
- Explain how the dispute would be handled in your country's legal system and the advice that you would provide to your client
- Understand specific information from your classmates' presentations

Steps for Completing the Exercise:

- Analyze the premises liability fact pattern under your country's laws
- Determine whether or not your client would have viable claims or defenses if the case were brought in your country's legal system
- Explain how the case would be handled in your country's legal system and what the probable outcome would be
- Explain what legal advice you would give your client if they came to you for legal advice in your home country

Research Required for the Exercise: The research you are required to do depends on your knowledge of these claims in your country's legal system. It is presumed that you are familiar with the law and with how you would approach this issue if SDA or Gateway West were a client of yours.

Grading: This presentation is not graded. Depending on the size of your class and your instructor's choice, you will present to your fellow classmates or to the entire class.

Handouts:

As part of your presentation, you must create a handout for your classmates, and the handouts must include fill-in-the-blank questions that your classmates must complete with information that you present during the presentation. Each handout must include at least five questions to complete.

For example, if a U.S. law student were giving a presentation about how the case would be litigated in the United States, he could include on his handout this question:

In complex litigation in the United States, a defendant can file a _____ complaint against another party for indemnity or _____ and the defendant becomes the _____ and the other party becomes the _____ _____.

As you are speaking, your classmates will have to listen, follow what you are saying and fill in the blanks. If you are listening to one of your classmate's presentations and are unsure about an answer, you should ask him or her to repeat so you can fill in the blank(s).

Grammar Review:

The basis of this exercise is hypothetical or conditional verbs: *if SDA or Gateway West were your client, what would you do?*

Remember the grammar when discussing hypothetical conditions.

Present: **IF + PAST SIMPLE, WOULD + BASE VERB**

*If Pamela **called** me to schedule an appointment, I **would tell** her to visit me at my office.*

NOTE: We use "were" for all tenses with the verb "to be" when using a conditional verb.

*If I **were** you, I **would not take** that class.*

*If Pamela **were** my client, I **would tell** her that she would likely be successful in defending against this claim.*

Past: **IF + PAST PERFECT, WOULD + HAVE + PAST PARTICIPLE**

*If Greg **had called** Pamela to clarify who was responsible for the water heater space, they **would have discussed** this and perhaps avoided any litigation.*

*If Pamela **had called** me before I left for the day, I **would have told** her to come to my office at 12:00.*

Information Pages

Office Memo: Premises Liability

Overview of the Assignment: For this assignment, you will write an office memo to the Senior Partner, summarizing your research on premises liability and providing your prediction of what will happen in the litigation.

Learning Objectives of the Assignment:

This assignment will build your skills to:

- Efficiently communicate in a written format
- Explain complex matters clearly and concisely
- Analyze and apply the rules of law regarding premises liability

Research for the Assignment:

You are not required to do any outside research for this assignment. You should base your analysis on the Massachusetts premises liability statutes and cases that you have read:

- <u>Young v. Garawcki</u>, 402 N.E.2d 1045 (Mass. 1980).
- <u>Humphrey v. Byron</u>, 850 N.E.2d 1044 (Mass. 2006).
- <u>Monterosso v. Gaudette</u>, 391 N.E.2d 948 (Mass. App. Ct. 1979).
- <u>Bishop v. TES Realty Trust</u>, 942 N.E.2d (Mass. 2011).
- <u>Chausse v. Coz</u>, 540 N.E.2d 667 (Mass. 1989).
- <u>The Great Atlantic and Pacific Tea Co. v. Yanofsky</u>, 403 N.E.2d 370 (Mass. 1980).

If you want to practice your legal research skills, you can look for and use other cases that you find. However, if you do search on Westlaw, LexisNexis or Bloomberg Law, be sure to limit your search and the cases you use to Massachusetts law and remember to change the citations to Jefferson as in indicated in the introduction.

Format of the Completed Assignment:

Your response should be in an office memo format and should include the following:

- Summary of the facts
- The relevant law
- Analysis of the law to the fact pattern
- Conclusion about how you think a court would rule if this matter were to go to court
- Your advice to the client about how to proceed

Follow the following format:

- 1 inch (2.54 cm.) margins (top/bottom and sides)
- 12 font, Times New Roman font
- Double spaced
- Maximum eight pages

Notes: This memo should be predictive and not persuasive. You are not trying to persuade the senior partner or the client about the strength of your arguments or urge him or her to take a particular course of action; you are only trying to inform about the law, how it applies to our case, how you think a court would rule and what advice you have.

In a memo, you can also use formatting like underlining, bold font or italics. You can also create headings and subheadings to organize your answer.

For additional information about office memos and e-memos, as well as samples, refer to the online additional resources.

Grading: This assignment is worth 102 points.

LEGAL CONTENT	0-6 points	8 points	10 points	12 points	Points
Issue statement (IS)	Document does not include an IS or includes IS that fails to properly identify the legal issue(s) and the applicable law	Identifies the legal issue(s) and correctly states the applicable law with minor mistakes	Identifies the legal issue(s) and correctly states the applicable law	Identifies the legal issue(s) and correctly states the applicable law in an exceptionally creative and concise way	_____/12
Short Answer	Document does not include a short answer or includes a short answer with significant mistakes	Responds to IS but with key facts or applicable legal principles missing	Responds to IS with key facts and applicable legal principles with no meaningful errors	Clearly and concisely responds to IS with key facts and applicable legal principles and no irrelevancies	_____/12
Facts	Few or none of the relevant facts are included; difficult to follow or understand	Most relevant facts are included as well as non-relevant ones; at times difficult to follow	Relevant facts are included with occasional irrelevancies; easy to follow	All relevant facts are included with no irrelevancies; story is clearly and concisely told to reader in objective way	_____/12
Rule	Hard to follow and understand; does not include relevant sources or cites inappropriate sources; no rule application	Cites to some relevant sources but is incomplete in covering all relevant aspects of the rule; includes some rule application	Cite only to relevant sources and mostly clear; rule application explains but not fully how rule has been applied	Clear and concise; includes only relevant sources and includes all parts of rule necessary for analysis; clear rule application	_____/12
Analysis	Contains conclusory statements and/or no case law; facts are analyzed in a conclusory or insufficient way	Uses some case law but does not analogize or distinguish or explain its application; some conclusory statements; facts briefly analyzed	Uses case law to show how rule applies to case; case law is compared and contrasted with success; most facts are analyzed	Analyzes case law completely, comparing it fully to client matter; facts are thoroughly analyzed in an objective way	_____/12
Conclusion/ Recommendations	No conclusion or recommendations are included in document	A brief conclusion is included but without sufficient client advice	Paper includes conclusion and recommendations	Paper includes full conclusion of the legal analysis and facts and presents creative and thoughtful recommendations	_____/12
Citations	No sources are cited in document	Some sources are cited, but inconsistently; citation format is inconsistent	All citations are present; correct format is mostly used	All citations are present; correct format is used throughout document	_____/12
WRITING	2	4	5	6	Points
Formatting	Document does not follow format instructions or the sample provided	Document attempts to follow instructions and sample provided	Document follows the instructions and sample provided with no meaningful errors	Document exactly follows the instructions and sample provided	_____/6
Organization	No structure or organization; free flow of ideas	Structure & organization present but reorganization or headings needed for full clarity	Document is clearly organized and structured with proper use of heading and subheadings	Document is exceptionally well organized and structured with proper use of headings and subheadings	_____/6
Syntax Mechanics	Contains numerous and distracting grammatical and mechanical errors that impede understanding	Contains some grammatical and mechanical errors that impede understanding	Contains few grammatical and mechanical errors but none that impede understanding	Contains no grammatical and mechanical errors; native-like use of English	_____/6
TOTAL					_____/102

Mock Client Meeting

Overview of the Assignment: This assignment simulates a client meeting between you and your client, Pamela Park of Stray Dog Advertising, LLC or Greg Blackman of Gateway West Development, Inc. For this exercise, you will meet with your client and explain to him or her the status of the litigation of <u>Gateway West Development, Inc. v. Stray Dog Advertising, LLC</u>, the results of your analysis about how a court might rule on the motion for summary judgment and your recommendations on how to proceed.

Learning Objectives of the Assignment:

This assignment will build your skills to:

- Explain and clarify the legal positions of the parties and describe potential outcomes to your client
- Respond to technical questions about litigation
- Incorporate technical legal English vocabulary that relates to commercial landlords and premises liability and use appropriate layperson explanations for client

Steps for Completing the Assignment:

- Read and be familiar with the Main Assignment File
- Be familiar with the premises liability cases that you have been assigned
- Recommended:
  - Anticipate the questions that you think your client might ask and prepare possible responses;
  - Draft an outline of what you would like to cover in the meeting.

Grading: This assignment is worth 102 points.

Note: Remember that part of the grading is also based on your professional demeanor. You are expected to arrive punctually, be dressed in professional attire and act as you would with a client in real life. You should play the part from when you come into the meeting room.

Punctuality: Student-attorney arrived on time to meeting: YES _____ (10 points) NO _____ (0 points)

Professional Attire: Student-attorney was dressed in appropriate professional attire: YES _____ (10 points) NO _____ (0 points)

Professional Demeanor: Student-attorney acted in a professional manner w/ client: YES _____ (10 points) NO _____ (0 points)

GRADING CRITERIA	0- 6 points	8 points (C or 75%)	10 points (B or 85%)	12 points	Points received
Engagement I (questions)	Attorney does not ask client any questions; engages in monologue	Attorney asks few questions; questions are hard to follow or show minimal preparation or understanding of matter	Attorney asks basic questions that demonstrate understanding of matter and preparation	Attorney asks thoughtful, insightful and creative questions that demonstrate deep preparation & understanding of matter	_____/12
Engagement II (answers)	Attorney does not respond to client's questions	Attorney responds to questions, but incorrectly or with hard to follow answers	Attorney responds promptly and correctly to all of client's questions	Attorney responds promptly and correctly to all of client's questions with creative, thoughtful and insightful answers that show a deep understanding of the issues	_____/12
Knowledge of Applicable Law	Attorney provides no explanation of the applicable law	Attorney provides explanation of with serious mistakes, or hard to follow (e.g. use of legal jargon)	Attorney provides clear explanation of with some mistakes; uses some legal jargon unnecessarily or without explanations that client can understand	Attorney provides clear, concise and correct explanation of the law with legal jargon when appropriate or w/ explanations client can understand	_____/12
Ability to Analyze Applicable Law	Attorney provides does not provide an analysis of the law for the client	Attorney attempts to analyze the law but provides incomplete or incorrect analysis	Attorney provides analysis of the law with no significant mistakes or misstatements of the law or facts	Attorney provides a clear, concise and correct analysis of the law as it applies to the client matter	_____/12
Advice and Recommendations	Attorney provides no advice or poor advice for client	Attorney provides not comprehensive or inaccurate advice	Attorney provides comprehensive and accurate advice to client on his/her legal matter	Attorney provides thoughtful and creative solutions for client	_____/12
Organization	Meeting is disorganized and hard to follow or lacks any organization	Meeting has some organization but is still confusing for client for how information is presented	Meeting is clearly organized and easy to follow	Meeting is clearly organized and is easy to follow; attorney takes extra steps to ensure client's understanding	_____/12
TOTAL					_____/72
TOTAL FROM PUNCTUALITY AND PROFESSIONALISM					_____/30

Total   ___/102

Client Advice Letter

• •

Overview of the Assignment: For this assignment, you will write a follow-up and advice letter to Pamela Park or Greg Blackman, summarizing your research on premises liability, as well as your meeting with him or her. You should also give recommendations to your client on how to approach this matter. Be mindful that even though your client is a sophisticated and experienced professional, he/she is not a trained attorney. Therefore you should avoid legalese in your letter.

Under Rule 1.4(a)(3) of the Model Rules of Professional Conduct, an attorney has the duty to keep his or her client "reasonably informed about the status of the client's matter." A thorough follow-up letter after a client meeting is one of the best ways to meet this duty, as well as regular phone calls, emails or meetings.

Learning Objectives of the Assignment:

This assignment will build your skills to:

- Efficiently communicate in a written format
- Explain complex matters clearly and concisely
- Incorporate technical legal English vocabulary that relates to commercial landlords and premises liability and use appropriate layperson explanations for client

Steps for Completing the Assignment:

- Review the predictive memo that you wrote to your senior partner about your client matter to ensure that the law and the issues are clear
- Be familiar with the case law regarding premises liability and summary judgment, as well as the fact pattern
- Conduct your client meeting with your client, Pamela Park or Greg Blackman
- Review the Business Correspondence online resources

Research Required for the Assignment: You are not required to do any outside research for this assignment.

Format of the Completed Assignment:

Your assignment should be written as a business letter, not as an email. Even though many firms and lawyers use email for much of the correspondence carried out, formal business letters are still an essential part of the practice of law.

Your law firm has the following policy regarding business correspondence. Your client letter must follow the policy guidelines.

LAW FIRM CORRESPONDENCE POLICY

The purpose of this policy is to ensure a uniform appearance of all business correspondence that is written by the attorneys and staff of the law firm and thus to increase the professional appearance of the firm's work product. All law firm attorneys and staff are required to employ the following guidelines when writing correspondence. Violation of the policy can result in disciplinary action, up to and including termination.

- The first page of all "traditional" letters must be written on law firm letterhead, which includes the firm's address and logo
- All letters must be written in a modified block letter format
- Letters must be written in Times New Roman, 12 font
- Letters must be 1.5 spaced and have 1" (2.54 cm.) margins, except for the initial page, which may have larger top margins to account for the logo, law firm address and sender's direct contact information
- Client letters must not exceed four pages

Grading: This assignment is worth 78 points.

Note: See the Online Additional Resources for examples of letters and for general information about business correspondence.

LEGAL CONTENT	0-6 points (failing)	8 points (C or 75%)	10 points (B or 85%)	12 points	Points
Introduction	Letter does not include an appropriate introduction or includes poorly constructed one	Letter includes introduction that states purpose with some irrelevancies or some relevant information missing	Introduction states purpose of letter and includes other relevant information	Introduction is engaging; states purpose of letter and includes other relevant information; written clearly and concisely	_____/12
Summary of Meeting	Letter includes no summary of the meeting	Letter includes summary but leaves out important information or states it unclearly	Letter summarizes the meeting but leaves out important information	Letter clearly and concisely summarizes the meeting, its core purpose and content	_____/12
Applicable Law	Student-attorney provides no explanation of the applicable law, or only uses legal jargon in explanation (inappropriate for audience)	Student-attorney provides explanation of with serious mistakes, or hard to follow (use of legal jargon)	Student-attorney provides clear explanation of with few mistakes; uses some legal jargon without appropriate explanations	Student-attorney provides clear, concise and correct explanation of the law with legal jargon with appropriate explanations	_____/12
Analysis	Contains conclusory statements and/or no case law; facts are analyzed in a conclusory or insufficient way	Uses some case law but does not analogize or distinguish or explain its application; some conclusory statements; facts briefly analyzed	Uses case law to show how rule applies to case; case law is compared and contrasted with success; most facts are analyzed	Analyzes completely case law, comparing it fully to client matter; facts are thoroughly analyzed	_____/12
Conclusion/ Recommendations	No conclusion or recommendations are included in letter	A brief conclusion is included but without sufficient advice or recommendations advice or next steps	Letter includes conclusion with recommendations and next steps	Letter includes full conclusion of the legal analysis and facts, presents creative and thoughtful recommendations and includes clear next steps	_____/12
WRITING	**2**	**4**	**5**	**6**	**Points**
Formatting	Document does not follow format instructions or the sample provided	Document attempts to follow instructions and sample provided	Document follows the instructions and sample provided with minor errors	Document exactly follows the instructions and sample provided	_____/6
Organization	No structure or organization; free flow of ideas	Letter includes organization and structure but is still confusing	Structure and organization but some reorganization is needed for full clarity	Document is clearly organized and structured	_____/6
Syntax Mechanics	Contains numerous and distracting grammatical and mechanical errors that impede understanding	Contains some grammatical and mechanical errors that impede understanding	Contains few grammatical and mechanical errors but none that impede understanding	Contains no grammatical and mechanical errors; native-like use of English	_____/6
TOTAL					_____/78

Section III

Advanced Legal Issues

Memorandum of Law
for Motion for Summary Judgment

Overview of the Assignment: For this assignment, you will write the memorandum of law in support of or in opposition to the third-party defendant's motion for summary judgment filed in the case <u>Gateway West Development, Inc. v. Stray Dog Advertising, LLC</u>.

Learning Objectives of the Assignment:

This assignment will build your skills to:

- Efficiently read and understand legal authority (statute and case law)
- Analyze the fact pattern by applying the relevant case law
- Employ the IRAC organization and the formal memorandum of law structure
- Communicate effectively and in a persuasive manner to convince the court and the reader that your client's position and argument is the one to follow

Research for the Assignment: You are not required to do any outside research for this assignment. You should base your analysis on the premises liability statutes and cases that you read and review in class:

- <u>Young v. Garawcki</u>, 402 N.E.2d 1045 (Mass. 1980).
- <u>Humphrey v. Byron</u>, 850 N.E.2d 1044 (Mass. 2006).
- <u>Monterosso v. Gaudette</u>, 391 N.E.2d 948 (Mass. App. Ct. 1979).
- <u>Bishop v. TES Realty Trust</u>, 942 N.E.2d (Mass. 2011).
- <u>Chausse v. Coz</u>, 540 N.E.2d 667 (Mass. 1989).
- <u>The Great Atlantic and Pacific Tea Co. v. Yanofsky</u>, 403 N.E.2d 370 (Mass. 1980).

If you want to practice your legal research skills and if allowed by your instructor, you can look for and use other cases that you find. However, if you do search on Westlaw, LexisNexis or Bloomberg Law, be sure to limit your search and the cases you use to Massachusetts law and remember to change the citations to Jefferson. law as indicated in the introduction

Format of the Completed Assignment:

For your completed assignment, you must follow Local Rule 5.2 of the Courts of Jefferson.

Local Rule 5.2 GENERAL FORMAT OF DOCUMENTS TO BE FILED

Format: All documents filed must be typewritten, printed, or prepared by a clearly legible duplication process. Document text must be double-spaced, except for quoted material and footnotes, and pages must be numbered consecutively at the bottom. Documents filed after the case-initiating document must contain—on the front page and above the document's title—the case number and the name or initials of the assigned district judge and magistrate judge.

Represented Parties. A memorandum of law filed by a represented party must be typewritten. All text in the memorandum, including footnotes, must be set in at least font size 12 (i.e., a 12-point font) as font sizes are designated in the word-processing software used to prepare the memorandum. Text must be double-spaced, with these exceptions: headings and footnotes may be single-spaced, and quotations more than two lines long may be indented and single-spaced. Pages must be 8 ½ by 11 inches in size, and no text — except for page numbers — may appear outside an area measuring 6 ½ by 9 inches.

Length: No memorandum filed with the court shall exceed the length of twelve pages, excluding caption and table of contents.

Grading: This assignment is worth 90 points.

Note: See the online resources for additional information about memoranda of law and persuasive writing.

LEGAL CONTENT	0-6 points	8 points	10 points	12 points	Points
Introduction	Document does not include an Introduction or includes issue statement instead	Introduction is not persuasive or does not include persuasive or relevant facts or the law	Student attempts to make introduction persuasive, to "put the spin" but does not include all facts or something...	Introduction is persuasive, clear and concise and clearly introduces reader to the client's story and position and identifies the relief sought	_____/12
Facts	Few or none of the relevant facts are included; difficult to follow or understand	Relevant facts are included as well as non-relevant ones; mostly clear	Relevant facts are included; factual background is mostly clear and easy to follow with few irrelevancies	Relevant facts are included with no irrelevant facts; story is clearly and concisely told to reader in persuasive way	_____/12
Rule	Hard to follow and understand; does not include relevant sources or cites inappropriate sources; no rule application	Cites to some relevant sources but is incomplete in covering all relevant aspects of the rule	Cite only to relevant sources; rule application explains but not fully how rule has been applied	Clear and concise; includes only relevant sources and includes all parts of rule necessary for analysis; clear rule application	_____/12
Argument	Contains conclusory statements and/or no case law; facts are analyzed in a conclusory or insufficient way	Uses some case law but does not analogize or distinguish or explain its application; some conclusory statements; facts briefly analyzed; student attempts to make persuasive arguments	Uses case law to show how rule applies to case; case law is compared and contrasted with success; facts are analyzed and argued in a persuasive way	Analyzes completely case law, comparing it fully to client matter; all facts are thoroughly analyzed and argued in a very persuasive way	_____/12
Conclusion	No conclusion is included in document	A brief conclusion is included but unclear relief sought	Paper includes conclusion with relief sought	Paper includes full conclusion of the legal analysis and facts and persuasively argues for relief sought	_____/12
Citations	No sources are cited in document or citation formats are incorrect and inconsistent	Sources are cited, but inconsistently; citation format has meaningful mistakes in format	Citations are complete; few meaningful mistakes in format	No mistakes in citations; correct format is used throughout document	_____/12
WRITING	2	4	5	6	Points
Formatting	Document does not follow format instructions or the sample provided	Document attempts to follow instructions and sample provided	Document follows the instructions and sample provided with minor errors	Document exactly follows the instructions and sample provided	_____/6
Organization	No structure or organization; free flow of ideas	Document includes some organization and structure but is still confusing; no use of headings or subheadings	Structure & organization present but reorganization needed full clarity; subheadings included but not effectively persuasive	Document is clearly organized and structured with proper use of persuasive heading and subheadings	_____/6
Syntax Mechanics	Contains numerous and distracting grammatical and mechanical errors that impede understanding	Contains some grammatical and mechanical errors that impede understanding	Contains few grammatical and mechanical errors but none that impede understanding	Contains no grammatical and mechanical errors; native-like use of English	_____/6
TOTAL					_____/90

Mock Oral Argument

Overview of the Assignment: For this assignment, you will carry out the oral argument for the motion for summary judgment in the <u>Gateway West Development, Inc. v. Stray Dog Advertising, LLC</u> case, currently docketed in the Hemings County District Court. Oral arguments are scheduled for the motion filed by Stray Dog Advertising, asking the court to enter judgment in its favor.

You will represent the party that your instructor has assigned to you.

Learning Objectives of the Assignment:

This assignment will build your skills to:

- Effectively and persuasively communicate legal rules and argument
- Conduct yourself orally in a professional courtroom setting
- Respond to questions about the relevant law

Steps for Completing the Assignment:

Before the oral arguments, review the following:

- Pleadings
- Notice of Motion and Motion for Summary Judgment
- Your Memorandum of Law, as well as that of your opposing counsel
- Cases cited in your memo and opposing counsel's
- Facts of the client matter

Research for the Assignment: Although no additional research is required for the assignment, you should review the memorandum of your opposing counsel and review the cases that he/she includes, consider how you can rebut the cases, or explain how they are inapposite to the matter at hand and address those cases in your oral argument.

Format of the Assignment:

Each side has 20 minutes for his or her argument. The moving party first presents his/her arguments and may reserve time for rebuttal. It is the moving party's decision to reserve time for rebuttal. After the moving party has presented his/her arguments, it is the non-moving party's turn. The non-moving party does not receive time for rebuttal since he/she can listen to opposing counsel and respond directly to any arguments made. After the non-moving party finishes, the moving party responds with rebuttal, if he/she previously asked the court to reserve time for it.

Be prepared to answer questions from the court, and part of your preparation should be anticipating the questions that the judge might ask and preparing answers. But in the event that the judge doesn't ask questions or asks few, be prepared to fill the time allotted with your argument.

Grading: This assignment is worth 90 points.

Premises Liability

Unit 4

Punctuality: Attorney arrived on time to oral argument: YES _____ (10 points) NO _____ (0 points)

Professional Attire: Attorney was dressed in appropriate professional attire: YES _____ (10 points) NO _____ (0 points)

Professional Demeanor: Attorney acted in a professional manner w/court and opposing counsel: YES _____ (10 points) NO _____ (0 points)

GRADING CRITERIA	0-6 points (failing)	8 points (C or 75%)	10 points (B or 85%)	12 points	Points received
Engagement	Attorney does not respond to the court's questions	Attorney responds to questions, but incorrectly or with hard to follow answers	Attorney responds promptly and correctly to all of the court's questions	Attorney responds promptly and correctly to all of court's questions with creative, thoughtful and insightful answers that show a deep understanding of the issues	_____/12
Knowledge of Applicable Law	Attorney provides no explanation of the applicable law	Attorney provides explanation of with few meaningful mistakes or with explanation that is hard to follow	Attorney provides clear explanation of the law with no meaningful mistakes	Attorney provides clear, concise and correct explanation of the law	_____/12
Analysis of Applicable Law	Attorney provides no analysis of the law or provides analysis that is incorrect or incomplete	Attorney provides analysis of the law but has some mistakes or misstatements of the law or facts	Attorney provides a clear, concise and correct analysis of the law as it applies to the client matter	Attorney present unimpeachable case for the client, analyzing persuasively, concisely and clearly the law as it applies to client matter	_____/12
Conclusion and Relief	Attorney does not identify relief sought or conclude argument	Attorney provides advice, but	Attorney provides advice but	Attorney clearly identifies the relief sought and summarizes the client's position	_____/12
Organization	Argument is disorganized and has serious faults of organization	Argument has minor faults of organization	Argument is clearly organized and easy to follow	Argument is exceptionally well organized and presents arguments in novel way	_____/12
TOTAL					_____/60
TOTAL FROM PUNCTUALITY AND PROFESSIONALISM					_____/30

TOTAL   _____/90

Section III

Advanced Legal Issues